Field Armies & Fortifications in the Civil War

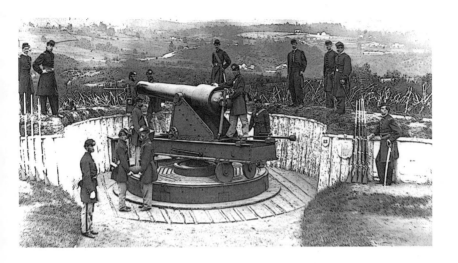

CIVIL WAR AMERICA Gary W. Gallagher, editor

Field Armies & Fortifications in the Civil War The Eastern Campaigns, 1861–1864

Earl J. Hess

THE UNIVERSITY OF NORTH CAROLINA PRESS   Chapel Hill and London

Set in Charter and Melior types
by Keystone Typesetting, Inc.
Manufactured in the United States of America

The paper in this book meets the guidelines for
permanence and durability of the Committee on
Production Guidelines for Book Longevity of the
Council on Library Resources.

Library of Congress Cataloging-in-Publication Data
Hess, Earl J.
Field armies and fortifications in the Civil War : the
Eastern campaigns, 1861–1864 / by Earl J. Hess
    p. cm. — (Civil War America)
Includes bibliographical references and index.
ISBN 978-0-8078-2931-8 (cloth : alk. paper)
ISBN 978-1-4696-0993-5 (pbk. : alk. paper)
    1. United States—History—Civil War, 1861–1865—
Campaigns. 2. United States. Army of the Potomac—
History. 3. Confederate States of America. Army of
Northern Virginia—History. 4. United States—
Defenses—History—19th century. 5. Confederate States
of America—Defenses—History. 6. Fortification, Field—
History—19th century. 7. Fortification—East (U.S.)—
History—19th century. 8. Historic sites—East (U.S.)
9. East (U.S.)—History, Military—19th century.
I. Title. II. Series.
E470.2.H47 2005
973.7′3—dc22   2004022010

cloth   09 08 07 06 05 5 4 3 2 1
paper   17 16 15 14 13 5 4 3 2 1

For Pratibha and Julie,

with love

Contents

Illustrations

Maps

Preface

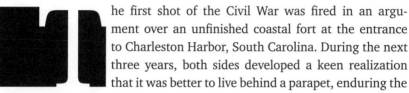he first shot of the Civil War was fired in an argument over an unfinished coastal fort at the entrance to Charleston Harbor, South Carolina. During the next three years, both sides developed a keen realization that it was better to live behind a parapet, enduring the dirt, mud, baking sun, and bitter cold, than to die in the open. Fortifications of some kind played a role in all campaigns of this immense conflict. Civil War soldiers became experts in the building of field fortifications, and earthworks came to play a vital role in determining the outcome of the conflict. The Civil War ended in the ditches around Petersburg, where Lee's Army of Northern Virginia was pinned to the earth in the most sophisticated system of field fortifications yet seen in the history of the world.

Surely, the topic of fortifications is one of the more important yet to be explored by historians. I did not become aware of this aspect of Civil War military history until I moved south to take up my first full-time academic appointment, at the University of Georgia, in 1986. Driving back and forth between Indiana and Georgia took me by many battlefields of the Atlanta campaign. I was amazed to find remnants of earthworks and became fascinated with them, how they came to be there, and who had built them. They are tangible links, of a quality different from that of letters, diaries, or memoirs, with the Civil War past.

What followed was a massive research project that took me to many places over the next fifteen years. During that time, I visited a total of 303 battlefields and fortification sites of the Civil War and found remnants of earthworks or masonry forts at 213 of them. Of the 303 sites visited, 136 are relevant to the eastern campaigns. I found remnants of earthworks or masonry forts at 94 of the eastern sites. Additional visits to non–Civil War military sites have helped to set the conflict in perspective. I have visited thirty-three places in the United States, most of which are related to pre–Civil War military operations. Further perspective was gained by examining sites outside the United States. I have been fortunate in seeing a large variety of earthen and masonry fortifications, as well as battlefields, in nine countries. Sites in Australia, Belgium, Denmark, England, France, Germany,

India, the Netherlands, Puerto Rico, and Sweden have proved to me that the similarities in fortification use and style are more important than the differences, when seen within a global context. The remnants of prehistoric earthen forts in England are similar to the remains of Civil War fieldworks, and the engineers of eighteenth-century India obeyed the same imperatives as American engineers in laying out their masonry forts to conform to the lay of the land.

By taking me to so many interesting places across the South, this project has given me the widest possible exposure to the varied climate, terrain, and vegetation upon which the drama of the Civil War was played out. Such a comprehensive view of the landscape of the war is necessary if one is to gain a full appreciation of its magnitude, the varied problems faced by field commanders, and the enormous difficulties surmounted by ordinary soldiers. While struggling through the swampy bottomlands of Mississippi, digging through the coastal sand near Charleston, or climbing up the vertical slopes of Rocky Face Ridge, the Civil War soldier of both sides mastered a wide variety of landforms.

There simply is no substitute for field visits to military sites. Examining the remnants of earthworks answered many important questions that are not addressed in the voluminous primary literature. While many officers and men described earthworks in their letters, diaries, and memoirs, they did not address all topics relevant to understanding how fieldworks were configured, how the diggers dealt with rocky outcroppings, and how they accommodated other features in the landscape. Existing maps often fail to detail the finer points of construction. I have found that, although a marvelous and valuable technological aid, even satellite positioning can only identify the area and general outline of trench systems. Details in a fieldwork small enough to accommodate a single soldier do not appear on maps or satellite images. One must walk through the woods, compass and notepad in hand, in all sorts of weather. Brambles and briars were my worst enemy; an obscure but interesting configuration of trench, seldom seen by a visitor in more than 130 years, was my reward. Such a find made up for the torn clothes, scratches, and thousands of miles traveled in search of a tangible connection with the war.

I do not attempt to cover the entire history of fortifications in the Civil War; this study addresses one theme of that history. The complexity of Civil War fortifications as a field of study can be appreciated by dividing them into six major categories based on their types and uses. They include coastal defenses, city and town defenses, railroad defenses, river fortifications, siege works, and field fortifications. This classification system focuses on the works themselves and offers a technical approach to the history of fortifications.

This study, instead, concentrates on the campaigns of the major field armies, North and South. I will fully cover the topic of field fortifications, as that type played the most central role in the story of the field armies and their campaigns, but I will also touch on all other categories of fortifications as needed. Some coastal forts (such as Fort Macon and Fort Sumter) were attacked by elements of field armies. Washington, Richmond, and a host of lesser cities and towns had to be defended or attacked by contending field armies. Railroad defenses were needed to protect lines of communication, especially for Federal armies. River defenses came into play in the campaigns of many commanders, especially Ulysses S. Grant. Siege operations were conducted by Grant, Nathaniel P. Banks, and the Army of the Potomac, among others.

This is not a technical study; the focus is on military operations. I introduce technical aspects only to make sense of the fortifications. To that end, a glossary of technical terms used throughout this volume is appended.

The purpose of the study is to see how much and why fortifications played a role in the success or failure of Civil War field armies. This is a unique approach to the subject, only partially taken by one other historian. Edward Hagerman's *American Civil War and the Origins of Modern Warfare*, published in 1988, examines fortifications, logistics, communications, and army administration in an effort to see how modernizing trends in military affairs affected the conduct of Civil War operations. Thus, Hagerman was forced to make only general points about the use of fortifications. To date, I am not aware of any other historian who has taken my approach to the topic in any conflict other than the Civil War.

A handful of army officers wrote articles on the use of fortifications by Civil War armies. These were published around the turn of the twentieth century and have remained obscure ever since. These authors based their conclusions on very limited research and tried to cover the entire war in a few pages. Also, there are a number of interesting articles and some books on individual forts used in the Civil War, but they focus mostly on the engineering perspective.

I hope my efforts will take the study of fortifications to a new level of understanding by incorporating the engineering aspects into the operational perspective. I will attempt to explain why fortifications are an important component of understanding how the Civil War was fought.

Even military historians who write detailed tactical studies of major battles in which field fortifications played a role simply mention the works in passing, without explaining how, why, or by whom they were made. This seems to be largely true of other American and European conflicts as well. For their part, historians of fortifications tend to focus on permanent or semipermanent works, writing books and articles on the structures themselves, not on military operations designed to attack or defend them. There is a real disconnection between those who study operations and those who study fortifications. This work will attempt to bridge that gap.

Therefore, I address a number of topics in this study. What did the soldiers and their commanders think about the use of fortifications? How did fighting behind earthworks affect their morale? How much were fortifications used? How were they constructed? How were they designed to conform to the landscape? Who laid them out and built them? How sophisticated and strong were they? How and why did the reliance on earthworks evolve? What role did fortifications play in altering the tactical outcome of a battle and the strategic course of a campaign? What were the factors that led to success or failure when troops attacked earthworks? What role did the presence of obstructions placed in front of the earthwork play in affecting the outcome of an attack? Were fortifications more important as a defensive or an offensive feature on the battlefield?

It became apparent in the course of my research that fortifications cannot be understood without recognizing how they related to the lay of the land and to the presence of vegetation. Trenches, parapets, and forts were features on the landscape of war just as were trees, hills, and ridges. Another complicating factor is that soldiers often used existing features on the battlefield for cover. A ridge line, a rocky outcropping, a railroad grade, a barn, or a sunken road could serve well in this regard. They were often used during engagements where no fortifications were built. Pre–Civil War engineering manuals recognized this use as a legitimate part of the art of fortification. Thus I discuss battles such as Second Bull Run, where no earthworks were dug, as the Confederate use of the unfinished railroad grade made that engagement a legitimate part of the story of fortifications in the Civil War.

Another related topic is military engineering. I found it necessary to understand something of the professional military engineer, both before and during the Civil War, in order to understand the topic of fortifications. Thus I include a certain amount of institutional and professional history in this study. Engineers were generally well regarded in mid-nineteenth-century America, but they labored under several handicaps during the war. Too few to handle all engineering duties and restricted in rank and pay scale, they often were ignored when credit was doled out for successful campaigns.

Engineer officers and enlisted men alike played quiet but essential roles in the operations of field armies, and they deserve their due.

During the past twenty years, a revolution in public attitudes toward battlefield preservation in the United States has occurred. There is a growing realization that, with further development and the passage of time, whatever remains of our Civil War landscape is threatened if not doomed to be eliminated in the coming decades. Preservation of the remnants of Civil War fortifications has been greatly advanced as a result of this new awareness. I hope that my efforts aid this worthy cause. To that end, I make full use of the insights gained from my field visits in describing various earthworks. Also, I give some indication of what remnants were found at various sites. Earthworks were being destroyed at several places when I visited them, and I know that remnants have been demolished since my visit to other sites as well. The joy of finding a well-preserved work at one site was often counterbalanced by neglect or destruction at other places. A precious relic callously denuded of its protective cover by tramping feet, or in some cases, being driven over by heavy logging equipment that left terrible gashes in the parapet, was a sad discovery that proved that we need to save everything possible.

The study of fortifications has been advanced by a number of dedicated scholars in the past twenty-five years. In his unpublished thesis on Civil War field fortifications, which mostly focused on Fortress Rosecrans at Murfreesboro, David Russell Wright made good points about the state of scholarship in 1982. "The study of field fortifications of the Civil War is a relatively unbroken ground," he wrote, "with most extant earthworks being overlooked by the scholar and amateur alike. Both field and library research and documentation have yet to be initiated on a large scale." Wright also noted the importance of on-site study of fortification remnants as an important way to rectify this situation, a point I discovered when those Atlanta campaign earthworks first attracted my attention in 1986. "Most Civil War writers neglect to mention or describe fortifications," Wright continued, "while others do so in passing and only then with great apprehension. The lack of justified recognition stems from the fact that most students of the Civil War do not understand nor have sufficient reference material concerning the study of fortifications."[1]

I would not say that the same is true today, for the study of earthworks has blossomed since Wright completed his thesis. Most of it has been done by talented and dedicated historians working for the National Park Service, using global positioning as well as intensive on-site examination of remnants. The results appear in reports that are seldom, if ever, published. I have used this material whenever possible, along with papers and reports written by historic archaeologists who also have devoted a growing amount of attention to Civil War earthworks. The publication of Clarence R. Geier Jr. and Susan E. Winter, eds., *Look to the Earth: Historical Archaeology and the American Civil War* (1994), highlighted the promise of this approach to understanding the history of Civil War fortifications. In addition, George G. Kundahl, *Confederate Engineer: Training and Campaigning with John Morris Wampler* (2000), sheds a great deal of new light on the professional military engineer in the Civil War.

Finally, the visual documentation of Civil War fortifications has been an important source of information for my study. There are hundreds of photographs of forts, trenches, obstructions, and siege works easily available to the scholar, and I have pored over them to gain insight into how earthworks were constructed and how they fit into the landscape of the battlefields.

In short, everything from a soldier's letter to an official report, a photograph, a conversation with a park ranger, or an obscure and lonely remnant of an earthwork has informed this study. All inquiries have been focused on the fortifications and the role they played in the operations of the major field armies, North and South, during the four years of war.

After fifteen years of research, I wound up with more than two filing cabinets crammed with material. The question then was how to organize and make maximum use of it. A multivolume series seemed the best approach. This initial volume will cover the eastern campaigns from Big Bethel in June 1861 to the Confederate capture of Plymouth, North Carolina, in April 1864. This period saw a transition to the habitual use of field fortifications in the Overland campaign, and thus one purpose of this initial volume is to explain how the Union Army of the Potomac and the Confederate Army of Northern Virginia came to rely on cover whenever possible by the time of the Spotsylvania phase of Grant's drive toward Richmond.

But this initial three-year period in the eastern campaigns is not important simply as a prelude to the Overland campaign. There is a widespread assumption that fieldworks were significant from the Wilderness on, but not before. A three-year period of open, fluid warfare, it is thought, was suddenly replaced by static, even stalemated operations. That is a misperception. There was no such sharp break between the Virginia operations of 1861–63 and those of 1864–65. This volume will show that the use of some kind of field fortification was common throughout the eastern campaigns and was not confined to a specific time period. The difference is one of degree. Fieldworks were less used in battles such as Second Manassas and Antietam but were heavily implemented during the Peninsula campaign, after Fredericksburg, and at Chancellorsville. They were also widely used at

Gettysburg. There was a trend toward more heavy reliance on field fortifications on both the Union and Confederate sides, but it was not inevitable or uniform. In fits and starts, by 1864 the armies in the East had intensified their use of quickly constructed fortifications, building on a long period of experience in their construction.

Two subsequent volumes will follow this story to its conclusion in the East. One will detail the use of fortifications in the Overland campaign, and the other will cover the Petersburg campaign.

In addition to detailing the use of fortifications in the major campaigns of the East, I follow several lines of interpretation in this book. First, as already mentioned, the campaigns from 1861 to the early months of 1864 saw the widespread use of fortifications. There is no clearly defined break between this period and that of the Overland campaign. Second, there has been some discussion about who initiated the construction of field fortifications. I argue that fieldworks were started by a wide range of people. Middle-level officers—regimental, brigade, or division commanders—usually initiated them, but on fewer occasions corps and army commanders ordered their construction. On still other occasions, the rank and file took it upon themselves to build them. A third line of interpretation identifies who actually did the digging. While engineer officers usually planned and laid out the works, there is no doubt that the men in the ranks did the vast majority of the labor. The engineer troops in both armies were far too few in number to do much in this regard. Slaves and free black laborers were an important part of the workforce only in constructing semipermanent defenses around Yorktown, Richmond, Petersburg, and a few other places.

The fourth line of interpretation relates to a slow evolution in the use of fieldworks and in their growing sophistication. Early in the war, soldiers usually dug a simple trench with a parapet. More sophisticated features gradually adorned it, including obstructions placed in front, traverses dug to offer flank protection, and headlogs. This trend toward more elaborate trench systems evolved into the sophisticated fieldworks at Spotsylvania, Cold Harbor, and Petersburg, which cross the line between a field fortification and the semipermanent earthwork systems that guarded important cities like Richmond and Washington, D.C. Defense in depth, in which one or more trench lines were constructed behind each other, was another more sophisticated design. It was relatively rare in the Civil War, simply because the number of men available to any field army was limited, yet one can see evidence of it at Cold Harbor.

A fifth line of interpretation identifies why armies had come to rely habitually on field fortifications by the time of the Overland campaign. The prevailing view has been that the full employment of the rifle musket, with its longer range, by both armies led to this heavy reliance. I strongly argue against this view, convinced that the shock of combat and continuous contact between the armies, or at least the imminent threat of continued fighting after a pitched battle, were the keys to either army's willingness to dig in. This can be seen in several engagements of the eastern campaigns during 1861–64, including First Manassas and Fredericksburg.

Finally, a sixth line of interpretation deals with whether the use of field fortifications helped or hindered tactical operations. Of course, the answer depends on which army and which campaign one refers to. Generally, the armies of the Civil War made effective use of fieldworks. There are only a few cases where they dug in unnecessarily, such as the Federal construction of an elaborate defense system to protect Suffolk, Virginia, a town of little strategic value. There are other instances where field armies failed to dig in widely or effectively, as with Lee's army at Second Manassas and Antietam. In both battles, more extensive use of fieldworks would have been fully justified. But in most other cases, the use of field fortifications was balanced and rational. Both sides built impressive fieldworks during the Chancellorsville campaign, deftly aiding their particular tactical needs (the only exception was the failure of the Eleventh Corps to properly fortify its position on May 2). Gettysburg saw the eventual construction of fieldworks that were appropriate to the terrain along nearly the entire length of each opposing line of battle.

The list of campaigns in which fieldworks played a significant role would include nearly all the campaigns addressed in this volume. Sometimes they failed to stop a vigorous attack, as at Gaines's Mill, but on other occasions they played the decisive role in abruptly deciding the outcome of the campaign, as at Mine Run. Sometimes they were poorly planned and built and were cracked open by smart attacks, as at Rappahannock Station and Plymouth. They were used both offensively and defensively. By and large, one is tempted to argue that American field armies made more effective use of field fortifications than did their European counterparts, although this a thesis in need of study.

Finally, a word about sieges is in order. The strong tendency among Civil War contemporaries to call any static positioning in a fortified field position a siege has largely been accepted by modern historians. There were many different kinds of siege operations; only a few were employed at Yorktown and Suffolk, while a fuller range was used against Fort Wagner on Morris Island. The latter is, in fact, one of the classic siege operations in American military history. I refrain from overusing the word "siege" but will deal with the varied components of siege operations as they were applied to these campaigns.

These six lines of interpretation will continue throughout the three volumes that are planned to cover the eastern campaigns of the Civil War. Further elaboration of all six are offered in the conclusion of this volume.

I wish to offer a special note of gratitude to the staff members at all the archives and libraries I visited or contacted for information. Additionally, several people have gone beyond the ordinary to offer help or encouragement. They include Christopher Calkins at Petersburg National Battlefield; Robert E. L. Krick and Joseph Kyle at Richmond National Battlefield; A. Wilson Greene at Pamplin Park; Jerry L. Bochek at Newport News Park; Richard Sommers and Arthur Bergeron at the U.S. Army Military History Institute; and Jane M. Sundberg at Yorktown Battlefield. The Harrisburg Civil War Round Table offered me a James F. Haas Fellowship in 1998 to aid in the completion of research at the U.S. Army Military History Institute. I would also like to thank William L. Shea for helpful ideas and encouragement.

A special note of gratitude is due the self-proclaimed "trench nerds" of the Civil War Fortifications Study Group. Formed in 1992, mostly by dedicated historians working for the National Park Service, this is the only organization devoted to the study of Civil War fortifications. It organizes yearly conferences centered around visits to the remnants of fortifications. The members of this small but vibrant group are the richest storehouse of information about Civil War fortifications. They are a sounding board for anyone interested in learning about the topic or anyone in need of reliable information regarding identification, preservation, and assessment of earthwork remnants. I would like to thank specifically several members of the study group who have been particularly helpful in influencing my thinking on the subject. They include Dale Floyd, Philip Shiman, Stacy Allen, and Paul Hawke.

I wish to thank Gary W. Gallagher and Robert K. Krick for their careful readings of the manuscript and their helpful suggestions for improvement. David W. Lowe of the National Park Service and the Civil War Fortifications Study Group read the manuscript as well. He offered many helpful suggestions and saved me from several embarrassing mistakes. His deep and comprehensive knowledge of Civil War earthworks, his enthusiasm for the subject, and his stylistic suggestions improved the manuscript a great deal.

Finally, as always, I am eternally grateful for the support, encouragement, and love of my wife, Pratibha. It would all be useless without her.

1 : **Engineering War**

Responsibility for fortifications in the pre–Civil War army rested with the Corps of Engineers, the elite of the military establishment. Created initially by the Second Continental Congress in 1779 and renewed in different form by the Congress of the new government in 1794, the corps was institutionalized in its current form in 1802. A separate group of topographical engineers, responsible for mapmaking, was created in the War of 1812 and given its own institutional status in 1838 as the Corps of Topographical Engineers. The U.S. Engineer Department was created immediately after the War of 1812 to serve the administrative needs of the corps. It was headed by the chief engineer.[1]

The Corps of Engineers owed its status to its role as keeper of a body of technical knowledge and its tight connection with the U.S. Military Academy at West Point. Created in 1802, the academy had a curriculum that was heavily oriented toward engineering. Political support for it stemmed largely from the assumption that West Point could produce a number of well-trained engineers who would eventually return to civilian life with their technical skills. The Corps of Engineers controlled the academy. Only engineer officers were appointed as superintendents, and most of the faculty were former or current members of the corps. Beginning in 1842, the assistant professor of engineering was required to participate in postgraduate training in military engineering under the academy's most famous faculty member, Dennis Hart Mahan, the acknowledged expert on fortifications in the United States. Mahan put his students through a rigorous pace in this course, requiring each one to design a fortification for a particular site and plan an attack against it.

Cadets also were exposed to practical experience in field fortification. In his third year at the academy, Cyrus B. Comstock took a course called Practical Engineering. He and his classmates spent two hours every day making fascines, gabions, and sap rollers. The class regularly visited Washington Valley, where the only company of engineers in the army maintained a demonstration site. Here the cadets watched as saps and parallels were made, inspected "a small lunette with palisaded gorge," or looked at the effects of

10-inch Columbiad fire on "different materials for embrasures." They used sticks to profile the shape of a parapet and studied examples of several different types of obstructions, from abatis to chevaux-de-frise. Civil engineering was a large component of the academy curriculum as well. The top graduates of the academy, roughly 12 percent, were commissioned directly into the engineers, the topographical engineers, or as ordnance officers.[2]

The prestige of the Corps of Engineers, as well as its connection to the academy, was the basis of its elevated status within the army, a status jealously guarded by the officers who headed the corps. The corps liked to throw its weight around during intramural conflicts, and it also was the most politically active branch of the army. Corps heads often fought with politicians over West Point and the other major aspect of the corps' existence, its responsibility for building and maintaining an ambitious and very expensive system of coastal forts. Approved in the wake of the army's dismal performance in the War of 1812, the Third System consisted of about twenty-five masonry forts of various sizes and designs strung out along the coastline of the United States. Costing millions of dollars and mostly complete by the time of the Civil War, it was "the centerpiece of national defense," in the words of historian William B. Skelton.[3]

The emphasis on coastal forts helped to justify the maintenance of the Coast Survey, created in 1807 to map the long coastline of the country. It operated under a limited budget and relied heavily on navy and army engineers for survey duties. The Coast Survey also hired promising civilians and gave them valuable topographical engineering experience. It provided another pipeline, besides West Point, for the training of engineers experienced in government-sponsored projects.[4]

As the primary repository of technical expertise in engineering, the corps had a heavy influence on the many U.S. military missions sent to observe European armies. American officers traveled to Europe more than 150 times from the end of the War of 1812 until the outbreak of the Civil War. While more than half of those trips were undertaken as private travel by officers on leave, the rest were officially financed observer missions. The Thayer-McRee Mission of 1815–17 was important in bringing to America the idea that all things French were the final word in military affairs.

But more important than the Thayer-McRee Mission was the Delafield Commission of 1855–56. Three officers took part: Maj. Richard Delafield of the engineers, Maj. Alfred Mordecai of the Ordnance Department, and Capt. George B. McClellan of the cavalry. All three had originally been commissioned into the Corps of Engineers upon their graduation from West Point. The object of the commission was to observe military operations in the

Crimean War, but the three officers traveled all over Europe, observing the gamut of military matters. They left on April 11, 1855, and visited England, France, Prussia, Poland, Russia, Berlin, Vienna, and Constantinople. Diplomatic red tape and military suspicions on the part of the French delayed their arrival at the theater of war until the siege of Sebastopol was over. The Americans reached Sebastopol a month after the city fell to the combined French and English armies on September 8, 1855. After a month of observation, they returned to Vienna and then toured Italy, the Rhine Valley, Waterloo, Paris, and London. By the time the three officers returned to New York on April 28, 1856, they had traveled 20,000 miles.[5]

The Delafield Commission was unique in that it was the first to survey several countries and the first to see the immediate aftermath of operations. Each commissioner wrote a separate, lengthy report. Delafield concentrated on engineering but did not complete his report until November 1860. Mordecai wrote on artillery and ordnance, while McClellan wrote on cavalry, to a degree, but mostly ranged widely across the whole spectrum of military matters.

The result of their labor was impressive; each man wrote with a fine degree of professionalism, detail, and evaluation. But none of them discerned very well how the early signs of technological innovation were beginning to change military operations. They noted a wide array of new developments, ranging from the use of processed foods and submarine torpedoes to the construction of a military railroad for the tactical support of the English army. But they failed to ponder the effect of the widespread use of rifles on tactical formations. The technological developments were eagerly described, often in minute detail, but there was no recognition that they might begin to challenge how armies traditionally fought.

Overall, the commissioners took away from their long tour of Europe an awareness that the scale of warfare had changed and that the mobilization of manpower and military resources had increased to create expanded field armies. But they also sensed a threat to American security from this and argued the need for strengthening the Third System of seacoast fortifications.[6]

It was a rather self-serving performance, however, and much of it reinforced old ways of doing things in the American military, despite some minor technical recommendations. Also, the commissioners unsuccessfully tried to portray the French model as outdated and the Russians as the truly admirable belligerent in this conflict. Objectively, the Russian nation and its army were hardly suitable models for intelligent professionals of a modernizing nation; the suggestion fell on deaf ears.

Delafield's comments on matters relating to fortifications were interesting. He focused intently on seacoast forts everywhere he went and provided extraordinary maps, sketches, and diagrams of dozens of works in several countries. Delafield also was impressed by the European art of protecting fixed assets on land with scientifically designed permanent fortifications. He emphasized the success of the huge masonry forts built by the Russians to protect the entrance to the harbor at Sebastopol in repelling an Allied naval attack in October 1854.

But Delafield paid some attention to field fortifications as well. Both he and McClellan lauded the Russians for the tenacity with which they defended a line of hastily constructed fieldworks to cover the southern approaches to Sebastopol. The Russians held out for eleven months, even though they were heavily outnumbered in both infantry and artillery in the latter stages of the siege. "Such was the efficacy and power of *temporary field fortifications*, with inexhaustible supplies of the munitions of war," commented Delafield. The Russians were the first to use what came to be called rifle pits, small holes dug for one to twenty men forward of their defense line. Soldiers armed with rifles harassed Allied work parties on a daily basis from these pits, which were typically protected by gabions filled with stone or dirt. Delafield felt this tactic of harassment was "unusual." He also gathered a number of photographs of the Russian works at Sebastopol and included exquisite line drawings based on them to illustrate his report. Few other visual documents convey the squalor of a small fortification that has endured months of bombardment better than these remarkable illustrations.[7]

All three reports of the Delafield Commission were widely distributed in the army and were well respected by officers and interested civilians alike. But these reports had limited impact on the thinking and doctrine of the American army. This was due in part to the onset of the Civil War soon after the reports were published, and to the fact that there were relatively few recommendations in the reports. Delafield's comments on the efficacy of field fortifications apparently had no influence on professional army officers, and the fact that the coming Civil War would be fought by an avalanche of volunteers who had never read the report made it even less influential. The significance of the Delafield Commission lies in the fact that the American army was obviously growing in its sense of professionalism and study. It still had a long way to go in terms of divining new trends that might affect how armies operated in the field and then moving aggressively toward meeting the challenges that change offered. McClellan sounded a plaintive note of despair in his report, which illustrated how far the army had to go to be a top-notch military force. He bemoaned the size of the American engineer establishment, calling it "ridiculously and shamefully small."[8]

Theory and Doctrine

To the extent that the pre–Civil War army had a set of theories that could be called a doctrine, prevailing thoughts on the role of fortifications in the operations of field armies centered on whether they should be used for offensive or defensive purposes. Dennis Hart Mahan was the only influential American theorist in this regard. A graduate of the West Point class of 1824, Mahan studied at the French School of Application for Artillery and Engineering at Metz from 1825 to 1830. He returned to West Point soon after he came home to teach engineering, and he held the position until his death in 1871. Mahan had an extraordinary influence on the creation of professional standards of military engineering in the United States, both through his classes at West Point and through his book *A Complete Treatise on Field Fortifications* (1836). He later wrote six more books on warfare and engineering. Mahan also was primarily responsible for establishing standards of professionalism in civil engineering. The several reprintings of his *Complete Treatise* not only informed regular officers, but they were widely read by the pre–Civil War militia and by volunteer officers during the war.[9]

Mahan revised prevailing French military thinking about the role of fortifications in field operations. Theorists of Napoleon's day had advocated maneuver and flanking, the indirect approach, to win battles quickly and decisively. This was largely rejected following Napoleon's defeat. Instead, theorists such as Antoine Henri Jomini favored the direct approach, or massing troops for frontal attacks. Napoleon himself had adopted such tactics on occasion during the later years of his career, most notably at the battle of Borodino during the invasion of Russia in 1812. Jomini and others even believed the spirited offensive could be successful against field fortifications. These post-Napoleonic writers were most influential until about 1840, during the period when Mahan was studying in France, and most American commentators adopted Jomini and his compatriots with enthusiasm.

One of these French theorists, Francis Gay de Vernon, a professor of fortification and the art of war at the Ecole Polytechnique, also urged the use of field fortifications to protect the army. Vernon argued that fieldworks should even be used to facilitate offensive action, as long as they were designed so the attacking force had an opening in the works to debouch and mass in the open for the assault. Vernon's book on war and fortification was used at West Point from 1817 through 1830.[10]

Mahan was dedicated to the direct approach, but he significantly revised how it should be conducted. He argued that the poorly trained volunteer force that the United States relied on to fight its wars could not conduct successful attacks on fortified positions unless the defending army was somehow damaged first. Even if U.S. volunteer troops were successful in attacking a well-fortified position defended by a fresh army, the losses would be prohibitive. Mahan believed the volunteers were more valuable to the country as permanent civilians than as temporary soldiers. Moreover, the small regular army was too valuable to waste in frontal attacks on strong positions.

Mahan instead advocated what he called an "active defense." First, use field fortifications to create a defensive position, entice the enemy to attack it, and damage him significantly. Then, follow up with a counterattack that would be sure to take the enemy position and scatter or decimate the opposing army. This was a smart adaptation of prevailing French theory to the peculiar conditions of the American military force. Whether it was practical in the field was another issue. The enemy would have to cooperate in developing such a scenario, and volunteers, who often were naively enthusiastic about attacking with little preparation, would have to be convinced of the need to dig in before the first shot was fired.[11]

Despite these obvious limitations, Mahan was the only American military theorist who offered an original twist on the European doctrine. Despite Mahan's prestige, his theory about the active defense was not uniformly accepted among American officers. It existed side by side with prevailing French theory about the need to mass and attack directly without using fieldworks. West Point cadets and serving officers were exposed to both theories. Mahan's followers made sure his views were kept active with the passage of time. Henry W. Halleck's solid book, *Elements of Military Art and Science* (1846), praised Mahan's theory as best suited to the peculiar characteristics of the American soldier. James St. Clair Morton, a brilliant young graduate of the academy, perpetuated Mahan's theory in publications such as *Memoir on the Dangers and Defenses of New York City* (1858) and *Memoir on American Fortification* (1859).[12]

Yet if one looks at the campaigns of the Mexican War from 1846 to 1848, one would have to conclude that few American officers paid attention to Mahan's theory. Repeatedly, American commanders assumed the tactical offensive without digging in, and they usually made successful attacks. Even on the rare occasion when American troops acted on the defensive, as at the battle of Buena Vista, they failed to fortify. It is true that the Mexican War could be taken as a sterling proof of the Jomini school of thought as it relates to offensive tactics and the role of fieldworks. But one would have to point out that the Mexican army was not as dangerous a foe as most European armies of the day, and not as dangerous as either the Northern or Southern armies would be in the Civil War. Historians have noted that the Americans came out of Mexico with a belief that a spirited attack can overcome field fortifications, for they had done so many times, but it must be noted that such a lesson was unequally learned. Thomas J. "Stonewall" Jackson seems to have come from the war with little regard for the usefulness of fieldworks, to judge by his lack of attention to them in the Civil War. But George McClellan and others served equally well in Mexico and yet often resorted to field fortifications in the bigger war to come. Both Union and Confederate armies in general used fortifications of all kinds far more frequently in the first half of the Civil War than their counterparts ever did in the Mexican conflict.[13]

Lessons learned from the introduction of rifle muskets in the 1850s and the experience of the Crimean War of 1854–56 were mixed. Mahan did not believe that rifles would significantly alter the validity of his theory, and he pointed to the siege of Sebastopol as proof that armies needed to entrench for protection even if they planned offensive action. Historian Edward Hagerman firmly states that the rifle musket revolutionized combat, and he also argues that it invalidated the direct approach to attacking an enemy position. He interprets McClellan's commission report as sensing this change in the reality of warfare. Hagerman believes that McClellan pointed out "that the first significant use of rifle infantry weapons in the Crimean War shifted the tactical balance from the open frontal assault to entrenched tactical deployment."[14]

The role of the rifle musket in affecting the nature of tactics in the Civil War is controversial. I disagree with Hagerman's assessment on this matter (see the Preface for my comments on the use of the rifle musket). In short, there is, in my view, no evidence that rifled small arms significantly affected the success or failure rate of frontal assaults or led to the increased use of field fortifications. Moreover, my reading of McClellan's report does not support the view that the young captain recognized such a shift. McClellan did note that the Russian fieldworks around Sebastopol were strong and well designed. But he also pointed out that they were little more than "inert masses" unless defended by highly motivated infantrymen and artillerymen. McClellan rejected the prevailing opinion of his day that Sebastopol demonstrated the greater value of temporary fieldworks over permanent works. It merely demonstrated that "temporary works in the hands of a brave and skillful garrison are susceptible of a longer defence than was generally supposed. They were attacked as field works never were before, and were defended as field works never had been defended."[15]

As a field commander in the Civil War, McClellan would practice much of what Mahan had taught. His Peninsula campaign is a model of the active defense, with the Federals entrenching before meticulously planning offensive action. He was never able to entice the Rebels into launching an ill-advised attack on his works, but McClellan also demonstrated in the Maryland campaign that he was quite able to launch fierce attacks without preliminary entrenching. It is difficult to find support for the argument that he believed the Crimean War had demonstrated the inevitable shift to greater use of fieldworks. His years in the pre–Civil War army and his innate caution probably accounted more for his use of fieldworks than did his one-month tour of the battlefield outside Sebastopol.

Did McClellan, Mahan, and Halleck fail to discern revolutionary changes in military affairs and therefore fail to teach Civil War armies how to fight better? That would be too harsh an accusation. The two most important changes in military affairs, as they affected the Civil War, were the widespread use of the rifle musket and the fielding of huge armies that dwarfed anything seen in previous American experience. If the rifle musket did not alter the tactical picture, then the massed levies of poorly trained men and officers were the key change. Thousands of civilian soldiers could not possibly be trained before the war, and after they enlisted, all that could be expected of them was that they would learn the basics of drill and linear formations. One of the key limitations of Civil War armies lay not in a lack of understanding of the impact of new weapons or the feasibility of using fieldworks, but in the struggle of commanders to effectively manage large concentrations of troops over battlefields that were covered with thickets, ravines, and many other obstacles that wrecked neat lines. Field commanders on both sides went into the Civil War with faith both in the tactical offensive and in the use of fieldworks. What had preceded their day—the French belief in the direct offensive and Mahan's concept of the active defense—was more influential in their thinking than any theoretical musings about the future.

Manuals

Whatever there was of doctrine in the pre–Civil War army was conveyed to cadets through Mahan's classroom instruction. The military manuals available to officers both before and during the Civil War were primarily technical treatises designed to convey detailed information about organizing and drilling troops, deploying them on the battlefield, and teaching them the rudiments of how to perform their military duties. The same was true of the handful of manuals that dealt with fortifications. Mahan's manual was by far the most important. It was to a large degree a distillation of Vernon's manual adapted to better suit the characteristics of the American military establishment. Mahan's was the primary treatise on fortifications in the U.S. army; all other writers who dealt with fortifications in their manuals mostly restated what he said.

Mahan defined field fortifications broadly: "All dispositions made to enable an armed force to resist, with advantage, the attack of one superior to it in numbers, belong to the ART OF FORTIFICATION." Fortification could be achieved by creating a barrier on the surface of the ground from materials quickly gathered from the local area (a breastwork), by digging into the earth to create a trench and parapet (an earthwork), or by taking cover behind existing features (such as a railroad grade, a stone fence, a sunken road, or a building). Mahan insisted that the fortification, no matter of what type, should be effective as a physical barrier to the attacker and give an opportunity to the defender to use his weapons most effectively. He briefly outlined his concept of the active defense in the manual and stressed that any work should be defended "to the last extremity." Mahan provided detailed advice on how to attack and defend works. He recommended methods of overcoming the physical barrier of the ditch and parapet and advised that defending forces be packed in numbers behind a defensive work, with improvised grenades consisting of loaded and primed artillery shells handy to roll into an attacker if he gained the ditch.[16]

But the vast majority of his treatise is devoted to the detailed technical information needed to construct field fortifications. This information is thoroughly and clearly explained, demonstrating Mahan's mastery of the principles of military engineering. Mahan dissected the earthwork into its component parts and suggested how to make it most effective by building traverses and shaping the parapet to shield defending troops. He favored the construction of bastions in keeping with his attachment to historical French principles and provided a formula for determining how many men and guns would be needed to defend works of varied sizes. Mahan provided information on defending mountainous terrain and bridge crossings. He spent a great deal of time detailing the construction techniques for a wide range of what he called "interior arrangements" inside a fieldwork. Mahan paid attention to the different kinds of revetments engineers could build to hold up parapets and traverses. He described the various obstructions that could be placed in front of works to delay and frustrate the advance of an enemy force, what he called "accessory, or secondary means of defense." Mahan correctly defined these as "artificial obstacles, so arranged as to detain the enemy in a position where he will be greatly cut up by the fire of the work." Mahan detailed the duties of topographical officers and provided instructions for the conduct of military reconnaissance. His treatise offered field officers several options when constructing long trench lines that connected detached field fortifications. He also defined the differences between permanent fortifications and fieldworks and provided a succinct overview of siege operations.[17]

Since Mahan was the author of the most widely used manual on fortifications, his prominence in the theory and construction of fieldworks in America was assured. Several other men wrote manuals that had far less influence and more limited circulation. One manual writer, Egbert L. Viele, produced a fine volume titled *Hand-book for Active Service: Containing Practical Instructions in Campaign Duties, for the Use of Volunteers*. It was published in 1861, when the outbreak of war created an enlarged demand for such instructional books. Although derivative of Mahan's, Viele's book is detailed but insightful. Viele did not like redoubts configured in circular outlines, as they were more difficult to build and did not lend themselves easily to flank defenses. Yet, they "enclose a greater space than any other redoubt with an equal length of parapet." He did not like berms, the narrow ledge of natural earth left at the foot of the parapet to prevent the dirt from sliding back into the ditch. Viele correctly pointed out that this ledge could offer an attacker a foothold to get out of the ditch and up the outer slope of the parapet. He thought berms were unnecessary if the parapet was no more than eight feet tall or the quality of the dirt was "very adhesive." It was not necessary to ram the dirt of a parapet, thought Viele, as "loose earth resists the penetration of shot just as well." Like Mahan, Viele advocated the use of material to fill in the ditch when attacking a fort, but he also suggested the attacking force approach in column and then spread out into a line when it reached the ditch. Obstacles could be dismantled by the use of tools, and sharpshooters should be posted as close as possible to the enemy work to keep the defenders down. Viele even suggested that if the attack took place at night, the line of approach should be delineated with stakes and the men should wear distinguishable marks on their clothing to prevent confusion.[18]

Henry D. Grafton, a captain in the 1st U.S. Artillery, prepared and published his own manual titled *A Treatise on the Camp and March, With Which is Connected the Construction of Field Works and Military Bridges* in 1861. It also was a distillation of Mahan, but with fewer new insights and less detail. Grafton did, however, correctly note that fieldworks do not have to be geometrically correct, "for it is the ground upon which this work is to be situated that must determine the shape." Adhering to Mahan's theory of the active defense and the need to suit fieldworks to the quality of the American military force, Grafton suggested that a continuous line of trench between field forts would be best for raw troops. It offered more thorough protection as there were no breaks in the line, but it inhibited the possibility of following up a repulse with a counterattack. Grafton advocated placing veteran troops in a line with breaks in it so they would have greater freedom of movement on the battlefield.[19]

This incomplete survey of manuals represents a devolution from the best to the lesser. There was one manual specifically written for military engineers, and it was superb. Capt. James C. Duane published *Manual for Engineer Troops* in 1862. While Mahan dealt with the construction and use of field fortifications, Duane provided a manual to instruct the professional engineer. He divided his book into sections called Ponton Drill, Rules for Conducting a Siege, School of the Sap, Military Mining, and Construction of Batteries. The book is devoted exclusively to practical information, how to make and use things related to the profession of military engineering. Duane also provided detailed information about how to manage troops who dig works of all kinds.[20]

In terms of technical information about how to construct field fortifications, the prewar and Civil War officer was well served by the several manuals available. Theoretical and doctrinal instruction about the relationship between fieldworks and the operations of field armies, however, was extremely meager. Many of Mahan's and Viele's suggestions about how armies should use field fortifications were unrealistic, based as they were on theories untested on the battlefield. Improvisation, therefore, would play as great a role in determining the conduct of operations as suggestions found in the manuals. While these books provided essential information of a technical nature, they had little impact on directing commanders who had to use fieldworks either offensively or defensively.

Yankee Engineers

The Corps of Engineers and the Corps of Topographical Engineers, like the rest of the U.S. army, were woefully unprepared to fight the Civil War. There were only forty-eight officers in the Corps of Engineers, and eight of them resigned at the outbreak of war. More than half the officers in the corps were on duty at coastal forts, and several were at various locations attending to administrative duties or public works projects. The lone engineer company was mostly at West Point training cadets, except a detachment of thirty men that was working on the Pacific coast. The Corps of Topographical

Engineers had only forty-five officers, who were scattered around the country, and no enlisted men.[21]

Efforts were immediately made to enlarge the size of both corps, but Congress hesitated due to financial constraints; engineers, both officers and enlisted men, received a higher rate of pay than other soldiers. But the shock of First Bull Run convinced congressmen that this was going to be a longer, more complicated war than imagined. The legislature authorized six new officers in each corps and three additional companies of enlisted engineers, plus a company of enlisted men for the Topographical Engineers. Congress, however, refused to authorize the officers to hold commissions at higher ranks. As a result, the engineers would constantly feel embarrassed at holding positions of great importance in the huge field armies while having commissions that reflected service in the tiny prewar army.

Officers were barely able to recruit enough troops to make up the additional engineer companies. Company A had been created in May 1846, at the start of the Mexican War, although engineer troops had been organized for both the War of Independence and the War of 1812, only to be disbanded when no longer needed. Company B was recruited in Portland, Maine; Company C was formed in Boston; and Company D was created in 1862 by transferring men from Companies A, B, and C. In the field, these four companies were designated the U.S. Engineer Battalion. The one company of enlisted men authorized for the topographical engineers, however, never materialized.[22]

The Engineer Battalion was used mostly to construct bridges and roads, although in a few cases it was pressed into duty on the battle line as infantry. As historian Philip Shiman has noted, it was "merely a collection of companies" without proper staff officers. This put pressure on company officers, who had to assume staff duties for the daily administration of the battalion. Since service in the battalion offered little chance of promotion, it did not appeal to ambitious engineer officers, who preferred positions on the staffs of corps and army leaders. Starting with Capt. James C. Duane, the battalion had six commanders during the war, and a total of twenty officers saw service as commanders of its four companies. In addition, the battalion hardly ever filled its ranks. By late 1863 it had less than half its authorized strength.[23]

Ambitious engineer officers also sought commissions in volunteer regiments as a way to gain higher rank, more pay, and greater opportunities for fame. Many of them even tried to retain their commissions in the Corps of Engineers to ensure they would have a place in the army when the volunteers were disbanded. The chief engineer resisted this ploy because it would have prevented him from having a full complement of working engineers. The small size of the corps and the drain of its few officers to other duties created a constant need for more trained engineers. Reluctantly, the corps tried to address this by hiring civil engineers on contract. Their training often was haphazard, mostly acquired on the job in civilian life, and thus an affront to the high sense of professionalism that characterized the Corps of Engineers. But necessity dictated tolerance, and the civilians were often hired to work on less vital installations far behind the lines.[24]

Brig. Gen. Joseph G. Totten ably headed the Corps of Engineers during the first three years of the war. Seventy-three years old when the war broke out, he had been the tenth graduate of the U.S. Military Academy in 1805. Totten had served in the War of 1812 and was chief engineer at the siege of Vera Cruz in the Mexican War. He had headed the corps since December 7, 1838, and his chief concern was the construction and maintenance of the coastal forts. During the war, he sought to maintain the administrative independence of the corps. He effectively ran the engineering establishment until pneumonia suddenly took his life on April 22, 1864.[25]

The Corps of Topographical Engineers, however, did not maintain its administrative independence. Col. John J. Abert, seventy-two years old when the war started, was well past his prime. A graduate of the West Point class of 1811 and a veteran of the battle of Bladensburg in the War of 1812, he retired on September 9, 1861. Yet his replacement, Col. Stephen H. Long, was unable to handle the demands made on his understaffed agency by the war. The maps on file when the war broke out were relevant mostly to coastal defense and frontier exploration, not to conducting major campaigns into the southern states, and the agency's officers often were drawn off to a variety of engineering duties other than cartography. The corps also failed to recruit the one company of enlisted men Congress had authorized in August 1861.[26]

Merging the two corps into one and pooling their available manpower and resources seemed to be the best solution. McClellan strongly urged this course of action in the middle of his Peninsula campaign. He had a number of engineer vacancies to fill in the Army of the Potomac and constantly had to deny the request of officers in the Engineer Battalion for commissions in volunteer regiments. Merging the two corps would add a substantial number of new engineer officers to the available pool of candidates. He called the situation "embarrassing" and noted that his engineer officers were badly overworked. Totten resisted the merger. He thought topographers were not true engineers and that adding them to his beloved corps would dilute its effectiveness. But most younger subordinates of both corps strongly supported the merger. Congress finally abolished the Corps of Topographical

Engineers on March 3, 1863. It also created a new rank, brigadier general, for the head of the enlarged Corps of Engineers. Higher ranks were opened for subordinate officers, too, including four colonels, ten lieutenant colonels, twenty majors, thirty captains, and forty lieutenants. Although 105 officers were authorized in the corps, it seldom had the opportunity to fill every slot with qualified men.[27]

The record of these Federal engineer officers was superb. They performed their varied tasks admirably, displaying a high degree of professionalism that often was sorely lacking in the volunteer service. Their duties while serving on the staffs of field units included scouting terrain, drawing road maps, locating campsites, and directing subordinate units along prescribed routes of march. When needed, they laid out lines of fieldworks and supervised the digging by infantrymen.

As the primary field army in the East, the Army of the Potomac enjoyed first choice in allocation of engineer officers. John Gross Barnard was its first chief engineer. Born in Massachusetts in 1815, he graduated second in the West Point class of 1833 and gained wide experience in varied construction projects before the war. He was given a commission as brigadier general of volunteers in September 1861 and ably directed the construction of the Washington defenses. His astute handling of engineering tasks in the Peninsula campaign was fully documented in his report, which could easily have served as a model for how engineer officers should record their activities.

Barnard was McClellan's chief engineer from the summer of 1861 to August 1862, but his place was filled by equally capable officers. Cyrus Ballou Comstock, although holding rank as lieutenant and captain and hindered by sporadic bouts of illness, served as chief engineer in late 1862 under Ambrose E. Burnside and in early 1863 under Joseph Hooker. Gouverneur K. Warren held the post in the summer of 1863 under George G. Meade, while James Chatham Duane ably filled it from October 1863 until the end of the war.[28]

Despite efforts to keep the engineer officers devoted to their duties, many of them obtained commissions in the volunteer service and commanded troops in battle. While some led regiments, a total of thirty-three engineer officers or former members of the Corps of Engineers held commissions as generals. Eight of them commanded field armies, and ten led corps. In contrast, eight Confederate generals had formerly been officers in the U.S. Corps of Engineers. All told, eleven engineer officers or former members of the U.S. Corps of Engineers were killed in battle.[29]

While the needs of the Army of the Potomac were met by its overworked engineer officers, the same cannot be said of the army's meager contingent of regular engineer troops. Congress had not authorized enough of them.

These four companies were supplemented with volunteer units that were recruited for engineer duties. At first this was resisted by Congress, which did not want to spend the extra money engineers normally received. State governments took it upon themselves to raise these units, and Congress finally agreed to accept them in October 1861. Three regiments and a company served, although the men did not receive the extra pay normally accorded engineers. The 1st New York Engineers was raised in New York City and was led by English-born Col. Edward W. Serrell. It served primarily along the Atlantic coast during the first half of the war. The 15th New York Engineers and the 50th New York Engineers constituted the Volunteer Engineer Brigade in McClellan's Army of the Potomac. A company of engineers was raised in Pennsylvania in the summer of 1862. It worked on the defenses of Washington, D.C., and later on the bridges at Harpers Ferry. The Pennsylvanians remained in service, obscurely, until June 1865. Another regiment, the 2nd New York Engineers, was authorized but never fully recruited. Its men were transferred to the 15th New York Engineers in October 1863.[30]

The volunteers attached to the Army of the Potomac did superb duty in the field. They greatly outnumbered the small regular engineer companies and were instructed by them in the technical aspects of their specialized duties. The Volunteer Engineer Brigade was led by Brig. Gen. Daniel P. Woodbury, a forty-nine-year-old graduate of West Point who had served in the Corps of Engineers before the war. He had been a topographical engineer at First Bull Run before promotion to his general's rank. Woodbury commanded the volunteers until his transfer to Key West, Florida, in March 1863. He was replaced by Brig. Gen. Henry W. Benham, who also had served in the Corps of Engineers after his graduation from West Point. Benham was a good engineer but had little facility for commanding troops. He demonstrated both traits in the Western Virginia campaigns of 1861, earning enough recognition to achieve promotion to brigadier general. But his handling of men in the battle of Secessionville, near Charleston, in the early summer of 1862 left a great deal to be desired. He was relegated to engineer duties and then given Woodbury's brigade. Benham led it as an administrator; he never accompanied it under fire to act as infantry in battle and thus turned in a respectable performance throughout the remainder of the war.[31]

In addition to the volunteer regiments raised as engineers, field commanders sometimes assigned line units to a specific engineering project or designated them to devote their energies toward engineering work for a given length of time. McClellan dedicated the 5th New Hampshire, 64th New York, and parts of the Irish Brigade to bridge building on the Chickahominy River during the Peninsula campaign. This sort of duty was given line units more frequently in the western armies, where there were far fewer engineer troops and a great deal more work to be done as well.[32]

In addition to the regular and volunteer engineer units, and the line units dedicated to engineer duties, commanders of the Army of the Potomac organized detachments of pioneers at least as far down the chain of command as the division level. These company-sized units consisted of men detailed from the ranks and were used mostly to remove obstructions and repair roads during a campaign. The pioneers also buried the dead after an engagement, although there were too few of them to complete the job after a major fight. At times black laborers were hired to do pioneer work as well.[33]

There sometimes seemed to be less distinction between engineer troops and line units than one would think. When one considers the varied amounts of engineering work to be done for a field army, either in camp or on the move, the number of engineer troops was far too small. One veteran estimated that details from infantry units performed most of the engineer work of the army; only about one-fifth of it was done by the organized engineer units. Only tasks that demanded specialized skills, such as pontoon work and laying out major forts, had to be done by the engineers. Other tasks, such as building small bridges and laying out simple earthworks, could either be improvised by experienced amateurs in the ranks or be directed by engineers who quickly gave directions and then went off to other duties. In an army with few trained specialists, improvisation was a common mode of operation.[34]

The engineer troops sometimes lent a hand in fighting as well, although their specialized skills meant that field commanders pushed them into harm's way only reluctantly, and then for short periods of time. The U.S. Engineer Battalion acted as infantry at Malvern Hill and in the Union advance to Shepherdstown following the battle of Antietam. It guarded Westminster, Maryland, against Confederate cavalry during the Gettysburg campaign. These few experiences, however, did not allow the engineer troops to gain a battle record, for they were brief and did not result in significant fighting. Fortunately for the sake of the engineering establishment, these troops were only used in emergencies to fill space until other troops could be brought up. They were far too valuable and few in number to waste as combat troops.[35]

Rebel Engineers

Stonewall Jackson believed that the Yankee engineers were better than the Rebel engineers. They had, he believed, found a gap in the Confederate line at the battles of Groveton and Fredericksburg. This offhand opinion, given to his topographical engineer in April 1863, indicates only one thing:

Jackson was tightly focused on what the engineers could do for him on the battlefield. Combat engineering hardly existed in the 1860s, at least when compared with what it would become by World War II. The vast majority of an engineer's labor in the Civil War was devoted to support services rather than aiding line units to find better ways to attack the enemy on the battlefield.[36]

Jackson failed to give the Rebel engineers their due. The truth was that Confederate engineers were every bit as competent and knowledgeable as their Northern counterparts, and they served the needs of Rebel field armies equally well. The Confederates received a few engineers at the start of the war when eight of the officers in the Corps of Engineers resigned; Maj. G. T. Beauregard was the most prominent of them. Seven officers from the Corps of Topographical Engineers also resigned. Each of them received commissions one or two ranks higher in the Confederate army.[37]

The Confederate government created a Corps of Engineers on March 7, 1861, consisting of five captains, four majors, and a colonel, with a company of sappers, miners, and pontoniers. Skimpy even for a peacetime establishment, it was less than adequate to meet the demands of war. Congress increased the corps in May 1861 by adding a lieutenant colonel, five more captains, and one more company of sappers and bombardiers. That brought the total number to twenty officers and 200 enlisted men, still far too few to meet the needs of Confederate field armies. In addition, Congress allowed a meager budget for the Engineer Bureau, which was created within the War Department to handle the administrative needs of the officers and troops. It received $1 million in September 1861, compared with $3.5 million for the Ordnance Bureau and $12 million for the Commissary General's Office.[38]

The officers who filled available slots in the Confederate Corps of Engineers were, like their Union counterparts, West Point graduates. The ranking engineer, Maj. William H. C. Whiting, was too busy in the field to run the bureau. After achieving the highest set of grades ever accumulated at West Point, Whiting served in the U.S. Corps of Engineers until Fort Sumter led him to resign. He was chief engineer in Gen. Joseph E. Johnston's army and facilitated its transfer from the Shenandoah Valley to victory at First Manassas. In his absence from Richmond, Maj. Josiah Gorgas, chief of ordnance, was expected to double as chief engineer. He disliked this assignment because it took too much attention from his ordnance duties.[39]

Whiting was promoted to brigadier general and given field command after First Manassas, opening the way for a permanent replacement as head of the Engineer Bureau. Maj. Danville Leadbetter was chosen. Graduating third in his West Point class of 1836, Leadbetter had served in the U.S. Corps of Engineers until he resigned in 1857 to become chief engineer of the state of Alabama. He took charge of the bureau on August 3, 1861, but led it for only three months. An uprising by Unionists in eastern Tennessee led to the burning of several railroad bridges, and he was sent to oversee their reconstruction on November 13, 1861.[40]

Capt. Alfred L. Rives filled in as temporary head of the bureau for the next ten months. He was thirty-one years old and had an impeccable resume. Born in France, he had attended the University of Virginia, Virginia Military Institute, and the Ecole Polytechnique in Paris when his father served as U.S. ambassador to France. He later was assistant engineer to Montgomery C. Meigs in construction work on the U.S. Capitol and entered the Virginia state engineers at the outbreak of war. There he served as assistant chief and, later, chief of engineers.[41]

As temporary head of the Confederate Engineer Bureau, Rives scrambled to meet the growing needs of his officers. The bureau contracted with private firms to manufacture a variety of equipment, especially shovels and other entrenching tools. It established workshops at Richmond, Charleston, Augusta, Mobile, and Demopolis to make as much of its own equipment as possible. When necessary, the bureau sent agents through the blockade to Europe to purchase "intrenching tools, technical books, and surveying and drafting equipment." Like many other departments and bureaus in the Confederate government, the Engineer Bureau had to be creative in its endeavors to supply the Southern war effort.[42]

Rives also was burdened by a number of applications from men who sought transfer from state engineer forces to the Confederate service. Secretary of War Judah P. Benjamin proposed they be accepted in a Provisional Corps of Engineers. Their services were too valuable to ignore, yet the government cringed at the thought of enlarging the permanent engineering establishment. The provisional corps, which was authorized by Congress in December 1861, was intended to exist only for the duration of the war. It had room for fifty officers, but at no rank higher than captain. The positions were filled by March 1862. The next month the number of slots was doubled, and ranks higher than captain were opened by the end of 1862.[43]

Benjamin persuaded the Confederate Congress to authorize the provisional corps by arguing that a number of civil engineers who were working as hired employees of the government deserved a chance at promotion. These were men "educated for scientific pursuits, not military engineers by profession, but whose services it has been indispensable to secure for engineering purposes." The Confederates were not so fastidious about utilizing the skills of civil engineers as the Federals. Lt. Claudius B. Denson praised the "hardy civil engineers" who came into the provisional corps. Their prewar experience "in building the railroads, water works, and similar internal improvements" had been good preparation for military engineering duties.[44]

Rives needed the extra help offered by the enlarged provisional corps, for the Confederate bureau became fully responsible for all fortifications previously under the charge of Virginia state engineers in November 1861. The state authorities in Richmond had created an army, the Virginia Forces, in April 1861. It included a sizable corps of engineers headed by Col. Andrew Talcott. Sixty-four years old and a graduate of the West Point class of 1818, Talcott had extensive military and civil engineering experience before the war. He laid out the works at Yorktown, Jamestown Island, and Gloucester Point. He also supervised three topographical survey parties to map the area around Richmond and began the Inner Line of defenses around that city. North and South Carolina had also created state engineer corps in 1861 to work on defenses within their boundaries. State engineers from all three states obtained commissions as engineers in the Provisional Army, Confederate States. When the state defenses were handed over to Rives's bureau, all paperwork also was shifted to his office.[45]

Rives's tenure was meant to be temporary. His permanent replacement was Lt. Col. Jeremy F. Gilmer, who would run the bureau for the remainder of the war. Gilmer was a solid engineer and a keen administrator, but he came to the bureau in a roundabout way. Forty-four years old when he assumed his position, he had graduated among the top five of his West Point class of 1839. He served in the Corps of Engineers and taught at the academy for a time. Gilmer worked at a variety of posts, was aide to engineer chief Totten, and served in the Mexican War. He saw service in Virginia in 1861 but then transferred to the West and was involved in the Fort Henry and Fort Donelson campaigns. Gilmer was Gen. Albert S. Johnston's chief engineer at Shiloh, where he was wounded. After recuperating, he reported for duty in August 1862. Lee wanted him to head the Engineer Bureau, but Gilmer persuaded the general to appoint him chief engineer of the Army of Northern Virginia, succeeding Maj. Walter H. Stevens.

The appointment never worked out. When Lee launched his Second Manassas campaign, he left Gilmer behind to supervise the construction of the Richmond defenses. Poor health frustrated his desire to engage in an active campaign, but Gilmer insisted on promotion to colonel before he would consent to head the bureau. President Jefferson Davis agreed, and he was named the new chief on September 25, 1862.[46]

Gilmer threw his energy into the job of revitalizing the engineering establishment. The bureau had barely managed to fulfill its role in the war effort thus far. Leadbetter and Rives were well-trained engineers but not good administrators. During his brief tenure, Leadbetter paid attention mostly to the coastal forts at Mobile. Rives tried very hard to do his job right but was limited by his own youth and lack of experience, as well as by the scant resources allocated him by Congress. His advice to engineers regarding field fortifications tended to be unrealistic; he often advocated detached works, or simple trenches that were ill suited to the topography of a given area. Also, as a scion of an old Virginia family, Rives paid almost no attention to any area outside that state. He made the bureau a regional, not a national, institution. His outgoing correspondence as temporary bureau head reveals a young man barely able to cope, scrambling to patch together mediocre solutions to problems and deflecting complaints about bureau inefficiency.

Gilmer brought much-needed maturity and professional experience to the job. He set out to increase the budget, selected the best men for available positions, sent letters filled with sound advice on field fortifications to subordinates, and served effectively as a spokesman for engineering concerns with the War Department and Congress. He was the indispensable man of the Rebel engineering establishment, and he transformed the bureau into an institution of national importance.[47]

Beefing up the ranks of the Engineer Corps was a high priority for Gilmer. He pushed for more officers and complained that many of the provisional engineers were not worth their pay. Twenty-four of the 100 officers were "worthless sons of broken down Virginia families," and 20 others belonged to South Carolina families of similar station. The exacting Gilmer found only 20 others who could "lay any claims to be called engineers." He wanted to enlarge the number of regular engineers allowed by Congress to compensate for this weakness, telling his wife that he hoped to recruit "a few more proper men who can do something."[48]

Gilmer was prepared to turn down ineffective applicants and to pursue men of worth. Capt. George W. C. Lee, Robert E. Lee's oldest son, did not want to give up his slot in the engineers even though he sought a field command. Gilmer refused to go along with this plan. George Gilmer Hull, his brother-in-law, applied for a commission in the engineers based on his experience as manager of the Atlanta and West Point Railroad. Gilmer turned him down. Col. Walter Gwynn applied for a commission as lieutenant colonel in the corps, "but we are a little afraid to trust him," Gilmer told his wife; "*he takes to[o] many drinks each day.*" Gilmer liked Lemuel P. Grant and George H. Hazlehurst and offered them captaincies in the corps. "We want all the intelligent help we can get," Gilmer told Grant. "The common man of the South is willing to expose his life for our independence, which we will certainly secure, if the willing efforts of the masses can be guided and assisted by the intellectual & professional men of the land. Intelligence and proud spirit will make any people free." Both Grant and Hazlehurst accepted.[49]

In addition to staffing the corps, Gilmer managed an increasingly large budget. The Engineer Bureau was allotted $10.5 million for 1863 and $20 million for 1864. In addition to the 100 officers in the provisional corps, he persuaded Congress to increase the number of regular engineers to 120 officers. He issued General Orders No. 90 on June 26, 1863, clearly spelling out the responsibilities of engineers in the field. Gilmer even was given a chance to engage in field duty. The president authorized him to help Beauregard defend Charleston in August 1863 and promoted him to major general. For a time he served as second-in-command of the Department of South Carolina, Georgia, and Florida. In his absence, Rives again acted as chief of the bureau until Maj. Gen. Martin L. Smith became available for duty and replaced him as acting chief. When Smith took over as chief engineer of Lee's army in 1864, Gilmer finally returned to Richmond after an absence of ten months.[50]

The Confederates never had a separate corps of topographers; its work was done by any available engineer. A map bureau, headed by Capt. Albert H. Campbell of the provisional engineers, was created in Richmond for the Army of Northern Virginia. Campbell relied on sketch maps and field notes supplied by men engaged in survey duty but did not have adequate information to provide useful maps for Lee during the Seven Days campaign. He received several assistants after that and a pile of much-needed tracing paper that Lee's army had captured in the campaign. By the end of 1862, Campbell had produced a number of good maps, mostly of Virginia counties. To resupply his wants, he sent an officer through the blockade to England to buy India ink, watercolors, drawing paper, pens, and pencils.[51]

The Confederate engineer officers struggled against many problems. In the early months of the war, Rives had to piece together an engineer component for the main Confederate army in the East. The young bureaucrat assured Joseph E. Johnston in February 1862 that his Army of Northern Virginia had gotten all the engineer officers he could find. Rives listed sixteen men he had sent to the army in the preceding months. Half were officers in the Provisional Army, Confederate States, and the rest detailed from artillery service, ordnance and quartermaster duties, and the staffs of other commanders. One even was an artillery private. All of the nonengineers had some previous engineer experience and could learn quickly on the job.[52]

Rives admitted to Johnston that he had difficulty finding someone qualified to serve as his chief engineer. He suggested detailing a brigade leader,
such as Robert E. Rodes, to fill that role. Eventually, two men would shoulder
the task of directing Lee's engineer operations during the first half of the war.
Walter Husted Stevens, born in Penn Yan, New York, in 1827, graduated
fourth in the class of 1848 at West Point. He was commissioned in the U.S.
Engineers and married the sister of future Confederate general Louis Hébert.
Stevens was an engineer officer on Beauregard's staff at First Manassas and
later served as acting chief engineer for Johnston. When Lee took over the
Army of Northern Virginia, Stevens was put in charge of constructing the
Richmond defenses. He served as Lee's chief engineer in the summer of 1862
before spending the next two years on the Richmond works. William Proctor
Smith was born in Virginia in 1833 and graduated from West Point in 1857.
He became a lieutenant in the U.S. Topographical Corps. Smith entered
Virginia state service as an engineer officer and then became a Confederate
artillery officer. He saw service in North Carolina before transferring to the
Army of Northern Virginia in June 1862. Promoted to the rank of lieutenant
colonel in the Confederate Corps of Engineers, Smith was working on the
Richmond defenses when Lee named him his chief engineer on April 9, 1863.
He served in that capacity until April 1864.[53]

The Confederate Congress allowed for an engineer officer to serve on the
staff of each division in the army, but brigade commanders had to borrow
division officers or work around the regulations by taking on volunteer aides
as engineers or by detailing line officers who had some experience in civil
engineering. A total of seventy-five men served as engineer officers on various staffs in the Army of Northern Virginia during the Civil War. John B.
Magruder had eleven, more than anyone else, while Lee had only five. Sixteen percent of the engineer staff officers in the army had attended West
Point; 37 percent had a university education; only .09 percent had attended
state military schools; 24 percent had experience as civil engineers before
the war; and 13 percent had no evidence of training or prewar civil experience. Engineers represented only .03 percent of the 2,284 staff officers who
served in the Army of Northern Virginia.[54]

The Confederates put a great deal of energy into collecting an impressive
number of engineer officers, but they failed to move forward on recruiting
engineer troops until the midpoint of the war. Two companies of sappers and
miners had been authorized for the Virginia Forces, but they were never
organized. At that stage of the war, Lee felt that the duties of engineer troops
were so specialized that recruits with experience in "ordinary mining &

excavation" were not qualified. A company of sappers and miners was created by the Confederate government in 1861, but this was far too little to meet the army's needs. Gilmer initially suggested the creation of a company to work on roads and bridges for the Army of Northern Virginia in October 1862 and then forwarded a more ambitious proposal in December 1862. He envisioned four engineer regiments: one to serve the Army of Northern Virginia, one to operate in middle and eastern Tennessee, one to serve the Mississippi Valley, and the last to work on the Gulf and Atlantic coast. The men could be recruited from the ranks of infantry regiments.[55]

Congress finally approved on March 29, 1863, and the Adjutant and Inspector General's Office issued General Orders No. 66 on May 22 to begin recruiting. The regiments were to be officered by men already holding commissions in the engineer corps or to line officers who had some engineering experience. Two companies in each regiment were to be trained as pontoniers, and there were to be forty artificers and forty-five laborers in the ranks of all other companies. Artificers were defined as carpenters, bricklayers, stonemasons, and cabinetmakers. Each company was to be recruited from a single division.[56]

The recruiting process went quickly in some units but met resistance in others. On July 17, 1863, Lee decided to stop recruiting engineer troops in his army, following his heavy losses at Gettysburg. He felt he could not spare men from the ranks. Lee also feared the creation of the engineer regiment would drain men from his existing pioneer companies. Secretary of War James A. Seddon refused to give up on the engineer regiments. He proposed that only fifty men be taken from each of Lee's divisions, while conscripts could be used to fill up the remaining positions in the new regiments. Seddon sweetened the deal by promising to supply more conscripts for Lee's army as well. This was an acceptable compromise, and Lee even agreed to promote Maj. Thomas Mann Randolph Talcott of his staff to colonel so he could command the regiment. The Adjutant and Inspector General's Office issued an order on July 28, 1863, outlining the duties of these new engineer regiments, and recruiting resumed. Talcott's 1st Engineer Regiment established a camp of instruction near Richmond that winter and reported to Lee for duty on April 12, 1864.[57]

The engineer regiments were never meant to duplicate the work of the existing pioneer troops. Units of pioneers had been around for some time. Robert E. Rodes's Alabama brigade of the Army of Northern Virginia had a "pioneer party" in each regiment as early as May 1862. Rodes was careful to select men with carpentry or ax skills whenever possible. The detailed men were told to do the normal duties of all men in the ranks whenever they were not performing pioneer duties. These units apparently were organized informally by individual brigade leaders. Secretary of War Seddon recommended to Davis on January 3, 1863, that the practice be institutionalized by creating a company for each brigade. Their task was to take care of any problems with roads and bridges to facilitate marching during campaigns. It was a good idea and was quickly implemented in Lee's army, where a company was created for each division rather than each brigade.[58]

Just as in the Federal army, most of the work of constructing fortifications in the Confederacy was done by infantry units. The engineers were responsible for laying out lines, or at least for selecting where lines should be laid out if there was little time available. Work on major and complex forts was reserved for engineer officers and troops. Black laborers were used mostly to construct semipermanent works around cities or other fixed assets, and even then they were not a reliable source of labor. Owners were reluctant to provide them because they had no control over how the slave was treated on the job. Coming from their isolated lives on the plantation, the blacks often fell victim to communicable diseases, and the army cared for them with no more attention than it treated its own soldiers. Owners also did not like to lose the services of their slaves, especially during planting and harvesting seasons.

The Confederate government tried to utilize this source of labor for work on fortifications as much as possible. Black men, both slave and free, were impressed early in the war, but Congress did not create regulations to govern the process until March 1863. It allowed for slaves to be drafted by the government for sixty days, with an additional thirty days added as punishment if the planter delayed in producing the laborers. Owners were allowed to send overseers, but the government had complete authority over the workers. Planters were paid twenty dollars per month for each slave they sent. In one of several sporadic attempts to utilize this labor source, President Davis authorized the secretary of war to hire or press as many as 20,000 slaves in February 1864. Owners were to be compensated if the slave was injured or died. Congress, in fact, appropriated well more than $3 million in early 1864 for that purpose. Each state was allocated a percentage of the 20,000 workers as its quota. While the Conscript Bureau was responsible for mobilizing this labor force, the Engineer Bureau was responsible for organizing the slaves into gangs and putting them to work. The implementation of this plan brought thousands of black laborers to fortification sites at Richmond and Atlanta, and in a more systematic way than in the past, but it was very unpopular. The impressment of slaves caused so much resentment that several state officials refused to cooperate.[59]

Geography of the Eastern Campaigns

The theater of operations in the East was mostly confined to the 100-mile space that separated Richmond from Washington, D.C. On only two occasions did the opposing armies venture out of this box: when Lee invaded Maryland in September 1862 and Pennsylvania in June 1863. There were a number of subsidiary campaigns in the Shenandoah Valley, in eastern North Carolina and southeastern Virginia, and along the coast of South Carolina. But the heart of the eastern campaigns took place in a relatively small arena, often traversing the same ground fought over in previous movements.

The theater of operations was divided into three geographic regions. The Atlantic Coastal Plain, or Tidewater, stretched along the coast. It was flat, sandy ground that supported the earliest settlements in Southern colonial history. At the time of the Civil War, the region had long since given up its economic and political dominance, but it was still the location of numerous large plantations and fine old mansions. The Coastal Plain constitutes 25 percent of the land mass of Virginia, averaging 100 miles wide. It rises from sea level to 300 feet in elevation. The soil is a mixture of sand and clay that supports a forest cover of mostly pine and cedar. The subsurface rock formations were created by erosional runoff from the Piedmont and other land areas to the west and then uplifted by the movement of the earth's crust. The uplift was uneven, making the Coastal Plain much wider in the southern states than in New England. In contrast, Chesapeake Bay, the largest embayment on the North American coast, was formed by submergence instead of uplift. This area had been drained by the Susquehanna River, which flowed all the way to the ocean near modern-day Norfolk, Virginia. The James, Potomac, and Rappahannock rivers had all drained into the Susquehanna. When the large area around the lower part of the river subsided, Chesapeake Bay was formed, and those three rivers drained into it.[60]

The next land area to the west is the Piedmont. The word "piedmont" means "at the foot of the mountains." The border between the Coastal Plain and the Piedmont is known in Virginia as the Fall Line, and it stretches from Washington, D.C. to Fredericksburg, Richmond, and Petersburg. The Fall Line is four to ten miles wide and includes, as the name implies, a number of waterfalls on the streams that cross it. Settlers planted towns along the Fall Line because it was a natural line of demarcation. Boats ascending the rivers from Chesapeake Bay could not proceed farther upstream. The Fall Line also provided a natural axis for the Virginia campaigns, as it directly linked the two opposing capitals.

The Piedmont covers about one-third of Virginia and averages elevations of 300 to 500 feet along the Fall Line. At the western edge elevations are 800 to 1,200 feet. That part of the Piedmont lying south of the James River is called the Southside. The tree cover across the Piedmont tends to be more oak than pine or cedar. The underlying rock strata are much older than that of the Coastal Plain and originally were marine sediments. The Piedmont has been exposed to weathering for more than 200 million years.[61]

The Blue Ridge constitutes the border between the Piedmont and the Appalachian Highlands. It is twelve to fourteen miles wide and has peaks that reach elevations of 4,000 feet. The ridge tends to get wider and higher south of Roanoke, Virginia. The ridge apparently was not formed by uplift; it has a particularly resistant layer of subsurface rocks and thus eroded more slowly than the land around it.

The same is true of the many ridges that dominate the Great Valley of Virginia, of which the Shenandoah Valley is a part. The weaker sedimentary layers that underlay the valleys allowed faster erosion. Limestone and shale lay under the valleys, and stronger sandstone and conglomerate support the ridges. The Valley of Virginia starts at the Potomac River and stretches to the Tennessee border. Some twenty miles wide at its mouth, the valley narrows to about five miles as one travels south. The Valley of Virginia is subdivided into six separate valleys. The Shenandoah Valley is the largest and most important, stretching from Harpers Ferry to Botetourt County south of Lexington. Massanutten Mountain runs through the valley for fifty miles as a high, dominating ridge. The other five valleys are smaller and are located in the south, out of the region of most Civil War campaigning. They include Fincastle Valley, Roanoke Valley, New River Valley, Holston Valley, and Clinch Valley. The ground in these regions is mostly fertile grassland produced from the decayed limestone that underlaid the topsoil.[62]

The western border of the Valley of Virginia is the Appalachian Plateau, which is the beginning of a much more expansive feature called the Appalachian Highlands. The plateau has layers of sedimentary formations under its surface that tilt toward the west. This means that the eastern edge of the plateau stands at a sharper angle than the western side. Elevations on the plateau are as high as 4,000 feet.[63]

Military operations in the East from 1861 to 1864 were concentrated in one or two regions. The Fall Line was the scene of many major battles, including Fredericksburg and Chancellorsville. The Coastal Plain also was traversed by several campaigns and witnessed fighting at Yorktown, Seven Pines, and the Seven Days. The Piedmont tended to be the scene of fewer operations because it drew invading Union armies away from Richmond, while the Shenandoah Valley saw a series of campaigns designed to distract Federal forces in the spring of 1862. The Confederate invasions of Maryland

and Pennsylvania took place in the western reaches of the Piedmont. The differing soils, tree cover, road conditions, and availability of clean water all had an effect on the nature of campaigning in the East.

Engineers could not take care of such problems, but they could and generally did facilitate the movement of field armies and enabled them to operate more effectively in the eastern theater. There was a strong tendency for both the Army of the Potomac and the Army of Northern Virginia to draw more engineering resources than any other field armies, and nowhere else can one see such a concentration of talent and numbers as in Virginia and surrounding areas.

2 : On to Richmond

lthough fighting with improvised armies, the field commanders of the Civil War often recognized the value of fortifications. At Big Bethel, First Manassas, and Ball's Bluff, field fortifications were used in peripheral ways that often had little impact on the outcome of the battles, yet field armies dug in deeper and more widely after each engagement. The capital cities of the opposing sides were ringed with the beginnings of massive earthworks designed to protect the political and administrative centers of the Union and Confederate war efforts. Even along the Atlantic seacoast, fortifications came to play a role in combined operations designed to close blockade-running ports and open the door to future Union incursions on the edges of Confederate soil.

Big Bethel

One of the first battles of the war occurred near Big Bethel, a rural church on the Yorktown Peninsula. The Federals had retained control of Fortress Monroe on the tip of the Peninsula after Virginia seceded from the Union on April 17. Monroe was one of three forts in the seceded states still under Union control. It was strategically located to serve as a jumping-off place for an advance up the Peninsula to Richmond. Such an attempt would be made by McClellan the following spring. In May 1861, Maj. Gen. Benjamin F. Butler occupied the post with a small garrison and easily controlled Hampton and Newport News as well.

The Confederates shifted troops to Yorktown, halfway up the Peninsula and the site of the American victory that had brought the Revolution to a close in 1781. Col. Daniel Harvey Hill's 1st North Carolina (six months) reached Yorktown on May 25 and began to dig in. "We worked all night throwing up fortifications," Hill wrote his wife, and "are now in a very strong position and I have not the slightest uneasiness." His men dug along the most advantageous ground outside town, which happened to be the same spot where Lord Cornwallis had planted his own works eighty years earlier. The British earthworks that protected the town were reworked and incorporated into Hill's new line. The diggers uncovered "human bones, powder, cartridges, bombshells," and other relics of the Revolution, according to Lewis Warlick of Hill's regiment. The Tar Heels dug day and night, a novel occupation for many of them. "We do all this work ourselves," bragged Francis Marion Parker, "have no negroes to help us; our boys say they intend going to ditching when they get back home; that they are getting to be experts at handling the shovel and spade. It goes right tough with some, who have never been used to any thing of the kind before." Soon the Rebels had a strong position that Hill was certain could withstand attacks by 10,000 Yankees.[1]

Hill led the 1st North Carolina to a forward post at Big Bethel, some thirteen miles from Yorktown and eight miles from Hampton, on June 6. Here the road between the two towns crossed the northwest branch of Back River. Hill built a mile-long infantry trench and placed a redoubt just south of the line to cover the bridge that crossed the branch. This redoubt was an enclosed artillery emplacement that also accommodated firing positions for infantry. It was designed by both Hill and Lt. Col. Charles C. Lee of the 1st North Carolina and was constructed on the night of June 7 and all day on June 8. The regiment had only twenty-five spades, six axes, and three picks. Two spots forward of the main position were fortified for artillery, one for a single gun to cover the right flank. The land around Big Bethel is flat, but the northwest branch of Back River forms a valley 150 yards wide just south of the redoubt. The Tar Heels, positioned mostly in the work, could easily cover the bridge with their fire. Col. John B. Magruder arrived on June 8 to take command of the Rebel forces, bringing with him several companies of Virginia infantry, cavalry, and some guns.[2]

Butler decided to eliminate this outpost, even though he knew it was well fortified. Among other reasons, he wanted to prevent the Confederates from rounding up slaves to work on the defenses of Yorktown. Butler sent 3,500 men and two guns under Brig. Gen. Ebenezer W. Pierce toward Big Bethel on the night of June 9. Magruder had 1,800 men and five guns to defend the position. The Yankee approach led to some hasty entrenchment by the 3rd Virginia, which was placed to cover Magruder's right. The men "worked with great rapidity," according to Hill, "and in an hour had constructed temporary shelters against the enemy's fire." The Federals pressed forward along Hampton Road to keep the Rebels occupied in front while troops tried to outflank the position. On the right, the 3rd Virginia evacuated its meager works, but a countercharge by a portion of the 1st North Carolina recovered the one-gun emplacement and forced the Federals to retire. Other companies of the 1st North Carolina stopped the Yankee threat to the left. There was a lot of noisy firing all around, but the Federals did not push home their advance on Magruder's front. After about an hour, the Yankees retreated to Hampton, and the battle was over.[3]

It was a meaningless defeat for the Federals but a stimulating victory for the Rebels. The 1st North Carolina, which made up the bulk of the Confederate troops under fire, had held the redoubt well. Balls flew over their heads and buried themselves in the nearby parapet. "We were greatly protected by our breastworks," crowed Lewis Warlick; "if it had not have been for them we would have been slaughtered by numbers." Only one man in John Thomas Jones's company was injured, and that was merely a scratch on his face.[4]

The battle taught members of the 1st North Carolina the value of earthworks. Hill's command returned to Yorktown and immediately strengthened the fortifications. "The men don't dislike it near so much as they did before the fight at Bethel, where they saw the necessity of building them," reported Egbert A. Ross to his sister. Francis Marion Parker, who still was proud that no slaves had been used to build the works, admitted the same to a friend. "Before the action our men seemed unwilling to use the spade and shovel so constantly; but seeing how effectually the trenches screened them from Yankee bullets, they are perfectly willing to do any amount of that kind of work." Hill reported that if all Confederate regiments dug as well as his Tar Heels, "there would not be an assailable point in Virginia. After the battle they shook hands affectionately with the spades, calling them 'clever fellows and good friends.'" What had seemed like formidable fortifications before Big Bethel now appeared inadequate, but the additional work transformed them into the kind of protection the Tar Heels required. The North Carolinians were convinced that at least 25,000 Yankees were needed to take them by storm.[5]

The story of Big Bethel illustrates a common tendency among Northern and Southern soldiers in the first half of the war. Their campaigns often involved some degree of earthwork construction even if the average soldier doubted the usefulness of the labor he expended. The first battle usually taught the men differently, and it was often followed by a spate of increased digging. The Tar Heels were unusually frank in their expressions following the battle of June 10, and their extra work demonstrated how seriously they took the lesson; but this attitude did not necessarily translate into consistent progress toward a full realization of trench warfare. The members of Hill's 1st North Carolina went home in November, after their six-month term of enlistment was over. Many eventually joined other, long-term units, especially the 11th North Carolina. None of these men indicated in their subsequent letters that they continued to feel so warmly about the value of fortifications. It was necessary for soldiers to be repeatedly taught that lesson in several campaigns before they were willing to dig in as they would do automatically by the spring of 1864. Long months of fighting, often in the open, were to follow before commanders and soldiers alike embraced fortifications fully and consistently.

First Manassas, Manassas Junction, and Centreville

First Bull Run was the first major battle of the conflict. The climax of the initial Union drive toward Richmond, it came to grief only thirty miles south of Washington near Manassas Junction. The Confederates were acting on the defensive, guarding the approaches to Richmond, and at first relied only halfheartedly on fortifications to block Union progress. The battle was an open field fight with no earthworks involved, but the Confederates hastened to dig in much more thoroughly after the engagement.

As commander of Virginia Forces, Maj. Gen. Robert E. Lee recognized the value of Manassas Junction as a forward line of defense for Richmond. He told local commanders in late May 1861 that it had to be held at all costs. Suggesting they dig in along Bull Run Creek, Lee promised to send entrenching tools. Brig. Gen. G. T. Beauregard took command of Confederate forces at the junction on June 1, 1861. He had graduated second in his West Point class in 1838 and had served as an engineer officer on Winfield Scott's staff during the Mexican War. Beauregard thoroughly examined the lay of the land around the junction. It was mostly a flat plain surrounded by rolling countryside, an ideal place for a railroad junction but less suitable for defense than the topography along Bull Run, a short distance to the northeast. Beauregard ordered Brig. Gen. James Longstreet's brigade to dig modest earthworks at the junction, but he intended to place most of his strength at the creek. Longstreet's men grumbled at doing hard labor, so Beauregard called on local planters. Claiming that his soldiers could not be spared from drill, he asked the civilians to send "such of their negro men, as they can spare," well supplied with spades and picks.

Beauregard placed most of his troops along the creek and at various points along the roads that approached Manassas. Six detachments of twenty-five men each, with axes, spades, and picks, were sent to cut trees and dig ditches across the roadbeds near Fairfax Court House, Centreville, and other spots well forward of Bull Run. Beauregard wanted to delay a Union advance long enough to give him time to concentrate his strength. Other than some slight defenses planned by Capt. Walter H. Stevens at Fairfax Court House, there were no works at these advanced places because Beauregard had no intention of defending them. Yet he did not build works along the west side of Bull Run either. He could well have done so, for there were numerous fords easily accessible to the Federals, and even a small, resolute force behind a well-built earthwork could have delayed a crossing for some time.

Beauregard changed his mind after the Federals approached his position. Brig. Gen. Irvin McDowell's 30,000 men were slowed by the road obstructions, but the Yankees launched a reconnaissance in force on July 18. Pressing forward against Blackburn's Ford and Mitchell's Ford, they fired a lot of artillery and skirmished with the Rebels, but they did not take advantage of a ridge on the north side of the stream that Beauregard called "an admirable natural parapet." It was nearly fifty feet higher than the ground occupied by the Confederates. Even this tentative Union advance was enough to propel the Confederates into a spate of entrenchment. All day of July 19 the troops dug in at the fords, constructing works designed by Lt. Col. Thomas H. Williamson and Capt. David B. Harris.

Erroneous reports that the Confederates were well fortified on July 18 contributed to an exaggerated fear of earthworks among the Federals. Northern newspapers had been filled with "columns of balderdash" about masked batteries, which supposedly were concealed artillery emplacements that could ambush the Yankees as soon as they appeared on a quiet road. "I doubt there was a soldier in our regiment," recalled Abner Small of the 3rd Maine, "who hadn't already written home tall tales of concealed rifle-pits, mined roads and bridges, and masked batteries, which had no existence except in the ink pots of the penny-a-line journalists."

The battle that took place on July 21, 1861, involved some 60,000 troops on both sides. The Federals held the Confederates in place along the creek while a strong flanking column used a ford upstream to cross and attack Beauregard's left. This assault was stalled by hard-fighting Confederates, especially Brig. Gen. Thomas J. Jackson's Virginia brigade on Henry House Hill, allowing more Rebel troops to gather for the climax of the engagement. Reinforced by troops newly arrived from the Shenandoah Valley under Gen. Joseph E. Johnston, the Confederates counterattacked and drove the Yankee army from the field, creating a panic that turned the retreat into a rout.[6]

Beauregard greatly increased the troop concentration at Manassas Junction and began to dig extensive earthworks after the victory. Nearly a dozen forts of all sizes were constructed around the junction with some connecting infantry trenches. The works covered all approaches to Manassas and straddled the two rail lines that ran to it, the Orange and Alexandria Railroad and the Manassas Gap Railroad. At least two works were constructed on high, commanding hills a half-mile and a mile to the east of the line, known today as Mayfield Fort and Signal Hill. In addition to the works at the junction, Beauregard maintained the older fortifications at the fords across Bull Run.

Confederate line, Manassas Junction. Note how the artillery emplacement and embrasure have been constructed. The connecting line on the other side of the railroad grade has a parados, and the Confederates have made extensive use of barrels for traverses in the works farther away. (The Western Reserve Historical Society, Cleveland, Ohio)

When members of the 21st North Carolina crossed the stream at Blackburn's Ford on their way to the junction in early November, they came across the Creole general inspecting the damage done to his works by rising waters. "It will require much labor to restore them," commented a soldier in the Tar Heel regiment, "since the water completely hid them from view at many places."[7]

The works at Manassas Junction were well designed. Some of the detached ones had a simple, circular configuration. The largest work was on top of Signal Hill. It had several bastions and was configured to cover the entire hilltop. At least nine photographs taken in the spring and summer of 1862, after the junction had been occupied by Federal troops, show the true nature and extent of the works. They had a post-and-plank revetment. Small saplings, many still with dried leaves, were interwoven along the tops of the posts. In some works, this hurdle extended only a few inches down the posts, but in at least one work it extended fully halfway down their vertical length. The hurdle provided rigidity for the top of the posts to help prevent them

Hurdle revetment in a Confederate fort, Manassas Junction. This is a superb example of hurdling that extends halfway down the revetment, to the bottom of the embrasures. Note the raised artillery platform in the center of the image and the two emplacements at ground level on either side. (Massachusetts Commandery, Military Order of the Loyal Legion and the U.S. Army Military History Institute)

from bending inward with the pressure of the parapet. This type of reinforcing with intertwined saplings was a clever way to strengthen the revetment and make it last.

The photographs show that the Confederates often used barrels to build traverses. One of the forts had a wooden palisades constructed to its rear to cover the road that led to the sally port. A photograph also shows a connecting infantry trench that has a well-formed parapet facing the front but a smaller parapet (called a parados because it was designed to protect the rear of the work) immediately behind the trench. This parados is also rare in Civil War fortifications, useful only if the designer expected the possibility of crossfire from the rear of the work.[8]

A stronger line was constructed at Centreville. The town sits on a high ridge that runs roughly north to south, about six miles north of Manassas Junction. The line of works lay to the east, northeast, and north of Centreville, slicing across six roads. The eastern line ran along the top of the ridge, a high and dominating position, for 1 ¾ miles. The northern line ran at a right angle to the eastern line and descended onto the flatter land northwest of Centreville. The best-preserved section of the eastern line still has a

Artillery emplacement in Confederate fort, Manassas Junction. Note the saplings and branches interwoven along the posts that support the revetment of the parapet. Note also the wooden gun platform consisting of stringers sunk below the surface and a solid floor of planks laid on top. The short posts at the embrasure have holes in them; the Confederates had secured metal hooks to use as leverage while pulling the guns forward with ropes after they were fired. Note also the remnants of a campfire and cooking pole immediately behind the platform. (Massachusetts Commandery, Military Order of the Loyal Legion and the U.S. Army Military History Institute)

large parapet, a well-dug ditch in front, and the remnants of a fire step in the trench, a rarely preserved feature of Civil War fortifications. There is also a parados behind the trench here, as at Manassas Junction. The eastern line had a total of seven works of all sizes, including two redoubts, two lunettes, two batteries, and "one bastion fort," with a total of forty embrasured gun positions. The northern line was two miles long and included thirty-one embrasured gun positions. Today most of this line is gone, but a well-preserved section crosses Stone Road. It has two artillery emplacements, one with four and the other with five embrasures. There is a ditch in front of the artillery emplacements but none in front of the connecting infantry trench. The land here forms gentle waves or ripples, and the line is placed on the highest wave.

Confederate works, Centreville. In this wonderful view of a connecting line, the works face toward the left; note the fire step and the hurdle revetment in the foreground. Note, too, the parados, which also has a hurdle revetment. There is a ditch in front of each parapet. The same construction can be seen in the continuation of the line in the midground on the other side of the road. Note that the photographer also is standing in a road. A massive work pierced with embrasures stands on high ground in the distance. Despite these details, it is difficult to pinpoint the location of these works on the map of the Centreville defenses. (Massachusetts Commandery, Military Order of the Loyal Legion and the U.S. Army Military History Institute)

These works at Centreville formed a more continuous line than those at Manassas Junction. One fort had embrasures for eight guns and parapets 10 to 20 feet thick and 6 feet tall. A wooden door and a loopholed palisades guarded the sally port in its rear. Ditches 6 to 10 feet deep and 12 feet wide circled the forts. The size of the fort and its configuration—circular, octagonal, or three-sided—varied. The Centreville line would have been a difficult target for any force approaching from the front.[9]

The availability and quality of entrenching tools was a problem for Beauregard's troops. David B. Harris reported on their scarcity and poor condition. By mid-January 1862 Harris had only 105 picks available, and "Several require[d] pointing." He had 23 spades in the depot, but 10 were borrowed from the 8th South Carolina and 5 more were damaged, leaving only 8 of these essential tools available for departmental use. Of 14 axes, 4 had not been returned by work details, and 1 of Harris's 7 saws apparently had been acquired from the enemy. Only 4 files and 1 grinding stone were in store for use in sharpening the tools. These problems were eased by more careful attention to the tool supply by infantry officers. Robert Rodes ordered each regimental commander in his Alabama brigade to have on hand one ax, one shovel, and one pick. All excess tools were to be turned over to the quartermaster. The Engineer Bureau in Richmond also sent sandbags for use on the Centreville works.[10]

The formidable works at Manassas Junction and Centreville were never tested in battle. The Confederates evacuated both places in March 1862 and moved to new positions along the Rappahannock River.

Defenses of Washington

The summer of 1861 also saw major efforts to fortify the two capitals of the opposing sides. Given their proximity and the natural tendency for armies to strike for their enemy's political center, the two cities became locked in a deadly contest of attack and defense.

Before the start of the war, the only formal defense of the Northern capital was Fort Washington, built after the War of 1812 some twelve miles down the Potomac River. This masonry work on a high bluff was designed to defend against a naval force armed with smoothbore guns sailing up the stream. The land approaches to the city were open and not easy to defend. It was located in southern Maryland, a slave state with divided loyalties and just across the Potomac from Confederate territory. Situated in a basin on the north side of the river, the city was surrounded by higher ground that ranged from 200 to more than 400 feet above the lowest river level. It is possible to see this if one stands at Fort Washington and looks toward downtown Washington on a clear day. The trees on the high ground just to the north of the city center are visible above the buildings and monuments.

The first Union effort to secure the city's defense involved gaining control of the transportation routes across Maryland that linked it to the free states, and in the process the Federals prevented Maryland from seceding as well. Federal troops then crossed the Potomac River to occupy Arlington and Alexandria on May 23, 1861. They began to fortify the next day under the supervision of Maj. John G. Barnard. Six major forts were constructed over the next seven weeks; they were nearly finished when McDowell left for Manassas on July 16. Military engineers began to survey the land and map out the roads north of the city in preparation for building similar works there.

McClellan took command of the Army of the Potomac on July 27 and was

Fort Totten, defenses of Washington. Officers of Companies A and B, 3rd Massachusetts Heavy Artillery, with the crew of a 100-pounder Parrott gun. Note the neatly whitewashed revetment, the sodded parapet, and the well-polished tube. (Library of Congress)

surprised that so little had been done to fortify Washington. Any reluctance to invest the time and money to dig in evaporated with the defeat at Bull Run. McClellan assigned Barnard to oversee the construction of works north of the river. He would devote his considerable expertise to this project for much of the war, and he justly deserves the title "Father of the Washington Defenses." Construction would continue for the rest of the war, involve thousands of troops and civilian workers as laborers, and cost $1.4 million. But all this effort and money turned Washington into the most heavily fortified city in the history of North America.

McClellan endorsed a plan developed at the instigation of the House of Representatives (since Washington was a Federal city, the U.S. government was responsible for its defense). The plan called for a system of forty-eight forts mounting 300 guns. Barnard likened the project to Wellington's Lines of Torres Vedras, which protected the approaches to Lisbon, Portugal, during

Magazine of Fort Totten, defenses of Washington. Gun crews demonstrate their readiness at pieces mounted en barbette. Note the heavy timber facing of the magazine on the right. Also note, in the foreground, the entrance to a tunnel (known as a postern) that goes under the parapet and gives access to the ditch. This is on the gorge, or rear, face of the fort. (Library of Congress)

the Peninsula War of the Napoleonic era. In both cases a system of field fortifications stretched for miles across the countryside. The idea was to place enclosed works on key ground and sweep the surrounding area with artillery fire. Curtains consisting of "light parapets" could later be built to connect these works and hinder enemy movement between them. Barnard cited Napoleon himself, who had asserted that all national capitals are natural targets and should be heavily fortified.

Barnard went to work in August 1861 enlarging the line of works south of the river as well. Names for the new forts were assigned the following month, and most honored famous officers, especially those recently killed. Barnard spent an average of more than $7,000 on each fort in his plan, employing a dozen engineers who were aided by civilian crew foremen. It took about eight months to complete this initial phase of the fortification plan. The line of works, thirty-three miles long, required a garrison of 20,000 men, while the guns typically were 24-pounders and 32-pounders. There was

Fort Slemmer, defenses of Washington. Like Fort Totten, Fort Slemmer guarded the northeastern approaches to Washington. Note the line of abatis outside the fort, the neatly packed but unsodded parapet, and the revetment made of sharpened, upright logs to support the entrance. (National Archives)

yet no complete system of connecting infantry lines—that was a development of the future—but the basic system of forts had been established. Twenty-three were on the south side of the Potomac, from where everyone expected the major threat, while fourteen forts and three batteries screened the west and north sides of the city between the Potomac and the Anacostia River. Eleven additional forts were constructed south of the Anacostia and east of the Potomac.

When he compared his handiwork with the Lines of Torres Vedras, Barnard noted that the Washington defenses had fewer but larger forts and far less auxiliary construction, such as abatis, palisades, and military roads. Fewer guns were mounted at Washington, but of course they were heavier and more powerful than those available to Wellington. In weight, the Federal artillery around the capital was double the tonnage at Torres Vedras.[11]

By the time McClellan was ready to launch his Peninsula campaign, Washington was secure. The line of forts would be greatly enhanced over the next three years so that it became an iron vise around the city, absolutely impenetrable if manned by sufficient numbers of troops. But the defenses also created a dilemma for Union commanders. To man them adequately required a lot of troops who could be better employed in the field armies that were taking the offensive into the heart of the Confederacy. The massive earthworks became a burden, creating the necessity for hard choices in troop deployment. But the political nerve center of the Union had the shield it needed in case of emergency. Washington required fortifications; it was wide open and potentially in the path of invading Confederate armies.

Defenses of Richmond

The defense of Richmond was not undertaken with such decisiveness or lavish expenditure of time, money, or manpower. Consequently, even though it needed protection, the Confederate capital was fortified in a haphazard fashion. Responsibility for the defenses was divided among three governmental levels—the city, the state, and the Confederate—as Richmond was the capital of both Virginia and the Confederacy. The city asked the state to begin fortifying, but initial efforts were later deemed inadequate by central authorities. Believing the works were too close, a more forward line was planned. When McClellan approached in the spring of 1862, another, more forward line was built. As a result, not one but three lines of works were constructed to defend the Confederate capital.

Richmond also was vulnerable to a drive up the James River by Federal gunboats. When Robert E. Lee commanded the Virginia Forces, he pushed for the construction of batteries below the mouth of the Appomattox River. The site of old Fort Powhatan, twelve miles south of the Appomattox, was the first location chosen. It was followed by works built on Jamestown Island, Hardin's Bluff, Mulberry Island, and Day's Point.

Lee also initiated the construction of forts just outside the city. When a committee of the Richmond City Council asked him on May 9, 1861, to consider fortifying Richmond, Lee ordered Andrew Talcott, the chief engineer of the state of Virginia, to look into the matter. Talcott initially recommended that four or five redoubts built along key roads outside Richmond would "afford all the protection required at this time, and be fully within [my] means to construct and of the State to defend." He envisioned the works as big enough to hold 600 men. Talcott proceeded in an unhurried fashion. First, he and his subordinates conducted a thorough topographical survey to decide where to place the redoubts. Then they traced the outline on the ground. Next, he placed an order for the ordnance to arm them. Lee reported that the work was slowed by a shortage of labor, and he wanted the city council to take action on the matter.[12]

The Committee on Defenses in the Richmond city government recommended that the mayor "impress the services of such free negroes he may think proper to work on the fortifications around the city." The committee also strongly suggested that "it is not alone the duty of our citizens to build them, but as this city is an important point to the Confederate Government," the Davis administration should take charge of the project and pay at least part of the expense. Secretary of War Leroy P. Walker agreed to share costs. Hundreds of free black and slave laborers were sent to the line, fed, and housed by state authorities.[13]

Meanwhile, Confederate authorities examined Talcott's line and found many faults. First, it was too close to prevent the Yankees from bombarding the city. Second, all the guns were to be mounted en barbette, so that they could fire over the parapet instead of through embrasures cut into it. This would expose the gun crews to enemy fire as they worked their pieces. Third, the line was too short, essentially covering only the eastern approaches to the city. The engineers recommended that a longer and more forward line be constructed, and that the first line be completed so it could serve as a support to the new line. They wanted to cover at least some of the northern and southern approaches to Richmond. Thus, the initial position came to be called the Inner Line, and the new position would be known as the Intermediate Line.[14]

Work on the Richmond fortifications proceeded at a slow pace, perhaps because of the victory at First Manassas, which promised to keep the Yankees some seventy miles north of the city. Little progress had been accomplished by the time Maj. Danville Leadbetter, acting chief of the Confederate Engineer Bureau, inspected them in October 1861. He found that serious problems impeded the arming of these works. Only six guns had thus far been mounted. Thirty more were available but lacked carriages due to a shortage of mechanics and skilled laborers to construct them. Talcott assured Leadbetter that the state authorities wanted the Confederate government to take charge of the defenses, and the acting bureau chief agreed. Even though he had no engineer officers to supervise the defenses full time, he hoped the civil engineers already working on them could handle the job for a while.[15]

Thus responsibility for the city defenses was shifted to the governmental authority with the best prospects for shouldering it. This did not speed up work. The slaves and free blacks earlier pressed into service were released after a reasonable amount of time, and black convicts were put to work on the fortifications. Even by late February 1862 the works were only "fairly well started," in Leadbetter's words. Eighteen forts or semi-enclosed works were under construction along the Inner Line, with seven outworks. The line was twelve miles long and between one and one and a half miles from the city. It needed 218 heavy guns, but there was little prospect of that number becoming available any time soon.[16]

Until an imminent threat appeared, there was no pressing need to complete the armament of the existing forts or to initiate the construction of new ones. Thus many months were wasted that winter that could have been used to perfect a defensive system that rivaled the one already surrounding Washington.

Ball's Bluff

Months of Federal inactivity followed the disaster at Bull Run. Confederate forces assumed positions in a wide arc along the south side of the Potomac River, with the far left at the village of Leesburg, thirty-five miles upstream from Washington. Leesburg was held by Col. Nathan G. Evans, whose Mississippi and Virginia brigade watched the fords and ferry crossings of the upper Potomac. He built Fort Evans, a sizable redoubt two miles east of town near the road linking Leesburg with Edward's Ferry. It enclosed one and a half acres and was used by Evans as his headquarters. The fort was situated on high ground, with a good view in all directions and gentle, irregular slopes surrounding it.

Another work called by the Federals the Masked Battery was built where the Edward's Ferry Road crossed Cattail Run. The emplacement was on the western bluff of the creek, about twenty feet above the bottomland. It straddled the road with a single parapet and a good ditch in front. The parapet, of which about seventy yards remain, had a protruding, angular bastion to protect the left wing.

Evans completed these two works before the Federals advanced against his position in October. While Fort Evans had big, well-made parapets, the Masked Battery was a minor fieldwork that nevertheless presented a good front to an approaching enemy. Both works were vulnerable to turning movements.[17]

On the Maryland side of the river opposite Evans's position, Brig. Gen. Charles P. Stone commanded a Federal division of three brigades. McClellan initiated a series of moves in late October designed to see if Evans could be compelled to evacuate Leesburg. The Rebels had just pulled back from their advanced positions along the rest of the Potomac River line, so McClellan sent a division under Brig. Gen. George A. McCall to occupy Dranesville, fifteen miles southeast of Leesburg. This move merely made Evans more watchful, so McClellan instructed Stone to move across the Potomac to threaten the Rebels more directly. Stone was to feint a crossing at Edward's Ferry while making his real strike at Smart's Mill Ford, near Harrison's Island in the middle of the river. Just downstream from Smart's Mill Ford lay Ball's Bluff, a steep, eighty-foot-tall eminence virtually unguarded by the Confederates. A series of events led the Federals to move a considerable number of troops over Harrison's Island and up the narrow path ascending Ball's Bluff. It became the main line of approach, despite its obvious difficulties.

The result of these moves was a Union fiasco. While Stone supervised the crossing of Brig. Gen. Willis A. Gorman's brigade at Edward's Ferry, Col. Edward D. Baker was to cross at Ball's Bluff to reconnoiter Evans's position on October 21, 1861. He soon was pushing his entire brigade up the bluff, and a sharp battle developed on top of the height. Evans realized that Gorman's crossing was a feint, so he sent all available troops to the bluff. They attacked the Federal line, which stretched across a small open field and was anchored on both ends at the edge of the bluff. It was one of the most undesirable positions to be in, backed up against a precipitous cliff with a winding trail leading to a narrow bottomland and a hazardous crossing of the river. Baker was killed, and Union attempts to break through the trap and retreat to Edward's Ferry were unsuccessful. Subsequent Confederate attacks forced the harried Unionists to retreat under fire. There were not enough boats for everyone to cross, so many Federals drowned, pelted by Confederate rifle fire. Of 1,720 men engaged, the Yankees lost 869 killed, wounded, and captured. The Confederates had almost the exact number engaged but lost only 155.[18]

The next day, October 22, the 13th Mississippi attacked Gorman's 2,000 men, who had dug in on the south side of the Potomac at Edward's Ferry. Gorman's skirmishers were driven into the works, but the Confederates failed to press home an attack due to the strength of the position. Nevertheless, Stone ordered Gorman to withdraw to the Maryland side that evening.[19]

Confederate reinforcements were rushed to Leesburg after the battle, but the Federals had no more heart for offensive moves in this area. The battle led to increased digging by the Rebels. Daniel Harvey Hill initiated the construction of two more redoubts, Fort Johnston to the north of Fort Evans and Fort Beauregard about a half-mile south of it. Some of the latter work remains, a straight parapet about 300 yards long. It has a good trench but no ditch in front of the parapet. Interestingly, the Confederates constructed a series of short traverses, only one yard long, placed every thirty yards along the extant line. It is the earliest surviving example of traverses dug for the protection of infantry in a field fortification of the eastern theater.[20]

Atlantic Coast

While the armies were fighting between Richmond and Washington, operations were taking place along the Atlantic coast that were designed to nibble away at the edges of the Confederacy. Its long coastline was vulnerable, and the Northern navy controlled the coastal waters. There was ample opportunity to exploit this advantage to close down seaports and open the way for incursions inland.

The first target was the most vulnerable: two Rebel forts on the thin line of barrier islands that protected much of North Carolina's coastline. Fort Hatteras and Fort Clark covered inlets through this line of islands that gave access to the wide, calm sounds that lay between the barrier and the mainland. The landscape here—narrow, flat, treeless, and sandy—did not allow for the deployment of large numbers of troops or much heavy ordnance. With little in the way of naval power, the Confederates were not able to offer much support to these forts.

The expedition against them, as well as subsequent operations along the coast for the rest of the fall, winter, and spring to come, was essentially an amphibious operation. Each of these expeditions had a greater or lesser number of infantry cooperating, but their role was primarily to occupy points blasted into submission by naval gunfire. The only exception to this rule was the invasion launched by Brig. Gen. Ambrose E. Burnside on the North Carolina coast, which will be discussed in more detail in the next chapter. Burnside waged a sustained campaign that not only penetrated the seacoast but drove some distance inland to occupy a number of points. All of the others merely seized toeholds on the coast that could be enlarged if future operations demanded it.

Maj. Gen. Benjamin F. Butler led the first of these expeditions against the barrier islands. He commanded 860 infantrymen; the main power lay in the guns aboard the seven warships, commanded by Flag Officer Silas H. Stringham. His ships bombarded Fort Hatteras and Fort Clark on August 28, 1861, compelling their surrender the next morning. The infantry landed to take control of the works.[21]

A much larger expedition was organized to take Port Royal and Beaufort, South Carolina, which were protected by two strong fortifications on coastal islands. Fort Beauregard, on St. Phillips Island, and Fort Walker, across the sound on Hilton Head Island, were major obstacles to a Union thrust up the Broad River. Brig. Gen. Thomas W. Sherman commanded 12,000 Federal infantrymen who accompanied the fleet of seventeen warships under Flag Officer Samuel F. Du Pont. The powerful fleet bombarded both forts on November 7, 1861, and compelled them to surrender. Sherman's men landed to occupy the fortifications, the islands, and the two port cities, but no incursion inland was planned.[22]

The Federal attack on Fort Pulaski, at the mouth of the Savannah River, involved very few infantrymen. Engineer Capt. Quincy A. Gillmore directed operations there. He planted batteries on Tybee Island under cover of darkness and opened a bombardment on April 10, 1862, with thirty-six guns. Nine of the cannon were rifled. The guns blasted the masonry walls of the fort for thirty hours, breached them, and compelled the garrison to surrender. One regiment of Federal infantry had helped Gillmore and the engineers to construct their batteries, and of course, infantrymen occupied the surrendered fort; but no movement inland was contemplated.[23]

The comparative ease with which the Federals reduced coastal defenses led the Confederates to evacuate their remaining forts on exposed islands in the winter and spring of 1862. The Yankees could bring their strengths—heavy naval guns and control of the waters—to bear against overextended Confederate resources. A better strategy lay in concentrating men and guns at key locations such as Charleston and the Cape Fear River approach to Wilmington and in strengthening individual earthworks so they could be a defensive match for offensive firepower. This strategy proved to be quite successful.

3 : Western Virginia and Eastern North Carolina

hile military operations unfolded in the corridor between Washington, D.C., and Manassas, Union forces also launched successful efforts deep in the western counties of Virginia and along the coastline of North Carolina. Field fortifications were used by both sides as the Federals achieved limited but important victories in these two regions.

Western Virginia

The first sustained, deep penetration of Confederate territory began in northwestern Virginia in June 1861. Situated across the Ohio River from free territory, this area was a vulnerable shoulder of the Confederacy. Union troops entered it initially to protect the Baltimore and Ohio Railroad and then enlarged their presence on Virginia soil to the degree that they were engaging in an invasion. Within the first year of the war, they would secure the first large section of Confederate territory liberated from the secessionists.

George McClellan gained his first public fame by commanding the troops that initially crossed the Ohio. Acting on reports that the railroad bridges were being destroyed by Confederate troops, he rushed several regiments into Virginia on May 27 and easily chased the Rebels away from the railroad. Col. Benjamin F. Kelley, who had recently organized a Union regiment at Wheeling, planned and led a strike against those Confederates who had fallen back to Philippi, thirty miles from the railroad at Grafton. The resulting engagement on June 3 sent the Confederates fleeing southward.

McClellan believed that the best line of advance into western Virginia was not here but farther south, along the Great Kanawha River Valley. Charleston and Gauley Bridge were key locations along that route. Yet he felt it was necessary to postpone an advance along that line in order to personally take charge of the growing Union concentration already operating along the line of the Staunton-Parkersburg Turnpike, which connected Grafton and Philippi. This pike was the major road through the northern portion of the Virginia mountains. It started at Staunton in the middle range of the Shenandoah Valley and ran to McDowell, then crossed Alleghany Mountain and Cheat Mountain and headed northward up the valley of Tygart's River

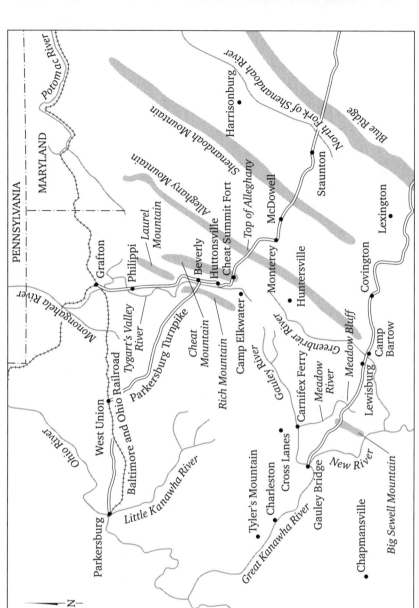

Western Virginia, 1861

between Cheat Mountain and Rich Mountain to Beverly. It then forked; one branch headed northwestward to the Baltimore and Ohio Railroad at West Union before going west to Parkersburg on the Ohio River, and the other branch led northward from Beverly to Philippi and Grafton.[1]

The Confederates were compelled to react. Gen. Robert E. Lee moved two columns into the region, advancing Brig. Gen. Henry A. Wise into the Great Kanawha River Valley and Brig. Gen. Robert S. Garnett up the Staunton-Parkersburg Turnpike. Garnett led 6,000 men to Rich Mountain northwest of Beverly, believing this to be the best place to stop the Union drive along the thoroughfare. The pike passed through a saddle of Rich Mountain; just to the west, Garnett deployed 1,300 men behind a fortification called Camp Garnett. It was made of log breastworks, as the thin soil of the mountain did not allow for a lot of digging. Trees were cut down for 150 yards in front to form an abatis and open a field of fire. Garnett similarly fortified the point where the other branch of the pike crossed Laurel Mountain north of Beverly. He personally commanded the majority of his force at Laurel Mountain, but twelve miles separated his two wings.

McClellan moved cautiously toward both positions with 20,000 men. When engineer Lt. Orlando M. Poe found a low ridge in front of Camp Garnett, McClellan hoped to place artillery there to shell the Confederates out of their works. This plan probably would not have worked without an accompanying infantry assault, but McClellan's subordinate Brig. Gen. William S. Rosecrans was willing to lead one. He found a local Unionist, twenty-two-year-old David Hart, whose family farm lay alongside the pike on the top of the mountain some distance behind Camp Garnett. Hart was willing to show Rosecrans a footpath up the mountain that would allow him to bypass the fortified camp and enter the pike in the saddle.

The plan worked well. Rosecrans carefully led 1,917 men along the path on the night of July 10 and struck the paltry Confederate force holding the saddle behind hastily constructed breastworks. Even though there were only 310 Rebel troops and one gun in position, the struggle lasted nearly all day on July 11. The woods surrounding the Hart farmstead were thick but clear of undergrowth, and the rude breastworks provided the only margin of advantage the Rebels enjoyed; yet Rosecrans gained possession of the Hart farmstead and the pike by evening. Lt. Col. John Pegram, who commanded the troops at Camp Garnett, evacuated the work that night and bypassed the Hart farm to escape. Garnett also evacuated the fortification at Laurel Mountain, but Pegram felt compelled to surrender his small force in Tygart's Valley on July 13, believing he had been cut off. Garnett was killed in a skirmish at Carrick's Ford that day as the Federals vigorously pursued his command.

It was a hard-won victory that garnered enormous, and largely unde-served, praise for McClellan. He demonstrated some of his later characteris-tics: extreme caution, indecision, and an abiding fear of failure on the bat-tlefield. John Beatty, an officer in the 3rd Ohio, pinpointed a reason for McClellan's waffling when he complained and explained in the same pas-sage: "We do not know the strength of our opponents, nor the character and extent of their fortifications. These mountain passes must be ugly things to go through when in possession of an enemy." It was reasonable for McClellan to be cautious when commanding a large force in the crowded mountains, where logistical problems were far worse than in other terrain, but nothing can excuse McClellan's refusal to advance on Camp Garnett when the sound of Rosecrans's hard-fought battle for the saddle could distinctly be heard on July 11. Rosecrans fought his way to victory despite McClellan's inaction. He demonstrated the best way to deal with fortified mountain passes; there always was a way to climb the mountain to right or left and outflank the enemy, difficult as that process might be.

W. C. Johnson and E. S. Hartshorn, two early historians of Civil War fortifications, noted the irony of this situation. They pointed out in 1915 that Garnett had worked for twenty-five days constructing his fortifications and lost them in a matter of hours without inflicting significant losses on his opponent. "This engagement furnishes an excellent illustration of the futility of expending much effort on works which can not meet the conditions for which they have been constructed."

Rich Mountain also demonstrated that the use of fortifications would be a key element of the western Virginia campaign. There seemed to be some-thing psychologically appealing in a fort located on the top of a mountain. The romantic image of a "mountain fastness," reinforced with earthworks, captivated the imagination of everyone. Beatty pondered the meaning of Rich Mountain and how the Confederates would defend their region when he wrote, "They will fight with desperation, I have no doubt. Nature has fortified the country for them. He is foolishly oversanguine who predicts an easy victory over such a people, entrenched amidst mountains and hills."[2]

Yet Union forces vigorously projected power into these mountains, and they eventually carried the day. McClellan paused after the victory at Rich Mountain and ordered the construction of a major fortification where the turnpike crossed Cheat Mountain. Six companies of the 14th Indiana started the work on July 16 and were later joined by the 15th Indiana, the 3rd Ohio, and some Ohio cavalry and artillery units. The men cleared the trees on both sides of the pike, where the land sloped west and east. The white pines were used as abatis in front of the parapet, which also consisted of logs covered with dirt. The parapet was eight feet wide at the base and four feet wide at the top. Two blockhouses were situated northeast and southwest of the point where the pike crossed the summit, and a covered way, or a communication trench with berms thrown up on both sides to protect against enemy fire, connected the blockhouses to the fortification. Cabins were built inside the fort as well, with lumber from a nearby steam sawmill. The huts measured twenty feet by forty feet, had a fireplace at one end, and housed up to one-fourth of a company of soldiers. Because a man named White owned the land, the spot often was called White Top. The soldiers more commonly called it Cheat Summit Fort, Fort Milroy, or Camp McClellan. At more than 4,000 feet above sea level, it was the highest Federal fort in the eastern theater.[3]

The Union drive along the Staunton-Parkersburg Turnpike ground to a halt because of logistical difficulties and McClellan's desire to push another column up the Great Kanawha Valley. He started 3,000 troops under Brig. Gen. Jacob D. Cox in mid-July. Cox easily won success against Henry A. Wise's 4,000 Confederates, outflanking their position at Tyler's Mountain on the north side of the river and forcing them to retire. Wise evacuated Charleston without a struggle, burned the bridge at Gauley, and retreated eastward. Cox occupied Charleston on July 25, but McClellan had left the region the day before, called by the authorities in Washington to take charge of the defeated troops streaming back from Bull Run. He had managed to use his success in western Virginia as a springboard to the top command in the East.

Rosecrans richly deserved his promotion to succeed McClellan as the Union commander in the mountains. He instructed Cox to stop at Gauley and fortify it as a forward outpost. Often called Gauley Bridge, this tiny community was the strategic gateway to the Kanawha River Valley from the east. The Great Kanawha, which cut as much as 800 feet into the rugged mountains, was formed by the confluence of the Gauley River from the northeast and the New River from the southeast. The two streams met at Gauley Bridge. Two miles south of town, the Falls of the Kanawha impeded riverborne traffic coming up from the Ohio. The bridge at Gauley was built across the Gauley River in 1822 on massive stone piers that remained after the wooden bridge was burned by the Confederates.

Two engineer officers arrived at Gauley Bridge on August 5 to supplement the one already serving with Cox, but the general felt they were not needed. There "was little fortifying to be done beyond what the contour of the ground indicated to the most ordinary comprehension." Cox, an amateur soldier, felt that West Point–trained engineers were not a sine qua non of field operations. He thoroughly and competently fortified Gauley Bridge.

The Federals put a gun emplacement on a nearby hillside and then ran an infantry trench along the Gauley River to a small creek that emptied into the stream. A redoubt was dug at the junction of the creek and the river. The trench was then run beside the creek up the mountain to a gorge. The parapet of this trench line consisted of barrels filled with earth, as there was little topsoil. Much labor was expended in cutting thousands of trees in all directions, up and down the slopes, to create fields of fire and to make a nearly impenetrable slashing. Cox also converted a sawmill below the Falls of the Kanawha into a blockhouse with loopholes for small arms.[4]

Wise was reinforced by Brig. Gen. John B. Floyd, bringing combined Confederate strength in the region to 8,000 men. The two generals bitterly despised each other, however, and each viewed the other as a rival. Wise advanced to probe Cox's position at Gauley Bridge, but Floyd took his men to Carnifex Ferry, a crossing of the Gauley River some twenty miles upstream from Gauley Bridge. Neither general tried to help the other. Floyd entrenched his men on the north side of the rugged stream atop a high river bluff. He formed a bridgehead in neutral territory between Cox and Rosecrans, but he did nothing to exploit that advantage. The only offensive action he took was to send troops to rout the 7th Ohio, which was positioned two miles north of the ferry at Cross Lanes, on August 26.

This small but embarrassing Union defeat and Floyd's inaction prompted Rosecrans to take the offensive. Floyd had 1,900 men in his fortified bridgehead, which was called Camp Gauley. The countryside was very wild, the bluff ascended to 450 feet, and the Gauley River wound through the hills like one's fancied image of a mountain stream. Floyd put an artillery emplacement on the first high ground inland from the ferry, with a long line of infantry trench attached to its left and a much shorter line appended to its right. Ravines some 30 feet deep lay in front of each wing, while the road continued northward from the artillery emplacement. The ravine in front of the right wing was deeper than the one on the left. Some 200 yards in front of the Confederate artillery was a slightly higher rise where Federal artillery could be placed to bombard the work. Apparently the Confederates had not cut the trees in front of the fortification far enough, and the Federals could approach under cover. But Floyd's greatest problem was that the formidable crossing of the Gauley River was just to his back. Bridgeheads are strategically important only if they are used for further offensive action into enemy territory, but Floyd displayed no intention of doing that.

Rosecrans reduced this bridgehead with a force of 5,000 men on September 10. His attacks were repulsed that day, but Floyd felt compelled to give up Camp Gauley that night and retreat across the river. Shortly after, Cox advanced from Gauley Bridge and forced Wise to retire without offering battle. Wise and Floyd combined their forces at Big Sewell Mountain, a commanding eminence thirty-five miles from Gauley Bridge. Here, on top of this enormous height, the Confederates would finally halt the Union advance along the line of the Great Kanawha, but only after much suffering and bitter feuding among themselves.[5]

The animosity between Floyd and Wise boiled over at Big Sewell Mountain. While Wise wanted to stay put and fight the Yankees, Floyd was convinced that Meadow Bluff was a better place to make a stand. The bluff was ten miles east of the mountain, and Floyd decided to take his command there even though Wise elected to stay at Sewell. This was a petty move by Floyd, conducted mostly because he wanted to get away from Wise, and it unnecessarily divided the small Confederate force. Moreover, Meadow Bluff was far less favorable as a defensive position than Big Sewell Mountain. After crossing the mountain, the road descended into Meadow River Valley and ran upstream along the bottomland. The river flows west and northwest to empty into Gauley River at Carnifex Ferry. After running along the bottomland for five miles, the road crossed Meadow River and ascended Meadow Bluff near the modern town of Crawley. The bluff ranges from 100 to 200 feet high and offers a good position for defense against a frontal attack, but high ground on the flanks would allow an attacker to turn the position. Floyd set his men to work digging a line of infantry trench nearly three miles long on top of the bluff. One company of the 22nd Virginia had only "one axe [and] two butcher knives to work with, so some idea may be formed of the efficiency of our defenses," noted a soldier.[6]

While Floyd fortified his position at Meadow Bluff, Wise played the hero at Big Sewell Mountain. It is a huge, elongated mountain with very steep sides that utterly dominates the surrounding countryside. The road crossed the mountain at an elevation of 3,021 feet. Only a couple of small remnants of the works remain, and there are no extant maps of the fortifications, so it is difficult to know how they conformed to the lay of the land. But Robert E. Lee found it a good place to make a stand when he arrived in mid-September to direct Confederate operations. He was largely unsuccessful, preferring to give advice to his feuding subordinates rather than taking command. Lee managed to draw most of Floyd's force, regiment by regiment, back to Big Sewell Mountain, so that he had 9,000 men there by October 1. Rosecrans had joined Cox by then, and both Union forces advanced on the mountain. The Federals endured rain, illness, and logistical problems but managed to bring 8,200 men to Sewell. They hovered near the mountain for several days in a vain effort to find a weak spot in the Confederate defenses. Then Rosecrans retreated on October 6 to a point near Gauley Bridge. Floyd followed up this retreat in early November by advancing to shell the earthworks at Gauley Bridge, but he made no serious effort to breach them before retiring. Thus the campaign along the Kanawha–Gauley Bridge–Big Sewell Mountain line came to an end. Both sides were stalemated in their mountain forts.[7]

Operations along the Staunton-Parkersburg Turnpike had been taking place during and after the period embraced by the battle of Carnifex Ferry and the maneuvering and digging at Sewell Mountain and Meadow Bluff. Lee had arrived in western Virginia in early August and had sent a small force under Brig. Gen. William W. Loring against the Federals at Cheat Mountain. The Federal commander, Brig. Gen. Joseph J. Reynolds, protected the approach to the rear of Cheat Mountain by digging a strong line of works across the Huntersville-Huttonsville Pike in Tygart's Valley. A Confederate force moving north along this road could get behind Cheat Mountain and take the summit fort in the rear. Called Camp Elkwater, Reynolds's line of works stretched 300 yards across the full width of the valley. The trench was six feet deep and fourteen feet wide with a firestep inside and gun emplacements at each end. It was a very strong and well-placed earthwork.

Loring struck at both Camp Elkwater and Cheat Summit. Like Rosecrans and Cox at Big Sewell Mountain, his men hovered around the two positions without mounting a major attack in mid-September; then they retired to a new defensive position where the Monterey Turnpike crossed the Greenbrier River. The Confederates dug in on a commanding bluff overlooking the river crossing and called their earthworks Camp Bartow. Their artillery emplacements were simple, semicircular parapets. They were yet incomplete when Reynolds attacked on October 3. The Federals exchanged artillery fire and tried unsuccessfully to outflank the position. Then Reynolds retired to Cheat Mountain. Once again, high ground with a good field of fire and reinforced with earthworks had stopped a strategic offensive. The stalemate achieved by the Confederates at Big Sewell Mountain, a worthy accomplishment considering the string of disasters they suffered in the early part of the fighting for western Virginia, was duplicated at Camp Bartow. But of course, the Federals also were able to consolidate their gains by fortifying high ground.[8]

Despite their defensive achievement, the Confederates abandoned Camp Bartow for fear that a larger, more aggressive Federal attack lay in the future. They retired all the way to the top of Alleghany Mountain, five miles east of Camp Bartow and ten miles east of Cheat Mountain. At an elevation of 4,400 feet, this entrenched Confederate camp was the highest fortification on either side in the eastern theater. It was built on both sides of the Staunton-Parkersburg Turnpike as it crossed the summit of the mountain. The fort was

Remnants of Confederate Camp Bartow, West Virginia. This artillery emplacement consisted of a simple parapet in a semicircular configuration. (Cohen, Civil War in West Virginia, *50)*

located west of the road, and several cabins and a protecting infantry trench were situated east of it. Like Cheat Summit Fort, the works at Camp Alleghany were built on a slope. There was no ditch in front of the modest parapet, which consisted of rock covered with dirt from the trench. Thousands of sugar maples were cut down to clear room for the camp and a field of fire. At least thirty-five cabins were constructed.

The works here were tested when Brig. Gen. Robert H. Milroy took command of Union forces at Cheat Mountain. An aggressive commander, Milroy was determined to capture Camp Alleghany before the most severe winter weather set in. He led a force against Col. Edward Johnson's Confederates on top of the mountain on December 13, 1861. The resulting battle was sharp and costly. Milroy tried to outflank the position; but his attack was repulsed, and another, separate column approaching the camp from the cabin side also was repelled. The Federals were forced to return to Cheat Mountain, effectively ending the campaign in western Virginia for the time being.[9]

Even though the Federal invasion of western Virginia had been undertaken haphazardly, it had developed into a major effort that was largely successful. The Yankees had advanced along both lines of penetration as far as they could, given their logistical difficulties and the limited number of troops that could be employed in the mountains. Cheat Mountain was more

Remnants of Confederate defenses at Camp Alleghany, West Virginia. The simple trench and parapet are placed below the military crest of the slope. (Cohen, Civil War in West Virginia, *52).*

than 100 miles from Parkersburg on the Ohio River, measured in a straight line, while Gauley Bridge was 75 miles from the mouth of the Great Kanawha River. The Confederates at Camp Alleghany were 30 miles west of the Shenandoah Valley, the eastern edge of the Appalachian Highlands, as measured in a straight line; Big Sewell Mountain was 65 miles from the valley. At least half of the mountainous western counties of Virginia had been denied to the Confederacy. Union forces had turned the tide in the struggle for this border region.

Fortifications played a large role in the western Virginia campaigns. Neither side could afford to commit enough power to gain a decisive advantage over the other, and several indecisive engagements were fought. The use of fortifications by both sides was among the key factors in creating this stalemate, on both the tactical and strategic levels. The Confederates relied on fortified positions to slow down and stop the Union advance, and the Federals relied on fortified positions to hold their offensive gains. Neither side had made much headway against the other by September, and from that point on it became a matter of deciding who could outlast the other. The better-organized and more numerous Federals eventually won this contest.

No fortified position on either side was taken by direct attack in the western Virginia campaigns. Most confrontations between an attacker and a fortified defender resulted in probing moves, artillery exchanges, and finally a decision not to attack at all. Both Rosecrans's assault on Camp Gauley at Carnifex Ferry and Milroy's attack on Camp Alleghany were repulsed. But several fortified positions were evacuated because the enemy outflanked the position, as at Rich Mountain, or because of a breakdown of willpower on the part of the defender, as at Carnifex Ferry and Camp Bartow. The strength of the individual earthworks and their high, commanding positions deterred vigorous attacks.

The weather and terrain affected the outcome of the campaign as much as did fortifications. Unusually heavy rains fell that summer and fall, with a twenty-day period of precipitation starting on July 22 followed by eight weeks of sporadic showers. It actually snowed on top of Cheat Mountain in August. Muddy roads made supply by wagon very difficult. The transportation system lay in the river and creek valleys, so flooding also became a problem. The normal round of communicable diseases that always afflicted new regiments was worsened by the weather. Floyd asserted that eleven days of cold rain in September had "cost more men, sick and dead, than the battle of Manassas Plains." Lee was forced to send most of his troops away from Big Sewell Mountain, after Rosecrans and Cox retreated from the area, due to his supply problems. The 14th North Carolina took 750 men into Virginia but had only 277 left for duty by spring. Charles Snead, a member of the regiment, found it impossible to describe the conditions. "Our men suffer from the want of blankets, and clothing," he complained. "This is a cold, wet country and unless we are attended to we shall surely die." The winter months were brutal. Benjamin Franklin Templeton, a member of the 2nd Rockbridge Artillery, arrived at Camp Alleghany in December to find that his mustache and beard were so frosted he could not open his mouth until he warmed them by a fire.[10]

Disease, logistical difficulties, and harsh weather severely reduced the combat effectiveness of the regiments involved in the western Virginia campaigns. The Confederates could not afford to outlast the Federals in the waiting game. When the spring campaigns heated up in the Tidewater, the Rebels were forced to withdraw most of their troops from the mountains. The fortified camps at Big Sewell Mountain and Alleghany were evacuated by April 1862. The Federals also shifted most of their troops from the mountains to other areas. Western Virginia became a separate state in 1863, but it remained the scene of sporadic fighting for the remainder of the war.[11]

The campaign in the mountains had given rise to two commanders who would figure prominently in the history of fortifications: McClellan and Lee. Both men were fortunate enough to leave western Virginia early, McClellan in late July and Lee in late October, before their reputations suffered irreparable damage. But it is difficult to determine if either commander or his troops learned lasting lessons about the value of fortifications in the western Virginia campaigns. McClellan's and Lee's attitudes toward earthworks will be touched on in subsequent chapters, but both men seem to have been guided by their natural temperament rather than by their mountain experience in deciding whether to use fortifications in the Peninsula campaign and in the Seven Days battles. The troops were equally ignorant of how valuable fortifications could be when they descended from the heights and went into the Army of the Potomac or the Army of Northern Virginia. It was as if new campaigns under new commanders and in different terrains erased any lessons learned in the wild and unusual environment of Appalachia.

Eastern North Carolina

Another unusual environment was the coastal plain of North Carolina, scene of the Union's first major attempt to use its control of the sea to project power onto the coastline of the Confederacy. North Carolina was an apt target. More than half of its long seacoast was shielded by a string of low barrier islands. Between these thin islands and the mainland were wide sounds that offered access to the major rivers of the state. Union armies could penetrate the coastal plain, a rich agricultural region. The vital rail line that connected Richmond with Wilmington could be interdicted, and a substantial chunk of Confederate territory could be reclaimed for the Union. The presence of Federal troops on the coast of North Carolina would force the Confederates to detach large numbers of soldiers to guard against raids farther inland. It was an effective strategy that utilized the Union's strength in numbers and naval power against a weaker flank of Confederate defenses.

Brig. Gen. Ambrose E. Burnside was put in charge of the strike force, consisting of 15,000 men supported by ten warships and numerous transports under Admiral Louis M. Goldsborough. The combined expedition assembled at Annapolis, Maryland, in the fall of 1861. Benjamin Butler's expedition had cleared the Outer Banks of Confederate troops the preceding August, and Burnside had the luxury of steaming into the sounds without opposition.[12]

His first target was Roanoke Island, the capture of which would open the mouths of several important rivers. Roanoke was historic ground, the site of Sir Walter Raleigh's first attempt to plant a permanent colony in North America. In 1585 more than 100 colonists had settled there and built an earthen fort for protection. Located in the northeastern corner of the island, it consisted of a deep ditch, a parapet, and about fifty square feet of space inside the work. A palisades guarded its sally port. Fort Raleigh, as it is now known in its reconstructed form, was built by Governor Ralph Lane as a defense against Spanish raids. The colonists gave up and evacuated the island the next year, but a second colony was established in 1587. The fort failed to protect the colonists from whatever fate befell them. When Governor John White returned to the island in 1590, he found that many houses had been dismantled and the logs used to build a palisades around the settlement, which was deserted. The only clue was the word "CROATOAN," the name of a nearby island. Subsequent searches failed to locate the "Lost Colony of Roanoake."[13]

The Confederates constructed five forts on the northern half of the island; three were large works on the northwestern shore to guard Croatan Sound. The rest were a small battery on the eastern shore and a three-gun battery in the middle of the island called Fort Defiance. Henry A. Wise commanded 1,914 men on the island. Goldsborough bombarded the three works on the northwestern shore on February 7. The largest, Fort Huger, mounted twelve guns, while Fort Blanchard had four guns and Fort Bartow had seven pieces. The parapets were eight feet tall and made of sand, with layers of sod to prevent erosion. Magazines inside the forts were constructed of logs covered with thick layers of sod. The batteries were well made, but forts have little hope of stopping ships unless they are situated much above water level. Roanoke Island is very low and flat, and Croatan Sound is wide and easily navigated. Goldsborough's ships had no difficulty pounding the forts.[14]

While the ships attacked, Burnside landed his troops at Ashby's Harbor halfway up the western coast of the island on the evening of February 7. The only road on Roanoke led northward from there and gave access to the rear of the forts. The Confederates had one work straddling the road at the narrowest width of the island. Fort Defiance mounted three guns behind a meager earthwork consisting of a simple parapet and a deep ditch in front. Located at a place called Suple's Hill, named for a local farmer, it was actually on flat land only a few inches above the marshes that crowded both flanks. The dimensions of the work were surprising: the parapet was 4 ½ feet tall, made of sand and sod, and only 100 feet long. D. H. Hill had recommended it be lengthened to stretch from one side of the island to the other, but that was not done and possibly was not even feasible, considering the low, marshy ground to either side of the "hill." Trees were cut in front of the work over an area 80 yards wide and 300 yards forward, all the way to a sharp curve that took the road due north toward the guns. The heaviest piece, an 18-pounder, was in the right of the battery and pointed directly down the road, while a 12-pounder and a 6-pounder were positioned in the middle and left. The Confederates did not site the guns to fire anywhere except down the road, since they assumed the marsh to either side was impassable for troops. Three Virginia companies and one company of the 8th North Carolina held the work, commanded by Col. Henry M. Shaw, but reserves were a short distance to the rear.

Burnside approached Fort Defiance on February 8 with six regiments. Artillery and skirmish fire forced the Federals off the roadway and into the marsh for cover. Burnside did not dare a frontal attack but sent troops to envelop the work by advancing on both sides through the marsh. The Federals encountered soft mud and standing water that often went up to their waists, and the tangle of vines repeatedly tripped them. Visibility was reduced to no more than twenty yards because of the marsh vegetation. As a result, the Yankees struggled for a couple of hours to move only a short distance. But the severe limitations of the Confederate earthwork doomed the defense, along with the gross disparity of numbers. As soon as enough Yankees had worked their way around the flanks, the Rebels had no choice but to evacuate Fort Defiance. Just as they were leaving, the 9th New York launched a frontal attack, easily covered the open space, crossed the ditch, and scrambled over the low parapet. Maj. Edgar A. Kimball of the 9th nearly drowned when he impulsively jumped into the flooded ditch. A short, stocky man, he lost his sword but somehow managed to get out before swallowing too much marsh water. All in all, it was a remarkably easy victory.[15]

The other forts fell after Fort Defiance was evacuated, and Roanoke Island was soon in Union hands. It became the base of further operations along the coast. Some time later, Charles Johnson of the 9th New York was wandering a mile east of his regimental camp in the northeastern part of the island and came across the remnants of the fort built 277 years earlier. The parapet was overgrown with vegetation, and he found arrowheads nearby. The "breastworks are not more than ordinary mounds now," he noted, "and any one who was not shown the place would probably pass over it a hundred times without discovering anything so unusual as to warrant the thought of a fortification."[16]

New Bern was Burnside's next target. One of the state's oldest cities and its second colonial capital, New Bern was located twenty-five miles up the Neuse River. Confederate efforts to fortify the town had been started by state authorities in late 1861, but when Col. Charles C. Lee of the 37th North Carolina arrived on January 9 to take command of the post, he found much of the work to be inadequate. The primary fortifications were a series of forts on the west side of the river several miles below New Bern. They were designed to interdict ship traffic, but some had parapets too thin to withstand naval gunnery. Lee worked diligently to improve the defenses. Brig. Gen. Lawrence O'Bryan Branch also bent every effort when he took charge of the area later in January. He increased the number of river forts to four, mounting a total of thirty guns. In addition, he planted two small batteries to cover the wharves of the city and another battery on the north side of the Neuse, opposite New Bern. Bundles of hoops and sandbags filled with dirt helped to increase the size of the parapets, and railroad iron was spiked to the timber frames of some casemated batteries. Branch hoped to plant underwater mines and prepared a flat with bales of cotton and barrels of turpentine to serve as a fire barge that could be set loose among the Yankee ships.[17]

The weakness of this defense was that it discounted the possibility of a land approach to New Bern. Burnside's combined operation threatened to bring not only a seaborne fleet but a large force of infantry against the city, so Branch constructed two lines of works. The first, called the Croatan Line, was located fifteen miles south of town, astride the Atlantic and North Carolina Railroad. Branch considered it the stronger of his two lines, as it stretched for a mile all the way from the river to a wide swamp. Fort Dixie anchored the line on the bank of the Neuse. The Confederates never had a chance to man this position adequately. Branch sent the 35th North Carolina on March 12 when news of Burnside's approach reached his headquarters, and he reinforced that lone regiment with the 26th North Carolina and a battery early the next day. But the Federals landed below the Croatan Line and swiftly marched toward it before this meager force could settle down. The two regiments and the battery barely escaped before being cut off by the Federals. Charles M. Duren of the 24th Massachusetts crossed the Croatan Line later that day and found it "not quite finished" but apparently "very strong."[18]

Branch now had to rely on the second and weaker of his two lines, anchored at the river's edge by Fort Thompson, nine miles south of town. This earthwork was the largest of the river forts, mounting thirteen guns, and its parapets were made of sand and sod. Only three of the guns were sighted to fire inland, sweeping the front of an infantry trench that extended west from the fort. This line was strong until it reached the railroad, a distance of one mile, but it did not extend beyond the tracks. Branch had to hastily push new works farther westward, but the lay of the land was difficult. Immediately west of the tracks, in line with the Fort Thompson Line, was Bullen's Branch, which flowed westward from the railroad into Brice's Creek, a north-to-south stream. The new works west of the railroad had to be constructed north of the branch, 150 yards farther north than the rest of the line. This created a substantial gap, and Branch inadequately filled it by building emplacements for two heavy guns at a brickyard just east of the railroad. But the guns were not yet in place when Burnside attacked. Branch also placed his least reliable men, 2,000 North Carolina militiamen, in this sector. Moreover, the new works west of the railroad consisted of a series of redans placed at the end of fingers of land that constituted the irregular northern bank of Bullen's Branch. To be able to build a connected line of works, Branch would have had to move the position at least a half-mile farther north, further enlarging the gap along the tracks. The redans were thirty yards from the stream and ten to fifteen feet above its water level, which had been raised by recent rains and a dam. The works had no ditch, just a good parapet and trench about forty yards long, and their faces were curved to the rear for some flank protection. The redans were dug by the 26th North Carolina on the rainy night of March 13.

The Fort Thompson Line was an interesting combination of strong and weak elements. The river batteries were designed by state engineers who "were excellent designers and erectors of forts," according to Daniel Harvey Hill, "but their civilian lack of military insight led to many a blunder in the location of these forts." The infantry line from the river to the railroad was well made. Its parapet was 6 feet wide at the top, 5 feet high on the interior slope, and 10 feet high on the exterior, from the bottom of the ditch to the top of the parapet. The ditch was 10 feet wide. The parapet consisted of logs covered with dirt, and the trees in front were cut down for a clear field of fire 350 yards deep. The land is flat and undulating, but it ascends moderately as one moves northward toward the Confederate position.

The gap at the railroad would prove to be fatal to Branch's hopes. Not only was the line west of the tracks 150 yards to the rear of the line that lay east of the railroad, but neither line of works was close to the tracks. The first redan was nearly 200 yards from the railroad. The line of at least eight redans that lay west of the railroad was surprisingly strong, considering its hasty construction. Bullen's Branch, with its three feet of water and banks cleared of trees, was a formidable obstruction. An obscure road on the far right of this line also was protected by a small artillery emplacement, but it was never tested, as Burnside did not extend his battle line far enough to reach it.[19]

The Federals brought 8,000 men against this hybrid line early on the foggy morning of March 14. Branch had 6,000 men to defend the position. The Confederates held firm for two or three hours, keeping the Federals who approached east of the railroad at bay. The 26th North Carolina easily held off the timid Union advance west of the railroad as well, but the center could not hold. Union forces advanced along the six-foot-high railroad embankment and penetrated the brickyard, scattering the frightened militiamen. Branch was able to rush more reliable troops in to contain the breech, but a further push cracked the line wide open. Most Confederate troops managed to get away before being trapped, but they abandoned their camp equipment and personal belongings. While some Rebels retreated directly to New Bern, others escaped westward across Brice's Creek and marched to Kinston. Burnside's victorious men occupied New Bern the next day.[20]

The battle of New Bern was the largest and most important engagement of Burnside's expedition. It was followed by the peaceful occupation of several coastal towns. The Confederates hurried reinforcements to Kinston and sent engineer officers to survey the countryside between it and Goldsborough to find places where defensive works could be built. Meanwhile, New Bern became the center of the Federal presence in North Carolina and was heavily fortified during the next several months. A short line was constructed straddling the railroad just south of town, and a longer, much stronger line was built to cover the western approaches. This western line was anchored on massive Fort Totten, built where the two major roads that entered New Bern from the west and southwest came close together one mile from town. It was a star fort with five bastions, enclosing seven acres of land. The parapets were 8 feet tall and 12 feet thick. Fort Totten had a deep, wide, and dry ditch and mounted five guns in each bastion (two of which were sighted to sweep the ditch), and emplacements for eight more guns and mortars were built elsewhere in the fort. A huge traverse was constructed in the middle of the work to protect against crossfire. It consisted of "faced timbers" placed endwise in a trench to form a well-fitted log wall. A second such log wall was constructed a few feet away and parallel to the first. The space between was partially occupied by a magazine at each end, and the rest of the space was filled with dirt. Emplacements for sharpshooters were constructed atop the traverse, giving the Yankees a high vantage point to see across the flat land. It was an engineering marvel, 400 feet long, 20 feet thick, and 25 feet tall. "This great traverse was a landmark to the country for miles around," recalled a member of the garrison.[21]

Burnside still did not have a good port to supply his expedition and meant to solve that problem by reducing Fort Macon, which protected Beaufort and Morehead City. The latter town was thirty-three miles southeast of New Bern and was the coastal terminus of the Atlantic and North Carolina Railroad. Fort Macon, a masonry fortification, was located on the east end of Bogue Island, one of the sheltering outer banks. Across Beaufort Inlet, which gave access to the two ports, Shackleford Banks lay to the east of Fort Macon. Col.

Moses J. White commanded the fort, which was garrisoned by 400 men with fifty-four guns and enough powder for only three days of heavy firing. The fort had five sides, with most of its artillery placed to fire at the sea and the inlet. A citadel inside the work also mounted several guns. A fortification on the counterscarp, the outside edge of the moat, was fitted with embrasures for muskets so the defenders could fire back into the moat. Artillery was mounted en barbette on top of the counterscarp and the walls.

The Southerners had been preparing Fort Macon ever since North Carolina seized the thirty-year-old work on April 14, 1861. The city of New Bern sent a force of slaves and "free negro volunteers" to strengthen the fort. Capt. Henry T. Guion prepared gun emplacements and leveled sand dunes over an area 1,000 yards from the fort to deny cover to an attacker. Engineer records indicate that on April 25, 1861, there were 207 blacks at the fort; 163 of them worked on the fortification, 32 cooked for the garrison, and 12 were on the sick list. The preceding night the chief engineer had placed a free black man named William Hazell in a cell and ordered him "well worked for talking saucily of Lincolns having set them all free." It probably seemed to Hazell that, although legally free, he was being treated as a slave, for it is doubtful that free black men truly had the luxury of "volunteering" for such labor. By August 20, 1861, when Confederate authorities took charge of the fort, it was nearly ready for action.

Burnside and his subordinate commanders planned a quick, efficient strike at Fort Macon. Brig. Gen. John G. Parke's brigade was assigned the task. Parke assembled his men and Burnside's siege train at Morehead City, occupied Beaufort, and crossed to Bogue Island by mid-April 1862. He then constructed three batteries along the southern edge of the island at a distance of 1,280 to 1,680 yards from the fort. Flagler's Battery contained four 10-inch mortars, Morris's Battery held three 30-pounder Parrotts, and Prouty's Battery had four 8-inch mortars. A covering line of detached rifle pits was placed 900 yards from the fort. Parke's men put each battery on a large sand dune, leaving the forward slope, toward the fort, intact and digging out the rest of it to make gun and mortar emplacements. Sandbag revetments held up the eight-foot-tall parapets, and the Parrott guns also had embrasures. White had no mortars to lob shells onto these batteries.

The Federals were ready to open fire on the morning of April 25, the climactic day of the siege. Joined by the fire of four ships, the bombardment did little damage at first. The Confederates had constructed a huge sand glacis around the fort to protect its masonry walls, and thus it had no prominent profile. When cannon smoke accumulated over the work, gunners had difficulty sighting their targets, and most rounds overshot the fort. White's return fire began to gouge out sections of the Union parapets; the gun crews in Flagler's Battery were almost exposed after a while and had to make repairs with gabions. White's success was temporary. Lt. William S. Andrews and Lt. Marvin Wait, signal officers, were on duty atop a hotel in Beaufort as part of a chain of signal stations Parke had established earlier. They happened to be perfectly placed to see how the Federal rounds were missing the target. Andrews began to signal information to Bogue Island that enabled the gunners to improve their aim. By 11:00 A.M., a majority of rounds were slamming into Fort Macon, and Federal accuracy improved even more as White's return fire decreased. White accepted the inevitable when the protective structure around his magazine began to deteriorate, and he raised a white flag at 4:30 P.M. Negotiations followed, and Parke took possession of Fort Macon on April 26. This was the second time in history that rifled artillery was used against a masonry fort.[22]

Burnside also sent a small force northward to attack the locks of the Dismal Swamp Canal in mid-April. It was a halfhearted effort to calm fears that the Confederates might use the canal to deploy ironclads they were building in coastal North Carolina. Brig. Gen. Jesse L. Reno led the strike, landing 3,000 troops near Elizabeth City on April 19. Col. Ambrose R. Wright defended the canal from his base at South Mills, but he had only his own 3rd Georgia and some cavalry and artillery. Although outnumbered three to one, Wright met Reno three miles south of town where the main road, known locally as Sawyer's Lane, ran through an open field a mile wide. Wright's men took position in a deep drainage ditch that ran along the northern edge of the field. They pulled down a rail fence and constructed crude breastworks on the edge of the ditch. Knowing that another drainage ditch 300 yards ahead might be used by the Federals, they piled rails in it and set the wood afire.

Reno's men came upon the Confederate position on the morning of April 19. While two regiments advanced through the woods on the Rebel left, another tried to turn the right. Before this was accomplished, the 9th New York launched a frontal attack that failed. Once again, as at Roanoke Island, flanking Unionists forced the Confederates out of their prepared position. Wright lost the battle of South Mills, or Sawyer's Lane, and pulled back to a previously prepared line of works behind Joy's Creek, one mile south of town. The creek itself, some ten yards wide, was a good obstruction, but the position could be turned. Wright therefore retreated another twelve miles to North West Locks, where he assumed a position that he was confident could not be turned. Reno did not pursue. He received false information that the Confederates were gathering reinforcements, and because Burnside had given him strict orders not to spend too much time on this minor operation, he retired to the boats and sailed away the next day.[23]

Burnside consolidated his initial gains by May 1862, but there was serious doubt about what to do next. He wanted to strike inland to disrupt Confederate rail communications with Virginia, but Burnside realized he did not have the strength to do that and hold the ports, cities, and countryside he had occupied. McClellan's Peninsula campaign was under way, and that general was calling for more troops to swell his army as it lumbered toward Richmond. Thus there was no prospect of reinforcements for Burnside. Moreover, the North Carolina expedition was short of wagons, cavalry, and artillery, and these resources could not be spared from McClellan's army. McClellan asked Burnside if he could send some troops, or at least strike for Goldsborough to divert Confederate attention from Richmond, but Lee's attacks during the Seven Days campaign curtailed any plans for further offensives in North Carolina. Burnside was ordered to bring all the troops he could spare to Virginia as soon as possible. He left behind his artillery and cavalry but took most of his infantry northward by late July.[24]

The Confederates relied heavily on fortifications in opposing the Union incursion onto North Carolina soil, but they consistently failed to use them properly. At both Roanoke Island and New Bern, the two most important engagements of the campaign, the Rebel earthworks were poorly designed and improperly constructed. Fort Defiance was far too short and too low, the guns were not properly sighted, and no provision was made to guard its flanks. A portion of the works at New Bern was impressively made, but Branch's inability to tie the line closely to the railroad created a gaping hole that the Federals exploited to win the battle. Fort Macon could not stand alone without massive works on Bogue Island or Shackleford Banks to support it, and the light works at South Mills played no role in determining the outcome of the engagement. The Federals had little difficulty overcoming the defenses at every turn.

Burnside's North Carolina campaign established a major Federal presence on the coast that would persist until the end of the war. The full possibilities of this achievement were never realized, however, because the Federals did not exploit them. They maintained troop strength in this enclave of Union control only at a level sufficient to hold it and, now and then, to threaten raids into the interior. This forced the Confederates to detach significant numbers of troops to contain them, but a decisive strike at vital supply lines farther inland was not mounted until very late in the war.

4 : The Peninsula

he Federals began their long-awaited second drive toward Richmond nearly one year after the fall of Fort Sumter. It would be a massive undertaking, involving more troops than had ever been assembled in a single field army in the country's history, and would bring a comparable response from the Confederates. The campaign saw the extensive use of fortifications by both sides for offensive as well as defensive purposes, but they never became the key factor in determining the outcome of the campaign. While the Confederates built complex works along the Warwick River during the Yorktown phase of the campaign, all the other earthworks on the Peninsula were much simpler and of more limited usefulness. No previous operation of the eastern campaigns had utilized fortifications so much, yet the ability of engineers, field commanders, and ordinary soldiers to use them as a weapon to achieve victory was still undeveloped.

Whether or not an army used earthworks was often determined by the attitude of its commander, and George McClellan was, by nature, inclined to rely on them. He had graduated second in the West Point class of 1846 and thus secured a coveted appointment in the Corps of Engineers. The young lieutenant quickly prepared for service in the Mexican War, where he helped plan and build the battery emplacements that softened the Mexican position at Chapultepec. McClellan was one of three members of a commission sent to observe operations during the Crimean War of 1854–56. He was impressed by the Russian defense of Sebastopol and came away from the Crimea a firm believer in the efficacy of field fortifications.[1]

McClellan's willingness to take fortifications seriously as a major element in operations was tied to his innate conservatism as a field commander. Not only did his political leanings lead him to admire elite Southerners and view the war as a conflict for the restoration of the status quo, with no interference in the institution of slavery, but he had an almost overwhelming fear of battlefield loss. McClellan conceived of warfare as an art, the aim of which was to outmaneuver his opponent so as to gain tactical and strategic advantage with minimal loss of men. He was cautious to a fault and prone to use earthworks as a substitute for action rather than as an aid to further advances.[2]

Confederate fort, Centreville. Photographer George N. Barnard called this the principal Rebel fort at Centreville. He exposed the view from atop the wide parapet. Note the earthen banquette and artillery emplacement on the opposite face and the loopholed stockade covering the gorge on the left of the view. Civilian houses and log barracks can just be seen in the background. (Library of Congress)

The Confederate works at Manassas and Centreville haunted him for months during the winter of 1861–62, and McClellan conceived of a strategic advance that would take the positions in flank rather than approach them from the front. The Federals would utilize their control of the Potomac River and the Chesapeake Bay to land troops at Urbanna, fifty miles east of Richmond on the Rappahannock River, and force the Confederates to evacuate their works or lose their line of communications with the capital. McClellan hesitated so long in setting this plan in motion that he gave the Rebels an opportunity to decide, for their own reasons, that Manassas and Centreville had to be evacuated. They were responding to a familiar problem: too few troops to defend too much territory. Gen. Joseph E. Johnston, commander of Rebel forces in northern Virginia, was convinced that a position closer to the Confederate capital would allow him to concentrate his limited manpower. In a meeting between Johnston, President Davis, and the cabinet on February 19, 1862, everyone came to the conclusion that a withdrawal from Manassas and Centreville was a foregone conclusion; the only question that remained was when it should be conducted. Davis wanted it to be at the last possible moment, but Johnston came out of the meeting believing it was entirely at his discretion.

On March 5, Johnston received word of increased Federal activity and immediately concluded it meant an advance on Manassas. He ordered an evacuation of the troops and all supplies that could be taken. The Rebels were gone by March 9. Johnston established a new defensive position on the south side of the Rappahannock River on March 11.

The Federals were surprised by this sudden evacuation. The increased activity that prompted Johnston to retreat was actually McClellan's limited moves to capture Rebel batteries along the Potomac River. A contraband reported Manassas and Centreville empty soon after word arrived at McClellan's headquarters that the Rebels had abandoned the upper Potomac. The general set his army out from Washington, D.C., on March 10 and occupied the railroad junction later that day. McClellan was suitably impressed by the works at Manassas and Centreville. The latter were "formidable," he thought, "more so than Manassas," even though "several dozen embrasures" were occupied by logs painted black. These "Quaker guns" caught the imagination of the public in a way that tended to belittle the danger of enemy fortifications and the excessive caution displayed by the Union commander.[3]

With the Urbanna plan now moot, McClellan dusted off another proposal, made as early as February 3, to outflank Richmond itself. He wanted to land his army on the tip of the Yorktown Peninsula, formed by the near convergence of the York River and the James River, and approach the capital from the southeast. It would take advantage of Union control of the coast, strike the enemy from an unexpected quarter, and avoid a lengthy overland approach to Richmond.[4]

The plan was approved, and the first troop movements began on March 17. Over the next three weeks, some 400 ships transported 121,500 men, 44 batteries, more than 1,100 wagons, and more than 15,600 animals to the Peninsula. The Union's immense resources were demonstrated by Abraham Lincoln's insistence that large numbers of troops be left behind to guard the approaches to Washington. Despite the huge army landed on the Peninsula, there were enough men remaining to position more than 35,000 soldiers in the Shenandoah Valley, over 10,000 at Manassas, more than 7,000 at Warrenton, and 18,000 to man the defenses of the capital.[5]

The Army of the Potomac also had a hefty engineer component, far larger than that of any other Union force. In addition to Capt. James C. Duane's three-company U.S. Engineer Battalion, the 15th and 50th New York

Quaker guns at Centreville. Painted black and stuck into embrasures, these logs could easily be mistaken for cannon when viewed from a distance. This work has three artillery platforms and a good hurdle revetment. Note the expansive countryside and the large parapet that angles across the open space. (Massachusetts Commandery, Military Order of the Loyal Legion and the U.S. Army Military History Institute)

Engineers constituted Brig. Gen. Daniel P. Woodbury's Volunteer Engineer Brigade. Thirty wagons carried entrenching tools for the engineers; tools for the line infantry had to be supplied by McClellan's quartermaster department. The army carried trains of bridging equipment, with a total of 160 pontoons capable of spanning up to 1,500 yards of water. In addition to his chief engineer, McClellan had the services of eight engineer officers of nearly all ranks and levels of experience. Never again would the Army of the Potomac have such lavish engineer assets for a campaign.[6]

McClellan landed this immense army on the Peninsula by utilizing a Union toehold on its tip. Fortress Monroe was garrisoned by a small force under Benjamin Butler, who had also fortified several points near the fort to create a substantial area for the Army of the Potomac to deploy.

The area of McClellan's operations was entirely in the Coastal Plain, or Tidewater, of Virginia. Most of the land on the Peninsula is below 100 feet in elevation, rising to as much as 160 feet the closer one moves to Richmond. The terrain is generally flat but cut by streams. What pass for hills and ridges are really little more than irregularities or undulations in the landscape. The Peninsula has a light and sandy soil that is easy to dig. A cover of mixed pines and hardwoods with thick underbrush characterizes the vegetation. The most serious obstacles in the landscape are sluggish, swampy rivers, such as the Warwick and the Chickahominy. Even in dry weather these streams could be a major impediment to an army; in wet weather, the entire land-scape of the Peninsula turned into cloying mud and the sluggish streams became deep, swift channels.[7]

When McClellan was ready to advance in early April, he sent two columns along the only good roads up the Peninsula. One paralleled the York River by way of Howard's Bridge to Yorktown, and the other skirted the James River to Lee's Mill on the lower reaches of the Warwick River opposite Yorktown. The smaller roads were unpredictable. The general hoped to reach Yorktown in "two rapid marches" and to use one column to cut off Rebel communications with Richmond and the other to invest the place. McClellan assumed heavy works circled the small town. The retreating Rebels felled timber on the roads north of Big Bethel, destroyed bridges, and abandoned a few small earthworks.[8]

McClellan's army moved almost imperceptibly through the first of three Confederate lines on the Peninsula as it marched from Big Bethel to York-town. The line was yet unfinished, and the Rebels never had a firm intention to make their stand there. Known as the Poquosin River Line, it was the shortest of the three defensive positions. Located four and a half miles north of Big Bethel and five miles south of Yorktown, the Poquosin River Line had two well-developed fortifications at Howard's Bridge on the east and Young's Mill on the west. Howard's Bridge lay near the head of the Poquosin River, which starts nearly seven miles inland and flows into the York River. Young's Mill lay near the head of Deep Creek, which starts about two and a half miles inland and flows into the James River. A space of nearly three miles, which Maj. Gen. John B. Magruder called "wooded country" that was defended by a very light line of works, lay between the two fortified posts. Magruder toyed with the idea of defending this line, but he later admitted that, even though anchored by substantial works on the flanks, the center was very weak. He estimated it would take up to 25,000 men to hold it adequately, and he had only 11,000 when he evacuated the line on April 5.[9]

Young's Mill had at least four small works for artillery located on the ends of fingers of land that lay between the ravines that drained into Deep Creek. The fortifications had been built by engineer Lt. Richard Lowndes Poor in

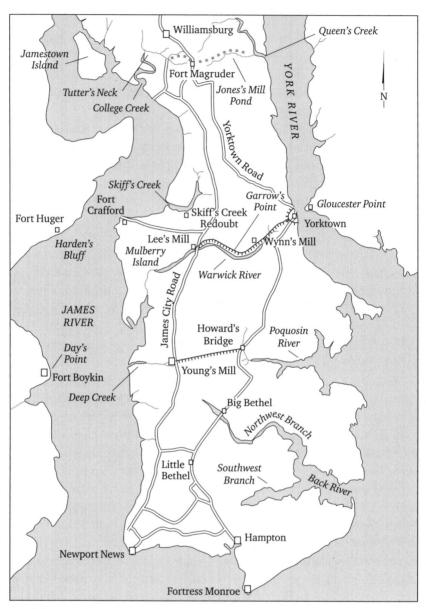

Confederate Defense Lines on the Peninsula, April 1862

October 1861. Poor was frustrated by the irregular terrain, for it allowed for "no regular system being used." He had to fit the works to the fingers of land and often was flustered by the troops assigned him as laborers. One infantry officer had his men raise a parapet only half as high as Poor required. Another officer did not understand what a redan looked like. Poor staked out the shape, explained it to the man, and then rode away to reconnoiter. When he returned, he found that the officer "had played the old boy with the lines"; instead of a sharp chevron, the redan had an irregular U-shaped curve.

Despite these irritations, Poor managed to get the works into proper shape. All were perched about twenty-five feet above the bottom of Deep Creek and followed a general plan. None of them had embrasures, traverses, or other flank protection for the field guns. There was a ditch in front of the artillery emplacements and borrow pits behind the parapet as well, where soldiers obtained more dirt to strengthen the parapet. The guns were placed on the natural level of the earth, not dug down or built up. One of the four works was semicircular, while the others were chevrons made by digging two linear parapets.

Howard's Bridge was defended by two redoubts on the north side of the Poquosin River. The work to the west of the road had embrasures for four guns, while the smaller work to the east had only one embrasure. South of the river, the Confederates had constructed a curved infantry trench west of the road. They cut down the timber within reach of all the works to form an effective abatis. Drawings by topographic draftsman Robert Knox Sneden show the works to be well made, with embrasures for the artillery and post-and-board revetments for the parapets.[10]

Yorktown

Yorktown was already heavily fortified, and Magruder had the beginnings of a good line that stretched across the Peninsula from that town and along the north side of the Warwick River. This line surprised McClellan when the head of his two columns encountered it. The cautious commander had no thought of breaking through without reconnaissance, so his advance halted. The presence of extensive fortifications on the east bank of the York River, opposite Yorktown at Gloucester Point, prevented the navy from sailing up the river to outflank the line. Thus, as McClellan informed Winfield Scott, "I find myself with a siege before me."

McClellan played a bit loose with terms, for he really hoped to avoid what he called "the tedious operations of a formal siege." Instead, he planned to bring up mortars and heavy artillery to batter his way through the Warwick Line. He knew that he had immense superiority of numbers over Magruder, believing the Confederates had merely 15,000 men in line, but rather than risk the lives of his soldiers, McClellan refused to act until he could use his heavy ordnance. "Instant assault would have been simple folly," he later reported. Preparation and the accumulation of an avalanche of resources was his plan. "The eclat of taking Yorktown will cover a delay of the few days necessary to get everything in hand & ready for action," he informed his wife.[11]

McClellan's preparations were hampered by his poor maps and the flat landscape of the Peninsula, which made the Confederate positions difficult to scout. His personal reconnaissance on April 6–7 convinced him that his plan to overwhelm the Rebels with weight of ordnance was correct. Engineer officers who were able to catch glimpses of the Rebel works confirmed McClellan's assumption that they were "formidable." The Warwick River itself was an effective obstacle, and the Confederates were rapidly reinforcing the line. By April 7, McClellan was convinced there were 100,000 men facing his 85,000 troops, a gross error that he nevertheless continued to accept. Even as his men went to work digging gun emplacements, McClellan began to call for more troops.[12]

The Federals spent roughly ten days preparing the groundwork for their operations against the Warwick Line, and McClellan was ready to begin building gun emplacements by April 17. Initially, six batteries were planned, situated from 1,500 to 2,000 yards from the Confederate works. Batteries No. 1 and 2 were constructed in three days, but the others took much more time and labor to complete. Connecting lines between these works were begun on April 25. The lines were laid out by engineer officers, and enlisted men dug them twelve feet wide and three feet deep. Most of the digging was done at night; the Rebels could hear the noise but fired only randomly at the workers.[13]

"It seems the fight has to be won partially through the implements of peace, the shovel, axe & pick," commented a New Hampshire man as the Federals dug into the sandy soil. The shape of things to come was apparent to Robert Knox Sneden when he saw "Hundreds of new picks and shovels" deposited near the headquarters of the Third Corps. The enlisted men worked in large groups. Ward Osgood of the 15th Massachusetts saw a gang of 100 soldiers building a gun emplacement behind a sheltering screen of trees. The Rebels had failed to cut the timber very far in front of their line, so the Yankees dug in on their side of the trees to obscure their work and cut down the timber when finished. On the far right, where most of the digging was done, the Federals were excited when they realized they were building works exactly where George Washington had entrenched during

Federal Battery No. 1, Yorktown. The only one of McClellan's batteries to open fire on the Confederates, it was located on the Farinholt property. Note the use of sandbags and gabions as revetment and the many ladders that gave access to the tops of the traverses. (Massachusetts Commandery, Military Order of the Loyal Legion and the U.S. Army Military History Institute)

the Yorktown siege. "The parallels which WASHINGTON had built, eighty years before, could be traced as easily as if erected only the day previous," noted the historian of the 2nd New Hampshire, "and oftentimes the same dirt which had been thrown up by our forefathers to establish the Union was shoveled over by us to perpetuate it." They found numerous bullets, bones, and other relics of the Revolution but carefully reburied the remains as they were uncovered.[14]

McClellan's engineer officers worked with a will, laying out battery emplacements, scouting the Rebel lines, drawing maps, directing work details, and sometimes placing themselves in danger. Lt. Orlando L. Wagner, an engineer on the staff of the Third Corps, was laying out a new work near Battery No. 7 when he was mortally wounded by enemy fire. Three enlisted men had helped him use a steel tape to mark out the location of the work, and Wagner had drawn sketches on a plane table shielded from the sun by a parasol. This probably drew Confederate attention, and a shell explosion so damaged his arm that it had to be amputated. He died four days later.

Capt. William Heine, a Prussian observer who served as a topographical engineer on the Third Corps staff, discovered long strips of freshly sawn lumber nailed to trees. The Confederates had apparently placed them to serve as artillery range markers. The boards, six inches wide, were nailed vertically on the tree trunks and could be seen from quite a distance. Heine and three enlisted men quickly tore them down.[15]

One of the reasons construction of the batteries was postponed until April 17 was McClellan's need to organize supporting elements for the work. The existing civilian roads were completely inadequate for the movement of supplies, heavy guns, and men up to the line; also, planking had to be cut to build revetments, and depots had to be established to feed and supply the huge army. The Federals were helped greatly by the discovery of a working sawmill less than two miles from the Rebel line along the Yorktown Road. The same machinery that had recently been used to cut lumber for Rebel barracks now was used to cut planks for Union earthworks. Other materials essential for the construction of fortifications were gabions and fascines, which made good revetments for gun embrasures or bulk for widening or increasing the height of parapets.[16]

The military roads required a large expenditure of manpower, for they had to be built for several thousands of yards in order to connect the new battery emplacements with civilian roads. Michigan soldier Perry Mayo reported that the roads "had to be graded as nice as a railroad" because guns weighing as much as twenty tons had to be hauled over them. By the time the artillery was ready to be emplaced, the spring rains had set in, turning the Peninsula into a quagmire and negating much of the fine grading. The heaviest artillery presented the worst problem. It had to be transported up to three miles from the landings to the batteries, and often the guns sank to the axles of their carriages; they had to be manhandled out of the mire by the unfortunate men of the 1st Connecticut Heavy Artillery and the 5th New York Heavy Artillery. Supporting infantry had to build a corduroy road, consisting of cut logs laid side by side, that was wide enough for two teams to pass each other.[17]

The Connecticut and New York artillerymen were responsible for McClellan's siege train, a special unit consisting of seventy heavy guns and mortars. The biggest of these guns were two 200-pounder Parrotts and twelve 100-pounder Parrotts. The rest of the ordnance in the siege train consisted of 20- and 30-pounder Parrotts, a 4.5-inch Rodman, and forty-one mortars ranging in caliber from eight to thirteen inches.[18]

Most of the immense amount of labor that took place in the Union lines throughout April was done willingly by the enlisted men, but a few Federals began to balk toward the end of the month as they grew tired of the heavy work. Sometimes the fault lay squarely with the officers, who did not take the work seriously enough to supervise their men properly. An engineer officer reported that some infantry officers in charge of work details preferred to lie in the shade of the trees rather than watch their men. Even when the officers were willing, administrative foul-ups sometimes delayed the work. If precise information about where the work parties were to go on a given day was not conveyed, the parties appeared where the engineer officers were not, and vice versa.[19]

But there was only one recorded instance of enlisted men refusing to dig. Capt. Wesley Brainerd of the 50th New York Engineers was in charge of a work detail at Battery No. 4 one rainy night when members of the 74th New York went on strike. "The Officers used any means in their power to get the men to work but to no purpose," Brainerd recorded. He had to postpone the planned work that night because the New Yorkers returned to their camp at 9:00 P.M. Brainerd reported the unit's dereliction of duty to headquarters, but nothing was done about it.[20]

Beyond this single instance of a refusal to dig, there were many cases of soldiers putting only partial effort into their labor. Engineer Lt. Miles D. McAlester reported near the end of the confrontation at Yorktown that "no interest whatever in the work could be excited in the officers, and that therefore the men were generally idle." At the same time, Barnard was forced to report that "officers and men from Hooker's division worked badly." To give them their due, the infantrymen were not used to such heavy labor, and it was expected of these green soldiers in a concentrated form under a spring sky that often deluged them with more rain than they needed. Robert Knox Sneden noted how the heavy labor taxed the infantrymen. "Those who work in the trenches grow thin," he wrote, "and officers and men complain of being overworked. The field hospitals show it." Orders went out to issue three gills of whiskey per day for the men, but the mud and rain often caused sickness even with this internal fortification.[21]

McClellan's management of the "siege" of Yorktown cannot be faulted. Once he had decided to emplace batteries and bombard his way through the Warwick Line, his men spent the right amount of time and labor preparing the works to achieve that goal. Yet the general felt compelled to explain why it was taking him so long to advance up the Peninsula. "I can't go 'with a rush' over strong posts," he wrote his wife. "I must use heavy guns & silence their fire—all that takes much time & I have not been longer than the usual time for such things—much less than the usual in truth." McClellan promised to attack "the first moment I can do so successfully—but I don't intend to hurry it—I cannot afford to fail." Meanwhile, he was quite prepared for any sallies by Magruder; "the more he does attack the better I shall be contented." With his emphasis on placing as much heavy ordnance as possible to batter the Rebels, McClellan was convinced he was "avoiding the faults of the Allies at Sebastopol."[22]

McClellan was content to act as his own supervisor of the siege until he slogged through the muddy trenches on the afternoon of April 27. "Went over the whole extent & saw everything with care," he informed his wife. McClellan discovered "so many blunders committed" that he appointed Brig. Gen. Fitz John Porter, commander of the Fifth Corps, as "Director of the Siege." McClellan admitted it was "a novel title," but the position was essential to the efficient running of the varied work needed to complete the fortifications. Porter, who enjoyed McClellan's complete confidence, would "save me much trouble, relieve my mind greatly & save much time." Before Porter's appointment, the daily details were supervised by the senior brigadier general of each division, who was given the title "General of the Trenches" for his division's sector. Now Porter could bring his talents to bear and exercise control over the entire line. With help from two of McClellan's aides, who served as an impromptu staff, Porter visited the line of works and acquainted himself with its configuration and state of readiness. Then he issued instructions for "united action under all circumstances on the whole front and for expediting the completion of the works."[23]

Despite the sporadic refusal to work, the Army of the Potomac was full of confidence during its stay in front of the Rebel works at Yorktown. Stephen Minot Weld, an officer on Porter's staff, expressed a view that was widely held. He felt assured that McClellan would never waste lives and was impressed by the enormous marshaling of resources. "The whole affair will be conducted on scientific principles applied by skilful engineers, and with a man at the head whose forte is in this kind of warfare, namely General McClellan. My idea is that he will take the place with the least possible sacrifice of life, and in order to do this, he must have sufficient time to carry out all his plans thoroughly."[24]

Magruder, Johnston, and the Warwick Line

The Warwick Line that gave McClellan reason to pause was incomplete when he confronted it in early April. By the end of the month, however, it would be transformed into one of the strongest defensive positions of the war. Credit for the construction of the line belongs to John Bankhead Magruder. Born in Maryland in 1807, Magruder graduated from West Point in 1830 and was commissioned into the infantry. The young officer was soon transferred to the artillery, where he served for the remainder of his time in the U.S. Army. He participated in the Second Seminole War and contributed greatly to the success of Winfield Scott's campaign to Mexico City in 1847. Magruder helped build the American siege works at Vera Cruz and commanded an artillery company in the bombardment of that strategic port city. He participated in the battle of Cerro Gordo and continued with Scott all the way to the Mexican capital. Service on the frontier followed in the 1850s.[25]

Magruder became familiar with the art of fortification through his experience in the artillery. Joseph L. Brent, who served on his staff as chief ordnance officer during the Peninsula campaign, thought the flamboyant general "had the faculty of an engineer in discovering strong and weak localities intended to be defended, and allowed no detail to escape him in the way of preparation."[26]

The works at Yorktown, Gloucester Point, and Jamestown Island were started in May 1861 when Robert E. Lee, then major general of the Virginia Forces, sent an engineer officer to initiate construction. Infantry regiments were given tools and told to dig in around Yorktown and at Gloucester Point, but there were never enough troops available to push the work forward as rapidly as desired. Magruder tried to employ slaves and free black laborers but was frustrated by many roadblocks. The secretary of war thought it unlikely the Federals would make a move against Yorktown that fall or winter, and he was reluctant to incur the expense of mobilizing civilian laborers of any kind. Moreover, he did not want to take slaves from plantations during harvest season. The Engineer Bureau also made it clear that holding free black laborers beyond the sixty-day maximum mandated by law was "cruel" and would not be allowed. Governor John Letcher of Virginia even worried that, in their zeal, labor press gangs might mistake a small population of Pamunkeys living in King William County and King and Queen County for free blacks. He strictly prohibited any effort to coerce these Native Americans into the work details at Yorktown, though he believed their chief might voluntarily provide workers if he were asked.[27]

Magruder was also frustrated when he tried to round up slave labor from local plantation owners. Thirty-two slaves arrived at Jamestown and worked one month before their release, but many planters were reluctant to send their men. William Jerdone of Charles City County complained that he had already sent eleven slaves in the summer of 1861, still had not been paid for their labor, and had even lost the tools he had sent with them. He could not spare any workers now. When Magruder issued a second call for slave laborers, Jerdone argued that proper accommodations for them had to be made before he would risk his valuable property.

Magruder persisted by ordering planters to send help in the spring of 1862. Jerdone was to provide half of his slave force but sent only nine hands. Several became sick on the job, and one died. Another planter, John A. Selden of Westover, sent six slaves to Jamestown. Two returned within one month, and he heard that two others were ill.

Jerdone's and Selden's reluctance to comply with the army's requests was not unusual. Magruder managed to gather no more than 1,000 slaves in December 1861 and worked them on semipermanent earthworks around Yorktown and Gloucester Point, but most were reclaimed by their owners after a short time on the job.[28]

By the time McClellan appeared, the fieldworks that constituted the Warwick Line barely existed. There were only 11,000 men available to hold a position that was thirteen and a half miles long. Six thousand Confederates were detailed to garrison Yorktown, Gloucester Point, and Mulberry Island. The remainder were stretched out along the rest of the line. Magruder had the services of a very good chief engineer, Capt. Isaac M. St. John, a Yale University graduate and prewar civil engineer. Alfred L. Rives dispatched eight additional engineer officers to help St. John push the works forward in early April. Despite the immense amount of labor Magruder's men expended on the Warwick Line, the commander never hoped it would be a permanent defensive barrier. He wanted to delay the Federals as long as possible while heavy reinforcements arrived from Joseph E. Johnston's army on the Rappahannock River. Magruder was eminently successful in fulfilling this limited objective.[29]

Half of the defensive power of the Warwick Line was the Warwick River itself. One of the more substantial streams on the Peninsula, it originated in the marshes half a mile west of Yorktown and flowed westward across the flat landscape to the James River. For the most part, the banks were low, swampy, and "covered with dense fringes of thickets and small trees," as Union brigade leader Oliver Otis Howard put it. In its lower course, downstream from Lee's Mill, the river ran through a hollow 400 yards wide, with forty-foot-high bluffs on either side, before emptying into the tidal basin formed by the James.[30]

Magruder enhanced the defensive power of this obstacle by strengthening two dams built by civilian millers—at Wynn's Mill and Lee's Mill—and building three new dams to flood the stream. Protected by earthworks, these dams turned a watercourse that naturally was about two feet deep and fifteen feet wide above Lee's Mill into a watery obstacle fifty feet wide. It could still be waded with some difficulty in places, but there were no longer any fords. Magruder estimated that at least three-fourths of the length of the river was completely impassable for infantry. The newly constructed dams were located one mile above Lee's Mill, two-thirds of a mile farther upstream at a place called Garrow's Point (which was called Dam No. 1), and a half-mile above Wynn's Mill, the uppermost location. Because spring rains washed chunks of earth away, the Confederates had to undertake enormous labor to maintain the dams. Brig. Gen. Howell Cobb complained that if more rain fell, Dams No. 1 and 2 "both will go. All that *ten engineers & several hundred negroes* could do *to day* has been done," he informed his superior on April 9.[31]

The Warwick Line was the most formidable field fortification built in the eastern theater of operations before the Chancellorsville campaign. It employed defense in depth, which was comparatively rare in the Civil War, at two key points. The Confederates made heavy use of traverses for flank protection of infantry as well as artillery, and they utilized communication trenches, covered ways, bombproofs, and water obstacles. As an added boon to researchers and students of the war, the best of these works are well preserved in Newport News Park and Colonial National Historical Park.

The heavy works at Yorktown itself wrapped around the place on three sides. These were semipermanent fortifications mounting a number of heavy guns, with thick parapets and deep ditches. They also, in many places, duplicated British defenses from the 1781 siege. Several water batteries had guns trained to fire on boats steaming up the York River. Across the wide stream at Gloucester Point, the Confederates had a smaller but equally strong complex of semipermanent works. These were principally designed to fire on Union boat traffic.

From Yorktown, a line of hastily constructed field fortifications took shape across the Peninsula with several strongpoints. While the Federals called the first two works on this line the White and Red Redoubts, the Confederates designated the former as Fort Magruder. Both were self-contained works connected to the line of infantry trench. They were located on the spine of high ground that served as the watershed of the Peninsula. This ground seemed the most likely spot for a Union attack, so a second line of infantry trench was dug to the rear, connected to the front line with communication trenches. Wynn's Mill was the next strongpoint, located at a significant bend in the Warwick Line and therefore demanding many traverses. Dam No. 1 at Garrow's Point also was studded with multiple artillery and infantry lines to create defense in depth, and Lee's Mill was treated with heavy artillery emplacements. Mulberry Island, on the north bank of the James River, was

Confederate artillery emplacement, Yorktown. Taken by George N. Barnard in June 1862, this view shows a carriage that had mounted a gun the Confederates named after D. H. Hill. Note the extensive use of sandbags and the log-and-post revetment. (Library of Congress)

the western anchor of the Warwick Line. Fort Crafford was located here to fire on river traffic.

Many Union engineers came to admire the work done by the Confederates at Yorktown. Naturally they could more easily see the impediments to an approach toward the line and caught only limited glimpses of the works themselves. John G. Barnard wrote that "every kind of obstruction which the countryside offered, such as abatis, marsh, inundation, & c., was skilfully used."[32]

The Confederates owed a debt of gratitude to John Magruder for his effective transformation of this meager line of works into a formidable position. But Magruder would soon be superseded. President Davis had decided early in April that Joseph E. Johnston should transfer most of his men to the Peninsula and take command there. The shift of troops began immediately, the object being to leave no more than 8,000 men on the Rappahannock. Johnston inspected the Warwick Line on April 14 to determine how long it would be advisable to hold at Yorktown.

Johnston brought to the task a great deal of experience, prestige, and careful attention to detail, but he seems to have been predisposed to abandon the Warwick Line from the beginning. A graduate of the West Point class of 1829, with Robert E. Lee, Johnston was commissioned into the artillery. As a member of Winfield Scott's staff, he helped to oversee the siege of Vera Cruz and later commanded troops in the battles outside Mexico City. Johnston was made brigadier general and held the post of quartermaster general of the U.S. Army in June 1860. He played a large role in the victory at First Manassas and was a natural selection for command of the army defending northern Virginia and Richmond.

Yet Johnston shared McClellan's conservative approach to military operations. Always ready to act on the defensive, he also felt more secure positioned close to the capital. Johnston now made a cursory inspection of Magruder's fortifications. He looked at the works surrounding the town and visited the Red and White Redoubts and Wynn's Mill. What he saw created a quiet sense of gloom, so he apparently canceled a planned trip to Gloucester Point and the third line of Rebel works on the Peninsula, at Williamsburg. Johnston noted the shortages of axes and ammunition, discounted the fact that already 31,500 troops were working feverishly on the line, and easily came to the conclusion that it would be unwise to hold at Yorktown. In a conference with the president, Johnston was opposed by Davis and Lee, both of whom wanted the army to delay McClellan as long as possible on the Peninsula. Johnston agreed to wait until the Federals were ready to open with their heavy artillery, but he had no intention of fighting for the Warwick Line.[33]

Johnston's decision meant that Magruder's earthworks would never really be tested in battle. Was this decision wise? It was based mostly on Johnston's aversion to risking everything in battle and his preference for winning his goals through maneuver. But it was also inspired by the incomplete nature of the earthworks themselves. Magruder's men literally were in the process of turning the line into a strong position. Two weeks later, when the Yorktown phase of the Peninsula campaign neared its end, that line was stronger, and Johnston would have 55,000 men to defend it. There is no doubt that he could have prolonged the stalemate at Yorktown by many days, if not weeks, if he had been willing to suffer casualties. But the ultimate outcome would probably have been a Union victory anyway. Brig. Gen. Jubal A. Early, whose brigade held the section that included the Red and White Redoubts, later noted that the Rebels could not have launched significant attacks on the Federals because of the obstruction posed by the Warwick River, and they were too thinly stretched to be certain of resisting a massive attack. Early thought that McClellan could have "shelled us out of" the works. It was, therefore, merely a matter of time before the Warwick Line would have to be abandoned, but, typically, Johnston was eager to do so early rather than late.[34]

Meanwhile, McClellan's engineer officers scanned what they could see of the Rebel line and concluded that the only weak area was around Dam No 1. The river just below the dam was shallow enough to be waded, and the works were not yet complete. The Federals launched a reconnaissance in force against the dam on April 16. Local commanders exceeded their instructions, and the push turned into a serious attack. It was preceded by a general bombardment by the field artillery; a total of twenty-two Union guns were in the vicinity of the dam, while only three Confederate pieces were in place to defend it. The bombardment started at 9:00 A.M. and lasted nearly all day. Two of the Rebel guns rarely fired, giving the Federals the impression that they had silenced them. The artillery at Wynn's Mill also participated in the exchange.[35]

Four companies of the 4th Vermont waded the river just below the dam, where the water was from two to five feet deep, at 4:00 P.M. They took the defending Confederates by surprise, driving the 15th North Carolina and the 16th Georgia out of the works. Reinforced by 600 men from their own regiment and the 6th Vermont, the Federals remained in the captured works for more than an hour before a Confederate counterattack drove them out. More troops of the 4th Vermont attacked along the dam, but they were easily repulsed. The 6th Vermont crossed farther downstream and made a brief lodgment on the other side, but it was pushed back by a Rebel counterstrike. The Federals gained nothing by this operation and lost 44 killed and 148 wounded. Two days later, a truce was arranged so the Confederates could deliver 29 of the Vermont dead to the Federals in the middle of the dam.[36]

Life in the Trenches

On the same day that the Rebels gave up the Yankee dead at Dam No. 1, Ward Osgood of the 15th Massachusetts offered his brother the opinion that "it will be quite a long siege—the taking of Yorktown probably two or three weeks." He was prescient about the schedule but naive at terming a three-week siege a long affair. Other than enduring heavy manual labor, the ordinary Federal soldier fared well, which contributed to Osgood's lack of concern about the outcome. The routine of the 1st Massachusetts was probably typical of that of other regiments. The men were up by 4:00 A.M., formed under arms for one hour in case of a Rebel attack at dawn, then ate breakfast and counted out the details for work on the fortifications. They returned by dark but often had their sleep interrupted by false alarms delivered by the pickets. Their daily routine was enlivened by the increasingly fierce sharpshooting that took place on both sides of the Warwick River and the extensive use of balloons for reconnaissance.[37]

Outnumbered two to one, the Confederates had more work, picket duty, and stress to endure. They vividly described the difficulties of the siege in letters home and in their postwar memoirs. High-ranking officers felt as much stress as the common soldier. Daniel Harvey Hill slept only three hours each night and admitted that his men slept as little. "They stay in the trenches in the rain & cold all night, & all day," he reported. "Sickness is making terrible havoc among them." The 8th Alabama was continuously in the trenches from April 3 through May 3, except for four days, and the men were constantly working. "During the Siege the men were much exhausted from the heavy duty and incessant watching," recalled Hilary A. Herbert, an officer of the 8th. "To add to our discomfort, a cold wintry rain was falling more than half the time." The rain was especially noteworthy, for it seemed to pour nearly every day. The trenches often were filled with water, men sank six inches into the mud, and clothing and blankets were soaked. The flat terrain impeded drainage, and the dams along the Warwick further lessened the flow. A morass formed along the stream that separated the two armies. Due to the close proximity of the Yankees, the Rebels could rarely afford to build fires to ward off the chilly weather, and rations often were reduced to a bit of salt meat and hard bread.[38]

Many Confederate regiments had to endure artillery fire or engage in minor operations to deny terrain advantages to the enemy. The 24th Virginia sallied forth on the evening of April 12 to cut down an orchard and burn some buildings used by Yankee sharpshooters. They were fired on by pickets, and one man was wounded. Two other regiments and a battery supported the Virginians as they finished their work in ninety minutes. All along the line the daily sharpshooting increased in strength and vigor, forcing the men to crouch low behind their parapets. "I have had to lay in water nee Deep all day and all Night to Ceep the yankey Balls from hiting me," complained Henry M. Talley of the 38th Virginia. Sometimes the firing reached an intensity that compelled regimental and brigade leaders to ready their men for an attack. One-third of the 23rd North Carolina were kept on guard at all times, and the rest were placed in the works at 10:00 P.M. on April 19, because commanding officers were worried about the increased firing near Wynn's Mill. The men were allowed rest later that night, but Orderly Sgt. Henry C. Wall had to waken them for duty at 3:00 A.M. on April 20; he had a very difficult time getting them up and into the works.[39]

Thus thousands of Union and Confederate troops were exposed to the peculiar dangers and duties of trench warfare, even though the attrition of manpower was limited and the length of line and frequency of combat were nothing like the coming Petersburg campaign. Despite all this, the morale of Johnston's troops remained high. They were as yet mostly green soldiers filled with a high level of motivation for the war, and everyone wanted to do his part for the cause. The growing strength of their earthworks increased their confidence, for without them the army could not have held its position at Yorktown. Long after the war, artillery officer Edward Porter Alexander would remember the Warwick Line as "mere ditches with dirt thrown out in front," but most Confederates were proud of their digging at Yorktown. A Tar Heel soldier named Joseph F. Gibson thought the place was "well fortified." The works were stronger than those at Manassas Junction, he rightly concluded. "We are so strongly fortified that they can't hurt *us* at all," crowed James Peter Williams of Brown's Chesapeake Artillery. Nathaniel Venable Watkins, a member of the 4th Virginia Heavy Artillery, was impressed by the strength and even the beauty of the works at Gloucester Point. "It is perfectly astonishing to see the great amount of work which has been done during the last two or three weeks," he wrote to his wife on April 18. "The whole face of things has been changed since I first came here, and our fortifications are I think twice as strong. It will be a most beautiful place when finished—the batteries are laid off so regularly & some of them turfed over so beautifully. I was standing guard this morning on the highest point of our works where I could have a full view of Yorktown, all of our works, York river, and the Yankee fleet. I often wished that you could be with me, and enjoy the beautiful scenery."[40]

The Fall of Yorktown

The tranquillity that Watkins so much enjoyed was interrupted on April 30 when the first Union artillery fire from the heavy batteries descended on Yorktown. McClellan wanted the guns to fire on the wharf to interrupt the flow of supplies to the Warwick Line. Battery No. 1, the heaviest of the Union gun emplacements, opened at 2:00 P.M. with five 100-pounder Parrotts and one 200-pounder Parrott. Half a dozen ships at the wharf immediately scattered. The heaviest Confederate ordnance able to return fire was an 8-inch Columbiad, no match for the monster Parrotts, and it was firing at its maximum range, 6,200 yards. Firing slowly because of the difficulty of reloading such huge guns, the Federals pumped thirty-nine projectiles—an assortment of solid shot, percussion shells, time fuse shells, and even four Greek fire shells—into the wharf area. They continued the shelling on May 1 despite a heavy fog.

That day, Johnston held a conference of his officers to express his decision to evacuate Yorktown. These few shells were enough to send his large army retreating up the Peninsula. Johnston was convinced that the heavier Union artillery would silence his guns and pave the way for an assault or siege approaches. The evacuation was ordered for the evening of May 2, but the Confederates had to endure a hail of sixty rounds on the wharf and the water batteries that day as they prepared to leave. Their 8-inch Columbiad burst trying to counter this heavy fire. Johnston had to postpone the evacuation one day, until the evening of May 3, due to administrative confusion regarding the organization of his trains. That day, Battery No. 1 fired thirty-four rounds, unanswered by the Confederates, and five other Union batteries were ready to open on May 4.[41]

The evacuation took the Federals by surprise. McClellan was happy that some of his guns were firing at the wharf and jubilant at the near prospect of a full-scale bombardment by all of his heavy batteries. "It will be a tremendous affair when we do begin & will I hope make short work of it." He expected the full bombardment to begin on May 5 or 6 and believed Yorktown would fall in two days. The Federals noticed their enemy was unusually quiet on the night of May 3, and McClellan suspected either an attack or a withdrawal. "I do not want these rascals to get away from me without a sound drubbing," he bragged to his wife.[42]

Despite McClellan's desire to test the batteries, everyone in blue received the news of Johnston's evacuation with joy and relief. Many units immediately crossed the narrow no-man's-land and entered the Rebel works. Some Unionists met with a terrible surprise: dozens of torpedoes planted in exposed places. American soldiers had never encountered such weapons before, and these explosives struck everyone as diabolical because they killed and maimed by surprise and seemed to take life for the sake of killing rather than to achieve some immediate tactical goal. Even many Confederates found their use distasteful.

The torpedoes were entirely the work of Brig. Gen. Gabriel James Rains, commander of an Alabama and Georgia brigade in Daniel Harvey Hill's left wing. A West Point graduate, Rains had experimented with explosives in the prewar army and had devised an especially sensitive detonation device. Without receiving permission from higher authorities, he had taken it upon himself to plant artillery shells in front of certain sections of the works at Yorktown but left them unarmed. Only when the order to evacuate was given did he prime the booby traps and order the planting of many more shells inside the works. In addition to delaying the Federal pursuit, Rains was motivated by a desire to avenge the shelling of his hometown of New Bern, North Carolina, just before it was captured on March 15.[43]

The first torpedoes were encountered more than 100 yards in front of the town defenses at Yorktown. They were 8- and 10-inch mortar shells rigged to explode when stepped on. Upon entering the works, the Federals were shocked to find primed shells concealed in a variety of places. They were planted in the streets of Yorktown, near springs and wells, under shade trees, near telegraph poles, under coats that appeared to have been discarded on the ground, or inside carpetbags and flour barrels. "In some cases," reported McClellan's artillery inspector, Brig Gen. William F. Barry, "articles of common use, and which would be most likely to be picked up, such as engineers' wheelbarrows, or pickaxes, or shovels, were laid upon the spot with apparent carelessness. Concealed strings or wires leading from the friction primer of the shell to the superincumbent articles were so arranged that the slightest disturbance would occasion the explosion." The most ingenuous arrangement was in a house in Yorktown, where a coffeepot under a table in one corner of a room was attached by string to a weight that would fall on a torpedo when moved. Several shells were placed at the foot of the cellar stairs, and another room of the same house had a large shell on the table. No one could see how it was to be detonated, so everyone avoided entering the room. Rains used some large projectiles for the 8-inch Columbiad and arranged for them to explode when someone stepped on a small piece of wood that would snap the percussion cap.[44]

Several Yankees were injured or killed by these devices. A telegraph operator attached to Third Corps headquarters was blown to bits when he entered Yorktown to send a message, touched the instrument, and exploded a shell. The 40th New York entered one of the gun emplacements around Yorktown and assembled inside. The command was given to "order arms," so the men grounded their rifle muskets. One of the butts came down on a percussion cap and detonated a torpedo. Two soldiers were killed instantly and seven were wounded; "the torn limb of one was thrown thirty feet from the body," according to the regiment's assistant surgeon. The New Yorkers immediately evacuated the work and posted guards to keep everyone out. Col. Edwin C. Mason of the 7th Maine went ahead of his column to look for torpedoes and crushed a percussion cap with his foot. Fortunately the shell failed to explode. When Mason moved the dirt away, he saw the "red wax at the top of the buried shell" and counted himself an extremely lucky man. Mason then called for volunteers, who scoured the road on their hands and knees and found more than a dozen torpedoes. Mason saved his men, but McClellan estimated that at least five Federals were killed and more than a dozen were wounded by these "infernal machines."[45]

The Federals quickly learned how to deal with this novel threat. "Wherever you could see the dirt thrown up loosely, look out for your feet, or else they would be catching in some string . . . under the dirt, and then shells would explode," wrote Peleg W. Blake of the 5th Massachusetts Battery. Once located, the shells were marked with small red flags. Oliver Otis Howard shouted himself hoarse telling his men not to stray off the road or to touch any small boards lying on the ground. As awareness of these devices spread and more were located and marked with flags, the casualties lessened. After the first day, no one around Yorktown was injured by Rains's land mines.[46]

Even as the troops chased Johnston toward Williamsburg, they discovered some torpedoes planted in the road. Many mines had a foot or two of telegraph wire sticking out of the ground, apparently designed to catch a foot or a horse's hoof and fire the shell. The red flags were brought out, and the officers detailed men to stay behind and warn upcoming columns when clusters of shells were found. Rains toyed with the pursuing Federals. They found several heaps of dirt on the road to Williamsburg and wasted an hour carefully digging them out but uncovered no torpedoes. Rains installed a more deadly surprise on the road near Williamsburg. He found an abandoned ammunition wagon with five loaded shells and planted four of them, armed with his sensitive primer, near some trees that had been cut to fall across the road. The shells were exploded "with terrific effect" by the first Federal cavalry to arrive on the scene. William F. Barry witnessed the "horrible mangling" of a Yankee cavalryman and his horse on Williamsburg Road.[47]

McClellan was outraged by the concealed torpedoes. He agreed with Barry that such devices located in the glacis or in the bottom of the ditch of an earthwork were legitimate tricks of war, but to sew them promiscuously where they would kill without defending a position was barbarous. "I shall make the prisoners remove them at their own peril," he reported to Secretary of War Edwin Stanton. Two companies of the 50th New York Engineers were also detailed to dig them up.[48]

Johnston knew nothing of these torpedoes until he saw McClellan's report printed in the *New York Herald*. He made inquiries on May 12 and found that Rains was responsible, but he did nothing to discipline him. Word had already filtered through the Confederate command structure. While retreating from Williamsburg to Richmond, James Longstreet made a point of writing to Rains that he absolutely forbid him from planting shells on any roads used by his Center Division. Daniel Harvey Hill apparently had no objections to their continued use and neither did Rains. But Secretary of War George W. Randolph disapproved, expressing the opinion that it was wrong to take life for the sake of killing if no other, larger purpose could be gained.[49]

Fortunately for the pursuing Yankees and for the reputation of the retreating Rebels, Rains did not plant any more infernal machines. He proved to be a failure as an infantry commander in the coming battle of Seven Pines, the only engagement in which he led troops, and was soon shifted into administrative positions. His greatest contribution to the Confederate cause was in fashioning and deploying hundreds of submarine torpedoes to protect coastal cities such as Charleston and Mobile. Yorktown was the first of at least nine instances in the Civil War in which land mines were used.[50]

The confrontation at Yorktown ended on an anticlimactic note. Only Battery No. 1, of the fourteen Union gun emplacements, had the opportunity to test its pieces in action. Barnard was convinced that, if all the batteries had had a chance to pound the Rebels, the defenses would have caved in after only six hours of firing. Johnston abandoned fifty-two heavy guns and mortars. A total of about 500 men were lost by both sides in the siege, most in the abortive Federal attack on Dam No. 1 on April 16.[51]

McClellan's disappointment at not testing his heavy guns was overshadowed by his joy at forcing the Rebels out of their stronghold. He made sure that his superiors understood the strength of the Warwick Line, telling everyone it was "very formidable and could not have been carried without shelling." He bragged to his wife that Johnston must "have been badly scared to have abandoned [the works] in such a hurry." McClellan knew he would be criticized for not attacking earlier and argued that it would have been easy to order an assault at any time that would have cost at least 10,000 lives to take the position. He assumed "the world would have thought it more brilliant." Yet the young Napoleon felt "very proud of Yorktown; it and Manassas will be my brightest chaplets in history." He felt so good about these two operations, which were overshadowed by subsequent events, because he felt he had "accomplished everything in both places by pure military skill. I am very proud and grateful to God that he allowed me to purchase such great success at so trifling a loss of life." Admirable as a humanitarian impulse and indicative of why his men loved him, McClellan's sentiment also illustrates why he was not a great field commander. This limitation would eventually doom his Peninsula campaign.[52]

The rank and file of the Army of the Potomac, however, were quite disappointed that the Rebels slipped away with so little punishment. They saw all their hard labor as wasted, forgetting that it was the key to convincing Johnston to abandon his position. "The whole army were much chagrined that the enemy had so cleverly 'skipped out' after giving us all the hard work to construct fourteen batteries, corduroy numerous miles of road, etc.," complained Robert Knox Sneden. "All the fine guns stood up in the different batteries with ammunition piled in them for a forty-eight hours continuous bombardment as monuments of Mcclellan's imbecility and 'fortification on the brain.'"[53]

For their part, the Confederates do not seem to have been inordinately depressed by the retreat. They knew that their digging had stopped an army twice their strength for a month. Referring to the Federals, Magruder's artillery chief wrote, "They seemed determined to forego the gallant charge, and went to the spade and their rifled guns, under the cover of intrenchments, to dislodge us from our position. No other course could have afforded a more ennobling tribute to our small force or a more damaging slur upon the boastful arrogance of the enemy."[54]

McClellan's engineers now had a chance to examine the Rebel works, and they were impressed. "The line is certainly one of the most extensive known in modern times," thought Barnard. That was a professional opinion. The view of volunteer officers was less than generous. Lt. Charles A. Phillips of the 5th Massachusetts Battery was impressed with the quantity of dirt thrown up by the Rebels, but he denigrated "the manner in which it is arranged." The dimensions and profile of the works on his part of the line were "nothing more than those of an ordinary field work." He was convinced that the Rebel guns would have been dismounted and the works would have been reduced by twelve hours of concentrated fire. Henry Abbott of the 20th Massachusetts agreed, noting that the Federal heavies would have "knocked them all to pie in no time." Abbott concluded that "none of the niceties which the books lay down as necessary for the preservation of earth works, & which McClellan's Report says were executed with the greatest finish at Sebastopol, were observed here."[55]

The earthworks at Yorktown still had some useful role to play in the war. The Federals would occupy the town for the rest of the conflict, and they reworked many of the Rebel lines so that a small force could defend the area. Many of the Union works were leveled to prevent their use in an attack on the Federal post, but the more remote trenches were still intact in June 1863. The Confederate works along the Warwick River were left in place by the Federals, who knew that a Confederate force would never be able to use them to strike at Yorktown.[56]

Yorktown was the first confrontation of the eastern campaigns that involved a comparatively large amount of digging, and soldiers and civilians alike used the term "siege" to describe it. This would be a common occurrence throughout the war, for many campaigns, such as Petersburg, Atlanta, and lesser-known operations involving extensive earthworks, would be given that label. McClellan planned a limited attempt at reducing the Yorktown position. He hoped to dig only minimal works to cover his heavy batteries and relied on their firepower to compel a retreat. He never contemplated advancing saps or attacking. He had planned a similar tactic at Rich Mountain, where he was confronted with a strong but much smaller entrenched position and hoped to reduce it with field artillery.

Given his desire to lessen bloodshed, this was the only course open to McClellan. Lt. John C. Palfrey served as an engineer throughout the war. He accurately sized up the tactical situation at Yorktown in a postwar paper presented to the Military Historical Society of Massachusetts. He agreed with McClellan that the navy could not have silenced the batteries at Yorktown or Gloucester Point, and that landing troops to seize the works at the latter place would accomplish nothing if the water batteries at the former were still in operation. Palfrey believed that a concentrated attack could have succeeded against the Red and White Redoubts or Dam No. 1 if McClellan had had the stamina to try one. But he did not think the heavy guns could have silenced the Rebel artillery and forced a determined commander to abandon the line. He was convinced by the Confederate experience at Vicksburg and Battery Wagner that they could have held out another month, even under the heaviest Union artillery fire, thus necessitating siege approaches by the Federals. McClellan was lucky, in other words, that Johnston rather than a more resolute commander was in charge on the other side of the Warwick River.[57]

Williamsburg

While Johnston was retiring to the outskirts of Richmond, an unintended battle took place to his rear. McClellan's subordinates launched a vigorous pursuit and caught up with the Confederates at Williamsburg, ten miles north of Yorktown, where the third line of Rebel works crossed the Peninsula. It was an unfinished line consisting of a string of thirteen redoubts and one large fort, but Johnston had long before decided not to defend it. Subordinate commanders took it upon themselves to make a stand and blunt the Federal pursuit on May 5, resulting in the first battle of the campaign. They made full use of the large earthwork, called Fort Magruder, but ignored the other, smaller works in the line.

The Williamsburg Line was started in the early weeks of the war when Col. Benjamin Stoddert Ewell assumed command of the area. Ewell, the older brother of Richard Stoddert Ewell, a future corps commander in Lee's army, had graduated from West Point in 1832. He taught mathematics and engineering at the academy and also worked as a railroad engineer. In 1848 he became president of William and Mary College. Professor Nathaniel Beverly Tucker led him in a thorough study of the topography around Williamsburg; Ewell knew that the town lay on the spine of the Peninsula, the divide that separated water drainage between the two rivers. At this point two creeks started to flow toward the James and the York. Thus the main road linking Yorktown and Richmond ran through the streets of Williamsburg.

When Lee put Ewell in charge at Williamsburg on May 1, 1861, he instructed him to build a defense line across this spine of land between the heads of Queen's Creek and College Creek. Ewell asked mathematics professor Thomas T. L. Snead to survey the land and then decided to place the works along the north side of both creeks to minimize the length of the line. Lee approved the plan after a cursory inspection, and Ewell issued a call to the citizens of James City, York, and Warwick counties for the use of their slaves. He also asked civilian officials to notify free blacks in the three counties that they were expected to work, too, and he threatened that "a severe penalty" would apply if they did not show up. Ewell also called for spades, hoes, and axes.

But the plan was altered by Lt. Col. Alfred L. Rives, who was sent by Lee to inspect the project in late May. Rives disapproved of Ewell's plan because it ran the line through the northern part of town and would have led to the destruction of many private houses. He advised keeping the right wing intact but moving the center south of Williamsburg and extending the left wing along a line farther south than originally planned. This nearly doubled the length of the line, but it avoided the town and still found advantageous ground. Lee and Magruder approved, and the work was commenced. Hundreds of slaves and free blacks helped the available infantrymen to dig the redoubts. They also rebuilt a mill dam on the left of the line to create a water obstacle and felled trees to make abatis where possible. Fort Magruder and the other works were nearly finished by August. Two months later, Magruder planned to use this line as his last defense on the Peninsula, but Johnston never considered such a possibility when he took charge in April.[58]

The line, as altered by Rives, was four miles long. Some of the redoubts were enclosed, but others were redans, consisting of two parapets that joined at an angle. Each was about 600 to 800 yards from its neighboring works. Redoubts 1 through 4, on the right wing, lay behind a deep ravine formed by a tributary of College Creek called Tutter's Neck. Fort Magruder was located at the junction of the James City and Yorktown roads south of Williamsburg and thus blocked the major route along the spine of the Peninsula. Redoubts 7 through 14 were on the north side of Jones's Mill Pond, a tributary of Queen's Creek. The line formed a giant Z across the breadth of the Peninsula.[59]

The redoubts were mostly square works with sides forty yards long and raised platforms for two or three field guns. Except Fort Magruder, there were no cannons in any of them when Johnston's army passed through on its retreat from Yorktown. Apparently there were some small, scattered infantry

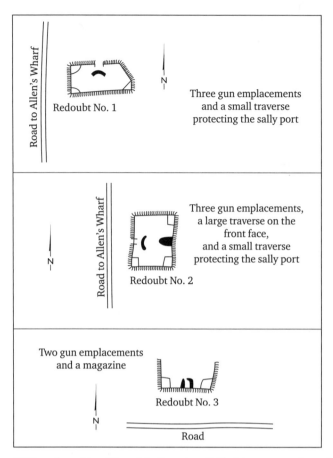

Williamsburg Line, May 1862 (based on field visits, 1994 and 1995)

trenches in front of a few redoubts and redans, but there were no connecting lines between the works. While the Confederates who fought there hardly noticed the fortifications, Union observers found them "well built. . . . The line in itself I think as strong as the one they held at Yorktown save that the flanks can be turned by water," thought artillery officer Charles Wainwright.[60]

Given its size and location, Fort Magruder was the only fortification that was occupied by the Rebels. It was "a large work," thought Union engineer Lt. Miles D. McAlester, but "irregular in *traci*," with "two fronts being bastioned." Trees had already been cut down for 100 yards in front of the work and constituted a superb abatis with limbs and trunks piled 10 feet high in places. The ditch around the fort, 9 feet deep and 9 feet wide, was filled with water from the incessant rains. The parapet was 6 feet high on the interior and 9 feet thick. The interior crest of the parapet measured a total of 600 feet in length. Fort Magruder was far bigger, more complex, and stronger than any other work on the Williamsburg Line. The rest had good ditches and parapets but no traverses for the artillery emplacements. Normally a small traverse was placed inside the work to cover the sally port in the rear, and most of the fortifications had a magazine.[61]

The engagement at Williamsburg was a bloody, pitched battle. Longstreet's division, acting as Johnston's rear guard, turned and took position. The Federals moved up to skirmish with the Rebels who held Fort Magruder, but they soon found that the earthwork was too strong to attempt an assault. Longstreet launched an attack on the Union left, south of the fort, and the Federal Second Corps responded with an assault on the Rebel left by Brig. Gen. Winfield Scott Hancock's brigade, which easily occupied the area around Redoubt No. 11 north of Jones's Mill Pond. Jubal Early's brigade counterattacked from the center of Williamsburg, exposed to a galling infantry and artillery fire, and was repulsed by Hancock with heavy losses. Longstreet's assault on the Union left, held by the Third Corps, was stopped in brutal fighting. This was enough for both sides. As the Confederates continued their retreat, the Federals were content to remain on the battlefield. More then 1,600 Confederate and 2,200 Federal casualties were the result, and Johnston was able to continue his retreat in peace.[62]

Benjamin Stoddert Ewell, who apparently did not participate in the battle, was convinced that his original plan for the Williamsburg Line had been better than Rives's alteration. He lamented the Union occupation of the town and argued that if "Fort Magruder had been where it ought the force in possession of it would necessarily have held Williamsburg." Given that Johnston had no intention of holding Williamsburg in any case, the question of how the line was placed was moot. Rives's line was just as strong as Ewell's line would have been, and it saved a good part of the old, historic town. Nevertheless, Benjamin easily convinced Richard, who bemoaned the interference with his brother's plan.[63]

By the morning of May 6, McClellan's army had marched, dug, and fought its way along the length of the Peninsula. It took more than one month to pass through the three lines of defense Magruder had constructed. This gave the Confederates time to reposition Johnston's army more than seventy miles to meet the developing threat to the capital. Arguably, McClellan could have made faster progress and increased his chances of capturing Richmond that spring, but he was by no means too late to achieve that goal. It would depend on how he approached the city during the coming few weeks.

5 : From Seven Pines to the Seven Days

hen Johnston evacuated the Peninsula, he also abandoned a large number of Confederate forts, water batteries, and defensive lines. The Rebels had expended a great deal of labor for many months perfecting several kinds of earthworks on the Peninsula and along the banks of the James River. Only the Warwick Line proved its mettle in a direct confrontation with McClellan's army. The engineering skill, time, and labor invested in most of the others were ultimately wasted.

Defenses on the James River

The lower James was defended by numerous works. The Confederates fortified six major positions: Fort Boykin at Day's Point, Fort Huger at Harden's Bluff, Mulberry Island (the western anchor of the Warwick Line), Jamestown Island, Fort Powhatan (near the mouth of the Chickahominy), and Drewry's Bluff. The works at Jamestown Island were the most extensive, while the defenses at Drewry's Bluff were the most important. The latter place was the last river defense site capable of preventing Yankee gunboats from steaming to Richmond.[1]

On Jamestown Island, as at Yorktown, the Rebels were digging in hallowed ground, the site of England's first permanent colony in North America. A small island off the mainland, on the north side of the James River about fifty miles downstream from Richmond, it was also the site of several colonial fortifications. The first was merely an abatis shaped like a half-moon, which was replaced by an earthen fort in June 1607. It was triangular in shape, mounted artillery, and enclosed one acre. The wooden components of James Fort burned in January 1608 and were rebuilt later that year. Capt. John Smith soon after enlarged the fort into a pentagonal shape. A blockhouse was added in 1609 to guard the isthmus that connected the colonists to the mainland. This isthmus eventually eroded, and the settlement was left on an island.

Two other colonial fortifications were built to protect the colony. About 1663 a detached work with four sides was constructed east of the settlement but was dismantled within twenty years. A second fort, built in the 1670s, mounted twenty guns within its crescent-shaped parapets but was deserted by 1716. Jamestown barely survived Bacon's Rebellion in 1676, and the colonial capital of Virginia was moved to Williamsburg by 1699. A battery mounting two guns was constructed on the island during the Revolution.[2]

Nearly three miles long, Jamestown Island was a strategic location because its bulk narrowed the width of the James River. The channel is almost four miles wide at the island's downstream end but narrows to slightly more than half that width at the upstream end. By 1861 there were only a few reminders of the colonial past. A church tower, the remnants of one of the forts, and a magazine were still there when Rebel engineers began to plan their own fortifications.[3]

They decided to place their major work 20 yards from the church tower and 100 yards from the site of the blockhouse built in 1609. Andrew Talcott was aided by Capt. Edmund Trowbridge Dana Myers and Lt. Catesby ap Roger Jones of the Virginia navy in laying out the work on May 3, 1861. It had six sides and was large enough for eighteen guns. Jones supervised the more than 100 slaves who built the fort. The workers dug up pieces of body armor and found timbers that probably were part of the colonial fortifications. Remnants of the fort show a raised, continuous platform on two sides facing downriver, with embrasures for three guns. There was an additional gun embrasure to the rear, pointing upriver. A long traverse in the middle of the work had a magazine in one end, and the ancient church tower stood directly in the line of fire. Jones christened the work Fort Pocahontas.[4]

Five other works were constructed on the island. The Sand Battery, sited by Talcott in late May near the river midway along the island, was built for five guns. The Square Redoubt was constructed in part by the 14th Virginia in early June. Two works were built that same month to guard the bridge connecting the island to the mainland. The Bridge Redan had three faces and mounted one gun, while the Bridge Lunette was designed for an infantry garrison alone. Finally, the Point of Island Battery, a semicircular emplacement for two guns, was built in July and August at the eastern tip of the island. It had two sides and connecting infantry trenches to left and right for a short distance.[5]

Fort Pocahontas is partially intact today, although the river has eroded the land close to its remaining parapet. The Square Redoubt, however, is magnificently preserved about three miles from the church tower. Its parapets are about fifty yards long and have deep, wide ditches. There are no remnants of traverses, magazines, or bombproofs in the work. A small traverse inside the redoubt covers the sally port, and four raised gun platforms are intact. Robert C. Mabry, an officer in the 6th Virginia, marveled at the skill used in constructing the Jamestown Island defenses. He called the Square Redoubt "one of the neatest pieces of work I most ever saw."[6]

Until work was pushed forward on the three defense lines on the Peninsula and at Drewry's Bluff, Jamestown Island was the key to the James River defenses. By the end of the summer of 1861, it had half the heavy artillery available southeast of Richmond. Magruder's works on the Peninsula and McClellan's campaign toward Yorktown focused Confederate resources away from the island. By the time Johnston decided to abandon the Peninsula, the defenses at Jamestown Island had become irrelevant.[7]

The river battery at Drewry's Bluff, however, remained important for the rest of the war. It was constructed long after work on the lower James River sites had started. In fact, before the winter of 1861–62, there were no major batteries upstream from Jamestown Island. When efforts to fortify the river close to Richmond began in February, Augustus H. Drewry led Confederate engineers to his farm at a bend in the river eight miles from the capital. Here a bluff that was 80 to 110 feet above water offered a magnificent site for heavy guns. Work began on March 17, after Johnston evacuated Manassas Junction, but proceeded slowly. An inspection report of April 28 warned that the fortifications would not be ready until August, so a concentrated effort to push the work was mounted. A company of sappers and miners, a battalion of artillerymen, some infantrymen, marines, and sailors from the Confederate navy were rushed to the site. They managed to get the defenses ready by mid-May.

A map drawn by Rebel gunner Horace Mann in 1914 shows Fort Darling, the main earthwork, to have been a bastioned work with a large magazine and a bombproof. It mounted six guns arrayed along two sides; one faced the river, and the other aimed downstream. The latter face also had four large traverses, with one end of the magazine acting as a fifth traverse because it extended all the way to the interior slope of the parapet. The complex at Drewry's Bluff was large enough for a barracks and additional batteries for six guns outside the fort. One of those outlying emplacements was a casemate.

Obstructions were placed in the river to delay Federal boats within range of the fort's guns, but work crews made slow progress, contributing to the growing anxiety of concerned citizens. Thomas H. Wynne, chief engineer of the city of Richmond, complained to Secretary of War George W. Randolph after he and several other citizens inspected the obstructions on April 29. Randolph ordered engineer chief Rives to push forward the work as quickly as possible.

The works at Drewry's Bluff were tested on May 15, two weeks after

Johnston evacuated the Warwick Line on the Peninsula. Five Union gunboats, led by the ironclads USS *Galena* and USS *Monitor*, steamed into view and bombarded the site. The artillery exchange lasted four hours and resulted in a decisive repulse. The hastily constructed battery emplacements proved their worth, not only by stopping the Federal advance, but by severely damaging the *Galena*. The ship was hit fifty times, and more than half of these rounds penetrated its armor.

Following this battle, additional gun emplacements were built at Fort Darling. Four raised platforms for field artillery were placed on the land face in June 1862, and a tunnel was dug under the middle of the land face to allow men to safely enter and exit the fort. But the works at Drewry's Bluff were not challenged again until May 1864 when the Union Army of the James approached them from the land side.[8]

Defenses of Richmond

Authorities at several levels of government had been wrestling with the problem of fortifying the capital since the war began, but they had not made a great deal of progress by the time McClellan's army arrived. The initial line, too close to the city and inadequately supplied with artillery, was nearly complete, but scant work had been done to build better lines. The Confederate House of Representatives passed a resolution on February 24, a couple of weeks before Johnston evacuated Manassas Junction, asking for information on the state of the capital's defenses. Alfred L. Rives waited until March 12 to write a report. By then, McClellan was well advanced in his plans to approach the city from the Yorktown Peninsula.

Rives detailed the defenses by dividing them into two categories. First, there were the James River defenses. Second, there were the land defenses just outside the city. Col. Danville Leadbetter, former chief of the Engineer Bureau, had already decided that the Inner Line was too near Richmond, but he declined to abandon it because so much work had already been done. Before Leadbetter left for other duties in Tennessee, he directed Rives to follow through with its completion according to the plans already laid down by Virginia state engineer officers under Andrew Talcott. Rives did the best he could, enclosing the open rear of some of the batteries and draining flooded magazines. He did not press forward with filling the empty gun emplacements because he believed it was unwise to concentrate "so many pieces on a contracted local defense." Rives also thought it injudicious at this time, before the Federals had fully developed their offensive plans, to begin building a new line farther forward of the existing, flawed position. That could be done quickly by the troops as necessity demanded.

Congress had also wondered about the feasibility of using the Chickahominy River as a line of defense, but Rives felt unable to offer an opinion on that issue. Andrew Talcott had already told Rives that he thought little of the scheme. Yet Rives suggested that a series of dams and protecting earthworks, similar to the system soon to be built along the Warwick River on the Peninsula, might be useful.[9]

Jefferson Davis forwarded Rives's report to the House and added a lengthy report of his own. The president, a West Point graduate with experience in the Mexican War, demonstrated in this report a remarkably firm grasp of the details and doctrine of fortifications. He was able to make intelligent and useful points about the river batteries on the lower James. Davis admitted that the Inner Line was too close to the city but noted that it was put there to minimize the amount of labor to build it and the number of troops to defend it. Davis discounted its weaknesses, however, by noting that the heavy guns would keep the enemy at bay.

Davis waxed eloquent when he argued against the need to build additional lines outside the city. Like Rives, the president wanted to wait until the Federals neared Richmond; then more digging could be done insofar as it was needed. Davis wanted to fight the enemy in the open rather than rely on heavy earthworks to save the capital. "Any system of fortification which could be constructed during the war for the defense of this city would only serve to gain time," he argued. "An army which allows itself to be shut up in a fortified city must finally yield to an enemy superior in numbers and munitions of war." In short, if an army cannot prevent itself from being trapped inside the city it is defending, it is doomed to lose the campaign anyway.

Rives further developed his views on Richmond's defense in letters to his engineer officers in the field. He was convinced by the battle between the USS *Monitor* and the CSS *Virginia* on March 9, 1862, that the Federal ironclads were too powerful to be stopped by the water batteries on the lower James River. He also thought that a well-handled field army needed only a few small fieldworks, open to the rear and "with a simple embankment" as a parapet, to defend the capital.[10]

True to their strategy, Davis and Rives pushed forward work on the Intermediate Line in late March only as McClellan showed signs of moving toward Richmond. The city council voted to release the city engineer from all other duties so he could help state authorities work on the fortifications. Additional batteries were built along the James River below Drewry's Bluff at a place called Chaffin's Bluff. The Confederate government took control of the city's defenses that spring and confirmed the opinion of the state engineers

about the Inner and Intermediate Lines. The former was pushed to completion and the latter was hurried along.[11]

A third line of defense would be initiated by Robert E. Lee after he took
command of the Confederate army defending Richmond in June. But until
that time, the citadel of the Confederacy was protected by only two imperfect lines of defense, neither satisfactory to any engineer who passed judgment on them. It was time to put Davis's strategy of an active defense of the
city to the test.

Seven Pines

The units of Johnston's Army of Northern Virginia stumbled through the
mud to the vicinity of Richmond by mid-May. They were tired, sick, and
hungry, but no orders were issued to dig in outside the city. Magruder's staff
officer, Joseph L. Brent, recalled that the men were quite happy about that
omission. After digging so extensively at Centreville, Manassas Junction, and
Yorktown, only to retreat from those places without a fight, they "seemed
falsely impressed with the idea that the use of the spade was mere labor
lost." Rumor had it that Johnston himself "sympathized with this idea." This
was not exactly true, but Johnston nevertheless laid no plans to build earthworks beyond those that were already under way through the efforts of state
and Confederate authorities. He positioned his units in the open field to
cover the approaches to the capital, well in front of the lines of earthworks
that were being built. The men received supplies from the Richmond depots,
rested, and were soon in fine trim.[12]

McClellan approached the city cautiously, faced with the daunting task of
crossing the Chickahominy River with its wide, alluvial bottomland. This
stream, which presented either a swampy morass or a raging torrent, de-
pending on how much rain fell, was Johnston's best hope to catch the Federals off guard. It would be a tedious and dangerous process to move the
Army of the Potomac across and to build suitable bridges to supply the
troops. The Confederates would have an opportunity to strike at isolated
units on the Richmond side and defeat McClellan in detail. The Young Napoleon started this process in late May by carefully moving Maj. Gen. Darius
Keyes's Fourth Corps and Maj. Gen. Samuel P. Heintzelman's Third Corps
across the river while keeping the rest of the army east of it as long as possible. He was motivated partly by a desire to make contact with Maj. Gen.
Irvin McDowell's First Corps, which had been held back in the vicinity of Manassas Junction and Fredericksburg thus far during the campaign. McClellan
had been calling for McDowell's men to reinforce him ever since and so far

was having little luck convincing Lincoln or Stanton of the wisdom of this transfer. Additionally, he needed to protect his principal supply base and the Richmond and York River Railroad, both of which were located east of the river. McClellan advanced his most trusted subordinate, Fitz John Porter, and the Fifth Corps to Mechanicsville, eight miles northeast of Richmond, to anchor his right flank. Thus, he unwittingly played into Johnston's hands by leaving some 36,000 men west and south of the Chickahominy and retaining roughly 70,000 east and north of it.[13]

Federal engineers worked hard to build secure links between the two wings. They rebuilt the line of the Richmond and York River Railroad, including its bridges, from the York River to Savage's Station, three miles west of the Chickahominy. More work was undertaken by the infantry of Maj. Gen. Edwin V. Sumner's Second Corps. The 1st Minnesota, 5th New Hampshire, and 64th New York built two wagon bridges over the river, cutting timber, floating beams to the bridge sites, raising piers and stringers, and building corduroyed causeways over the wide bottomland to connect the bridges with dry land. Although the channel was only forty feet wide, the bridges were one-quarter of a mile long. The upper span, called the Grapevine Bridge, had a causeway whose rough log flooring was softened by a layer of dirt. The building of these spans involved an enormous amount of labor, but they were finished by May 29.[14]

The transportation links across the river were finally opened when Johnston launched his attack against the left wing of the Army of the Potomac on May 31. He planned to hit Keyes and Heintzelman with twenty-one brigades totaling 55,000 men, giving him a decisive numerical advantage if he could throw all of the troops into a coordinated assault. But the inexperience of the Army of Northern Virginia at all levels of command hampered the attack so badly that only nine of the twenty-one brigades, about 14,000 men, were heavily engaged. A combination of poor maps, bad staff work, and poorly written orders robbed Johnston of an opportunity to drive the Federals away.[15]

The Army of the Potomac was deployed in a line that stretched for twelve miles, from Porter's Fifth Corps position at Mechanicsville through Maj. Gen. William B. Franklin's Sixth Corps and Sumner's Second Corps positions north and east of the Chickahominy. South and west of the river, Keyes's Fourth Corps held a forward position in the vicinity of Seven Pines, an important road junction eight miles from the center of Richmond. Brig. Gen. Silas Casey's division was located in front, west of Seven Pines, with Brig. Gen. Darius N. Couch's division positioned around the junction and along Nine Mile Road northward to Fair Oaks Station on the Richmond and York

Approach to Grapevine Bridge, Chickahominy River. Taken by Brig. Gen. Daniel P. Woodbury, this photograph depicts men of the 5th New Hampshire and 64th New York putting down a layer of dirt on the wooden causeway leading to one of the bridges spanning the Chickahominy River in June 1862. (Massachusetts Commandery, Military Order of the Loyal Legion and the U.S. Army Military History Institute)

River Railroad. Heintzelman, who was given overall charge of the troops west of the river, had his Third Corps positioned five miles to Keyes's rear.

Casey and Couch were partially fortified. McClellan had ordered Barnard to lay out a defensive line at Seven Pines, which was done a half-mile west of the crossroads on May 28. Barnard ordered the construction of an enclosed work with connecting trenches, and Lt. Miles McAlester designed what would be called Casey's Redoubt, a prominent feature in the battle. Digging started on May 29 or 30, but McAlester could not get enough men to work on it. As a result, the redoubt was "quite incomplete" when Johnston struck on May 31. Casey placed his division line on the east side of a cleared field and cut a considerable amount of timber on the west side to create a dense slashing. The redoubt was positioned near the center of his division line. Casey advanced his picket line into the belt of trees on the far side of the field, beyond the forty-yard-wide slashing. The pickets, hidden in another belt of trees, were separated from the Confederate position by an open field that was 500 yards wide. East of Casey's position, Couch dug in at a clearing near Seven Pines and built a third line one and a half miles east of the junction. The infantry works of Couch's position originated as a breastwork, made by piling logs on top of the earth, and then a ditch was dug in front. The dirt was thrown over the pile to make a parapet four feet thick at the top.

Heintzelman later recalled that persistent rain slowed the work of fortifying and filled the ditches with water by the time Johnston attacked on May 31. Several details from Casey's division were out slashing more timber that morning when signs of enemy activity led officers to recall them to their units. One battery occupied Casey's Redoubt, two infantry regiments were north of the fort in a connecting line, and three were south of it, but Casey poorly disposed of the rest of his division. He put a forward line in front of his works in the open field, 200 yards from the slashing. Not only was this line exposed, but the obstructions should have been within close musket range to be effective. He also separated units from two of his three brigades, making it difficult for brigade leaders to control their troops under fire. The fortifications constituted Casey's second line.[16]

Johnston's attack was greatly impeded by the terrain of the battlefield. The landscape is flat, or as Maj. Gen. Gustavus W. Smith put it, "slightly undulating," and lies at about 160 feet elevation. The sandy soil quickly became "soft and spongy" when soaked with rain, while the woods tended to have thick underbrush "matted with tangled vines, and the luxuriant foliage, in the full bloom of spring, rendered it in many places impossible to distinguish objects ten paces distant." When a heavy rain set in at 5:00 P.M. on the evening of May 30, "the face of the country was literally flooded." The rain stopped the next day, but the Chickahominy began to rise between McClellan's two wings. Pools of standing water, some more than knee deep, pockmarked the landscape. The attacking Rebels had to struggle across this terrain and then contend with the wide belts of slashing, "hundreds of treetops with the ends of limbs pointed and sharpened," as Henry C. Wall of the 23rd North Carolina put it.[17]

Daniel Harvey Hill hit Casey's 6,200 men with 9,000 screaming Confederates and, after tough fighting, drove them away, capturing Casey's Redoubt and its artillery at 3:00 P.M. Then Hill hit Couch and was stopped. He worked units around Couch's right flank and gained the rear, forcing the second Union line to evacuate under fire, but the third line held on. Fugitives from the first two positions took shelter in this unfinished trench one and a half miles east of Seven Pines until the Rebel attacks ended at dusk. Farther north, Brig. Gen. William H. C. Whiting's division struck the Fair Oaks section of the Union line, but the Federals held firm without earthworks. The Confederates launched a series of disjointed attacks on Union positions to the north and east of Nine Mile Road, none of which succeeded in driving the Yankees. The only thing accomplished by either Confederate wing was Hill's success in bending the extreme Union left back like a fish hook with Fair Oaks Station as the anchor. Further Confederate assaults on June 1 failed to accomplish any more. The Rebels retired, nursing more than 6,100 casualties while the Federals suffered 5,000 losses. The highest-ranking casualty was Johnston himself, who was hit by shell fire on May 31. Gustavus W. Smith took charge of the army for the useless attacks the next day and for the retreat.[18]

Johnston's plan, to attack while the Federals were struggling across the Chickahominy, was ruined by poor handling, by the terrain and weather, and by the Federal fortifications. The works were modest in size and strength and failed to stop the Rebels, but the extensive slashing disrupted their formations and robbed them of momentum. The Confederates should have learned that enthusiasm would not necessarily compensate for terrain difficulties and that there was no substitute for efficient control and detailed, thorough planning. Rebel survivors of the battle of Seven Pines, also known as the battle of Fair Oaks, did not brag about capturing two lines of Yankee earthworks. They more often moaned about the difficulties of the terrain and occasionally about stiff Union resistance. Johnston was now out of the picture, and Robert E. Lee was named his permanent replacement.

McClellan began shifting the bulk of his army across the Chickahominy in June as the Federals dug in more extensively to defend their forward position. Soon a continuous line of infantry trench, studded with several forts, took shape to defend Seven Pines and Fair Oaks. McClellan was preparing for a repeat of Johnston's attack; the works were primarily defensive in nature, although they could be used as the base for a continued advance toward Richmond.

Soon after the battle, Barnard instructed McAlester to finish Casey's Redoubt and "extend the defensive line to the right, to embrace Fair Oaks, and to the left, to connect with the White Oak Swamp." The line started as little more than a row of breastwork, to be later transformed into a proper parapet by dirt thrown up from the digging of a trench. Initially there was a shortage of axes and shovels, but work picked up as necessary tools became available. On June 7, Barnard laid out a large fort on the right flank near the river, on Golding's Farm, which became Redoubt No. 6. Intermediate works—

Federal Fort Sumner, Fair Oaks. Several of the redoubts on Barnard's line seem to have been given other names as well. While these are not listed in the official reports, it is likely that Fort Sumner was Redoubt No. 4. Note the use of timber and sandbags to make the revetment and the yet-unused sandbags lying around. (Massachusetts Commandery, Military Order of the Loyal Legion and the U.S. Army Military History Institute)

Redoubts No. 4 and 5—arose between it and Casey's position. McAlester, Cyrus B. Comstock, and Lt. Francis U. Farquhar completed the connecting lines between the forts. South of Casey's position, Redoubts No. 1 and 2 extended the line to White Oak Swamp.

The completed line was more than three miles long. A total of forty embrasures graced the parapets that were twelve feet thick, fronted by a deep, wide ditch. Most of the six works were open to the rear; Nos. 3, 4, and 5 had five sides, while No. 6 was square and No. 2 was triangular. From left to right, Barnard identified Redoubt No. 1 as a lunette with eight guns; Redoubt No. 2 as a redan with six guns located south of Seven Pines; Redoubt No. 3 (Casey's Redoubt on May 31) as an "irregular pentagon" with five guns a few hundred yards south of Williamsburg Road; Redoubt No. 4 as having nine guns north

Federal artillery position at Fair Oaks. Identified as Battery C, 1st Pennsylvania Light Artillery, the location of this view is uncertain. The configuration of the works matches that of the large artillery emplacement at Robert Courteny's, but the only battery to occupy those works was Capt. J. Howard Carlisle's Battery E, 2nd U.S. Artillery, and only on June 28. The location of Battery C, 1st Pennsylvania Light Artillery, is unknown. Note, however, the raised timber platforms, the neatly dug parapets and ditches, and the gunners' tents stretched between the artillery pieces. (National Library of Medicine)

of Williamsburg Road and south of the Richmond and York River Railroad, due west of Fair Oaks Station; Redoubt No. 5 as containing six guns north of the railroad; and Redoubt No. 6 as mounting six guns on the right.

A photograph of No. 5, taken by James F. Gibson, shows a large, communal gun platform at the natural level of the earth. It has a border made of logs and a ditch around the sides and back of the platform, in which the ammunition chests could be safely placed. The parapet had a post-and-plank revetment reaching to about waist high, with a layer of sandbags several feet on top of that for ease in forming embrasures. Some of the redoubts also were fixed with magazines.

While the Seven Pines Line was taking shape, Capt. James C. Duane of the U.S. Engineer Battalion constructed four batteries on the east side of the Chickahominy River to defend the bridges that McClellan relied on to keep

Federal engineers corduroying a road, Peninsula campaign. A rare photograph of engineer troops engaged in road repair. Four hundred men of Brig. Gen. Daniel P. Woodbury's Volunteer Engineer Brigade lay corduroy along the road leading to the railroad station at Fair Oaks and the road linking McClellan's headquarters with that of Brig. Gen. William F. Smith's Sixth Corps division at Golding's Farm on June 17–19. Woodbury is the bearded officer on the right standing next to his horse. (Library of Congress)

his line of communications open to Fortress Monroe and to fire on Confederate positions on the opposite bank. Batteries No. 2 and 3 were to the left and right of the road that approached New Bridge, while No. 1 was located farther north, near Dr. Gaines's house. No. 4 was south of New Bridge, near Hogan's House. Each battery contained six guns.

In late June, Barnard authorized additional work on the Seven Pines Line. Lt. Col. Barton S. Alexander broke ground for another artillery emplacement big enough for thirty guns on the farm of Robert Courteny to the southwest of Golding's Farm. Placed between Redoubts No. 5 and 6, two regiments worked hard enough to erect substantial cover by dawn as two other regiments stood guard. Although Confederate pickets were within firing range, the work was undisturbed. This huge concentration of ordnance was to serve an offensive purpose, driving the Rebel artillery away from several prepared positions in the vicinity, but it was never finished. Lee's success in the coming

Seven Days campaign forced Alexander to stop work on it. Only one battery was emplaced on June 28 before the army pulled away from its advanced position west of the Chickahominy.[19]

Lee Takes Command

Neither Johnston nor Lee would rely primarily on earthworks to defend the city. Both commanders wanted to strike at the approaching Federals and decide the fate of the capital in open battle. The chief difference lay in the manner of executing that strategy.

Fifty-five years old when he took command of the Army of Northern Virginia, Lee had graduated second in the West Point class of 1829 and had won a coveted appointment in the Corps of Engineers. He worked extensively at Fort Pulaski and Fortress Monroe, performed administrative work in Washington as assistant to the chief of the Engineer Department, and applied his talents to civil projects such as improving navigation on the Mississippi River at St. Louis. He helped to plan and build the siege works at Vera Cruz during the Mexican War and performed superbly as a topographical engineer throughout Winfield Scott's advance on Mexico City.[20]

Lee determined on June 5, four days after assuming command of the army, to take the offensive against McClellan. He would adopt a more bold, comprehensive, and aggressive plan than Johnston's. As McClellan shifted troops across the Chickahominy River in June, he retained a sizable force east and north of the stream. Lee wanted to attack north of the river, throwing a force as heavy as that used by Johnston on a wide flanking maneuver, while leaving the minor part of his army to block the major part of McClellan's force due east of Richmond.

There were two prerequisites to make this plan work. First, Lee had to finish building the defenses of Richmond. Only by sheltering behind strong earthworks could the comparatively small force hold off McClellan's huge army east of the city. Second, Lee needed all the additional help he could find. Marginally used brigades were called northward from the coast of North Carolina, and a small but highly successful army under Maj. Gen. Thomas J. Jackson also had to be shifted from the Shenandoah Valley. The pressure on the capital was so great that these theaters of secondary importance could be depleted, for the time being, to save the heart of the Confederate nation.

Completing the Defenses of Richmond

Rives and Davis had argued earlier that any additional lines of defense protecting the city could quickly be dug when the need arose, and now Lee and his men set out to prove them right. Engineer officers scurried across the countryside laying out a forward line of defense just behind the positions already assumed by Lee's units following their repulse at Seven Pines. This position would become the Outer Defense Line of Richmond. Adjustments had to be made, but the line essentially was straight. The next step was to cut thousands of trees that stood nearby. "Forests were felled and new roads were made, and old ones obliterated," recalled Joseph L. Brent, "so that the entire face of the country was changed." Civilians in the area moved away, if they had not already done so, certain that the activity meant heavy fighting. Many of their houses and outbuildings had to be burned or dismantled to clear fields of fire. Lee rode along the developing line every day, "making suggestions to working parties and encouraging their efforts to put sand-banks between their persons and the enemy's batteries," recalled James Longstreet.[21]

The Engineer Bureau frantically tried to supply Lee with all that he needed. Rives dispatched a dozen engineer officers and civilian assistants, but it was far more difficult to find proper tools. Lee clamored for shovels, picks, axes, and spades. Rives took some axes from the navy and contracted with the state penitentiary to make five dozen per day for the government. Regimental leaders in Lee's army were ordered to search for any spare tools hoarded by the men for camp chores. Rives also arranged for thousands of sandbags to be sent to the army.

As June wore on, the need for more efficient labor by the soldiers became paramount in order to finish the work on time. Within Rodes's Alabama brigade, a schedule was worked out so that each regiment, in sequence, devoted its entire strength to the brigade's defenses for three hours at a time. When Walter H. Stevens, who was in charge of the defenses, asked Rives for 300 black laborers, the bureaucrat could not supply them. The numerous shortages led Stevens to complain about inefficiency at the Engineer Bureau. Rives explained to Lee that he could not personally compensate for the Confederacy's lack of resources. "In addition to my other duties," he confessed, "I find my position of general supply & disbursing agent for Major Stevens exceedingly onerous."[22]

Yet the works took shape despite tool shortages and ruffled feathers. Supervision of the digging fell to infantry officers, most of whom were un-tutored in the art of fortification. Brig. Gen. William Dorsey Pender, commander of a North Carolina brigade in Maj. Gen. A. P. Hill's division, wanted the works to be as uniform as possible. He sought "to make them look pretty I suppose," commented John Wetmore Hinsdale, his staff officer. Hinsdale knew that it would be more effective to curve the line to take advantage of each undulation in the land, and he also knew that it was important to cut down all the trees immediately in front of the trench. Yet Pender wanted to keep many trees intact to serve as forward observation posts. When Hinsdale offered his advice, Pender assured him he "knew all about it," so Hinsdale kept quiet and concluded that his leader was a conceited fool. It was a harsh judgment, for Pender would soon prove his ability as an aggressive battlefield commander.[23]

After the war, several Confederate officers argued that the rank and file enthusiastically supported Lee's plan to dig in around Richmond. Joseph Brent remembered that the men were shocked by the casualties suffered at Seven Pines. They had come to "appreciate the advantages of entrenched position, and their approval of Gen. Lee's policy was very cordial." Longstreet also claimed that the men had started to know the value of earthworks. But contemporary evidence seems to indicate that the opposite was true. The soldiers apparently complained loudly about the hard work, believing that attack was the only way to save Richmond. Their initial view of Lee was decidedly uncomplimentary. Noting his relatively advanced age, they called him "Granny Lee" or the "King of Spades."[24]

Lt. Robert G. Haile of the 55th Virginia, in Brig. Gen. Charles W. Field's brigade of Hill's division, apparently spoke for many soldiers when he expressed disgust at the digging. Haile could see the Federals constructing earthworks across a stream in front of his regiment. "That is the system that they are going to persue," he concluded, to hold every inch of ground they could. "I don't think it should be allowed[.] I go for attacking them at once and never stop untill they are driven from our soil. The very idea of two large armys only separated by a small stream to be entrenching themselves is out of the question. I go in for their meeting each other in open ground and fight it out and be done with it."[25]

Civilian observers also castigated Lee for his policy. John M. Daniel, editor of the *Richmond Examiner,* spared no vitriol in denouncing Lee as incompetent. West Pointers knew only how to dig, to fight the war on "scientific" principles, and lacked the visceral need to destroy their enemy. Daniel wrote out of frustration; after Johnston's dilatory strategy and failed attack at Seven Pines, the citizens of Richmond were understandably worried and hoping for a savior. At first, Lee did not seem to fit the bill.[26]

While outwardly unfazed by the criticism, Lee took quiet notice of it and made haste to defend himself. McClellan would dig his way into the city, Lee warned Jefferson Davis, by taking and fortifying position after position under cover of his heavy guns. Lacking the same weight and quantity of ordnance, the Confederates could only win by storming his works. Waiting on the defensive to resist a siege would only prolong the campaign, not change its outcome. Davis understood that Lee wanted to build works so he could hold the city with minimal manpower while using the rest for offensive action, but Lee wanted to make sure the president would support this policy in the face of widespread criticism. "Our people are opposed to work," Lee complained. Officers, soldiers, and civilians alike ridiculed it as unnecessary. Yet work was "the very means by which McClellan has and is advancing. Why should we leave to him the whole advantage of labor[?] Combined with valour fortitude & boldness, of which we have our fair proportion, it should lead us to success."[27]

Within a month of taking command, Lee had the defenses of Richmond ready to serve his strategic needs. As they were improved over the course of the war, the works became an impressive system of fortifications.

The Inner Line consisted of sixteen detached redoubts about one mile from the edge of the city. Twelve works lay north of the James, stretching all the way from the eastern to the western side and anchored on the river. Four redoubts lay south of the James. The works were open to the rear, but their outline often was complex, incorporating several bastions. In fact, many people today refer to them as "star forts" because of their pointy appearance on maps.

The Intermediate Line was a continuous line of works from one and a half to three miles from the edge of the city. It also stretched from one side of Richmond to the other, anchored on the James. A forward extension of the line ran to the Outer Line north of the city, forming a short corridor connecting the two lines at this point and protecting the Mechanicsville Pike and the Virginia Central Railroad. The Intermediate Line stretched south of the James, covering about half the southern approach to the city.

The Outer Line was the one most heavily dug by Lee's men in June 1862. It started at Chaffin's Bluff and extended northward to the Chickahominy River at New Bridge, five miles northeast of the city's edge, and covered the eastern approaches to Richmond. This stretch was a continuous line. Then a line of detached works ran along the south bank of the Chickahominy from New Bridge for nearly four miles to the Chickahominy Bluffs due north of town. This part of the line was continuous for about one and a half miles, and here also was the extension connecting the Outer and Intermediate Lines. From this point, the line ran continuously another mile to the junction of Brook Run and the Chickahominy. The run flowed west to east into the river, due north and four miles from the city's edge. From this junction, there was a line of detached works for six miles along the south bank of Brook Run, before the line angled southward to end at the James River west of Richmond.

This represented an enormous amount of digging. The Inner Line ran for eight miles, the Intermediate Line stretched for fourteen miles, and the Outer Line totaled some twenty-six miles. A more efficiently planned system could have reduced this labor significantly, for the Outer Line was the most important, while the Intermediate Line was, arguably, necessary as a fallback position. The Confederates were lucky to have come up with enough ideas, labor, guns, spades, and strong backs to construct a workable, although redundant, system of defense for the capital.[28]

The Outer Line was anchored at Chaffin's Bluff, a fifty-foot-high eminence on the north bank of the James River one and a half miles downstream from Drewry's Bluff. The construction of river batteries had already been started by May 16. Eight heavy guns were in place by the time Johnston attacked at Seven Pines, but there were still no works for either infantry or field artillery by the time Lee started the Outer Line. The new commander ordered the additional work at Chaffin's immediately, and a feverish pace of activity was begun that would extend well beyond the immediate campaign.

Engineer Lt. William Elzey Harrison laid out the works, while Henry A. Wise's Virginia brigade provided most of the labor, with help from a force of black workers. Harrison's line began near the bluff and crossed Osborne Pike, one of several good roads leading to the southeast sector of Richmond. It angled to take advantage of a ridge up to 140 feet tall. The first segment of the line was made up of five detached batteries and stretched to a private house called Mountcastle. From there the line consisted of an infantry trench studded with ten more batteries. The whole line stretched for a mile and a half and crossed two other approaches to Richmond. Battery No. 11 covered the Varina Road, and Batteries No. 12, 13, 14, and 15 covered New Market Road. They were completed by early August 1862 despite a break by Wise's men to take part in the battle of Malvern Hill. This line would be heavily strengthened, and many additional works would be added in the vicinity to better protect the river batteries at Chaffin's Bluff. Batteries No. 7, 8, and 9 would later be transformed into Fort Harrison, a key target of the Federal Fifth Offensive of September 1864 during the Petersburg campaign.[29]

The only remnants of Richmond's defenses are a few bits and pieces of the Outer Line. East of Richmond and a few hundred yards south of Williamsburg Road, the line was straight and consisted of a large parapet fronted by a deep ditch. There was no trench or traverses along the infantry curtain, but several two-gun emplacements were made with raised platforms. A traverse separated the two emplacements within each bastion. North of Richmond, along the Chickahominy Bluffs, a more complex and stronger artillery position was constructed just east of Mechanicsville Pike. Three two-gun emplacements were made with protecting traverses and parapets, the latter thickened by digging a ditch in front. A trench was dug along the connecting infantry line, which was curved to conform to the edge of the bluff. The infantry parapet was only half as large as the traverses that protected the artillery. The crossing of the river along Mechanicsville Pike was long and vulnerable, hence the fairly elaborate earthworks. The road stretched along a causeway over the wide, swampy bottomland. The bluffs are about 100 feet above the river level.

An artillery emplacement on the south bank of Brook Run, five miles north of the state capitol and just west of Brook Road, overlooked the wide, gently sloping ground to the stream. It stands about fifty feet above the brook level. This was a historic spot, the rendezvous point for Gabriel's Conspiracy, an abortive slave uprising in 1800. Gabriel, from nearby Brookfield Plantation, planned to gather hundreds of fellow slaves here, attack Richmond, capture Governor James Monroe, and seize arms at the state arsenal. The plot fell apart when a storm flooded Brook Run and two plotters revealed the scheme to their masters. Gabriel and more than thirty followers were executed. The spot also was the scene of three separate cavalry attacks on Richmond later in the war. Maj. Gen. George Stoneman's Federals skirmished here on the night of May 4, 1863, and Brig. Gen. Hugh Judson Kilpatrick captured the artillery emplacement on March 1, 1864, with 3,500 troopers. He shelled the Intermediate Line for a while before retreating. Finally, Maj. Gen. Philip Sheridan's 12,000 troopers unsuccessfully attacked the position on May 11, 1864, hours after winning the battle of Yellow Tavern and mortally wounding Maj. Gen. J. E. B. Stuart two miles north of here.

The works at this spot were quite strong; their capture by Kilpatrick was merely the result of a surprise. The massive artillery position has three gun emplacements, two on the natural level of the earth and the third on a sunken platform. Each platform has a large traverse to its left, an embrasure to its front, and a ditch in front of the large parapet. A stretch of remaining infantry line to the east side of Brook Road shows that the Outer Line also was massive. There was no trench, but the line consisted of a large parapet and a deep and wide ditch.[30]

The Outer Line would be the primary defense of Richmond for the rest of the war, yet it might not have been built at all except for Lee's decision to entrench in June 1862. Unlike Washington, the Confederate capital was primarily shielded by a line that was initiated for the purpose of making an offensive against the enemy more certain of success. In both cases the earthworks freed the defending armies and gave them the flexibility to strike at the enemy. In the case of the Federals, that meant a four-year series of

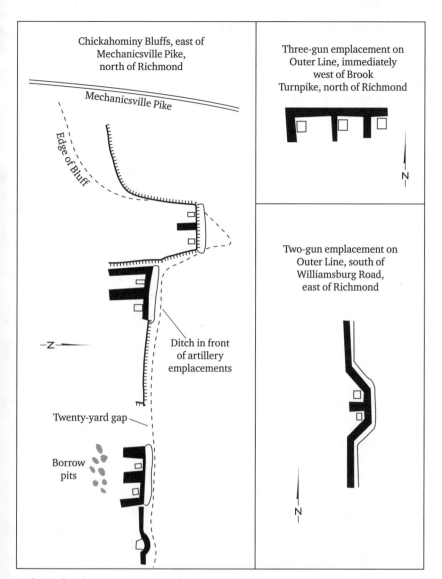

Richmond Defenses, Spring 1862 (based on field visits, 1994 and 1997)

campaigns to take Richmond; in the case of the Confederates, it meant the much more limited goal of driving the enemy from the gates of the capital in the summer of 1862. Both systems of defense served their purposes well until Grant's relentless drive to Richmond forced Lee to shelter his army in the works and adopt a strategy that Lee and Davis had always feared would result in the eventual loss of the city.

Jackson's Shenandoah Valley Campaign

Besides completing the defenses of Richmond, the Confederates had to bring Jackson's army from the Shenandoah Valley in preparation for Lee's Seven Days campaign. Jackson had already created a name for himself at First Manassas, but his claim to military genius was established by a short, brilliant campaign in the Valley of Virginia that tied down more than 50,000 Federal troops while using 15,000 of his own. Jackson took advantage of the good roads and generally level landscape of the valley and employed a Napoleonic strategy of maneuver between three widely separated columns of Union soldiers. He had the advantage of interior lines of march and good troops. It was a combination that baffled the Yankees for weeks and led Lincoln to refuse McClellan's persistent calls for more men in favor of defending the capital against a possible strike by the Confederates.[31]

Jackson, a graduate of the West Point class of 1846, had gone immediately to war in Mexico. Commissioned into the artillery, he had participated in the siege of Vera Cruz and in many other actions throughout Scott's campaign to Mexico City. Jackson was exposed to the use of fortifications but never seemed to have developed a special knowledge of them. His attitude toward operations, fully developed in the Valley campaign of 1862, emphasized maneuver and open field fighting to attain his strategic goals. Jackson seems to have disdained fortifications either for offense or defense, for they hardly played a role in the campaign. His Federal opponents, still inexperienced in operations, also paid scant attention to them.[32]

The landscape of the region, as already noted, well suited Jackson's needs. The Shenandoah Valley, on the margin between the Piedmont and the Appalachian Highlands, is one of Virginia's unique geographic features. The eastern extent of the highlands is the western boundary of the valley. The lower part of the valley is so wide that the bordering mountains are out of sight. The valley slowly narrows as one proceeds upriver, to the southwest, and ends near Lexington, 160 miles from Harpers Ferry, where the Shenandoah empties into the Potomac River. West of the Valley, however, one enters a true Appalachian landscape, with high, dominating ridges stretching from the northeast to the southwest, rugged and often narrow valleys between, and jumbled mountains stretching west as far as the eye can see.[33]

The Federals had already conquered much of this mountainous western side of Virginia but were as yet quiet in their occupation duties some fifty miles west of the Valley. Jackson initiated operations in the Shenandoah in March 1862, when he attacked another occupying force at Winchester, in the wide, lower end of the Valley. The resulting battle of Kernstown, fought just outside Winchester on March 23, was a Confederate failure. Jackson's men were repulsed in open field fighting, some of which swirled around a stone fence on the end of a dominating ridge outside Kernstown. It was one of the few battlefield defeats that Jackson suffered during the war, yet the Valley remained quiet for more than a month as McClellan launched his drive up the Peninsula.[34]

By early May, when the Army of the Potomac was beginning to close in on Richmond, the need to divert Yankee attention had become paramount. Jackson initially moved against a force under Brig. Gen. Robert H. Milroy that was advancing eastward across the Appalachian Highlands. Milroy had rested in winter quarters ever since his failed attack on the Confederate garrison of Camp Alleghany in December 1861. By the early spring, Southern commanders had given up hope of retaining the western mountains of Virginia, and Brig. Gen. Edward Johnson evacuated Camp Alleghany in early April. Milroy immediately moved forward to occupy it. "I was greatly surprised at the great extent and immense strength of the reble fortifications and winter quarters here," he informed his wife. Most of the existing works had been built following his attack. "The place is now almost a Gibralter for strength both by nature and art." Fortunately for Milroy's men, the Confederates left their forage, winter huts, and stables intact; a heavy snowstorm hit the mountaintop on April 7, the day after the Federals occupied the camp.[35]

Milroy pursued Johnson on April 8, advancing along the Staunton-Parkersburg Turnpike, one of two major avenues of invasion into the mountains of western Virginia. He hoped to push all the way to Staunton in the middle part of the Shenandoah Valley, completing the nine-month series of moves along that mountain road, but Johnson began to fortify on top of Shenandoah Mountain. The pike crawled across this rugged barrier, which was twenty-six miles from Camp Alleghany and twenty-two miles from Staunton. Like many features named "mountains" in Appalachia, this landform is really a huge ridge that stretches for dozens of miles. Where the road crosses the ridge through a narrow and shallow gap, Johnson's men built a fortified camp named Fort Edward Johnson. Like most fortified posts in the Appalachians, it was a superb defensive position unassailable by frontal approach but vulnerable to a flanking movement. The works are well preserved. North of the pike, they consist of a thin infantry parapet that conforms to the edge of the narrow ridgetop. A one-gun emplacement is located 400 yards north of and 100 feet higher in elevation than the pass. A similar parapet lies south of the pike, but there are no artillery emplacements. Neither work has a traverse or a ditch. The Confederates were lucky to have scratched even a modest parapet and trench from the rocky soil. But the dominating view for thirty miles in all directions and the nearly vertical sides immediately in front of the position compensated for the meager size and profile of the works.[36]

Milroy was not deterred by these fortifications. "I will hist them out of that as soon as I get the ballance of my forces up," he crowed to his wife. His men pushed past the village of McDowell and advanced nine miles farther east to the foot of Shenandoah Mountain, where they skirmished with Johnson's pickets. Milroy climbed a high ridge two miles away on April 18, a clear day, and could see the Confederate fortifications with the naked eye. Johnson also saw him and worried that the Federals could easily outflank his strong position. He evacuated Shenandoah Mountain on April 19 and retired to Staunton. The Federals continued their pursuit the next day and skirmished with Rebel cavalry for ten miles. The van of Milroy's column reached nearly to Staunton itself before the aggressive general finally pulled back to McDowell to await reinforcements from other Union columns still moving through the mountains.[37]

News of Milroy's advance alerted Jackson to the need to safeguard his western flank. He feigned an evacuation of the Valley, moved his men to Staunton by rail, and then marched across the mountains. One can truly appreciate this accomplishment by driving along Highway 250 from Staunton, which is the route of the old Staunton-Parkersburg Turnpike. Jackson crossed Great North Mountain, the western edge of the Valley, through a wide and deep gap about twelve miles west of Staunton. Then he crossed Calfpasture River. Milroy had moved most of his command back to the west side of Shenandoah Mountain by May 5, but he left the 32nd Ohio at the foot of the east slope. Part of Jackson's command skirmished with the Ohioans on May 7 and forced them to head for McDowell. This alerted Milroy to Jackson's presence. Brig. Gen. Robert C. Shenck joined Milroy at McDowell with three infantry regiments and a battery on the morning of May 8. The Confederates continued their advance over Shaw's Fork, Shaw's Ridge, and Cowpasture River and onto the top of Bullpasture Mountain. McDowell lay in the next valley, formed by Bullpasture River.[38]

Milroy shelled the Rebels for much of the day and then attacked. Bitter fighting took place on top of Sitlington's Hill, which was connected to Bullpasture Mountain on the east side of the valley. It took place in a cleared field and through the woods and ended in a draw. The Federals conceded defeat, retreated from the battlefield, and prepared to retire to Franklin. About 256 of 6,000 Federals fell at McDowell, while Jackson lost 500 of his 9,000 men.[39]

McDowell was the only engagement of the Shenandoah Valley campaign that was fought on Appalachian terrain; the remaining battles took place inside the Valley. Jackson next turned his attention to a Union force under Maj. Gen. Nathaniel P. Banks, stationed in and around Strasburg near the lower end of the Valley. The Federals had built a redoubt on a commanding hill just outside town, but it was not designed to accommodate Banks's 9,000 men. Jackson outflanked the Federal position by moving through Front Royal on May 23 and drove Banks from Strasburg to Winchester, twenty miles away. Further operations drove the Federals into Maryland.[40]

The drive to McDowell and the strike at Strasburg were the only two instances where fortifications played a role in Jackson's Valley campaign, and in both instances that role was marginal. In neither case did earthworks affect the outcome of the engagements. The rest of the Valley campaign that year saw Jackson's greatest triumph in the battles of Cross Keys and Port Republic, on June 8 and 9. Here Jackson defeated two converging Federal columns in classic Napoleonic fashion. Soon after, his jubilant men were ordered to Richmond and left the Valley on June 17. In thirty-five days he had marched 245 miles, fought four battles, and won them all.[41]

The Seven Days

Lee mustered 85,000 men for his planned offensive, the largest number ever to serve in the Army of Northern Virginia, while McClellan had 104,300 men at his disposal. The Confederates accomplished an admirable goal, bringing the majority of their strength against the enemy's weakest point. Lee launched 56,100 men against Porter's 28,100, while leaving 28,900 Rebels south of the Chickahominy to oppose McClellan's four corps, consisting of 76,200 troops. Only the Union general's innate caution and the heavy earthworks recently constructed by the Confederates made this plan feasible.[42]

The receipt of Lee's plan, issued in General Orders No. 75, "profoundly impressed" Joseph L. Brent, Magruder's staff officer. "Here, thought I, is the most momentous act of war ever revealed to me. This is the opening of the great game which will probably decide the fortunes of the Confederacy." After their lengthy retreat, failed attack at Seven Pines, and month-long spate of digging, the men of Lee's army were desperate for a chance to whip the Yankees, and Granny Lee now seemed to be made of bolder stuff than anyone had imagined.[43]

McClellan spent the month of June improving his defensive works. His own plans to enter Richmond were similar to those employed at Yorktown: to rely on earthworks and his superior artillery to minimize casualties. Dennis Hart Mahan had called such a tactic an "'active defense'—in effect, an advance toward battle from behind his own field fortifications." It promised a long campaign, but one that Lee and Davis thought eventually would be successful. McClellan believed he was outnumbered two to one and used that fallacy to justify his entrenchment to Lincoln. He wanted to "bring the greatest possible numbers into action & secure the army against the consequences of unforseen disaster." The general viewed his objective as a daunting one. "The rascals are very strong," he wrote his wife, "they are well intrenched also & have all the advantages of position."[44]

In the days preceding Lee's attack, orders went out from McClellan's headquarters to strengthen the works south of the Chickahominy. The Second and Third Corps were to "cut as much timber as possible in front of their positions." Parapets were strengthened and ditches were deepened. The 19th Massachusetts, in the Second Corps, had a parapet that was four feet high, three feet wide at the top, and seven feet wide at the bottom. There were enough men to place two ranks behind this respectable barrier. Manning these works while the generals developed their strategy was boring, thought Lyman Blackington, but the men spread their rubber blankets over poles for shelter from the sun and rain.[45]

The Seven Days campaign began when Lee made his initial strike against Porter. His plan called for a frontal and flank approach to the Union position, which had been strongly fortified. The Federals had constructed a line of works on the east side of Beaver Dam Creek, one mile east of Mechanicsville. The line covered the western approaches, which were flat, open fields between the creek and the town. At least two artillery emplacements covered crossings of the creek over the dam at Ellerson's Mill and the main road from Mechanicsville to Bethesda Church. Porter called this position "naturally very strong." The banks of Beaver Dam Creek were steep and some sixty feet high, and the water in the stream was waist deep. The bottomland was 200 yards wide and very swampy near the mouth. The creek valley narrowed and became more shallow as one went northward, upstream from its junction with the Chickahominy River.

The creek was a good obstruction that constituted the main feature of the battlefield, but the works themselves were modest by later standards. The line was placed at the lower end of the creek bluff, near the edge of the bottomland, and had a parapet that was chest high with a post-and-plank revetment. The trees in the creek valley were cut down to clear a field of fire and create a slashing. One of the artillery emplacements remains; it is a simple work, a straight parapet 20 yards long with a good ditch. Faint evidence of two embrasures can be seen. There is a 30-yard remnant of a supporting infantry line to the left of this emplacement, with a parapet and a shallow trench, but no ditch in front. This artillery emplacement is to the rear of Porter's main line, about 150 yards from the irregular lower edge of

Federal works at the battle of Mechanicsville. This dramatic illustration shows the Union line of battle fighting from behind modest works. Note that there is no protection for the upper part of the body. (Johnson and Buel, Battles and Leaders, *2:327)*

the slope and about 50 yards down from the top of the creek bluff, which has a very gentle incline. The line of works was one and a half miles long on the east side of Beaver Dam Creek and manned by three brigades of Brig. Gen. George A. McCall's division of Pennsylvania Reserves, some 9,500 men, supported by thirty-two guns.[46]

Lee hoped to flank Porter out of his position. Jackson was to accomplish this task, but for reasons that still intrigue historians, he failed to do so. Jackson's column struggled to a point within a few miles of the battlefield before bivouacking on the evening of June 26. Impatient to go in, Lee's men launched frontal attacks that afternoon. Some 11,000 Confederates eagerly stormed the works and were ripped to shreds. First they struck McCall's right wing, upstream. Then Daniel Harvey Hill sent two brigades under Pender and Brig. Gen. Roswell S. Ripley against Porter's left wing, with equally devastating results. The green troops thought little of the danger and exposed themselves unnecessarily. Nowhere did they come close to penetrating the line. A Virginia officer who crossed the battlefield the next day wrote that it was "literally covered with our dead soldiers." Many bodies lay within twenty yards of the works, but most littered the swampy bottomland. The Confederates lost 1,475 men, while the Federals tallied a loss of only 361 men. "It was not war," one Pennsylvania infantryman later remarked, "it was murder."[47]

"We were lavish of blood in those days," Daniel Harvey Hill was to admit, "and it was thought to be a great thing to charge a battery of artillery or an earth-work lined with infantry." The men of Pender's and Ripley's brigades had no idea how strong Porter's works were, or of the difficulties they would encounter while struggling across Beaver Dam Creek. Not only were many good men wasted, but the battle "had a most dispiriting effect" on the survivors. With hindsight, it became easy for Hill and others to see that Lee should have waited until June 27 to allow Jackson more time to turn Porter's flank.[48]

The irony is that although the Confederates suffered a tactical defeat, they won a strategic victory at the battle of Mechanicsville, also called the battle of Beaver Dam Creek. McClellan had visited Porter's fortified position early in the afternoon of June 26. When he left just before Lee attacked, he still had not decided whether to evacuate the position. At 3:00 A.M. of June 27, the order to pull out reached Porter. McClellan ignored the bloody repulse and decided the Fifth Corps should retreat six miles eastward to the vicinity of Gaines's Mill, where a semicircular line had already been sketched out by Barnard. The new position better protected several crossings of the Chickahominy, thus securing the connection between the two separated wings of McClellan's army.[49]

McClellan threw away a superb defensive position and all the morale advantages gained by Porter's victory. James Longstreet, whose troops had wasted themselves in the attack, thought the Federals should have rushed up reinforcements and dug additional works to cover Porter's flank during the night of June 26–27, to make the strong position impregnable. Longstreet noted that only the bloody attacks at Malvern Hill dispirited his troops more than the drubbing they received on June 26. The Federal withdrawal reinspired them, and they fought ferociously the next day at Gaines's Mill. Although light in nature, Porter's earthworks and the obstruction presented by Beaver Dam Creek had played key roles in determining the outcome of the battle of Mechanicsville. The true waste was committed by McClellan with his decision to retreat.[50]

Porter's new position at Gaines's Mill was strong in many ways. It embraced "a largely open, oval-shaped plateau" from 40 to 80 feet above the surrounding countryside and at 150 feet elevation. The position was two miles wide and one mile deep. Most of the land inside the Union semicircle was open and cultivated. Elder's Swamp shielded the right, and Boatswain's Swamp screened the left. The center was high and open. Porter had more than 27,000 men and ninety-six guns to defend this bridgehead. Brig. Gen. George W. Morell's division was placed on the left to defend Boatswain's Swamp, Brig. Gen. George Sykes's division was put on the right, and Mc-Call's division was held in reserve.[51]

Lee brought more than 54,000 men to this position but faced a terrain feature that was almost as formidable as Beaver Dam Creek. Longstreet occupied the far right of Lee's line and thus had to contend with Boatswain's Swamp, which was actually a small stream that cut deeply through the landscape. His men had to attack across an open plain to reach the swamp, then descend its western slope. There was little water in the bottom that day, but the slopes were covered with trees and patches of underbrush.[52]

To strengthen their position, the Federals hastily threw up fieldworks. Porter's infantrymen had few axes, so they borrowed some from the artillery units and cut down trees in the valley of Boatswain's Swamp to create an irregular abatis. They rolled some logs into place as a crude breastwork and piled on rails from nearby fences, a few sandbags, and "felled timber and rubbish" to raise the work to about waist height. Morell deployed his men in two lines. The first stood partway down the eastern slope of Boatswain's Swamp, and the second was forty feet higher, on the crest of the slope. Longstreet later referred to the defenses as "a good breastwork," but Porter's men had little time and minimal tools to make a strong fortification. These were what a post–Civil War generation of military theorists liked to call "hasty entrenchments," works thrown up "on the spur of the moment by troops just deployed and awaiting the hostile advance." In fact, it was the first time that the Army of the Potomac constructed such works. All of its previous fortifications, like those at Beaver Dam Creek, had been made "more or less at leisure, at some time previous to the day when they were to be used." Lacking the experience at hasty entrenching that produced the fieldworks of 1864, Porter's men threw up fortifications that had little chance of stopping a determined assault. Morell also erred in placing his men in two lines so close to each other, for if one fell back, it would mask the fire of the second and endanger the whole position.[53]

The decision to fortify seems to have been made on the regimental and brigade levels. Maj. William S. Tilton of the 22nd Massachusetts thought that the ravine of Boatswain's Swamp was a good defensive feature, but he ordered his men to throw together a breastwork "by felling great pines" and smaller trees. Col. Jesse A. Gove, temporarily commanding the 22nd Massachusetts and 13th New York of the First Brigade in Morell's division, suggested this be done. Col. Charles W. Roberts ordered his 2nd Maine in the same brigade to pile knapsacks onto a rail fence for better protection. The

U.S. Engineer Battalion helped to build works on Porter's right. But one wonders if some units were too hasty in constructing their defenses. Colonel Roberts reported that his Maine boys waited for two hours after building their knapsack-lined fence before the Confederates attacked. These troops did little more than create a false sense of security.[54]

Porter held on from 2:30 P.M. until dusk of June 27 against repeated and vigorous assaults, not so much because of his works but because of the firepower he had packed in his bridgehead and the physical obstruction of Boatswain's Swamp. Not until late evening did the Confederates crack open the line. Brig. Gen. John Bell Hood personally led the 4th Texas and 18th Georgia of his brigade, a part of Brig. Gen. William H. C. Whiting's division, in a slashing advance across Boatswain's Creek. There were few trees at the bottom of the valley here, just to Longstreet's left, and Hood's men easily clambered across the small piles of logs. Rather than stopping to return Union fire, Hood pushed them forward without pause. The Federals abandoned their first line and crowded over the second, causing immense confusion that ensured the success of Hood's attack. As it emerged onto the open fields around the Watt House, the 4th Texas captured four Federal guns. The rest of Hood's men and those of Col. Evander M. Law's brigade, also of Whiting's division, widened the break to the left.

The Union perimeter collapsed, but Porter managed to withdraw most of his men to the south side of the Chickahominy. He lost more than 6,800 troops and twenty-two guns, compared with 7,993 Rebel losses. Although his retreat from Beaver Dam Creek to Gaines's Mill foreshadowed his intentions, McClellan gave up his drive against Richmond and retreated to a new base on the James River in the wake of Porter's defeat.[55]

Gaines's Mill was the decisive engagement of the Seven Days. Could Porter have held indefinitely, despite being heavily outnumbered? He had a good position that could have been strengthened by better fortifications. Lt. Colonel Adoniram Judson Warner of the 10th Pennsylvania Reserves was highly critical of the works and of the deployment of the infantry in two lines. Porter could have saved many lives if his lines had "been better posted and entrenched, as we afterward learned to entrench when in the presence of the enemy." Warner considered, with the benefit of hindsight, that his generals had been "ignorant" in June 1862; two years later, there would have been no hesitation to dig in vigorously despite the shortage of time and entrenching tools. If Porter had held his position on June 27, his effort would have been wasted unless McClellan had been willing to reinforce him and make a determined stand north of the river. Without that kind of support, the Fifth Corps would not have lasted another day at Gaines's Mill even with stronger earthworks.[56]

The Seven Days campaign now became a race for the James. McClellan issued orders for all of his units to evacuate their positions and head for Harrison's Landing, thirty miles southeast of Richmond, where the navy could supply and support his army. Lee tried to move his scattered units to cut off the Federals. A sharp battle resulted at Savage's Station on the Richmond and York River Railroad on June 28. Confederate attacks were repulsed without the aid of fortifications, and the retreat continued.[57]

At first, the Federals south of the Chickahominy reacted to the defeats at Beaver Dam Creek and Gaines's Mill by strengthening their fortifications. Traverses were added to the works occupied by the 19th Massachusetts in the Second Corps line. Then McClellan's order to retreat came through. Advancing Confederates of Huger's division entered the Union works along Williamsburg Road on June 29 and were astonished to find all manner of equipment and personal belongings left behind. North Carolina band leader Sam Mickey scavenged through abandoned knapsacks and was shocked to find playing cards and bottles of liquor; he concluded that the Yankees "must have been a hard set of men." Mickey also thought the abandoned works were "very dirty and filthy, and it seemed as if a human being could not stand [to] be at such a place any length of time." His regimental commander, Lt. Col. Henry K. Burgwyn Jr. of the 26th North Carolina, had the foresight to order his men to reform as soon as they entered the works so they would not disperse and plunder the camps. A wagon was stuck in the mud; artillery projectiles, canteens, axes, spades, and other tools were scattered about; and the carcass of an artillery horse was found lying in the open. South Carolina infantryman Robert Wallace Shand was greatly impressed by the strength of the Yankee works near Fair Oaks Station. He believed the parapet was twenty feet wide at the top and fifteen feet high, with ditches fifteen feet deep and twenty feet wide. Shand must have described an artillery emplacement rather than the infantry parapet. He also found lots of food and a quantity of personal letters, many of which were written in German. There was ample evidence that the works had been evacuated in a hurry.[58]

Lee came close to cutting the Army of the Potomac in two at a crossroads called Glendale. While Longstreet attacked this junction from the west, Jackson moved from the north against another portion of the Federal army posted in a strong position behind White Oak Swamp to the northeast of Glendale. While Jackson again failed to press home his part of the advance, contenting himself with heavy artillery fire, Longstreet's men conducted slashing attacks across level, heavily wooded terrain. In this engagement commonly known to the Confederates as the battle of Frayser's Farm, Longstreet did not have to contend with fortifications. Even though they occupied the ground for several hours, the Federals failed to build even crude works. Most of the troops were from the Second and Third Corps, which had not yet been engaged save for some of the Second Corps men in the open field fight at Savage's Station. McCall's Fifth Corps troops occupied the Union center and at least one regiment, the 12th Pennsylvania Reserves, built a hasty entrenchment. Its crude breastwork adjoined two log huts that sheltered six companies, which had to retreat when outflanked. Otherwise the battle of Glendale was a vicious slugging match with seesaw fighting across a landscape littered with scrub timber and marked by an occasional open field. Both sides suffered more than 3,500 casualties, but the Federals managed to hold the junction and allow their comrades to retreat from Jackson's feeble efforts at White Oak Swamp.[59]

This set up the climactic engagement of the Seven Days, the battle of Malvern Hill, on July 1. McClellan had not exercised personal control over any of the battles in the campaign, and now he told Fitz John Porter to organize a rear guard position on a gentle rise of ground one mile north of the James River. Porter positioned Morell's division on the left and Couch's division on the right, 17,800 men all told. They were supported by thirty-seven guns. Porter's front was narrow, only 1,200 yards wide, but it was shielded by Turkey Run to the west and Western Run to the north and east, forcing the Rebels to approach on an equally narrow front. Lee's men had to advance for half a mile up an open, slightly rising piece of ground. At 150 feet elevation, Porter's line was 60 feet above the sheltering bottomland of the two creeks. Malvern Hill was a nearly perfect battlefield for the Unionists, but there was little time or inclination to dig in, despite the Fifth Corps experience at Beaver Dam Creek and Gaines's Mill.

Lee tried to soften this position with an artillery barrage, but the Rebel guns could not master the Federal pieces. A series of uncoordinated, piecemeal attacks began in the afternoon. Brigade after brigade went forward across the open fields. Four hundred yards in front of the Union guns lay a swale about ten feet deep that drained toward the Union right. Some Rebel units were able to take shelter there and reform their ranks, but no one was able to push on closer than about forty yards from the belching guns. Firepower and careful selection of terrain advantages ruled the day at Malvern Hill. By the time the attacks stopped at dusk, Lee had sacrificed more than 5,600 men to no purpose. Porter lost barely 3,000.[60]

As with his victory at Beaver Dam Creek, McClellan threw away any advantage gained here except to complete his change of base to the James River. Safely ensconced at Harrison's Landing, he secured this new base with heavy works. Harrison's Landing was a stopover for river steamers on the grounds of Berkeley Plantation, which had been established in 1619 and was reportedly the site of the first Thanksgiving celebration in North America that year. The current mansion had been built in 1726. The plantation was the ancestral home of the Harrison family, which had produced a signer of the Declaration of Independence, Benjamin Harrison V, and the ninth president of the United States, William Henry Harrison. Another member of the family, Benjamin Harrison, was currently serving as an officer in an Ohio unit and would become president twenty-three years after Appomattox. McClellan's line included nearby Westover plantation, a former Harrison house that later was the home of the famous Byrd family of Virginia.[61]

McClellan's fortified camp was four miles wide and one mile deep. It protected 90,000 men, 288 guns, 3,000 wagons and ambulances, 2,500 beef cattle, and 27,000 horses and mules for the next two months. Barnard scouted the terrain on July 2 and gave general directions to Barton S. Alexander, who superintended construction. Alexander was aided by McAlester, Comstock, and Farquhar in laying out the line on July 5–7. Trees were cut and pinned together for the revetment of the infantry line; then a ditch was dug eight feet deep, and the dirt was piled up against the logs to form a parapet four feet wide at the top. A shallow trench was dug behind the parapet.

The defensive perimeter stretched in a great bow. Both flanks rested on natural features, and gunboats on the James River provided fire support. On the left, Barnard's line ran along the left bank of Kimage's Creek, which flowed through "a deep ravine" and had a wide and marshy outlet to the river. Cleared fields lay west of the creek, but woods were on the Union side. Upstream, nearly at the head of this short creek, the line veered off to the east at a right angle and ended three-quarters of a mile away at the dam of Rowland's Mill Pond. Barnard relied on the water itself to cover the next half-mile of the perimeter and resumed the line at the southeastern edge of the pond. It continued through woods for half a mile, then veered to the southeast for one and a quarter miles across the cultivated fields of Westover Plantation. Then the line headed due south for half a mile to Herring Creek. Barnard felt that the only weak area of this otherwise strong position was the most forward portion, to the left and right of the mill pond.

This forward part of the line was studded with enclosed works for artillery and infantry. The engineers put one work near Kimage's Creek, where the line made its right angle turn to the east, and two smaller works flanked both of the roads that crossed the line to left and right of the mill pond. The portion of the line that faced Kimage's Creek had several gun emplacements with flank protection to fire on an enemy approaching over the cleared fields to the west. Trees were slashed in front of the line, except across the open fields of Westover.

The connecting infantry trench was soon finished, but the redoubts took a couple of weeks. The regular and volunteer engineer troops did the specialized work on them, but infantry were employed in the rough construction. Alfred Bellard, a soldier in the 5th New Jersey, worked on one redoubt for seven guns and on another for six guns. He and his comrades cut all the trees for 200 yards in front of the line. The next day, the slashing caught fire, and a strong wind blew the flames across the works. The blaze scorched logs in the revetment and burned a lot of equipment and personal belongings in the unit's camp, located just behind the line. The redoubts, with parapets double the thickness of the infantry line, had embrasured artillery emplacements.[62]

These works prevented Lee from attacking the Federals. He scouted McClellan's position on July 4, even before the fortifications were complete, and decided it was not worth chancing an attack. Yet the Seven Days campaign ended with a Southern victory and the saving of the capital. Curiously, Lee suffered tactical defeats at Beaver Dam Creek, Savage's Station, White Oak Swamp, Glendale, and Malvern Hill, but his only tactical victory, at Gaines's Mill, was the turning point of the campaign. The price was high on both sides. Lee lost 20,204 men, or 22 percent of his army, while McClellan posted losses of 15,855. An additional 10,246 Confederates were lost from Yorktown to the beginning of the Seven Days, and McClellan lost 9,515 men during that period.[63]

Much more than the end of the Peninsula campaign and the saving of Richmond had been accomplished by July 1, 1862. Lee had established himself as the preeminent Southern general of the war, and the Army of Northern Virginia had been transformed into the most effective field army of the Confederacy. During the next six months, Lee would win spectacular victories exceeding the costly, blundering triumph of the Seven Days. During this period the morale of his men soared to extraordinary heights; they and their commander would disdain all fortifications, whether their own or the Federals'. Troops could hardly learn that fieldworks are important if they futilely attacked them one day, only to have the enemy abandon them in the night. Lee's men went to battle in the last half of 1862 having learned from the Seven Days that digging was not necessary, and that enemy fortifications were not impregnable.

The Peninsula campaign was representative of how field armies used fortifications during the first half of the war in the East. They used them both offensively and defensively; they dug semipermanent works to defend major, fixed assets; and they experimented with hasty fortifications to meet a specific tactical need. More commonly, both sides constructed fieldworks that lay somewhere between these two categories, works that were made with relative leisure for defending one stage in a strategic advance or defense, and that were occupied for several days or weeks at a time. The quality of engineering, the seriousness with which soldiers approached this work, and the reliance that commanders placed on fortifications varied widely. Both armies consisted of green volunteers who were learning the art of war by hard experience.

6 : Second Manassas, Antietam, and the Maryland Campaign

he Seven Days battles saved the Confederate capital for the time being, but McClellan's large army was still entrenched only twenty miles from the city. Lee refused to accept that his own army had to remain inert in the outskirts of Richmond to guard against another Union thrust. He intended to take the war northward, to enlarge the area of operations, and to confront another Union force, the newly created Army of Virginia under Maj. Gen. John Pope, which was hovering north of the Rappahannock River. This move would shift the focus of the war away from Richmond for some time to come.

Defenses of Richmond

Lee had to arrange for the city's defense while he was away. He ordered increased work on its growing ring of fortifications. The southern approaches were strengthened, more guns were ordered for Drewry's Bluff, and works at Petersburg, an important rail junction thirty miles south of the capital, were also pushed forward.[1]

Lee's newly appointed chief engineer, Col. Jeremy Francis Gilmer, began to inspect the lines and suggest improvements. "The greater anxiety is felt for pressing forward defensive works now," Gilmer wrote his wife, "because a large part of our forces in & about Richmond have been sent northward to *whip* Pope, leaving the reduced forces here in need of aid from the much abused pick and shovel." When Lee shifted his army to the Rappahannock River, he left all of his engineer officers behind to see to the defenses of the capital. Only one officer returned to field duty by August 25, on the eve of the campaign against Pope.[2]

Much work was done at Chaffin's Bluff that summer and fall as Lee ordered improvements on the Outer Line of the city defenses. Two brigades and all of A. P. Hill's division worked on the fortifications there in late July and early August until those troops were shifted to field duty elsewhere. Maj. Gen. Gustavus W. Smith took charge of the Richmond defenses on August 30, while Lt. Col. William Proctor Smith took over from William Elzey Harrison as engineer in charge of the works at Chaffin's Bluff. Responding to recommendations by Gilmer, Smith used Henry A. Wise's Virginia brigade to improve the defenses. These troops would spend the next several months digging earthworks near Richmond. Smith connected Batteries 2 through 5 of Harrison's line with an infantry trench, completed gun emplacements all along the line to Williamsburg Road, and slashed timber to create fields of fire.

He also laid out a secondary line that branched off from a point on Harrison's line between Battery 9 and 10 to cover the area between Battery 11 and New Market Road. W. P. Smith's line was built in October and November 1862 and had two artillery redans. One, Smith's Battery, was a redoubt with five faces. The other, overlooking the valley of Coles Run, was constructed the same way and had four gun platforms. If the enemy broke through the left wing of Harrison's line, Smith's new position would still protect the bluff batteries at Chaffin's. Brig. Gen. Junius Daniel's North Carolina brigade did the work on Smith's line.[3]

As troops were sent to reinforce Lee or left for garrison duty in North Carolina and South Carolina, less labor was available to work on the Richmond fortifications. Noting that Lee was "excessively anxious to push rapidly to completion" the defenses around Richmond, Alfred L. Rives received authority from the War Department to impress one-fourth of all male slaves in several Virginia counties as laborers. Their masters were to be paid twenty dollars per month for each slave, and the government was to provide rations. Rives also enlisted the aid of the Richmond and Danville Railroad to transport the workers. He rounded up shovels, picks, and axes and even impressed 30,000 feet of three-inch lumber from a privately owned company and a grove of 100 pine trees from a family farm to make revetments. In October, Jefferson Davis called on Governor John Letcher of Virginia for 4,500 additional black laborers. Gilmer, now head of the Engineer Bureau, worked out a system to mobilize this labor force, fixing quotas for nearby counties and assigning agents of the county governments the responsibility of organizing the crews and delivering them to Confederate authorities. Gustavus Smith planned to allocate at least 200 blacks to the Chaffin's Farm works, which he hoped to complete as rapidly as possible. Half of Daniel's brigade was at work on them all the time, and Smith urged Wise to put as many men on the project as possible. The slaves produced some controversy among local residents. Reports soon circulated that they started work late each day and cut privately owned timber for their firewood. But the large slave population was one of the few sources of workers the Engineer Bureau could call on to supplement the meager number of soldiers left behind by Lee.[4]

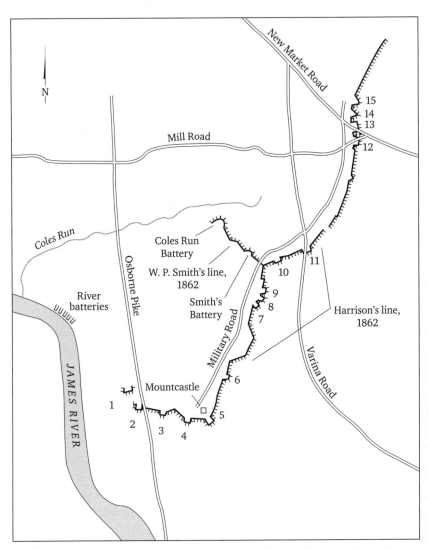

Chaffin's Bluff Defenses, 1862 (based on maps in Dickinson, "Union and Confederate Engineering Operations at Chaffin's Bluff," 17, 30, 66, RNB)

The crisis that developed when McClellan drove to the outskirts of Richmond had taught Confederate authorities a hard lesson; it was foolish to ignore a system of semipermanent defenses for the nation's capital. Even as Lee took the war dozens of miles from Richmond, military and civilian leaders worked hard to perfect the ring of works guarding the city. They wanted to be ready the next time a Yankee army threatened the capital.

Second Manassas

Lee's decision to move north represented a watershed in the eastern campaigns. The Confederates had been compelled to fight a desperate series of battles close to Richmond during the spring and early summer, but they had not been able to clear Federal troops from the vicinity of the capital. When Lee deftly took the war away from Richmond, he kept the theater of operations either along the Rappahannock River or in Maryland and Pennsylvania for the next twenty months.

Fortifications would play a relatively modest role in his campaigns. Lee's army came away from the Seven Days with a palpable disdain for fieldworks. They had beaten the Army of the Potomac despite its use of temporary defenses, and they felt little need to resort to earthworks when an open field fight was possible. But the dangers of ignoring fortifications became apparent to many of Lee's soldiers during the upcoming campaigns, especially during the vicious battle of Antietam, where the Confederate army was badly outnumbered and fought in largely open, rolling terrain. Lee's command probably came closest to being crushed in the field here than at any other time in its history, and the lesson forced a grudging appreciation of fieldworks that would become evident in the battle of Fredericksburg. The summer and fall campaigns represented a slow but real evolution toward greater reliance on field fortifications, at least among Lee's hard-bitten soldiers.

As the Army of Northern Virginia set out to deal with Pope in August 1862, the lessons of Antietam and Fredericksburg, let alone the Wilderness and Spotsylvania, were in the future. Coming from the bloody but victorious engagements of the Seven Days, Lee's men were brimming with confidence in their commander and eager to capitalize on their success outside the gates of Richmond. A hard-won victory over elements of Pope's army at Cedar Mountain on August 9, in the piedmont of Virginia, helped to boost their confidence. It was fought without the aid of fortifications on either side and took place in a largely open, agricultural landscape in the shadow of the mountain.[5]

Lee and Pope faced each other along the Rappahannock River until late August; both commanders failed to cross and catch the other in the flank. Lee then decided to break the stalemate with a bold and powerful stroke. He sent Jackson and 24,000 men on a wide flanking movement to get well to Pope's rear and draw the Federals north. Longstreet was to follow, with the two wings reuniting somewhere east of the Bull Run Mountains. Jackson started on August 25 and marched fifty-four miles in two days, crossing the Bull Run Mountains through Thoroughfare Gap. He reached Manassas Junction on August 27 and plundered the rich store of supplies Pope had left there. By now the Federals were fully aware of his whereabouts and were on the move northward. Jackson assumed a defensive position near the old Bull Run battlefield and waited for the Federals to attack. He was confident his men could hold on long enough for Longstreet to duplicate his flanking march and support him. Jackson took up a position ten miles southeast of Thoroughfare Gap along the line of an unfinished railroad grade, the best defensive ground in the area.

This risky strategy gave Pope an opportunity to strike Jackson's isolated corps with 50,000 men before Longstreet made it to the field, but the Federal commander neglected to hold Thoroughfare Gap. Longstreet reached the pass by August 28. Jackson made his first contact with Pope that same day. The Confederate commander launched a surprise attack on a Federal division as it moved eastward on Warrenton Turnpike near Groveton. The attack was stopped by fierce Union resistance as the afternoon gave way to evening. Pope formed opposite the railroad grade, while Longstreet delayed his link-up with Jackson until the last minute.[6]

The railroad grade was the proposed Independent Line of the Manassas Gap Railroad, one of two railroads that met at Manassas Junction. The Independent Line was meant to bypass Manassas and link Gainesville with Alexandria. Work had started in the mid-1850s, but financial difficulties forced a postponement just before the war broke out. The grade was nearly complete; it had a number of cuts and fills, but saplings and brush had already begun to grow on them.

Like most civilian projects, the railroad grade was not an ideal military fortification. The cuts were roughly 100 yards long and ranged in depth from 1 to 10 feet. Many of the cuts were too deep for the soldiers, as they could not fire over the rim, and some of the fills were too high for them to fire conveniently over the top. None of the cuts had firing steps, and none of the fills had revetments, so it was difficult to snuggle up closely to the earthen barrier and gain maximum coverage. Woods screened the approaches on many parts of the line, although on others, such as that occupied by the Deep Cut, there was open ground. The land in front of the Deep Cut was especially good for defense, as it was level for about fifty yards and then gently lowered into a series of swales. The ground to the rear of the grade rose gently to Stony Ridge. At a maximum elevation of 330 feet, the ridge was only about 80 feet higher than the railroad grade. The railroad "provided an inconsistent—and hence vulnerable—bulwark," according to a recent historian of the battle.[7]

Jackson did not put complete faith in it. Each of the three divisions divided its strength. A. P. Hill's on the left was arrayed in two lines. His left wing was

Railroad cut at Second Manassas. It was at this point that Fitz John Porter launched an attack by 10,000 Federals on August 30, 1862. (Earl J. Hess)

sixty yards to the rear of the grade, while his right wing was immediately behind it. Ewell's division, now led by Brig. Gen. Alexander R. Lawton, also was positioned with one line to the rear and another at the grade. Brig. Gen. William E. Starke's division on the right positioned its skirmishers in the grade and its main line 200 yards to the rear on Stony Ridge. Jackson's line was nearly two miles long, and its right flank was open, screened only by two brigades, so that Longstreet could move up and extend it.[8]

The first Federal attack on Jackson's position was made on August 29 by Brig. Gen. Robert H. Milroy's brigade. Milroy hit a section of the grade called the Dump, one of the larger fills that lay unfinished when work on the railroad ended two years earlier. The Dump also marked the boundary between Starke's and Lawton's divisions. Milroy's piecemeal attack by regiments actually took the Federals across the grade, but lack of support on either flank prevented them from exploiting their success. The Unionists had to repulse a small Confederate counterattack as Milroy's men pulled back. Another Federal attack, this one against Hill's division by Brig. Gen. Cuvier Grover's brigade, also captured a section of the railroad grade. Grover's five regiments hit a gap 125 yards wide between two of Hill's regiments, but they had to withdraw in the face of a counterattack by Hill's second line. A local Rebel counterattack hastened the Yankees on their way.[9]

Soon after Grover was repulsed on the Confederate left, Col. James Nagle's brigade attacked the center. His three regiments started from Dogan Ridge and crossed several hundred yards of open ground to a patch of woods that fronted this sector of Jackson's line. The Federals threw out skirmishers and pressed on to the grade. Lawton had two brigades on the railroad grade and two more in a second line 400 yards to the rear. The cut was so deep that Nagle's men were able to get within point-blank range before being seen. They marched right up to the lip of the cut and fired their muskets into the excavation. Of course, the Confederates could not stand this encounter and fled. Nagle's elated soldiers pushed on about 100 yards beyond the grade before they were met with counterthrusts by several Rebel units. As with Milroy and Grover before him, Nagle was unsupported on either flank. His men had to retreat under difficult circumstances, and other units back in the Union line had to be repositioned to stop a spirited Confederate counter-attack across no-man's-land.[10]

The last major Union strike at Jackson on August 29 was the most massive, involving ten regiments under Maj. Gen. Philip Kearney. It was launched just after Nagle's repulse, about 5:00 P.M., and it threw several units of Hill's division into disorder. Kearney's men pushed the Rebel skirmishers out of the railroad grade on the far left of Hill's line, where Brig. Gen. Maxcy Gregg's brigade was positioned on a rocky knoll well behind the railroad. Farther to the right, Brig. Gen. James J. Archer's Tennessee brigade was positioned in the grade itself and received a devastating volley at point-blank range. At least a part of Archer's command retreated in haste, and the rest held on grimly until help arrived from Brig. Gen. Lawrence O'Bryan Branch's North Carolina brigade. When Early counterattacked on Gregg's front, Kearney was forced to retire. The railroad line continued to hold despite this very close call.[11]

Pope had his best chance to crush Jackson on August 29, but he threw away every opportunity by launching uncoordinated, small-scale assaults and by failing to find and exploit Jackson's exposed flank. He was given one more day to try, because Longstreet took a great deal of time positioning his corps to Jackson's right. Maj. Gen. Fitz John Porter organized an assault by 10,000 men on August 30 with Starke's division as the target. The Confederates were positioned in two lines, 200 yards apart. The open ground in front of Starke's division was dominated by Confederate artillery to the Union left. This was the heaviest assault on the railroad grade, and it was not too late, even at 3:00 P.M., to accomplish some good for Pope. Hundreds of Federals braved the intense artillery fire and lodged themselves at the foot of the Dump, where the large earth embankment alone separated them from the

Rebel defenders. For at least thirty minutes a static firefight at very close range thundered across the grade. As their ammunition gave out, many of Jackson's men threw rocks onto the heads of their opponents, who often threw them back. Reinforcements arrived from Hill, and their counterattack was enough to force the Unionists to retire. The predictable Rebel counterattack was launched, and it was just as predictably thrown back.[12]

Late that afternoon Longstreet launched his long-delayed assault. It was unexpected and resulted in a crushing defeat for Pope. The only terrain feature in Longstreet's way was Chinn Ridge, and outnumbered Federal troops fought a heroic action there that delayed the Rebels for ninety minutes. Another Union line was formed between the ridge and Henry Hill on the old First Bull Run battlefield, and part of the line was placed in the cut of Sudley Road. Milroy called it "a splendid covert for my men. . . . They could be entirely protected while loading and only expose their heads while firing over the bank." A remnant of the cut today is about twenty yards long and five feet deep, with a ravine in front of it. This was a better defensive position than most of Jackson's railroad grade, but the momentum was on Lee's side. Longstreet's advance broke the line, and Pope's army conducted a fighting retreat to Washington.[13]

Neither side dug earthworks or constructed breastworks during the Second Bull Run campaign. While some postwar commentators were surprised at this, believing that the value of fieldworks had already been demonstrated on the Peninsula and during the Seven Days, the truth was that the Union failure in the latter campaign had dispelled any illusions that fieldworks were indispensable to victory. Most of Pope's units had not participated in the Seven Days and, with his focus on destroying Jackson, Pope had no intention of immobilizing his army by digging in. Longstreet, likewise, intended to win through offensive action. Jackson is the one who could be criticized for failing to fortify. The railroad grade was an imperfect defense that needed work to be transformed into an effective fortification. Jackson's men defended this position by forming two lines, by hard fighting, and by the fact that the Union thrusts were wasted in small-scale, unsupported efforts. Although he fought a purely defensive battle, Jackson maintained his mobility, moving units from the rear line to threatened points on the front line, something that would have been difficult if he had dug in.[14]

Defenses of Washington

In early September, when the glow of Rebel victory still burned brightly after Second Manassas, the Confederate Map Bureau in Richmond prepared a series of maps of the area around Washington, D.C. Alfred L. Rives also provided statistics on the ranges of several landmarks in Washington—such as the White House and the Capitol—from across the Potomac River at Arlington. Apparently he hoped Lee would invade Maryland, invest the Northern capital, or at least shell Washington—anything to pay back the Yankees for the threat they had pressed against Richmond the preceding spring.[15]

While Lee had no intention of attacking Washington, he hatched plans for a bold invasion of Northern-held territory. Maryland had never formally seceded from the Union, but this border slave state was vulnerable now that Pope's army was streaming back to the capital and much of McClellan's army was still en route from the Peninsula. The authorities, not privy to Lee's plans, naturally became alarmed for the safety of the city. Not since the aftermath of First Manassas had Washington been thrown into such a panic.

The city became a refuge for Pope's defeated army, but organization was soon brought out of chaos when McClellan assumed command of the city defenses on September 3. He moved the rest of the Army of the Potomac to the region and organized a campaign into Maryland, leaving Maj. Gen. Nathaniel Banks in charge of the city defenses. There were plenty of men, some 46,000 veterans of Pope's army and more than 15,000 garrison troops. The equivalent of an entire field army hovered around the capital for the rest of the fall, providing labor for a massive expansion of the defense system and needed improvement of what had already been built.

With so many resources and the apparent need for protection, Secretary of War Edwin Stanton appointed a commission in October 1862 to recommend what should be done on the works. Consisting of Engineer Chief Joseph G. Totten, John G. Barnard, Quartermaster Gen. Montgomery C. Meigs, and George W. Cullum, Halleck's chief of staff, the commission studied the problem for two months and issued a report on Christmas eve. The commission approved what had already been done but recommended half a dozen new forts and improved infantry lines between the works. It also recommended a permanent garrison of 25,000 infantrymen, 9,000 artillerymen, and 3,000 cavalrymen. Barnard reported that $100,000 had been spent on the works during the last five months of 1862, and he believed another $200,000 would be needed to complete the work recommended by the commission. This was a large sum when added to the $550,000 spent before the summer of 1862, yet the government readily endorsed the commission's suggestions.[16]

Even as the commission deliberated, Barnard set the soldiers to work. They cut timber to clear fields of fire and improved the existing works. Alfred Bellard of the 5th New Jersey helped to build a new fort using the method outlined by the engineer manuals. Light pieces of wood were used to construct a frame exactly outlining, in three dimensions, the shape and size of the parapet. The soldiers dug a deep and wide ditch and used the dirt to fill this frame, tamped it to make the parapet solid, and then sodded it. The ditch eventually filled with water from rainfall, and obstructions were fitted in front of the work.[17]

Barnard supervised additional work on the fortifications in early 1863. By then there were far fewer soldiers available, and the engineer had to hire squads of civilian laborers (and foremen to oversee their work)—as many as 1,000 at a time. The civilians were paid more than a dollar per day. He also hired up to forty carpenters to manufacture wooden structures. This was the last phase in the creation of the Washington defenses. A total of sixty-eight forts and batteries, ninety-three unarmed field gun batteries, three block-houses, and twenty miles of infantry trench constituted the most extensive system of fortifications to guard a single location in American history. The line around the national capital totaled thirty-seven miles in length. Not only in their massive size but in their precision and adherence to regulations were the Washington defenses "the showpiece effort of the Engineers," according to a modern historian.[18]

The works created such a huge demand for troops that the Department of Washington was organized in February 1863. The personnel were termed the Twenty-Second Corps, and Maj. Gen. Samuel P. Heintzelman was put in charge. He had nearly 62,000 men at first, but the number had dwindled to 44,000 by April and to 32,000 by June due to transfers to the Army of the Potomac. The defenses tied these men to safe but monotonous duty in a position that was far too strong for any sane general to contemplate an attack. The works protected the capital well, but they were bigger, more extensive, and more demanding of troops than necessary. When Grant came east to command all Union troops, he stripped the defenses of their man-power to maximize strength for the spring campaign against Lee in 1864.[19]

Lee's Maryland Campaign

Lee crossed the Potomac River on September 4 and occupied Frederick. He expected the Federals holding the lower end of the Shenandoah Valley at Harpers Ferry and Martinsville to retire so he could use the Valley as his line of communications, but Halleck ordered those men to hold on. It was the decisive factor in the coming campaign, for the rest of Lee's movements would be oriented around clearing the Valley path for his supplies.

Lee's plan to eliminate the roadblock in the Valley was issued to his commanders on September 9. He divided the army into four parts, three of which were to make rapid movements to Harpers Ferry, reduce the place, and rejoin him at Boonsboro about twenty miles north of Harpers Ferry. They had three days to accomplish the task. Jackson led one of the three columns, 14,000 men, from Frederick on September 10. He was to occupy the high ground called Bolivar Heights on the west side of Harpers Ferry, while Maj. Gen. Lafayette McLaws and 8,000 men occupied Maryland Heights on the north side of the Potomac River. The third column, 2,400 men under Brig. Gen. John George Walker, was to take Loudoun Heights east of the Shenandoah River.[20]

Harpers Ferry

Few other engagements of the war would be so dominated by the terrain of the battlefield as this one. Harpers Ferry, an old and important arsenal town at the confluence of the Potomac River and the Shenandoah River, was nestled among some of the most imposing mountains in the eastern theater. The Potomac River was the only waterway powerful enough to cut through the mountains as plate tectonics created them millions of years ago. Thus the gap at Harpers Ferry is the only deep-water gap in the Blue Ridge. The flow of the Shenandoah River, the largest tributary of the Potomac, was diverted when the Blue Ridge rose up. All other smaller streams in the area also were redirected by the rise of the mountains to flow into the Shenandoah or the Potomac, leaving many so-called wind gaps in the mountaintops. They are the remnants of stream erosion, cut slightly into the emerging mountaintop before the water was diverted. The combination of plate movement and hydrography created a rugged, natural arena with the town of Harpers Ferry as the stage.

The most important high ground is Maryland Heights, which is part of the Blue Ridge. The heights are the end of a long, wide, and high ridge that stretches many miles from the north. The elevation of Maryland Heights ranges from 1,300 to 1,400 feet, almost 1,000 feet higher than the land beside it. The end of Maryland Heights points directly toward the junction of the two rivers. On the other side of that junction, the Blue Ridge continues with Loudoun Heights, which constitutes the modern boundary between Virginia and West Virginia. West of Harpers Ferry, Bolivar Heights is a ridge some 700 feet tall, about 300 feet higher than the town itself. Bolivar Heights is a superb defensive position screening the approach to Harpers Ferry. All this high ground surrounding the town would be a wonderful defensive position if adequately fortified and manned, but that would require thousands of troops. If left unguarded, the high ground on each of the three sides can doom the position by allowing enemy forces to dominate the town with artillery fire. This would be the key to Confederate success.[21]

Loudoun Heights and Maryland Heights, Harpers Ferry. Note the timber stockade and signal station on Loudoun Heights on the right and the commanding position of Maryland Heights in the background. The naval battery was located on the plateau on the left. (Johnson and Buel, Battles and Leaders, *2:608).*

The mountaintops had a thick layer of original trees until the 1840s, when extensive cutting took place to produce charcoal. By the time of the war, the heights were covered by a second growth of scrubby timber and underbrush. Confederate troops commanded by Jackson occupied Harpers Ferry in April 1861, and 500 of them took possession of Maryland Heights on May 9. They cleared an area on top and erected a stockade, but Gen. Joseph E. Johnston evacuated Harpers Ferry in mid-June 1861. Union captain John Newton scouted the heights when the Federals took possession and reported that the vegetation was so thick as to be "difficult of penetration." This led Federal commanders to defer extensive fortification on the high ground, but they could hardly ignore the strategic significance of the heights. When Jackson's Valley campaign was in full swing in May 1862, Federal engineers hastily laid out the naval battery, manned by gunners from the Washington Navy Yard. It was located on a plateau one-third of the way up Maryland Heights and could fire on almost any spot in town as well as on Bolivar Heights. It had seven gun emplacements, and the parapet was made mostly of sandbags. An old road built before the war by charcoal and quarry workers was used to gain access to the site, some 400 feet above the Potomac.[22]

In September, Jackson would be greatly aided by the incompetence of his opponent, for Harpers Ferry was under the command of Col. Dixon S. Miles. Born in 1804 and a graduate of West Point, Miles already had a checkered war career. Hit with dysenteric diarrhea just before First Bull Run, he took quinine, opium, and brandy and was visibly inebriated during the engagement. A court of inquiry failed to find evidence to convict him, so he remained on duty. Miles was shifted to the quiet post in March 1862, but he did little to fortify it beyond constructing the naval battery. Under pressure from department commander John E. Wool, Miles also erected a line of infantry trench on Camp Hill, a modest elevation between Bolivar Heights and the town. Wool's instructions to build a blockhouse on Maryland Heights, lay abatis in front of the work on Camp Hill, and entrench a camp on Bolivar Heights were never followed.

Miles had 11,000 men at Harpers Ferry, organized into brigades, but most were green troops who had never been tested in battle. As the three Confederate columns converged on the place, Brig. Gen. Julius White brought an additional 2,500 men from Martinsburg on September 12. Although White outranked Miles, he gave up command of the post and its threatened garrison to the colonel.[23]

The faulty dispositions of this incompetent officer gave Jackson his opportunity to seize the heights. Miles put three of his four brigades west of town, two on Bolivar Heights and another on Camp Hill to support a battery of fourteen guns. The last brigade, under Col. Thomas Ford, was placed in an isolated position on Maryland Heights. Ford constructed a line of breastworks consisting of logs and rocks, and he cut trees to form an abatis in front. Loudoun Heights was left unoccupied.[24]

On September 12, the day that White reached Harpers Ferry, McLaws ascended Maryland Heights. He advanced to Ford's line of breastworks and stopped for the night. Although his forces greatly outnumbered Ford's, McLaws gingerly advanced on the morning of September 13, outflanked the line, and forced the Unionists to retreat. The Federals regrouped a quarter of a mile away while McLaws halted. A stalemate ensued for several hours. Then, at midafternoon, Ford apparently misunderstood an order from Miles and took his entire brigade off Maryland Heights. McLaws most likely would have taken the high ground anyway, but Ford's withdrawal offered Jackson the key to Harpers Ferry.

September 13 was a momentous day for many commanders in this campaign. As McLaws secured Maryland Heights, Jackson's column approached Bolivar Heights and Walker's column ascended Loudoun Heights. Many miles to the east, McClellan received a copy of Lee's Special Orders No. 191, which outlined the Harpers Ferry operation and showed that Lee himself commanded what little remained of the Army of Northern Virginia in western Maryland. A copy of the order had been found wrapped around three cigars in an abandoned Rebel camp. McClellan decided to push westward, force his way through the passes of South Mountain (the continuation of the Blue Ridge north of the Potomac River), and hit Lee before Jackson could rejoin him. He also dispatched Maj. Gen. William B. Franklin's Sixth Corps to relieve Harpers Ferry. McClellan delayed the start of his movements until the next day, giving both Lee and Jackson more time to accomplish their goals.[25]

With Jackson's column blocking Miles's escape on the west and McLaws busily planting guns on Maryland Heights, it was up to Walker to complete the investment of Harpers Ferry. He reached the foot of Loudoun Heights at 10:00 A.M. on September 13 and dispatched two regiments to the top. They found the summit unoccupied. That evening Lt. William G. Williamson and another engineer officer scouted the rocky top for good artillery positions. Williamson sketched a map and sent it to Jackson by courier, and he supplemented it with another sketch and verbal information when he saw Jackson the next morning. The commander approved, and Williamson again ascended the heights to supervise the construction of battery emplacements on September 14. Walker placed five Parrotts on Loudoun Heights that day, and McLaws planted six guns on top of Maryland Heights. Jackson established his batteries on School House Ridge, a lower but well-defined feature about 1,000 yards in front of Bolivar Heights.

Jackson used signal flags to communicate with McLaws and Walker, intending to coordinate the opening of his bombardment, but Walker grew impatient and opened without orders at 2:00 P.M. on September 14. This compelled Jackson and McLaws to commence firing. The Confederate artillery dominated the poorly placed Union guns, but the Federal infantry was well protected by ravines and suffered comparatively little. While the guns roared, A. P. Hill's division moved forward to find an opening on the south end of Bolivar Heights. A shelf of bottomland along the river allowed him to flank the Union forces on the high ground and plant some guns in preparation for an attack the next day. Only a line of abatis stood in Hill's way.[26]

On September 14, after a day of hard fighting, McClellan broke through three passes in South Mountain. This development compelled Lee to plan a retreat to Virginia. He sent orders to McLaws to give up the siege of Harpers Ferry and rejoin the army in the vicinity of Sharpsburg. But Jackson assured

Lee that he could compel the surrender of the garrison on September 15, and the army commander relented. McLaws dispatched some units northward to block Franklin's advance toward Harpers Ferry, and fifty cannon resumed the bombardment of Miles's isolated command on the morning of September 15. Soon the Federal guns ran out of long-range ammunition, and Miles surrendered. White flags were raised, but one of the last Confederate shells mortally wounded Miles. White assumed command and negotiated the surrender. Jackson captured 12,500 men and seventy-three guns but lost only 286 men. Only 217 Unionists were killed and wounded. The Northerners were outnumbered, inadequately fortified, and ineptly led, and their loss of supplies and prestige was enormous.[27]

South Mountain

After Lee dispatched the three columns to take Harpers Ferry, he moved his remaining three divisions—two of Longstreet's and one commanded by D. H. Hill—to Hagerstown and Boonsboro. The loss of Special Orders No. 191 gave McClellan the information needed to move on these divisions, but the Union commander delayed half a day before acting. He did not expect much resistance at the passes of South Mountain and thus was unprepared for a major battle. Lee received word from his cavalry on the night of September 13 that the Federals were beginning to move, so he dispatched D. H. Hill to take charge of the position on South Mountain. Hill had only two of his five brigades in place when the battle started the next morning.

South Mountain, which rises from 1,000 to 1,300 feet above the valleys to either side of it, is the eastern edge of the Appalachian Highlands north of the Potomac River. Between Frederick and Hagerstown there are four crossings: Turner's Gap, through which the National Road traversed the mountain; Fox's Gap; Crampton's Gap; and Brownsville Gap. The first two are less than a mile apart, while Crampton's and Brownsville gaps are about five miles south. The slopes of South Mountain are steep and rugged, especially near the top. This was the only battle in which the Army of the Potomac had to contend with Appalachian terrain, even though units of that army had fought in the mountains of western Virginia and most regiments that surrendered at Harpers Ferry would later join the army as well.[28]

The Ninth Corps of McClellan's army tried to force its way through Fox's Gap, the second pass from the north, at 9:00 A.M. The slope there ascended sharply for about 300 yards and then gave way to a more moderate slope before a sharper ascent was resumed. The gap itself is wide and deep, cutting through about half the height of the mountain. The Federals found remarkably open terrain, much of it farmland, as they neared the top. Regular battle lines could be drawn here, and Brig. Gen. Samuel Garland's North Carolina brigade fought well. The Rebels eventually were pushed back to the crest and beyond, where Garland's men took shelter in a road that was sunken a couple of feet deep and bordered by a stone fence. This was an effective fortification even though it allowed the Rebels to see only about fifty yards to their front; beyond that point, the natural crest of the mountain shielded the attackers. Garland was killed, and one-third of his command, which was outnumbered three to one, fell; even some hand-to-hand fighting took place. Additional brigades from both Hill and Longstreet stalled the Federal advance in the afternoon and prevented the Ninth Corps from exploiting its advantage, but the gap was essentially in Union hands.[29]

Farther to the south the Sixth Corps was assigned to crash through Crampton's Gap and relieve Harpers Ferry, but Franklin dithered. Initially only four regiments, aligned behind a stone fence near the base of the mountain, defended the pass. The land in front of Crampton's Gap is open, rolling, and pastoral; but the slope is very steep, and the gap itself is comparatively shallow, cutting down through about one-fourth of the eminence. The Rebels were placed at the base of the mountain where the lowest part of the slope met the surrounding countryside. They should have been farther up, to force the Federals to traverse the steep slope, but there was no good terrain feature like a stone fence on the mountainside. Franklin bombarded the position for two hours and then launched an infantry assault at 4:00 P.M. that easily pushed the Confederates up the mountain toward the gap. The Federals occupied the pass as dusk descended, but it was too late to go farther.[30]

Turner's Gap, on the far north, presented the most difficult terrain. The National Road approached the gap through a deep gorge that was wide and spacious at the bottom but quickly narrowed, with steep sides, as it neared the top. The gap itself is also narrow, cutting down through one-fourth of the mountain. When the First Corps approached this imposing obstacle, Brig. Gen. George G. Meade's division was sent up a road that ascended a spur to the north of Turner's Gap. Meade was to outflank the gap by gaining access to the mountaintop just to the north. He was separated from the rest of the corps by a deep ravine, so Brig. Gen. John P. Hatch's division advanced up the same spur but south of the ravine. A lone Alabama brigade, led by Brig. Gen. Robert E. Rodes, faced both Yankee divisions. Rodes put up a hard fight and lost one-third of his men, but he delayed Meade and Hatch for some time. While this slow ascent was taking place, Brig. Gen. John Gibbon's brigade launched a spirited attack up the National Road toward the gap. Brig. Gen. Alfred H. Colquitt's Georgia brigade blocked the way at a stone fence and stopped Gibbon near dusk before he could capture the gap. That successful defense would soon be wasted, for Meade and Hatch had nearly completed their turning movement by pushing Rodes back to the mountain-top. The next morning, they would be in position to seize Turner's Gap.[31]

By the time the fighting had ended, all of McClellan's army was on the battlefield. If he could have accomplished this at dawn and then moved swiftly, the passes probably would have been forced more easily. McClellan's half-day delay after he found Lee's lost order had given the Rebel commander time to shift large numbers of men to the passes by midafternoon, and the swift movement to a decisive showdown with Lee west of South Mountain was no longer possible. Instead, McClellan was forced into a heavy battle merely to secure possession of the gaps.

More than 2,000 men were lost by both sides in this battle on September 14, the day that Jackson was getting the upper hand on Miles at Harpers Ferry. When one surveys the battlefield today, a question naturally arises: Why did the Confederates not use this immense natural feature to block McClellan's advance indefinitely? In short, why did Lee not dig in before September 14? Even small detachments behind good works could have delayed any Union force moving westward and given him more time to concentrate his army west of South Mountain. Rather like Pope and Thoroughfare Gap at Second Bull Run, Lee neglected to use earthworks at a natural bottleneck that could have paid rich strategic dividends.

Antietam

Lee fought a defensive battle at Sharpsburg even though the terrain offered few advantages to his outnumbered army. With only 35,000 men at the start of the engagement, he arrayed his divisions so as to reap every possible benefit from the landscape. The ground between Antietam Creek and Sharpsburg is open, rolling farmland, with numerous limestone ledges and outcroppings. The inequalities in the land are relatively modest. The bed of Antietam Creek lay at an elevation of 320 feet, Sharpsburg was at 480 feet, and the tops of the rolling hills did not exceed 520 feet. It was more wooded in 1862, when significant patches of trees dotted the northern section of the battlefield, than it is today, but the ground offered opportunity for artillery concentrations and for the rapid movement of large masses of infantrymen.[32]

Lee did not dig in, although there was time and opportunity to do so. Good fieldworks would have been amply justified, considering the disparity of numbers and the open nature of the terrain. It is true that the topsoil is shallow—only five inches in some places—but there were fence rails and stones that could have been used to make breastworks. Historian Edward Hagerman has suggested that Lee demonstrated his adherence to "an extreme tendency in American tactical thought that opposed all fortifications in the open field of battle" because it would hinder "the resumption of the offensive." This is probably true. Lee wanted to keep his tactical options open when the clash took place. Antietam fits nicely into the trend many Civil War commanders displayed. They were eager to dig in during the first half of the war only when they occupied rough terrain that in itself inhibited tactical movement, but in open ground they did not want to tie their forces down unnecessarily to the defensive. McClellan also did not fortify when he reached the vicinity. Hagerman wonders if he was "intimidated by the criticism" of his reliance on fortifications during the Peninsula campaign, but it is more likely that he intended to assume the tactical offensive as soon as possible. McClellan knew he had to attack, and there was no reason to dig works. Even on the Peninsula and in the Seven Days, he had always demonstrated a tendency to dig in only when needed.[33]

The battle fought on September 17 was one of the most costly of the war, and the Confederates tried to make good use of existing topographical features as cover. The rocky outcroppings, the ravines, and the woods themselves offered some protection. The fight started on the northern part of the field when the First Corps of the Army of the Potomac emerged from North Woods and struck Jackson's men, newly arrived from Harpers Ferry, in the area of farmer Miller's cornfield. The Federals crossed a ravine that separated the woods from the field and entered the ripening stand of corn. The only fortification thrown up on this part of the field by the Confederates was a small breastwork in the pasture south of the field. The fighting swayed back and forth through and around this patch of corn until the stalks were shot down, broken over, and trampled by thousands of feet. Attacks and counterattacks failed to result in a decisive advantage for either side but littered the countryside with casualties.

Soon after the First Corps started, the Twelfth Corps supported it to the left by attacking from East Woods. This corps was led by an engineer officer, Maj. Gen. Joseph K. F. Mansfield, who had never commanded in combat. Mansfield had lobbied for a field assignment for some time and took over the Twelfth Corps on September 15. Half of his 7,200 men were just as green as he was, but they all fought well, duplicating the tactical experience of their comrades to the right. The Rebels on this part of the line found several opportunities to take advantage of the inequalities of the ground. Capt. Thomas M. Garrett of the 5th North Carolina reported that his men came up to "a ledge of rock and earth, forming a fine natural breastwork," and held there until they were outflanked and forced to retire. Mansfield was shot in the chest early in the advance and died the next day.[34]

Sunken road, Antietam. Taken shortly after the battle, this view demonstrates how the roadbed could serve as a makeshift field fortification. It also movingly illustrates the aftermath of combat in the Civil War. (Library of Congress)

In the Confederate center, D. H. Hill's men found a farm road that started from Hagerstown Pike and went southeast, zigging and zagging, until it reached Boonsboro Pike between Sharpsburg and Antietam Creek. Wagon traffic to a gristmill on the creek had worn down sections of it, and erosion had hastened the sinking of those sections several feet. A recent historian has called it a "natural trench," although that is an overstatement. The sunken section that would play a role in the battle is about 500 yards long, and its depth ranges from one to four feet, barely deep enough for a fortification. Like all such features, the sunken road lacked a parapet, and the view from it was restricted. On the left, one can see a couple of hundred yards ahead, but in the center the rising ground to the front restricts the view to no more than thirty yards. On the right one can see a long distance, except that anyone in the bottom of the rolls in the landscape is hidden from view. The Sunken Road, or Bloody Lane as it would become known, offered two brigades of Hill's division a line of demarcation to form along, and it did cover them to a limited extent from enemy fire; but it was far less effective than a well-made earthwork or even a good breastwork would have been.[35]

These limitations did not prevent the fighting in the Rebel center from reaching a level of intensity hardly equaled on other battlefields. The Union Second Corps sent 5,700 men rolling across the open landscape to slam into this position. Rodes's Alabama brigade was on the left, and Brig. Gen. George B. Anderson's North Carolina brigade was on the right, totaling 2,500 men. Hill sent three more brigades to support these two, but the Confederate position in the Sunken Road fell when Anderson's right flank was turned. About the same time, the left flank of Rodes's brigade collapsed. Here the road angled sharply and was so shallow as to be almost on the natural level. The 6th Alabama was exposed to a deadly enfilade by the Federals who had lodged themselves on the rising ground just in front of the center of the Sunken Road, so the 6th was ordered to move to a deeper part of the road. The commander misunderstood his instructions and retreated from the road altogether, and the Federals exploited this mistake to hasten all Rebel troops out of the lane. The Confederate defenders held the Sunken Road for three hours but lost nearly a third of their number.[36]

On the Confederate right, the Union Ninth Corps was stymied for a long while by Antietam Creek. Maj. Gen. Ambrose E. Burnside tried to force a passage across one of several stone bridges in the area, the Rohrback Bridge, soon to be known as Burnside's Bridge. It was 125 feet long and 12 feet wide. The creek valley was narrow with a steep western bluff that rose about 100 feet above the bridge. Col. Henry L. Benning and 400 men of the 2nd Georgia and 20th Georgia took position overlooking the crossing. They took shelter in shallow quarry pits and behind a stone fence and piles of cordwood, and supplemented the civilian features with a small breastwork made of fence rails and logs. A Union veteran recalled after the war that these were "rude but substantial breastworks."[37]

For three hours Burnside's men tried simultaneously to push their way across the stone bridge and to find a usable ford nearby. Benning's badly outnumbered soldiers on the creek bluff demonstrated their advantage of position, supplemented by a few minor fortifications. Five hundred Yankees were lost in effecting the crossing, while only 120 Confederates fell. Finally the Ninth Corps crossed and began to move against Lee's right wing. The Army of Northern Virginia faced a terrible crisis. It was exhausted, and there were no reinforcements except A. P. Hill's division, which arrived just in time from Harpers Ferry to block Burnside. The Ninth Corps barely made it out of the creek valley before Hill's men took position on the high ground behind a stone fence half a mile from the bridge. Here the Union advance ground to a halt.[38]

Despite the loss of more than 12,000 men in each army, the fighting was a tactical draw. Lee evacuated Maryland, so in that sense Antietam was a major Union victory. Like Second Manassas, the battle was notable for the absence of prepared fortifications and the use of existing terrain features. But unlike Second Manassas, Antietam nearly wrecked the Army of Northern Virginia. Lee would be much more cautious in the next encounter at Fredericksburg.

Defenses of Harpers Ferry

McClellan responded slowly to Lee's retreat from Maryland as subordinate commanders saw to the safety of Harpers Ferry. The post had demonstrated its strategic usefulness by hindering Lee's communications, but its defenses had been neglected by previous Federal commanders. Now a major effort was made to erect the kind of works that would secure the post against a large attack such as the one Jackson had unleashed. It was a scenario typical of the Civil War; field commanders responded to a battle by digging in.

Lt. Cyrus B. Comstock surveyed the area in early October and recommended that a lot of work be done, but his recommendations fell short of what was needed to thoroughly secure the post. Comstock correctly noted that holding the peninsula west of the junction of the Shenandoah and Potomac rivers was the key to the position, and he recommended extensive earthwork construction to guard against an attack from the west. Bolivar Heights should be fortified with a line nearly two miles long, consisting of an infantry trench and three battery emplacements. The heights should be held by 6,000 men and twenty-seven guns. Comstock wanted the line placed a bit down the forward slope of the height and continued all the way to the Shenandoah, where a redoubt would be constructed on the bottomland. This was to prevent the enemy from flanking the line, as A. P. Hill had done the preceding month. Comstock also recommended the construction of a redoubt on a hill north of the Potomac big enough for 500 men and with artillery that could command the northern end of Bolivar Heights.

Comstock noted that all the high ground within one and a half miles of the peninsula had to be securely held if Harpers Ferry was to be safe. Log blockhouses could be erected on the crests of Loudoun Heights and Maryland Heights as a first step while artillery emplacements were hewn out of the rocky soil, and the extensive tree cover could be cleared to open expansive fields of fire. The next step should be to erect a line of redoubts or stone blockhouses to protect a permanent camp big enough to house up to 3,000

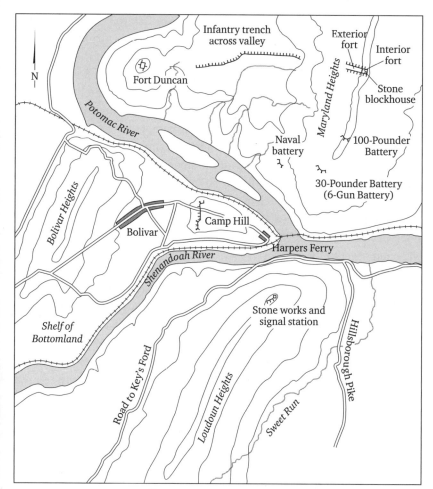

Harpers Ferry Defenses, 1863

men and eight guns on top of each crest. The camps could be supported by artillery fire from Camp Hill, firing up the slopes of both mountains, a difficult task for gunners that the engineer never fully appreciated.[39]

The proposal was partly implemented. Bolivar Heights was not fortified according to Comstock's plan until two years later, in the middle of Sheridan's Shenandoah Valley campaign, but Maryland Heights became the focus of immediate construction efforts. Seared by McLaws's occupation of that eminence and how it had doomed the garrison in September, the Federals started work on October 15, 1862, according to Comstock's plan. The foundation of a stone blockhouse was started that day on the crest of Maryland Heights. It was 40 feet by 100 feet with a bastion on each end. The work straddled the crest at an elevation of 1,448 feet. Before it was completed, engineers had second thoughts about the feasibility of a stone fort. This material was initially chosen because of the rocky nature of the soil, but it would not stand more than a few rounds from even a small field piece. In September 1863 the structure was converted into a supply warehouse.

More effective fortifications were built around the stone structure. The Interior Fort, consisting of an earth and rock parapet for infantry, was built in June 1863 when Lee's Pennsylvania campaign threatened Harpers Ferry. It had a rectangular configuration, with the stone blockhouse at one corner of the rectangle. Five embrasures for 30-pounder Parrotts were included in the parapet, which also had a ditch in front. The Exterior Fort was constructed at the same time. It extended the Interior Fort westward, 550 feet down the slope of Maryland Heights. The parapet consisted of stone and was 5 feet wide and 3 feet tall.

Two major gun emplacements were built on Maryland Heights. The 30-Pounder Battery, also known as the 6-Gun Battery, was dug in October 1862. Its fire covered the tops of Loudoun Heights and Bolivar Heights. The work had four sides but was open to the rear. The 100-Pounder Battery, built in June 1863, had a 9-inch Dahlgren whose fire could cover nearly everything— Loudoun Heights, the valleys east and west of Maryland Heights, and Bolivar Heights. It was located on the crest of Maryland Heights between the Stone Fort and the 30-Pounder Battery. The Dahlgren piece was replaced with a 100-pounder Parrott in August 1863, and the gun platform was raised to provide a wide traverse of fire.[40]

The Stone Fort complex was the left anchor of a line extending westward from Maryland Heights to the Potomac River. Fort Duncan, built on the hill that Comstock identified as needing a redoubt to cover the north end of Bolivar Heights, lay in advance of this continuous line of infantry trench. It was a rectangular work with parapets fifteen feet thick, a ditch, and sixteen guns. The old naval battery was reinforced as well in June 1863. The sandbag parapet was replaced by earthworks, the emplacement was enlarged and embrasured, and four magazines were added. Loudoun Heights received its share of attention, but that paled in comparison with the work on Maryland Heights. Units of the Twelfth Corps occupied Loudoun on September 22, 1862. They cut trees and built stone works and a signal station on its crest.[41]

The work at Harpers Ferry in late 1862 and early 1863 was far more extensive than anything that had been done before Jackson captured the place, and it essentially mastered the difficult engineering problem of defending this mountain post. The modest garrison would use the works on Maryland Heights as a citadel. When Lee invaded Pennsylvania in June 1863,

10,000 Federals evacuated the town and fled to the works. They readied for an attack, but Lee bypassed the post rather than reduce it. The same thing happened in July 1864 when Jubal Early raced down the Valley and raided into Maryland. This was not an unusual plan, for dozens of small towns throughout the occupied South were guarded by small garrisons with a modest earthwork on the outskirts of the village. The garrison was expected to take refuge in the fort, leaving the town occupied temporarily until the enemy—usually cavalry raiders or guerrillas—grew tired of their failure to take the earthwork and left. Thus the fortification plan implemented by the Federals for Harpers Ferry allowed them to maintain the post even though it exposed the town to periodic occupation by the enemy.

The final part of Comstock's plan, to fortify Bolivar Heights and close the most accessible door to Harpers Ferry, was not implemented until August 1864. Officers apparently had believed that with a modest garrison, Maryland Heights was the only essential real estate to hold in the area. But after two episodes of giving up the town and taking refuge on the heights, Sheridan completed the ring of fortifications around Harpers Ferry. Planning for his drive up the Shenandoah Valley to deal with Jubal Early, Sheridan ordered the digging of nearly two miles of trench on the ridge, connecting not three but six redoubts. As Comstock had recommended, the line was placed some thirty yards down the forward slope, which is very steep and utterly commands the valley below. A well-preserved stretch of this Sheridan earthwork contains a lot of gravel, and a ditch lies in front of what little remains of one redoubt on the left. Sheridan's defeat of Early in the coming campaign eventually cleared the Valley of Rebel troops.[42]

7 : Fredericksburg

ee went on the defensive after Antietam, and Lincoln replaced McClellan with Ambrose Burnside. The new commander devised a plan that might well have worked. The army was concentrated at Warrenton and would dash for Fredericksburg thirty miles southeast, cross the Rappahannock River, and head for Richmond, another fifty-five miles away. Burnside arranged for supplies and pontoons to be shifted to Fredericksburg in preparation for his move. Maj. Gen. Edwin V. Sumner's Right Grand Division reached Fredericksburg on November 19, the same day that the leading elements of Lee's army arrived, but the logistical support was not there. The wharf facilities at Aquia Creek and the railroad from that place to Fredericksburg would not be operational for another week, and the pontoons also were missing due to a staff mix-up. These delays and mistakes forced Burnside to halt at Fredericksburg without crossing the river. Soon he was confronted by Lee and most of the Rebel army.[1]

The two armies would face each other in this spot for the next five months. Fredericksburg, nestled in the valley of the Rappahannock, was one of the oldest towns in Virginia. On the east side of the river rose Chatham Heights to an elevation of 100 feet. The small town of Falmouth also was here. The river lies at 60 feet elevation, and Fredericksburg is laid out on the bottomland of the west side, only 20 feet above the river. While the valley is comparatively narrow, it quickly widens on the west side as one travels south of town. The line of bluffs that ranges along the western edge of the bottomland made a superb defensive position, and the Confederates occupied it. Taylor's Hill, on the north, anchored the Rebel left and is as high as Chatham Heights. Marye's Hill is three-quarters of a mile from the river and directly west of Fredericksburg. Telegraph Road runs along the base of Marye's Hill and is sunken in places, with a stone wall holding up the eastern bank. A drainage canal ran north to south outside the town some 200 yards east of Telegraph Road. Farther south, Telegraph Hill offers a high and commanding view of the town and the bottomland below. The line of heights continues south to Howison's Hill and beyond, until a wide and deep ravine cuts into the bluff line. Here the Richmond, Fredericksburg, and Potomac

Railroad curved west. Hamilton's Crossing was the name of the spot where a wagon road crossed the rail line as it curved.[2]

Both sides were given plenty of time to fortify their positions, but neither did a thorough job. The Confederates concentrated on digging battery emplacements on the high ground but neglected to provide protection for the infantry. Lee sent his artillery chief, Brig. Gen. William N. Pendleton, to select battery sites soon after he arrived at Fredericksburg on November 23. Pendleton noted that the Federals were already fortifying their gun emplacements. "On our own line a few hurried works were in progress" as well. Pendleton recommended places for two 30-pounder Parrots on December 1, and Lee approved his recommendations the next day. One was emplaced on Howison's Hill and the other on Telegraph Hill. Pendleton ordered the dense tree cover on Telegraph Hill cut down, staked out the gun emplacement, and directed the digging. Lee realized what a grand view the hill now afforded and made it his headquarters site; afterward it became known as Lee's Hill.[3]

Confederate activity quickened after this start. Lee not only used Pendleton but sent two other artillerymen and engineer Capt. Samuel R. Johnston to site and fortify most of his remaining guns. Col. Edward Porter Alexander was put to work soon after his battalion reached Fredericksburg. One of Lee's most skillful artillerists, Alexander took pains to place the guns far enough down the forward slope of the bluffs so they could hit targets on the bottomland below—in short, so they could fire on advancing infantry and field batteries. Lee complained about it, for he wanted the guns sited farther up the slope so they could achieve sufficient elevation to fire on Union guns across the river, but he relented when Alexander told him the digging had already begun. Lee would realize the value of this adjustment when the Federals attacked nearly two weeks later. Orders also went out to measure the distance from each gun position to probable targets, and traverses were constructed where necessary to protect the cannon against enfilade fire.[4]

There are remnants of three artillery emplacements on Lee's Hill. None have a regular ditch in front, just a line of holes where the soldiers dug dirt to make the parapet. One emplacement has an L-shaped parapet with the gun platforms on the natural level of the earth. The others are different in design. One has a dug platform with a long traverse on the left but no parapet in front, and the other has a traverse on both sides.[5]

Lee committed himself to a limited policy of fortifying in order to keep his options open. Digging in all along the line, infantry as well as artillery, would have represented a decision to stay put. It might have averted a Federal offensive, but with the huge terrain advantage he possessed, perhaps Lee wanted to induce rather than deter a Union attack. There were alternative

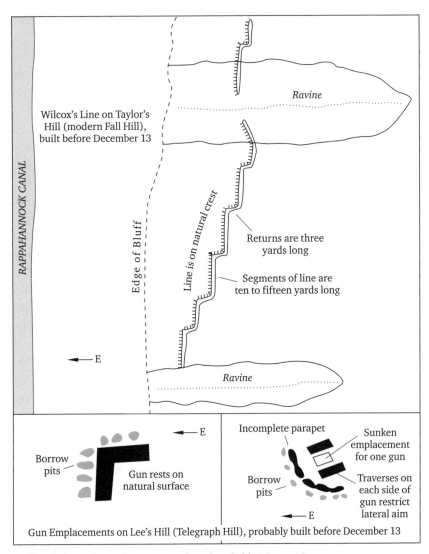

RAPPAHANNOCK CANAL

Wilcox's Line on Taylor's
Hill (modern Fall Hill),
built before December 13

Ravine

Line is on natural crest

Edge of Bluff

Returns are three
yards long

Segments of line are
ten to fifteen yards long

E

Ravine

Borrow
pits

E

Gun rests on
natural surface

Incomplete parapet

Sunken
emplacement
for one gun

Borrow
pits

Traverses on
each side of
gun restrict
lateral aim

E

Gun Emplacements on Lee's Hill (Telegraph Hill), probably built before December 13

Fredericksburg, December 13, 1862 (based on field visit, 1995)

crossing points downriver that Burnside wanted to utilize, and Lee had to
retain his mobility in case it became necessary to shift his army to those
points. He knew there would be time, if needed, to construct hasty works on
the heights if a crossing took place at Fredericksburg. All in all, Lee handled
the situation quite well.

Burnside was stymied in his efforts to find a less dangerous crossing
downstream, for Lee effectively used Jackson's corps, which reached the vicinity of Fredericksburg by December 1, to block all possibilities. He assumed

a defensive line thirty-five miles long, with Longstreet covering the area upstream from the town and Jackson stretched out downstream to Port Royal. Fully aware of the difficulty of crossing at the town and of Lee's terrain advantage, Burnside also knew the Rebels were not heavily dug in, so he decided to cross at Fredericksburg. He announced this decision to his subordinates on December 9. Three spots were selected on a two-mile sector of the river where five bridges some 440 feet long would be set up. There would be 147 guns, divided into four groups on Chatham Heights, to cover the crossing. Maj. Gen. William B. Franklin's Left Grand Division would strike at Hamilton's Crossing, where the Rebels were weakest, and Sumner's Right Grand Division would hit Marye's Hill. When the plan was relayed to the engineers, Capt. Wesley Brainerd "came to the conclusion that we might now return to our quarters and with great propriety execute our last Wills & Testaments." The proposed movement "seemed like madness."[6]

The way was clear for the most dangerous forced crossing of a river to take place during the war. Brig. Gen. William Barksdale's Mississippi brigade and the 8th Florida were detailed to hold the town of Fredericksburg. These 1,500 men took shelter in houses and behind makeshift barricades. In one place they dug a rifle pit behind a board fence, piercing portholes through the boards. Three streets parallel to the river—Sophia, Caroline, and Princess Anne—were similarly fortified. The U.S. Engineer Battalion took charge of one bridge while Woodbury's Volunteer Engineer Brigade handled the other four. Fog helped to screen the movement when it began at 1:00 A.M. on December 11. Captain Brainerd noted that the upper bridge was at midstream by 3:00 A.M. An hour later, at dawn, his men received the first fire from Barksdale's troops. Brainerd acted on Woodbury's order to pull back his men and let the Federal artillery silence any opposition. Unfortunately neither the engineers nor their infantry support had any cover on the eastern bank, and the Union artillery failed to drive the Mississippians out of Fredericksburg. Brainerd sent his engineers out again, but they refused to expose themselves on the half-finished bridge. Two hours later Brainerd led ten men onto the span; five were shot before they reached the end of it, and the rest were hit soon after. Brainerd also was wounded but managed to make it back to shore. At 10:00 A.M. Woodbury led eighty volunteers from the 8th Connecticut to the bridge, but they refused to work as soon as the first man fell.

The fog cleared off by noon, and the bridge was still only two-thirds of the way across the Rappahannock. The engineers had earlier suggested that infantrymen cross the river in boats to clear a bridgehead on the west bank, but no one took that recommendation seriously until now. Preceded by concentrated artillery fire, 120 men of the 7th Michigan set out in six pontoons rowed by men from the 50th New York Engineers. Several were hit in crossing, but the rest landed and took a number of buildings. Another contingent of infantry from the 89th New York went over to help, and soon the way was clear to finish the bridge. Woodbury lost 7 killed and 43 wounded bridging the river.[7]

The other bridges were less costly and time consuming to build. One of them was nearly finished at 8:15 A.M. when Rebel fire forced a delay, but the artillery managed to clear enough Confederates from that part of the west bank to allow the engineers to finish it by 9:00 A.M. Two bridges were built the next day, making a total of five to cross Burnside's army.[8]

The Confederates strengthened their artillery emplacements on December 11, building embrasures and raising parapets and traverses a bit higher. "The engineers objected, and said they were 'ruining the works,'" recalled William Owen of the Washington Artillery, "but the cannoneers said, 'We have to fight here, not you; we will arrange them to suit ourselves.'" Longstreet agreed with his gunners, saying, "'If you save the finger of a man's hand, that does some good.'"[9]

But the guns could do little to hinder the bridge builders as Barksdale's men provided most of the resistance that delayed the laying of the pontoons. They made good use of cover. General Woodbury found a house that had loopholes cut into it only a few yards from the spot where the upper bridge reached the west bank. A stone wall nearby had been used by the Mississippians, and cellars with windows cut through stout masonry foundations made good blockhouses. The Rebels "could load and fire in almost perfect safety" from the Union artillery fire. The initial halt to the building of the upper bridge at 4:00 A.M. was caused by only two companies of the 17th Mississippi, which rose from its cover to deliver a volley at the engineers.

Even after the Federals secured the crossing, they had to fight hard before Fredericksburg was cleared of enemy troops. Barksdale's men resisted street by street, in one of the few instances of urban combat in the Civil War. Across several streets they erected "considerable barricades" made of "barrels and boxes, filled with earth and stones, placed between the houses, so as to form a continuous line of defense." The 19th and 20th Massachusetts crossed the river to join the 7th Michigan. Battle lines were formed in the streets and advanced against the barricades as both sides fought at close range. William L. Davis of the 13th Mississippi reported, "We killed lots of them in back yards and out houses." Rebel soldiers could hear Union officers urge their men forward with shouts of "Come on" as they fired at muzzle flashes in the darkness. Barksdale was only supposed to delay, not stop, the Yankees, but his spirited stand lasted longer than his commander expected. He finally gave up Fredericksburg and retired to the heights an hour after dusk.[10]

As Burnside's army crossed the river on December 12, Lee's men again strengthened their positions. On the far left, Brig. Gen. Cadmus M. Wilcox's Alabama brigade dug in on Taylor's Hill. Because their position was enfiladed by Federal guns on the opposite side of the Rappahannock, they worked numerous angles into the line. The work had a trench and parapet but no ditch. Each return in the line was three yards long, while the length of each section between the returns varied. It was not the first zigzag earthwork dug during the Civil War, as some modern commentators have asserted, but a cremailliere, or indented, line well established in both European fortification history and all the fortification manuals.[11]

While most Confederate guns were already fortified, Lee did not order the infantry to dig in even though an attack on his position along the bluffs was imminent. Lafayette McLaws's division, however, erected works along its part of the line in the Rebel center. Arrayed along the foot of the bluffs, the men dug a modest infantry trench and erected breastworks through a patch of woods with abatis in front. Brig. Gen. Joseph B. Kershaw's South Carolina Brigade, composing the left of McLaws's line, built its works on the night of December 12, finishing them by 8:00 the next morning. William L. Davis of the 13th Mississippi claimed that Barksdale's soldiers took it upon themselves to grab a few axes and erect "some fine breast-works of logs" in the patch of woods. "There was no orders to do this—it was a suggestion of our own," he contended. But McLaws and Kershaw reported that their units dug in, implying that an order was given on the division level.[12]

On the far right, Jackson's Second Corps took charge of the area around Hamilton's Crossing on December 12. Maj. Gen. John B. Hood's division of Longstreet's First Corps had held this area before and had dug a trench near the railroad big enough to hold one and a half brigades. Hood's men had also cut a military road 500 yards to the rear of this work. Jackson placed fourteen pieces of artillery just behind this little trench and used its modest parapet as cover for the gunners. After the war, one of Jackson's veterans remarked that the Federals had the impression Jackson was strongly fortified. The truth was that none of the Corps was dug in. "We had no time to construct anything like fortifications," he later wrote. That was not truly the reason for the lack of earthworks at Hamilton's Crossing, for Jackson's men could have worked on the night of December 12. Jackson wanted to assume the tactical offensive. He had level ground in his front and a vulnerable position to defend, a good justification for attacking. But Lee decided this would be purely a defensive battle and refused to unleash Jackson's corps.[13]

Remnants of Confederate artillery emplacements at Prospect Hill, Fredericksburg. These emplacements were constructed by Jackson's men just before the battle of December 13. They were improvised in a simple trench dug earlier to accommodate one and a half brigades of infantry. (Earl J. Hess)

Thinking of Fredericksburg with postwar hindsight, Longstreet's staff officer G. Moxley Sorrel was surprised that so few fieldworks were constructed before the engagement. "Later in the war such a fault could not have been found," he wrote. "Experience had taught us that to win, we must fight; and that fighting under cover was the thing to keep up the army and beat the enemy." As good as it was, Lee's position at Fredericksburg could have been even stronger with the addition of more earthworks.[14]

Jackson, especially, needed fortifications at Hamilton's Crossing, for the ground favored a Union attack. Franklin deployed the First and Sixth Corps on the Union left to punch through at the crossing and turn Lee's right. Jackson was positioned a half-mile away on the other side of the open bottomland. The only impediments were some ditches and fences that could disrupt formations. Meade's division of the First Corps conducted the assault with John Gibbon's division to its right in close support. The last division of the First Corps was held in reserve. The entire Sixth Corps was assigned the task of guarding the pontoon bridge, Franklin's only lifeline to the east side of the Rappahannock. He hoped Burnside would relieve the Sixth Corps with troops from the army's reserve so he could use more men in the attack, but that did not happen. Nevertheless, Franklin committed a grievous error in relying on only one division to break through Jackson's line while assigning an entire corps to guard a bridge. The situation called for a massive assault with all available men.

Meade attacked at 9:00 A.M. on December 13. His men stumbled across the obstructions posed by ditch and fence and smashed into the Rebel line north of the artillery at Hamilton's Crossing. The defending troops, Archer's Tennessee brigade, were partially covered by the small work, but the weight of the attack forced them back. Meade penetrated an undefended marshy area to Archer's left, captured the crest of the low bluff to Archer's rear, and disrupted several other brigades; but he lost connection with Gibbon to his right. Rebel counterattacks drove Meade back in a larger repetition of the failed Union assaults against Jackson's line along the unfinished railroad at Second Manassas. Gibbon's division hit the Rebel line a few minutes later but was repelled. Franklin had no heart for continuing the offensive and halted further operations on the left.[15]

Burnside had hoped that Franklin would draw enough Confederate strength so that Sumner could assault Marye's Hill, but the attack on the left was not big or prolonged enough to achieve that goal. Nevertheless, Burnside sent Sumner's men in at noon. He stated in testimony before the Joint Committee on the Conduct of the War that the position was strong but not well fortified, and he therefore hoped to break through immediately opposite the town. Aiming points to the right or left of Marye's Hill might have been better. Alexander believed the Federals would attack just north of the height, while Longstreet expected an assault on McLaws's front just to the south. By striking the face of the hill, Burnside upset these expectations but hit an almost impregnable section of the line.[16]

The Federals emerged from Fredericksburg and assembled some 300 yards from the Confederate position at the foot of Marye's Hill. Before them was a mostly open and gently ascending ground, cluttered here and there with a few houses, fences, and gardens, especially at the fork of Telegraph Road about 150 yards in front of the Rebels, but a fold of ground from one to six feet deep offered some protection. Alexander had assembled nine guns to bear directly on the Union line of approach, and there were eight more on Lee's Hill and Howison's Hill.[17]

The Confederate position at the foot of Marye's Hill made good use of existing structures. The famous stone wall was 600 yards long and held up the eastern embankment of Telegraph Road. It was about 4 feet high in most sections, but in others the top was even with the natural level of earth. The road was some 25 feet wide and partly cut into the base of the hill. At its best,

The stone wall, Fredericksburg. A photograph taken soon after the war shows the Innis house next to the stone wall. (Massachusetts Commandery, Military Order of the Loyal Legion and the U.S. Army Military History Institute)

the stone wall was "just the height convenient for infantry defence and fire," according to Longstreet. At its worst, the wall needed a little work. On December 12, Confederate troops had taken dirt from behind the wall and put it outside to make firing positions and a firmer parapet.[18]

The corps commander, however, admitted that no one thought it an important feature before the Federals attacked. McLaws claimed credit for first suggesting troops be placed there. He had wanted to pull Barksdale's brigade out of Fredericksburg on the evening of December 10, a few hours before Burnside's engineers started to bridge the Rappahannock. McLaws was convinced Barksdale would be outflanked and overwhelmed if the Federals crossed. Longstreet wanted the Mississippi brigade to delay the Yankees as long as possible, so he asked McLaws if there was a good defensive position just outside town for Barksdale to fall back to. McLaws identified the sunken road. So when Barksdale had to evacuate Fredericksburg on the night of December 11, he retired to the stone wall. Brig. Gen. Thomas R. R. Cobb's brigade relieved him later that night as Barksdale's men moved to the patch of woods and built their breastwork the next day. Longstreet kept Cobb in the sunken section of Telegraph Road but assumed Burnside would bypass him and ascend Marye's Hill.[19]

The Second Corps was primarily responsible for attempting to take this position. Maj. Gen. William H. French's division led just after noon with piecemeal attacks by three brigades. The first, Brig. Gen. Nathan Kimball's, got no farther than the fork in Telegraph Road. Then Maj. Gen. Winfield S. Hancock's division weighed in with similar piecemeal assaults by three brigades, two of which got closer than any of French's men. Corps commander Maj. Gen. Darius N. Couch then ordered Maj. Gen. Oliver O. Howard's division into the fray, two brigades of which tried unsuccessfully to flank the left of the stone wall position. When French and Hancock asked for support, Brig. Gen. Samuel D. Sturgis's division of the Ninth Corps sent two brigades into action. Each attack was stopped well short of the stone wall, about 100 yards from the Rebels, although individual soldiers managed to get as close as 30 yards.[20]

Cobb's Georgia brigade was the target of this concentrated fury, and it needed help. McLaws sent Kershaw's South Carolina brigade from his fortified line to assist. Two brigades from another division—Brig. Gen. Robert Ransom's and Brig. Gen. John R. Cooke's North Carolinians—also reinforced Cobb's line. In places, the combined manpower made a formation four ranks deep. Kershaw's men either knelt or stooped while waiting for the Yankees to approach, then they rose, fired, and reloaded. Despite the heavy and prolonged firing, no one was reported injured by their comrades in these crowded conditions because men in the rear ranks passed loaded guns forward to be fired. Some men reported firing more than 100 rounds during the battle, and they had to stop periodically to swab out gun barrels with pieces of their own clothing. "The boys were as black as cork minstrels" because of biting so many cartridges while sweating. "Our shoulders were

Modern view of the stone wall, Fredericksburg. This view shows the reconstructed Innis house, the stone wall, and Telegraph Road. (Earl J. Hess)

kicked blue by the muskets and were sore for many days," reported Charles Powell of the 24th North Carolina.[21]

The final round of assaults took place just after 4:00 P.M., when Couch received an erroneous report that the Rebels were evacuating the top of Marye's Hill. He ordered Brig. Gen. Andrew A. Humphreys's division to strike, and two brigades went in over the same ground where the shattered remnants of other troops lay as mute testimony to the futility of Burnside's plan. Federal officers who participated in this last attack on the sunken road later told McLaws that the Confederate fire "seemed to *'come out of the ground,'* and the bullets went over them in sheets." The men plopped down for safety and retired after a half-hour. Brig. Gen. George W. Getty's division of the Ninth Corps attacked to the north of the stone wall but made no headway. Dusk finally ended the slaughter. The Federals used 27,000 troops to attack Marye's Hill and lost 3,500 of them during the course of the afternoon. Only 800 of the 3,500 Confederates who defended the stone wall were lost.[22]

Burnside's army slept on the field, but Lee ordered his elated men to strengthen their position "by the construction of earthworks at exposed points." Exactly what was accomplished in this way is not clear, but most of the work seems to have been done on the artillery emplacements. Alexander recalled that his gunners "worked some on our pits, strengthening & repairing damages" caused by accurate Federal shelling on December 13. Brig. Gen. Maxcy Gregg's South Carolina brigade of Jackson's corps cut trees to make a breastwork. Brig. Gen. James L. Kemper's Virginia brigade had not participated in the fighting that day, but it relieved Kershaw's Carolinians in the sunken portion of Telegraph Road. The Virginians worked all night to raise the height of the protective wall, and by dawn they were "pretty well hidden." Barricades were erected where streets penetrated the line of the stone wall. Lee was quite pleased with what his men had accomplished during the night. "My army is as much stronger for their new intrenchments as if I had received reinforcements of 20,000 men," he commented the next morning.[23]

Burnside considered resuming the offensive on December 14. Capt. Alanson M. Randol of the 1st U.S. Artillery was consulted regarding the feasibility of knocking down the stone wall with artillery fire, but he advised against it. Randol had found out it was a retaining wall and told the council of war that crumbling the wall from the front would do little good as long as the sunken road was intact. So a stalemate ensued as Couch's men constructed defensive works at the edge of town opposite Marye's Hill. The men no longer felt "very pugnacious" and feared a Rebel counterstrike. The exact nature of these defenses is unknown, but they probably consisted of breastworks made of whatever material was handy. The scattered houses on the edge of town also served as blockhouses for sharpshooters, and a lively exchange of skirmish fire was kept up all day between Couch's men and the Rebels who continued to hold Telegraph Road. The council of war finally convinced Burnside to order a withdrawal, but it would not begin for twenty-four hours.[24]

More digging took place on December 14 as Jackson's men extended their meager earthwork at Prospect Hill. Entrenching tools were rushed to the site, and railroad ties were pried loose to serve as the foundation of an enlarged parapet. The night of December 14 was illuminated by an aurora that helped the Rebels see as they worked. They dug an infantry trench on top of Marye's Hill to connect the artillery emplacements. Elsewhere on the line, Cooke's North Carolina brigade received tools and collected logs and rocks to build a work with a ditch three feet deep and five feet wide. The Tar Heels "felt ourselves quite safe for another fight." Brig. Gen. James H. Lane's North Carolina brigade took an exposed position on the Confederate right the next day, December 15, and the men built "a very good temporary breastwork of logs, brush, and dirt." That night the 20th North Carolina of Brig. Gen. Alfred Iverson's brigade, Jackson's corps, took position on the right wing behind the railroad embankment. Oliver E. Mercer thought the grade "afforded not much protection at the place that our Regt. was, so as soon as dark we went at it with the bayonets and grabbing with our hands." They had only three spades in the regiment, so "you may believe our finger nails were black next day." The night of December 15 was dark and windy; but the direction of the wind was west to east, and the Confederates did not hear the noise of Burnside's evacuation. The Army of the Potomac pulled back to the east bank of the Rappahannock under cover of night.[25]

When the Rebels advanced to recover lost ground, they were amazed by the debris of battle. The town was sacked, with many burned and looted buildings, but most attention was drawn to the area in front of the stone wall. The houses at the edge of town, used by the Federals as refuge and blockhouses for three days, were filled with dead and wounded. Lots of dead were clustered around the corners where Yankees had exchanged long-range shots with the Confederates, but the largest concentration of bodies lay behind a board fence that enclosed a lot filled with peach trees. Bullets had easily passed through the boards, and Edward Porter Alexander found enough corpses behind the fence to form "a double rank of the length of the fence." The boards were "a perfect honeycomb," in the words of a Virginian in Brig. Gen. William Mahone's brigade. Another soldier found that he could push every finger of his hand through a different hole at one time. There was a sickening accumulation of blood, brains, caps, and equipment behind the fence as well.[26]

During the battle of December 13, only a few units of Lee's army were protected by minor fortifications. Most of the artillery, Wilcox's brigade on Taylor's Hill, McLaws's three brigades in the center, Cobb's brigade behind the stone wall, and Archer's brigade at Prospect Hill completed the list. But long after Burnside recrossed the river, Lee's army began to construct some of the most extensive field fortifications it had yet dug in the war. Next to the fortifications on the Warwick Line of the Peninsula campaign, and the defenses of Richmond and Petersburg, the Army of Northern Virginia had never engaged in anything like it. Whether Lee ordered it or Longstreet initiated it on his own corps front is unclear, but soon the entire army was engaged in fortifying the line. The effort involved clearly signaled Lee's intention of remaining on the bluff for an indefinite period of time as Burnside mulled over his next move across the river.[27]

All units fell to digging. Work parties were detailed, and axes, spades, and other tools were shared. Lee had plenty of engineer officers—too many in the opinion of Capt. James Keith Boswell, Jackson's chief engineer. He recommended that one be sent west and another be relieved, as the latter possessed no engineering experience and was afflicted with boils. Enough engineers were left so that each division commander had one on his staff, a unique circumstance in the Confederacy, enjoyed only by Lee's army.[28]

Daniel Harvey Hill thought he could do his own engineering; consequently, "no one will stay with him," according to Boswell. Hill, who commanded a division in Jackson's Second Corps, insisted on placing a line of works along River Road quite close to the bank of the Rappahannock. Boswell inspected it and advised him to move back to the bluffs, about half a mile to the rear. The Federals had a commanding position on the other side of the river, and the flat land behind Hill's advanced line would allow Federal artillery to punish any reinforcements sent to him. Two other engineer officers agreed, but Hill stubbornly refused to move until Jackson himself intervened on the side of the engineers. "So that nearly two weeks work was thrown away on an untenable line," complained Boswell.[29]

Lt. William G. Williamson of the Provisional Corps of Engineers was one of the three who advised Hill to move his line. He supervised the work done by Hill's division from December 29 to January 23, then spent the rest of the month inspecting works constructed by Brig. Gen. Jubal A. Early's division and Brig. Gen. William B. Taliaferro's division of the Second Corps.[30]

The resulting line stretched for thirty-five miles along the Rappahannock River with a trench five feet wide and two and a half feet deep in many places. The works "follow the contour of the ground and hug the bases of the hills . . . , thus giving natural flanking arrangements." On the far left of Lee's line, the works were extended upstream to United States Ford. Longstreet wanted to stretch them even farther with a huge refused flank from there southward so as to cross the roads leading from Chancellorsville to the rear of Lee's Fredericksburg position. Engineers scouted the terrain for this refused section of the line, which would have been about eight miles long, and decided where it should be laid out, but the work was never built. There were shortages of tools and manpower. Had it been built, however, it would have played a significant role in the Chancellorsville campaign the following May.[31]

On any part of the long Confederate line there were technical and tactical problems to work out. Jackson asked Longstreet for advice about how to protect his men from enfilade fire. "The problem that you speak of is the one that I was trying to solve," replied Longstreet. "It occurred to me that we might protect our men along your line of rifle trenches from the flank fire of the batteries . . . by good traverses for that purpose, with a good traverse on the right flank of each pit." This exchange of letters has prompted many scholars to assume Longstreet was an expert on fortifications. But historian Edward Hagerman correctly notes that Longstreet's solution was obvious, clearly spelled out in the fortification manuals, and that Jackson was merely uninformed about the art of field fortification. Through friendly advice such as this, the Army of Northern Virginia was learning how to dig in.[32]

"The world has never seen such a fortified position," wrote Maj. Alexander S. Pendleton of Jackson's staff. "The famous lines at Torres Vedras could not compare with them." That was an expression of pride and of historical myopia, for Wellington's fieldworks at Torres Vedras were far heavier and stronger. The system Lee's men built on the bluffs overlooking Fredericksburg consisted of comparatively light fieldworks. McLaws fortified his division on the crest of the bluff with a mostly straight line of trench and parapet, but no ditch or traverses. A one-gun artillery emplacement near Howison's Hill has a semicircular parapet that incorporates the connecting infantry trench into its ditch. Ten yards to the rear and left of this emplacement is a two-gun emplacement, detached from the infantry line, with two semicircular and connected parapets and a ditch in front. Howison's Hill itself has a two-gun emplacement with retrenchments on both flanks and a deep ditch in front.

South of Howison's the line descended onto the flat land near the foot of the bluffs. Here Lee's fortified position expanded to front and rear as three lines were either entirely or partially dug in to create defense in depth. There was a fortified skirmish or picket line at the railroad embankment, the main line along the foot of the bluff (mostly paralleled by the modern park service road), and a few short segments of a third line and a collection of regimental camps about 400 yards to the rear of the main line. Half a dozen covered ways connected all three lines. Only here, on the right wing, was there room to expand the position across the flat bottomland of the Rappahannock River.

Maj. Gen. George E. Pickett's division dug in just north of Deep Run, a wide and deep cleft in the side of the bluff. The line has a trench behind the parapet but no ditch. Pickett's position forms a salient several hundred yards forward of the main line. A long, covered way extending forward of the salient with a parapet that faces north leads to the skirmish line at the railroad. There are two one-gun emplacements at the junction of the covered way and Pickett's salient. These emplacements are sunken and have retrenchments on both sides, but no ditch in front. A second gun emplacement is designed to fire both east and north. The ground in this flat bottomland has much clay, making for well-preserved earthworks, but there are also a few rocks in the soil.

John B. Hood's division was positioned south of Deep Run. He also constructed a covered way that extends several hundred yards eastward with a

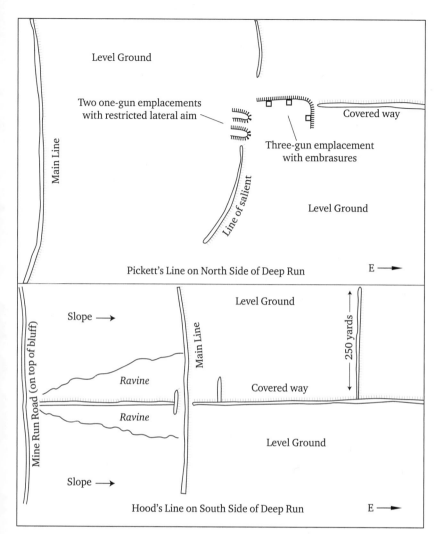

Confederate Works at Fredericksburg, Built after December 13, 1862 (based on field visit, 1995)

parapet that faces north. Two shorter lines run north and south, intersecting the covered way at intervals of 250 and 400 yards each, to create intermediate holding positions between the skirmish line and the main position. The covered way also extends westward from Hood's main line to connect to some short lines and the regimental camps to the rear.

At Hamilton's Crossing, Jackson's engineers sank battery emplacements for the guns that guarded Lee's right flank. Traverses protected their flanks, and the infantry trench was incorporated into the battery emplacements, providing them with a parapet and a trench in front. Some of the one-gun emplacements are twenty yards apart, while others are adjacent and touching one another.[33]

The Confederate defenses at Fredericksburg were among the more extensive created by the Army of Northern Virginia during the first part of the Civil War. They exhibit a unique system of defense in depth with trenches and artillery emplacements that are strongly and uniformly built. This is typical of works planned by engineers and constructed at relative leisure by troops taking direction from their superiors. Once the basic trench was finished, there was no need for further embellishments such as obstacles or restructuring of the design.

The Fredericksburg campaign was significant but not crucial in the evolution of trench warfare. Hagerman believes that Lee "accepted the primacy of the entrenched tactical position over the open frontal assault" following the battle. In the future, Lee "used the frontal assault only when he had the advantage of surprise . . . or when he believed dire strategic circumstances left no alternative." Francis Augustin O'Reilly also has asserted that Lee's army "became inculcated in the use of fieldworks as a result of Fredericksburg" and that this "altered the course of the war." Both scholars stretch the point too far. Lee hardly lost his aggressiveness after Fredericksburg. He indulged it at Chancellorsville, where he had ample opportunity to retreat, and at Gettysburg, where his chief subordinate fervently counseled a turning movement rather than frontal assaults. He more consistently adopted the defensive after Gettysburg even though he often expressed a desire to attack. Lee's decision to dig in after the battle owes more to a general attitude among Civil War commanders, which was an inclination to use earthworks in the field only if they intended to remain on the defensive. It did not mean that Lee would automatically dig in or act on the defensive in future engagements. The stumbling way in which Jackson approached the order to fortify indicates how little thought and experience many officers and men of the Army of Northern Virginia had invested in the art of field fortification to this point in the war.[34]

The campaigns of the last half of 1862 gave the Rebels plenty of experience at fighting without fortifications. They grew adept at using existing civilian structures and even the smallest inequality of the ground for protection. This was less often the case on the Peninsula or in the Seven Days. Even so, the terrible battle of Antietam set the stage for the defensive battle of Fredericksburg. That engagement on December 13 led to Lee's decision, readily supported by the rank and file, to fortify the bluffs after Burnside retreated. By 1863 the Army of Northern Virginia was beginning to accept that fieldworks were a useful weapon in its arsenal.

The attack and defense of the stone wall position at the foot of Marye's Hill demonstrated the effectiveness of using a civilian feature as a field fortification. The strength ratio between the Federal attacker and the Confederate defender was a staggering 7.5 to 1. Yet the assaults were repulsed with a loss ratio of 4.5 attackers to 1 defender. And this occurred with a feature that needed but little effort to become the equivalent of a breastwork, far less sophisticated and complete in its coverage of the defender than would be typical of the massive fieldworks of 1864.

Burnside did not fortify his position on the east side of the Rappahannock River after the battle of Fredericksburg, but the U.S. Engineer Battalion began protecting the army's supply line on February 8, 1863. The depot at Aquia Creek and several stations on the Richmond, Fredericksburg, and Potomac Railroad were fortified with earthworks and stockades. The ten-mile-long line was fully protected by March 13.[35]

Defenses of Richmond

After Lee took the war away from Richmond in August 1862, there was a persistent problem in finding manpower to work on the defenses of the capital. Progress in their construction lagged by the new year, so Jeremy Gilmer resumed efforts to round up African Americans as laborers. His January 13, 1863, request for the city of Richmond to provide 550 slaves was poorly received. Gilmer urged Governor John Letcher to persuade the city to comply as late as March 11. The Engineer Bureau had to proceed carefully in any efforts to call up slave labor, for owners were always touchy on the subject. Lee wanted the city defenses to be completed in time for the spring campaign season, and Gilmer bent every effort to get black laborers to the works.

In March, Gilmer issued a major call for slaves from twenty-nine counties in Virginia. The number required ranged from 20 to 307 slaves from each county for a total of 2,832. To soften the impact of this draft, Gilmer pointed out that most of these counties had not yet fulfilled calls made the preceding autumn. This draft would be for sixty days and, added to the unfilled quota, would amount to no more than 5 percent of the slave population of these counties. Gilmer also issued a call for 1,029 free blacks in twenty-four counties to labor on the defenses, a request Lee fully endorsed. These men were drafted in exactly the same way as slaves, by notifying the justices of the peace in each county that they were responsible for rounding up the men.[36]

Gilmer had to pay a price for acquiring this workforce. Mobilizing slave and free black labor was far more complex than simply detailing soldiers to do the work. The soldiers were a captive labor force with preexisting systems of supply and command. Orders to work, along with detailed instructions about what was to be done, simply had to be conveyed to officers. To utilize slave labor, Gilmer had to deal with owners who were reluctant to release their valuable property to the government's care. Slaves were exposed to camp diseases and often did not receive adequate medical attention; they could be mistreated or ignored by incompetent overseers, or they could run away because of lax supervision.

A segregated system of support had to be created, for slave or free black workers could not mix with white soldiers. They had to be organized into gangs, tents had to be found to shelter them, food had to be supplied, contract surgeons had to be hired to look after their medical needs, and white overseers had to be hired to manage them. Political problems were nonexistent in mobilizing free blacks, for they had no powerful spokesmen to intercede on their behalf. Yet Confederate authorities preferred to tap into the far larger slave population and called on the free blacks only when necessity required it.

When the call went into effect, Gilmer was besieged with requests from slaveowners for exemptions from the draft. He also had to deal with numerous claims from owners for government compensation when slaves ran away or died on the job. Fortunately for Gilmer, there was legislative authority for impressment of both slave and free black labor, mostly by the Virginia state government. The Confederate government and its departments readily accepted this legislation and governed their actions by it, so there was ample legal authority behind attempts to settle claims. The burden of proof lay with the government agents to, in Gilmer's words, "relieve themselves from liability to the owners of slaves that die, escape to the enemy or are injured" in government work. In cases where slaves died due to "gross negligence on the part of the overseers" while working on the Richmond defenses, Gilmer readily compensated the owners. In all other cases, he gave the claims to a special commission of three army officers who gathered evidence to protect the government from fraud in future legal action. Gilmer admitted that the total amount of the claims was huge, and he advised waiting for congressional action to cover them if it was ever decided the government had to pay.

Thus there were many headaches associated with using slave labor. It was by no means the most efficient mode of building fortifications, but in many cases slaves were the only available workers. They were normally used only on semipermanent works away from the threat of imminent action. As the largest Confederate defense system in the eastern theater, the Richmond fortifications absorbed the lion's share of slave and free black labor. Gilmer hoped the works would be nearly finished before owners began to clamor for their property. He informed President Davis's staff that there probably would be no need for more than a small workforce after April 20. Acting on public pressure, the War Department arbitrarily decided that all slaves should be dismissed from work on the Richmond defenses by April 10. The complex of forts and infantry trenches that girdled the capital would never truly be completed until 1865, but a mixture of soldiers, slaves, free blacks, professional engineers, and civilian engineer assistants, mobilized by city, state, and national governmental efforts, eventually protected the city nearly to the end of the war.[37]

8 : Chancellorsville

Burnside committed a tragic error of judgment in attacking Lee's strong position at Fredericksburg. It was compounded by a failed attempt to march around Lee's left and cross the Rappahannock in January, a good move spoiled by unexpected weather that turned the flanking movement into the infamous Mud March. Burnside was replaced by Maj. Gen. Joseph Hooker on January 26, 1863, and the Army of the Potomac was rejuvenated by improved living conditions, more frequent furloughs, the introduction of corps badges, and Hooker's infectious optimism. When the spring brought good campaigning weather to Virginia, the Federals were ready for another try at Lee. Considering the digging that followed the battle of Fredericksburg, this next campaign was sure to involve field fortifications.

Hooker devised a plan very similar to Burnside's flanking movement. Lee had too many earthworks guarding possible crossing sites downstream from Fredericksburg, so Hooker attempted to cross well upstream of the town. He left the First and Sixth Corps at Falmouth to keep Lee occupied and took the rest of his army on a long flanking march. Hooker conceived of his campaign as one of maneuver, not one involving head-on assaults on entrenched positions. If he succeeded in flanking Lee, he hoped the Rebel commander would evacuate the heights at Fredericksburg and retreat southward. Yankee hopes for victory were bolstered by the knowledge that Longstreet had taken two divisions to southeastern Virginia and eastern North Carolina to gather supplies and possibly recapture some occupied towns. Hooker outnumbered Lee with 134,000 men, compared with 40,000 Confederates.

The flanking column started out on April 27 and made its way upstream. Meanwhile, the First and Sixth Corps, under Maj. Gen. John Sedgwick, crossed the river and established a bridgehead on the open bottomland opposite Hamilton's Crossing to divert Rebel attention. That same day, April 29, Hooker's flanking column began to cross the Rapidan River above its junction with the Rappahannock. The several crossings here, including Germanna Ford and United States Ford, had been fortified by the Confederates with artillery emplacements and infantry works, but these defenses were lightly held. The next day, Hooker advanced four corps from the fords to occupy Chancellorsville, a key crossroads ten miles west of Fredericksburg and four miles south of the junction of the Rapidan and Rappahannock. It was one of the most successful flanking maneuvers of the war. Hooker ordered his men to halt at the crossing so he could take stock of the situation and determine his next move.[1]

The Federals were in the eastern area of a region known as the Wilderness, which lay from 200 to 300 feet in elevation on the eastern edge of the Piedmont where it borders the Coastal Plain. Most of the timber had been cut for charcoal production, and the landscape was covered with a dense second growth of small trees and brush. Two roads traversed the Wilderness. Orange Plank Road was paved in many spots with two-inch-thick planks laid on two rows of logs. It forked halfway between Fredericksburg and Chancellorsville; Plank Road curved in a southwesterly direction toward the latter place, while Orange Turnpike went directly west to Chancellorsville. The two roads rejoined here and continued about two miles west before splitting again at Wilderness Church. The turnpike continued northwest to Wilderness Tavern, and Plank Road went southwest to Orange. The Wilderness was a most unwelcome place to fight a battle, for the thick vegetation severely limited visibility and provided few places to deploy artillery.[2]

Hooker's order to halt around Chancellorsville led most of his men to construct some form of field fortification on the night of April 30. Brig. Gen. John W. Geary's division of the Twelfth Corps simply cut abatis in front of its position for a distance of some 300 feet. The engineers laid out works on other parts of the semicircular line, and the soldiers used axes and shovels to build them. "To most of us this was an unfamiliar effort," recalled Rice C. Bull of the 123rd New York, a regiment in Brig. Gen. Alpheus S. Williams's division of the Twelfth Corps. Bull's unit was relatively new and had not yet been under fire. "But as farm boys we all knew how to handle both an ax and shovel and by ten that night had a good defense in our front. There was a lot of fallen timber that we gathered and placed lengthwise, then dug a trench behind, with the dirt thrown over the logs. The trench was over two feet deep, wide enough for the line to stand in and with the embankment the total depth was five feet." The green soldiers slept in their trench that night, the first line of battle the 123rd had ever established.[3]

Hooker's chief topographical engineer, Brig. Gen. Gouverneur K. Warren, thought little of this defensive position. It was "a bad line, and had several commanding positions in its front for the enemy to occupy." Yet, he admitted, it was the best available. The next day, May 1, they continued to dig in. The 123rd New York cut abatis in front of its earthwork until midmorning. Then Hooker ordered a cautious advance toward Fredericksburg and neared a low ridge that lay just outside the eastern edge of the Wilderness, near a Baptist meetinghouse called Zoan Church. By now Lee was well aware of the danger. He quickly dispatched Jackson's corps to the area, and the Rebels managed to occupy the ridge just before the Federal vanguard took it. Some Confederates began to dig in as Jackson pushed ahead and forced Hooker's column back toward Chancellorsville.[4]

This effectively blocked any Federal assault on the rear of the Fredericksburg fortifications, but it appears that Hooker still believed that Lee might evacuate those works and slip away to the south. Rather than try to block him, the Federals dug in more strongly around Chancellorsville. Hooker's men used bayonets, tin plates, boards, pointed sticks, and their hands if axes and shovels were not available. Some regiments dug two lines, and everyone worked until the early hours of the morning. They constructed a line six miles long, enough to accommodate two-thirds of Hooker's infantry and thirty-one batteries. The left rested on the Rappahannock River one mile downstream from United States Ford, and the right rested on Orange Plank Road west of Chancellorsville. There was no natural defensive feature here, where Maj. Gen. Oliver Otis Howard's Eleventh Corps held the right. The modern remnants of Hooker's defensive line have no ditch in front, but the Federals dug a good trench unadorned by traverses, even at the angles where those features could have been useful.[5]

The most prominent section of this line, held by the Twelfth Corps, was the angle that protected the road junction at Chancellorsville. It curved south, then west, and then north to make a half-circle around the crossroads. The Eleventh Corps continued the line westward along Orange Turnpike. The eastern and southern stretches of the Twelfth Corps line have slight remnants that show a trench and parapet but no ditch. Despite the long curves in the line, there are no traverses. On the right of the Twelfth Corps line, just south of Orange Turnpike, remnants of the earthwork also show a trench and parapet but no ditch. There are two features that may be termed firing bays; these are large enough for a couple of men and were made by building short traverses across the trench. The right end of this line stops 100 yards short of the turnpike. An extension runs forward of the end, toward the west, for about ten feet.

The Twelfth Corps continued the line north of Orange Turnpike as well. Again, there is a trench and parapet but no ditch in front. A ravine lies in front of the work, and in this generally low-lying ground, the line runs along a slight rise that is both the natural and military crest. The Federals constructed six traverses at the end of this line, just before it crossed a ravine. The traverses join the main parapet at an angle, and the earth is banked to protect the men from an enfilade fire from the right. There are a couple of detached sections of works on the other side of the ravine, apparently signifying some confusion about how far the line should continue.[6]

Two Confederate engineer officers scouted the Union earthworks that curved around the road junction at Chancellorsville and reported them too strong to risk a frontal attack, but Jackson still wanted to take the offensive. When Confederate cavalrymen reported Howard's right flank in the air, he and Lee planned a turning movement to roll it up. This was a bold and crucial decision in shaping the course of the battle. Lee demonstrated that he had no intention of giving up his entrenched position on the bluffs outside Fredericksburg and retiring south. He meant to fight it out here, ten miles west of that town in the confusing environment of the Wilderness, and hold the line of the Rappahannock at all costs.

Field fortifications would help him. Maj. Gen. Richard H. Anderson positioned three brigades of his division between Hooker and Fredericksburg, three and a half miles from Chancellorsville. Lee sent his chief engineer, Lt. Col. William Proctor Smith, to help Anderson lay out a defensive line. "Set all your spades to work as vigorously as possible," Lee instructed Anderson. It was the first time that Lee ordered his infantrymen to dig in on the eve of a major battle. They constructed what a Mississippian called "ample rifle pits." The works were probably no stronger than the ones Hooker's men had built at Chancellorsville, and they were closer to Chancellorsville than the line started on May 1 at Zoan Church. While Anderson and a portion of McLaws's division held this line, Lee would send Jackson and 29,400 men, accompanied by 108 guns, on a long flank march. That left only 14,000 men and 24 guns to hold the Federals in check. Maj. Gen. Jubal A. Early commanded 12,400 Confederates holding the works at Fredericksburg against Sedgwick. Only through the use of fieldworks, and blessed by Hooker's caution, could Lee take such a calculated risk as dividing his already outnumbered army in the face of the enemy.[7]

There are interesting remnants of the far left end of this Confederate line. No evidence of a ditch or of traverses remains, but the line conformed to a low ridge with sloping and often open ground in front. An artillery emplacement on Anderson's front was dug for one field gun; it consisted of a semicircular parapet with no ditch in front and no connection to the infantry trench line. Brig. Gen. Carnot Posey's Mississippi brigade held the extreme left of the line as it crossed Furnace Road. The far left of Posey's position was refused at a right angle to the rear. This refused line ran straight, like the rest of the trench, for a few yards; then the Mississippians dug zigzags for about 100 yards until the line ended at a dry stream bed. Each zig and zag is about six feet long.[8]

Lee was using fieldworks as a pivot for an attack, a classic tactic taught by Mahan in his prewar courses and in his influential manual. The works held by Anderson and McLaws were meant primarily for defensive purposes, to protect the approach to the rear of the positions at Fredericksburg, but they also gave Lee the opportunity to mass the majority of his available manpower for an offensive strike.

Jackson's flank march was one of the most thoroughly successful maneuvers of its kind. The Rebels marched in tight formations along the narrow roads, choked by the encroaching growth of the Wilderness. It took them almost all day to reach the starting point of their assault on Howard. Meanwhile, the Federals discovered the movement but thought it signified a general retreat southward. The Third Corps made a heavy reconnaissance in force that pressured Anderson and McLaws but failed to discover or disrupt Jackson's plans.[9]

The rest of Hooker's army continued to dig in on May 2, unaware of the impending disaster. Soldiers in the 118th Pennsylvania of the Fifth Corps used the largest logs they could find to build a breastwork at least three feet high. "The men worked with the energy of despair to erect this covering," reported Capt. Francis Adams Donaldson. Two days earlier, when everyone realized they had gained an advantage over Lee, they were optimistic. Now that orders clearly indicated a defensive battle rather than a grand sweep to exploit the opportunity, they had become resigned to failure. "The backing and filling plan of action, substituted for the bold aggressive one, had made them timid and panicky," Donaldson wrote. The 118th Pennsylvania had never built fieldworks before, but the men expended a lot of time and energy on them.[10]

Too bad for Howard that his Eleventh Corps did not emulate the moody Pennsylvanians. New to corps command but with a good record as a brigade and division leader, Howard failed to protect the right flank adequately. Hooker's staff members were aware that the Eleventh Corps was not secure, and there was talk at army headquarters about pulling it back to connect to the river. This would have greatly altered the Federal position but firmly protected both flanks. Howard, however, assured everyone he could hold, and the decision was made to bolster the right "with breastwork and abatis." But Howard's men failed to fortify sufficiently. The works in Howard's front were light and intermittent, and he refused his extreme right only in the most perfunctory way. Two regiments and two companies of a third regiment continued the line at a right angle to the rear. They only had a bit of abatis in their front. The terrain along Orange Turnpike is irregular with a lot of uneven rolls, and it offered no advantage for the Federals. They needed good

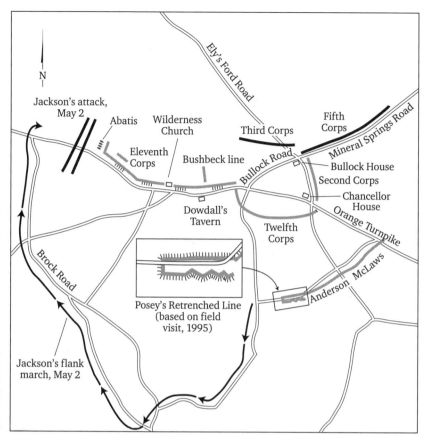

Chancellorsville, May 2, 1863

works to make this ground defensible. The only substantial work they had was the so-called Bushbeck Line, named after brigade leader Col. Adolphus Bushbeck. It ran north from the main line at Dowdall's Tavern, about one and a half miles from the western end of the line. The Bushbeck position was quickly dug on the morning of May 2 and was not yet finished when Jackson struck late that afternoon. The trench was so shallow that soldiers had to kneel or lie down to be protected, and there were no artillery emplacements; yet the line was a good traverse that could have played a large role in stopping Jackson had it been long and deep enough. After Jackson attacked, the Bushbeck Line quickly filled with large numbers of troops, and a battery took position near it. The men were so crowded, in fact, that they got in one another's way, and the potential advantages of the work evaporated.[11]

Despite the complete surprise achieved by Jackson and the relatively poor state of readiness and morale in the Eleventh Corps, the Rebel flank attack could have been stopped earlier than it was if proper earthworks had been constructed by Howard's men. One can only assume that Howard's position seemed to be out of the main area of danger on May 2, that everyone believed the Rebels were retreating southward, and that even if they did attack, they would most likely hit the center or the left. That complacency and the consequent lack of proper fortifications endangered Hooker's right wing. The Eleventh Corps was shattered and pushed back the entire length of its line. The Confederates even captured the rightmost one-third of the Twelfth Corps line, which straddled Orange Turnpike north and south, before darkness stalled their attack. Jackson was accidentally wounded by his own men in the darkened thickets while reconnoitering the battlefield.

The Federals worked hard to protect their shattered right flank that night. Twelfth Corps troops hastily constructed a new line of works along a slight ravine facing west, directly in the path of the Confederates, and south of Orange Turnpike. This new line was continued north of the pike by Maj. Gen. Hiram G. Berry's division of the Third Corps. The Yankees worked until 3:00 A.M., cutting abatis for at least fifty feet in front of their works and using the largest trunks to build the parapet. Division commander Williams later reported that his men were "well sheltered behind logs and a slight depression of the ground behind the woods. This artificial and natural protection saved me hundreds of lives."[12]

Efforts apparently were made that night to connect the Twelfth Corps line with the reserve troops to the north. Hooker had kept the First and Fifth Corps idle that evening. The latter remained along Mineral Springs Road, while the former was just coming onto the battlefield after its march from Fredericksburg. The First Corps reached its position along Hunting Creek late that night and hastily dug in. The Fifth Corps spent the night constructing a line of works southward from Ely's Ford Road toward the right end of the Twelfth Corps line. In the darkness, however, the diggers could not determine where the right of the Twelfth Corps line ended. They extended their works about halfway between Ely's Ford Road and the point where the Twelfth Corps line had existed before Jackson's attack. The Confederates, however, had already captured that line on the evening of May 2. As soon as this became apparent in the confusing darkness, probably when they discovered Confederate skirmishers, the Fifth Corps men stopped extending southward.

The remnants of this putative connecting line south of Ely's Ford Road are well preserved. The line has a good ditch, a rare find on the Chancellorsville battlefield. A long retrenchment was dug just before the line reached a

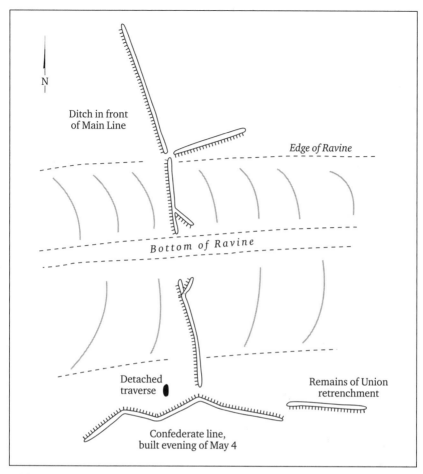

Fifth Corps Line, South of Ely's Ford Road, Built Night of May 2, 1863, in Attempt to Connect to Twelfth Corps Line, Chancellorsville (based on field visit, 1995)

ravine. Curiously, the Federals left six feet of natural earth between the main line and the beginning of the retrenchment, presumably to allow for the movement of guns and troops, but they failed to dig a ditch in front of the retrenchment. The main line continues across the shallow ravine but ends abruptly halfway to the next ravine. On the south side of this second ravine is the position already occupied by Jackson's men. There is evidence of a retrenchment, facing south toward the Rebel position, but this connecting line did not extend any farther south.[13]

Fortifying continued on other parts of the field. The 1st Delaware of the Second Corps was ordered up to support other troops and made "a temporary breastwork formed of knapsacks, fence rails, and bags of earth." Another Second Corps regiment, the 145th Pennsylvania, took great comfort in the protection afforded by its earthwork and abatis. The men felt they could hold their position "by remaining calm and determined." These units, ironically, were not tested by battle that morning, but they demonstrated the growing tendency to dig in when threatened and to value the emotional support offered by earthworks when battle was imminent.[14]

Maj. Gen. J. E. B. Stuart took temporary command of Jackson's corps and sent it into a series of poorly coordinated attacks against the Third and Twelfth Corps on May 3. The rest of Lee's little army also attacked that morning in an effort to regain contact with Stuart's men. The result was one of the most vicious battles of the war; in the worst day of fighting at Chancellorsville, several of Lee's best units were shredded. The attacks began about 6:00 A.M. and lasted all morning. The thick vegetation disrupted formations and prevented the massing of large numbers of units, so the fighting on May 3 devolved into a series of violent charges by unsupported Rebel brigades with little artillery support. An officer serving on the staff of Brig. Gen. John R. Jones's Virginia brigade called this the worst battle he had ever seen due to the woods and the stout Union fortifications. The "enemy, with their usual industry, had erected four lines [sic] of fortifications, in strong and well selected positions, constructed of large logs and earth," he reported to his wife. Jones's men were stopped by these defenses, and they refused to resume the attack.[15]

The famous Stonewall Brigade now came up to try. Its advance also was disrupted by the terrain, especially the abatis laid down by the Yankees. In hard fighting the Virginians managed to capture a section of the Twelfth Corps works south of Orange Turnpike, but their brigade was "chopped to pieces," in the words of a modern historian. Stonewall's old command lost more this day than on any other day of its history; 493 men fell while capturing one line of Union works, and the "survivors did not aggregate a full-sized regiment."[16]

Brig. Gen. Stephen D. Ramseur's North Carolina brigade now came up to exploit the limited penetration achieved by the Virginians. Lt. Weldon Davis of the 30th North Carolina wrote, "We had to charge that breastwork over the tops and logs of those trees," and they lost heavily in the process. Davis saw infantry fighting at point-blank range across the works for the first time. The Rebels lodged themselves just outside the parapet, but the Yankees refused to budge; "each man would stoop down to load his gun and then poke it over the top to shoot, then dodge back to load again, nothing between them but the thickness of the works," Davis reported. Whichever side displayed more tenacity would win a contest like this, and the Federals gave way first. Ramseur's brigade lost more than 700 of its 1,500 men, but it cracked open the Twelfth Corps line. The newly constructed work that ran north and south, connecting with Berry's line north of Orange Turnpike, was captured.[17]

On other parts of the Twelfth Corps line the abatis also tore apart Rebel formations. When the attackers managed to gain a section of works near the 27th Indiana, the Hoosier regiment counterattacked and pushed the Confederates back into the abatis. They "were soon thrown into the utmost confusion," noted regimental commander Silas Colgrove. "While endeavoring to retreat through the brush and tree-tops, they became mixed up in a perfect jam, our men all the time pouring in the most deadly fire." On another part of the Twelfth Corps line, Posey's brigade captured a section of Federal works, and at least one Mississippian admired their construction. The line was "well made of logs and earth with an abatis of from fifty to one hundred fifty yards in front."[18]

The Confederate artillery had a difficult time finding suitable terrain on which to deploy. There were relatively few open spaces in the Wilderness, and the tangle of short, thick trees obscured the view. Edward Porter Alexander found only four small places where his guns could be deployed on the night of May 2. One was only 100 feet by 200 yards in size, another was the Plank Road itself, another was described as "only a thin place in the woods" (a farm lane large enough for four guns), and the last was "an isolated little clearing" only 100 feet in diameter. From the latter location, Alexander could fire indirectly at Hazel Grove, a larger clearing occupied by the Federals, only because he knew the direction and distance.

Hazel Grove was a glittering prize for Alexander. He could see it on the morning of May 3 and called it "a beautiful position for artillery, an open grassy ridge, some 400 yards long, extending N.E. and S.W." The Twelfth Corps line went through it. Directly in line with Hazel Grove, looking northeastward, one could see a similar open space called Fairview. Located southwest of the Chancellor House, it was the concentration point for thirty-seven Union guns that had helped to stop Jackson's attack on the evening of May 2. Later that night the Federals dug emplacements for the guns. The work was begun by the artillerymen themselves, "when not engaged in firing." Capt. Charles W. Squier, chief engineer of Berry's division of the Third Corps, brought up a pioneer company to take over the job near dawn. The works were a series of one-gun emplacements in a line across the clearing, following the crest of a slight rise in the ground. The parapets are semicircular, and the gun platforms show evidence of having been dug slightly into the ground. The main line of emplacements is long, and each position immedi-

Federal artillery emplacements at Fairview, Chancellorsville. This photograph, taken in the 1930s, shows unrestored remnants of the Union gun emplacements. It was one of hundreds of photographs on display at the Virginia Room Exhibit of the 1939 World's Fair in New York. (Courtesy of The Library of Virginia)

ately adjoins the other. A forward line some seventy-five yards ahead has fewer emplacements that are about a gun's width from each other. No ditches are apparent at any of the emplacements. All of this indicates hasty work in the dark and under pressure.[19]

Hazel Grove was the key to the fighting on May 3. It gave the Federals the opportunity to split Stuart from the rest of Lee's army and to exploit the disadvantages suffered by the two isolated wings. The Confederates had to occupy Hazel Grove in order to reunite the Army of Northern Virginia (or at least these two portions of the army), and they had to occupy it in order to have a good artillery platform. Today, one need only drive south from Hazel Grove toward Catharine Furnace to see how the grove dominates the area to the west and south.[20]

One of the major Union mistakes of the campaign was to give up Hazel Grove about two hours after the fighting started on May 3. Stuart told Alexander to put thirty guns there. Alexander surveyed the open corridor to the northeast and saw the Federal artillery dug in at Fairview, and beyond them the Chancellor House about 2,000 yards from his cannon. Now began an artillery duel that the Confederates won, partly because their infantry advanced on both flanks of the Fairview position and forced the Union guns to retire. Alexander then moved his artillery forward and used Fairview as a platform to bombard the area around the Chancellor House. The occupation of both open areas and Alexander's quickness in exploiting them broke the back of Union resistance. The Federals were driven from the crossroads by midmorning, and the two wings of Lee's army reunited.[21]

After this signal and bloody success, Lee wanted to pursue the retreating Federals northward. But he was diverted by news that Sedgwick had sprung into action that morning. The Sixth Corps had moved out of Fredericksburg and captured the bluffs held by Early. Hooker's withdrawal gave Lee an opportunity to shift much of his army eastward to contain the Union drive. This gave Hooker's large force much-needed time to reform north of the crossroads in order to protect access to United States Ford, the army's lifeline with the North.[22]

The collapse of the Fredericksburg line must have come as a surprise to Lee, despite how thinly Early's men were spread along the bluffs. Ironically, the rupture occurred precisely where the easiest Confederate victory had taken place on December 13: the stone wall at the foot of Marye's Hill. The Federals had learned how few Rebels crouched behind the wall and were determined to break through. Only one regiment, the 18th Mississippi, and three companies of the 21st Mississippi held the wall previously defended by more than two brigades. With the rest of the 21st stationed on top of the

View from Hazel Grove to Fairview, Chancellorsville. The Confederates positioned thirty guns at Hazel Grove to bombard a line of Federal guns behind hastily constructed fieldworks at Fairview. When the Yankees withdrew, the Rebel gunners replaced them so as to bombard the area about the Chancellor House in a key move that helped to win the battle. (Earl J. Hess)

height, there were no more than 1,200 men and eight guns defending the hill. Early thought the main threat would be on his right, at Hamilton's Crossing, and he stationed half of his 12,700 men there. Three regiments were on Lee's Hill, and Wilcox's brigade guarded Taylor's Hill and Stansbury's Hill to the north.

Sedgwick used his Sixth Corps and one division of the Second Corps, as the First Corps had already been ordered to join Hooker. He arrayed his 27,100 men and sixty-six guns along the same line held by Burnside's army on December 13. The small Rebel force was divided into two lines. Even though covered by the stone wall, the forward line was heavily outnumbered. The second line farther up the slope to the rear would have little ability to hold if the first line gave way.

Sedgwick organized three columns of attack. The northernmost would start first, a signal for the other two to begin. It consisted of four regiments, one behind the other, headed by the 61st Pennsylvania and the 43rd New York. Advancing from town along Orange Plank Road, this column was pounded by eight cannon of the Washington Artillery. The Rebel gunners lay

Federal artillery emplacements opposite Fredericksburg, Chancellorsville campaign. Capt. Andrew J. Russell exposed this view of three guns of Capt. Franklin M. Pratt's Battery M, 1st Connecticut Heavy Artillery, behind emplacements on Stafford Heights. (Library of Congress)

down such an effective fire that the first two Federal regiments were stopped in their tracks and the following two could not get by the tangle.

The second column started a few minutes later and consisted of only two regiments: the 7th Massachusetts and the 36th New York. They aimed at the left end of the stone wall, held by three companies of the 21st Mississippi. The fire of these men, plus that of the 18th Mississippi to their right, stopped this column before it came close to the wall.

The third column, however, broke through. It consisted of four regiments arrayed in a combination of column and line. The 5th Wisconsin, 31st New York, 23rd Pennsylvania, and 6th Maine hit the 18th Mississippi and overwhelmed it. By hand-to-hand fighting at the stone wall, the Federals secured Telegraph Road. With retreating Confederates streaming up the slope, the 21st Mississippi also retired, and the hill was cleared.[23]

At least one occupying Yankee thought little of the works that had protected Marye's Hill for five months. Capt. Henry Livermore Abbott of the 20th Massachusetts examined the Confederate fortifications after the bluffs were captured and thought them "of the meanest description. Nothing whatever but rifle pits for the infantry, . . . which are in fact better suited for an infantry

The stone wall at Marye's Hill, Chancellorsville campaign. This famous Andrew J. Russell photograph was taken on May 3 and shows the dead of the 18th Mississippi, which unsuccessfully defended the position against the 5th Wisconsin, 31st New York, 23rd Pennsylvania, and 6th Maine. Note how the wall forms a good breastwork at this location. (Massachusetts Commandery, Military Order of the Loyal Legion and the U.S. Army Military History Institute)

fire, particularly down a slope, than the most elaborate intrenchments." The artillery epaulements "covered the pieces well enough, but didn't pretend to be works. It was evident they depended on the position & not on the works. It is certainly, both for artillery & infantry fire, the best position that can be imagined, being just the right slope & having spines which run out from the hills & enfilade a great part of the slope." Yet the Federals captured this position with one decisive stroke.[24]

The fighting became fluid after the collapse of the bluff line, and earthworks played little role in it. Early retreated southwest along Telegraph Road to regroup, while Sedgwick pushed westward along Orange Plank Road toward Chancellorsville. Wilcox managed to evacuate Taylor's Hill soon enough to get ahead of Sedgwick's column at Salem Church, some four miles west of Fredericksburg, where a slight ridge offered a viable position. Wilcox was joined by elements of McLaws's division that had been rushed eastward by Lee. The fighting swirled around Salem Church. No breastworks or earthworks were employed, as this was a pitched battle and there was no time to fortify, but Wilcox's men used the brick church as a blockhouse. The Federal drive west was stopped here.[25]

That night, Wilcox's men dug in at Salem Church. There was hardly a spade or pick in the brigade, so the Alabamans used whatever they could find. While some loosened the earth with bayonets, others used tin plates and even their hands to pile it into a parapet. Sedgwick did not dig in that night. The next morning, May 4, Early adroitly moved back to the bluffs outside Fredericksburg, which were lightly held by the Federals, and easily recaptured most of them. This placed Sedgwick in a quandary. He could not retreat to the town, and the way west was blocked by Wilcox and McLaws. The alternative was to retreat northward and secure Banks's Ford as a link across the Rappahannock to the North, as Hooker had already done with United States Ford farther west. Sedgwick repositioned his men to form a bridgehead protecting access to Banks's Ford. It was a long line that included Taylor's Hill, but there is no indication that it was fortified.[26]

Lee was desperate to strike in order to take advantage of his success. He wanted both Federal forces pushed across the river as soon as possible and was frustrated with the delay consequent on repositioning troops during the course of May 4. Finally, near evening, a large Rebel force attacked Sedgwick's left wing. Although his line held, the Federal commander pulled back and shortened his defensive perimeter. He also ordered his troops to dig in. Sedgwick received no assurance of support from Hooker and did not know if holding his bridgehead was worth sacrificing his men. It is unclear whether any fortifying began along the shortened perimeter, but Sedgwick abandoned it and retreated across the river on the night of May 4.[27]

The other bridgehead, laboriously built by Hooker's men, was a much tougher objective. It had been laid out on the night of May 2 by Gouverneur K. Warren and Capt. Cyrus B. Comstock. The line created a bulge three and a half miles long and three miles wide; the right rested on the Rapidan, and the left remained on the Rappahannock to cover the pontoon bridges at United States Ford. Hooker placed six corps, some 50,000 men and 106 guns, in this position. The line was well placed to take advantage of the terrain. On the right it ran behind Hunting Run, which became a deep and imposing valley the closer it flowed to the Rapidan. It turned and paralleled Ely's Ford Road to its junction with Bullock Road; then it veered off sharply along Mineral Springs Road to run toward the Rappahannock.[28]

The Federals worked on this line for the rest of May 3 and May 4 while Sedgwick was fighting near Salem Church. They were annoyed a great deal by Confederate sharpshooters. Brig. Gen. Amiel W. Whipple, commander of a division in the Third Corps, was killed while supervising the construction of works on his part of the line. Pioneers of the Third Corps also cut a military road three miles long through the woods to give easier access to United States Ford. Work on the fortifications never really ended until the campaign itself came to an end, which illustrates how thoroughly the Federals had learned the value of field fortifications. Charles Mattocks of the 17th Maine in the Third Corps reported that three Rebel shells smashed into the new parapet in front of his regiment on May 4 but harmed no one. He compared this to what had happened the day before, when a single shell exploded in his company and killed two men and wounded five more. "I am strongly in favor of fortifying now," he recorded.[29]

This fortified bridgehead far exceeded anything dug before in the campaign. In fact, it was better than any fieldworks dug by either army in 1861–62, with the possible exception of the Warwick Line at Yorktown. One must look to the Confederate fortifications at Mine Run and to the 1864 campaigns in Virginia to find comparable works, although Chancellorsville provided the precedent.

The 29th Pennsylvania, a Twelfth Corps regiment commanded by Lt. Col. William Rickards Jr., was responsible for a length of line 200 paces long. Rickards's men first made a breastwork of logs and earth four feet tall and then placed a headlog on top, raising it four inches above the parapet. This is the first recorded use of a headlog in the eastern campaigns and predates the well-known headlogs on the Twelfth Corps line on Culp's Hill at Gettysburg by two months. Rickards's men had only "six old worn-out axes" and "three or four picks and spades," so most of them used bayonets and tin plates to build this work in twenty-four hours. They were quite pleased with the result, "making a very secure defense, and from behind which we felt confident that we could defend ourselves from a much superior force to our own."[30]

All along the line, Hooker's position was impressive, and much of it is well preserved. Starting with the apex of the bridgehead at the junction of the three roads, the Yankees dug a small but strong V-shaped earthwork so that one wing could fire down Ely's Ford Road and the other could aim down Bullock Road. Three traverses, 15 feet long and spaced 15 feet apart, adorn the right wing to protect against enfilade fire. There is an artillery emplacement next to the third traverse, but the rest are designed to protect infantry. There is a good trench and parapet here, but not a good ditch, while a short retrenchment covers the left flank of this little work.

Along Ely's Ford Road, the Federals placed several traverses from 6 to 20 yards apart behind the line. Most of these traverses are 20 feet long, but some are only 6 feet long, and all were made by digging earth on both sides

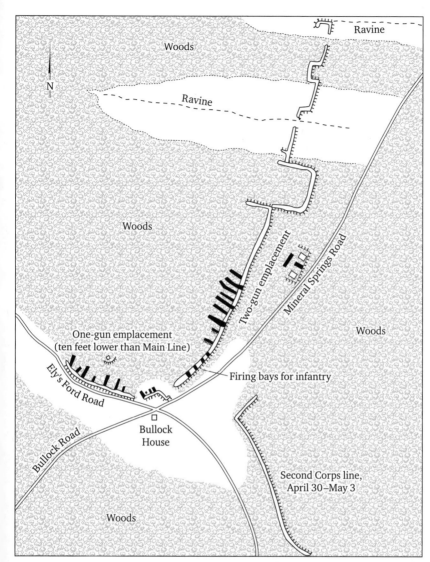

Union Fortified Bridgehead Covering United States Ford, May 3–5, 1863 (based on field visit, 1995)

and piling it up to make a thick, tall bank. The Federals planted a one-gun artillery emplacement just to the rear of this section of the line, angled so it could fire toward the apex, but it is on ground about 10 feet lower than that of the main line.

The most impressive remaining section lies along Mineral Springs Road, from the apex stretching northeastward. The remnants begin about 50 yards from the apex, where there is a series of bays in the trench created by small traverses made inside the trench itself. This is a feature common to fieldworks in 1864, especially in the Atlanta campaign, but unusual for the first half of the war. Each bay is about 10 feet wide. Then there is a section consisting of two traverses, 10 feet long, each with the earth banked toward the apex, and a third section follows with seven huge, long traverses dug on both sides. These are 20 yards long and are spaced about 20 to 75 yards apart, and some connect with the parapet of the main line while others end at the trench.

The Federals dug a two-gun artillery emplacement about 200 yards from the apex, but they placed it 40 yards in front of the main line, not behind it. The emplacement has a good parapet in front, long traverses for flank protection, a third traverse separating the two gun platforms, and even a short traverse to the rear. Farther along the line the Federals constructed a bulging salient that protrudes 30 yards forward of the main line and is 60 yards wide. The reason for this and the forward artillery emplacement probably lies in a desire to cover a small flat area in the landscape that lies before the main line. A substantial ravine is located just north of this flat area, and the salient allowed the Yankees to deliver enfilade fire into any Rebels who tried to approach the line along its bottom. On the other side of the ravine, the line is indented to allow oblique fire. Another 250 yards farther north, the line approaches another ravine where a short retrenchment was dug on the shoulder of the ravine slope.

The innovative, even quirky, configuration of this line is another characteristic of field fortifications dug in 1864. Warren and Comstock were not responsible for this; they simply identified the ground on which the line was to take shape. The diggers—the men in the ranks and their noncommissioned and commissioned officers—were responsible for these little nuances. The line appears to have been dug quickly by men who nevertheless invested a lot of thought into how the work could help them. It looks like something patched together by several different people who did not always coordinate their efforts. For example, the protruding bulge appears to have been built separately, and the men who dug the main line simply attached the parapet wherever they happened to approach it. Both sides of the bulge extend some distance to the rear of the main line, the right side much farther than the left. It is unlikely this was planned, but it is effective. The rearward extension on the left side of the bulge offers soldiers the opportunity to fire to the left, toward the ravine, although over the heads of friendly troops. The fact that the traverses are dug differently—some have a trench with all the dirt thrown on one side, while others are dug equally on both sides, and several have different lengths—also indicates that individuals or squads or perhaps even companies had different ideas about how to make a good earthwork. All of these characteristics are typical of the extensive field fortifications dug in the last year of the war and uncharacteristic of those dug before the end of 1863, with only a few exceptions. In short, what we can see of the fortified bridgehead today reveals it to be an exceptionally strong field fortification, an assessment fully supported by all surviving descriptions of it in the primary literature.[31]

On the Confederate side of the battlefield, Stuart's men do not seem to have fortified their position until the evening of May 4, in response to a report that the Federals might be ready to attack. There was the usual shortage of proper tools. The men used "bayonets instead of picks and mattucks and their hands instead of shovels and spades," recalled a soldier named John Wood. The 12th Georgia of Brig. Gen. George Doles's brigade received orders to dig in at 5:00 P.M. that day. There were only one or two axes in the regiment and a few bayonets, but the men built a rough work of planks and logs. They were able to improve it later that night when a supply of spades and picks arrived.[32]

The line these men built was exactly like most of the field fortifications at Chancellorsville, quite strong and serviceable, but not as impressive as Hooker's fortified bridgehead. Much of the captured Union line was incorporated into Stuart's work. The line started at the far right end of the Twelfth Corps line that had been dug on May 1 and 2 and curved eastward across Bullock Road. Here it connected with Berry's Third Corps Division line at a rather sharp angle, wrapping around the north end of Berry's work. The Rebels dug three traverses at this angle. Each one is ten feet long, dug on both sides, and attached at right angles to the parapet. These were constructed for infantry protection, as there are no artillery emplacements nearby.

One can easily see how the Confederates merged their defenses with Berry's. Their line curved around the end of Berry's line, and the extreme right end of the Union work still exists just behind the newer Confederate work. Then the Rebels moved their line a bit to take advantage of Berry's parapet. They dug a trench on the west side of it, the outside of the Union work, and used the Federal trench as a ditch in front of their newly claimed parapet. As a result, the parapet is much thicker than usual. Few other fieldworks at Chancellorsville have the benefit of an exterior ditch.[33]

Stuart's line was intended for defensive purposes, to enable the Confederates to hold the ground they had won on May 3, but Lee had no intention of remaining on the defensive near Chancellorsville. As soon as it was clear that Sedgwick had retired across the Rappahannock, Lee initiated plans to attack Hooker's fortified bridgehead and drive his men across the Rapidan. Edward

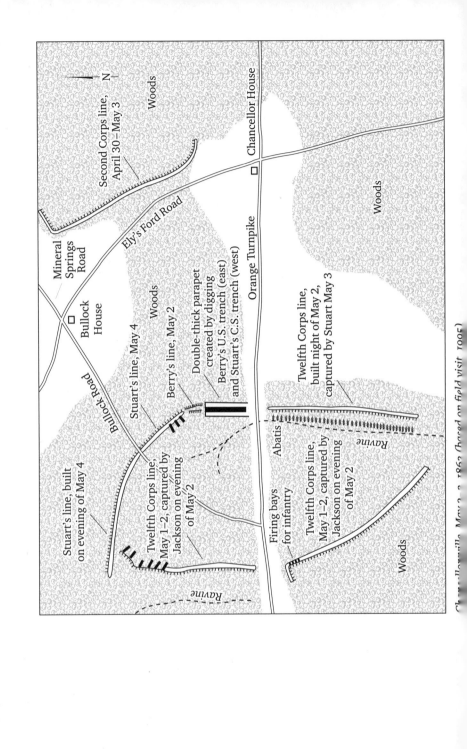

N

Woods

Second Corps line,
April 30–May 3

Mineral
Springs
Road

Ely's Ford Road

Chancellor House

Bullock
House

Woods

Stuart's line, May 4

Berry's line, May 2

Double-thick parapet
created by digging
Berry's U.S. trench (east)
and Stuart's C.S. trench (west)

Orange Turnpike

Woods

Bullock Road

Twelfth Corps line,
built night of May 2,
captured by Stuart May 3

Stuart's line, built
on evening of May 4

Twelfth Corps line,
May 1–2, captured by
Jackson on evening
of May 2

Abatis

Firing bays
for infantry

Ravine

Twelfth Corps line,
May 1–2, captured by
Jackson on evening
of May 2

Ravine

Woods

Chancellorsville, May 2–3, 1863 (based on field visit 1995)

Porter Alexander received orders to scout the area for positions from which he could obtain an enfilade fire on the bridgehead. He found a place for a half-dozen guns near the extreme left of the Union line, but it was impossible to get a good enfilade fire from there or anywhere else. Alexander was certain any attack on this field fortress was doomed, but he used 100 men to dig emplacements and had the six guns ready by dawn of May 6.

Fortunately for the Rebels, Hooker evacuated his bridgehead. Warren and Comstock laid out a shorter line inside the position on May 5. It was three miles long and ran from the Rappahannock to the mouth of Hunting Run on the Rapidan. A continuous parapet with abatis in front was constructed by two divisions of the Fifth Corps, and Warren used pioneers from several different corps to put the finishing touches on the line. He placed timber barricades across each road after the troops had passed through the line. Hooker's men crossed the river that night as the Fifth Corps held this shorter line; the rear guard made it to the north bank by 8:00 A.M. of May 6.

Lee was disappointed by this move. He seems to have thought his army, although bloodied and depleted, could take the fortified bridgehead. His assessment was not shared by any of his subordinates who left an opinion for posterity. Alexander was sure the army would be mauled if it attempted the charge. He later wrote that the greatest Federal blunder of the campaign was the retreat on the night of May 5, as Hooker's entrenched line was "'impregnable.'" If Lee had attacked and lost, Hooker likely would have retreated across the river anyway. But then the battle of Chancellorsville would have ended with a Confederate tactical defeat similar to the repulse of Pickett's Charge at Gettysburg.

The Confederates had many opportunities to examine the bridgehead in detail after the Yankees retreated. They found works of the most intricate design, lines "crossing each other like the squares on a checkerboard," remarked Capt. W. L. Fagan of the 8th Alabama in Wilcox's brigade. Fagan had never seen such formidable works. "They were carefully constructed of fresh green logs piled upon each other, longitudinal pyramids as high as a man's shoulders. Above, on stakes, with a crack between for muskets, was a large head-log." Carefully constructed abatis lay for 100 yards before the works, and the tree cover was so thick beyond the abatis that artillery could hardly be emplaced to support the infantry attack. Foot soldiers would have found it nearly impossible to breach the abatis anyway, thought Fagan, and the captain concluded that, if defended with spirit, the bridgehead could not have been taken.[34]

The battle cost the Federals 17,304 casualties, while Lee's army lost 13,460 men. The battlefield was strewn with debris, personal belongings of soldiers, and lots of army equipment. Staff member Henry E. Young found that small details poorly supplied with shovels and picks had managed to bury most of the Confederate dead by the evening of May 5, but they continued to bury the Federal dead for days afterward. Often these details used the trenches as graves, piling the corpses in and pulling down dirt from the parapet. The thick tree cover was shivered by artillery and intense small arms fire; trunks were shredded, and limbs were broken and scattered in all directions. The earthworks remained as stark reminders of the battle. William J. Reese, an Alabama artilleryman, found Union works made of "knapsacks filled with sand" and any other material that could stop a bullet. Three months later, a clerk on Longstreet's staff named Lancelot M. Blackford rode around the battlefield and was impressed by the maze of earthworks. "On either side of the road for 5 or 6 miles, the whole country is cut up with trenches and fortifications," he wrote. "The positions of the enemy's lines and ours, during the days of the battle, were so often exchanged, . . . that it is often impossible now, even for one with some familiarity with the field, to distinguish the enemy's & our rifle-pits."[35]

The Chancellorsville campaign introduced the extensive use of rapid field fortification to the eastern theater, but one wonders if the battle of Chancellorsville was necessary. Lee could have retreated from Hooker's grasp on May 1 and retired to a defensible position farther south, such as Spotsylvania, from which Hooker would have had difficulty maneuvering him just as Grant would have a similar difficulty in 1864. Lee could have avoided fighting a battle at great cost to his small army, but he would have had to give up the line of the Rappahannock, something he was determined not to do. The result was a spectacular victory for the Confederates, often described as Lee's finest moment on the battlefield and among the best fighting done by his army. It instilled a renewed confidence among the men and a conviction in Lee's mind that his army could do anything. Gettysburg was one of the direct results of this overconfidence.[36]

Another result of their victory at Chancellorsville was, ironically, a return to the old mood of the last half of 1862, to discount the value of earthworks. Even though Lee's men were impressed with Hooker's field fortifications and awed by the fortified bridgehead, they realized that spirited drives and hard fighting had overcome defensive works. The Twelfth Corps and Third Corps line had fallen on the morning of May 3 even though they were shielded by earthworks. The fact that Lee was more than ready to strike at the bridgehead indicates that he had learned no lesson about the tactical strengths of well-made fieldworks. Lee had reached the peak of his aggressiveness in the late spring and early summer of 1863.

The landscape of the Wilderness played a significant role in shaping the course of the battle. The thick vegetation limited visibility for everyone, it hindered a commander's ability to mount large-scale infantry assaults, and it severely hampered the artillery's efforts to support attacks. Confederate sources often noted the effectiveness of the abatis constructed by the Federals and imply that it was a better barrier to their assaults than the works themselves. Alexander recognized that it was easy to quickly construct lines of defense in this forest, for simply by cutting the small trees and brush, "an entanglement would result which only rabbits could get through."[37]

A year later, when Lee met Grant in the Wilderness to open the spring 1864 campaign, many commentators justified that move by arguing that the tangled vegetation offered the Rebels an advantage. They could meet the Federals in a landscape that nullified the greater Union weight in men and cannon. There is little basis for such an argument, for the vegetation affected both armies. It was difficult terrain to operate in whether one wore blue or gray, and Lee's attacks on May 3, 1863, were greatly disrupted by the trees. Rebel artillery officer David Gregg McIntosh perceptively noted this while touring the battlefield decades later. "At times there was much demoralization," he wrote of the infantry attacks.

> Organized bodies of troops left the Federal front, and withdrew after firing a few rounds. Some of the Confederate commands after two or three unsuccessful assaults upon the enemy's lines became discouraged, and it required the utmost efforts of their officers to keep them up to their work. The lines of battle when organized for attack, would soon be broken in passing through the undergrowth and woods; one organization would lose touch with those on its flanks before the force of the assault could be delivered, and the consequence was a series of disjointed attacks without flanking support, and without reserves sufficiently strong to render support and renew the attack at the opportune moment.[38]

Later commentators failed to understand that Lee won at Chancellorsville not because of the terrain but because Hooker failed to take advantage of his many opportunities to beat Lee. The vegetation of the Wilderness hindered Confederate chances of tactical success as much as it limited Union chances. The Confederates won despite the tree cover, not because of it, and they were lucky that Hooker never engaged his large reserve. They were also fortunate to have captured Hazel Grove, which offered them the only good ground on which to deploy and make use of their guns against the Yankees.

If the landscape offered Lee little advantage, what role did the fieldworks play for each side at Chancellorsville? The Army of the Potomac had dug hasty entrenchments only once before, at Gaines's Mill, and it had done a poor job there. The works dug quickly at Chancellorsville were not only much more extensive but much stronger than those at Gaines's Mill. The Federals were on the defensive most of the time at Chancellorsville, which accounts for their extensive digging. Infantrymen and pioneers did all of the labor. Hooker had 1,700 engineer troops available in the U.S. Engineer Battalion and the 15th and 50th New York Engineers, but their primary task was to lay fourteen pontoon bridges in nine days. Most of the fieldworks constructed by Hooker's men were far better than anything the Army of the Potomac had made before. Hooker's fortified bridgehead was exceptionally strong, foreshadowing the works of 1864 that cross the boundary between hasty entrenchment and fixed earthworks in terms of their sophistication and protective power. Despite this, the Third and Twelfth Corps position failed on May 3 even though all observers agree that the line was well made. James Johnson Kirkpatrick of the 16th Mississippi, in Posey's brigade, thought that "troops of any courage might have held them." Rather than a lack of courage, one can only point to the quality of troops, the difference in experience between the Federals and the Confederates who were fighting on this part of the field, and the spirit of aggressive offense and passive defense that animated either side. Lee's men simply outfought the Federals that morning and overcame the Union advantage of fieldworks. Additionally, earlier in the campaign, the Federals had erred in not fortifying Howard's Eleventh Corps line. This was another mistake Lee did not hesitate to take advantage of when given the opportunity.[39]

Lee's use of fieldworks at Chancellorsville was judicious and wise. He relied on good entrenchments to allow Anderson and McLaws to hold Hooker on May 1 and 2, and he used those works as part of his plan to attack Howard's poorly fortified line. His reliance on the Fredericksburg works for a similar purpose failed because of an effective Union attack plan and the fact that Early had too few men to hold the line. The Confederates refused to allow the Third and Twelfth Corps position to forestall slashing attacks on the morning of May 3, thus demonstrating that the increased reliance on fortifications at Chancellorsville would not bring about trench stalemate, a condition seen later in 1863 at Mine Run. Whenever strong earthworks prevented an enemy from either attacking or outflanking a position, trench stalemate set in. Lee's only mistake regarding fortifications at Chancellorsville was to plan an assault on Hooker's fortified bridgehead.[40]

William D. F. Landon of the 14th Indiana had the good fortune to survive the battle of Chancellorsville. He saw the bloodied field again a year later while recuperating from a wound he received at the Wilderness. It was strewn with bones and equipment, and earthworks crisscrossed the landscape. "Both armies adopted the McClellan plan," he mused, drawing a parallel with the Peninsula campaign. That plan was to " 'fortify as you go'—a few shovels full of earth and a log or two save many lives."[41]

9 : Goldsborough, New Bern, Washington, and Suffolk

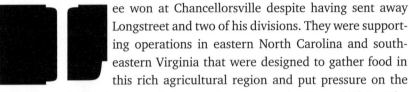ee won at Chancellorsville despite having sent away Longstreet and two of his divisions. They were supporting operations in eastern North Carolina and southeastern Virginia that were designed to gather food in this rich agricultural region and put pressure on the Federal garrisons that occupied several towns on the Coastal Plain. The Yankees had established their presence in this region in early 1862 with the Burnside expedition, but they had failed to use it effectively as a springboard to attack vital lines of communication. More important operations in Virginia, most notably McClellan's drive on Richmond and Lee's subsequent efforts to mass troops for the Seven Days battles, had forced both sides to recall units from eastern North Carolina. The war had therefore stagnated on the Coastal Plain, with both sides content to watch each other from their respective towns.

The stalemate ended in mid-December 1862 when Maj. Gen. John G. Foster launched a raid from New Bern to Goldsborough to cut the Weldon Railroad. It was organized as a support for Burnside's offensive at Fredericksburg. Foster gathered a sizable force, four brigades with 10,000 infantrymen, forty guns, and 600 cavalrymen. He left New Bern on December 11, the same day that Burnside's engineers bridged the Rappahannock River, and encountered trees felled by the Rebels for several hundred yards along the road. Foster's pioneers, helped by details from the infantry regiments and even by freed blacks from the surrounding area, cut a path through the roadblock.[1]

Foster neared Kinston on December 13 to find Brig. Gen. Nathan G. Evans's South Carolina brigade of 2,000 men holding the town. Evans had also placed the 61st North Carolina in a forward position at Southwest Creek, four miles south of Kinston. The Tar Heels were entrenched along the north bank of this stream a short distance from the creek bluff and straddling the road to Kinston. The line consisted of a simple trench with a ditch but no traverses. Two artillery emplacements reinforced the line. A one-gun emplacement was located just to the left of the road; the other emplacement, for three guns, was on the far right of the line. It was a strong position but vulnerable to a flanking movement. Foster easily found a way to ford the creek nearby and forced the Rebels to evacuate their works.[2]

The next day, December 14, Foster continued his advance toward Kinston and found Evans close to town. The rebels were not dug in, but Foster noted that the ground on which they were positioned "formed a natural breast-work." A swamp lay to their right, and the Neuse River was on their left. Foster nevertheless outflanked their right and forced Evans to pull back across the Neuse and through Kinston. The Confederate repositioned his harried brigade two miles outside town, but he pulled back farther when Foster sent troops to the north side of the river.[3]

Foster sent part of his force a short distance downstream along the north side of the Neuse to a point where the Confederates had some gun emplace-ments to fire on Union boats trying to ascend the river. These entrenchments had been sited and built by Col. Walter Gwynn, a West Point graduate and prewar civil engineer, just two months earlier. Chief Engineer Gilmer had wanted Gwynn to design one or two large enclosed works to minimize man-power needs, but the ardent colonel designed a line of works that would have required 10,000 men for its defense. The ordnance did not arrive until a few days before Foster appeared. The Federals took possession of these works after the Rebels evacuated them. They found "a sort of half circular fort, with breastworks a mile and a half long," according to one Yankee. Modern remnants of these works include the large, semicircular work with a ditch in front and open to the rear. The work is about fifty yards wide. The riverbank is low here, not more than fifteen feet high. The remnants of an attached infantry line stretch for about fifty yards to the right of the semicir-cular work. It is a straight, simple trench. On the western end of this line of river batteries lies another artillery emplacement for two or three guns; it consists of two L-shaped parapets with no remnants of a supporting infantry trench. The Confederates left seven guns in these river batteries, including an 8-inch Columbiad, two 32-pounders, and four 6-pounders.[4]

The Confederate defenses of Kinston, although flawed, were adequate as long as the static nature of military operations prevailed during the last half of 1862. But Foster surprised everyone with his large and aggressive cam-paign. Evans was badly outnumbered, so his evacuation of the town was understandable. Foster recrossed the Neuse on the morning of December 15 and moved upstream on the south bank, intending to cross at White Hall sixteen miles to the northwest. He pushed his men to a point about three and a half miles short of that goal by nightfall.

On December 16 Foster realized that the Confederates had burned the bridge at White Hall, yet he demonstrated on the south bank and pretended to rebuild the span while exploring alternate crossing points. Foster deployed two regiments along the southern bluff and opened a heavy artillery bombardment of the north side that lasted for six hours. The Confederates under Brig. Gen. Beverly H. Robertson had four regiments, a section of artillery, and 600 cavalrymen, but the brunt of this Yankee shelling was borne by the 11th North Carolina. It deployed along the low, swampy northern bank of the Neuse and took shelter behind logs, tree stumps, and piles of timber at a steam sawmill. By evening Foster was satisfied that there were no feasible crossing points. He broke off the engagement and moved upstream along the south bank of the river.[5]

The Confederate authorities had not constructed works at White Hall or Goldsborough. Both places seemed far beyond the Federals' reach in the contested area between New Bern and Kinston. Foster reached Goldsborough just when the few Rebel regiments there were being reinforced, and he gained the bridge that took the Weldon Railroad over the Neuse River. It was defended only by the 52nd North Carolina, and Foster sent five regiments to drive it off and set fire to the bridge from the south bank. He then covered the area with intense artillery fire to prevent the Rebels from extinguishing the flames and prepared to withdraw. He was about seventy miles from New Bern and did not feel strong enough to take and hold Goldsborough. The Confederates attempted to punish Foster as he left. A poorly coordinated movement sent the 51st and 52nd North Carolina into an assault up the open slopes of a hill into the teeth of two Union batteries supported by a full brigade. The Tar Heels were easily repulsed, and Foster escaped.[6]

The Goldsborough Raid succeeded on a tactical level, for Foster was able to cut the railroad that linked Lee's army with the important blockade-running port of Wilmington. But the breakage was temporary; Rebel engineers repaired the bridge and got the trains rolling again. On the strategic level, the raid did nothing to help Burnside's disastrous attack at Fredericksburg.

Instead, the Goldsborough Raid raised the awareness of Confederate authorities about the dangers in eastern North Carolina. They shifted additional troops to the area to prevent any more Yankees from touching the Weldon Railroad. Five brigades were stationed at various points along or east of the line by early 1863. They could be rapidly shifted by railroad cars to threatened places. Foster's move had forced the Confederates to divert more troops to this region, but the diversion was not large enough to impair Lee's combat readiness in Virginia.[7]

Soon Confederate commanders turned their thoughts to taking the offensive. On February 13 Maj. Gen. Samuel G. French sent Brig. Gen. James J.

Pettigrew's North Carolina brigade from Magnolia toward Union-occupied Plymouth. Pettigrew was to force the Federals to take shelter behind their defenses while he gathered food in Washington, Martin, and Tyrrell counties. Along the way, he was to demonstrate to local farmers that they would be protected as they prepared to plant their spring crops. Logistical considerations were driving strategy in eastern North Carolina as the war continued to devastate large parts of Virginia or to deny the Confederate government access to rich agricultural areas in the western states. Pettigrew had made it as far as Goldsborough when French, unaccountably, called off the expedition on February 17.[8]

But French's strategy would be adopted by other Confederate authorities. Lee sent Longstreet and two of his divisions to the south side of the James River, initially to guard against a possible Federal advance on Richmond from the southeast. Longstreet took command of the Department of Virginia and North Carolina and laid plans to gather food and threaten Union-occupied towns in his department. He would approach Suffolk, Virginia, while Daniel H. Hill, the commander in North Carolina, would strike at New Bern and Washington. Longstreet planned to protect the Weldon Railroad through aggressive action, reap a logistics benefit for the Confederate army, and more effectively utilize the large numbers of troops deployed along the coastal plain of both North Carolina and Virginia. With Longstreet's two divisions, the Confederates had thirteen brigades in the region.[9]

New Bern

Daniel Harvey Hill gathered 12,000 men to strike at New Bern in three columns. James J. Pettigrew's North Carolina brigade would attempt to capture Fort Anderson, a small work on the north bank of the Neuse River opposite the town. Then Pettigrew was to shell New Bern and the Union gunboats on the river. Beverly H. Robertson's cavalry brigade was to move south of the Trent River and tear up the Atlantic and North Carolina Railroad south of New Bern, while Hill would accompany Brig. Gen. Junius Daniel's North Carolina brigade as it advanced north of the Trent River toward the western defenses of New Bern. Pettigrew's role in this plan was crucial, for the line of fortifications around the west side of town was far too strong to be attacked without some diversion or crossfire being laid on the town.[10]

Pettigrew left Goldsborough on March 9 and reached Fort Anderson five days later, after tough marching over muddy roads. The work was garrisoned by 350 men of the 92nd New York under Lt. Col. Hiram Anderson Jr. Pettigrew described it as "a simple *pan coupe*" with an interior crest of nine feet. The ditch was eight feet deep. Fort Anderson was well sited with a swamp to the right, a creek to the left, and the river to the rear. It could only be approached from the front. The work was on top of a slight rise of ground with an open field in front.

Fort Anderson seemed too strong, and Pettigrew did not attempt an immediate attack. He thought he could take it at the cost of 100 men, but he preferred to bombard it awhile. Then he asked the Federals to give up, and Anderson requested half an hour to think it over. Meanwhile, the Northerners positioned a gunboat to provide fire support for the earthwork. Pettigrew found himself in an unequal duel because his four 20-pounder Parrotts proved to be defective. The axle of one broke, the tube of another burst, and about half the shells exploded prematurely. The Confederates could not win this duel, so Pettigrew eventually gave up and retired.[11]

Robertson contributed nothing to the expedition. He advanced only far enough to send out some patrols to the railroad and withdrew. Daniel, however, encountered Union pickets ten miles from town on the lower Trent Road. He pushed them to Deep Gully, a crevasse spanning the road only two miles from the main line of works, on March 13. Four Confederate companies crossed the gully and broke through the fortified Union line on the east side. The Federals unsuccessfully tried to retake the position the next morning. This resulted in the withdrawal of all Yankee troops into the fortifications, which were anchored in this sector by Fort Totten. Hill waited all day for the sound of Pettigrew's fire on New Bern, but he could tell by the noise coming from Fort Anderson that the Federals had not evacuated the north bank of the Neuse. Hill ordered Daniel and Robertson to fall back.[12]

This would not be the last Confederate attempt to take New Bern, but all subsequent efforts would encounter the same problem that stymied Hill. The Federals had the place so well fortified that it would take a large army and a siege to dig them out. Pettigrew nullified any possibility that Hill's scheme could work by timidly refraining from an attack on Fort Anderson, the only way the work might have been taken. Hill had no stomach for a protracted effort at New Bern. He called off the operation at the first sign of failure.

Washington

Hill next turned his attention to Washington, North Carolina, and mounted a more sustained and vigorous effort to retake that smaller but no less well fortified town. Washington is located on the Tar River just before it widens into a broad, tidal stream renamed the Pamlico River. The Federals had begun digging in on June 25, 1862, when engineers laid out a semicircular line of works that covered the town completely on the north side of the river.

Black laborers cut the timber and assisted in digging the works, which consisted of a simple trench bolstered by four blockhouses and a large, square redoubt in the center. No fortifications were dug south of the river.[13]

Hill reached the vicinity of Washington on March 31. He positioned Pettigrew's and Daniel's brigades on the south side of the river to block any Federal effort to relieve the town from New Bern. Three hundred men of the 26th North Carolina dug gun emplacements at Rodman's Point, on the south bank of the Tar just downstream from Washington, on the night of March 31. That same night, other troops occupied an abandoned Confederate work at Hill's Point, seven miles downstream. They mounted guns and christened the place Fort Hill. The field guns at both positions were to stop Federal river traffic to Washington. Daniel covered the southwestern approach to Washington while Pettigrew covered the southeastern quadrant. Key locations at Chocowinity Crossroads, due south of town, and Blount's Mill, the only crossing point of Blount's Creek along the best road between Washington and New Bern, were securely held. Longstreet loaned some troops so Hill could complete his encirclement of the town. Brig. Gen. Richard B. Garnett's Virginia brigade invested Washington north of the Tar River, while Brig. Gen. Henry L. Benning's Georgia Brigade collected food in the area.[14]

All of this fortification required a considerable amount of digging, and Hill was inadequately supplied with engineers. Col. William Gaston Lewis, commander of the 43rd North Carolina in Daniel's brigade, was detailed to help. "When the regiment marches I go with it," he reported; "when it rests, I am on engineering duty for Genl's Hill & Daniel." He did topographical work and laid out several fortifications. The works at Rodman's Point and Hill's Point were offensive in nature, but the fortifications at Blount's Mill and additional works constructed at the crossing of Swift Creek, southwest of Chocowinity Crossroads, were defensive. Garnett's works north of the Tar were also offensive. They protected the Rebel guns that pounded the defenses of Washington. Little is known about these works, but they appear to have been hastily constructed gun emplacements, with little if anything in the way of supporting infantry works. By the time all his dispositions were complete, Hill had Washington almost completely cut off from the outside world. Garnett fully invested the north side, while Pettigrew and Daniel did the same on the south side. The only channel of communication left to the Federals was the river. Although the journey was dangerous, they were able to run boats past the Rebel batteries at Fort Hill and Rodman's Point.[15]

John G. Foster reached Washington with a few staff members on March 30 before the Confederates arrived. With only 1,200 men, he wisely relied on the spade as his main defense. The works around Washington were already strong, but Foster greatly improved them with additional labor. Beginning on April 2, his men built traverses along the line. The only detailed map of the Union works at Washington indicates that at least twenty-eight traverses were constructed. These were an essential feature in a curved line. Foster also directed that the ditch in front of the works be deepened and flooded wherever possible—that meant on the right and in the center, where swampy land neared the works. He built Fort Hamilton for three guns on the far right, near Blockhouse No. 4, to fire on the Rebel guns at Rodman's Point. Other redoubts were constructed to cover the bridge over the Tar River and inside town, the latter in case the Confederates broke through the defenses.

Most of this work was finished by April 6, when Foster began to place abatis before the gun emplacement that covered the road to Plymouth and on the edge of a creek on his right flank. He built Fort Cerris near Blockhouse No. 1, mounted a 30-pounder Parrott, and manned it with sailors. The Federals also started some works on Castle Island, in the river opposite town. While all this was going on, Garnett's daily artillery fire grew heavier as he emplaced at least six batteries, most of which were concentrated opposite the Federal right wing. Details had to stop work on the Castle Island defenses due to Confederate fire. Foster reported that the daily exchange of artillery rounds usually resulted either in a draw or in the silencing of at least some Rebel guns.

A detailed map of the Union defenses at Washington, drawn by C. M. Allis of the 27th Massachusetts, indicates that Foster's men did their work well. From Blockhouse No. 1 on the left to Fort Hamilton on the right, there was a continuous and strong trench laced with numerous traverses. Fort Washington was a large work in the center of the line, due north of town. The four roads leading into Washington were covered by artillery emplacements, and large swampy areas helped to shield the center and right wing. The trees had already been cut for a half-mile in front of the works. Garnett never attempted a strike against these heavy defenses.[16]

The Federals tried to relieve Foster but failed miserably. Brig. Gen. Henry Prince was in charge of these efforts. He scouted the south bank of the Pamlico but could find no suitable place to land troops from their transports. Moreover, Fort Hill and the works at Blount's Mill would block his approach even if he could embark successfully. So Prince sent Brig. Gen. Francis B. Spinola with a relief column of 6,400 men overland from New Bern by way of Blount's Mill. Neither he nor Spinola had much hope of success, and Spinola was a rank amateur who had little, if any, combat experience. He cautiously probed the defenses at Blount's Mill on April 9. The works were small but

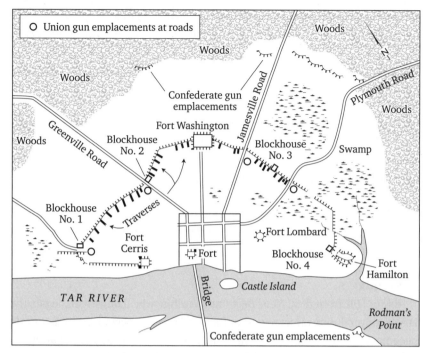

Woods

Woods

N

Woods

Confederate gun
emplacements

Jamesville Road

Plymouth Road

Woods

Fort Washington

Greenville Road

Blockhouse
No. 2

Blockhouse
No. 3

Swamp

Woods

Blockhouse
No. 1

Traverses

Fort
Cerris

Fort Lombard

Blockhouse
No. 4

Fort
Hamilton

Fort

Bridge

Castle Island

TAR RIVER

Rodman's
Point

Confederate gun emplacements

Union Defenses of Washington, N.C., April 1863 (based on wartime map by C. M. Allis, 27th Massachusetts, published in Chase, Battery F, 85)

well placed, and only 2,800 troops and four 6-pounders were in the area. The antagonists skirmished and exchanged artillery fire for two hours, then Spinola hastened back to New Bern.[17]

The easy victory at Blount's Mill encouraged the Rebels mightily. Capt. Stephen Wiley Brewer of the 26th North Carolina believed that Washington would fall. If his comrades did not "whip them we Can Starve them out and they will be Bound to surender." But Brewer was wrong. The siege was not airtight. Enough Union ships slipped past the Rebel batteries to bring in supplies, reinforcements, and news from New Bern. Hill's efforts were hampered by the poor quality of his field artillery; the tubes were weak, and the ammunition was often defective.[18]

Foster was disgusted with Prince's weak effort to relieve his men. He believed Washington was strong enough to withstand a lengthy siege, but he also wanted to punish the Confederates as much as possible. Therefore he left town on the *Escort*, a boat that had run the blockade several times. His plan was to organize a proper relief expedition from New Bern. But there would be no need for this, because Hill gave up. After fourteen days of siege, he accepted the fact that he could not starve Washington into surrender, and he had no intention of wasting valuable manpower by attacking such a strong position. The Confederates pulled out on the night of April 15. The Federals sent out black laborers to level the Confederate batteries north of the Tar and occupied Rodman's Point.[19]

Despite his greater efforts at Washington, Hill was no more successful than he had been at New Bern. Again, the superior Union earthworks were the key. The Confederates did not feel that recapturing either town was worth the huge investment of time and resources needed to construct siege approaches. They primarily wanted to collect food. Any offensive victory over the Union garrisons would have to be bought at little cost. When Federal defensive measures raised the ante too high, the Southerners gave up their efforts. In a situation like this, all the advantages lay with the defending Yankees.

Suffolk

While Hill fretted at New Bern and Washington, Longstreet began the largest Confederate effort to gather food and seize an occupied town. Suffolk became the chief focus of his effort. It had been occupied shortly after the Rebels evacuated Norfolk and Portsmouth on May 9, 1862, and lay twenty miles northwest of those port cities. Suffolk had barely 1,400 residents, half of whom were black, and it lay on the Nansemond River just north of the Dismal Swamp. The Nansemond emptied into the James twenty miles downriver. Jericho Canal, big enough for small skiffs, ran east of town and connected the Nansemond with the Dismal Swamp. The land around Suffolk was "flat, intersected by swampy streams, and half grown up in woods, mostly the Southern pine," according to Union staff officer Hazard Stevens. Two railroads ran through town, and Petersburg was only thirty miles to the northwest.

Suffolk was too far from the important coastal towns the Federals needed to occupy and too exposed to Rebel strikes in the middle ground between Petersburg and Norfolk. The Yankees maintained a tiny garrison there until Maj. Gen. John J. Peck took command on September 22, 1862. He increased the troop strength to 9,000 and set the men to work fortifying the place. The Confederates made no serious move against Suffolk, as they were preoccupied with more important objectives to the north of Richmond. Following the defeat at Fredericksburg, Burnside's Ninth Corps was detached from the Army of the Potomac and temporarily encamped at Newport News. This was another reason Lee sent Longstreet with Hood's and Pickett's divisions to the Richmond area. Longstreet had 14,000 men, and Samuel G. French added his division, another 4,000 men, to that force. News of this transfer led the Federals to detach Brig. Gen. George W. Getty's division of the Ninth Corps to reinforce Peck, while the other two divisions were sent to the Mississippi Valley under Burnside. Peck now had nearly 15,000 men and the support of three small gunboats in the Nansemond.[20]

Peck, a West Point graduate, had been commissioned in the artillery and had fought in Mexico and on the frontier. He had resigned from the army in 1853 to enter business in Syracuse, New York, but participated in the Peninsula campaign and the Seven Days. His division of the Fourth Corps remained at Yorktown following the latter campaign, and Peck wound up at Suffolk. The exposed nature of the post and the fact that his huge garrison had little else to do accounts for the large amount of labor he expended on its defense. Suffolk has no naturally defensible ground; the landscape around it is utterly flat. Peck laid out a rectangular line of works that surrounded the town on the south side of the river and included nine forts and several batteries. Connecting infantry works enclosed the circle, which totaled eight miles in length and required seven months of hard labor. Peck ignored the stretch of river from Suffolk downstream, assuming the gunboats would protect that area. There were several older Confederate works along the river. The most important was constructed during May and June 1861 at Hill's Point, where the Western Branch flowed from the west into the Nansemond about eight miles downriver from Suffolk. The river narrows here considerably as one steams upriver. The Confederate fort was a reworking of a redoubt called Old Fort because it dated to the War of 1812. The Confederates renamed it Fort Huger.[21]

Longstreet originated the plan to strike at Suffolk in March 1863 and convinced Lee of its propriety. His objectives were to protect Richmond from a possible thrust from the southeast, to gather food, and to recapture Suffolk and other towns if the opportunity presented itself. Longstreet reached the Suffolk area by April 11. After reconnoitering, he felt certain he could take the place by assault at a cost of 5,000 irreplaceable troops. Suffolk was not important enough to justify that cost, but Longstreet explored the stretch of river downstream from town, thinking he might be able to maneuver the Federals out.[22]

The Confederates dug in two to three miles from the Federal lines, with Pickett on the south side of town, French on the west, and Hood on the north. Hood also was responsible for probing toward the Nansemond River east of town, and his moves prompted Getty to scout the riverbanks and urge Peck to dig new works to prevent the Rebels from crossing. Peck approved, and Getty masterminded, a project of earthwork construction that effectively closed the only open door to Suffolk in the nick of time. Peck shifted troops to these works, which were built over the course of several days. They consisted of a line of detached works along the south bank of the river, linked by a ten-mile military road that connected Suffolk with the area opposite Hill's Point. Many of the detached works seem to have been eventually connected by lines of infantry trench. Hood's division constructed less extensive, detached works at key locations near the north bank of the Nansemond, as the Confederates gradually realized that there were no good crossings of the river that the Yankees had not already fortified.[23]

Meanwhile, Peck used the rest of his force to strengthen the already substantial works around Suffolk. His men grew tired of the incessant digging. A veteran of the 16th Connecticut recalled after the war that Peck "kept fortifying and refortifying until his soldiers had become regular mud-diggers, and he had spent no end of labor and money in constructing works of immense magnitude, to defend a position not worth holding. There was digging and basket-weaving to an extent that went far toward developing the talents of the soldiers for farm work." His men, sick of fashioning gabions, called themselves "The Basket-Makers of the Nansemond."[24]

By the time both sides had finished exploring each other's positions on opposite sides of the river, the strategic character of the campaign for Suffolk had already been set. Longstreet gave up the possibility of forcing his way through the ring of earthworks, and his only hope was to completely encircle the town and starve the garrison out. Getty's quick action in fortifying the river line prevented him from doing that, and the Confederates essentially ran out of options. They busied themselves digging extensive lines of earthworks—Pickett's division alone manned a line seven miles long—that covered Suffolk on three sides, from the Dismal Swamp westward, northward, and eastward to Hill's Point. Only the eastern quarter, south of the Nansemond River and east of Jericho Creek, was open to the Federals, and it was more than enough to deny Longstreet his encirclement of the town. A strategic stalemate ensued, with Peck relying on the strength of his earthworks to win the campaign and Longstreet contenting himself with penning the Yankees in town and gathering food. It fulfilled the minimum needed to make his campaign worthwhile, but he had obviously hoped for more.[25]

The Confederates were hampered in their digging by the usual shortage of tools. Brig. Gen. Lewis A. Armistead, commanding a brigade in Pickett's division, complained that he did not have enough spades to work on his infantry line and his artillery emplacements at the same time. Lt. Turner Vaughan of the 4th Alabama was ordered to dig two pits for pickets, but his thirteen-man detachment could manage only one. A lack of spades and "roots in the ground" delayed work on the other pit, even though it only had to be big enough for two men. Vaughan's men made their beds "inside the entrenchment so as to sleep without being disturbed or without being in danger." He apparently meant they slept in the bottom of the trench at night. Even when not on duty in the works, the Rebels often were called on to rush to the line in expectation of an attack, only to find out it was a false alarm.[26]

The Rebels began to gather food on April 14 and continued to do so until the campaign ended more than two weeks later. Brigade-sized forces were sent to scour the area from the James to Albemarle Sound, and from the Blackwater River to the Nansemond and the Dismal Swamp. Most of the food was found in eastern North Carolina counties where the Federals had not yet made a significant presence, in the large gray area where neither side completely controlled the land. Transportation was a problem, for the Confederates often did not have enough wagons to haul the food.[27]

The strategic stalemate altered when the Federals decided to seize Fort Huger. The Confederates had planted some field artillery there that, along with the other batteries along the north bank of the Nansemond, harried Federal shipping. Five gunboats managed to run past the fort on April 16, but they were trapped by its guns and could not return downriver. An attempt to take the fort was launched on the night of April 17. Two hundred Yankees landed on the north bank but withdrew after two companies of Alabama troops advanced as skirmishers against them. The fort was manned by Companies A and B of the 44th Alabama, while the 55th North Carolina, a green regiment, was encamped one mile to the rear as a reserve. Capt. Robert M. Stribling's Virginia Battery had five guns in the fort. The gunboats kept up a desultory fire at the fort on April 18, but it did little harm, as the Rebels had constructed a bombproof.[28]

Three Federal officers devised a plan for the next attempt to take Fort Huger. To avoid the confusion of a nighttime operation, they decided to land troops in daylight as close as possible to the rear of the fort, which was inadequately fortified. The river bluff was twelve feet high, and the fort was fifty yards from the stream; a plowed cornfield lay between. If the boat steamed as if it had every intention of running past the fort but then veered sharply to the bank, the garrison could be taken by surprise. Three hundred men from the 8th Connecticut and the 89th New York were loaded on the *Stepping Stones*, and canvas was draped around its sides to hide them.

The boat sheered sharply to the bank some 300 yards from the fort on the evening of April 19. Unfortunately, its prow grounded on a sandbank 30 feet from the shore. About 100 of the infantrymen clambered off and waded to the riverbank, while the captain swung the boat's aft to unload the rest closer to shore. They climbed the bluff and rushed the surprised garrison, which had time to turn only one gun around to fire a shot at the attackers. The Federals captured 140 men, nine officers, and the five guns in an operation that lasted only ten minutes. One Federal was killed and fourteen were wounded.

The 55th North Carolina was posted too far away to be of any use. Col. John Kerr Connally initially wanted to counterattack but changed his mind when he was informed that the Federals already held the fort. He moved his men half a mile closer to the captured work; they endured a hail of gunboat fire but then fell back for better cover. Seven hundred Union troops were landed at Hill's Point that night and dug a new line of works to cover the fort's rear. The blockade was opened, allowing the boats free transit up and down the Nansemond. Yet the Federals did not mean to hold Fort Huger permanently, as they were too exposed on the north bank of the river. The Confederate earthwork was leveled and abandoned on the night of April 20, upon Getty's recommendation.[29]

Longstreet blamed French for the loss of Fort Huger. Longstreet had earlier offered command of his artillery to the general, but French saw this as a way to deny him command of his division, so he refused to formally accept it. Instead, French agreed to help by passing information to the artillery chiefs of each division. It was French's understanding that he was not responsible for placing the guns or for defending the emplacements, but Longstreet apparently thought that French had accepted these responsibilities. Hood assumed he had no accountability for the river batteries, and the result was that no higher officer paid attention to affairs at Hill's Point. At lower levels of command, accusations of cowardice and incompetence against Connally were made by two officers on the staff of Brig. Gen. Evander Law's Alabama brigade. The hotheaded Connally challenged them to a duel, but his subordinate officers stepped in to take responsibility for it. After much negotiation, Maj. Alfred H. Belo of the 55th North Carolina fought the duel with Capt. John Cussons of Law's staff on April 21. Each fired two rounds with rifle muskets, piercing the other's hat and clothing; then their seconds negotiated an end to the affair.[30]

The capture of Fort Huger was a turning point of the siege, for it demonstrated the vulnerability of the Confederate river batteries. The failure of the Rebel ironclad CSS *Richmond* to support Longstreet meant that he had little opportunity to challenge Federal control of the Nansemond. The Confederates dropped all aggressive moves along the river and concentrated on gathering as much food as possible, especially after Peck received 9,000 reinforcements. With the additional strength, he conducted several large demonstrations over the next few days. Five thousand Yankees drove the Rebels out of their advanced picket lines on April 24. Another 5,000 men crossed the river on May 3 to advance along Providence Church Road and drive Hood's picket line even farther. They stopped when they realized how strong was the main Confederate line.[31]

Pressure like this merely hastened Longstreet's departure, which became imperative when Lee ordered him to rejoin his army on April 30. Longstreet planned the withdrawal well. Orders were issued on May 1, and the movement started on the night of May 3, a few hours after the worst fighting at Chancellorsville. The earthworks were abandoned, and the gray columns marched toward Petersburg along roads lined with partially cut trees. Longstreet's pioneers waited until the column passed before they applied the final cuts to block the roads. Peck offered no pursuit, content to have won the campaign through the use of the spade and the pick. French's division stayed along the Blackwater River, while Hood's and Pickett's divisions returned to Lee. The Federals lost about 260 casualties, and Longstreet lost about 1,400 men.[32]

The Federals were eager to examine the Confederate earthworks, and everyone was impressed by them. They included log and sod revetments, good abatis, embrasured artillery emplacements, covered ways, and parapets up to 15 feet thick. There was defense in depth, with up to five lines in some sectors. On the Union side, Getty estimated that 3,434 yards of infantry trench and 308 yards of battery parapet were constructed, 7 feet tall and 7 feet thick on top, around Suffolk. An additional 4,398 yards of infantry line and 1,944 feet of battery parapet, 8 feet tall and 10 feet wide at the top, were constructed along the south bank of the river from Suffolk to Hill's Point.[33]

Capt. Hazard Stevens of Getty's staff put it well when he wrote that "the siege was more distinguished for digging than for fighting." The Federals were fatigued by all the work, added to the emotional strain of a siege and the constant rounds of picket duty and skirmishing. Yet Peck's strategy "was strictly that of the passive defensive, although he was equal in numbers to the enemy before the siege ended." A modern historian has argued that the "foundation of [Union] success was laid long before the siege began, during the months of diligent [toil] on Peck's well-conceived defenses." Captain Stevens related "a good joke" about Peck, "a regular old granny" who "works his men to death on the fortifications." One of Peck's soldiers told a comrade he "hoped he wouldn't die until about a fortnight after Gen. Peck did. 'Why so?' 'Because by that time he will have Hell so fortified that nobody can get into it." Stevens related that Peck "takes the story as a great compliment to his engineering powers."[34]

It is ironic that after proving the importance of well-made earthworks, Peck recommended that Suffolk be abandoned. He argued that it was bad enough to cram so many thousands of troops into Suffolk to hold the huge rectangular line of works that protected the town, but several thousand more would be needed to garrison the line of works along the south bank of the Nansemond to Hill's Point. It was too much for a post of such relative insignificance. He suggested the works be leveled before the Federals gave up the town, and it was done. That did not end the fortifying in southeastern Virginia. Captain Stevens sent several letters to his family complaining of the heavy work that was done in the Portsmouth area along the Elizabeth River and the Dismal Swamp Canal. "Every change of command produces a change of lines," he snorted, and digging continued well into November 1863.[35]

Longstreet failed to employ all the techniques of siegecraft at Suffolk. He never attempted an assault or regular approaches but relied on a futile attempt to invest the town. The campaign also did not influence the development of trench warfare. Neither Longstreet nor his men were more prone to resort to field fortifications after Suffolk, despite their undeniable skill at constructing them in a short time. Unfortunately, the leveling of the Federal earthworks by Peck and the destruction of the Rebel earthworks by postwar agriculture have not left us any remnants whereby we can see if the design and construction of the Suffolk lines advanced the technique of fortification. Moreover, Suffolk quickly became a forgotten campaign because it resulted in no significant battle.

The secondary campaigns in Virginia and North Carolina from December 1862 through May 1863 demonstrated that, even in a relative backwater, fortifications played a significant role in operations. As activity increased, troop strength multiplied, and confrontation became more regular, digging increased as well. The Federals intended to retain all their captured towns and used the spade as their chief weapon. New Bern, Washington, and Suffolk withstood attack because of superior Union engineering and the hard labor of their garrisons.

10 : Gettysburg and Lee's Pennsylvania Campaign

he ending of the Suffolk campaign allowed Lee to concentrate his army once again. With the addition of Longstreet's two divisions, he could resume offensive movements given up in the wake of the Maryland campaign. This time Pennsylvania was the goal. Lee hoped to take the scene of operations away from the Rappahannock River, where it had been planted for six months. Gathering food was another consideration, and generally causing havoc on free soil was yet another. The Pennsylvania campaign shook up the North. It was the Confederacy's biggest incursion into free territory during the war.

Lee planned to enter Northern soil by way of the lower Shenandoah Valley, but a modest Union garrison at Winchester barred the way. An old city in the middle of the expansive lower end of the Valley, Winchester was the scene of two battles fought during the preceding year as part of Stonewall Jackson's Valley campaign. Its strategic location meant that the town would change hands more than a dozen times during the war and three more battles would be fought in and near its rows of substantial houses.

Second Winchester

Winchester was not an easy post to fortify. The landscape is generally level with a few prominent hills and ridges, but they are no more than about 200 feet high and are not arrayed in a manner to allow a defending force to construct a systematic line of works. It was not possible to build a cohesive system of defenses with no holes in its perimeter.[1]

Federal troops had first entered Winchester on March 11, 1862, but Jackson drove them out in late June near the end of his Valley campaign. After Jackson evacuated the Valley to join Lee for the Seven Days, Col. Abram S. Piatt's Federal brigade reoccupied the town and began to fortify. Fort Garibaldi (later renamed Fort Milroy) was the major work constructed just west of Winchester on a prominent hill. Wood from the nearby home of James S. Mason, of the Mason-Slidell affair of 1861, was used in its construction. Trees between the fort and the town were cut down for a clear field of fire. Julius White replaced Piatt as Federal commander at Winchester on July 28, but he blew up the magazine in Fort Garibaldi when he evacuated the town on September 2 to take refuge with Dixon Miles at Harpers Ferry. Lee's Maryland campaign and Jackson's capture of Harpers Ferry gave the Confederates control of the Lower Valley until October. A small Confederate cavalry force continued to occupy Winchester until John W. Geary's troops retook the town without a fight on December 4.[2]

Robert H. Milroy took command of Winchester on January 1, 1863, and began to strengthen its defenses. Capt. W. Angelo Powell, Milroy's chief engineer who had also worked on Fort Garibaldi under White's direction, now enlarged and rebuilt it. The work commanded the western and southern approaches to Winchester and mounted four 20-pounder Parrotts and two 24-pounder howitzers. Renamed the Flag Fort, it finally was designated Fort Milroy by the time Lee's army approached in June 1863.

Star Fort, big enough to hold eight cannon and 400 men, was built one mile north of Winchester. Its gun platforms reportedly were constructed of both stone and wood. West Fort, described as "an unfinished lunette," stood half a mile northwest of town. It was open to the rear, mounted six guns, and had an infantry line and a smaller work extending northward from its right flank.[3]

If General in Chief Henry W. Halleck had had his way, Winchester would not have been held at all. He believed it was too exposed to maintain a sizable garrison there. Halleck told Maj. Gen. Robert C. Schenck that it was more effective to protect the Baltimore and Ohio Railroad by concentrating at Harpers Ferry and other vital points on the line, not by holding forward posts such as Winchester. Schenck had placed 6,900 men under Milroy at the town, mainly to act as an early warning force. This was a task better left to cavalry. Milroy did not have enough men to halt a serious Confederate move into the lower Valley by Lee, and he could not quickly evacuate the artillery and the supplies needed to feed so may soldiers. Schenck had set up an opportunity for Lee to capture a sizable force of Yankees while he cleared an invasion route to Pennsylvania.[4]

Lt. Gen. Richard S. Ewell moved Lee's Second Corps from Fredericksburg on June 4 to take Winchester. He sent one division under Maj. Gen. Robert E. Rodes to Berryville, east of town, where Milroy had posted a small brigade, while approaching Winchester from the south with the other two divisions. Jubal Early and Edward Johnson skirmished near the town on the evening of June 13, forcing Milroy to pull back into the three main forts. The Federal commander remained confident that his fortifications were strong enough to allow his men to hold out for at least five days, even though they were outnumbered.[5]

Brig. Gen. John B. Gordon's brigade of Early's division occupied Bowers Hill, just south of Fort Milroy, on the morning of June 14 and continued to skirmish for the rest of the day. Gordon was to occupy Milroy's attention while Early took his other three brigades on a wide flanking march to the west. Scouting reports and visual observations across the generally level landscape had allowed Ewell to determine that Milroy's forts were isolated and could be reduced one by one. West Fort was the most vulnerable. It was dominated by higher ground to the west called Little North Mountain. Early would need almost all day of June 14 to march ten miles with twenty guns. Johnson's division remained southeast of town, and Rodes's division approached Winchester from the east, following the evacuation of Berryville by Milroy's outpost. Early began his flank march at 11:00 A.M. as Confederate artillery fired from Bowers Hill and Gordon and Johnson sent out skirmishers.[6]

While Milroy prepared to retake Bowers Hill, Early's marching column was shielded from Federal view by Little North Mountain. At midafternoon the Confederates began to roll their guns up the shallow slope of the ridge, and Early deployed his infantry behind heavy timber three-quarters of a mile from West Fort. The artillery also used a low stone fence for added protection; the gunners tore out rocks to make embrasures for some of the pieces. When the artillery opened fire, officers saw the projectiles throw up chunks of dirt from the fort's parapet. Early used Brig. Gen. Harry T. Hays's Louisiana brigade as his strike force. The Confederate guns dominated the field as Hays deployed his men in two lines. After a forty-five-minute bombardment, he gave the order to advance at 5:00 P.M.[7]

West Fort was garrisoned by only one battery, one regiment, and a company from another regiment, all under Col. J. Warren Keifer. These units had little chance of holding off three veteran brigades of Lee's army. Only two Union guns managed to fire at Hays, and Keifer's infantry opened up at a range of 150 yards, just when the Louisianians hit a thin patch of abatis. Resistance melted quickly as Hays's men pushed through the abatis and ascended the parapet. The Federals also abandoned the smaller work to the north and its connecting infantry parapet. This smaller work held two guns and was three-quarters of a mile north of West Fort. Timber still stood fifty yards in front of the smaller work, and the slope to its rear was quite steep, making it difficult to evacuate the guns. Hays lost sixty-six men in taking this position, and Keifer lost fifty.[8]

As Keifer's command streamed back three-quarters of a mile to Fort Milroy and Star Fort, Early's guns advanced to the low ridge on which West Fort was located and began to bombard those two Union positions. His three brigades aligned on the guns and prepared to continue the attack the next day. Hays's men reversed West Fort and made connecting trenches to each side of the work that night. Dusk put an end to the fighting as Gordon's brigade began to dig a redoubt on Bowers Hill. Engineers marked the outline, and picks and shovels were issued. The Georgians worked until dawn.[9]

The fall of West Fort convinced Milroy that he could no longer hold the town. He had enough artillery ammunition left for only three more hours of firing, and a council of war advised evacuation. Since Gordon was so close on Bowers Hill, Milroy ordered all artillery and wagons left behind. The Federals spiked the guns and took all the ammunition they could carry and left at 1:00 A.M. on June 15. Ewell sent Johnson's division toward Stephenson's Depot, several miles north of Winchester, to cut off Milroy's retreat. A sharp battle was fought there at dawn on June 15—a confused, open field fight in which the poorly handled Union column barely managed to bypass Johnson's men. About 3,500 Federals were captured, while the rest escaped to Harpers Ferry and Bloody Run, Pennsylvania.[10]

Ewell's capture of Winchester opened an invasion route for Lee, nabbed a large haul of prisoners and guns, and demonstrated how a poorly fortified post could be quickly overcome with the right tactics. Ewell lost only 266 men in taking the town, but Milroy lost 4,443 (of whom 413 were killed and wounded), twenty-three guns, and 300 wagons. "I feel most miserable about it," Milroy confessed to his wife. "There is so much disappointment and anguish in my defeat and retreat from Winchester that it is painful for me to think of it and relate the facts to you." Milroy was beset by almost every disadvantage imaginable. He was outnumbered and outmaneuvered. His fortifications were inadequate against a force of three divisions, he had no outside help, and his men did not fight to hold West Fort. A board of inquiry, held to investigate the disaster, absolved Milroy of blame even though his lack of inspired leadership contributed to the failure. For their part, the Confederates celebrated a brilliant victory. Fort Milroy was renamed Fort Jackson, making it perhaps the fortification with the largest number of aliases in the Civil War.[11]

Lee started the rest of his army toward Pennsylvania at the same time that Winchester fell into Ewell's hands. By late June his eager veterans were crossing the Potomac River, traversing western Maryland, and entering the state. The North was aflame with anxiety and uncertainty. Lee's exact target was unknown, and the authorities and the public alike scrambled to prepare for any eventuality.

Pittsburgh and Harrisburg

Pittsburgh was the first to feel the grip of fear, despite its distance from the theater of war. Already known as the Iron City, it produced 15 percent of the Union's cannon and 80 percent of its heavy guns. Reports that Confederate guerrillas might raid southwestern Pennsylvania from western Virginia sparked efforts to defend the place. The Department of the Monongahela, with headquarters at Pittsburgh, was created on June 9, 1863, to be headed by Brig. Gen. William T. H. Brooks. Brooks found only one militia regiment and a battery with no guns, but the engineers sent Capt. William P. Craighill to help fortify the city. Brooks called a public meeting for June 14, the day Early captured West Fort at Winchester. Here he asked the citizens for up to 5,000 volunteers. Business leaders agreed to provide their employees as laborers to build the works and pay their salaries while they were doing it, if the government agreed to provide them a subsidy of $1.25 per man each day.

Brooks readily agreed, and more than 2,000 men gathered for work on June 15. They broke ground at three places around Pittsburgh, and many other sites were opened during the next few days. A wide variety of people worked on the fortifications: industrial workers, tobacconists, photographers, carters, stonecutters, and students of the Iron City Business College, Jefferson College, and Duff's College. The city's free blacks offered their help; at first it was rejected, but then the authorities allowed them to participate. All told, more than 11,000 people helped build the defenses of Pittsburgh. They were still working on July 2 when the temperature reached 111 degrees and the battle of Gettysburg was in full swing. Brooks hired boys to haul water to the workers.

A surviving time-and-pay book for laborers who built one redoubt, called Fort Mechanic on Coal Hill, shows that it was begun on June 15. A total of 121 workers spent a week building it, and they received $699.20 for their time. The water boys were paid seventy-five cents per day.

News of the battle of Gettysburg cooled the ardor in Pittsburgh, so the extensive ring of fortifications was never completed. Only one fort was ever garrisoned, and it is doubtful if any were armed; but the defenses of the city were impressive. They totaled sixteen redoubts, sixteen batteries, and one work large enough to be termed a fort. About twelve miles of defenses circled the city. Superb postwar photographs show the works to have been well made and very well sited on the high ground that surrounded Pittsburgh. The threat of cavalry raids had sparked the building frenzy, yet Craighill planned and the citizens executed a defensive arrangement that was designed to protect Pittsburgh against a major threat, such as Lee's army. But the Confederate commander gave no indication of contemplating such an absurd plan as moving his army through the mountains of northern Appalachia to attack this important but isolated city. Such a move would have endangered his own men more than Pittsburgh. As it were, the well-made forts served as monuments to the war for decades to come, until most fell prey to urban expansion.[12]

Harrisburg, on the other hand, had plenty of reason to worry. The state capital, located on the Susquehanna River in south central Pennsylvania, was vulnerable to a strike from Virginia and Maryland. South Mountain, the continuation of Virginia's Blue Ridge north of the Potomac, curved north and east directly toward the city, while Cumberland Valley, just to the north of South Mountain, offered a ready-made avenue of invasion for Lee. The Confederates apparently intended to capture or at least threaten Harrisburg, and the citizens went into a frenzy of digging to protect their homes.

The city lay on the east bank of the Susquehanna, which greatly aided its defense, but a good ford and two bridges offered easy access across the stream. In September 1862, Army engineers had recommended that defenses be constructed in response to Lee's invasion of Maryland, but the plan was never implemented. It called for eight redans and a connecting line of infantry trenches, built in a four-mile-long semicircle, to cover all approaches to the river crossings. The plan also called for a large redoubt inside the semicircle. Lee's approach prompted action in 1863. As in Pittsburgh, a public meeting was held during which 1,000 volunteers were summoned. The 1862 plan was utilized, and a huge work called Fort Washington was started on Hummel Hill, also known as Bridgeport Heights. John H. Wilson, a Pennsylvania Railroad engineer, helped Capt. Richard I. Dodge of the 8th U.S. Infantry lay out the fort on June 15. Although shale made the digging difficult, as many as 600 volunteers nearly finished it by June 20. Fort Washington encompassed sixty acres within its semicircular configuration, its rear facing the river. Abatis was placed before it on the slopes of Hummel Hill, artillery emplacements were built, and a military road was cut up the hill to its rear. A telegraph line also was stretched up the hill to the fort. The remnants of the work show a deep, wide ditch in front of large parapets, and there are ample supplies of the gritty shale that made up the substance of the hill.

Dodge and Wilson also laid out Fort Couch on top of Hummel Hill, half a mile in front of Fort Washington. The hill actually is a long, commanding ridge running lengthwise along the valley. Designed by Maj. James Brady of a Pennsylvania artillery regiment, Fort Couch was built to deny the Rebels access to the ridgetop and thus was a support and protection for Fort Washington. Its remnants include a large and wide parapet laid out in a zigzag configuration. Open to the rear, it is much smaller than Fort Washington; perhaps it was designed to be more extensive but was never finished. In addition to Fort Couch, several smaller earthworks were built at different locations along the route of the Cumberland Valley Railroad west of Harrisburg and along the Susquehanna River. A number of infantry and artillery officers thought the defenses were weak due to the loose shale that made up the parapets, which they feared would fly through the air when hit with projectiles, but Harrisburg was well fortified despite that possible danger.[13]

Gettysburg

The Harrisburg defenses were almost tested in battle. The vanguard of Ewell's corps approached within two miles of Fort Washington on June 29, when Lee ordered his army to concentrate in the general vicinity of Gettysburg. Two days later, fighting broke out west of that town, forcing the generals to accept battle where neither had planned it. Maj. Gen. George G. Meade, who replaced Hooker on June 28, devised a contingency plan based on fortifying a strong position that blocked Lee's path to Washington, D.C., and Baltimore. That plan was nullified by the developing battle at Gettysburg, but it was a sound approach to dealing with the Confederate threat.

On the evening of June 28, Meade began moving the Army of the Potomac from its bivouac near Frederick, Maryland. He established an extended position near Emmitsburg, Taneytown, Union Mills, and Westminster so as to block Lee's possible moves south and east. The First Corps probed toward Gettysburg on June 30, hoping to determine more accurately where the Confederates were located. That same day Lee's cavalry under Stuart rode through Meade's scattered position, passing Union Mills on its way to join Lee at Gettysburg. The next day, July 1, fighting started at that crossroads town.

Also on July 1, Meade issued a directive to establish what became known as the Pipe Creek Line. The directive became irrelevant a few hours later when the scale of the fighting and the need to consolidate the army at Gettysburg became clear. Meade's engineers had scouted the location of the line the day before, enlisting the aid of local resident Peter Koons. A Union sympathizer, Koons told the officers everything he knew of the local topography and promised not to reveal to anyone what they were doing. The line was laid out along the south bank of Big Pipe Creek, which started west of Manchester and flowed westerly past Union Mills. The creek then veered southwest between Taneytown and Middleburg to join Little Pipe Creek. Now named Double Pipe Creek, the stream continued westward to the Monocacy River. The line was to stretch from the origin of Big Pipe Creek for nearly twelve miles, almost to Middleburg. Union Mills would be just to the right of the line's center. The creek valley was narrow and bordered by hills on what would be Meade's right, upstream from Union Mills, but it was wide and flat downstream from that tiny community. The terrain on both sides consisted of "high sloping wooded hills" about 100 to 200 feet above water level. These constituted superb positions for infantry and artillery. Baltimore was thirty-two miles to the southeast, and Washington, D.C., was about fifty miles due south.[14]

The earthworks were never dug because developments at Gettysburg turned everyone's attention to the north. Meade was compelled to send Second Corps commander Winfield S. Hancock with authority to decide whether to stay and fight or fall back to Pipe Creek. Hancock arrived at 4:00 P.M. on July 1 and decided the army must concentrate at Gettysburg. Meade then ordered it done. By dawn of July 2, all units of the Army of the Potomac had left Pipe Creek except the Sixth Corps, and it would soon set out as well. Meade continued to view Pipe Creek as a possible fall-back position during the battle. When he asked a council of war on the night of July 2 whether the army should remain at Gettysburg or retire, he had the Pipe Creek position in mind. Fortunately, there was little desire on anyone's part to give up the good ground at Gettysburg. Because it remained unfortified and untested, the Pipe Creek position was obscure in the minds of observers and historians of the campaign. Brig. Gen. Henry J. Hunt, Meade's artillery chief, had thoroughly inspected it on the morning of July 1 and believed it was a better position than the one assumed at Gettysburg. But First Corps division commander Maj. Gen. Abner Doubleday had little faith in Lee's willingness to follow Meade's plan. He thought that Lee probably would have avoided the Pipe Creek Line by leaving one corps to occupy the Federals while he used the other two to attack Harrisburg, perhaps even to strike at Philadelphia.[15]

Whether Meade's position at Pipe Creek would have been stronger than the hills and ridges outside Gettysburg will never be known. Gettysburg was an encounter battle, initiated without plan by either commander but taken advantage of by both to concentrate their respective armies and accept the flow of events. Lee brought two of his corps to the battlefield, Hill's west of town and Ewell's north of town, while the Federals pitted their First Corps under Maj. Gen. John Reynolds against Hill and Howard's Eleventh Corps against Ewell.

The fighting on July 1 was grand and bitter, and there was little time for even hasty fortifications. Many First Corps units literally deployed from marching column into battle line while loading their rifle muskets on the run. Reynolds was killed early in the engagement, and his successor, Doubleday, ordered Brig. Gen. John C. Robinson's division into reserve on Seminary Ridge. Doubleday instructed Robinson to build "some slight entrenchments." Brig. Gen. Gabriel R. Paul's brigade dismantled fences and used the rails to create a semicircular line covering the west side of the Lutheran Seminary building. The First Corps line was soon advanced to McPherson's Ridge 400 yards forward, but the breastwork would come into play as a defensive position later that day.[16]

Meanwhile, elements of the First Corps tangled with Brig. Gen. Joseph R. Davis's Mississippi and North Carolina brigade of Heth's division in and around one of three cuts of an unfinished railroad grade that paralleled Chambersburg Pike, the major artery entering Gettysburg from the west. Brig. Gen. Lysander Cutler positioned three regiments to the right of this cut, but they were outflanked by Davis's advance. Ordered to retire, two of the regiments managed to do so in orderly fashion, but the leftmost unit, the 147th New York, stayed on the field due to a mix-up of orders. It finally had to retreat, and part of the regiment fled across the cut to the south side of Chambersburg Pike as Davis's men took position in and near the excavation.

Three fresh regiments, led by the 6th Wisconsin of Brig. Gen. Solomon Meredith's Iron Brigade and Cutler's 14th Brooklyn and 95th New York, counterattacked the Rebels. It was a magnificent advance across a long stretch of open ground. The Wisconsin regiment lost 160 men but managed to close on the waiting Confederates. Davis's men found that this civilian feature, like that at Second Bull Run and Antietam, was at best an imperfect fortification. A. L. P. Vairin of the 2nd Mississippi recalled that "our men thought [the cut] would prove a good breastwork but it was too deep." They could not see, much less fire, over the top of it. What seemed at first like a good shelter turned into a trap. "I did not go into the cut, seeing its danger," recalled Vairin, "and cautioned all I could to get out by the right flank." Davis's position collapsed as the 6th Wisconsin alone captured 232 Confederates.[17]

The Federals reconstructed their position near the railroad cut but later evacuated it when Ewell's corps arrived on the battlefield north of Gettysburg. Ewell's artillery enfiladed Cutler and the other Yankee regiments, so they fell back. Cutler's 56th Pennsylvania, along with the 76th and the 147th New York, took up several positions during the day on and near Oak Ridge, the continuation of Seminary Ridge north of Chambersburg Pike. At the first of these locations they built a slight breastwork of fence rails. Col. J. William Hofmann of the 56th Pennsylvania commented that he had seen Confederates at Antietam who had "picked up rails and fought very stubbornly behind them," so he encouraged other regimental commanders to do the same. Soon after, Brig. Gen. Alfred Iverson's North Carolina brigade of Ewell's corps attacked. Its extreme right faced Cutler's left, but Brig. Gen. Henry Baxter's brigade, to Cutler's right, did most of the work of ripping apart Iverson's ranks and decisively stopping this Confederate advance.[18]

Maj. Gen. Oliver O. Howard's Eleventh Corps moved through Gettysburg to confront Ewell's veterans north of town. These unlucky victims of Jackson's flank attack at Chancellorsville had no well-defined terrain features to use as natural fortifications. Brig. Gen. Francis C. Barlow's division occupied Blocher's Knoll, the only high ground conveniently situated, yet it is clear that no one in the corps had the time or inclination to construct fieldworks of any kind. After the war, Capt. Alfred Lee of the 82nd Ohio explained that this lack of attention contributed to the crushing defeat suffered by the corps. Barlow's position was outflanked and overrun, and the corps suffered a fiasco that was nearly as bad as that of May 2.[19]

The final action on July 1 involved a fierce struggle for the position partly shielded by Paul's breastwork around the Lutheran Seminary building. The Federals were forced to fall back to this position because Heth's division had pushed them off McPherson Ridge in heavy fighting. Maj. Gen. William D. Pender's division replaced Heth's exhausted men. The semicircular breastwork did not cover the entire 700 yards of the First Corps line on Seminary Ridge. It was only two feet tall, and the ends connected with a stone fence that stretched along the top of the low ridge for about 200 yards south of Chambersburg Pike. The Iron Brigade and Col. Chapman Biddle's brigade, both worsted in the fight for McPherson Ridge, held the breastwork with tenacity when Pender advanced. The left wing of Col. Abner Perrin's South Carolina brigade and the right wing of Brig. Gen. Alfred M. Scales's North Carolina brigade fronted the fieldwork. Scales's line was raked by fire from a cluster of Federal guns north of the seminary building, but Perrin managed to break the Federals through inspired leadership. He detected a weakly held segment of the Union line just south of the breastwork. Advancing the 14th South Carolina to Biddle's front to hold his attention, he ordered the 1st South Carolina to advance laterally toward that spot. The Carolinians smashed through, and the position collapsed, sending the First Corps streaming to the high ground south of Gettysburg.[20]

It is not surprising that the Confederates, since they were on the offensive, paid no attention to constructing breastworks on July 1. Rather than fortifying, their pioneers spent the day on other duties. Thomas Bailey of the 47th North Carolina in Pettigrew's brigade had been assigned to the pioneer corps of Heth's division on June 10 and was given "a very sorry spade." The corps stayed one and a half miles from the battlefield on July 1, moving on to bury the dead that evening. Then it picked up abandoned arms and equipment the next day when the fighting resumed.[21]

While it is understandable that so little fortifying was done on July 1, there were no excuses on July 2. Even though the fighting did not start until the evening, very few units on either side dug in. Only the Twelfth Corps and some regiments of the First Corps took advantage of the lull to construct earthworks on Culp's Hill, the anchor of the Union right. Eight hundred yards southwest of Culp's Hill lay Cemetery Hill, with Stevens's Knoll between. Culp's Hill has two crests, one much lower than the other, with a saddle between the two. While the west and south slopes are gentle, the north and east slopes of both crests are quite steep and rocky. Those slopes were effective obstacles to an attacking enemy.

The Twelfth Corps and elements of the First Corps dug in here on the evening of July 1. The 6th Wisconsin of the Iron Brigade had twelve spades and shovels, quite a lot in comparison with many Civil War regiments. Lt. Col. Rufus R. Dawes told his men to dig in, and they did it "with great energy. A man would dig with all his strength till out of breath, when another would seize the spade and push on the work. There were no orders to construct these breastworks, but the situation plainly dictated their necessity."

The Iron Brigade line ran along the north slope of Culp's Hill from Stevens's Knoll. It was placed on the military crest a few feet forward of the natural crest. The line incorporated rocky outcroppings whenever possible, even angling back to the natural crest to do so. Two gaps in the line resulted from hasty construction. A small opening three feet wide existed between the left of the 6th Wisconsin and the right of the 2nd Wisconsin, and a gap of forty yards lay between the left of the 2nd Wisconsin and the right of the 7th Wisconsin. The latter hole was less dangerous than it appears, for the 7th was positioned forty yards behind the line of the 2nd. The parapets consisted of logs, fence rails, rocks, and earth. The dirt came from a trench, for there is little evidence that a ditch existed. Photographs taken the following November show that some units used posts stuck in the parapet to support the logs and rails.[22]

The Twelfth Corps works, to the right of the Iron Brigade, were constructed in a similar manner. Logs and rocks were the main components of the parapets. In fact, in a photograph taken about July 15, 1863, one section of the line appears to have no trench or ditch and no earth on the parapet. Some units took apart a nearby stack of firewood to revet the works. Several Twelfth Corps regiments also added headlogs to their parapets. They raised the log above the work to create slits through which they could fire their rifle

Federal fieldworks on Culp's Hill, Gettysburg. Taken about July 15, 1863, this is a view of works built by the 102nd New York of Greene's brigade. Note the absence of a trench or of dirt on the parapet. In places, it appears that the fieldworks of the Twelfth Corps were simply rock, timber, and rail breastworks. (Massachusetts Commandery, Military Order of the Loyal Legion and the U.S. Army Military History Institute)

muskets, duplicating the type of protection at least one Twelfth Corps regiment erected on Hooker's fortified bridgehead at Chancellorsville. All of this construction was done in about four hours of hard labor; the men often used cups, plates, and bayonets to compensate for the shortage of entrenching tools.

Since these works played a significant role when the Confederates attacked Culp's Hill on July 2, there was lot of postwar argument about who deserved credit for them. Maj. Gen. Henry W. Slocum, commander of the Twelfth Corps; division leader Brig. Gen. Alpheus S. Williams; and brigade leader Brig. Gen. George S. Greene were all credited with the idea. It also appears that John W. Geary left the option of fortifying up to his brigade leaders. Geary was said to have remarked that he did not like the idea personally, as he thought it might dull the offensive spirit of the men, but Greene disagreed and dug in anyway. Williams later wrote his daughter that he ordered his division to build works, for he had "experienced their benefits at Chancellorsville." It seemed "almost absurd" to do so, given the rough nature of the slope in front of his men. "Still, though ridiculous the work, we were there, and our men had learned to love entrenching with logs. So at it they went and in a couple of hours had covered themselves with a good, substantial breastwork."

It made little difference who was credited for initiating the fieldworks at Culp's Hill, for all signs pointed to their construction. The Iron Brigade was already fortifying its line before the Twelfth Corps began. Slocum's men had ample experience with earthworks at Chancellorsville, so it would have been surprising if they had lolled about on the hill all evening doing nothing.[23]

On Stevens's Knoll the 5th Maine Battery was protected by small lunettes consisting of semicircular parapets. Similar works shielded the artillery on Cemetery Hill. Capt. Michael Wiedrich's Battery I, 1st New York Light Artillery, made low, semicircular parapets. These did not interfere with the traversing of the muzzle but offered little protection for the gunners. No additional construction of artillery defenses took place after Capt. R. Bruce Ricketts's Batteries F and G, 1st Pennsylvania Light Artillery, arrived on Cemetery Hill at 4:30 P.M.

At the very least, small earthworks helped to shield the artillery on Cemetery Hill during the fighting of July 2, and they probably were improved the next day. A photograph taken about July 12, 1863, of the eastern side of the hill shows much more elaborate works for Lt. James Stewart's Battery B, 4th U.S. Artillery. It had three guns on the north side of Baltimore Pike and one on the south side. The photograph shows substantial log revetments supporting the stone and earth parapets. There was one such work, wrapping around three sides but open to the rear, for each gun.

While the artillery on Cemetery Hill was at least partially protected, the infantry manning this sector of Meade's line was not. Eleventh Corps units simply relied on existing stone fences along the bottom of the eastern and northern slopes. These fences were only a couple of feet high and thus offered scant protection, but they provided a ready-made line of demarcation for the battle and were better than nothing. Why the Eleventh Corps did not follow the example of its sister corps to the right and dig in is unknown. Its experience at Chancellorsville and on July 1 should have been a guide.[24]

The Second Corps did not dig in on Cemetery Ridge, mostly because flinty rock just below the surface made it difficult to do so. A low stone fence offered some protection for infantry and artillery alike. The Third Corps, responsible for holding the southern end of Cemetery Ridge, not only failed to dig in but advanced its line without authorization from Meade. Corps commander Maj. Gen. Daniel Sickles liked the lay of the land some distance ahead, where Sherfy's Peach Orchard occupied some of the highest ground in the valley between Cemetery and Seminary ridges, rather than the ever-lowering crest of Cemetery Ridge. It meant his Third Corps formed a salient rather than a straight line, and salients are always vulnerable to concerted attacks from different directions. Moreover, Sickles now had too few men to occupy Little Round Top and Big Round Top at the southern end of Cemetery Ridge, which should have been the anchor of the Union left. Sickles did not have time to dig in even if he had been inclined to do so.

The Confederates did even less fortifying on July 2. Col. David Lang's Florida brigade of Maj. Gen. Richard H. Anderson's division, Hill's Third Corps, took position behind a low stone fence on the crest of Seminary Ridge, "which our men improved with rails & dirt which protected us from stray balls and shells." Fully intending to drive the Yankees from their position, no other Confederates seem to have constructed fieldworks of any kind that day.[25]

The Rebel offensive on the evening of July 2 was a powerful thrust. Longstreet threw two divisions against the Union left. Vicious fighting led to the capture of Sherfy's Peach Orchard, the Wheatfield, and Devil's Den. The latter was a relatively small area of jumbled boulders eroded from the end of a granite outcropping known as Houck's Ridge, at the foot of Little Round Top. A relatively steep slope and a low stone fence at the military crest offered the Federals some terrain advantages, but they were overcome by the ferocity of the Rebel attack. Another stone fence at the edge of the Wheatfield also offered a slight advantage to Sickles's troops, but the Confederates overcame that edge with determined fighting. Possession of the Round Tops proved to be the key to this part of the battle. Sickles's men held the Rebels off long enough for some Fifth Corps units to occupy the smaller hill just before Law's brigade of Hood's division struck it. Law's Alabamians crossed the large hill unopposed but were stopped by Col. Strong Vincent's brigade, which held Little Round Top against not only Law's men but Brig. Gen. Jerome B. Robertson's Texas and Arkansas brigade.[26]

Anderson's division cooperated with Longstreet by attacking the Federal center on Cemetery Ridge. Ambrose R. Wright's Georgia brigade initially hit the 15th Massachusetts and 82nd New York, which were in position along Emmitsburg Road some 200 yards in front of the Union line. The two regiments hastily threw together a breastwork. Some men yelled out, " 'Put those two fences into one,' " meaning the post-and-rail fences that lined both sides of the road. Regimental commander Col. George H. Ward also told them to gather rails from a fence to the rear. The Massachusetts men responded with a desperate energy. Pvt. Roland E. Bowen made two trips to the rail fence, which was easy to dismantle, but the two post-and-rail fences were another matter. The ends of the rails were firmly wedged into holes in the posts, making the stoutest fence used in nineteenth-century America. "We tried to break it down with our boot heels," recalled Bowen; "we tried the breech of our muskets. We tryed to shove them one way or the other so as to get out one end, but we could neither do the one thing nor the others. Then we formed parties of 5 or 6 all seizing the rail in the center. . . . We all pulled together and with a loud crack, out she would come." With the few rails they were able to pry loose, the Yankees made what Bowen exaggerated as "quite a formidable breast work, almost bullet proof," that was two feet high. All this did little good. Wright's Georgians outnumbered the two regiments, which fired a few rounds then fell back. Other Federal troops stopped Wright at the ridge.[27]

On the Union right, Ewell's corps struck Cemetery Hill and Culp's Hill. At the former, the Union artillery and infantry held firm even though Rebel attacks forced several units back up the slope. Farther to the right, the Twelfth Corps made good use of its fieldworks. Confederate attacks captured the lower crest and forced the Federals back some distance, but Slocum's line held firm. The Yankees were helped by a fortuitous circumstance. When Geary's division occupied the upper crest, it refused its right flank a bit in the saddle. Later, when Williams's division extended the line to the right, this short refused line became a traverse. When Williams's men were driven from the lower crest, the traverse came into play as a ready-made protection for Geary's right flank, which helped the Federals to limit the Rebel penetration.[28]

After about three hours of fighting, both sides were more inclined to fortify on the night of July 2. On the Confederate right, rock barricades sprang up in Devil's Den. The 4th Alabama built such a work facing Big Round Top on the morning of July 3, and the 4th and 5th Texas followed its example. Available stone fences were used and improved as defensive features by other Rebel units in this sector over the course of July 3, as both sides remained inert for the rest of the battle.[29]

On the Union left, opposite this activity, the Federals were even more interested in finding some protection. Brig. Gen. John C. Caldwell's division piled up rails and threw some dirt over them during the night of July 2 and the morning of July 3. On the Round Tops, with their enormous granite outcroppings, it was only possible to pile up stone breastworks. Brig. Gen. Henry L. Benning, commander of a Georgia brigade in Hood's division, could hear the clink of rocks dropping into place on the hills. Photographs taken within two weeks of the battle accurately depict what these works looked like during the latter stage of the battle. They are low in profile and often

Rock breastworks on Little Round Top, Gettysburg. This photograph, taken on July 6, 1863, shows the Federal breastwork on the south side of the crest. Note how the Federals have incorporated a large rock outcropping as a salient. (Massachusetts Commandery, Military Order of the Loyal Legion and the U.S. Army Military History Institute)

swerve to incorporate large rocks into the parapet. One such boulder forms the apex of a V in the line, and several short breastworks are located a few yards behind one another as the battle line became bunched on the hillside. These breastworks on the Round Tops have quirky angles and took advantage of anything in the rocky ground to enhance their strength.[30]

The fighting on July 3 started with a flurry of action on the Union right. Ewell's men resumed their attacks soon after dawn, in an attempt to widen the bulge they had created in the Twelfth Corps line. Three attempts failed, and a Union counterattack reclaimed the works on the lower crest of Culp's Hill by midmorning.

Besides that, Confederate efforts were concentrated on a massive strike against the center along Cemetery Ridge, preceded by a huge artillery bombardment. Pickett's division of Longstreet's corps, Heth's division (commanded by Brig. Gen. James Johnston Pettigrew), and two brigades of

Pender's division (commanded by Maj. Gen. Isaac R. Trimble) made up the attacking force, about 12,000 men. Some Confederate units built slight breastworks, often with shallow trenches, to shelter themselves from the rain of shells to come in the bombardment. Lang's Florida brigade did this, using rails and dirt scratched out by bayonets, when it and another brigade were positioned in the valley to support the Confederate line of artillery.

Roughly 6,000 Federals held the center of the Union line where these Confederates were to strike. As already noted, the ground was too rocky for extensive earthwork construction. Moreover, Brig. Gen. Alexander S. Webb's brigade of the Second Corps, which held the angle in the stone fence near the copse of trees, had no entrenching tools. Col. Norman J. Hall's brigade, to Webb's left, had one shovel. Hall's men found enough topsoil to dig a trench 200 yards long, connecting the southern end of the stone fence with a wooden fence farther south. An observer called it "a large cart rut" no more than a foot deep. The dirt was piled on fence rails to make a parapet one foot high. Brig. Gen. William Harrow's brigade, to Hall's left, shared this meager fortification.

Farther to the left, the 14th Vermont, 80th New York, and 151st Pennsylvania effectively used breastworks made of fence rails as shelter during the bombardment. Some Federal artillery units also had modest protection. While the Eleventh Corps gunners on Cemetery Hill could not dig in, due to the graves of the cemetery, several batteries under Maj. Freeman McGilvery to the left of the point of attack had a parapet of dirt-covered rails 380 yards long and 2 feet tall.[31]

Thus three forms of fieldworks were used in the July 3 fight: the employment of existing civilian features, earthworks, and breastworks, all concentrated on a narrow sector of the battlefield. The artillery bombardment, which started at 1:00 P.M. and lasted one hour, was unprecedented in scope, but it failed to prepare the way for the infantry. Pickett, Pettigrew, and Trimble launched one of the most famous assaults in American history. The open, ascending terrain allowed their men to become good targets. Pettigrew and Trimble, especially, had difficulty dealing with the stout post-and-rail fences along Emmitsburg Road, still largely intact on the left wing of the Rebel force. The road was about 175 yards from the waiting Yankees, who opened fire when the Confederates were struggling over the fences. The effect of the fire and the disruption caused by the fences threw formations into disarray, and only fragments of Pettigrew's and Trimble's commands ventured beyond Emmitsburg Road. Some managed to get within a few yards of the stone fence but failed to penetrate the Union position. Pickett's division had an easier time, for most of the fences had already been torn

Confederate breastworks on Seminary Ridge, Gettysburg. A well-publicized photograph of Confederate prisoners taken about July 15, 1863. It shows a Confederate breastwork made of building timbers and rails, and some dirt appears to have been thrown in front and on top of the pile on the far left. (Library of Congress)

down during the fight of July 2. But Pickett's men stopped and massed in front of the stone fence, which offered an irresistible line of demarcation between the two armies and provided some shelter for the exposed Confederates. Flanking fire and fierce resistance doomed the attack, and Pickett's men had to retire. Although slight, the fortifications played a significant role in enabling the Federals to hold on. Many Yankees gave credit to the fences as well. "We saw the fences and knew their alignment would be broken," remembered Color Sgt. John M. Dunn of the 1st Delaware. "Once the touch of elbow was gone the confidence of the charge was destroyed." Many members of the Second Corps repeatedly yelled "Fredericksburg!" while firing at the Rebels.[32]

Lee gave up the fight after this bloody repulse, and the armies remained quiet for some time. Much of the Confederate position along Seminary Ridge was fortified, to a degree, now that offensive action had been canceled. Robert E. Rodes's division of Ewell's corps erected works on the morning of July 4. Just north of the unfinished railroad cut northwest of town, faint remnants of his earthwork show that it was placed forward of the natural crest of the shallow ridge, here called Oak Ridge, allowing for a good field of fire for about fifty yards before the profile of the ridge sloped sharply downward. The line, however, offered a wonderful view of the flatter land that Gettysburg occupied. Rodes built a log-and-rail breastwork to the south of Chambersburg Pike on the grounds of the Lutheran Seminary. A photograph taken about July 15 depicts three captured Confederates standing before this work. It is probably the best photographic depiction of a Civil War breastwork. The work consisted of timbers taken from a building, lumber, and rails and was about waist high. Farther south along Seminary Ridge, the Confederates built rock parapets for their artillery emplacements. These were low and offered little protection.[33]

Williamsport and Falling Waters

Although these defensive works were slight, Meade did not intend to test them. He felt the Confederates were trying to trick him, "expecting that, flushed with success, I would attack them when they would play their old game of shooting us from behind breastworks—a game we played this time to their entire satisfaction." Instead, Lee's army pulled away from Gettysburg on the evening of July 4 and began its retreat to Virginia. Hampered by heavy rains and Union cavalry, the Confederates faced the swollen Potomac River and were forced to wait until it subsided. Engineer officers and division pioneers worked hard to prepare the crossings. Planks were hauled to a point near Williamsport opposite the mouth of a stream called Falling Waters, one of the crossing places. Pontoon boats were constructed at Williamsport and floated downstream; a total of twenty-three were assembled at Falling Waters to make a bridge more than 500 feet long. Boxes filled with stones anchored the boats firmly in the rolling current. The pioneers also constructed a dirt causeway across the Baltimore and Ohio Canal, which ran along the bottomland, and dug an approach to the pontoon bridge. The crossing was ready by July 13 when the pioneers dug some small artillery emplacements along the approach road a couple of miles inland from the bridge.[34]

While this feverish activity was taking place, the rest of Lee's army prepared to defend the bridgehead. There was already a small Union work at Williamsport, the largest town along this stretch of the Potomac. It had been built by Abner Doubleday in 1861 on a bluff overlooking both the river and

Gettysburg and Lee's Pennsylvania Campaign 233

the canal, and it consisted of three artillery emplacements with good traverses. But of course it was designed to cover the river crossing and fire on Virginia. Lee needed a lengthy fieldwork, facing east, to protect two crossing points of the river south of Williamsport. He sent his chief engineer, Col. William Proctor Smith; several subordinate engineer officers; and Edward Porter Alexander to select a location for this work on July 7. The group scouted for three days. "There was no very well defined & naturally strong line," Alexander remembered, and "we had to pick & choose, & string together in some places by make-shifts & some 'little work.'" At one point Alexander and the engineers argued about one of these points, and Lee settled the matter in Alexander's favor.[35]

The group was aided by many other officers. On July 8 the three corps commanders and their staff members joined Lee in scouting the terrain. Part of the group continued scouting on the morning of July 9, but by noon the commanders had seen enough and left the work to the engineers and to Alexander. On July 11, with the ground decided upon, Ewell and his three division commanders accompanied the corps topographer, Capt. Jedediah Hotchkiss, to minutely inspect their section of the line. The various units were assigned their places and began to dig in. The Second Corps held the left; the Third Corps, the center; and the First Corps, the right. The works were in good shape by July 12, when it became obvious that the Federals opposite were digging in as well.[36]

The Confederate line followed the crest of some ridges only fifteen to thirty feet high. In places they offered good, sloping fields of fire, but the ridges were irregular, with breaks and rocky outcroppings. The defensive position needed good works, placed far enough from the river to prevent Union artillery from firing on the two crossings. "Picks & shovels seem to be the order of this day," commented Capt. Charles E. Waddell of the 12th Virginia on July 11. His men improved their works on July 13 by cutting trees for abatis in a drizzly rain while the pickets continually skirmished.[37]

The men had a very good attitude toward the digging. The heavy losses and failed attacks at Gettysburg, and their desperate situation north of the swollen Potomac, created a willingness to seek all the protection they could find. They also hoped the Federals would attack. Lee was more than normally concerned about the strength of his position, and he asked Alexander many questions in a "very personal & confidential mood" until he was satisfied that all was being done correctly. Lee seemed "to take satisfaction in the confidence I felt that we could hold them," Alexander proudly remembered.

Unfortunately, there are no easily accessible remnants of Lee's line at Williamsport to allow us to gauge its design and sophistication. The weak points received special attention from Alexander and those units responsible for holding them. Alexander considered the village of Downesville to be "the key point of our right flank," and he assumed Meade would concentrate his efforts there. Thus Alexander posted a heavy force of guns at Downesville and on the nearby campus of St. James College. He also planned to use the college buildings as blockhouses if necessary. A painting of an unidentified section of Lee's line, done by an anonymous artist, shows two lines of infantry trench, with the forward line reinforced by several traverses designed to protect artillery. There are a number of one-gun emplacements with semicircular parapets.[38]

Lee's Williamsport line was essentially a fortified bridgehead, although it was not configured in the traditional design of a semicircle with both flanks resting on the river. Instead, the line was constructed as a nine-mile-long fieldwork in open ground, but it effectively covered the crossings of the Potomac River. Meade was very impressed by these works and hesitated to attack. His corps commanders agreed. In fact, few members of the Army of the Potomac had any heart for assaulting the line. Capt. Henry L. Abbott of the 20th Massachusetts wrote that it was "the unanimous opinion of every officer I heard, that an attack on those works, built high of logs and earth, with wide open sweeps in front, would have been certain defeat, even if held by a third of our own force."[39]

So the Federals dug in opposite Lee, while Meade tried to devise a plan to pry the Rebels out of their stronghold. The Yankees selected ridges similar to those upon which the Confederates dug, and they used logs and rails as the base of their parapets. The picket line and the artillery also were fortified. While the vast majority of Meade's men dug without complaint, Capt. Francis A. Donaldson of the 118th Pennsylvania disapproved of fortifying just now. He thought it would make the men "timid." With the general impression that the Confederate army was crippled, he thought the proper course was to cross the Potomac elsewhere and cut Lee's line of communications.[40]

But Donaldson ignored the fact that the swollen river was a barrier to the Federals as well as to the Confederates. The water receded enough so that Lee began to ferry some of his wagons over the stream on July 12. The engineers finished the pontoon bridge at Falling Waters the next day, and the artillery began to cross at dusk; the infantry started moving in the middle of the night. The First and Third Corps crossed the pontoon bridge, but the Second Corps forded at Williamsport. These movements were made without the knowledge of the Federals. Meade had earlier decided to conduct a reconnaissance in force, to involve a division from each of four corps, at 7:00 A.M. on July 14. Word of the Rebel withdrawal reached his headquarters barely a half-hour before the start of this movement, so Meade ordered the whole army forward at 8:30 A.M. The Federals found nothing but empty and thoroughly muddy trenches, for it had rained heavily the night before. Nevertheless, everyone was impressed with Lee's line. "It is a strong position," noted an officer of the 80th New York.[41]

Heth's division covered Lee's crossing that morning. It aligned itself two miles from the pontoon bridge, where six small artillery emplacements had been dug along the road, but there were no guns to fill the works. Heth's men were surprised by Federal cavalry and had to conduct a fighting retreat to the bridge. They lost several hundred prisoners but cut the bridge before the Yankees could force a passage. Lee's men were finally on Confederate soil, and the Pennsylvania campaign was over.[42]

Previous patterns associated with the use of field fortifications continued with the battle of Gettysburg. Lee wanted to maintain his grip on the tactical offensive and refused to close his options by ordering earthworks constructed, and the Federals seem to have been content with occupying the high ground and waiting to see what happened. Only the Twelfth Corps and a few units of the First Corps dug in before they were engaged. Only after heavy fighting did the rest of both armies follow their example and try to fortify. In some cases they had little material to work with except rocks, but the desire to find protection led them to build whatever they could. The Federal line had some sort of fieldwork along nearly its entire length by dawn of July 3, and Lee's army had at least the semblance of fieldworks along most of its line by the next day. None of these defenses were extraordinary except for the headlogs on the Twelfth Corps front and the intricacy of the lines of rock breastworks on the Round Tops. Gettysburg saw relatively extensive use of protection, compared with Second Manassas and Antietam. Historians have estimated that there were twenty-five miles of stone fencing on the battlefield and that more than three-quarters of it was used as protection by various units.[43]

In the immediate aftermath of Gettysburg, few men in Lee's or Meade's armies were ashamed of seeking cover on the battlefield. Their actions at Williamsport prove this. J. J. Renfroe, a chaplain in the 10th Alabama of Wilcox's brigade, was the odd man out. He was not a fighter, and his unusual comment, written soon after the battle, seems archaic. "I have just finished reading an old history of some ancient campaigns," he wrote to a fellow prelate; he was "forcibly struck with the remark that, 'The army that fights on horse back and behind breastworks, will, in time, become a hord of cowards, while those who fight in the open plain will grow in every gallant virtue.' This has been true in this war. The Yankee infantry and artillery have fought behind breastworks and they are a hord of cowards." Renfroe was desperately trying to explain the defeat at Gettysburg by noting the Federal use of fieldworks and attacking Yankee character in the process. He spoke for an old-fashioned attitude about battlefield élan, the virtue of the spirited assault, and what he thought was a cowardly craving for artificial advantages based on terrain. By the summer of 1863, his attitude was fast becoming a relic of the past.[44]

Defenses of Richmond

The failure of this campaign had repercussions throughout the Confederacy. Among them was a renewed interest in strengthening the Richmond defenses. D. H. Hill surveyed the works and recommended improvements. He found that parts of the Outer Line west of Brook Turnpike were unconnected and the detached batteries had no works for infantry support. "As the city may have to be defended by local troops, the importance of infantry cover cannot be overestimated," he informed Secretary of War James A. Seddon. Hill also found that several batteries at Staples's Mills and along River Road were too close to tree cover, and he recommended that these woods be cleared and additional infantry works be built to support the guns. Chief engineer Jeremy Gilmer ordered Col. Walter Husted Stevens to do what Hill suggested, using soldiers from Hill's command if possible. Gilmer also urged Governor John Letcher and the mayor of Richmond to impress free blacks in the capital to work on the fortifications. "The labor asked for is essential to a vigorous defense of Richmond, should the enemy advance in force on the city."[45]

The complex of fortifications near Chaffin's Bluff needed additional work. Henry A. Wise, whose Virginia brigade had primarily built the works, had hoped to finish the job by the end of December 1862. But the senior engineer of the Richmond defenses inspected the area in late May 1863 and found that more timber had to be slashed in front of the lines. Additionally, he recommended that ditches be dug in front of the works, ordnance heavier than field artillery be placed in several batteries, and a secondary line be constructed to the rear of a portion of the first line that had been built a year earlier.[46]

This report spurred work on three major additions to the complex of fortifications at Chaffin's. Gilmer personally laid out an extension of the Intermediate Line from the junction of Osborne Pike and New Market Road southward to Coles Run Battery. The digging started in August 1863, and a major work soon to be called Fort Gilmer was laid out along this extension. The timber was slashed for a good distance around the fort, whose parapets

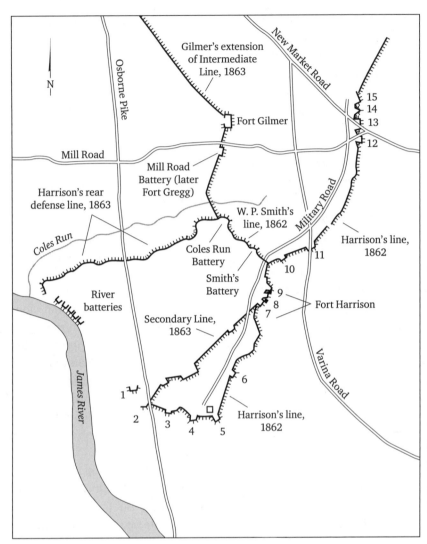

Chaffin's Bluff Defenses, 1863 (based on maps in Dickinson, "Union and Confederate Engineering Operations at Chaffin's Bluff," 17, 30, 66, RNB)

rose to a height of eight feet. A deep ditch and a banquette strengthened the work, and a stockade covered its open rear. Gilmer added a culvert under the parapet at the south end of the fort to drain water. Another work, initially called the Mill Road Battery but later designated Fort Gregg, was constructed with positions for four guns.[47]

Engineer William Elzey Harrison, who had laid out the first line at Chaffin's the preceding year, undertook the second major project. He started a new line from the bank of the James River, upstream from Chaffin's, to the Coles Run Battery. It provided cover for the north side of the batteries at the bluff, in effect enclosing those gun emplacements on all sides north of the river.[48]

The third project reinforced Harrison's original line, which stretched from Osborne Pike to the northeast in a great bulge toward the approach of the enemy. It involved the construction of a new line to the rear of the old, stretching from Batteries No. 7, 8, and 9 toward Battery No. 2 at Osborne Pike. It had three battery emplacements and was much shorter than the stretch of the original line that fronted it. This Secondary Line of 1863 was on ground as much as twelve feet higher than that of the original line. The guns could therefore fire over friendly troops in the front. At the left end of the Secondary Line, Batteries No. 7, 8, and 9 were reconfigured into a single fort and called Fort Harrison. It was a formidable work with four artillery platforms and one large and five small traverses. Barracks were built behind the fort to house the gunners and garrison. Work on the fort itself was done relatively quickly, but the engineers did not have time to complete the preparation of the work. A year later, when Fort Harrison was attacked as part of Grant's Fifth Offensive at Petersburg, there was no stockade to its rear, and the numerous trees that had been slashed in its front had not been crafted into an abatis. Most of the Secondary Line was dug by Brig. Gen. Eppa Hunton's Virginia brigade of Pickett's division, which replaced Wise's Virginians when the latter were sent to Charleston in mid-September.[49]

The Richmond authorities also turned their attention to strengthening the defenses of key railroad bridges on lines leading into the capital. Those across the North and South Anna rivers had been threatened during a Federal cavalry raid in late June as Lee was heading toward Pennsylvania. In fact, the South Anna bridge had been captured after a fight with defending Confederate troops. The War Department wanted small, enclosed works at these points, defensible by "a few companies" that could hold off enemy horsemen and light artillery. Jeremy Gilmer provided detailed instructions for the work near Belfield, Virginia, where the Weldon Railroad crossed the Meherrin River. It needed to be big enough for three companies, and he insisted that one enclosed work was better than "extended lines of rifle pits" because a small force needed comprehensive protection. If the little work was commanded by higher ground nearby, Gilmer wanted the engineer in charge to raise the height of the parapet facing that threat. The little fort should be as close to the bridge as possible but could be as far away as 500 yards if necessary.[50]

In addition to dispatching engineer officers to take care of bridge defenses, Walter Husted Stevens tackled the persistent problem of finding laborers to work on the Richmond defenses. The War Department waited as long as feasible before pressing 5,340 slaves in late August, although harvest season was by no means ended. With slave laborers slowly trickling in, Stevens had to contend with the consequences of yet another call-up of workers, this time from among the free black population of Virginia. He was deluged with requests for exemptions and circulated rules for dealing with this issue. His guidelines were authorized by Gilmer. About the only exception he allowed was for workers already employed by the government. A proposal was made by a Virginia senator to use black convicts as laborers on the Richmond defenses. Stevens was not enthusiastic about it, and Alfred L. Rives thought it would drain available manpower to provide enough guards to prevent escapes, so the proposal was rejected.[51]

By the beginning of 1864, it was time for the government to settle accounts with slaveowners who claimed to have lost their bondsmen because of working conditions at fortifications. Stevens estimated that 250 slaves had died or had run away while working on the Richmond defenses. At an average value of $2,000, that amounted to half a million dollars. Alfred L. Rives estimated that 104 slaves had been lost while working on other defenses in the state; he could only guess that the number lost outside Virginia while working on various fortification projects amounted to 1,200 slaves. In total, 1,554 bondsmen were lost in the Confederacy because their masters responded to the call for workers. Rives asked for a congressional appropriation of $3,108,000 to cover the loss.[52]

Despite this enormous cost, the War Department and the Engineer Bureau issued a new call for workers on February 17, 1864. Officers were to press free blacks first, then slaves if needed. Stevens was willing to allow substitutes for men who were employed in important civilian work, but he refused to grant exemptions. These laborers were kept on the job throughout the winter but needed to return to their civilian work by late April, especially the slaves owned by planters. The Engineer Bureau sought permission to press more free blacks as an alternative. It was a never-ending problem because the huge fortification system ringing the capital demanded endless labor. Thousands of African Americans who had little personal interest in the survival of the Confederacy were forced to support it, one shovel of dirt at a time.[53]

11 : Charleston

One week after the battle of Gettysburg, Federal troops began a campaign against Charleston, South Carolina, that would be the largest land attack on the defenses of that important city. Not only was it a highly visible symbol, the place where the first shots were fired in the Civil War, but Charleston was an important port for blockade runners. The operations against the city in the summer of 1863 involved extensive fortifications for both offensive and defensive purposes. In fact, Charleston was one of the most heavily fortified cities in America. Confederate authorities had sought to protect the place as soon as the Yankees had evacuated Fort Sumter in April 1861, and Union commanders had pondered how best to tackle this citadel of the South.

Various Federal officers had proposed plans for operations against Charleston for some time. Brig. Gen. Thomas W. Sherman commanded the expeditionary corps that cooperated with the navy in the capture of Port Royal in November 1861. He passed on the recommendation of his chief engineer, Capt. Quincy A. Gillmore, who proposed a plan for taking Charleston. Gillmore advised seizing Morris Island and Sullivan's Island, which flanked the throat of Charleston Harbor south and north. Gillmore then recommended using rifled artillery to reduce Fort Sumter, which was located on a sandbar near the middle of the throat. He also thought a similar strategy could be employed against Fort Moultrie on the southern end of Sullivan's Island and Fort Johnson on the northern shore of James Island. This latter island comprised much of the land south of the harbor. Then Gillmore recommended bombarding Charleston itself. Alternatively, Gillmore noted that the Federals could advance up the Stono River, which constituted the western and southern border of James Island. Once the island was in Union hands, the forts at the entrance to the harbor would eventually fall like ripe apples. Gillmore thought it would take 14,000 men, a dozen field guns, and twenty siege guns to take James Island. Sherman agreed with his engineer but thought more resources were needed to accomplish either of the two plans. Almost the same proposal was advanced a few weeks later by Lt. Col. Daniel P. Woodbury, aide-de-camp to John G. Barnard.[1]

The Confederates had invested a great deal of time, energy, and resources in preparing Charleston's defenses. Col. Roswell S. Ripley took charge of the project after the fall of Fort Sumter. A West Point graduate who had been commissioned into the artillery, Ripley was a good engineer. He strengthened the masonry forts guarding the harbor, put sand against the sea face of Moultrie, and erected earthworks around it. He protected James Island by strengthening Fort Johnson and constructed batteries at the mouth of the Stono River to block Federal ships. These works were sited on Coles's Island, and they not only protected the entrance to the Stono but also blocked the approaches to Folly Island and Morris Island.

Fort Johnson was the oldest fortification at Charleston. Its site was first fortified in 1704, and the current work was initially erected in 1780. That year the British bypassed the harbor altogether, ascended the Stono River, and compelled the surrender of Charleston by investing the city. Ripley extensively renovated the fort, building a giant earthwork mounting fifteen guns and mortars with supporting infantry trenches.

The War Department created the Department of South Carolina, Georgia, and Florida in November 1861, and Robert E. Lee was named its commander. Port Royal fell to a combined Union force the day before he assumed command. This and other Federal strikes along the Atlantic coast convinced Lee that he did not have enough resources to hold all points. He adopted a strategy of concentrating his strength at key spots and planned to use the railroad to shift men to threatened areas.[2]

Pemberton and the Defenses of Charleston

Maj. Gen. John C. Pemberton replaced Lee in March 1862. Born in Pennsylvania and with little experience in the field, Pemberton had no engineering background and brought a weak staff to Charleston. He did not trust Ripley, who eventually went to Virginia to command a brigade, and sometimes borrowed the state engineer of Georgia for consultation.

Pemberton essentially furthered Lee's policy of consolidation. He abandoned the outlying defenses of the Stono River, including Coles's Island, and built new works farther up the river. This exposed Folly Island, Morris Island, and the southern half of James Island to Union operations. It was a controversial move that provoked criticism from Governor Francis W. Pickens. Pemberton took a gloomy view of his prospects. "What under the old system of warfare was our strength is now our weakness," he complained. "The many approaches by water and the recent proof of the practicability of their gunboats passing our batteries have made the defense of this city a very difficult problem to solve." He feared the Federals could bring so much power to bear on the harbor entrance that it was only a question of time before they broke through the protecting ring of forts.[3]

Yet the works that Pemberton initiated proved to be strong. On the upper reaches of the Stono River, Fort Pemberton took shape on James Island to protect access to Elliot's Cut, which led directly toward Charleston. The work was an enclosed, five-sided fort mounting twenty-one guns. It had supporting infantry trenches, and the Stono was obstructed with tree limbs and torpedoes. The fort was completed in the spring of 1862.[4]

To the northeast of Charleston, Pemberton constructed a line of infantry and artillery works near Mount Pleasant in Christ Church Parish. It was seven miles from town and spanned the higher ground between Copahee Sound and the headwaters of Elliott's Creek. Fort Palmetto anchored the right flank of this line. It was a circular parapet that was little more than thirty-five yards in diameter, with two magazines inside. The land is very flat here, and the Mount Pleasant Line consisted of a simple trench and parapet. The engineers tried to place the line on any slight rise of ground they could find; but it often lay on completely flat terrain, and the small remnants seem to indicate they were successful in keeping the line as straight as possible. The woods were not cut far enough in front of the Mount Pleasant Line, however, and Pemberton's engineers failed to cut embrasures for the artillery emplacements. Both defects were remedied more than two years later.[5]

The northwestern approach to Charleston was sealed before Pemberton's arrival, when "a range of low fortifications, running across the neck of land from Cooper to Ashley Rivers," was constructed soon after the fall of Sumter. This line was two miles from the city. It had a ditch ten feet wide and a parapet with fifteen feet of relief. Southwest of Charleston were two lines of works covering the Charleston and Savannah Railroad. The first was two miles beyond the railroad bridge over the Ashley River. It consisted of an infantry trench reinforced with artillery redans, and its left rested on Wappoo Creek. The second line was six miles beyond the bridge and consisted of a large redoubt near the railroad with a wet ditch in front. Several other detached redoubts were constructed to the left of this one along the north bank of Ashley River.

To the southeast of Charleston, James Island offered the easiest approach for an attacking army. Pemberton's works here consisted of two lines and two concentrations of forward, detached works. One line covered the western portion of the island between Wappoo Creek and James Island Creek. This continuous line incorporated several small artillery redans and stretched for a mile and a half. Another line of similar length stretched eastward from James Island Creek to Lighthouse Creek. It consisted of six redoubts, five redans, and one lunette, all detached. East of Lighthouse Creek, low, marshy islands stretched out to the sea. The two lines covered the higher ground that made up two-thirds of James Island. Fort Pemberton essentially was a forward work in front of the right wing of these two lines, and the works at Secessionville were a forward post in front of the left wing.[6]

Criticism of Pemberton for inadequately fortifying Charleston was only partly deserved. He made a serious mistake in abandoning the works guarding the mouth of the Stono River. That forced him and his successors to build more massive works closer to the city, which required a lot of labor and large garrisons. Besides that mistake, Pemberton actually built on Ripley's good work to cover all possible approaches to the city.

Secessionville

In early April 1862 Maj. Gen. David Hunter replaced Thomas W. Sherman as commander of what was called the Southern Expedition. Still based at Port Royal, elements of the expeditionary corps reduced Fort Pulaski near Savannah in mid-April by establishing rifled batteries near the work and bombarding it.

Soon after, Brig. Gen. Henry Benham devised a plan to strike at Charleston. Since Pemberton had abandoned the mouth of the Stono River, it was possible for Union forces to gain access to the southern half of James Island. Benham called for one division under Brig. Gen. Isaac Stevens to sail into Stono Inlet and land on Sol Legare Island, which was connected to James Island by two causeways. Another division under Brig. Gen. Horatio Wright would land from Edisto Island to Johns Island, march over it, and cross the Stono onto James Island. These toeholds would lead to further movement toward the northern shore of the island overlooking the harbor.

The operation was successful at first. The Federals started out on June 2, 1862, when Stevens landed on Sol Legare Island and Wright crossed the water from Edisto Island and began to march across Johns Island. Some of Stevens's men skirmished with Confederate troops at one of the causeways connecting Sol Legare to James on June 3. Nearly a week later, on June 9, Wright crossed the Stono and encamped at Grimball's Plantation on the western edge of James Island. He built a fortified camp consisting of a line of infantry trench and battery emplacements more than 1,200 yards long, which was designed by Col. Edward W. Serrell of the 1st New York Engineers. The Confederates sought to push troops close to this post to contain the Yankees at Grimball's Plantation. The resulting fight on June 10 was an open field engagement fought outside the works and resulting in a Confederate repulse. But this battle convinced Hunter to call off the operation. He ordered Benham, who commanded the two divisions in the field, to retain his toehold on James Island. Benham far exceeded his orders and took the offensive.[7]

Hunter instructed Benham to do all that was necessary to secure his camps, and Benham decided that taking the Tower Battery, about two miles away, was necessary. He later wrote that the Confederates fired heavily from the fort as far as his picket lines and that they could use the work as a base to harass his encampments. Under the guise of conducting a reconnaissance in force, Benham made a major effort to take the battery on June 16. Laid out by Col. Lewis M. Hatch near the village of Secessionville, and guarding a road toward Charleston Harbor that ran along a narrow neck of land, the Tower Battery was a strong fortification that earned its name because of an observation tower erected just to the rear. The work had four faces, and the indented front faced the direction of approach from the southwest, rendering the configuration of the fort a giant M. Its parapets, which ranged from nine to sixteen feet high, mounted seven guns. The Tower Battery's greater strength lay in its location. Marshes swept up to the ditches of the work on both flanks, leaving a stretch of solid land only about 200 yards wide in its front. A sandy, flat cotton field stretched before the battery. The rows of the previous crop were still high, which made for some rough marching but provided a modicum of cover if one lay flat behind them. Moreover, a hedge ran a couple of hundred yards from the fort and parallel to its front face. The Tower Battery was a good work in a superb defensive position.[8]

Benham made his arrangements on the evening of June 15 and set out early the next morning. Stevens's division, some 3,500 men, would attack frontally while Wright advanced along the solid ground north of the marsh that flanked the fort's right wing. The most Wright could do was to occupy any Confederate forces that might threaten Benham's left and deliver long-range musketry at the fort. In a last-minute conference Benham's subordinates advised not making the attack at all, but he was determined.[9]

Despite his misgivings, Stevens took some care to organize his assault. He told his men to advance quietly, each regiment immediately behind the preceding one. It was still dark, and Stevens wanted surprise to be his chief ally. The Federals captured an outlying picket post but were discovered by the time they were within artillery range of the Tower Battery. The 8th Michigan led the way with two of its companies a few yards ahead to act as a forlorn hope. The regiment managed to climb the parapet at the angle where the left face joined the front and shot down some of the gunners, but the 9th South Carolina Battalion raced into the fort just in time to save the 100 Confederate gunners who were desperately trying to stop the Michigan troops.

When the Federals were pushed off the parapet, most took shelter in the ditch or retreated.

It proved impossible to bring up troops fast enough to help the 8th Michigan exploit its brief hold on the parapet. Soggy ground, the severely restricted approach, and inexperienced regimental commanders disrupted the flow of help. The left wing of the 7th Connecticut became bogged down in the marsh to the north, and the unit halted well short of the fort. A third regiment, the 28th Massachusetts, essentially duplicated the performance of the 7th Connecticut. Then the 79th New York conducted a spirited attack, bypassed the two stalled regiments, and gained a tenuous hold on the parapet exactly where the 8th Michigan had almost succeeded; but the 79th, too, was pushed off the work because no support came up. Two more regiments tried, but neither was able to lend timely aid to the 79th. The 100th Pennsylvania made it as close as thirty yards from the fort, but the 46th New York halted among the fragments of previous regiments that littered the cotton field. By 5:30 A.M., only an hour after the start of the attack, the battle was over.

Wright failed to offer effective support. The 3rd New Hampshire advanced to a point opposite the Tower Battery but remained separated from it by 150 yards of marsh. The regiment fired on the fort and was blistered with return fire by Confederate infantry that had rushed into the work. In addition, more Rebel infantry and artillery, positioned to the north of the 3rd New Hampshire, opened fire on the regiment. As the 3rd Rhode Island Heavy Artillery advanced against this northern threat, the New Hampshire men pulled out, and Wright beat a hasty retreat. Unaware of this, Stevens worked to reform his shattered division behind the hedge in anticipation of a second charge on the fort, but Benham lost his nerve and ordered everyone to return to their camps.[10]

Col. Thomas G. Lamar of the 1st South Carolina Artillery commanded the Confederates that day. He called up infantry support and directed the gun crews as they opened fire when the Federals were 700 yards away, personally sighting an 8-inch Columbiad. All told, there were no more than 500 infantrymen inside the Tower Battery during most of the battle, but an additional 1,000 came up near its end. They had only an hour's sleep the night before, having exhausted themselves in preparing the fort for action. Because of the colonel's successful effort, the Tower Battery was renamed Fort Lamar.[11]

Federal losses amounted to 685 men, while Lamar lost 204. Hunter arrested Benham for exceeding his orders. For the next two weeks the Federals maintained their tenuous hold on James Island and Sol Legare Island. Wright strengthened his defense at Grimball's Plantation, adding emplacements for twenty-seven guns and building a detached work called Battery Wright for nine guns. On the eastern end of Sol Legare Island, well within range of Fort Lamar, a previously constructed work named Battery Stevens was strengthened, and a new fort, Battery Williams, was built for four guns. All of this labor came to nothing, however, for Hunter, distraught that higher authorities could not send him reinforcements, abandoned James Island. The evacuation began on July 1. Benham's culpability for this disaster was widely known, but political influence saved his career. He led the Volunteer Engineer Brigade in the Army of the Potomac from 1863 to the end of the war, but his command of that unique organization was undistinguished.[12]

The attack on Fort Lamar failed because Benham and Stevens inadequately scouted the terrain to determine what obstacles lay in the path of the division, and Stevens could not move his regiments quickly enough across the confined battlefield. The distance between each regiment increased as obstacles slowed progress. As a result, the two units that gained the parapet had no support to exploit their advantage. Lamar brought up Confederate infantry in time to repel them. Finally, the work itself was a major factor in Lamar's victory. Its design and location could not have been more suited to Rebel needs. Hazard Stevens, who served on his father's division staff, believed the Federals lost at Secessionville because of "the strength of the work[,] manned as it was by a resolute garrison, and the destructive fire of its heavy guns."[13]

The elder Stevens had planned to make good use of Capt. Alfred F. Sears's Company E, 1st New York Engineers. Assigned to follow the forlorn hope, the two advanced companies of the 8th Michigan, Sears ordered his men to sling their rifle muskets over their backs and armed them with tools to remove obstructions. For some reason Stevens changed his mind and ordered the company to the rear just before the assault began. Sears then helped the artillery cut its way through hedges and other natural obstacles. He reported that the slung muskets interfered with the men's ability to work and suggested that combat engineers be armed with pistols or sabers. "The sabers would form a useful implement also in clearing entanglements, abatis, and hedges," he added. As it was, some of his men dropped their tools when they thought at one point that they would be ordered to take part in the attack, and he lost these implements that habitually were in short supply.[14]

Beauregard and the Defenses of Charleston

Pemberton tried to take credit for the victory at Secessionville by arguing that his abandonment of the defenses at the mouth of the Stono River lured the Federals into attacking James Island, but the Charleston public remained dissatisfied with their Northern-born commander. He did not have the personality to inspire confidence, appeared indecisive as well as inattentive to the public mood, and was inept in handling politicians. President Davis replaced him with his opposite in every way, G. T. Beauregard, on August 29, 1862.

Beauregard was not satisfied with Pemberton's work. The system of outer defenses that he had partially devised in 1861, with Ripley's help, had been abandoned, and the newer works Pemberton had started closer to the city demanded much labor and armament to complete. Beauregard found many faults with the placement and design of Pemberton's fortifications. The works on James Island were "not very properly arranged and located," he thought.

His subordinates also found fault. Wilmot G. De Saussure, the state's adjutant and inspector general, considered the James Island fieldworks "little more than heavy breastworks, which may give confidence to raw troops, but as they cover a great extent, and run through a country nearly the whole of which is a natural road, masses may be thrown upon any particular point, and the works are not strong enough to resist such an attack." Brig. Gen. States Right Gist wanted to reinforce the line of detached works between James Island Creek and Lighthouse Creek by filling in the empty spaces with infantry trenches. Gist also wanted to thicken the parapets of the continuous line between James Island Creek and Wappoo Creek, as the work had eroded considerably.

The line between the Cooper and Ashley rivers northwest of Charleston had a strong profile and was "elaborately constructed, but badly located, . . . not being well adapted to the ground," wrote Beauregard. Woods in front partially commanded them, and the line could be enfiladed by gunboats in either river. "Adaption of 'means to an end' has not always been consulted in the works around this city," he concluded. "Much unnecessary work has been bestowed upon many of them." Moreover, there were far too few resources; a mere 6,500 infantrymen and 1,700 artillerymen were all he had, while both Pemberton and Beauregard thought the department needed more than 43,000 men.

Roswell Ripley returned from duty in Virginia to help Beauregard, and Lt. Col. David B. Harris was also available. On Beauregard's staff since First Manassas, the Virginia-born Harris was his chief engineer. The Creole general also appointed Capt. William H. Echols as chief engineer of South Carolina and Capt. John McCrady as chief engineer of Georgia.[15]

Beauregard felt that his weakest sector was James Island. Because of Pemberton's abandonment of Coles's Island and his slow construction of new

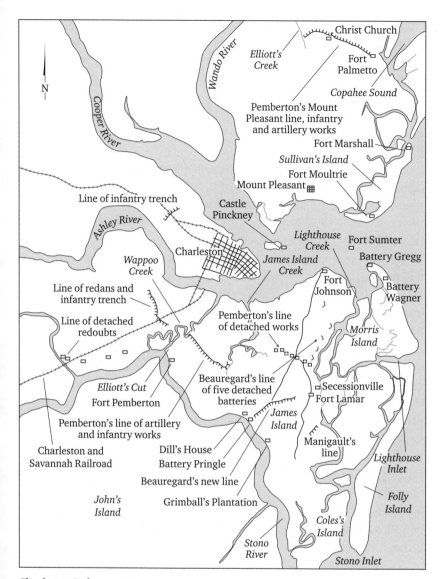

Charleston Defenses, 1863

works in the area, the island was poorly defended and too large for the available manpower. Ripley was convinced that maintaining the defenses at the mouth of the Stono would have been the most economical plan for defending the island.

Beauregard considered strengthening Pemberton's lines on James Island. Captain Echols worked up estimates of time and labor needed to build two new redans, extend one battery, and raze more than 200 yards of existing earthwork on the line of detached works from James Island Creek to Light-house Creek. It would have involved employing 100 black laborers for four-teen and a half days to move 7,384 cubic yards of dirt. The proposed changes to the continuous line of works between Wappoo Creek and James Island Creek involved creating three new redans with a total of 25,395 cubic yards of earth. One hundred blacks would be needed for fifty-one days. Echols did not calculate the time and labor needed to revet and sod the parapet or build gun platforms.

Beauregard hesitated to invest so much effort on a defective line, but he strengthened the harbor defenses of Charleston. Harris was primarily re-sponsible for reinforcing the walls of Sumter and Moultrie and obstructing the entrance to the harbor. He also placed torpedoes in every navigable stream that gave access to the harbor.

The work was hampered by a shortage of labor. Beauregard and his subor-dinates constantly complained that the soldiers did not have their hearts in heavy work. Langdon Cheves thought the problem was that "neither officer nor men were taught . . . by their superiors to regard this work as an impor-tant part of their duty." Beauregard had seen this problem before First Ma-nassas. "Our Southern soldiers object most strenuously to work with spades and shovels," he explained to Governor Francis Pickens. "They will do it in very pressing emergencies, but on ordinary occasions do more grumbling than work; they prefer decidedly to fight." The commander suggested orga-nizing a company of 100 black laborers for every two regiments, but the Confederate use of slave labor around Charleston was characterized by prob-lems. Officers reported illness and chronic shortages of shelter, firewood, bedding, and food among the black workers. Soldiers provided the most efficient labor supply for work on fortifications, but the number of troops available had to be large enough so that they were not overworked. It also helped a great deal if there was some imminent threat or the immediate prospect of a battle to spur the soldiers to greater exertion.[16]

Throughout the last half of 1862 and the first half of 1863, the Federals made no serious move against Charleston. Hunter was content with the status quo and downplayed the suggestions of every subordinate who of-fered ideas for an offensive. As the navy made plans to attack the harbor defenses, Brig. Gen. Truman Seymour proposed establishing batteries on Morris Island to breach Sumter's walls, but Hunter ignored him. Maj. Gen. John G. Foster came up with a similar plan, but Hunter transferred him due to a conflict over other matters. The result was that the army did virtually nothing when the navy attacked. A fleet of seagoing ironclads steamed up to Sumter on April 7, 1863, and bombarded the masonry fort. Exaggerated

Northern faith in the power of these new weapons was shattered. The iron-clads lacked the firepower to overcome the armament of Charleston's harbor forts. Battered, they retreated without doing any appreciable harm.

Hunter allowed Seymour to land a brigade on Folly Island during the navy attack but refused to let this force do anything more. It continued to maintain a toehold on the outlying islands near the entrance to Charleston Harbor. Pemberton's abandonment of Coles's Island allowed Seymour this latitude. Little stood in the way of a Union landing on the southern end of Morris Island, which was just a few hundred yards north of Folly.[17]

Gillmore's Operations on Morris Island

The repulse of the ironclads created a lot of bad publicity in the North, which motivated the Lincoln administration to renew efforts to strike at Charleston. Hunter was replaced by Brig. Gen. Quincy A. Gillmore, who had recently led an infantry division in Kentucky but had not yet commanded infantry in battle. He had graduated at the top of his West Point class in 1849 and had worked on the nation's coastal forts as an officer in the Corps of Engineers.[18]

Federal authorities called Gillmore to Washington in late May 1863 and asked him if he could neutralize Sumter to let the fleet steam into the harbor. Gillmore answered in the affirmative. He proposed landing on the southern end of Morris Island, capturing the two forts at the center and the north end of the island, and reducing Sumter by long-range fire. Rear Admiral Samuel F. Du Pont, the leader of the April 7 attack, would command supporting naval vessels.

Gillmore took charge of the Department of the South on June 12, 1863. His command consisted of eleven occupied posts along a strip of seacoast in South Carolina, Georgia, and Florida. He abandoned some of the less important posts and shifted resources around to organize a force of 11,000 infantry, 350 artillerymen, and 400 engineer troops to attack Morris Island. The latter came from the 1st New York Engineers. Gillmore also had four newly raised black regiments. The force assigned to the Morris Island operation was half of the available manpower in his department. Beauregard had only 650 infantrymen and 350 artillerymen on Morris Island and 2,000 infantrymen, 3,800 artillerymen, and 550 cavalrymen deployed at various points on James Island.[19]

The Federals would employ fortifications at nearly every opportunity. Engineer troops broke ground for the construction of emplacements on the north end of Folly Island on the night of June 17; they finished works for thirty-two guns and fifteen mortars by June 26. Confederate pickets were stationed on the other side of Lighthouse Inlet, which separated the engineers from Morris Island, but the sound of the surf drowned out most of the construction noise. The Federals covered their progress with trees and brush during the day and even sprinkled dry sand over the newly turned, wetter sand. The parapets of these batteries were twenty feet thick and eight feet high. To lessen the work of cutting planks, the men built embrasures and sturdy platforms large enough to serve two guns each. Heavy pine logs roughly hewn on one side served as sleepers. It was necessary to provide a firm foundation for the platforms because of the wet sand underneath the surface. The Engineer Department in Washington, D.C., shipped thousands of sandbags to revet the parapets and traverses. Gabions reinforced with hoop iron and fascines wrapped with hides were used to revet the embrasures. The sand was particularly fine at one battery site, and the engineers had to use palmetto logs to revet the parapet up to two and a half feet high. The Federals also built bombproofs by leaning heavy logs against the parapet and covering them with two feet of sand.[20]

All this labor was done to provide artillery support for the landing on Morris Island. While the works were under construction, Gillmore shipped Brig. Gen. Alfred H. Terry's division and Brig. Gen. George C. Strong's brigade to Folly Island under cover of darkness. Terry moved his division onto James Island as a diversion on July 8. His division skirmished with the Confederates and effectively drew their attention away from Morris Island. Meanwhile Strong, covered by the massive fire of Gillmore's batteries and four ironclads, landed on the southern end of Morris on July 10. The infantry boarded boats the night before and waited behind marsh grass in Lighthouse Inlet. They tied white ribbons on their left arm so they could be easily identified. After a two-hour bombardment the next morning, Strong's men landed and easily captured the Rebel works, which consisted of eleven detached, one-gun batteries with no supporting infantry works nearby. The Federals occupied three-fourths of the island and were within musket range of Battery Wagner by 9:00 A.M. Gillmore decided the heat and the confusion of his landing were too great to allow an immediate attack on the work.[21]

The Confederates were not taken by surprise. Pickets had heard the sound of chopping on Folly Island during the night of July 8, but they could not see anything in the daytime. When the move occurred, Beauregard realized he did not have enough strength on Morris Island to repel Strong's brigade, so he evacuated the batteries on the south end of the island and relied on the two forts on the upper half. For the same reason, he could not shift troops from Morris to James Island to meet Terry's threat, nor could he move the troops on James to Morris. Beauregard continued to view James Island as the most vulnerable sector of his defense. Morris Island was comparatively isolated and a threat only to the safety of Fort Sumter if it was in Union hands. If James Island were occupied, it could lead to the fall of Charleston. The Rebels planted more torpedoes in front of Wagner and rushed reinforcements to the battery.[22]

The fort and its companion, Battery Gregg, had been built long before. Gregg was constructed soon after the abandonment of Coles's Island in 1862. It protected the wharf on the north end of Morris, which was the only link the island had with Charleston. After the battle of Secessionville, Pemberton ordered the construction of a larger work at the narrowest point of the island to protect Gregg from a northward attack. Capt. Langdon Cheves and Capt. Francis D. Lee, who had worked on Fort Walker and Fort Beauregard at Port Royal, designed it. Initially called the Neck Battery, it was started in the summer of 1862 about 1,200 yards south of Fort Gregg as an emplacement for artillery, with guns sited to fire down the length of the island. The Confederates renamed it Battery Wagner in November 1862 to memorialize Lt. Col. Thomas M. Wagner of the 1st South Carolina Artillery, who had been killed in the explosion of a gun at the work the previous July.[23]

When Beauregard inspected the work in the fall of 1862, he ordered it converted into a fort with infantry firing positions as well as artillery. The rear was closed by a parapet, and a battery of three heavy guns was built to fire at shipping. He added traverses between the gun emplacements on the land face and erected a large bombproof in the angle of the work. As an additional support, Beauregard ordered the construction of detached one-gun batteries on the south end of Morris Island in March 1863; these positions had been abandoned when Gillmore landed on Morris Island.[24]

By the time the Federals came within reach, Battery Wagner was impressive. The sea face measured 210 feet along the interior crest. The bombproof, 20 by 20 feet in dimension, was positioned as a traverse protecting the three guns on the sea face from fire by land-based artillery. A second bombproof was parallel to the sea face and measured 30 feet by 130 feet. It could hold 900 men if they were willing to stand "elbow to elbow and face to back." One-third of this large bombproof was used by the medical personnel as a hospital. The land face was 600 feet long with reentering angles and emplacements for five guns. Heavy traverses protected each one. An extension of the left flank, forming yet another angle in the work, stretched out to the high-tide mark of the beach. It was embrasured for two field guns that could sweep the front of the sea face. On the right a short, 300-foot-long retrenchment protected the flank. The deep ditch in front of the work could be filled with salt water from Vincent's Creek at high tide and retained by sluice gates.

The parapets were 15 feet high and 12 to 14 feet thick at the top. Battery Wagner mounted a 10-inch Columbiad and two 32-pounders on the sea face, with field guns and 32-pounders in the other emplacements.[25]

Morris Island was an inhospitable place to conduct operations. A low-lying barrier island, it ranged from 1,000 yards at the southern end to only 25 yards wide just south of Battery Wagner. The sand hills rose to no more than 36 feet above the high-water mark in the south, and to only 2 feet above it just south of the fort. The sea was a constant enemy. Spring tides often washed across the narrow neck south of Wagner, and Gillmore noted that they ate away one foot of the island every day during the campaign. To the west, a stratum of muck made up the salt marsh that separated Morris Island from James Island, and Gillmore noticed that this mud was often exposed between the high-tide and low-tide marks on the beach. "The island, in fact, is simply an irregular mass of sand, which, by the continual action of wind and sea (particularly the former), has been accumulated upon the bosom of the marsh." There was essentially no dirt on the island, only "a fine and almost white quartz sand."[26]

Gillmore attacked on July 11, hoping to avoid a protracted campaign on the island. The move was hastily planned and poorly coordinated. Four companies of the 7th Connecticut led, followed by the 76th Pennsylvania and 9th Maine, all of Strong's brigade. The push started at dawn from a distance of 500 yards. A thin line of 150 Rebels stationed in a forward position, a shallow trench on top of a slight rise of sand about 300 yards in front of the battery, fired a volley before retiring to the work. The Connecticut troops broke into a run and got into the ditch before the Rebel artillery opened up; several managed to cross the parapet and bayonet two Confederate gunners. The rest remained on top and on the exterior slope of the parapet or in the ditch, which had one foot of water in it, waiting for the 76th Pennsylvania to come up. That regiment had drifted some 200 yards behind the Connecticut unit. It was further delayed when the men dropped to the ground as the Rebel artillery opened fire. The Pennsylvanians screwed up their courage and rushed forward; some managed to make it to the ditch, but the rest retreated. Pelted with hand grenades from the interior slope of the parapet and harassed by flank fire because the reentering angles of the land face allowed the defenders to enfilade them, the Connecticut soldiers finally gave up their toehold on the battery. They suffered from Rebel fire all the way back. Only 88 of the 191 men in the four companies of the 7th Connecticut survived the attack.[27]

Three Union regiments were used in the assault, which cost Gillmore 339 casualties. It had been an opportunistic move, made without artillery support, to catch the Rebels by surprise. The major problem was coordination. The narrow approach to Wagner meant that only one regiment at a time could throw itself at the work; all supporting units had to follow. There was ample opportunity for those units to be delayed by a number of factors. The Connecticut companies needed help from the 76th Pennsylvania as soon as they reached the ditch; but ten or more minutes probably transpired before the vanguard of the Pennsylvania unit got there, and most of the regiment never made it that far. Col. Robert F. Graham of the 21st South Carolina commanded Wagner that day. He had 1,190 men in the fort. The 18th Georgia Battalion fought off the few members of the 7th Connecticut who mounted the land face. Graham lost 12 men that day.[28]

Gillmore was determined to try a second assault with substantial artillery preparation and more men. He constructed four batteries on Morris Island and named himself chief engineer to oversee the work. Forty-one guns were mounted on July 15. Gillmore planned to attack the next day, but a series of heavy rainstorms hit the area. The batteries were flooded, and a lot of powder was spoiled, forcing the Federals to delay their attack two days.[29]

Meanwhile, Beauregard had his hands full. He was forced to send reinforcements arriving at Charleston to James Island, for Terry's division remained there as a serious threat. These reinforcements, under Brig. Gen. Johnson Hagood, took the offensive and forced Terry to evacuate James Island by July 17. Beauregard held a conference to determine the feasibility of taking the offensive on Morris Island, but the participants concluded it would not work. The Union fleet covered the whole island with its fire, and the thin line of boats connecting the wharf at Battery Gregg with downtown Charleston could not ship large numbers of troops quickly enough to overcome Gillmore's strength. The Confederates resigned themselves to a grim defensive strategy on Morris to buy time for Sumter.[30]

When Gillmore opened his bombardment on July 18, Battery Wagner was manned by 1,620 men. In addition to the fire from his land batteries, Gillmore had the support of five monitors, the USS *New Ironsides*, a large wooden frigate, and six mortar boats. Altogether, some 9,000 rounds were pumped into the fort during nearly twelve hours of shelling. The Confederates lost no more than four killed and fourteen wounded in this hail of iron because most of the garrison remained in the bombproofs; only the Charleston Battalion stood fire at their stations. The units sheltering in the bombproofs were assigned sectors of the parapet so there would be no confusion when it came time to rush to their posts. The Charleston Battalion was on the right wing of the land face, the 51st North Carolina was in the middle, and the 31st North Carolina was on the left, holding the crucial angle. The guns were manned by two companies of the 1st South Carolina Heavy Artillery and Company B and Company K of the 63rd Georgia, acting as artillerists. Some members of the 51st North Carolina, which had served in Wagner for the preceding six days and had gotten little sleep, fainted from heat exhaustion in the crowded bombproofs. The parapets were hardly damaged by the Union bombardment, but the roof of the magazine began to deteriorate. Fortunately for the Rebels, the shelling stopped about dusk before this problem became critical.[31]

The attack, scheduled for dusk, was a duplicate of the failed assault seven days earlier, although on a larger scale. Strong's brigade led the attack supported by Col. Haldimand S. Putnam's brigade. Strong's advance unit was the 54th Massachusetts, which had been raised from among the free black population of the North. It was deployed in two lines so as to negotiate the narrow defile. Even so, the regimental formation extended so far down the beach that some men had to wade in the surf and others had to drop back and wait until the formation passed by. The Massachusetts men ran to the fort in the dusk; many climbed the parapet of the land face, while others tried to climb the sea face. The 51st North Carolina fired at point-blank range as the Federals struggled up the sand slope. They hung on for nearly an hour as their commander, Col. Robert G. Shaw, was killed.[32]

The Confederate garrison responded in time to man the parapet, although not uniformly. The 51st North Carolina raced out of the bombproof and took its position when there were still a few Federal shells falling, leaving only a handful of men behind who did not have the nerve to expose themselves. The entire 31st North Carolina, however, remained in the bombproof when ordered to take its position. The emotional hammering that accompanied the bombardment was too much for them. The regiment had been in service since September 1861, but it had been captured wholesale at Roanoke Island in February 1862 and had seen little combat since then. Lt. Col. Charles W. Knight reported that he could not get his men into position. A sympathetic artillery officer explained that it was "caused by the demoralizing effect of a new and strange experience." Yet the 51st North Carolina had seen as little combat as the 31st, and it performed very well. Beauregard thought the action of the 31st shameful, but Brig. Gen. William B. Taliaferro, who commanded Wagner that day, glossed over the incident in his report.[33]

The absence of the 31st North Carolina left a gap on the left wing of the land face that was exploited by the next wave of Yankees. The 6th Connecticut and 48th New York next hit Wagner, climbing the sea face. The Connecticut men made their way into the angle where the 31st North Carolina should have been and effected a lodgment, supported by many members of the 48th

New York. The rest of Strong's brigade hit the center of the land face, although their formations were disrupted by the retreat of some members of the 54th Massachusetts. But three additional regiments, the 3rd New Hampshire, 9th Maine, and 76th Pennsylvania, climbed the land face to reinforce those men of the 54th Massachusetts who remained on the parapet.[34]

Putnam's brigade was late in coming to Strong's support, and this helped doom the assault. Division leader Truman Seymour rode with Strong's brigade. He sent an aide, Maj. Josiah I. Plimpton, back to fetch Putnam as soon as he saw help was needed. Plimpton found Putnam's men lying down 200 yards to the rear of the Union batteries. When told to move forward, Putnam said Gillmore had told him to stay put. Plimpton reported back to Seymour, but the brigade commander could do little more than reiterate his order. Putnam responded to this second entreaty after having halted his brigade for some twenty to thirty minutes. As the brigade moved forward, its progress was delayed by a stream of men from Strong's brigade, most of whom had given up their precarious foothold on the parapet and retreated in the darkness. Fragments of the 54th Massachusetts, 6th Connecticut, and 48th New York still clung to the angle.

Although late, Putnam's men came closer than anyone to taking the fort. Part of his brigade attacked the sea face while Putnam and about 100 of his men entered the angle. Here they were protected from Confederate fire by the bombproof and the traverses, which also trapped the Federals in a corner. For a while neither side could accomplish anything. Putnam's men climbed to the roof of the bombproof and fired into the fort, but they lacked the strength to push forward. Taliaferro ordered the Charleston Battalion to counterattack and recapture the angle; but its captain was killed, and the battalion stopped in its tracks. The Federals did not know what to do. Putnam consulted with Maj. Lewis Butler of the 67th Ohio. Butler advised holding on until Brig. Gen. Thomas G. Stevenson's brigade, next in line of support, should come up. Then Putnam was killed, and Butler took command of what remained of his brigade. He held on in the angle longer than he estimated it would take Stevenson to come up, all the while pelted by fire from the 51st North Carolina to the left. The angle Butler's men occupied was like a well into which the Rebels were dropping small arms fire. Finally, Taliaferro organized another counterattack through the opening to the angle, and Butler retired at 10:30 P.M.[35]

Stevenson's brigade never made it to the work. Seymour had sent Plimpton to bring it up, but Gillmore, evidently concluding the assault was a failure, ordered the brigade to halt before it came within supporting range of the other two units. Again the primary problem was the narrow approach and the difficulties it caused in coordinating the movements of supporting troops. No more than about 500 men in line could pass through the defile. Each supporting wave of troops was too late to help the 54th Massachusetts exploit its minor advantage or to help Putnam's brigade take advantage of its significant toehold. Gillmore made this problem worse by halting Putnam's brigade at least twenty minutes. An additional problem was the confusion inherent in using the same narrow defile for retreat as well as advance. Supporting units had to breast the flow of defeated remnants of previous assaults streaming to the rear.[36]

Gillmore was a superb engineer, but he was far less experienced as an infantry commander. "It may be said," he later wrote, "that in making this assault the traditions and maxims of the engineer and his reverence for the spade and shovel as weapons of war were placed in abeyance." It was Gillmore's way of saying he was out of his element. The attack of July 18 electrified the nation because it was the first well-publicized use of black troops in combat during the war, and the 54th Massachusetts had not only led the assault but had performed as well as any white unit could have done in its place. Yet the attempt to capture Wagner by a coup de main utterly failed, despite the greater degree of preparation, the massive artillery bombardment, and the much larger force employed. Some 5,000 Federals participated in the operation, and 1,515 were lost. Beauregard reported that his men buried 800 bodies the next day, while a member of the 32nd Georgia, which had been rushed into the fort that night, counted 115 dead in a section of the ditch that measured only 100 feet long. Putnam was killed, Strong was mortally wounded, and Seymour was injured. Taliaferro lost 222 men.[37]

Improved assaults would not work against such a strong position, protected as much by nature as by the engineering art. It was now time for Gillmore to exercise his own mastery of siegecraft.

12 : The Reduction of Battery Wagner

fter the repulse of July 18, Gillmore decided to reduce Wagner by siege approaches and to begin bombarding Sumter at the same time. His position was close enough to the latter work to allow Parrotts to strike the masonry walls. It was believed that the siege approaches might not have to be run all the way to Wagner, for if Sumter's guns could be dismounted, the navy might be able to run in and cut off boat communication between Charleston and Morris Island. This would accomplish a complete investment of Wagner and starve the garrison into surrender.[1]

The result was one of the classic siege operations of the Civil War. The reduction of Battery Wagner was the largest, most significant offensive against Charleston. It involved the use of several modern devices, from land mines to calcium lights, and was directed by a gifted engineer who also served as commander of the Federal army conducting the siege. The Confederate defending force was badly outnumbered and nearly cut off from the outside world, but it held Wagner for two months under conditions that became appalling.

While Gillmore continued to act as his own engineer, he had several engineer officers to supervise the construction of works. Col. Edward Wellman Serrell, Maj. Thomas Benton Brooks, and Lt. Peter S. Michie were among the best engineers in the Union army. Serrell and Brooks had been commissioned in the 1st New York Engineers. The latter was put in charge of the saps and the batteries that supported them.[2]

For his part, Beauregard fully realized what was to come. "Contest here is now one of engineering," he wrote Adj. Gen. Samuel Cooper in Richmond. "With sufficient time, labor and long range guns, our success is probable, owing to plan of defense adopted. Otherwise, it is doubtful in proportion to the lack of those three elements." To that end, Beauregard ordered Wagner to be held until its parapet was so badly damaged it could no longer protect the garrison, and then the infantry was to defend each sand hill between Wagner and Gregg. The latter work could hold out for a few days on its own, he thought. Like Gillmore, Beauregard was a fine engineer, and he had a slate of good subordinates under him. Col. David B. Harris headed a contingent of

Reduction of Battery Wagner, July 18–September 7, 1863

Confederate and state engineers (some of the latter were state officers and others were hired civilians). Normally Harris reported to Ripley; but Beauregard wanted to be kept minutely informed of developments, so he he asked for Harris's direct report. Later in the siege, Beauregard requested that Chief Engineer Jeremy F. Gilmer come to Charleston to offer his counsel.[3]

The first parallel was opened 1,300 yards from the fort on the night of July 19. Gillmore packed it with defensive features. A palisades was built across the entire island to its front, and wire entanglements were placed in front of the palisades. A Requa battery was placed on the left flank of the parallel. This was an experimental gun that mounted twenty-five barrels of a similar caliber as a rifle musket on a horizontal platform. The barrels could be loaded quickly by using a bar to work cartridges into all of them simultaneously, and another bar adjusted the barrels laterally so that the bullets would scatter for a width of 120 yards at the weapon's maximum range. It could deliver a barrage by all the barrels at one time.[4]

The second parallel was opened on the night of July 23 by the flying sap (sending men into the open under cover of darkness to dig in before the Rebels discovered their presence). It was about 600 yards in front of the first and only 200 yards from the Confederate picket line. While the first parallel was 225 yards long, this second was 175 yards long, since the width of the island narrowed on the approach to Wagner. A battery of field guns was planted on the right of the second parallel, and inclined palisading and more wire entanglements were placed about 100 yards in front. The parallel was opened by 425 men of the 4th New Hampshire and 75 men of the 1st New York Engineers. It was not an easy task, as there often was not enough sand dug up before they reached the water table, and materials had to be hauled forward to build up the parapet. Worse than that was the discovery right behind the parallel of an old cemetery used by the city of Charleston to bury victims of disease. Some were in coffins, but many were simply wrapped in blankets or had no covering at all. Because there was so little space on the island, the Federals placed the corpses in the parapet. Zigzag communication trenches connecting the two parallels were dug on the night of July 24, again using the flying sap under cover of darkness, while the parapet of the parallel was revetted with sandbags. Traverses and the banquette tread were built on July 25. The second parallel was ready for use by that night, and the first parallel was evacuated as Gillmore's siege force moved forward. The Federals took up the inclined palisades in front of the first parallel and used it in the advanced position.[5]

Gillmore placed eleven Parrott rifles in the second parallel and planted seven more to the left and rear of the first parallel in preparation for the bombardment of Fort Sumter. A bombproof was built on the site of the cemetery just behind the second parallel; it was used by the infantrymen until needed as a magazine. The headquarters of the general of the trenches was placed in this parallel, too.[6]

The third parallel was opened on the night of August 9, a month after the initial Union landing on Morris Island. It lay 330 yards in front of the second parallel and 540 yards from Wagner. This time only 124 engineer troops were used. They started a communications trench to link the second with the third parallels. The sand was of a consistency that allowed them to dig down as far as 8 feet without revetting. A line of pickets was thrown out 30 yards in front of the engineers, with the Rebel picket line only 30 yards in front of the Union pickets. But the engineers dug so quietly on their hands and knees, using short-handled shovels, that hardly a sound could be heard above the pounding surf. The opening was done by the textbook. An engineer officer took one end of a rope with knots tied at 6-foot intervals and stretched it along the line of the proposed parallel. Then the men dropped to the sand, held onto the knot with their left hand, and dug with their right, throwing the sand over the rope. They dug laterally to connect their pits with the men to right and left. Sandbags were used to build loopholes for the sharpshooters, who took their places at dawn. The engineers then built the banquette and revetted the parallel, built an emplacement for the Requa battery, and erected the inclined palisades on the night of August 10.[7]

Gillmore decided not to push farther until the breaching batteries opened on Sumter, and that would take several days. Meanwhile the engineers worked to consolidate the position. The communication trench between the first and second parallels was revetted with sandbags so it would last longer and serve as a splinterproof shelter. It also would prevent the infantrymen from digging holes in the walls for their personal use, a practice that had been weakening the trenches for some time. Brooks preferred to use wood for this revetment, but it could not be obtained on the island. Unlike the first, the second parallel was not abandoned. Maintenance work on all the fortifications was constant. Officers in charge of each duty rotation inspected everything twice to see if repairs were needed. Iron rods were used to measure the sand covering the magazines, which had to be at least 8 feet deep. Gillmore and Brooks devoted a lot of time and attention to defensive features. The second and third parallels had a 10-foot-wide trench for easy movement of troops, and the banquette was 2 feet wide. The obstacles in front were so strong that they would have disrupted attacking formations even without firing by the defenders. A cover of at least 2 feet was kept on the splinterproof shelters, the communication trench was 10 feet wide, and parapets were at least 6½ feet high and 3 feet thick on top.[8]

The breaching batteries opened fire on August 17, delivering about 450 rounds per day at Fort Sumter. Its gorge and southeast face were hit the hardest, with overshoots punching the interior of the north and northwest faces. Soon Sumter was "a mere infantry outpost," in Gillmore's words, because the Confederates dismounted their guns and held it with a small garrison. The intense bombardment eased on August 23 when Federal gunners fired only a few rounds per day to prevent repairs to the walls. Then they resumed pounding the fort on August 30 and 31 in preparation for a proposed navy push into the harbor. That attack, however, was canceled.[9]

Brooks would have to abandon the flying sap, the quickest and most decisive way to advance his approaches. He used the full sap (digging an approach trench forward) beyond the third parallel. Unprotected diggers could not be sent into the darkness because Battery Wagner was too close. A sap roller (a rolling obstruction to protect the head of the approach trench) was constructed. The engineers advanced toward the desired spot on which to plant the fourth parallel on the night of August 18. A Requa battery was emplaced to cover the head of the sap. Initially the engineers had to work in mud and water as they traversed the edge of the marsh, yet ten men of the 1st New York Engineers dug sixty feet in six hours before they were relieved by another rotation of men. The second shift dug seventy feet during the daylight hours of August 19. Confederate sharpshooters fired constantly at the sappers, who lost one man from a shell explosion that day. Brooks decided it was worth risking the flying sap on a limited basis and ordered it done that night. The engineers were able to advance the sap 160 yards, to a point only a few yards in front of the Rebel picket line. Brooks detailed 300 men to guard the sap. He complained that it was very difficult to maintain a good parapet close to the sap roller, for the recent rains had left water standing only two feet below the surface.[10]

Brooks now encountered his most difficult problem: a small sand ridge directly in the path of his sap. The Confederates pulled their picket line back to this ridge. Sharpshooters stationed there harassed the sappers unmercifully. An attempt by the 100th New York to attack this position failed on the night of August 21, so Brooks built a fourth parallel 150 yards in front of the ridge and massed troops to capture it. He boldly used the flying sap again, placing his diggers immediately behind a line of skirmishers who kept the Rebels busy, only 300 yards from Battery Wagner. After furious digging, the Yankees were deep enough for temporary shelter. The sap was advanced quickly without using a sap roller to connect with the new parallel that night. All this digging was done by only 100 infantrymen and 15 engineers. The parallel was strengthened during daylight hours on August 22, with sandbagged loopholes, a banquette, and a widened trench. Empty powder barrels were also used to revet the fourth parallel.[11]

The attack on the sand ridge took place on the evening of August 26 after a heavy bombardment of both the ridge and Battery Wagner. This fire dismounted an 8-inch howitzer in the fort and shredded the sandbagged loopholes of the sharpshooters on the ridge. The 24th Massachusetts, 400 strong and supported by the 3rd New Hampshire, sallied from the fourth parallel at dusk amid volleys of musketry. It captured 76 of the 89 men there, who belonged to the 61st North Carolina. Most of the captured Tar Heels were afraid to run back to the fort because of the torpedoes scattered across the sand. Officers in Wagner quickly sent out 175 reinforcements, but they were too late to help. Col. George P. Harrison, who commanded Wagner that night, considered a counterattack but concluded from the reports of survivors that the Federals were too strong. Moreover, he was not certain of the location of all torpedoes planted in front of Wagner. This was not much of a problem when moving small groups back and forth to the ridge, but a determined counterattack would involve many more men who could be endangered by their own torpedoes. Brooks was not impressed by the captured works on the ridge. He called them "rude rifle-pits" with sandbag traverses and loopholes.[12]

The last major barrier to the siege approach had been breached, but the sapping grew more difficult beyond the sand ridge. There were dozens of torpedoes in front of Wagner, and the decreasing range meant that more lead and iron of all kinds could be delivered on the sap head. The fifth and last parallel was opened on the sand ridge the night of its capture. It would be the launching point for the push to cover the last 300 yards to Battery Wagner. This, the most narrow approach to the work, had been the key to the failure of both Union attacks. What could not be crossed by a wide frontage of troops could more easily be traversed if the sap were dug at sharp zigzags, worming its way across the neck of low-lying sand until the ditch of Wagner was within reach.[13]

Gillmore's men had already constructed an impressive series of siege works by the time they reached the sand ridge. According to the manuals, but in contrast to the Union siege approaches at Vicksburg, they had many defensive features. The Federals had the use of five Requa guns. Altogether, nineteen positions were constructed for these guns: four in the first parallel, five in the second, two in the third, five in the fourth, two in the fifth, and one in front of the fifth. Two of the guns were fired in a skirmish on the evening of August 25, but the Requas were never tested in a major attack.[14]

The second parallel remained the base of Gillmore's advance, and it was

Federal bombproof, Morris Island. Note the heavy use of sandbags as revetment and the rich display of tools and debris. A sandbagged lookout post is on the top left of the structure, and a Confederate torpedo sits on the ground with a bottle on top of it. (Massachusetts Commandery, Military Order of the Loyal Legion and the U.S. Army Military History Institute)

the most heavily fortified line of the siege works. Splinterproofs were built not only to protect the men but to shield the latrines as well, and a lookout post was made of sandbags on top of the magazine. Brooks had a tough time figuring out how to construct an effective obstacle to a Rebel sortie on the beach at low tide, for when the tide rose, the surf would wash over anything that was placed there. He built an emplacement for a Requa gun at the edge of the high-water mark and embrasured it so the gun could sweep the open beach at low tide. Whatever timber was used at the second parallel had to be hauled from Folly Island, as there were only two trees on Morris. There was little space at the second parallel, too. Brooks noted that he had to cram everything into an area only nine acres in size. "There is not room enough, nor earth enough, to make suitable traverses, epaulements, and bomb proof shelters for the protection of guns, ammunition, and garrison," he complained.[15]

Engineer troops constructed 460 yards of inclined palisades covering the first and second parallels. Made of pine saplings four to seven inches in diameter, the palisades was assembled at the engineer depot and divided into panels of five poles each for easier transportation. The engineers also

Federal splinterproof, Morris Island. Made of barrels, timber, and planks, with brush as a screen, it was designed to protect occupants from shell fragments but would have collapsed if directly hit. (Massachusetts Commandery, Military Order of the Loyal Legion and the U.S. Army Military History Institute)

made abatis to fill the gaps created in the palisades by Confederate artillery fire. Of course, the material for both palisades and abatis had to be hauled three miles from Folly Island.[16]

Given the nature of the soil on Morris Island, sandbags were used almost entirely for revetting. Sandbags also were useful in filling gabions, making foundations for mortar platforms, and constructing banquettes, traverses, and splinterproofs. When empty and flat, the bags measured six by ten by twenty-four inches; they weighed eighty-five pounds when filled. But the Federals preferred them only three-fourths full because when completely filled, they tended to burst if too much pressure was exerted on them. The open end of the sandbag was twisted and tucked underneath, rather than tied closely. Brooks discovered that he had to secure sandbags in place with stakes and wire only when he used them to revet the batteries of the heaviest guns. The muzzle blasts sometimes tore the cloth or even set the bags on fire, but both problems were solved if the gunners kept the bags wet during firing. Normal wear and tear created holes in all sandbags and dry sand escaped, but Brooks noticed that a new sandbag revetment could last about two months before this became a problem. He reported that 46,175 sandbags were used in the reduction of Battery Wagner.[17]

Other types of revetting material did not work so well with the fine Morris Island sand, which quickly leaked through the large cracks in gabions. Empty powder barrels filled with sand were useful to raise the parapet of approaches in front of the second parallel, but there were not enough of them. Strong sea breezes quickly weathered the parapets, which "are half destroyed in a week, and the trenches are correspondingly filled up," reported Brooks. This forced the Federals to constantly repair the works. At another location they might have put a layer of sod or even mud on them, but time and materials were not available.[18]

Brooks experimented with the embrasures of the heavy batteries, tying rawhide covers to shield the sandbag revetment, but the blast simply carried away the hides. Iron coverings were the answer, so Brooks salvaged iron from the wreck of a blockade runner at Light House Inlet. He made mantlets (protective covers) for the embrasures out of the same iron. Not all heavy guns were fixed in this way, but a bit of ingenuity served Brooks well. The Russians had used the same kind of iron to revet the embrasures of their batteries at Sebastopol.[19]

The wire entanglements used in front of the parallels were a relatively new feature of warfare. Stakes three and a half feet long, with two feet in the ground, were placed seven feet apart "in quincunx order"—that is, in a square with a fifth stake in the middle. Number 12 wire was wrapped in notches cut in the stakes from twelve to eighteen inches above the ground. Additional wire was stretched between the quincunxes and even from the quincunxes to the top of the palisades. Brooks was quite pleased with this obstacle. It was quickly and easily built and was a very good substitute for an abatis. Even Federal troops who knew of its existence often tripped over it, and the wires were seldom disturbed by Rebel artillery fire.[20]

Considering the small garrison of Wagner, the Federals expended a great deal of energy and material on defensive measures in their siege works. The labor needed to make all this was enormous for the relatively small force, about 10,000 men, available to Gillmore. Brooks estimated that three-fourths of the manual labor in the siege was expended in shoveling sand, and half of the rest was used in carrying material. About three-fourths of the work was done at night and nine-tenths of it under fire. Rebel sharpshooters seldom fired in the dark, but during the day they were quite active. Brooks reported that thirty-five artillery rounds per hour was considered heavy fire, but they sometimes received double that rate. That is why up to 150 men were hit in the advanced working parties and guard detachments during the

Federal Battery Rosecrans, Morris Island. This is one of four breaching batteries on the second parallel. Note how the revetment is constructed, and note the palisades on the far right. Also note the clutter of material behind the three 100-pounder Parrott rifles. (Massachusetts Commandery, Military Order of the Loyal Legion and the U.S. Army Military History Institute)

course of the siege. Illness was a serious problem. At the worst phase of the siege, nearly 22 percent of Gillmore's troops were sick. His 2,000 black troops were particularly pressed for work details, while white troops were usually used as guards. Eight-hour shifts were best for the work details, and the officers justified the use of black troops for heavy labor with the widespread belief that they worked more willingly. White soldiers sometimes skulked and complained when assigned manual labor. The problem was worsened by the fact that regimental officers often detailed their worst subordinates to supervise work details.[21]

The defensive power of these siege works was undeniable. The defenses would have held against almost any attack the Confederates could have mounted. The offensive power of the Federal works was immense as well. The whole point of the siege was to reduce Wagner and destroy Sumter, and Gillmore's artillery tried to accomplish both goals. Seven batteries were constructed among the siege works: one behind the first parallel, two on the right wing of the abandoned first parallel, and four at the second parallel.

Federal Battery Stevens, Morris Island. This was one of nine breaching batteries lo-cated well to the left and rear of the first parallel, where Morris Island was much wider. Two 10-pounder Parrotts were planted snugly behind a well-made sandbag revetment. The embrasures were formed with gabions. The gunners have hung their coats on poles and on pegs fastened to the sandbags. (Massachusetts Commandery, Military Order of the Loyal Legion and the U.S. Army Military History Institute)

Nearly all were named for officers prominent in the Union army, some of whom had been killed at Gettysburg. Nine more batteries were constructed well to the left and rear of the first parallel, where the south end of Morris Island was much wider. Altogether these works mounted thirty-eight guns, and the ironclads added their fire as well. As noted earlier, the bombardment of Sumter started on August 17 and continued on and off for several weeks. Col. John W. Turner, Gillmore's chief of artillery, worked out shifts for the gun crews. The breaching batteries on Morris Island fired more often on Sumter than the guns that were trained on Wagner, so their crews were on duty four hours and then took eight hours off. The fire on Sumter was very effective, far exceeding the damage done to Fort Pulaski by Gillmore's guns in April 1862. Soon the masonry walls of the fort were reduced to rubble so jagged that Turner saw through his field glasses that some projectiles did not strike squarely enough on a surface to detonate the fuse. "The lines were entirely destroyed," recalled a Federal artillery officer, "and it appeared a shapeless mass of brick and mortar."[22]

The Union fire on Battery Wagner had less obvious effect. The sand parapets often absorbed or even deflected projectiles, and they deteriorated more grudgingly when shells exploded on or inside them. Duty in the batteries firing on Wagner was, in some ways, more onerous. Turner established twelve-hour shifts for the gunners in these batteries because they fired less often, and the "dry, hard, flinty sand" blew all over the place and severely annoyed the men. Turner believed that the unusually large number of burst guns was caused by sand blowing into the barrels. It was necessary to locate the guns behind the Federal troops, who therefore suffered from premature explosions. The Rebels in Wagner lost up to seven men per day from the Union artillery fire.[23]

The Federals were positioned close enough to fire on Charleston with the right kind of ordnance, and Gillmore had the best available. Colonel Serrell suggested emplacing a heavy gun one mile from Morris Island, believing a suitable platform could be constructed on the marsh where the muck was sixteen feet deep. Gillmore put him in charge of the work. He and Michie developed a plan for what became the Swamp Angel Battery, or the Marsh Battery. They started on August 10 and drove pilings deep into the marsh by manual labor. Then they bolted two layers of pine logs onto the top of the pilings. The parapet was constructed entirely of 13,000 sandbags, filled on Morris Island and transported to the site. The gun platform consisted of marsh grass, canvas, sand, and planks. The whole emplacement supported an 8-inch Parrott rifle and weighed a total of twelve tons, while a plank causeway connected the site to Morris Island. The gun was hauled by boat to the emplacement in one night and was ready to open fire on August 17. At a range of 8,800 yards and thirty-five degrees elevation, the Swamp Angel shocked the citizens of Charleston with its fire. It was the first time in the war that a major city of the Confederacy was bombarded. Only at Fredericksburg did Federal guns deliberately fire into residential areas of a Southern town on a large scale. Gillmore's gunners used compass readings to aim at the steeple of St. Michael's Church, and they discharged shells filled with a chemical mixture designed to set fires. Fortunately for the residents, the extreme elevation weakened the gun, and it burst on the thirty-sixth round on August 23. Gillmore did not replace it for the duration of the siege, but a second Parrott was installed at the site in November 1863.[24]

Several superb photographs were taken of the Union siege works on Morris Island, providing an invaluable look at life in the trenches. The huge guns, ranging from 30-pounder to 300-pounder Parrotts, were protected by massive parapets. One can easily see how the sandbags and gabions were aligned to shore up the sand. Photographs of bombproofs show construction details

The Swamp Angel. This is the dismounted first Swamp Angel, which burst on August 23, 1863. Gillmore did not replace it until the following November. One can see the logs that constituted the base of the emplacement; the parapets were made entirely of sandbags. Its construction in the middle of the marsh west of Morris Island was an engineering achievement. (Massachusetts Commandery, Military Order of the Loyal Legion and the U.S. Army Military History Institute)

as well as the litter of equipment, even a disarmed Confederate torpedo. The 300-pounder Parrott burst, but enterprising gunners simply chipped back the jagged edges and continued firing. Several photographs of batteries Brown, Hays, Kirby, Meade, Reynolds, Rosecrans, and Strong give a sense of the clutter and debris lying about on the ground. The men had to pick their way around this mess much as a craftsman had to walk around the cast-off pieces of his handiwork. There was limited time and energy to maintain a spotless battery, and Gillmore's gunners hardly bothered to try.[25]

Clean or not, the Federal batteries severely punished the Rebels. Confederate officers did all they could to respond to the Union fire. They added two howitzers, two heavy guns, and a mortar to Wagner's armament and kept the garrison at a steady strength of 1,000 infantrymen and 180 gunners. The artillerymen exacted a price among the Federal guards and working parties. Wagner was so close that they had little time to take cover when lookouts yelled, "Cover, Wagner"; the shell often exploded before the warning was given. Colonel Harrison at times ordered his gunners to cease fire for a bit to draw out the Yankee working parties; then they resumed. "I found this to work well," he reported, "as my pickets report many shrieks from the

Burst Parrott rifle, Morris Island. This 300-pounder gun was chipped back and made ready for continued firing. The revetment appears to be a wall of sod, while gabions, fascines, and planks form the embrasure. (Massachusetts Commandery, Military Order of the Loyal Legion and the U.S. Army Military History Institute)

enemy's wounded." The Rebels were good at filling the embrasures with sandbags after each firing of the heavy guns to shield themselves from Union sharpshooters. They even ran a field piece out of the fort one night to fire on a working party, then ran it back before the Federals could return fire.[26]

Beauregard ordered the construction of five batteries along the southern edge of James Island to fire on the Federals besieging Wagner. They were poorly constructed because of the low-lying ground and the necessity for haste. When a rainstorm hit the area in late August, it flooded five gun platforms in Battery Haskell alone. The engineers had to drain them by cutting through defensive parapets and digging ditches that later interfered with the movement of guns. Maj. Edward Manigault, who was in charge of the heavy guns at Charleston, also noted that many rounds either exploded prematurely or failed to detonate at all. Of eighteen shells fired at one of Gillmore's batteries, three burst short, two broke prematurely, and only four landed on or near the target. These scattered the Yankee workmen only for a few minutes. Nevertheless, Gillmore lost four or five men each day from the fire of these James Island batteries. This was little more than an annoyance for a determined force such as Gillmore commanded.[27]

The small Confederate garrison of Wagner was just as determined, and it was managed with enough skill to endure the siege. The Rebels rotated commanders and regiments on a regular basis; this was probably the best solution to the problem of using a small force in a dangerous position. But Ripley complained that the frequent change of commanders caused inefficiency and confusion. He particularly referred to the management of the ammunition supply, but his comments could apply to all aspects of command in the fort. At least six officers were identified as commanding the fort during the course of the siege. The regiments were relieved regularly, from every two days when the bombardment was severe, to as many as eight days. Brig. Gen. Thomas L. Clingman argued that four days was the optimum. His 8th North Carolina was worn out by its week-long tour of duty at the fort. The 4th Georgia remained at Wagner for five days and lost one killed and eight wounded. The line of communications was tenuous. All supplies and troops had to be shipped from the forward depot at Fort Johnson to the wharf at Battery Gregg during the night.[28]

Under almost constant fire and distress from the heat while cooped up in a small place, the defenders of Wagner suffered physically and emotionally. Officers noted that fatigue parties often worked slowly and that the men took catnaps or slipped away into the darkness, even when good commissioned officers supervised their work. Many suggested relying on slave labor instead of soldiers. As the pressure of the siege mounted, discipline and attention to detail suffered. Engineer Capt. J. T. Champneys complained that the fort was becoming a mess. The bombproofs were "quite unpleasant," and the ground around the commissary building was "very offensive." Much "splintered wood" and "shattered timber" lay scattered inside the fort. Morale was affected by the common belief that if Sumter fell, the garrison on Morris Island would be cut off and sacrificed. The frequent Union artillery fire during the night also demoralized the garrison. Thomas Grange Simons of the 25th South Carolina could get no more than a half-hour of sleep at a time during his five-day rotation on the island, due to the noise and the constant call for repair parties. The well inside Wagner yielded salty water, and the hospital was overcrowded. Many wounded had to be placed outside the work behind sand hills.[29]

The large bombproof barely protected the garrison. There was not enough room inside it because the hospital took up a lot of space. Many soldiers were forced to remain out in the open, clinging to the interior slope of the parapet for protection even during the heaviest bombardment. Johnson Hagood experimented with sending half the garrison out of the battery to take shelter among the sand hills to the rear, believing they could rush back in time if an attack took place. John Harleston of the 4th South Carolina Cavalry acted as

Bombproof in Battery Wagner. Taken soon after Wagner fell, this photograph shows that many of the sandbags that constituted the Confederate bombproof were shredded by artillery fire and deteriorated by weathering. The Federal troops, some of whom apparently are members of the 54th Massachusetts, have a collection of shovels and picks leaning against the bombproof wall. (Massachusetts Commandery, Military Order of the Loyal Legion and the U.S. Army Military History Institute)

a courier between Gregg and Wagner. He recalled that when a shell caved in the entrance to the smaller bombproof one night, it trapped the men inside. An officer organized the rescue effort and assigned a man to dig for five minutes at the narrow opening. He was relieved by another until those inside were saved. Shells continued to fall every few minutes. One of them exploded in the entrance and nearly cut a man in two. His comrades had to dig out his body in order to continue the rescue effort.[30]

Harleston saw much more during his tour of duty as a courier. When he arrived on Morris Island on the night of August 31, he met an acquaintance who was leaving. "I thank God I am getting away from this place," the man told Harleston. "I tell you it is hell, hell." The couriers had only five worn-out horses, all of which were scratched by artillery fire, to cover the three-quarters of a mile that separated Gregg from Wagner. Even the corral had to be protected by an earthwork. It was worth a man's life to ride between the two forts along the beach, exposed to artillery fire the whole distance and to Union sharpshooters near Wagner.[31]

The garrison was exposed to the "burning sun of a Southern summer, its heat intensified by the reflection of the white sand," wrote Robert C. Gilchrist, an artillery officer in the battery. It "scorched and blistered the unprotected garrison," while rainstorms soaked the men unmercifully. "An intolerable stench from the unearthed dead of the previous conflict, the carcasses of cavalry horses lying where they fell in the rear, and barrels of putrid meat thrown out on the beach, sickened the defenders. A large and brilliantly colored fly, attracted by the feast, and unseen before, inflicted wounds more painful, though less dangerous, than the shot of the enemy. Water was scarcer than whiskey." The meat spoiled because of the long delays often encountered in shipping provisions from Charleston to Battery Gregg. Sometimes the barrels would be on the docks or in the holds of ships forty-eight hours in transit.[32]

Repair work on Wagner was constant and demanding, and the little garrison could barely keep up with it. They were hampered by a shortage of sandbags, which were especially useful in constructing loopholes for sharpshooters. Engineer Champneys directed a series of repairs during his time at Wagner, including replacing boards that held up the banquette, repairing revetments, and replacing sand blasted away from the bombproof, parapets, and traverses. Return artillery fire often was postponed or canceled entirely because of the need for workers to repair gun embrasures. Sometimes planned work was canceled because of ignorance. The engineers wanted to plant obstacles in the ditch of the land face one night but decided not to when no one could recall for certain whether torpedoes had been planted in the ditch. The work details were organized into two squads of seventy-five men each night. Garrison commanders often found the work so poorly done that it had to be redone later. Col. Lawrence M. Keitt reported on August 18 that the "men were greatly fatigued last night, and it was difficult to keep any but the willing men at work."[33]

The most unique and innovative feature of Wagner's defenses was the torpedo field planted along its land face. The Confederates began installing it on July 11 when fifty-seven shells were placed from 5 to 20 yards in front of the ditch. Capt. M. M. Gray, who had charge of them, examined the field after the assault of July 18 and found that twenty had been exploded, many by Federal artillery fire. Others were damaged by heavy rains that fell before July 18. Gray then planted an additional forty-seven shells, ranging from 20 to 250 yards in front of the fort. More and more were emplaced right up to the end of the siege until there was a minefield stretching far and wide along the approach to Wagner.[34]

This minefield was a significant obstacle for the Federals. It would have claimed many lives if a third assault had been planned, and it forced the sappers to slow down as well. But as Gillmore pointed out, it also protected the Federals because it inhibited sorties by the garrison against the head of the sap. In fact, several Confederates were killed by the torpedoes during the siege. When a flag was raised to pass communications between the lines on July 27, two Rebel artillerymen wandered in front of the fort and were killed by mines. One wonders if they were trying to desert. Another Rebel was badly wounded when he crawled over a torpedo one night when out on a detail to plant more of them. Perhaps the fact that the wind blew sand that covered the torpedoes accounts for the accidents that sometimes happened to the Confederates.[35]

When Federal sappers advanced beyond the sand ridge that had been captured on August 26, they encountered the first torpedo some 200 yards from the battery. Throughout the rest of the siege, the Yankees dug up more than sixty mines as they pushed their sap forward. Brooks divided them into three types. He found twenty that were fully armed 24-pounder shells with a tin covering. They were buried just beneath the surface with a percussion fuse on top that could be detonated by a footfall. More than thirty mines were made of ten-gallon kegs with conical additions on the ends. Brooks assumed these were normally used as underwater mines. The Rebels had placed boards on the ground with one end resting on the fuse so that anyone stepping on the board, even a few feet from the mine, would set it off. Finally, the sappers encountered three huge 15-inch Navy shells buried in the sand with detonation devices similar to those on the wooden kegs. They dug underneath these mines to dislodge them. The wooden kegs were rendered harmless by drilling small holes through the casing and pouring water in to soak the powder. Six torpedoes, however, exploded accidentally during the process of removal, causing twelve casualties. Some of the mines apparently had wires strung from the fuse to the fort so they could be exploded by the garrison.[36]

The torpedoes were not the only impediment to the final advance toward Wagner. The Federals established their fifth parallel on the sand ridge and immediately resumed sapping. The approach started from the right wing of the parallel, 245 yards from the Rebel work, and traced a huge zigzag, first toward the marsh and then to the beach. At that point, the head of the sap was only 100 yards from Wagner, but that last short distance was the most difficult to traverse. "The dark and gloomy days of the siege were now upon us," wrote Gillmore; "our progress became discouragingly slow and even fearfully uncertain." The head of the sap was so close that converging fire from different points in Wagner could be delivered on it, and the combination of clear skies and a full moon created so much light that Rebel sharpshooters were able to inflict heavy casualties among the sappers on the night

Federal engineers demonstrating how to sap, Morris Island. Members of the 1st New York Engineers show how the sapping operation worked. This photograph was taken after the fall of Battery Wagner, which can dimly be seen in the right background, and probably was exposed at a spot on the fifth Union parallel. (Massachusetts Commandery, Military Order of the Loyal Legion and the U.S. Army Military History Institute)

of August 29. The approach was stalled. Meanwhile, Brooks consolidated his hold on the fifth parallel. He established a Requa battery and built sandbagged loopholes and a banquette. Gillmore wanted him to construct more protected spaces using traverses so that he could mass infantry for an attack on Wagner.[37]

The sappers now became the key elements of Gillmore's command, for they had to take the army across the last 100 yards of sand to the ditch. Brooks divided the eight artificers and two noncommissioned officers of his sapping brigade into two squads to alternate duty at the head of the approach. They were responsible for moving the sap roller, a one-ton monster that protected the diggers. It was rolled forward only a few inches at a time, using hooks on the end of twelve-foot poles. The sappers quickly piled up sand to cover the flanks and then dug a trench four feet wide and two feet deep. The profile of the parapet could be smoothed out with a drag shovel, an instrument specially designed to be used from behind cover. The Confederates employed as many as 100 sharpshooters to harass the sappers during the day, but they caused little damage as long as due precautions were taken. Soon, however, the numerous torpedoes forced Brooks to stop using the sap roller.[38]

Gillmore intensified his efforts. He planned a concentrated artillery barrage by his batteries and the USS *New Ironsides* day and night to keep down Rebel fire and allow the sappers to dig across the last 100 yards. Two calcium lights would be used to illuminate the fort at night. These devices were invented by Robert Grant in 1850 and used a combination of oxygen and hydrogen as a heat source. Parabolic reflectors then directed the resulting light as far as eight miles. Gillmore set them up 750 yards from Fort Wagner, out of effective small arms range for the Confederates, and had a laboratory staffed by forty people to produce the oxygen and hydrogen. The Yankees were also helped by the fact that the James Island batteries ceased firing for fear of hitting the fort. Gillmore had earlier asked for a huge shipment of supplies, including 100,000 sandbags, fifty coils of assorted wire, and additional shovels, from the Engineer Department in Washington, D.C. Two coils of Gomez safety fuse, normally used in springing underground mines, were part of the shipment, indicating that Gillmore wanted to be prepared for all contingencies as he closed in on Wagner.

The plan went into operation on the morning of September 5, and it ushered in the most intense phase of the siege. Brooks's sappers had been able to advance the approach only about twenty-five yards the preceding few days. Now, in one day alone, they dug 150 yards in a series of short zigzags, ending up very near the beach. At dawn on September 6, the fort lay silent and badly damaged by the heavy Union fire. "It looms over the head of the sap, a huge, shapeless sand bluff," as Brooks put it. He ordered a U.S. flag flown at the head of the sap so gunners on the *New Ironsides* could better direct their fire. Brooks noticed that the Navy projectiles often hit the parapet and ricocheted into the fort, but fragments sometimes fell back into the ditch and even into the head of his sap. One Federal was injured this way. When the army projectiles exploded in the parapet of Wagner, they usually gouged a hole in it that was filled by the loose, shifting sand rolling downhill. The sappers found one torpedo in their path on September 5 and seven more the next day. Peering to the left, they could see many plungers on the ground in front of the land face. They also cut into several decaying bodies of their comrades who had been killed on July 18 and whose remains had been buried in front of the fort. The night before, some sappers had managed to crawl to the ditch of Battery Wagner and look around.[39]

These last few hours of the siege were the most impressive to observers. Charles Colcock Jones, a Rebel officer stationed on James Island, looked through his field glasses and plainly saw the Federals digging during the day, "as busy as bees, in full view and just in front of the Fort, working away with a steadiness and a rapidity, perfectly remarkable." During the night, Jones tracked the burning fuses of shells as they arched through the sky and exploded in and around the battery, illuminating it with a weird light that supplemented the shining moon. Both Wagner and Gregg remained silent.[40]

From the Union perspective, the view was a bit different. Officer William Eliot Furness observed the bombardment from a mortar battery. "It seemed like tossing heavy balls into a great sand-hill, which the explosions after the dropping of each ball converted into a hell's mouth. The air was thick and murky with smoke, the gunners were grimed and dripping with sweat from excitement and work, and the shells as they left the mortars described the most beautiful curves. Beyond the flag on the Rebel stronghold, no sign of life appeared in Wagner."[41]

Gillmore waxed poetic in describing the final bombardment. "As a pyrotechnic achievement alone, the exhibition at night was brilliant and attractive, while the dazzling light thrown from our advanced trenches, the deafening roar of our guns, and the answering peals from James Island added sublimity and grandeur to the scene. The imagination was beguiled and taken captive, and all the cruel realities of war were for a time forgotten in the excitement of this novel spectacle."[42]

Keitt commanded Wagner at this time and seemed more perturbed by the naval gunfire than by the land-based guns. He ordered nearly all of his infantry into the bombproofs, leaving only a few men on the parapet. Gun crews were kept at their posts on the land face but not on the sea face. Artillery officer Robert C. Gilchrist noticed that the navy projectiles often skipped on the water before slamming into or across the parapet. One ball hit a school of mullet and threw one into the fort.[43]

Wagner's condition slowly deteriorated during this intense bombardment. It had become a mess even before September 5, with broken gun carriages, odd pieces of lumber, splinters torn from wooden revetments by previous shelling, and thousands of projectile fragments littering the interior. Now the increased tempo of shelling diminished parapets and traverses, and the roof of the bombproof was furrowed like a plowed field. A traverse that protected the entrance to the hospital and one of the magazines was broken, and sand filled the passages to both. A relay of men had to dig the entrance out as shells continued to land in the area. "I could hear the frequent cry 'Call the ambulance corps,'" remembered Capt. Thomas A. Huguenin of the 1st South Carolina, "and presently some poor fellow would be brought in horribly mangled from the dangerous spot." But the job was eventually done, and light, air, and help could enter the hospital once more.

More than forty men were hit on September 5, and the killing continued the next day. The calcium light shone all night, virtually stopping repairs on the fort, and Union sharpshooters fired so much during the day that work details could not perform their duties.[44]

Living conditions in Wagner deteriorated faster than the fort itself. The Rebels had been tried to the utmost even before the concentrated bombardment began on September 5. They subsisted on raw bacon and biscuit and had no opportunity to bathe or sleep, night or day, when Captain Huguenin observed them on September 3. The water was nearly gone, so small wells were dug in and to the rear of the fort; but the liquid in these was so tainted by decaying bodies that it could not be used. The naval fire "was a novelty" for them, according to Keitt, and many men were demoralized by it. They were fainting from the heat, tension, and stifling air in the crowded bombproofs. His sharpshooters could do nothing to slow the work of the Federal sappers, which further diminished the morale of his men.[45]

An anonymous chaplain of one of Keitt's regiments offered an evocative description of life in Wagner during those last two days. The bombproofs were amazing, in his view. They saved the lives of so many men, yet they were hellish places. The chaplain felt "dazed by my long stay in the darkness, and weakened even to exhaustion by the toils and griefs of my work; head throbbing loud and hard, mental faculties almost benumbed." The bombproof walls were made of pine logs placed upright, with horizontal logs and a thick layer of sand for the roof. Rainwater constantly seeped through the sand and dripped onto the plank floor of the enclosure; the sound was audible even above the noise of the shelling. The drips also taunted the thirsty occupants. The chaplain gave a service on the afternoon of September 5 and forever remembered that the candle burned a "dirty yellow" flame because of the foul air. He could see the faces of the garrison, "ghastly, squalid, smirched—lips parched, tangled hair, eyes glittering with fever, watching and toil." They soaked up the religious message like men desperate for hope.[46]

This chaplain remembered the bombproofs of Wagner as the most salient experience of the war. "The sickening smell of blood, as from some foul shambles in a dungeon; the reeking, almost unbreatheable air, away from the skylight; the bare-armed surgeons, operating by candle-light; the floor, crowded with anguish and death; the grim, low walls, and the steady drip, drip, drip, ticking aloud; all these must come into the picture of the hospital bomb-proof of Battery Wagner."[47]

Early on the night of September 6, after the sap reached the fort, Federal captain Wheelock Pratt made a thorough inspection of the sea face. He found a fraise of sharpened stakes planted in the wall of the ditch, and about 200 pikes left over from the War of 1812 were stuck among them. Pratt was able to pull out the pikes and lay them in the bottom of the ditch, but the stakes were too firmly embedded. Meanwhile the sappers had completed the approach by running it along the glacis, the forward crest of the ditch, along the sea face. They even threw dirt into the bottom of the ditch to cover the stakes. The head of the sap stopped at the flanking wall that connected the sea face to the beach. The Federals did not have to worry about naval gunfire, for the *New Ironsides* fired only during the day. After a month and a half of digging, the siege of Battery Wagner had reached its climax.[48]

Gillmore planned his assault and briefed his subordinates on the night of September 6. The attack was to take place at 9:00 A.M. the next morning, when low tide would allow more room along the beach. The 3rd New Hampshire and 97th Pennsylvania would lead the attack by scaling the sea face, crossing the roof of the bombproof, and sealing its entrance to trap the garrison. Stevenson's brigade was to use the beach to bypass the fort altogether and attack the low-lying infantry parapet that covered its rear. Col. William W. H. Davis's brigade was to follow Stevenson but deploy facing north so it could block any movement of Rebel troops from Battery Gregg. Gillmore passed out drawings of the fort to brigade commanders at the conference. It was a good plan of attack, involving some 3,000 men. The companies assigned to scale the sea face were also issued shovels. The Federal artillery would fire until the last minute before the assault.[49]

Beauregard pulled the garrison out only hours before the attack was to take place. He sent David B. Harris and Capt. Francis D. Lee to Wagner on September 6 to inspect the battery and recommend a course of action. Harris advised evacuation. He found the men so discouraged by the stress of the final bombardment that a determined attack probably could not be repulsed. The fort was silent; it offered virtually no artillery fire or sharpshooting to impede the Yankees, and the angle was badly damaged. Harris thought the fort would be untenable in a couple of days.[50]

The pullout went smoothly, considering the constant artillery fire and the calcium lights that continued to shine on the fort. First the wounded and sick were removed, then companies were marched in small detachments to the wharf at Battery Gregg. The powder magazines were rigged with explosives. Two companies remained behind to light them and do other odd jobs before emptying the place; but the fuses were defective, and the magazines were never fired. No one in the garrison regretted giving up the fort. "It was a veritable deathtrap," recalled H. S. Fuller of the 23rd Georgia, "and it was a relief to us when we learned that the island was to be evacuated." John

Harleston was among the last to leave. On the boat going to Fort Johnson, he overheard a North Carolina soldier pronounce a final assessment of the place. "I have heard the preachers talk abut Hell, a great big hole, full of fire and brimstone, where a bad fellow was dropped in, and I will allow it used to move me at times, but Gentlemen[,] Hell can't be worse than Battery Wagner. I have got out of that, and the other place ain't going to worry me any more!"[51]

The evacuation was conducted so well that the Federals had no inkling of it until the first streaks of dawn on September 7. A deserter brought the first news of the pullout, and the Federals sent skirmishers who found the garrison had gone. Only seventy errant Rebels were caught. The work was littered with personal baggage, spiked guns, and commissary stores. "It looks almost impossible that what we have done could be done," marveled George Benson Fox of the 75th Ohio. The Confederates had lost 125 men during the final bombardment, and they evacuated Battery Gregg as well as Wagner. All of Morris Island was in Gillmore's hands.[52]

Gillmore was eager to see the work and inspected it immediately after the evacuation. He was a bit disappointed, for the damage to key points, like the large bombproof, was not as great as he had expected. Gillmore concluded that the sand protected it more effectively than dirt. Brigade commander Davis also inspected the work. "The filth was in keeping with the ruin that prevailed; and the heap of unburied dead without the sally-port showed how hasty had been the flight of the enemy."[53]

The Federals quickly cleaned up Battery Wagner and occupied it for the remainder of the war. Photographs show Yankee troops on review inside the work, their tents and artillery neatly positioned where once a deadly hail of fire had made life miserable for the former occupants. The bombproofs were repaired and kept in order. One photograph shows how well the gun positions on the land face were made. The sand traverses were formed with board-and-post revetments, and a covered way existed between them and the parapet to allow safe communication from one artillery piece to another. The Federals finished up Wagner as a model earthwork.[54]

Davis later noted the unique aspects of Gillmore's reduction of Battery Wagner. "The operations were carried on along a narrow strip of land less than one-half the front of the work, a thing of rare occurrence in besieging a strong work." Both sides had lines of communication across water—Charleston Bay for the Confederates and the coastal waters for the Federals. The heavy Parrott rifles proved their superiority. Davis argued that this campaign saw the first significant use of guns larger than 100-pounders. While Fort Pulaski had been breached by rifles at a range of a few hundred yards the preceding year, Sumter was turned to rubble at a range of two miles. All in all, not only the fire on Sumter but the siege approaches to Wagner were remarkable technical achievements. "A more difficult problem than the reduction of Battery Wagner has seldom been presented to the engineer for solution," Davis mused, and he gave full credit to Gillmore. The general should be considered the war's "foremost engineer, and his operations on Morris Island considered one of its most creditable performances."[55]

Although Wagner had been taken with consummate skill, a triumph of the engineering art, the capture of Morris Island hardly changed the strategic picture at Charleston. The Federals had a platform from which they could continue to bombard Sumter, and they launched a poorly coordinated effort to seize it as well. Both the navy and the army planned separate attacks for the night of September 8 without informing each other until late in the day. They decided to go through with both plans. Both contingents were to be transported in small boats, the navy from ships to the south of Sumter and the army from the streams and marshes that separated Morris Island from James Island. The navy boats struck first, with 500 sailors and marines. Only a portion managed to land on the rocky beach of the sandbar that Sumter occupied, where they were subjected to a devastating hail of small arms fire from the 300 defenders of the fort. The Confederates had been forewarned and were ready for the attack. They used hand grenades and threw broken masonry and bricks. Turpentine balls were ignited and tossed toward the attackers to light up the area. It was a disaster, especially when the guns of Fort Moultrie opened fire on the boats. The Federals lost 125 men. The army boats turned around when they heard the firing, for the officers were under orders not to cause confusion if the navy beat them to the fort.[56]

Although easily repulsed, the boat attack forced the Sumter garrison to take extra precautions. The Rebels anchored a boom of heavy logs just offshore to interfere with boats attempting to land. They stretched wire entanglements at the base of the crumbling walls and placed fraises of sharpened stakes set in wooden frames on the crest of the rubble pile. The garrison had to remove these obstructions on the wall every morning to prevent them from being destroyed in the daily bombardment. Log and sandbag barricades were built inside the fort so sharpshooters and field guns could fire on any Yankees who managed to enter the enclosure. In case of another, successful attack, the garrison could take refuge in the casemates while Rebel guns from the other forts bombarded the interior.[57]

Gillmore responded to this failure by emplacing guns on the north end of Morris Island to continue battering the fort. The batteries opened fire on October 26 and pounded Sumter for forty consecutive days. The fire was

Federal Fort Putnam, Morris Island. After the capture of Morris Island, the Federals planted 30-pounder Parrott rifles in Confederate Battery Gregg and renamed it Fort Putnam. Note the use of gabions, sandbags, and barrels as revetment, and the palisades outside the parapet. (Massachusetts Commandery, Military Order of the Loyal Legion and the U.S. Army Military History Institute)

directed mainly at the southeastern face on the basis of a deserter's report, later found to be false, that the Confederates were remounting guns there. Only a desultory fire was kept up on Sumter during November and December. Gillmore resumed his bombardment of Charleston on November 17, having remounted a gun in the Marsh Battery and erected new batteries to reach the target. Thirteen shells a day were tossed into the city, and on some nights the methodical rain of projectiles continued until morning. One 30-pounder rifle fired at an elevation of forty-two degrees and burst on March 19, 1864, after 4,615 rounds.[58]

Sumter would never fall until the city itself was evacuated, but Gillmore was right to assume it had been neutralized by the incessant Federal fire. The masonry walls were turned to piles of rubble, and the guns were removed to be repositioned in more tenable locations. A small garrison was maintained to prevent a surprise attack from capturing the place, but there was little defensive or offensive power left on the island. Louis Manigault, secretary to a Confederate surgeon in Augusta, Georgia, who visited his family farm outside Charleston in late November 1863, could see Sumter through his field glasses from the roof of the farmhouse, seven miles away. It "resembles now, in its cragged outlines, rather the ruined form of some Ancient feudal Castle than the far-famed Key-stone fortification of Charleston Harbour." Observers could also see the Federals on Morris Island from downtown Charleston if they peered across the harbor with good telescopes. After every fire from the breaching guns, "numerous heads would be seen above their works watching where the shell would strike."[59]

Sumter would stand as a symbol of Rebel resistance to the national government, although its possession had some real military value as well. Fearful that the Rebels might have hidden guns in the rubble to open on his fleet at close range, Admiral John Dahlgren continued to hesitate about taking his ironclads into the harbor as long as the Confederate flag flew over the fort. New Confederate batteries along the north shore of James Island also deterred him from this risky move. Gillmore was disappointed. The original plan called for the ships to sail in and neutralize the harbor as a blockade-running port, but it became clear that Dahlgren would never do this. The army might have captured the batteries on James Island, but that would have required a new expedition on an order larger than that which had captured Morris Island, and no one in Washington had any stomach for such a commitment.[60]

For their part, the Confederates were proud of their tenacious defense of Sumter. They dug holes five feet deep in the parade of the fort to obtain sand for strengthening the battered walls, and they freely used gabions to shore up the rubble where needed. The place was transformed into a weird object bearing no resemblance to its originally graceful shape. Engineer Jeremy Gilmer thought it could hold out forever. He did not worry about the Union navy, for firing heavy guns from the deck of a rolling ship prevented pinpoint accuracy. Only if Gillmore managed to establish batteries close enough to hit Fort Moultrie would the Confederates have to be concerned that the defenses of the outer harbor might crack.[61]

In the end, very little was accomplished by the Union siege operation on Morris Island. The harbor defenses were weakened but held firm, Sumter was battered beyond recognition but did not fall, and Charleston was treated to the horrors of bombardment, but nothing was achieved that could further the Union cause. A tactical success with little strategic gain, the capture of Battery Wagner nevertheless showcased the Union engineering establishment at its best.

Beauregard's New Line on James Island

On August 4, 1863, when the reduction of Battery Wagner was in full swing, William B. Taliaferro recommended that the fortifications of James Island be extensively renovated. Beauregard disagreed. He thought them so defective that renovation would be a waste of time. Instead, the department commander ordered David B. Harris to lay out and supervise the construction of a new line on James Island. Beauregard had contemplated this earlier but did not have the labor to do it. He wanted the line placed farther south of Pemberton's, stretching from the marsh near Secessionville to Dill's House on the Stono River where Battery Pringle anchored its right flank. It was only half as long as Pemberton's James Island defenses, thereby achieving economy of manpower. Beauregard envisioned a series of lunettes with closed gorges, each located at intervals of one-half to three-quarters of a mile, all connected with a cremailliere or indented line of infantry trench. He described a traditional line recommended in Mahan's treatise on field fortification.[62]

The digging essentially was done by the end of August, but the sodding of parapets and traverses was only half-finished. There were five batteries along the line, which was slightly more than two miles long, and four or five guns were mounted in each. Battery No. 1 occupies an angle in the line with a curved parapet ten feet high. Traverses twenty-five feet high protect each gun emplacement. Consequently, the ditch is wide and deep. Most of the traverses are triangular, but the one in the middle of the curve is rectangular and twice as wide as the others. It has a small emplacement on top, today about four feet deep and a couple of yards in diameter, for the protection of lookouts.

Battery No. 2 has two wings and occupies one of the indentations of the cremailliere line. Unlike Battery No. 1, the traverses are a bit lower than the parapet but still triangular in shape. Harris constructed an extension of the connecting infantry parapet to protect the battery's right flank. The infantry line between the batteries consists of a parapet about six feet high with a modest ditch in front, and the indentations are about fifty yards apart. There is no trench, for the landscape is very flat and infantrymen needed to be as high as possible. Even today, after more than 130 years of erosion, the line is uniform and graceful.[63]

Beauregard's new line was never tested in battle, for Federal operations against Charleston essentially ceased after the fall of Morris Island. It was an incredibly strong position that most likely would have held against anything Gillmore could throw at it, and the line represented the best in Harris's practice as an engineer. The sand traverses of Battery No. 1 are unusual; only the massive mounds of Fort Fisher at the mouth of the Cape Fear River in coastal North Carolina are bigger. On flat terrain, with immense amounts of sand available, it made sense to elevate the defenders as much as possible to achieve command over the approach to the work.

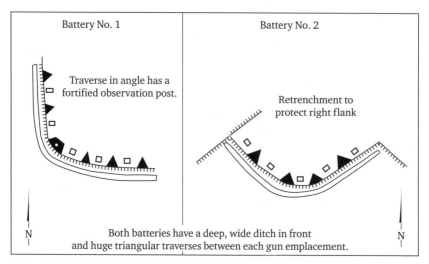

Beauregard's New Line on James Island, Built August 1863 (based on field visit, 1987)

Edward Manigault also designed a cremailliere line when he was ordered to fortify a position for pickets stretching from Grimball's Causeway to Rivers Causeway in August 1864. Manigault, an artillery officer in charge of Beauregard's siege train, dug the line forward of Beauregard's new line and to the southwest of Secessionville. It was 1,300 yards long and needed to protect thirty-six men. Since the line was on the edge of the solid ground next to the marsh, Manigault configured it as an indented line with faces sixty yards long and indentations of twenty yards. Eighty-eight black laborers, three overseers, and two lieutenants started work on the night of August 19. It took them an hour to dig each indentation, even though Manigault told the crew to dig only forty feet of the face and fifteen feet of the flank for now, "so that there may be some immediate shelter for the pickets, and the intervening portions may be dug when we have more time and labour."[64]

The city of Charleston itself bristled with artillery emplacements. A number of photographs taken after the Federals occupied the place show many large, well-made works. A battery on the Charleston waterfront consisted of two gun platforms on sand mounds that rose several feet, with a tall traverse between the emplacements. All the battery positions appear to have a good growth of grass on them, evidence of sodding to keep the parapets from eroding. Even on days when they did not dodge Federal shells, the citizens of Charleston were constantly reminded of the war every time they walked their streets, for there were Rebel guns everywhere.[65]

While the Confederates continued to expend labor on the defenses inside the city, at the entrance to the harbor, and on James Island, the works guarding the land approaches to Charleston were allowed to deteriorate. Robert Knox Sneden, a topographical draftsman for the Third Corps who had been captured during the Mine Run campaign, was transported to Charleston for exchange in late November 1864. He closely examined the works at the southern end of the railroad bridge over the Ashley River. "The red clay earthworks were washed down to a few feet high by the recent rains," he recalled. "The corduroy roads leading to them were broken up and rails stuck up in all directions. . . . The embrasures were all badly washed out by rain, no platforms for guns were visible, and loose sand was everywhere."[66]

The operations around Charleston during the war involved a commitment of forces on both sides that was modest compared with the campaigns in Virginia, but they included relatively large amounts of guns and troops compared with operations against other coastal ports. The city's symbolic value increased the public attention paid to these operations. As a result, few other campaigns saw so much publicity focused on the handiwork of engineers. The forts were the chief strength of the Confederate defense, for neither Pemberton nor Beauregard commanded enough troops to adequately defend the city without extensive earthworks. Despite Gillmore's siege of Battery Wagner, one is forced to conclude that the Confederates won the engineering contest at Charleston in the long run. The city never was captured by siege-craft or assault. It fell by default when Sherman's huge field army crossed its lines of communication in February 1865 during the march through the Carolinas.

13 : From Bristoe Station to the Fall of Plymouth

By the time Battery Wagner fell, the Army of the Potomac and the Army of Northern Virginia were resting quietly from the exertions of the Pennsylvania campaign. Lee settled his men around Culpeper Court House in the Piedmont, between the Rappahannock River and the Rapidan River. Meade took position near Warrenton north of the Rappahannock. Both armies used the Orange and Alexandria Railroad as their line of communications, but Meade realized that this area was not the true line of advance toward Richmond. The railroad led southwestward from Alexandria, away from the Confederate capital. This bucolic region between Fredericksburg and the Shenandoah Valley was a strategic backwater.

Both Lee and Meade were forced into active operations because of developments in the west. Gen. Braxton Bragg's Army of Tennessee lost Chattanooga, and Lee dispatched two divisions of Longstreet's First Corps, leaving but 45,000 men under his command. Lee also fell back to the south side of the Rapidan. Meade learned of this transfer and slowly advanced to the north bank of the Rapidan to prevent the Confederates from detaching more men. Soon after, news of Bragg's victory at Chickamauga arrived. Longstreet's contingent played a large role in this crushing defeat, and the Union Army of the Cumberland was forced to seek refuge in Chattanooga. The news compelled Lincoln to send the Eleventh and Twelfth Corps of the Army of the Potomac to reinforce the besieged Tennessee city, leaving Meade with 76,000 men. Lee seized the opportunity to strike at his opponent.

It began on October 8 when A. P. Hill's corps crossed the Rapidan to flank Meade's position. Hill's men shielded themselves by moving west of the ridges and taking back roads, while pioneer detachments rebuilt several bridges. Despite these precautions, Meade learned of the movement and retired toward Centreville near the old Bull Run battlefields. Most of his army crossed Broad Run along the track of the Orange and Alexandria Railroad on October 14. The Second Corps brought up the rear and was about to cross when the van of Hill's corps appeared on the scene only one and a half miles north of Bristoe Station, a small depot that lay just west of the run. Hill could see the tail end of a Union column east of the stream but had no idea that the Second Corps was near the track to the south. He impetuously ordered an assault on the column east of Broad Run by Maj. Gen. Henry Heth's division.

The resulting battle of Bristoe Station was a dismal Confederate mistake. Only two of Heth's brigades, totaling 4,000 men, were able to get into action. The head of the Second Corps came up just before Heth launched his attack, and the Federals sent skirmishers northward. They annoyed the two brigades so much that the Rebel commanders conducted a right wheel to confront the unknown force advancing along the railroad. Two Federal brigades of 3,000 men bore the brunt of this attack, but they were supported by three batteries and had all the terrain advantages on their side. While the Rebels advanced across an open, rolling landscape, the Yankees found that the railroad embankment was a ready-made breastwork. A ridge slope just behind the track provided an ideal platform for the artillery, and the entire Second Corps came up to extend the hastily formed line. Heth thought the Union position could have been stronger only with the addition of earthworks.

His two brigades were met with a hailstorm of fire as they approached the railroad embankment and were brought to a halt close to the blazing guns. Some Confederates managed to push onto the track while others wrapped around the Union right flank, which was in the air, but both attempts were quickly repelled. The survivors retreated under the same heavy fire that had stopped the advance, leaving more than 1,300 casualties on the field.

This "ill-judged" and "imprudently ordered" assault was entirely Hill's fault. He received a tongue-lashing from Lee that evening and the next morning. The Second Corps quietly evacuated the battlefield that night and rejoined Meade's army at Centreville. Nothing had been accomplished except to hasten the Army of the Potomac on its retreat. Lee retired on the evening of October 15, wrecking the Orange and Alexandria Railroad as far south as Rappahannock Station, where he established a defensive position. The battle of Bristoe Station involved no earthworks, but it demonstrated the effective use of existing terrain features. Once again a railroad embankment came into prominence as a defensive feature, and the ridge was well utilized by the Federal artillerymen to gain height advantage over their targets.[1]

Rappahannock Station

The pressure on Meade to do something after Bristoe Station was enormous, but he had to wait while the Orange and Alexandria Railroad was rebuilt. When that task was completed, Meade devised a plan to cross the Rappahannock. He divided the Army of the Potomac into two wings, the Fifth and Sixth Corps under Sedgwick and the First, Second, and Third

Corps under Maj. Gen. William H. French. Sedgwick was to advance from Warrenton directly toward Rappahannock Station, some sixteen miles, early on the morning of November 7. French was to move seventeen miles to Kelly's Ford, cross, and rush to Rappahannock Station to help Sedgwick.

Lee's defensive posture along the Rappahannock River was flawed. Hill's corps was posted to the left of the railroad crossing, while Ewell was positioned to the right. Five miles downstream, Kelly's Ford was the most vulnerable point because the land on the north side of the river there was high. Lee therefore established a fortified position some distance south of the ford.

He also established a bridgehead on the north side of the river at Rappahannock Station. The bridge had been destroyed by the Federals when they retreated early in October, and no fords were closer than Kelly's; so the Confederates erected a pontoon bridge 800 yards upstream from the charred piers. Two redoubts already existed on high ground west of the railroad and north of the river. These works had initially been built by the Confederates to defend against an advance from the north, but the U.S. Engineer Battalion had reworked them from September 3–22 to defend against an approach from the south. Now Lee had to remodify them to face a northern threat once again. One fort was 100 feet from the railroad, and the other, larger work was 400 feet to the left of the first. A mile-long line of infantry trench connected the two and continued east and west along the top of a low ridge, with both ends connecting to the riverbank. The line was vulnerable on both flanks. An attacker could use the railroad embankment as a cover to approach the smaller fort, and the infantry trench on the left wing was placed too far on the Confederate side of the ridge crest, permitting attackers to close in before they could be detected. This may have been a reversed Union trench positioned on the military crest. There were no obstructions in front of the line.

Moreover, the position was lightly held. Only Brig. Gen. Harry T. Hays's Louisiana brigade of Ewell's corps was in position. Under the temporary command of Col. Davidson B. Penn while Hays was on court-martial duty, the Louisiana Tigers were deployed in two lines. Two regiments occupied a ridge a quarter-mile in front of the works, while the rest were thinly spread out in the forts and the infantry trench. Penn had only two guns in each of the two forts.

More help arrived when it became apparent that something was afoot. Sedgwick's 30,000 men closed in on Penn's advanced position at 2:00 P.M. on November 7 and easily pushed the 900 Louisianians off the ridge. The Federals planted artillery there and began to bombard the forts. Two hours later, Brig. Gen. Robert F. Hoke's North Carolina brigade crossed the pontoon bridge and filled up the left wing of the position. Hays also returned and resumed command of his brigade.

Meanwhile, French captured Kelly's Ford with relatively little trouble. He posted his artillery on high ground north of the river and sent one brigade, preceded by a strong skirmish line, across the river. This small force captured the works, secured the crossing, and enabled the engineers to lay two pontoon bridges. The Third Corps was across the Rappahannock by dusk, but French could not push on to offer assistance to Sedgwick.

As it turned out, Sedgwick needed no help. He demonstrated on both flanks of the Confederate position but made his main attack in the center, led by Col. Peter C. Ellmaker's brigade of Brig. Gen. David A. Russell's division of the Sixth Corps. The 6th Maine spearheaded the assault, supported by the 5th Wisconsin. The quarter-mile distance was open, but several natural obstacles were in the way. The worst was a ditch some fourteen feet wide and six feet deep; beyond it, a field covered with standing water, mud, stumps, and brush had to be traversed. Several men of the U.S. Engineer Battalion advised Sedgwick about the terrain and the defensive works they had helped to build less than two months before. The Confederate line bent back so much on the left that it was almost parallel to the Union line of advance, and Hoke's North Carolinians could not fire on the attackers due to the faulty placement of the trench behind the ridge crest. The assault took the Rebels by surprise when it was launched at dusk, and the 6th Maine managed to get into the redoubts. A counterattack nearly reclaimed the works, but the rest of Ellmaker's brigade came up to secure the prizes.

The Confederate position collapsed. Of 2,000 defenders, only 461 escaped, and they set fire to the southern end of the pontoon bridge to prevent the Yankees from pursuing. Lee lost an additional 360 men at Kelly's Ford. Meade's losses were small, 42 at the ford and 419 at the station, but he captured seven Confederate flags and four guns.[2]

The next morning, Capt. Francis Adams Donaldson stood on the parapet of one of the captured Rebel forts. He could plainly see the open ground over which his comrades had assaulted and noticed that the forts were not in good shape. They "showed every sign of the battering they had received, especially about the embrasures." Lee and Ewell argued that the works at Rappahannock Station, though flawed, were good enough to have held, but Maj. Gen. Jubal Early disagreed. His division had supplied the garrison for these works, and he reported them to be "very inadequate, and not judiciously laid out or constructed." In a sense, both assessments were correct. There is no doubt that the fortifications were poorly planned and built, but the garrison contributed to the defeat as well. There were too few troops and too little artillery, and they were taken by surprise, even though they knew for half the afternoon that a large force of Unionists was only a quarter-mile away. The ground around Rappahannock Station did not lend itself to an effective system of defense, and ultimately the blame rests on Lee for deciding to hold the position. It could resist small attacks but not the massive weight of two corps. Rappahannock Station was one of the more embarrassing Confederate defeats of the war.[3]

Mine Run

Lee did not retire very far after the fall of Rappahannock Station. His army constructed a five-mile-long defensive line, using bayonets and tin cups in the absence of entrenching tools, between Brandy Station and Culpeper Court House. The right of the line was anchored by Pony Mountain; Hill was once again on the left and Ewell was on the right. But this was nothing more than a temporary measure, for the position had no natural obstacle in front and could easily be turned. Late on November 8, after Meade had crossed the Rappahannock, Lee retired to a new line eighteen miles long on the south side of the Rapidan. His right rested at Morton's Ford, where the line was refused four miles. The left rested at Liberty Mills, and Orange Turnpike and Orange Plank Road ran roughly parallel to the rear of the Confederate line.

Meade spent two weeks developing a plan for the next phase of his campaign. He would use fords downstream from Morton's to gain access to the turnpike and plank road and turn Lee's right. Meade's forces still outnumbered Lee's, 80,000 to 50,000, and might be able to gain a decisive advantage. The movement began on November 26, but the roads were muddy and the Rapidan was flooded, making it impossible to keep to Meade's timetable. Moreover, Lee learned of the movement as soon as it started. He sent Ewell's corps, temporarily under Jubal Early, to move eastward on Orange Turnpike while dispatching Hill along the plank road.

The initial clashes took place on November 27 several miles east of Mine Run, as the Second Corps met Early and the Fifth Corps skirmished with Hill. Lee ordered both columns to pull back that night to the west bank of Mine Run and dig in. The Rebels once again were forced to use their bayonets and even sharpened oak poles to break up the soil so it could be piled onto logs.

Meade spent November 28 scouting this fortified line. Warren recommended turning the Confederate right, so Meade sent him with 18,000 men to try. The movement began at dawn on November 29. Warren marched eleven miles and crossed Mine Run, but it was too late in the day to attack.

Meade prepared a massive assault for the morning of November 30. He wanted Sedgwick to hit Lee's left with the Fifth and Sixth Corps while Warren struck the right with the Second Corps and two divisions of the Third Corps. Warren would command 28,000 men and be responsible for the major part of Meade's plan. Positioned south of Orange Plank Road, his command straddled an unfinished railroad grade, opposed mostly by Maj. Gen. Cadmus M. Wilcox's division and Henry Heth's division of Hill's corps. The Rebels worked hard to strengthen their works, using boards to move dirt where spades were not available.[4]

The Mine Run campaign demonstrated how much Lee and his men had come to value field fortifications. Some units dug three different lines in three days. Lee's staff officer, Col. Walter H. Taylor, marveled at the men's facility with the spade and ax. The line on the west side of Mine Run was sited and constructed "in the course of an incredibly short time (for our men work now like beavers)," he reported. Lee gave his personal attention to the work, "directing important changes here and there." The sound of chopping could be distinctly heard in the Union camps on the night of November 29.[5]

"The rapidity with which an army can construct a line of breastworks is truly amazing," wrote Capt. William J. Seymour, an aide on Harry Hays's brigade staff. "When trees are near at hand, they are felled in an inconceivably short space of time, the limbs stripped off, and their trunks are placed lengthwise & on top of each other to the height of a man's breast; the interslices are filled with dirt—the whole forming an impenetrable barrier to minie balls and fragments of shell. A top log is often placed on the works, each end resting upon a block, thereby forming a crack of three or four inches through which the men can fire and keep their heads protected by the log." All in all, Seymour was quite impressed by the Mine Run fortifications; "the works were more elaborately and substantially made than any our army had previously constructed."[6]

Seymour was right. The men of Lee's army had never built such a field-work as this one at Mine Run. In addition to headlogs, a first for the Army of Northern Virginia, they constructed traverses where needed. Early ordered their construction on his part of the line to protect his men from a possible enfilade fire where the stream curved to the rear and forced the line to curve also. Early noted as well that the Federals occupied slightly higher ground on his front, stimulating additional labor on the part of his men. "We at once went to work like beavers and when the sun rose we were behind works that could not be taken," bragged Samuel D. Buck of the 13th Virginia.[7]

Two segments of Lee's Mine Run line are preserved and easily accessible, offering insight into its design. A 200-yard segment south of modern County Road 602, held by a portion of Maj. Gen. Edward Johnson's division of Ewell's corps, has a good parapet, ditch, and trench. There are no traverses

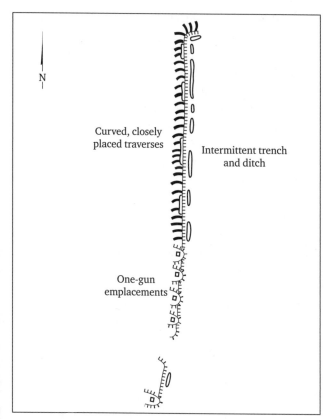

N

Curved, closely
placed traverses

Intermittent trench
and ditch

One-gun
emplacements

*Confederate Works at Mine Run, Segment of Line Held by
Rodes's Division, November 30, 1863 (based on field visit, 1996)*

on this segment of the line, which is located on the military crest of the
gentle slope that constitutes the creek bluff.

The other segment is more extensive and well preserved. It is three-
quarters of a mile long and on the part of the line held by Maj. Gen. Robert E.
Rodes's division of Alabama and North Carolina troops. This segment has
thirty-one traverses and five artillery emplacements. The traverses range
from ten to twenty-five feet in length and are crammed close together, and all
are connected to the parapet. Virtually all are curved to the right, and they
are placed farther apart as one walks from left to right of this line. On the far
right, about one-third of the preserved segment has no traverses at all.

There are signs of hasty construction along the entire line. Most of the
preserved segment has a shallow ditch, but it is not continuous throughout.
The same is true of the trench. Both the ditch and the trench are irregularly
dug; at one point, the ditch curves so far from the parapet that there is a two-

foot-wide berm between them. The traverses are irregularly dug as well; some are well formed, while others are unfinished or simply dug on one side with the dirt banked to the left of the excavation. Curved traverses are comparatively rare at other fortification sites. All of the artillery emplacements are for one gun and shaped like a horseshoe. Called demilunes, they are connected to the parapet and have natural earth as a platform.

Rodes's line is on the military crest of the slope, about fifty yards in front of and two feet lower than the natural crest. The slopes east and west of Mine Run are irregular, and the terrain is generally level but cut up by numerous streams that, through erosion, have formed low hills and ridges. The ground appears easy to dig.[8]

The Rebels placed abatis in front of their line wherever possible, but Mine Run itself was the chief obstacle for Meade's men. It was deeper and larger in 1863 than it is today; some observers estimated it was fifteen feet wide. Several reports indicated that the Confederates constructed small dams to increase the depth to five feet in places, and more than one Federal later reported seeing sharpened stakes, some under water, in the stream.[9]

The Confederates changed an obscure land formation into one of the strongest defensive positions of the war. Warren's Second Corps moved into position 300 yards from the Rebels on the morning of November 30. Sgt. George D. Bowen of the 12th New Jersey gazed across the landscape at dawn and saw a deep railroad cut in front and Confederate artillery sited to fire down its length. He could even see the headlogs on top of the parapet through field glasses. Bowen decided it was useless to attack and promptly made out his will. A member of the 1st Minnesota thought the planned attack was " 'a damned sight worse than Fredericksburg' " and vowed to go as far as he could, " 'but we can't get more than two-thirds of the way up the hill.' "[10]

Charles A. Upson of the 14th Connecticut endured an anxious morning as he contemplated the assault. He thought the compact lines of the Second Corps were beautiful.

> It was a splendid sight, . . . stretched a mile in length & one line behind the other, bayonets glistening in the sun, waiting anxiously for the word— "Forward, double quick." But still, beneath those blue jackets was many a fluttering heart, and although every man would obey orders, still when they looked on those lines of rifle pits and breastworks as far as the eye could reach, which it seemed impossible to take, their cheeks blanched, I know I felt my heart beat as audibly as the ticking of a clock, and the color came and went on my cheek. I looked on the sun[,] on the beautiful land around me as I thought for the last time.

Upson wanted to cry but thought his comrades would consider him cowardly. Instead, he quietly resolved to kill "one rebel at least before I bit the dust."[11]

M. R. Johnson of the 15th Massachusetts in the Second Corps remembered that the men were too experienced to have any doubts about what they were up against. "To a soldier who has seen two and a half years of active service engineering becomes a study, and the most of us knew that when our line should reach a certain point it would melt away like snow." Third Corps brigade leader Robert McAllister scanned the Confederate position that morning and believed his men could take it, but he would lose at least half of them in a few minutes. He called the Confederate line a "worthless prize." With Rebel soldiers standing on their works and taunting the Yankees to come on, many Federals "marked their names on slips of paper and pinned them to their blouses, should anyone survive to deliver the message to their families," according to John Haley of the 17th Maine. This practice seems to have been most common among those Second and Third Corps troops slated to make Warren's attack on the Confederate right, but men in the 118th Pennsylvania in the Fifth Corps, opposite the Confederate left, also labeled themselves. One officer of the regiment "took a fools cap sheet and in bold characters gave his name & address, ending with 'was this day mustered out the service, Nov. 30th, 1863.' He placed this length wise over his breast, pinning it fast and buttoning his coat over it." Francis Adams Donaldson wrote a more modest but equally sardonic message, "a few lines to the effect that I was killed in this impending assault and asked the finder of my body to kindly send this paper to my friends."[12]

Fortunately for these nervous soldiers, Warren hesitated to order the assault. He was up early and scouted the Confederate line. Perhaps no other corps commander in Meade's army was as well prepared to assess the strength of these works. Having graduated second in the West Point class of 1850, he had served in the topographical engineers. Warren's role in laying out Hooker's fortified bridgehead at Chancellorsville has already been noted, and he had also been Meade's chief engineer at Gettysburg.[13]

Warren clearly saw the situation in the same light as his men and postponed the attack, which was scheduled for 8:00 A.M. Fifty minutes later, his dispatch regarding this development finally reached Meade. The army commander flew into a rage, angry that his massive assault had been derailed and not knowing just how grim were the prospects. He also fumed that the young Warren, who had been a member of his staff only a few months before, was commanding the largest portion of his army and he was essentially at his mercy. Knowing that Sedgwick's attack would be worse than murder if it was not supported by Warren, Meade canceled his movement just before it was due to start at 9:00 A.M.[14]

Meade could not come up with an alternative plan. There appeared to be no opportunity to outflank Lee's position, and it was obvious a frontal assault was impossible. For two days, November 30 and December 1, the two armies stared at each other at close range without moving. "Our men remain night & day behind the breastworks," reported commissary officer Benjamin Wesley Justice of the 47th North Carolina. "At night one fourth of the entire army remains awake all night, one fourth relieving another fourth at the end of a given period, each fourth taking its turn during the night. Directions for cool, deliberate fighting in case of a night assault by the enemy, are issued to the troops just before night." The temperature dropped, causing much discomfort for the men on both sides of Mine Run.[15]

On the evening of December 1, Meade finally decided to give up the campaign and slip away. His army quietly retired under cover of darkness to the north side of the Rapidan and went into winter quarters. Lee, however, had grown restless. He was determined to attack even if the Federals were not, so he planned to advance two divisions of Hill's corps against Meade's left wing early on the morning of December 2. They found the Yankees gone but mounted no pursuit. Many Rebels were disappointed. "We all agreed that we would have carried their line, for they had scarcely any works, and our artillery would have very much commanded theirs." Later that day, word reached the Army of Northern Virginia about Bragg's defeat at Missionary Ridge, outside Chattanooga, on November 25. That important gate city to the Deep South was securely in Federal hands. The victory at Chattanooga would later propel its architect, Ulysses S. Grant, into command of all Union armies and lead him to direct operations against Lee. Meade would no longer have to face the South's best general alone.[16]

The Mine Run campaign resulted in about 800 Confederate casualties and double that number of Federal losses. It was the culmination of the fall efforts in Virginia that have been sadly overlooked by contemporaries and historians alike because they resulted in no major battle. The campaigns demonstrated how much the eastern armies embraced the construction of field fortifications. The line at Mine Run was the strongest fieldwork built to date by the Army of Northern Virginia. The only fieldwork constructed by the Army of the Potomac that matched it in strength and detail was Hooker's fortified bridgehead at Chancellorsville. The works at Mine Run foreshadowed what was to come in the next phase of the eastern war, beginning at Spotsylvania and extending to the end of the Petersburg campaign.[17]

Francis Walker, who served on Warren's staff at Second Corps headquarters, marveled at the Rebel works along Mine Run, calling the line "by far the most striking instance which had, down to that time, been given of the capability of this species of defence." Walker noted surprise at finding Lee so heavily entrenched, for it did not fit his previous habit. In the early part of the war, "stone walls or rail fences were considered good enough for anybody." Now the mood of commanders and men had changed. Walker correctly pointed out that in the campaigns of 1864, "it was to become almost impossible to get a fair fight anywhere in open ground."[18]

Mine Run also demonstrated a unique phenomenon of the war, what might be called trench gridlock. Lee's fortified line was so strong it deterred a Union attack, and the Federals could find no way to sidestep it. There are few better examples of how a strongly fortified position can alter a campaign and decide its result. The fortification itself became the key to the tactical and strategic result of Meade's offensive; it was so good that the would-be attacker was left with no alternative but to withdraw. In a sense this was not what a fortified line was supposed to do. The ideal was to strengthen a position enough so that the defender could punish the attacker as much as possible while holding it. If the work was so daunting that it deterred an attack, then nothing beyond checkmating the opponent could be accomplished. Lee's men hoped Meade would attack, and they were very disappointed that he did not try. Instead the troops were treated to two days of facing the enemy at close range without fighting.[19]

The armies remained in their winter camps except for a brief Union attempt to threaten the fortified crossings of the Rapidan in February. Meade was then on sick leave in Philadelphia, and Sedgwick was temporarily commanding the Army of the Potomac. Maj. Gen. Benjamin F. Butler came up with a plan and coaxed General in Chief Henry W. Halleck into pressuring Sedgwick to cooperate. Butler heard that Lee had dispatched 8,000 men to help in an attempt to recapture New Bern that winter. If Sedgwick threatened Lee's army along the Rapidan, enough Confederate troops might be drawn from Richmond to enable Butler to enter the city and free Union prisoners of war. Sedgwick thought the plan unworkable, but Halleck forced him to go along with it.

While two cavalry divisions demonstrated on the flanks, the First and Second Corps marched to Raccoon Ford and Morton's Ford, well to the east of Mine Run. Sedgwick only wanted them to make noise on the north bank of the river for two days, but Brig. Gen. John C. Caldwell, temporarily commanding the corps while Warren recuperated from illness, ignored those instructions and sent a sizable force across the river to seize the Confederate works on the south side on February 6. Three hundred men from Brig. Gen. Joshua T. Owen's brigade easily captured the ford itself, but they were then confronted by a fortified line, with artillery, ranged along a ridgetop about a mile from the crossing. Owen took the rest of his brigade across, and then the other two brigades of Brig. Gen. Alexander Hays's division also crossed. These men were held in readiness, but Hays realized the Rebel position was too strong to risk an attack.

When Warren arrived to reassume command of his corps, he wanted to withdraw Hays's division. It would be too risky to do it in daylight, as the Rebels were gathering more men and artillery on the ridge and could command the crossing with their guns. Ewell had reached the scene as well, and he ordered an attack at 5:00 P.M. It was poorly pressed, and Owen was able to stop it with spirited skirmishing on the Union right, where Ewell had hoped to cut through and capture the ford before Hays could retreat. Warren rushed another division across to reinforce Hays, but the Confederates skirmished until 10:00 P.M. Then Warren successfully withdrew his two divisions.

The affair at Morton's Ford demonstrated the value of planting fortifications at the fords that peppered the line of the Rapidan River, but it failed to help Butler's strike at Richmond. His column made it from Yorktown as far as the crossing of the Chickahominy River, where the Rebels put up enough of a stand to compel the Union commander to retreat. Sedgwick lost 260 men at Morton's Ford, compared with only 50 Confederate casualties.[20]

Mine Run and Morton's Ford were followed by a winter of recuperation as Grant took command and prepared for the coordinated offensives of 1864. The line of the Orange and Alexandria Railroad would no longer be the axis of advance, but Grant instructed Meade to erect defenses at all bridges between Bull Run and Rappahannock Station. It was important to supply the garrisons occupying that region of Virginia. The U.S. Engineer Battalion did most of the work. Lt. Andrew Jackson Crossley supervised the construction of two stockades at Bristoe Station to protect the bridge over Broad Run, one on each side of the track, that were 80 by 25 feet in dimension. He dug a trench 3 feet deep and put 13-foot-long logs upright in it. Two sides of the logs were hewn beforehand to form a tight union, and loopholes for muskets were cut in every third log. The works protected the garrisons from guerrillas or cavalry and covered the bridge to prevent its burning. Other defenses were made at Catlett's Station and Kettle Run by April 28. The regular engineers then finished a stockade started at Rappahannock Station by the 50th New York Engineers just before Grant launched his campaign against Lee.[21]

New Bern

Butler's intelligence that Lee had sent 8,000 men to North Carolina was exaggerated, for only Hoke's Tar Heel brigade, the 43rd North Carolina, and the 21st Georgia were sent to the region. Rebel forces were on the move in North Carolina in another effort to recapture towns occupied by the Yankees for the past two years. As in 1863, an ancillary purpose was to gather as much food from the Carolina coastal plain as possible.[22]

Lee had suggested operations against New Bern as early as January 2, based on a report that the Federal garrison could be easily surprised. He had wanted Hoke to command the attempt; but President Jefferson Davis preferred someone of higher rank, so Maj. Gen. George E. Pickett was chosen. Pickett would have 13,000 men, supported by fourteen Navy cutters under Commander John Taylor Wood on the Neuse River. He started from Kinston on January 30 in three columns. Brig. Gen. Seth M. Barton, with three brigades and twelve guns, was to cross the Trent River and advance to Brice's Creek. He was then to force a passage, capture any Federal forts along the south side of the Trent and along the west side of the Neuse, and enter New Bern across the railroad bridge. Col. James Dearing led a second column consisting of three regiments and three guns against Fort Anderson, on the north side of the Neuse. This was the same work that Pettigrew had failed to take nearly a year before. Pickett and Hoke led the remaining men against New Bern by advancing north of the Trent River. They planned to cross Batchelder's Creek and enter town from the west.

This was a complicated movement of widely separated columns, all of which were to strike the Federals on February 1. Wood's naval contingent was also to attack and capture Union gunboats on the Neuse that day. Lee had high hopes for the expedition. He urged Pickett to follow up the capture of New Bern with further strikes at Plymouth and Washington. In addition to capturing supplies and prisoners, the campaign would "also have the happiest effect in North Carolina and inspire the people," he wrote.[23]

The Yankees, not as complacent as Lee was led to believe, had strengthened the defenses of New Bern since Maj. Gen. John J. Peck took command of the city in August 1863. Peck, who had been responsible for the fortifications at Suffolk, believed the Trent River was the weak point of the defenses, as it divided them into two sectors and made it difficult to shift troops from one side to the other. The navy, however, did not want to send gunboats up the narrow stream to help. Despite Butler's reluctance to authorize new works, Peck built extensively along the more exposed parts of his defense perimeter.[24]

Pickett thus found a stronger target than he was led to expect. Most of Peck's new fortifications appeared along Barton's line of advance. Although he had been told that there would be no earthworks in the way, Barton encountered several citizens who reported just the opposite. He reconnoitered and saw the works for himself, describing them as "of the most formidable character." There was a line of works on the east bank of Brice's Creek, and the timber had been cut down on the west bank to create a clear field of fire. The Federals had also erected a blockhouse on the east side, a redoubt with ten guns where the creek entered the Trent River, and a battery for eight guns only 300 yards east of the confluence. A mile away, a large redoubt was built near the railroad bridge. Barton also heard of other works north of the Trent River. He decided to await instructions from Pickett, who ordered him to give up the attempt and move to the north side of the river. It would take several days for Barton to complete the redisposition of his command.[25]

Pickett's column fared little better. The Union earthworks at Batchelder's Creek were lightly held, but the bridge was dismantled. Hoke crossed some men on an improvised log bridge and drove the Yankees back while the wagon bridge was repaired. Then Hoke pushed on to within a mile of New Bern. Pickett halted to listen for the sound of Barton's advance south of the Trent River, for the western defenses of New Bern were far too strong to assault unaided. But Pickett never heard a sound from Barton, only the discouraging message that he was faced with equally strong defenses at Brice's Creek. Dearing also reported that Fort Anderson was too strongly held to risk an attack. There was little else to do but call off the operation, so Pickett fell back on February 3. He had taken twenty-two prisoners on the expedition and impulsively decided to hang them because they had deserted from Confederate units. This would brand Pickett as a war criminal after the conflict and force him to flee the country temporarily to avoid arrest and prosecution.[26]

Pickett had had no better luck with New Bern than Daniel Harvey Hill had in March 1863. All sectors of the town's perimeter were thoroughly covered with fieldworks that probably could have withstood any assault directed against them.

Plymouth

Other towns were not so well prepared as New Bern, however, and the Confederates wasted no time in attempting to take them. Pickett returned to Virginia immediately after the failure of his New Bern expedition and was succeeded by Hoke. The North Carolinian planned a strike against Plymouth, a small town on the south bank of the Roanoke River. Fort Branch, about forty-five miles upriver at Rainbow Banks, was still held by the Confederates. The sleepy little town had not been as thoroughly fortified as New Bern, and the garrison was less vigilant. Hoke still had a sizable force, including his own Tar Heel brigade now led by Col. John T. Mercer, Col. William R. Terry's Virginia brigade, Brig. Gen. Matthew W. Ransom's North Carolina brigade, and Col. James Dearing's cavalry regiment.[27]

Brig. Gen. Henry W. Wessells had commanded the garrison of Plymouth since the spring of 1863. He had 3,000 men, but the defenses were flawed. Fort Gray was detached two miles upstream from town to defend against an approach by Confederate gunboats. Fort Wessells, also known as the 85th New York Redoubt, was placed half a mile southwest of town and one mile southeast of Fort Gray. It was detached well forward of the main line of defense and mounted a 32-pounder and a 6-pounder. Fort Wessells also had a ditch, drawbridge, abatis, and forty-two infantrymen from the 85th New York. Twenty-three men of the 2nd Massachusetts Heavy Artillery worked the guns. Fort Williams lay at the center of the defense line, due south of Plymouth, and the right wing was defended by a continuous line of infantry trench from Fort Williams to the river upstream from town. Battery Worth anchored the right flank with a 200-pounder Parrott on the riverbank. The eastern side of town was loosely covered by Fort Comfort and Conaby Redoubt, detached works on either side of Columbia Road. The swampy bottomland of Conaby Creek was believed to be a sufficient obstruction to the approach of a Confederate force from the east.[28]

Hoke came within range of Union guns on April 17 and began to dig artillery emplacements that night. The next day he opened a bombardment of Fort Wessells while Terry haltingly approached Fort Gray. Ransom's brigade advanced east of Fort Williams, reaching within 800 yards of the work, and Mercer attacked Fort Wessells after nightfall. The Rebels began to enter the abatis but fell back when the Federals used 6-pounder shells "with special ignition fuses" as hand grenades. The Tar Heels suffered heavy losses, and Mercer was mortally wounded. After the repulse, Hoke intensified his artillery fire on Fort Wessells and punished the garrison severely. Rebel gunners obtained a crossfire on the work from positions as close as 100 yards, according to Yankee Lt. Lucien A. Butts. At this close range, even field artillery could break down a parapet. Shells gouged out chunks of sandy soil, and the sandbags "were broken and thrown off the parapet, so as to destroy the loop-holes" used by sharpshooters. Fort Wessells also was accidentally hit by Union naval gunfire. The garrison surrendered at 11:00 P.M.[29]

That night, as Fort Wessells was reduced, the CSS *Albemarle* descended the Roanoke. One of the best ironclad vessels the Confederacy produced, it

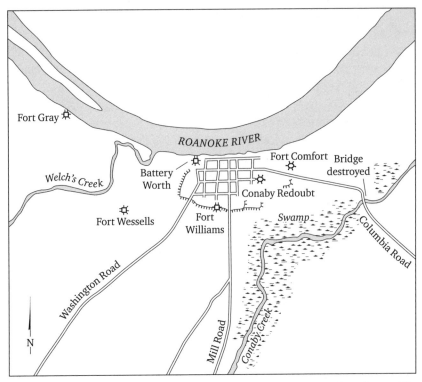

Union Defenses of Plymouth, N.C., April 1864 (based on wartime map by Solon E. Allis, 27th Massachusetts, published in Ballard, "Good Time to Pray," 20)

broke through a line of obstructions three miles upstream from town at 2:30 A.M. and easily passed Fort Gray. The *Albemarle* then steamed to Plymouth, rammed and sank the USS *Southfield*, and chased away the USS *Miami*, both wooden gunboats. By dawn of April 19, the Rebel ironclad controlled the riverfront at Plymouth. Its crew prepared to support Hoke's renewed efforts on land with naval gunfire.[30]

Plymouth might have fallen even without the success of the *Albemarle*, but the fire support of the ironclad proved decisive for the rest of the operation. The Federals now felt vulnerable, and they began to build bombproofs and traverses along the interior of their defense line. There was simply not enough time, however, to do this adequately. As a result, the interior of the whole line was exposed to a devastating artillery fire.[31]

Hoke shifted the focus of his operations to the Union left, now that the *Albemarle* had chased the Federal gunboats from that area. Ransom's brigade crossed Conaby Creek on a pontoon bridge during the night of April 19.

It was a "narrow but deep stream" and utterly impractical as an obstruction to an advancing enemy unless there were earthworks and a defending infantry force nearby.

Ransom attacked on the morning of April 20, firing a signal rocket to let Hoke know he was on the move. Fort Comfort was pounded by the guns of the *Albemarle* and then taken by the 35th North Carolina, but the garrison of Fort Conaby put up stiffer resistance. The 8th North Carolina, loaned to Ransom from Clingman's brigade, got into the ditch, where it was pelted with hand grenades. The Federals also fired through the loopholes cut into the palisades at the rear of the work. Surrounding the fort, the Tar Heels managed to fire back when the loopholes were empty, and they broke down the gate in the palisades, forcing the garrison to surrender.[32]

As Ransom's brigade shattered the left wing of Wessells's line, the rest of Hoke's command concentrated on the right wing. Battery Worth on the far right fell, and the Rebels concentrated their artillery fire on Fort Williams in the center of the line. Wessells was inside the fort and witnessed the tremendous pounding. "The breast-height was struck by solid shot on every side," he reported; "fragments of shells sought almost every interior angle of the work, the whole extent of the parapet was swept by musketry, and men were killed and wounded even on the banquette slope." Wessells surrendered Fort Williams at 10:00 A.M.[33]

Fighting continued to the right of the fort because Col. Enrico Fardella, who commanded this section of the works, had not received orders to give up. His men were isolated and hemmed in between the line and a hastily built parapet several yards to the rear, thrown up to defend against the shells of the *Albemarle*. Fardella's men were hit from all sides. Ransom's Tar Heels had by now entered Plymouth and were using houses at the edge of town, only 100 feet from the imperfect parados, as sharpshooter posts. Naval shells pounded the parapets of both lines. The feisty Fardella held a council of war in which he proposed an attack to break through, but his subordinates had no stomach for such a desperate endeavor. When Hoke sent in a request for surrender at 2:00 P.M., Fardella agreed. The surrender of Fort Gray soon followed, and Plymouth was completely in Rebel hands.[34]

The Federals lost 2,834 men in this fiasco, while Hoke's losses were estimated to be as high as 1,800. In his report to Peck, filed four months later, Wessells claimed that the losses due to enemy fire were not so heavy because he sheltered his men in bombproofs hastily constructed along the line. But Peck, the master earthwork builder of Suffolk fame, was not fooled. He bemoaned the loss of Plymouth and blamed it on faulty engineering. The fire delivered by the *Albemarle* was the key to Confederate victory, he thought, for it took the entire Union position in reverse. "Had all the works been inclosed, the results would have been very different," he informed Butler.[35]

Ulysses S. Grant was uncertain that these towns in eastern North Carolina needed to be garrisoned at all. When he received news of Hoke's attack on Plymouth, he urged it to be held "at all hazards, unless it is of no importance to hold." He thought it useful to detain Confederate strength in North Carolina but was certain Lee would recall Hoke as soon as the spring campaign started. The more he thought of it, the more Grant believed it best to give up smaller towns like Washington as "unnecessary to us," and he advised against any attempt to retake Plymouth. New Bern, however, obviously needed to be retained, as it could serve as a blockade-running port if it were once again in Southern hands.[36]

Hoke did not rest on his laurels after the fall of Plymouth. He besieged Washington on April 27 but hesitated to order an attack because of rumors that the Federals were preparing to evacuate the town. Brig. Gen. Edward Harland had indeed received orders to give up Washington the day before, but it was April 30 before he finally loaded his small garrison onto boats. Half the town was torched by the Federals as they left.

New Bern was Hoke's next target. He moved along the south side of the Trent River to a point due south of town, where he exchanged artillery fire with the Yankees on May 5. Hoke planned to attack the next day, but orders arrived from Beauregard, newly appointed commander of the Department of North Carolina and the Cape Fear, to return his units to Virginia. The order was prompted by Federal moves against Richmond: Benjamin Butler's Army of the James was landing at Bermuda Hundred, where it could threaten either the capital or Petersburg. Yet Beauregard had believed all along that minor operations against the Carolina towns were a waste of effort. The Federals could not be decisively hurt even if all of the towns were recaptured.[37]

It is doubtful that Hoke could have retaken New Bern or any other Federal post in North Carolina, but before Beauregard's order arrived, he had had every intention of trying. Hoke developed plans for an expedition against Roanoke Island, and J. G. Sills of the 66th North Carolina reported that much work was expended on revising the defenses of Plymouth. "Our men are kept very busy now all the time working on fortifications," he informed his father. "I think if the Yankees ever take this place they will lose more men than Gen. Hoke did." All plans for future success fell apart with the transfer to Virginia and the demise of the *Albemarle*. The ironclad was on its way through Albemarle Sound to assist Hoke's attack on New Bern when it was stopped in a fierce battle with Union gunboats, particularly the USS *Sassacus*. Then the *Albemarle* was sunk while docked at Plymouth on the night of October 27, 1864, by a daring raid conducted by Commander William B. Cushing. The Confederates evacuated Plymouth, and Federal forces once again occupied the town on October 30.[38]

The period between Gettysburg and the Wilderness saw a great deal of movement and many small battles in both Virginia and North Carolina but no major engagement or decisive victory for either side. Yet this transition period demonstrated the growing reliance on fortifications by both Union and Confederate commanders. Mine Run was the most salient example of this development, but it is evident in the backwater of North Carolina, too. With a lot of time on their hands, occupying Federals lavished work on New Bern, the citadel of their position on the coastal plain, and the town withstood all Confederate attempts at its reduction. Plymouth fell because its defenses were flawed. A weakening of Federal will prompted the evacuation of Washington; the defenses of that town were so strong that Hoke probably could not have broken through. Even Plymouth was given back to the Yankees six months after it was taken. The campaigns in eastern North Carolina were oriented around fortified posts, and the Federals usually won because of their engineering efforts.

Conclusion

By the time Plymouth fell, the armies in the East were on the eve of the Overland campaign and its intensive use of field fortifications. The preceding campaigns from Big Bethel to Plymouth were in one sense a preparation for the habitual use of fieldworks in 1864–65. Commanders on many levels relied on breastworks, earthworks, or preexisting features on the battlefield during almost every significant engagement from 1861 through 1864. There was a definite trend toward greater reliance on fortifications, but it was not steady or inevitable.

The evolution of trench warfare was centered, in part, on the problem of balancing the desire for offensive action with the need for assuming the defensive. If commanders wanted to take the tactical offensive, they often refused to dig in. Entrenching was, by definition, a sign that the commander wanted to hold his position and fight a defensive battle. Unless they were specifically designed to maintain one position while the commander attacked from another, trenches locked soldiers into a static defensive mode. Often, if the commander were undecided, he would refrain from entrenching in order to keep open all his tactical options until the last minute.

There was an ebb and flow in the growing reliance on field fortifications in the eastern campaigns. They were used from the beginning but did not necessarily play a decisive role in the outcome of either campaigns or battles. They were often used right after an engagement rather than before or during it. One can see many examples of this, especially after First Manassas and Fredericksburg, where the shock of combat led to a greater desire for cover in case battle was offered again quickly.

The Peninsula campaign saw a great deal of digging by both sides. McClellan recognized that the use of earthworks could help him achieve strategic results while lessening casualties. The Confederates relied on strong earthworks to delay him during his advance up the Peninsula. Lee also relied on extensive fortifications as a preparation for his offensive against McClellan in late June.

Ironically, the success of the Seven Days made the average Confederate soldier, and Lee himself, less appreciative of earthworks. Their offensive victory at Second Manassas increased their disdain for field fortifications, even though Jackson's men barely hung on while defending the unfinished railroad grade, which was an inadequate substitute for a fieldwork. The result of Antietam tended to prove that earthworks did have value for an outnumbered army defending an open position, and several of Lee's units took it upon themselves, especially the artillery, to dig in and repel Burnside's frontal attacks at Fredericksburg.

The tendency to rely on earthworks deepened at Chancellorsville, which became a pivot point in the development of field fortifications in the East. The Federals and Confederates used fieldworks at almost every turn in the flow of events. Hooker dug in as soon as he reached the crossroads, and Lee ordered his men to dig in on the eve of battle for the first time in the war. Hooker's men constructed heavy defenses to protect their bridgehead and line of retreat. Gettysburg represented a temporary reversion to the heady days of the summer and fall of 1862, when Lee's men were convinced that nothing the Yankees would dig could stop them. Rather like the aftermath of Antietam, the post-Gettysburg period saw a reversion to the tendency to take fieldworks seriously. Lee's men fully accepted them at Mine Run, which became the first instance in the eastern campaigns where fieldworks altered the tactical course of a campaign. The stage was effectively set for the Overland drive to Richmond in May 1864.

The Overland drive was a watershed in the use of fieldworks during the Civil War, with every phase of the campaign from the Wilderness to Petersburg seeing employment of large-scale defensive systems. In contrast, the use of fieldworks from Big Bethel to Plymouth was more modest. Fifty-seven battles and campaigns are discussed in this book; field fortifications were employed in 47 percent, and 43 percent were open field engagements. In addition, semipermanent works were involved in 22 percent of these encounters, permanent works were involved in only .03 percent, and soldiers used preexisting terrain features for defensive purposes in 12 percent. Siege operations were scarcely represented in the eastern campaigns of 1861–64, with siege works employed in three operations and mining in none.

Even if the first half of the war in the East pales in comparison with the campaigns of 1864–65 in the employment of fortifications, these early engagements in Virginia nevertheless saw more use of field fortifications than is evident in American warfare prior to 1861. A total of 108 major battles and campaigns of the French and Indian War, the War of Independence, the War of 1812, and the Mexican War were surveyed. Fieldworks were employed in 31 percent, and 30 percent were open field engagements. Semipermanent works were involved in 26 percent, permanent works were involved in 12 percent, and soldiers used existing features for defensive purposes in 9 percent of the engagements. Siege operations were more prominent, with siege works employed in 12 percent of the operations and mining taking place in 3 percent.

These percentages for pre–Civil War American conflicts are probably similar to those for the use of field fortifications in Europe. From the early sixteenth century, when fieldworks first appear in modern European warfare, until the Crimean War of 1854–55, field fortifications were used occasionally and usually in limited ways. The Sebastopol campaign in the latter conflict presaged Civil War operations such as Petersburg in its heavy reliance on fieldworks. The eastern campaigns of the Civil War from 1861 to 1864 saw a significant rise in the use of fortifications, and this period was, therefore, a transition phase to their increasing use after 1865. In fact, the half-century from the Civil War to World War I witnessed more attention by military engineers to the subject, and the Western Front of 1914–18 was the culmination of this trend, producing the most extensive and sophisticated field fortification systems ever constructed in history.[1]

Exactly where the tendency to entrench originated in the American Civil War has been a source of controversy. Early twentieth-century military authors argued that the common soldier was the wellspring of it. While men who used fieldworks were denigrated as "dirt-diggers" during the early part of the war, the latter part of the conflict saw the widespread use of fortifications because ordinary soldiers had a change of heart. "Great necessity and the stern experience of war drove erroneous notions from the heads of the combatants," wrote O. E. Hunt. "It was the good common sense of the troops that led them to understand the value of even slight protection. The high intelligence of the individual American soldier made it a simple matter for him to grasp this fundamental truth of his own accord." Other commentators noted the "education and intuition of the American soldier" as keys to his ability to understand the need for fortifications, and they cited soldiers' "inventive genius" as the tool that allowed them to improvise design features. Arthur L. Wagner even made the unfounded assertion that troops defended works they made for themselves more stubbornly than they defended works that had been built for them.[2]

Edward Hagerman has more recently argued against the view that ordinary soldiers commonly initiated entrenchment on the battlefield. He believes that since fortifying a line was a big project, the decision to do so must have been made on a relatively high level of command, at least as high as the division. Hagerman also asserts that most of the digging was done by engineer and pioneer troops.[3]

The truth lies somewhere between these two views. It is wrong to assume that privates routinely took it upon themselves to dig in; instructions to do so must have come from an officer, but it most likely was a regimental, brigade, or division officer. There is no evidence that corps or army leaders were routinely responsible for the field fortifications dug in the battles of the eastern theater during the first half of the war, but it is true that common soldiers did initiate some of them without orders from their officers. The problem in proving any point on this issue is that orders to dig in would likely be verbal rather than written, and one must judge by circumstantial evidence. By and large, the early twentieth-century writers were closer to the truth than Hagerman. Even if fortifying was not always initiated by the rank and file, their increasing willingness to dig in signifies a recognition that it was not just necessary but desirable to do so. One can be more definite about who did the digging: the vast majority of it was done by the infantry troops. There were not enough engineer troops available, and Confederate authorities used slave and free black laborers only on a few large semipermanent defense systems.[4]

The role of the rifle musket has also been a prominent theme in previous literature on field fortifications in the Civil War. Postwar writers were fascinated with the new weaponry, and they wanted to divine its impact on late nineteenth-century tactics. In the process, they had a strong tendency to emphasize its impact on Civil War tactics as well, ignoring the fact that the rifle musket of the 1860s was still a single-shot muzzle loader. They overlooked the idea that rapidity of fire might be more important in fostering changes in tactics than the presence of rifling in the barrel. The rifle musket of the Civil War could not be loaded any faster than a smoothbore. Its only advantage over the older weapon was a range that was about three times longer, but Civil War combat was usually fought at short ranges, similar to those of previous conflicts. In other words, although armed with rifle muskets, Civil War armies continued to fire at ranges generally consistent with the use of smoothbore muskets.[5]

Yet most modern historians have continued to assume that the rifle musket was the key factor that led to the widespread use of field fortifications. Hagerman has written that it was essential in driving the shift "from the primacy of the frontal assault to fortified field positions." Assumptions about the impact of the rifle musket on Civil War military operations have been questioned by Paddy Griffith. The role of the weapon has been exaggerated; the rifle musket did not foster the tendency to dig in by the latter part of the Civil War. The argument has always been made that the armies were fully armed with rifles by early 1864; since the widespread use of field fortifications began then, most commentators have connected the two as cause and effect.[6]

The widespread use of fieldworks was the result of continuous contact between opposing armies. Even during the first half of the war, when most infantrymen had smoothbores, lots of digging was done. The fact that entrenching often took place right after a battle indicates that the shock of combat affected the minds of commanders and men alike. They naturally wanted to find protection. Long periods of peace between battles and the offensive victories of Lee's men in the Seven Days and Second Manassas tended to suppress these feelings temporarily, but they resurfaced with Fredericksburg and subsequent battles. When the armies remained within musket range of each other for several days, officers and men indulged their desire for protection by digging elaborate fieldworks. Proximity to the enemy and exposure to danger were key factors driving the use of field fortifications.

There was also a slow development toward a more sophisticated form of trench defense during the eastern campaigns of 1861–64. Whenever possible, engineer officers laid out lines and specified design details. In most cases, the works that resulted tended to be straight, simple, and uniform. But in cases where the design details were left up to commanders of infantry units or the rank and file, one sees innovative and quirky features. Hooker's fortified bridgehead at Chancellorsville is the best early example of this phenomenon. The more often fieldworks were constructed, the less control military engineers had over the details, and the more one can see the impromptu genius of ordinary officers and men in devising details that suited their tastes.[7]

One example of this is the use of headlogs as an added protection. The first completely documented use of headlogs appears in May 1863. At least a few Twelfth Corps regiments used them on Hooker's fortified bridgehead at Chancellorsville. The same type of headlog was utilized by the Twelfth Corps on Culp's Hill at Gettysburg and much more extensively by both armies in 1864. The men simply placed a log lengthwise atop the parapet and raised it a few inches by using blocks. Federal troops in the siege of Vicksburg devised a different kind of headlog about the same time. It was made of two logs with loopholes cut halfway into each log and flattened sides laid together. When completed, a full loophole was formed. These took time and energy to make, and they resembled the loopholes in the wooden stockades of frontier forts and in Civil War blockhouses. The headlogs at Vicksburg were designed to be used by sharpshooters during a lengthy siege, while the headlogs at Chancellorsville and Gettysburg were designed to be erected quickly and used temporarily by an entire line of battle. Col. John T. Wilder claimed in a postwar article that his men used headlogs at Munfordville, Kentucky, during Bragg's invasion of that state in September 1862, but the evidence is inconclusive. Whenever the first headlogs were used, however, the fact remains that there was a clear trend toward making earthwork defenses stronger through innovation by individuals and small units by the middle of 1863 in both theaters of war.[8]

The tendency to dig in within striking distance of the enemy, called hasty entrenching by postwar military writers, was a true innovation of the Civil War. Field fortifications were used in many previous conflicts in both North America and Europe, but they were usually prepared before battle was imminent. True hasty fortifications were constructed under pressure, often literally under fire. I am not aware of any examples in American or European warfare before 1861.

The battle of Gaines's Mill was the first engagement during which either army in the East dug hasty works, "constructed on the spur of the moment by troops just deployed and waiting the hostile advance," in the words of Johnson and Hartshorn in the early twentieth century. Other examples included many of the works dug during the Fredericksburg, Chancellorsville, and Gettysburg campaigns and, of course, Mine Run. They would come to be the most common form of entrenchment in the brutal Overland campaign and throughout many phases of the Petersburg campaign as well. Arthur L. Wagner, a prominent military writer of the early twentieth century, noted that the use of hasty entrenchments "constituted the most marked characteristic of the rebellion."[9]

Finally, the terms and conditions defining a field campaign were being transformed in the Civil War, and much of that redefinition was taking place in the East during the campaigns of 1861–64. Field campaigns sometimes took on some of the attributes of a siege, as at Yorktown and Suffolk. There were classic sieges in the Civil War at Vicksburg and Port Hudson and in the reduction of Battery Wagner on Morris Island, their character hardly changed from past experiences in American and European history. But the size of field armies and a willingness to experiment with certain elements of siegecraft in static confrontations were marked features of warfare from the Crimea to World War I.

Likewise, the terminology of field operations became blurred in the Civil War. It was a peculiarly American, even a peculiarly Civil War, phenomenon to call any static confrontation in field campaigning a siege. This did not happen in American wars before 1861 or after 1865 and was rare in European warfare, too. The Civil War was fought mostly by civilian soldiers who were not overly careful in their use of terminology.

Whether to fight, retreat, or dig in: these were questions a Civil War field commander had to answer, often under great duress and with woefully inadequate information. Dennis Hart Mahan sought to guide future American commanders with his doctrine on the use of field fortifications as offensive tools. With volunteer soldiers, poorly trained but highly motivated, earthworks could be used to hold a position more effectively. Even a green soldier can steady his nerves while crouched behind a parapet. But Mahan was influenced by the French example to urge the offensive also, and he taught that fieldworks could aid the attack as well as strengthen the defense.

It is always difficult to assess the impact of a book or an idea on the practice of everyday life. Hagerman has argued that McClellan was a firm disciple of Mahan, that the professor had the biggest impact on the operations of the Army of the Potomac. The best graduates of West Point and those who adhered most stringently to the institutional model of the academy tended to find their way to the ranks of that army. One can argue that McClellan's Peninsula campaign was an example of putting Mahan's theory of the defensive-offensive to the test, and it worked until Lee took command and decided to attack in the Seven Days.[10]

It is doubtful, however, that other field commanders in the eastern campaigns of the first half of the war thought a great deal about Mahan's theory or pored over his writings or mused on his lectures delivered on the banks of the Hudson River. Field commanders usually thought they had to be on either the defensive or the offensive and then decide whether or not to dig in. A useful lesson learned by early 1864, through hard experience rather than reading, was that the two were not mutually exclusive. Commanders did not have to give up the offensive when their men dug fieldworks. The reliance on earthworks certainly did increase the power of the defense, but it did not necessarily create tactical stalemate. If commanders used fieldworks the right way, they could add offensive power to their armies. The key was not to butt one's head against strong defensive works but to outflank them while holding the enemy's attention with equally strong earthworks in their front. Grant would use this strategy as the only feasible way to pry Lee's tough army out of its long trench line at Petersburg.

Civil War officers on all levels of command had to learn how to incorporate the use of fieldworks into their repertory of skills as a soldier. To ignore the value of trenches was to deny their men a significant element in the array of advantages every commander seeks to accumulate in the deadly contest of war. The eastern armies, North and South, came through hard experience to fit themselves technically and mentally for their use of fieldworks in the Overland campaign and at Petersburg by the time Grant took command of all Union armies in March 1864.

Appendix 1

The Design and Construction of
Field Fortifications at Yorktown

The works at Yorktown were the most significant field fortifications of the eastern campaigns before the battle of Chancellorsville. Complex and strong, they call into question the previously held idea that reliance on fieldworks started in 1864. Large portions of them are well preserved, although the Confederate remnants are more easily accessible than the Union remnants.

Federal Works

McClellan's engineer officers conducted their preliminary survey of the Confederate line on April 6–12, while Barnard chose the site for the engineer and artillery depots. He also scouted the ravines and the road system to the rear of the proposed Union line. The heavy artillery emplacements received first attention. Batteries No. 1 and 2 were started on April 17 and essentially were completed in three days. No. 3 was begun, and sites were selected for Nos. 4, 5, 6, and 7. By April 22 at least four heavy artillery works were ready for guns, and No. 3 and No. 6 already had been armed with 20-pounder Parrotts and 10-inch seacoast mortars, hauled to the works by 100 horses.[1]

Eventually fourteen heavy batteries, five redoubts, and an unknown number of emplacements for field guns were constructed by McClellan's men. Battery No. 1, near the York River opposite the heaviest Confederate gun emplacements at Yorktown, consisted of a layer of logs with a layer of gabions on top, then a thick layer of sandbags topped the parapet and formed embrasures for the guns. Long, thick traverses were made of the same material as the parapet. The emplacement was located in the orchard of the Farinholt homestead, and the large frame house, just to the rear of the guns, made a superb observation post.[2]

Many engineers and infantrymen were impressed with the construction of Battery No. 4 because it was placed on the bank of Wormley's Creek. Capt. Wesley Brainerd and a party of the 50th New York Engineers cut the emplacement into the sloping bank, throwing dirt into the creek until they had room for as many as ten 13-inch mortars. The 1st Connecticut Heavy Artillery was responsible for placing and manning them. The entire floor of the emplacement was leveled, and a wooden platform was built for each mortar. The undulating creek bank was five to twenty

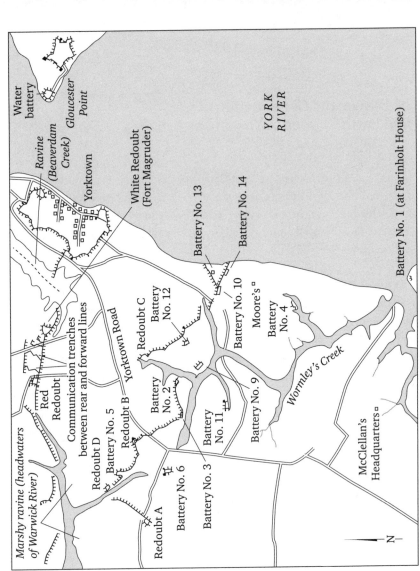

Water
battery

Gloucester
Point

*Ravine
(Beaverdam
Creek)*

Yorktown

White Redoubt
(Fort Magruder)

Battery No. 13

Battery No. 14

*YORK
RIVER*

Communication trenches
between rear and forward lines

Red
Redoubt

Yorktown Road

Redoubt C

Battery
No. 12

Redoubt D

Battery No. 5

Redoubt B

Battery
No. 2

Battery No. 10

Moore's □

Battery
No. 4

Battery
No. 11

Battery No. 9

*Marshy ravine (headwaters
of Warwick River)*

Redoubt A

Battery No. 6

Battery No. 3

Wormley's Creek

McClellan's
Headquarters □

–N–

Battery No. 1 (at Farinholt House)

Union and Confederate Works, East End of Warwick Line, Yorktown, April 1862

Federal Battery No. 4, Yorktown. This mortar battery was uniquely dug into the bank of Wormley's Creek, and access to it was gained by a footbridge over the stream, seen on the far left of this stereoscopic view. Ordnance was shipped to the site in the barge on the right. (Library of Congress)

feet above water. A small ravine that drained into the creek exposed the gunners to Rebel view, so the engineers built a stockade across it. The battery was accessible only from the rear, across the creek, so the engineers spanned the stream with a footbridge. The gunners hauled in their weapons and supplies by barges, which were pushed up the stream and anchored just behind the battery.[3]

Emplacements for field batteries on the center of the Union line received much less attention. Remnants of a position for eight guns, divided into two four-gun emplacements, are located opposite the Rebel position at Dam No. 1. It is the right wing of a work that curved around the Garrow house, which was burned at the start of the confrontation at Yorktown. The two emplacements have traverses and a continuous platform for all four guns on the natural level of the earth. They are also flanked by a much thinner infantry parapet.[4]

McClellan's artillery chief, Brig. Gen. William F. Barry, recommended that infantry and field artillery be deployed near the heavy guns. He believed No. 3 and No. 6 were "particularly exposed to sorties of the enemy." Apparently no one had planned to connect the heavy gun emplacements with curtains or even to construct flank protection for them, but Barry's recommendation spurred efforts to connect the batteries with infantry lines on April 25. First, a line was started between Batteries No. 2 and 3, and another was started from the Yorktown Road toward No. 5. That night the line between 2 and 3 was quickly finished across open, exposed ground. This section was dug four feet deep and six feet wide. Also on the night of April 25, a line was dug from Redoubt C, which lay forward of the heavy batteries, toward the southeast to cover the approaches to No. 9 and No. 12. This line was later completed all the way to the York River. From this latter section, a branch was run diagonally to a point 200 yards farther upstream than the original end of the line. Completed on the night of April 29, this branch allowed the Federals to observe much of the area between the Union and Confederate positions.[5]

By the end of the confrontation at Yorktown, engineers and soldiers had run another line from Redoubt A to Battery No. 5 and had started a line westward from A toward Batteries No. 7 and 8. Improvements on earlier lines continued even as new lines were opened. A banquette, made of logs in some sections and earth in others, was added to them.[6]

At first the Confederates fired very little on the Federals when they dug in opposite the Warwick Line, but they let loose an 8-inch gun on the diggers who worked on the line stretching from Battery No. 10 to the York River. Barnard reported that it did not delay the project, but he found it surprising that the Rebels did not harass his engineers and the infantry more systematically. He also noted that they failed to fire into the ravines and woods behind the Union position to disrupt support efforts. Barnard estimated that no more than a dozen Federals were hit by Confederate artillery fire while working on the fortifications.[7]

Although Barnard and everyone else called these lines parallels, they were, in fact, not like the work traditionally given this term. The concept was initially developed by French military engineer Sebastien Le Prestre de Vauban in the mid-seventeenth century. As used by him in many sieges conducted to further the strategic goals of Louis XIV, they were dug parallel to the enemy's line of defense and served as the starting point for all future siege approaches. At Yorktown the Federals dug them as an afterthought to connect existing batteries. Gillmore's men dug genuine parallels on Morris Island, but Barnard's subordinates erected curtains to connect enclosed works. The result was a system of fieldworks, dug in different sections and at different times, that constituted an irregular line.

The Yorktown system of works was the first major entrenchment project conducted by the Army of the Potomac in the field. Inevitably, problems were encountered. "There is great difficulty about tools," Fitz John Porter recorded in the "Journal of the Siege." The quartermaster department issued them to the troops but failed to keep accurate records of how many were given to each unit. Infantry officers neglected to keep track of them, and soldiers often kept them for use in camp or simply threw them away. This often caused delays for work details. Big shipments arrived by boat up the York River, and tools for 10,000 men were available in the depots by April 27; but proper implements came and went with frustrating uncertainty. Despite the huge quantity of tools issued during the campaign, Barnard had to rush a new shipment to the army to build the Harrison's Landing Line at the end of the Seven Days battles.[8]

Even though McClellan had a large number of engineer officers, Barnard asked that artillery officers help to design and construct the works. At least eight officers and several more who served as their assistants were regularly detached from their units. In addition, the men of two field batteries were sent to the Volunteer Engineer Brigade for three days of instruction to learn how to make gabions and fascines.[9]

Woodbury's engineers were primarily responsible for constructing thousands of gabions and fascines needed to shore up parapets and traverses in the growing system of fieldworks. Not only did they teach the artillerymen how to do this, but they instructed the 5th New Hampshire and 69th New York as well. From April 17 to May 4 Woodbury put an average of 283 men per day on this work. They made at least 2,888 gabions and several hundred fascines. In addition to these wooden components constructed in the depots to the rear of the line, a total of 113,500 empty sandbags were shipped to McClellan's army for use as revetment material.[10]

A more specialized article was the mantlet, a protective device to cover the embrasure of a gun to shield the crew from enemy observation and fire. Mantlets could be lifted when firing, or a circular hole could be cut in them to allow the gun tube to stick through. McClellan asked for 100 rope mantlets, inspired by their use on the Russian line at Sebastopol. Col. Richard Delafield, who had been one of the commissioners on McClellan's trip to Europe seven years earlier, took the responsibility of making them in New York City. He had difficulty finding the right kind of rope and thus made only twenty-five. The rest were constructed of half-inch wrought iron attached to oak planks that were three inches thick. Delafield thought iron was more effective than rope anyway, as it added a greater degree of protection against sharpshooters. Both types of mantlets were made in layers; the rope had three layers to make a total thickness of six inches, and the metal consisted of two layers of quarter-inch iron. Both types were shipped to the Peninsula. They were installed in fifteen embrasures of Battery No. 2 on April 29, and three more went to Battery No. 3 a short time later. By the end of the confrontation at Yorktown, these were the only artillery emplacements with such protection, but they were never tested in battle. Barry's artillerymen were innovative in protecting the gabion revetment of their embrasures, stretching green hides across the woodwork.[11]

Labor on the Union system of fortifications intensified as April neared its end. Merlons of sandbags were built atop the parapet of Redoubt A to create embrasures for the gunners. A covered way, or protected road, was dug between Batteries No. 7 and 8. Abatis was placed in front of at least some segments of the infantry line. Redoubt C, one of the more exposed works, received a lot of attention. Its ditch was widened by successive work details until it was twelve feet wide and six feet deep. Work continued on all projects until the morning of May 4, when it was discovered that the Confederates had evacuated the Warwick Line. There was still more work to be done. Several heavy batteries needed more traverses or thicker parapets, curtains needed to be completed, and revetting had to be finished in some works. Redoubt D was only started the night before, and a mortar battery to enfilade the cluster of Confederate works at Wynn's Mill was under way.[12]

The ordnance for these works was also in place by May 4. A total of 120 pieces (13 heavy, 45 mortars, 44 medium, and 18 field guns) were ready for action. More than 17,000 projectiles were stockpiled, 33 of which were 30-pounder shells filled with "Greek fire." The weight of ordnance was astonishing. Maj. Alexander Doull, the ordnance officer of McClellan's siege train, noted that the heaviest gun at Sebastopol was an English 68-pounder that weighed 10,649 pounds. The 200-pounder Parrott at Yorktown weighed 16,570 pounds. Doull proudly concluded that the weight of Federal artillery at Yorktown amounted to 50 percent more metal than "any guns that have ever before been placed in siege batteries."[13]

Barnard and Barry were convinced that they could have pounded the Rebels out of the Warwick Line with their combination of fieldworks and artillery, but Barnard was confident that he could have pried them out even with siege approaches if McClellan had allowed him. There were several ravines that originated between the lines and drained toward the Federal position. The Rebels could only see imperfectly into the heads of these drainage features, and therefore the Yankees could have worked in them in relative safety. Barnard had already chosen one ravine that could have allowed his men to dig a sap toward the ditch of the Yorktown city defenses. Admittedly he could not see this so clearly until the Rebels gave up their defenses, but Barnard seemed eager to try siege approaches. On the opposite side of the pending battlefield, Confederate Brig. Gen. Jubal Early thought his part of the Warwick Line was vulnerable to siege operations. He held the area encompassing the Red and White redoubts, on the spine of land that was the watershed of the Peninsula. This high, level ground, he thought, offered a good opportunity for siege approaches.[14]

Confederate Works: The Warwick Line

All along the Warwick River, from Yorktown to Mulberry Island, the Confederates transformed a meager line of works into one of the more impressive field fortifications of the war. It intimidated McClellan into a month-long digging competition.

The defenses around Yorktown were a citadel, a self-contained work inside a larger fortification; they were extensive, heavy, and studded with large guns. The line enclosed Yorktown on three sides, with the heaviest parapets and ordnance located on the south facing the Yankees. The parapet was 15 feet thick with a ditch up to 10 feet deep. Barnard thought these southward-facing works were the oldest of the Warwick Line. The works that circled west and north of town had probably been constructed the preceding winter, he guessed. They had equally thick parapets and deep ditches. In addition to these city defenses, there were seven water batteries to impede river traffic. These had parapets 18 feet thick with ditches 10 feet deep and were located about 80 feet above the water level. Sod covered the parapets of the water batteries, while sandbags and cotton bales were used to build traverses and embrasures in all the works around town. Most of the revetting consisted of log-and-post construction. The water batteries were armed with twenty-three guns, mostly 8-inch Columbiads and 32-pounders. Most of these works were located exactly where the British had built their own defensive works in 1781.[15]

Supporting the Yorktown city works were the defenses across the river at Gloucester Point. The York River is 1,000 yards wide at this point and demands a heavy work mounting sufficient guns to command the tidal stream. The Confederates constructed a water battery mounting twelve heavy guns. Shaped like a U, with its rear enclosed, it was barely 2 feet above high tide and had parapets 20 feet thick and nearly 8 feet high on the interior. Like the water batteries across the river, the parapet was protected by a layer of sod, and the embrasures were made of stacked layers of turf. A much larger fieldwork was constructed on the bluff, 40 feet above the water, to the rear of the water battery. Its parapet was also 20 feet thick and 7 to 10 feet high, with a ditch that ranged from 7 to 15 feet deep. This large fort had several bombproofs in the center for the protection of the garrison and a layer of sod on the parapet, but it only mounted three guns in barbette positions. The water battery was the main defense against Union ships; the huge fort to the rear was built for its protection.[16]

Stretching westward from Yorktown, the Warwick Line first took advantage of a short stream called Beaverdam Creek that flows into the York River just north of town. Then it crossed the spine of the Peninsula, which was a few feet higher than the land to either side, along which the major road to Richmond was laid. This was the most favorable ground for a Union advance, and the Rebels had no natural obstacles to help them. Two heavy redoubts were constructed, called by Federal observers the White and Red Redoubts. The former, also known as Fort Magruder, was an enclosed work 850 yards from Yorktown. It was shaped like an arrowhead that pointed west, and the connecting infantry line was attached to its front face. Fort Magruder had a stockade to cover its rear and mounted a 9-inch Dahlgren, a 4.5-inch rifle, and an 8-inch howitzer. With emplacements for field guns, the fort had room for twenty-two artillery pieces. Two embrasures were protected by mantlets. There were also emplacements for a few guns along the curtain connecting Fort Magruder to the Yorktown city defenses. Fort Magruder was an older work, constructed, Barnard reasoned from the settling and erosion, during the preceding winter.

The Red Redoubt, 525 yards west of the White Redoubt, was square, and the connecting infantry line was also attached to its front face. Barnard thought the fort started as a section of the curtain and then additional faces were added to make an

Remnants of Confederate fort, Gloucester Point, Yorktown campaign. This is a portion of the large star fort that protected the water battery. The view shows a part of the east face, pointing away from the water battery and toward an inland approach. (Earl J. Hess)

enclosed work. It was not as strong as Fort Magruder. The guns were mounted en barbette, and Federal observers from Battery No. 13 could see into its interior. To strengthen this area, the Confederates built a secondary line of infantry trench to the rear of both forts and dug five communication trenches to connect both lines. The communication trenches had to be dug in a zigzag configuration because the land gradually sloped up from the Confederate front line to the rear, exposing the rear areas to Union artillery fire. Barnard was not impressed with this arrangement and noted that these infantry works were not well placed to allow soldiers to fire from them.[17]

From the White and Red Redoubts the Warwick Line ran to the upper reaches of the Warwick River and followed that stream all the way across the Peninsula. Wynn's Mill, about 3,000 yards west of the Red Redoubt, was one of the most heavily fortified points on the line because the river bends in a right angle, necessitating extensive works to protect against enfilade fire. The complex of works at Wynn's Mill is 650 yards wide and about 100 yards deep. The first line curves to stay within 10 to 20 yards of the water's edge. It contains thirty-five traverses designed to protect both artillery and infantry positions. These traverses vary in size and

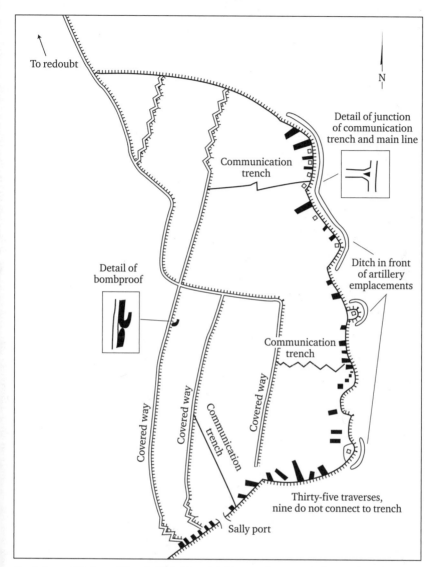

Confederate Works at Wynn's Mill, Warwick Line, Yorktown, April 1862 (based on field visit, 1995; OR Atlas, pl. 19, no. 29; and "Map of Yorktown and Vicinity," YB)

length, but most are either 10, 15, or 20 yards long. Some have dirt dug on only one side, while a minority are dug on both sides to make a wide, thick bank of earth. Ditching exists only in front of artillery positions, not infantry posts, to make a thicker parapet to resist counter battery fire. Wynn's Mill has five artillery positions with a total of eight gun emplacements. Most of the emplacements have raised

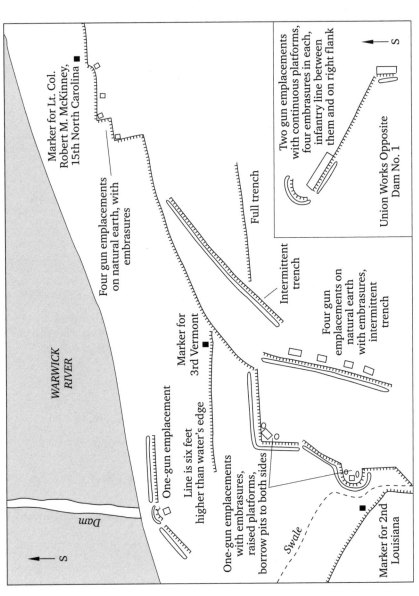

Confederate Works at Dam No. 1, Garrow's Point, Warwick Line, Yorktown, April 1862 (based on field visit, 1995)

The following labels appear on the map:

WARWICK RIVER

Dam

S

Marker for Lt. Col. Robert M. McKinney, 15th North Carolina

Four gun emplacements on natural earth, with embrasures

One-gun emplacement

Line is six feet higher than water's edge

Marker for 3rd Vermont

Full trench

Intermittent trench

Four gun emplacements on natural earth with embrasures, intermittent trench

One-gun emplacements with embrasures, raised platforms, borrow pits to both sides

Swale

Marker for 2nd Louisiana

Two gun emplacements with continuous platforms, four embrasures in each, infantry line between them and on right flank

Union Works Opposite Dam No. 1

S

platforms to lift the guns a few inches above the natural level of earth. Two emplacements are in bastions, which enabled the Rebels to construct two embrasures for one gun position, allowing for a greater degree of lateral aiming.

A system of covered ways and communication trenches connects the main line to a large redoubt northwest of the angle. It was located to the rear of the main line. These covered ways have a good bank of earth on the side facing the enemy, while three smaller communication trenches that branch out from them at different points have dirt banked on both sides. Two of the covered ways have zigzag segments at their ends because they approach the Union positions across the river head-on. Each zig and zag is about six yards long. Two of the communication trenches also have zigzag configurations. One of the communication trenches joins the main line with a bit of natural earth left at the junction to shield men in the communication trench from enemy fire down its length. An oddly shaped bomb-proof, consisting of a sharply curved parapet that literally wraps around to provide shelter on three sides, exists on one of the covered ways.[18]

Despite the danger of enfilade fire at this angle of the Warwick Line, the Confederate position at Wynn's Mill would have been very difficult to reduce. The next strongpoint downriver was Dam No. 1 at Garrow's Point, about six miles from Yorktown. While a bit smaller than Wynn's Mill, it was a formidable position. The natural width of the Warwick at this point was 15 feet, but the dam turned it into a lake 100 yards wide. The outlet for drainage of excess water was located on the Confederate end of the dam. Trees were cut for about 75 yards in all directions from the dam, whose top was wide enough for artillery and wagons to cross the river.

The works were built in layers. The first is a short line protecting an emplacement for one gun 20 yards from the water's edge and aimed along the length of the dam. The second layer is the main line of defense, a portion of the continuous line that links with Wynn's Mill to the left and the other positions to the right. It ranges from 40 to 150 yards from the water's edge and lacks traverses. The line makes several sharp turns and contains six artillery emplacements, four of which are located in angles and one in a bastion. All of these emplacements have embrasures; some of them also have raised platforms, while in others the guns rested on the natural level of the earth. Two gun positions have borrow pits to both sides, as the gunners needed extra dirt to strengthen the parapet or raise the gun platform, and two gun positions have a good ditch in front as well.

In addition to these artillery emplacements along the main line, the Confederates built a four-gun artillery position immediately to the rear. It consists of a single, large parapet with a good ditch and an irregular trench between the gun emplacements. The latter was dug simply to obtain more dirt to strengthen the parapet, which is fifteen feet wide at the base. The gun positions have embrasures and platforms at the natural level of the earth but lack traverses. The entire four-gun

Confederate Dam No. 1, Garrow's Point, Yorktown. Taken by photographer H. G. Houghton of Brattleboro, Vermont, this rare view shows Battery F, 5th U.S. Artillery, crossing the Confederate dam. The regular unit was one of four batteries attached to the Second Division, Sixth Corps. In the distance one can see the one-gun emplacement close to the Confederate end of the dam, and the main line behind it. The four-gun emplacement behind the main line is visible because of its pronounced embrasures. All of these works are well preserved today. (Vermont Historical Society)

position aims to the left oblique and supports the main line as it refuses several yards away from the river to cross a wide swale. After crossing, the main line returns toward the river.

To the rear of the four-gun position, and the main line as well, are two short, supporting trenches that constitute a third layer of defense. These are for infantry only, and one appears to have been started but abandoned in favor of the second. The first has a ditch and intermittent trench that stretches for only two-thirds of its length. The second short line has no ditch but a very good trench and a better parapet than the first. The second line also is positioned more effectively to support the main line.

The works that lay to the left and right of the position at Dam No. 1 were also strong. Between Garrow's Point and Wynn's Mill is a fully excavated artillery posi-

Remnants of Confederate one-gun emplacement, Dam No. 1, Yorktown. This photo shows the one-gun emplacement in the angled salient on the main line. (Earl J. Hess)

tion. The Confederates dug a rectangular space 3 feet deep, 15 yards wide, and 5 yards to the rear. It is 125 yards from the water's edge and has three embrasures, two facing the river and one facing to the right. Immediately to the left of this position they also dug two more artillery positions for one gun each, with embrasures pointing straight ahead.

Substantial remnants of the Confederate fortifications allow us to glimpse the nature of the works between Dam No. 1 and Lee's Mill, which lay three miles from Garrow's Point. The main line between these two locations approaches the water in some spots and lies 150 yards away in others. The Confederates were aware that they needed to allow water to drain through swales toward the river when it rained, and they altered their works to accommodate that need. Across a swale just to the right of the complex at Dam No. 1 they left a 6-yard-long gap in the main line and built a short traverse 10 yards from the gap for flank protection. As we have seen, the Rebels refused their line to cross the swale just to the left of Dam No. 1 as well, and they built artillery emplacements to fire obliquely across the swale in case the enemy chose to test this returned section of trench. They did similar things to the right of Dam No. 1. Two artillery emplacements exist in well-preserved form on both sides of a swale. Both are built in a shallow V so guns could fire forward across the river and obliquely across the swale. They have embrasures and a large, strong parapet.[19]

Remnants of Confederate four-gun emplacement, Dam No. 1, Yorktown. This photo shows the well-preserved ditch of the four-gun emplacement behind the main line. (Earl J. Hess)

The western end of the Warwick Line was anchored on the works at Lee's Mill, which were comparatively simple but very strong. The Confederates had the advantage of a deep valley in their front and an elevated position for their works, obviating the need for extensive, in-depth defenses. A good parapet, a trench, and ditching in front of the guns, the whole configured in either straight lines or rectangular bastions, constituted the works. One remaining artillery position, in the form of a large bastion, contains three raised gun platforms and one short traverse.

Lee's Mill was located six miles up the Warwick River, but a highly irregular shoreline along the James was created by numerous small islands hugging the west side of the Peninsula. As a result, the Confederates were compelled to build a number of outlying works to deny Yankee boats access to streams that could outflank the Warwick Line. Fort Crafford and several other smaller redoubts on Mulberry Island were among these works. Several had been built in 1861 as part of the effort to defend the lower James, and Magruder incorporated them into his Warwick Line. Fort Crafford was a large, five-sided work built to defend against both a land attack and a waterborne approach.

Another outlying work was built to deny the Federals access to Skiff's Creek, which lay to the rear of the Warwick Line. The Skiff's Creek Redoubt is only forty yards long and twenty-five yards wide. It has three raised artillery platforms on its

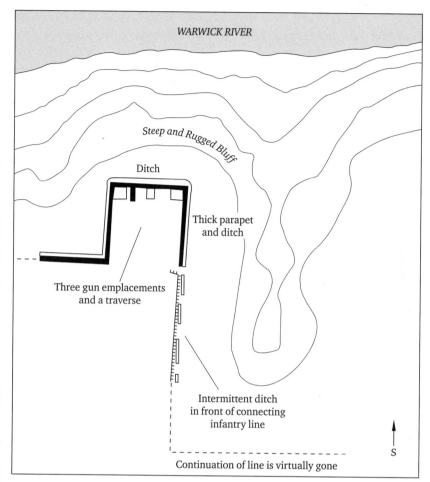

WARWICK RIVER

Steep and Rugged Bluff

Ditch

Thick parapet
and ditch

Three gun emplacements
and a traverse

Intermittent ditch
in front of connecting
infantry line

S

Continuation of line is virtually gone

Confederate Works at Lee's Mill, Warwick Line, Yorktown, April 1862 (based on field visit, 1995)

western side, one of the shorter faces, and an unguarded sally port in the middle of its eastern face. The work has a good ditch and parapet but no traverses or trenches.[20]

Barnard's evaluation of the Warwick Line was mostly positive, although he did note deficiencies in the system when he saw them. Lt. Cyrus B. Comstock also evaluated the works, but he did so before the Rebels evacuated them, by detecting what he could through field glasses. He noted the large number of traverses and a few bombproofs at Wynn's Mill and observed the size and profile of parapets at various parts of the line. Comstock could also tell that the rectangular bastions at Lee's Mill predated the siege; they were "well and neatly built," while the more hasty works thrown up recently had "no pretensions to finish or good construction—revetment being absent or poor, and embrasures formed by piling a few sand-bags near the interior crest." He probably would have agreed with the assessment of Henry L. Abbott, a volunteer officer in the 20th Massachusetts, who reported that the Warwick Line was "considered tolerably elaborate for temporary fieldworks, though of course nothing like the field fortifications before Sebastopol that the allies were so long in taking."[21]

Far less information is available on Confederate efforts to make or ship the necessary tools and material for earthwork construction than is available for McClellan's army. The Confederate Engineer Bureau in Richmond was active in procuring what was needed, arranging for 20,000 sandbags to be shipped to the Peninsula in mid-April. The end result proves that the Rebels did not allow whatever shortages they suffered to delay the completion of their strong works.[22]

Appendix 2

Preserving the Field Fortifications at Gettysburg

The fieldworks at Gettysburg are probably the most famous of any campaign in the East from 1861 through early 1864. The Twelfth Corps fortifications on Culp's Hill garner the lion's share of the attention. This is a curious circumstance, considering that Chancellorsville saw much greater use of fieldworks and all the fortifications at Gettysburg are very simple, modest constructions. The earthworks used in the Peninsula campaign also were more extensive and complex than those at Gettysburg. But the reason for this disparity of attention is not difficult to ascertain: the public's view of Gettysburg as the preeminent engagement of the Civil War. If something was done at this battle, it automatically gained more attention regardless of its intrinsic value, or lack of it, in the general course of the war. In addition, Gettysburg was fought in the midst of a relatively wealthy population that could afford to expend the resources to preserve relics of the battle.

Local residents initiated efforts to preserve the field fortifications soon after Lee left their town. "These works, for the most part, yet remain as they were at the close of the battle," wrote Professor Michael Jacobs of Gettysburg College in February 1864. He "hoped that they may continue untouched, as a memento of the battle, and as objects of grateful wonder, until time itself shall cause them to decay." More than a year later, journalist John T. Trowbridge found at Culp's Hill a "rude embankment of stakes and logs and stones, covered with earth." He also discovered "little private breastworks consisting of rocks heaped by a tree or beside a larger rock, or across a cleft in the rocks, where some sharpshooter exercised his skill at his ease."

The Gettysburg Battlefield Memorial Association was created in 1864 to oversee the preservation of the battlefield. It existed until the federal government took over in 1893. The association engaged in what would be questionable work by modern standards, rebuilding artillery lunettes and rock breastworks without strict regard to accuracy. It reconstructed the gun emplacements on Cemetery Hill, adding some in places where veterans of the battle did not remember works at all. It built others up so that they "seemed to me larger and more elaborate than my recollection would make them at the time of the battle," thought Capt. R. Bruce Ricketts. Local civic leader David Wills wrote to Governor Andrew Curtin in March 1864 that the artillery emplacements on Cemetery Hill "have already been very much defaced. They were made, first by piling up rails and then throwing up earth on top. The farmers have in most instances dug out their rails and the effects of the rains have settled the earth very much." The association worked hard to rebuild them as low, uniform parapets that look very different from the works depicted in photographs taken right after the battle. Today's visitor to Gettysburg sees the remnants of these association fieldworks, not the remains of the works used by the men who fought the battle.

The breastworks on the Round Tops received attention from the association as well. The small earthwork that protected McGilvery's artillery line was entirely reconstructed, having disappeared over the years due to agricultural activity. But the association rebuilt it straighter and aligned it to a postwar road constructed for touring vehicles.

The War Department took charge of the battlefield and created the Gettysburg National Park Commission, which administered the battlefield from 1893 to 1922. It infused a greater degree of scholarship and accuracy into the process of preserving the fieldworks, hiring Col. Emmor B. Cope as its engineer and mapmaker. Cope rebuilt 30,000 feet of stone fencing from 1898 through 1906. He rebuilt the artillery lunettes on the Confederate line and placed some guns along Seminary Ridge to mark positions. Relatively little restoration work was done after the commission was replaced by the Gettysburg National Military Park, until the New Deal stepped in. The Civilian Conservation Corps repaired and rebuilt stone fences at various points on the battlefield between 1936 and 1939, even though the general strategy of the Park Service has been to stabilize, not rebuild, historic resources. The visitor must always wonder, given the early postwar history of the battlefield, how much of the fortification remnants are authentic artifacts of the Civil War and how much are monuments to early, misguided preservation efforts.[1]

Glossary

Because the terminology used to describe fortifications is technical in nature, much of it deriving from the French language, it is often necessary for historians to include a glossary of terms for the reader's use. I include only those terms used in this volume; no attempt is made to provide a comprehensive dictionary of fortifications. I have made every attempt to be accurate in defining my terms, but I do not claim to have produced definitions that would satisfy an engineer. My purpose is simply to explain in common language what I think a term signified to a contemporary of the Civil War and to provide a common sense explanation readily understood by the reader of this book.[1]

A word about the meanings of key words and phrases is in order. Civil War contemporaries paid relatively little attention to the proper use of terminology, unless, of course, they were trained engineers. The average soldier used "rifle pits," "breastworks," and "ditches" to signify the same thing: earthworks made for infantry use. Specialists in military engineering recognized that each of these terms meant something different, but most soldiers did not care about such fine distinctions.

Like the specialist, we should try to differentiate between these terms. "Rifle pits" refers to individual holes dug for skirmishers, similar to twentieth-century foxholes. The term originated in the Crimean War when Russian riflemen dug similar holes in front of their earthworks so they could harass the Allied soldiers who were advancing siege approaches. Chaplain A. M. Stewart of the 102nd Pennsylvania recognized the misuse of this term and commented on it in his book, published in 1865. The phrase had "become a rather general one, designating almost any military construction, for offence or defence." It referred to "not merely a round or square hole in the ground, but a ditch, breastwork or embankment miles in length." Stewart was absolutely right. "Rifle pits" is probably the most commonly used phrase by Civil War soldiers to refer to infantry earthworks.[2]

I use the term "breastworks" to refer only to an accumulation of material on top of the ground—usually logs, rails, or stones—that does not involve any digging. This term ran a close second to "rifle pits" in its common usage among Civil War soldiers. The word "ditches" was much less commonly used, although it has a direct, earthy tone that leaves no doubt about what the writer was thinking. I use the word to refer only to the ditch dug in front of a parapet, for the purpose of both serving as an obstruction to an attacker and of acquiring dirt to thicken a parapet. The word "moat" more properly refers to a ditch in front of the parapet of a permanent work. The excavation behind, or on the friendly side, of a parapet should be called a trench.[3]

Abatis: An obstruction placed in front of an earthwork. Its purpose was to delay an attacker well within range of the defender's rifle and artillery fire. It was made of felled trees; the name comes from the French *arbes abattus*. The cut trees were lined up, and their butts were secured firmly to the ground, usually by digging a trench to receive the ends. Chains could also be used to secure the trunks to the ground. The branches were pointed toward the enemy and intertwined to present a solid front. If time and opportunity allowed, the points of the branches would be sharpened. If still green, the supple branches could be more easily moved aside by an attacker; when dried, they were hard and immovable. Losses would be heavy as attackers spent time trying to cut through with axes. An abatis was different from a slashing in that an abatis was arrayed in a line, while a slashing was created by cutting many trees over a wide area and letting them lie where they fell.[4]

Banquette: A raised platform at the bottom of a trench for infantrymen to stand on and gain enough height to fire over the parapet. The best trench was deep enough to completely cover the infantryman while he was standing straight. The banquette (also called a firing step) also allowed him to use the trench as a defensive position, not just a convenient hole to hide in.

Barbette: An artillery position fixed so that the gun tube could project, or at least fire easily, over the top of the parapet. It was quick and easy to construct but exposed the gun crew to enemy fire. Understandably, it was less popular than the embrasured artillery position, although it was often used.

Bastion Fort: An enclosed work, either square or polygonal, with protruding sections on all sides to deliver fire on all angles of approach to the work. The bastions were angular in shape and designed according to a mathematical formula; they transformed a basic redoubt into a stronger fortification with no areas around it uncovered by fire. Originally developed in the late fifteenth century, the term "bastion" was used loosely in the Civil War.

Berm: A separation between a ditch and a parapet. This feature takes care of a problem associated with piling dirt next to a hole: it will slide back in. Piling the dirt up so the bottom of its slope will be a few inches from the edge of the hole will create an "empty" space called a berm. If it is too wide, it could be used by an attacker to gain a foothold while climbing out of the ditch and up the outer slope of the parapet.

Blockhouse: A wooden defensive structure often used on the frontier before the

Civil War. Usually made of logs in a square or rectangular configuration and often with two stories, the blockhouse was quickly built and widely used to guard railroad bridges. Sometimes blockhouses were built inside or adjacent to earthworks. They were quite effective against small arms fire, but artillery fire could demolish them. That is why they were more commonly used to guard lines of communication from guerrilla raids rather than in the major operations of field armies.

Breastwork: A fortification created by piling material, usually logs, rails, or stones, in a line. It involved no digging into the earth and was quickly built "breast" high so that men could fire over the top. Most earthen parapets were made by piling logs or rails and then digging a trench, throwing the dirt on top of the pile to gain additional height.

Casemate: A completely enclosed artillery emplacement with walls and a roof. Rarely constructed during the Civil War because of the labor involved and because they seldom proved their worth in a bombardment.

Chevaux-de-Frise: An obstruction consisting of a shaft through which wooden spikes were pushed halfway. Both ends of the spikes were sharpened. With another row of such spikes set at a different angle, you have a wooden fence. It apparently originated as a defense against cavalry and was widely used in siege works to temporarily defend breeches in walls. It was also used in eighteenth-century British fortifications in North America as well as during the Civil War.

Citadel: A self-contained work inside a larger work. It was used as a defense of last resort if the larger work was penetrated by an attacker. In principle it was similar in purpose to the donjon, or keep, in medieval fortresses and castles.

Command: The height of the parapet above the original grade of the site.

Counterscarp: The outside wall of a ditch that lies in front of a work. The scarp is the opposite wall, the one that lies on the inside of the ditch below the parapet.

Cremailliere: A line of parapet that was indented, with a series of projections forward and continuations along the original line, to look like a series of steps. David Russell Wright well describes it as "a line or curtain that contained alternating long faces and short flanks which allowed the defenders to fire direct and flanking fires."[5]

Curtain: An infantry parapet that connected bastions or self-contained works in a line of fortifications. It protected the flanks of the works and unified the whole fortification system. A curtain could be adorned by trenches, ditches, traverses, or other embellishments, or it could be a simple parapet.

Demilune: A smaller or reduced version of a lunette.

Ditch: The linear excavation in front of a parapet. If it is filled with water, it is called a wet ditch, but that was rare in Civil War earthworks. It was sometimes called a moat.

Embrasure: An opening cut into the parapet to allow a gun to fire through. Its purpose was to protect the gun crew as much as possible. The sides had to be revetted, and it had to be large enough to allow the gun adequate play, but not so large as to allow the enemy to fire through it easily. The interior opening of the embrasure was called the mouth; the sides were termed cheeks; the bottom was called the sole; and the splay referred to how far the embrasure widened from the mouth to the outside edge.

Fascine: A bundle of sticks tied together. It could be used to help build a parapet or to revet the cheeks of an embrasure. It was also piled in the ditch of an enemy work so that attackers could cross the ditch quickly.

Field Fortification: An earthwork or breastwork usually constructed during a campaign and meant to be temporary, to be used only as long as the battle or campaign lasted. The difference between it and a semipermanent work was based on how long the defensive feature was meant to be used. The works defending Washington, D.C., New Bern, Suffolk, and Richmond were all technically field fortifications, but they were semipermanent because they were designed to last for the duration of the war. The only truly permanent fortifications were the masonry coastal forts constructed before the Civil War. Good examples of field fortifications include the Warwick Line at Yorktown, the hasty entrenchments at Gaines's Mill, and Hooker's fortified bridgehead at Chancellorsville.

Flying Sap: A sap constructed quickly by sending men out at night to dig a parallel before dawn. This method can only be used at comparatively safe distances from the enemy work. See also Sap and Full Sap.

Fort: An enclosed work. The technical difference between it and a redoubt, or a lesser work, is difficult to pin down. Generally, the term "fort" was used to denote any sizable or important work, even if it was little different from a redoubt.

Fraise: A line of stakes placed at or near the berm and pointed either horizontally or at an angle. Its purpose was to obstruct an attacker trying to climb from the ditch and up the outer slope of the parapet.

Full Sap: A sap constructed the hard way, by pushing a sap roller ahead while sappers dig an approach trench behind it. It was time consuming, as the dirt had to be quickly shaped into a parapet along the edge of the trench to protect the diggers. It was a necessary method, however, when the approach neared the enemy work and was vulnerable to small arms fire. See also Sap and Flying Sap.

Gabion: A cylinder open at both ends and made of twigs interwoven around sticks, used to revet parapets or the cheeks of embrasures. They were very commonly used in the Civil War, but the method of making them had to be taught by trained engineers.

Glacis: Raised earth on top of the edge of the counterscarp. The object was to form an imaginary line from the top of the parapet to the forward edge of the ditch. If a man could see entirely along that line, there would be no cover for an attacker to lie down just outside the ditch. The glacis also helped to prevent artillery rounds from hitting the scarp of the ditch.

Hurdle: A revetting material made in panels by interweaving twigs around sticks. It was less commonly used than other revetting material, such as posts, planks, logs, and sandbags. During the Civil War, it seldom was made as panels. Saplings or small branches were simply interwoven along the tops of posts supporting the revetment to give them more rigidity, enabling the posts to better withstand the pressure of a slowly collapsing parapet.

Mantlet: A covering across an embrasure to protect the gun crew. Mantlets were only used in the eastern campaigns at Yorktown, Morris Island, Cold Harbor, and Petersburg. Consisting of rope or iron, they were made with a small opening for the tube to stick through or could be moved aside when necessary, and they were effective only against small arms fire. McClellan saw them at Sebastopol and urged their use in the Civil War.

Merlon: In ancient and medieval fortifications, the raised segments atop the wall that formed half of the outline known as a crenellation. The open segments next to the merlons were the embrasures for archers to fire through. The term continued to be used in the modern era.

Moat: The ditch in front of a permanent fortification, usually filled with water.

Obstruction: Anything placed in front of a work to trip up or delay an attacker. Abatis, slashings, fraises, palisades, chevaux-de-frise, and even torpedoes were classified as obstructions.

Palisade: A stick (or pale) placed in front of the work. It could be pointed and angled toward the attacker or placed vertically to serve only as a barrier to movement. A line of such pales was called a palisade or palisades.

Parallel: A trenchline dug parallel to the enemy's work. The term referred to the line from which siege approaches were started toward the target.

Parados: The raised, linear mound of dirt to the rear wall of a trench. It protected the occupants from a fire to the rear.

Parapet: The raised, linear mound of dirt on top of the front wall of a trench. It was the primary component of a Civil War earthwork. The dirt had to come from either a trench behind the parapet or a ditch in front of it. Soldiers often piled the dirt on logs, rails, or in some cases, the bodies of fallen men, to raise the parapet even higher.

Profile: The shape of the exterior of a parapet, when viewed from the side. The better made the parapet, the sharper the profile. A good profile both had aesthetic appeal and offered better protection.

Redan: A small work consisting of two parapets joined to form an angle that protruded toward the enemy. It was often used to protect artillery.

Redoubt: Mahan defined it as "any enclosed work of a polygonal form, without re-entering angles."[6]

Refused: When the end of a line of works was bent toward the rear to protect the flank, it was a refused line.

Relief: The height of the parapet combined with the depth of the ditch in front of it.

Return: Any parapet that angled toward the rear. In an irregular earthwork, there may be many returned sections of parapet.

Revetment: The wall that shores up a mound of earth. It was made of varied material but most commonly logs, sandbags, posts, planks, and gabions. Also refers to layers of sod placed across the parapet of semipermanent earthworks to keep the dirt from washing or blowing away.

Rifle Pit: A single pit dug for one or more skirmishers or pickets. First used in the Crimean War, the term was widely used by Civil War contemporaries to refer to any earthwork constructed for use by infantry.

Sally Port: The opening in a parapet to allow the garrison to enter and exit. The term comes from the need to sortie or to sally: to send troops out of the enclosed work to attack the besieging enemy. It was usually placed in the gorge or rear of the work and was often protected by a gate or a short parapet placed across the opening and just inside the work.

Sap: A trench dug toward an enemy work. A key element of siege warfare, it enabled the besieger to approach the defended work while protected from fire. It was usually dug in a zigzag pattern to prevent the enemy from shooting along the length of the trench. Engineering manuals went into great detail about how saps were to be constructed. See also Flying Sap and Full Sap.

Siege: The oldest military operation in history that involved fortifications. It included cutting off the enemy garrison from outside sources of food, water, and reinforcements; bombarding the works to breach them and pave the way for a successful assault; or constructing aboveground approaches toward the works. Approaching underground is termed mining. The techniques of siegecraft evolved over centuries to reach a peak of scientific excellence in the eighteenth century.

Siege Works and Siege Approaches: Any earthwork designed to facilitate a siege, such as a parallel, is referred to as a siege work. Saps and mines are referred to as siege approaches.

Slashing: An obstruction made by cutting a large number of trees in a given area and letting them lie where they fall, mostly pointing toward the enemy. It was less systematic than an abatis but faster to make. With a thick growth of trees, it could be much more effective than an abatis.

Sortie: A sally or attack from a besieged work to raid the enemy. Usually used to disrupt his siege approaches by filling in saps, destroying artillery emplacements, or ransacking his camp.

Stockade: A wooden fortification consisting of logs placed upright, the ends stuck in a trench, with loopholes cut in the joints between logs for soldiers to fire through. The most common type of frontier fort before the Civil War, it was also used to protect railroad bridges during the war.

Torpedo: An explosive device planted in the ground before a work, or even in the berm or parapet. The modern term is "land mine." The earliest recorded use of a type of torpedo dates to 1277 in China, while the first "target-activated" mine dates to 1573 in Europe. The Confederates usually used artillery shells with percussion caps and planted them at Yorktown and Battery Wagner.[7]

Traverse: A bank of earth at an angle to a parapet, designed to protect a gun or a group of infantrymen from flanking fire. Their use demonstrates a more sophisticated understanding of earthwork construction than reliance on a simple parapet. The remnants of traverses at modern Civil War sites show that they varied widely in length and size. They could connect to the parapet at almost any angle, and some did not connect at all. They were built by digging along the sides of the traverse—on both sides or on only one side. Large traverses also could be built in the middle of a work to protect an entire parapet or to protect a portion of the area enclosed by the work from enfilading fire.

Trench: A linear hole in the ground that constituted another basic component of an earthwork, along with the parapet. Field fortifications did not always have a trench; often the diggers got the dirt to make the parapet by excavating a ditch in front rather than a trench. Trenches were seldom included in forts and other self-standing works.

Water Battery: An artillery emplacement located on the edge of a river, lake, or bay and designed to fire on ships.

Notes

Abbreviations

AHC	Atlanta History Center, Atlanta, Ga.
ALLM	Lincoln Memorial University, Abraham Lincoln Library and Museum, Harrogate, Tenn.
BCPL	Burke County Public Library, North Carolina Room, Morganton, N.C.
CHS	Chicago Historical Society, Chicago, Ill.
CinnHS	Cincinnati Historical Society, Cincinnati, Ohio
CWM	College of William and Mary, Special Collections, Williamsburg, Va.
ECU	East Carolina University, East Carolina Manuscript Collection, Greenville, N.C.
EU	Emory University, Robert W. Woodruff Library, Special Collections, Atlanta, Ga.
FB	Fredericksburg Battlefield, Fredericksburg, Va.
FSNM	Fort Sumter National Monument, Sullivan's Island, S.C.
GNMP	Gettysburg National Military Park, Gettysburg, Pa.
HU	Harvard University, Houghton Library, Cambridge, Mass.
ID-ISL	Indiana State Library, Indiana Division, Indianapolis
LC	Library of Congress, Manuscript Division, Washington, D.C.
LOV	Library of Virginia, Richmond
MC	Museum of the Confederacy, Richmond, Va.
MDAH	Mississippi Department of Archives and History, Jackson
NARA	National Archives and Records Administration, Washington, D.C.
NCDAH	North Carolina Division of Archives and History, Raleigh
N-YHS	New-York Historical Society, New York, N.Y
NYPL	New York Public Library, New York, N.Y.
OR	*The War of the Rebellion: A Compilation of the Official Records of the Union and Confederate Armies*. 70 vols. in 128. Washington, D.C.: Government Printing Office, 1880–1901. Unless otherwise noted, all citations are to series 1.
OR Atlas	*The Official Military Atlas of the Civil War*. New York: Fairfax Press, 1983.
PEM	Peabody Essex Museum, Andover, Mass.
RNB	Richmond National Battlefield, Richmond, Va.

SCL-DU	Duke University, Special Collections Library, Durham, N.C.
SHC-UNC	University of North Carolina, Southern Historical Collection, Chapel Hill
SHSI	State Historical Society of Iowa, Des Moines
SP-MA	Moravian Archives, Southern Province, Winston-Salem, N.C.
UA	University of Alabama, William Stanley Hoole Special Collections, Tuscaloosa
USAMHI	U.S. Army Military History Institute, Carlisle Barracks, Pa.
UVA	University of Virginia, Special Collections, Charlottesville, Va.
VHS	Virginia Historical Society, Richmond
VMI	Virginia Military Institute, Archives, Lexington
WLU	Washington and Lee University, Special Collections, Lexington, Va.
YB	Yorktown Battlefield, Colonial National Historical Park, Yorktown, Va.

Preface

1. David Russell Wright, "Civil War Field Fortifications," 1, 251–52.

Chapter 1

1. Abbott, "Corps of Engineers," 111–14; Katcher, *Building the Victory*, 1–2.

2. Skelton, *American Profession of Arms*, 168, 172, 247; Hagerman, "From Jomini to Dennis Hart Mahan," 202; Sumner, *Diary of Cyrus B. Comstock*, 155, 163, 193, 195–96.

3. Skelton, *American Profession of Arms*, 104–5, 243–45, 292.

4. Kundahl, *Confederate Engineer*, 13–18.

5. Skelton, *American Profession of Arms*, 240–41; Moten, *Delafield Commission*, 84, 89, 108, 112, 114, 119, 123–24, 135–37, 139, 146–47, 155, 157–58, 160–61, 165–66.

6. Moten, *Delafield Commission*, 154–55, 169–73, 198; Delafield, *Report on the Art of War in Europe*, 90–91, 109.

7. Moten, *Delafield Commission*, 195; Delafield, *Report on the Art of War in Europe*, 18–19, 48–50, 52–53.

8. Moten, *Delafield Commission*, 202–3; *Report of the Secretary of War Communicating the Report of Captain George B. McClellan*, 37.

9. David Russell Wright, "Civil War Field Fortifications," 9–11; Hagerman, "From Jomini to Dennis Hart Mahan," 201–3.

10. Hagerman, "From Jomini to Dennis Hart Mahan," 197–98, 200; McWhiney and Jamieson, *Attack and Die*, 43; Hagerman, *American Civil War*, 3–27.

11. Hagerman, "Tactical Thought of R. E. Lee," 24–26; Hagerman, "From Jomini to Dennis Hart Mahan," 203–4.

12. Hagerman, "From Jomini to Dennis Hart Mahan," 205–6, 210–11; Hagerman, "Tactical Thought of R. E. Lee," 26.

13. McWhiney and Jamieson, *Attack and Die*, 35–36.

14. Hagerman, "From Jomini to Dennis Hart Mahan," 206–9; Hagerman, "George B. McClellan," 116.

15. *Report of the Secretary of War Communicating the Report of Captain George B. McClellan*, 16–17.

16. Hagerman, "From Jomini to Dennis Hart Mahan," 204; Mahan, *Treatise on Field Fortification*, xv, 1–2, 9, 92.

17. Mahan, *Treatise on Field Fortification*, 2–4, 11–68, 76–91, 104–35, 143–44, 146–49, 151–52, 154.

18. Viele, *Hand-book for Active Service*, 95, 101, 105, 145–47.

19. Grafton, *Treatise on the Camp and March*, 24, 34–35.

20. Duane, *Manual for Engineer Troops*, 55–83, 150, 207, 234–37.

21. Shiman, "Army Engineers," 1–2, 6–7; Thompson, *Engineer Battalion*, 2.

22. Abbott, "Corps of Engineers," 115–17; Turtle, "History of the Engineer Battalion," 5; Thompson, *Engineer Battalion*, 3–4; Shiman, "Army Engineers," 11–12; Katcher, *Building the Victory*, 2–3.

23. Shiman, "Army Engineers," 24–27; John G. Barnard to Randolph B. Marcy, January 26, 1863, *OR* 11(1):108.

24. Shiman, "Army Engineers," 10, 29–30.

25. Ibid., 16–19; Warner, *Generals in Blue*, 509–10; Abbott, "Corps of Engineers," 125.

26. Shiman, "Army Engineers," 13–15; Holcombe, "Col. John James Abert."

27. George B. McClellan to Henry Wilson and Francis P. Blair Jr., May 15, 1862, in Sears, *Civil War Papers of McClellan*, 266; Shiman, "Army Engineers," 14–15; Katcher, *Building the Victory*, 13.

28. Warner, *Generals in Blue*, 19–20.

29. Abbott, "Corps of Engineers," 119–20.

30. Shiman, "Army Engineers," 35–36; Katcher, *Building the Victory*, 3–4, 14; Thienel, "Engineers in the Union Army," 37.

31. Turtle, "History of the Engineer Battalion," 5; Katcher, *Building the Victory*, 4, 9, 13; John G. Barnard to Randolph B. Marcy, January 26, 1863, *OR* 11(1):108; Warner, *Generals in Blue*, 30, 570–71.

32. Shiman, "Army Engineers," 38.

33. Ibid.

34. Billings, *Hardtack and Coffee*, 426.

35. Turtle, "History of the Engineer Battalion," 6–7.

36. Jedediah Hotchkiss Journal, April 15, 1863, in *Supplement to the Official Records*, 4:509.

37. Kundahl, *Confederate Engineer*, 143.

38. Nichols, *Confederate Engineers*, 9–10; Jackson, *First Regiment Engineer Troops*, 1; Steven B. Rhodes, "Jeremy Gilmer," 157.

39. Nichols, *Confederate Engineers*, 10, 23; Warner, *Generals in Gray*, 334; Vandiver, *Ploughshares into Swords*, 59–60.

40. Nichols, *Confederate Engineers*, 24; Warner, *Generals in Gray*, 176, 334; Steven B. Rhodes, "Jeremy Gilmer," 117.

41. Nichols, *Confederate Engineers*, 24; Steven B. Rhodes, "Jeremy Gilmer," 118–19; R. E. L. Krick, *Staff Officers in Gray*.

42. Beers, *Confederacy*, 205; Danville Leadbetter to Leroy P. Walker, August 26, September 13, 1861, and Jeremy F. Gilmer to James M. Robinson, February 26, 1863, M628, RG109, NARA.

43. Nichols, *Confederate Engineers*, 28–29; Kundahl, *Confederate Engineer*, 143.

44. Nichols, *Confederate Engineers*, 28; Danville Leadbetter to Judah P. Benjamin, September 20, 1861, M628, RG109, NARA; Denson, "Corps of Engineers," 409.

45. Talcott, "Reminiscences of the Confederate Engineer Service," 256, 258; Nichols, *Confederate Engineers*, 117–21; Beers, *Confederacy*, 207; Danville Leadbetter to Secretary of War, November 5, 1861, M628, RG109, NARA.

46. Steven B. Rhodes, "Jeremy Gilmer," 5–6, 9–10, 16–17, 25–26, 53–92, 94–95, 98, 101–3; Denson, "Corps of Engineers," 415.

47. These two paragraphs are based on a survey of correspondence in Letters and Telegrams Sent By the Engineer Bureau of the Confederate War Department, M628, RG109, NARA.

48. Steven B. Rhodes, "Jeremy Gilmer," 125; Kundahl, *Confederate Engineer*, 143; Jeremy F. Gilmer to wife, October 12, 1862, Gilmer Papers, SHC-UNC.

49. Gilmer to wife, October 12, 1862, Gilmer Papers, SHC-UNC; Steven B. Rhodes, "Jeremy Gilmer," 128; Gilmer to Grant, June 23, 1863, Grant Papers, AHC.

50. Steven B. Rhodes, "Jeremy Gilmer," 36, 144, 146, 156–58; General Orders No. 90, Adjutant and Inspector General's Office, June 26, 1863, *OR*, ser. 4, 2:609–10; Nichols, *Confederate Engineers*, 25.

51. Nichols, *Confederate Engineers*, 80, 82, 85–87.

52. Alfred L. Rives to Joseph E. Johnston, February 25, 1862, M628, RG109, NARA.

53. Ibid.; Warner, *Generals in Gray*, 292; R. E. L. Krick, *Staff Officers in Gray*, 271; "Stevens, Walter Husted"; records and William Proctor Smith to Samuel Cooper, July 8, 1861, William Proctor Smith service record, M258, roll 109, RG109, NARA; Jeremy F. Gilmer to Robert E. Lee, April 7, 1863, M628, RG109, NARA.

54. R. E. L. Krick, *Staff Officers in Gray*, 16, 36, 389, 392–93. The five engi-

neers who served on Lee's staff were Walter Husted Stevens, William Proctor Smith, Samuel Richards Johnston, Thomas Mann Randolph Talcott, and Martin Luther Smith.

55. Robert E. Lee endorsement, May 22, 1861, on letter of W. J. March to John Letcher, M998, RG109, NARA; Jeremy F. Gilmer to George W. Randolph, October 6, 11, 1862, and Gilmer to James A. Seddon, December 26, 1861, M628, RG109, NARA; Nichols, *Confederate Engineers*, 92; Steven B. Rhodes, "Jeremy Gilmer," 125, 127, 167; Jackson, *First Regiment Engineer Troops*, 2.

56. Jackson, *First Regiment Engineer Troops*, 3–5; Denson, "Corps of Engineers," 412–13.

57. Jackson, *First Regiment Engineer Troops*, 10–13, 15–27, 30; Steven B. Rhodes, "Jeremy Gilmer," 169–70; Nichols, *Confederate Engineers*, 93–95.

58. General Orders No. 40, May 12, 1862; General Orders No. 50, June 4, 1862; and General Orders No. 62, August 9, 1862, in Orders, Rodes's and Battle's Brigades, RG109, NARA; Jackson, *First Regiment Engineer Troops*, 2–3, 10.

59. Trexler, "Opposition of Planters to the Employment of Slaves," 213–16, 220, 224; Nichols, *Confederate Engineers*, 37–39.

60. Simkins, Hunnicutt, and Poole, *Virginia*, 9, 12, 14; Winters, *Battling the Elements*, 115–17, 119, 122–23; Calver, *Guidebook to the Coastal Plain*, 1; Zen and Walker, *Rocks and War*, 11.

61. Simkins, Hunnicutt, and Poole, *Virginia*, 13–14; Zen and Walker, *Rocks and War*, 11, 14; Winters, *Battling the Elements*, 118.

62. Simkins, Hunnicutt, and Poole, *Virginia*, 15–18; Winters, *Battling the Elements*, 118, 120.

63. Winters, *Battling the Elements*, 115–18; Simkins, Hunnicutt, and Poole, *Virginia*, 9, 19.

Chapter 2

1. Daniel Harvey Hill to wife, May 28, 1861, Hill Papers, CWM; Lewis Warlick to Cornelia, May 29, 1861, McGimsey Papers, SHC-UNC; Francis Marion Parker to Mrs. S. J. Parker, May 28, 1861, and Parker to wife, June 3, 1861, in Michael W. Taylor, *To Drive the Enemy from Southern Soil*, 29–30, 35.

2. Kimball, "Little Battle of Big Bethel," 28, 30; Hale, "Bethel Regiment," 83–86, 90–91; D. H. Hill to John B. Magruder, n.d., *OR* 2:93–94; field visit to Big Bethel, October 16, 1995. There are no easily accessible remnants of earthworks at Big Bethel; in fact, the battlefield is not well preserved. The old Hampton Road is now a well-used highway, and there are two monuments, both erected in 1905. One commemorates the battle generally, and the other marks the spot where Pvt. Henry Lawson Wyatt of the 1st North Carolina is believed to have been shot. Wyatt is

widely identified as the first Confederate soldier killed in the war. There apparently is a short section of an infantry trench extant on the battlefield, but it is quite difficult to find; the redoubt that sheltered the Tar Heels is completely gone.

3. Benjamin Butler to Winfield Scott, June 10, 1861, *OR* 2:77; D. H. Hill to John B. Magruder, n.d., *OR* 2:94–95; Emerson Gifford Taylor, *Gouverneur Kemble Warren*, 52–56; Kimball, "Little Battle of Big Bethel," 30, 32; Casdorph, *Prince John Magruder*, 124–31; Kennedy, *Civil War Battlefield Guide*, 6.

4. Lewis Warlick to friend, June 11, 1861, McGimsey Papers, SHC-UNC; John Thomas Jones to father, June 12, 1861, Jones Papers, SHC-UNC.

5. Ross to sister, June 20, 25, 1861, Ross Papers, SHC-UNC; Francis Marion Parker to wife, June 16, 1861; Parker to Mr. Nicholson, June 23, 1861; and Parker to wife, July 14, 1861, in Michael W. Taylor, *To Drive the Enemy from Southern Soil*, 43, 51, 62; E. B. Bristol to brother, August 12, 1861, Bristol Letters, BCPL; Lewis Warlick to friend, June 16, 1861, McGimsey Papers, SHC-UNC; D. H. Hill to John B. Magruder, n.d., *OR* 2:97. See Bryan, Kelly, and Lankford, *Images from the Storm*, 33–34, for interesting maps of the area around Big Bethel and the Confederate fortifications.

6. Robert E. Lee to Milledge L. Bonham, May 24, 1861, M998, RG109, NARA; William C. Davis, *Battle at Bull Run*, 51, 59–62; request by Beauregard to citizens, June 6, 1861; Thomas Jordan to D. B. Harris, June 8, 1861; and D. B. Harris to Philip St. George Cocke, June 29, 1861, Harris Papers, SCL-DU; receipts for entrenching tools, July 2, 4, 7, 9, 1861, Walter Husted Stevens service record, M331, roll 236, RG109, NARA; Beauregard to Samuel Cooper, August and [October 14], 1861, *OR* 2:440–42, 444, and 502; Jubal A. Early to Thomas Jordan, July 31, 1861, *OR* 2:465.

7. *OR Atlas*, pl. 10, no. 9; Dr. John Francis Shaffner to C. F. Pfohl, November 3, 1861, Pfohl Papers, SHC-UNC.

8. George B. McClellan to Lorenzo Thomas, August 4, 1863, *OR* 5:53; Davis and Wiley, *Photographic History of the Civil War*, 1:821–25, 846–48; field visit to Manassas, March 22, 1996. There is comparatively little left of the earthworks at Manassas. The principal remnants are Mayfield Fort, the works on Signal Hill, a Union battery at Cannon Branch, and the meager remnants on Battery Heights.

9. George B. McClellan to Lorenzo Thomas, August 4, 1863, *OR* 5:53; *OR Atlas*, pl. 10, no. 7; map of Confederate works at Centreville, RG77, G443, vol. 4, p. 20, NARA; William J. Pfohl to Crist, November 15, 1861, Pfohl Papers, SHC-UNC; diagrams of forts at Centreville in Pendleton Papers, SCL-DU; "A war-time photograph of the Confederate line at Centerville," 1939 World's Fair Photograph Collection, LOV; field visit to Centreville, March 22, 1996. See Bryan, Kelly, and Lankford, *Images from the Storm*, 128, for a good drawing of Centreville from the east that well illustrates how the town's perch on top of the ridge provided opportunities for defense. There are several sections of the works at Centreville, ranging from slight

to superb remains, that are preserved and accessible, but one has to search for them among the houses and shopping developments.

10. List of tools, January 20, 1862, Harris Papers, SCL-DU; General Orders No. 36, February 27, 1862, Orders, Rodes's and Battle's Brigades, RG109, NARA; Alfred L. Rives to Edward P. Alexander, January 25, 1862, M628, RG109, NARA.

11. Cooling, *Symbol, Sword, and Shield*, 8, 47, 64, 66, 69–71, 113, 239; Hagerman, "George B. McClellan," 119; Wilson, "Defenses of Washington," 261, 268; Cooling and Owen, *Mr. Lincoln's Forts*, 3, 5–7; John G. Barnard to Randolph B. Marcy, January 26, 1863, *OR* 11(1):106–8; maps of Washington defenses, RG77, Dr. 171-91 to Dr. 171-102, NARA. I have visited some of the remnants of the Washington fortifications, but there are a number I missed. Cooling and Owen, *Mr. Lincoln's Forts*, is a superb guide to the remnants as well as an impressive history of the defenses, complete with many engineer drawings and period photographs. See Bryan, Kelly, and Lankford, *Images from the Storm*, 25, for a drawing of Fort Washington.

12. Robert E. Lee to Andrew Talcott, April 29, 1861; Lee to Committee of City Council, May 11, 1861; and Lee to John Letcher, June 15, 1861, M998, RG109, NARA; Richard M. Lee, *General Lee's City*, 171; "Talcott, Andrew," in *National Cyclopaedia of American Biography*; "Talcott, Andrew," in *Dictionary of American Biography*; Andrew Talcott to Robert E. Lee, May 15, 1861, *OR* 2:851; Talcott to Lee, May 21, 1861, *OR* 2:864; Lee to John Letcher, June 14, 1861, *OR* 2:926.

13. Thomas, *Confederate State of Richmond*, 85; Thomas H. Wynne to Leroy P. Walker, July 11, 1861, *OR* 51(2):160–61; Walker to Wynne, July 12, 1861, *OR* 51(2):163–64; Robert S. Garnett to John P. Wilson, May 31, 1861, and Robert E. Lee to Mayor of Richmond, July 12, 1861, M998, RG109, NARA.

14. Hunt, "Defending the Citadel of the Confederacy," 306–12.

15. Danville Leadbetter to Secretary of War, October 9, 1861, *OR* 51(2):338–39; see also manuscript copy of this report in Letters and Telegrams Sent By the Engineer Bureau of the Confederate War Department, M628, RG109, NARA.

16. Hunt, "Defending the Citadel of the Confederacy," 306–12; Alfred L. Rives to John Winder, December 2, 1861, and John J. Clarke to Mr. Gleeson, December 2, 1861, M628, RG109, NARA.

17. William F. Howard, *Battle of Ball's Bluff*, introduction, 1, 3; Holien, "Battle of Ball's Bluff," 11–12, 17, 56; Farwell, *Ball's Bluff*, 38; field visit to Ball's Bluff, June 27, 1997. The remnants of the Masked Battery are easily accessible, but the remnants of Fort Evans are on private property. See Holien, "Battle of Ball's Bluff," 56, for a good modern photograph of its parapet.

18. William F. Howard, *Battle of Ball's Bluff*, 4, 9–18, 26, 33, 35, 40–46, 48, 50–51, 55–56; Holien, "Battle of Ball's Bluff," 13–14, 18, 52; field visit to Ball's Bluff, June 28, 1997. A portion of the battlefield is protected in a small regional park.

19. William F. Howard, *Battle of Ball's Bluff*, 60–61; Holien, "Battle of Ball's Bluff," 53.

20. Holien, "Battle of Ball's Bluff," 12, 56; field visit to Ball's Bluff, June 27, 1997. The remnants of Fort Beauregard are accessible.

21. Reed, *Combined Operations in the Civil War*, 11–15; Sauers, *"Succession of Honorable Victories,"* 17–21; Hawkins, "Early Coast Operations in North Carolina," 632–33. See also two superb illustrations of Fort Hatteras and Fort Clark in Hawkins, "Early Coast Operations in North Carolina," 635.

22. Reed, *Combined Operations in the Civil War*, 23–32; Ammen, "Du Pont and the Port Royal Expedition," 682–83, has good illustrations of a gun emplacement and of the exterior of Fort Beauregard.

23. Brown, "Fort Pulaski"; Reed, *Combined Operations in the Civil War*, 55; Gillmore, "Siege and Capture of Fort Pulaski," 1, 11, has good illustrations of the damaged fort after its surrender.

Chapter 3

1. Cox, "McClellan in West Virginia," 126–28.

2. Ibid., 128–31; copy of Confederate map showing Camp Garnett and Rich Mountain, RG77, US393-3, NARA; "Sketch of the Site of the O[pe]rations of the 10th, 11th, & 12th, July 1861, at *Rich Mountain*," RG77, G63, NARA; Fleming, "Northwestern Virginia Campaign of 1861," 17, 48; Zinn, *Battle of Rich Mountain*, 2, 5; Boehm, "Battle of Rich Mountain," 7–8, 12–14; Johnson and Hartshorn, "Development of Field Fortification in the Civil War," 573; Beatty, *Memoirs of a Volunteer*, 23–24.

3. Fleming, "Northwestern Virginia Campaign of 1861," 61; Catherine Merrill, *Soldier of Indiana*, 78; Lesser, "Preliminary Archaeological and Historical Investigations of Cheat Summit Fort," 31, 33; McKinney, *Robert E. Lee and the 35th Star*, 21, 48.

4. Cox, "McClellan in West Virginia," 137–43; Cox, *Military Reminiscences of the Civil War*, 1:80–82, 88–90; visit to Gauley Bridge, March 23, 1994. There appear to be no remnants of Cox's earthworks at Gauley Bridge, although the 1822 masonry piers of the old bridge are still in place.

5. Cox, "McClellan in West Virginia," 142–45; McKinney, *Robert E. Lee at Sewell Mountain*, 17–18; Lowry, *September Blood*, 69–70, 89; *OR Atlas*, pl. 9, no. 1; map of Carnifex Ferry battlefield, RG77, G274-2, NARA; visit to Carnifex Ferry, March 23, 1994. The battlefield is well preserved in a state park. No earthwork remnants are here; but the road from Camp Gauley to the ferry is intact, and one can easily understand the lay of the land on the battlefield and in the surrounding countryside.

6. McKinney, *Robert E. Lee at Sewell Mountain*, 27–29, 33; see Morrison, *Memoirs*

of Henry Heth, 151–59, for a good description of the bitter feud between Floyd and Wise; visit to Meadow Bluff, March 23, 1994. Tim McKinney, in a letter to the author dated April 1, 1994, stated that the Meadow Bluff earthworks are extant, although I did not have an opportunity to see them.

7. McKinney, *Robert E. Lee at Sewell Mountain*, 46, 86; Cox, "McClellan in West Virginia," 146–47; Tim McKinney to author, April 1, 1994; see Cohen, *Civil War in West Virginia*, 48, for a good modern photograph from the top of Big Sewell Mountain toward the Union approach, offering a superb view of the landscape and the dominating position of the Confederates; visit to Big Sewell Mountain, March 23, 1994.

8. Fleming, "Northwestern Virginia Campaign of 1861," 62–63; Cox, "McClellan in West Virginia," 147; McKinney, *Robert E. Lee and the 35th Star*, 48, 100; Catherine Merrill, *Soldier of Indiana*, 78. There is an interesting and rare map of the defenses of Camp Elkwater, apparently drawn by Lee, in Lee Papers, VHS. For a superb modern photograph of one Confederate artillery emplacement at Camp Bartow, see Cohen, *Civil War in West Virginia*, 50.

9. Fleming, "Northwestern Virginia Campaign of 1861," 63–64; there is a superb modern photograph of the remnants of earthworks at Camp Alleghany in Cohen, *Civil War in West Virginia*, 52.

10. McKinney, *Robert E. Lee and the 35th Star*, 28, 42–44; Cox, "McClellan in West Virginia," 147–48; McKinney, *Robert E. Lee at Sewell Mountain*, 108, 111; Charles Snead to Thomas, October 10, 1861, Snead Papers, SCL-DU; Templeton to brother, December 8, 1861, Templeton Papers, WLU.

11. Fleming, "Northwestern Virginia Campaign of 1861," 64–65.

12. Sauers, *"Succession of Honorable Victories,"* 49–50, 115, 122.

13. Kupperman, *Roanoke*, 22–26, 89–93, 112–15, 122–24, 130–33, 137–42.

14. Sauers, *"Succession of Honorable Victories,"* 151–53, 165–73; Valentine, "Transcript of Letters and Diaries, 1861–1864," 32, Valentine Papers, PEM; *OR Atlas*, pl. 12, no. 6; Charles Johnson, *Long Roll*, 100.

15. Sauers, *"Succession of Honorable Victories,"* 166, 173–77, 182–96; Hill, *Bethel to Sharpsburg*, 205–6; Welch, *Burnside Expedition*, 33–35, 37–38; Duren to parents, February 24, 1862, Duren Papers, EU; Charles Johnson, *Long Roll*, 96, 99–100; Valentine, "Transcript of Letters and Diaries, 1861–1864," frontispiece map, Valentine Papers, PEM; Sprague, "Burnside Expedition," 435–36; Dix, "'And Three Rousing Cheers,'" 73; "Sketch of the action at Roanoke Island, N.C., February 8, 1862," RG77, H81-2, NARA; Hawkins, "Early Coast Operations in North Carolina," 644, has a good illustration of the Union attack on Fort Defiance; field visit to Roanoke Island, December 2, 1995. Little is left of the forts on Roanoke except a small portion, only about ten yards long, of Fort Defiance. The remnant is well worth visiting, as it is the left end of the parapet and offers a wonderful view of the marsh

that still crowds the work today. While a modern road has replaced the corduroy road that approached the fort in 1862, one can still stand at the remnant and face east to see the same kind of environment that the Federals had to struggle through to outflank the work. The marsh stretches all the way to the eastern side of the island and has expanded into the deep ditch of Fort Defiance, the parapet of which is only about half as high today as it was in 1862.

16. Charles Johnson, *Long Roll*, 128, 156–57.

17. Charles C. Lee to sister, January 22, 1862, Ticktin Papers, NCDAH; Valentine, "Transcripts of Letters and Diaries, 1861–1864," 39–40, Valentine Papers, PEM; Lawrence O'Bryan Branch to Henry T. Clarke, January 28, 1862, Branch Letter, N-YHS.

18. Hill, *Bethel to Sharpsburg*, 217–18; Hess, *Lee's Tar Heels*, 12; Duren to parents, March 20, 1862, Duren Papers, EU.

19. Hill, *Bethel to Sharpsburg*, 219–21; Hess, *Lee's Tar Heels*, 12–13; Valentine, "Transcripts of Letters and Diaries, 1861–1864," 39–40, Valentine Papers, PEM; Sprague, "Burnside Expedition," 439; Duren to Parents, March 20, 1862, Duren Papers, EU; Hopkins, "Battle of Newbern as I Saw It," 143; visits to New Bern, February 24, 1994, and October 4, 1995. There are only a few earthwork remnants at New Bern. I could not find anything of the Croatan Line, and any remnants of Fort Thompson are inaccessible on private land. A well-preserved, 200-yard section of the infantry line east of the railroad is easily accessible, in about the middle of the line, and offers a view of the huge parapet and ditch much as it was in 1862. There are a few scattered, meager remnants of the line closer to Fort Thompson as well. The redans west of the railroad are well preserved, but this area is not easily accessible, as a thick stand of young pines covers the ground.

20. Sauers, *"Succession of Honorable Victories,"* 261–307; Hess, *Lee's Tar Heels*, 13–16. Hawkins, "Early Coast Operations in North Carolina," 649, 652, has two good illustrations of the Union naval bombardment of Fort Thompson and of the Federal infantry attack on the Fort Thompson Line. Burnside, "Burnside Expedition," 667, has a good illustration of a Confederate gun emplacement on the wharf at New Bern.

21. Sauers, *"Succession of Honorable Victories,"* 344–45; Special Orders No. 58, Department of North Carolina, March 22, 1862, William Proctor Smith service record, M258, roll 109, RG109, NARA: Burlingame, *History of the Fifth Regiment*, 181; *OR Atlas*, pl. 131, no. 2; visit to New Bern, August 12, 1995. There is nothing left of Fort Totten or its connecting line of works, but there are photographs of the fort taken in 1884 in the Reed Papers, SCL-DU.

22. Sauers, *"Succession of Honorable Victories,"* 308–40; Fort Macon Records, 16–19, Justice Papers, SHC-UNC; Branch, *Fort Macon*, 85, 87–88, 91, 97, 105, 128, 131–32, 138, 140–41, 148–49, 151, 154–56, 160–62, 166, 168; Hawkins, "Early Coast

Operations in North Carolina," 653, has a good illustration of the damage done to Fort Macon by Parke's artillery fire; field visit to Fort Macon, September 9, 1995. The fort is well preserved in a state park, and the site of Parke's batteries is indicated by historical markers.

23. Sauers, *"Succession of Honorable Victories,"* 377, 380, 384, 387, 390–91, 397, 400–405; visit to South Mills battlefield, October 3, 1995. The battlefield of Sawyer's Lane is not preserved, although the open area of 1862 is generally intact. There are now many modern drainage ditches in the area, and it is difficult to pinpoint exact locations of the action. The place where the road crosses Joy's Creek one mile south of South Mills is the location of Wright's fortified line, but there are no apparent earthwork remnants.

24. Sauers, *"Succession of Honorable Victories,"* 373, 441–45.

Chapter 4

1. Sears, *George B. McClellan,* 13, 23, 44, 46–47.

2. Moten, *Delafield Commission,* 187, 191; Rowland, *George B. McClellan,* 103–29, 198–232.

3. Symonds, *Joseph E. Johnston,* 145; Sears, *To the Gates of Richmond,* 13–17; McClellan to Stanton, March 11, 1862, in Sears, *Civil War Papers of McClellan,* 201; Sears, *George B. McClellan,* 162–64. In his report, McClellan tried to use the engineers' survey of the Confederate works at Centreville and Manassas Junction to justify his reluctance to approach these strong defenses; see McClellan to Lorenzo Thomas, August 4, 1863, *OR* 5:54. See Bryan, Kelly, and Lankford, *Images from the Storm,* 19–20, for sketches and a map of both Union and Confederate river batteries along the Potomac downstream from Washington; on pp. 24 and 128 the artist, Robert Knox Sneden, also drew a Confederate fort at Manassas and two Quaker guns at Centreville.

4. Sears, *George B. McClellan,* 164; Sears, *To the Gates of Richmond,* 23–24.

5. Sears, *George B. McClellan,* 167–68; Cooling, *Symbol, Sword, and Shield,* 115.

6. John G. Barnard to Randolph B. Marcy, January 26, 1863, *OR* 11(1):108–9.

7. Hicks and Schultz, *Battlefields of the Civil War,* 62; field visit to the Peninsula, October 12, 1994.

8. Oliver Otis Howard, *Autobiography,* 1:206; McClellan to Winfield Scott, April 11, 1862, in Sears, *Civil War Papers of McClellan,* 236; Laughton to parents and brothers, April 14, 1862, Laughton Papers, SCL-DU.

9. Johnson and Buel, *Battles and Leaders,* map, 2:188; John B. Magruder to Samuel Cooper, May 3, 1862, *OR* 11(1):405.

10. R. Lowndes Poor to Rives, October 12, 1861, Rives Papers, SCL-DU; field visit to Young's Mill, October 18, 1995; Bryan and Lankford, *Eye of the Storm,* 38. There are three good colored maps of the Confederate works at Howard's Bridge in Bryan,

Kelly, and Lankford, *Images from the Storm*, 34, 36, 38. The remnants at Young's Mill are easily accessible, but I could not find remnants of the infantry line between the mill and Howard's Bridge along Highway 17.

11. McClellan to Winfield Scott, April 11, 1862; McClellan to Edwin Stanton, April 3, 1862; and McClellan to Mary Ellen, April 3, 1862, in Sears, *Civil War Papers of McClellan*, 236, 227, 225; McClellan to Lorenzo Thomas, August 4, 1863, *OR* 11(1):10–11; Reed, *Combined Operations in the Civil War*, 143.

12. McClellan to Lorenzo Thomas, August 4, 1863, *OR* 11(1):8, 10–11; McClellan telegram to Lincoln, April 5, 1862; McClellan to Louis M. Goldsborough, April 5, 1862; and McClellan to Edwin Stanton, April 7, 1862, in Sears, *Civil War Papers of McClellan*, 228, 229, 232.

13. John G. Barnard to Joseph G. Totten, May 6, 1862, *OR* 11(1):318–19; Oliver Otis Howard, *Autobiography*, 1:214; Haynes, *History of the Second Regiment New Hampshire*, 43–44. Bailey, *Forward to Richmond*, 122–23, has a good reproduction of a watercolor by the Prince de Joinville, a French observer with the Army of the Potomac, depicting Federal troops building a heavy battery.

14. Sears, *To the Gates of Richmond*, 58; Bryan and Lankford, *Eye of the Storm*, 47; Ward Osgood to brother, April 18, 1862, Osgood Papers, SCL-DU; Haynes, *History of the Second Regiment New Hampshire*, 46–47.

15. Bryan and Lankford, *Eye of the Storm*, 41–43, 51, 53. Robert Knox Sneden's drawing of Battery No. 7 shows it to have six gun emplacements, each with barbette mounts. The work had a low, flat parapet, a log-and-post revetment, and no flank protection. See Bryan, Kelly, and Lankford, *Images from the Storm*, 51.

16. McClellan to Lorenzo Thomas, August 4, 1863, *OR* 11(1):17; Stephen M. Weld to father, April 25, 1862, in Weld, *War Diary and Letters*, 100; Guiworth, *History of the First Regiment*, 142.

17. Mayo to parents, April 25, 1862, in Hodge, *Civil War Letters of Perry Mayo*, 204; William F. Barry to Seth Williams, May 5, 1862, *OR* 11(1):348.

18. Sears, *To the Gates of Richmond*, 58; William F. Barry to Seth Williams, May 5, 1862, *OR* 11(1):339.

19. Fitz John Porter to Seth Williams, May 8, 1862, *OR* 11(1):314; Barnard, "Journal of the Siege," *OR* 11(1):325–26, 330.

20. Malles, *Bridge Building in Wartime*, 61; Barnard, "Journal of the Siege," *OR* 11(1):327.

21. Barnard, "Journal of the Siege," *OR* 11(1):336; Bryan and Lankford, *Eye of the Storm*, 52–53.

22. McClellan to Mary Ellen, April 19, 1862; McClellan to Edwin Stanton, April 18, 1862; and McClellan to Mary Ellen, April 23, 1862, in Sears, *Civil War Papers of McClellan*, 243–44, 241, 245.

23. McClellan to Mary Ellen, April 27, 1862, in ibid., 249–50; General Orders

No. 1, April 23, 1862, in Malles, *Bridge Building in Wartime*, 321–25; Fitz John Porter to Seth Williams, May 8, 1862, *OR* 11(1):313.

24. Stephen M. Weld to father, April 25, 1862, in Weld, *War Diary and Letters*, 101.

25. Casdorph, *Prince John Magruder*, 6, 24, 27, 38–42, 65–68, 72–78.

26. Brent, *Memoirs of the War between the States*, 159.

27. Danville Leadbetter to John B. Magruder, November 9, 1861, and Alfred L. Rives to Robert Ould, January 4, 1862, M628, RG109, NARA; Robert E. Lee to William B. Taliaferro, May 25, 1861, and George Deas to John B. Magruder, September 21, 1861, M998, RG109, NARA.

28. John B. Magruder to Samuel Cooper, May 3, 1862, *OR* 11(1):405; Riggs, *Embattled Shrine*, 58–60, 62.

29. John B. Magruder to Samuel Cooper, May 3, 1862, *OR* 11(1):405; Warner, *Generals in Gray*, 267; Alfred L. Rives to Samuel Cooper, April 8, 1862, M628, RG109, NARA.

30. Lafayette McLaws to wife, March 31, 1862, in Oeffinger, *Soldier's General*, 136; Eugene Janin to father, April 11, 1862, Janin Papers, SHC-UNC; Oliver Otis Howard, *Autobiography*, 1:206; John G. Barnard to Joseph G. Totten, May 6, 1862, *OR* 11(1):318.

31. John B. Magruder to Samuel Cooper, May 3, 1862, *OR* 11(1):406; Palfrey, "Siege of Yorktown," 108; Howell Cobb to Lafayette McLaws, April 9, 1862, McLaws Papers, SHC-UNC.

32. John G. Barnard to Joseph G. Totten, May 6, 1862, *OR* 11(1):318; "Reconnaissance of Secession Works and Plan at Siege of Yorktown," RG94, Civil War *Atlas*, Manuscript Series, NARA; *OR Atlas*, pl. 14, no. 1.

33. Symonds, *Joseph E. Johnston*, 21, 56–58, 70, 91, 148–50; Newton, *Joseph E. Johnston and the Defense of Richmond*, 88–92.

34. Early, *War Memoirs*, 65–66.

35. Cyrus B. Comstock to John G. Barnard, April 12, 1862, in J. G. Barnard, *Report of the Engineer and Artillery Operations*, 198; Palfrey, "Siege of Yorktown," 145–47; John B. Magruder to Samuel Cooper, May 3, 1862, *OR* 11(1):406; Perry Mayo to parents, April 25, 1862, in Hodge, *Civil War Letters of Perry Mayo*, 205; Miles C. Macon to unknown, April 17, 1862, in "Daily Consolidated Reports of Artillery," MC.

36. Palfrey, "Siege of Yorktown," 145–47; Coffin, *Full Duty*, 94–95; Erastus Buck to wife and friends, April 20, 1862, in Balzer, *Buck's Book*, 27–28. The United Daughters of the Confederacy erected a small monument at Dam No. 1 in 1967 to commemorate this little fight, and there are also markers relating to the positions of the 15th North Carolina, 7th Georgia, 2nd Louisiana, and 3rd Vermont.

37. Ward Osgood to brother, April 18, 1862, Osgood Papers, SCL-DU; Guiworth, *History of the First Regiment*, 143; Sears, *To the Gates of Richmond*, 48–56.

38. Daniel Harvey Hill to wife, April 22, 1862, Hill Collection, NCDAH; Hilary A.

Herbert, "A Short History of the 8th Alab. Regiment," enclosed in Herbert to McLaws, August 8, 1869, McLaws Papers, SHC-UNC; April 19, 1862, Wall Diary, NCDAH; John B. Magruder to Samuel Cooper, May 3, 1862, *OR* 11(1):408; Gary W. Gallagher, *Fighting for the Confederacy*, 75; James Peter Williams to Aunt Mary, April 27, 1862, Williams Letters, LOV.

39. April 12, 17, 19, 1862, Wall Diary, NCDAH; Henry M. Talley to mother, April 27, 1862, Talley Papers, VHS; Gary W. Gallagher, *Fighting for the Confederacy*, 75. See Bryan and Lankford, *Eye of the Storm*, 54, for a good description of sharpshooting along the Warwick Line.

40. Gary W. Gallagher, *Fighting for the Confederacy*, 75; Joseph F. Gibson to uncle, April 15, 1862, Overcash Papers, SCL-DU; James Peter Williams to Aunt Mary, April 27, 1862, Williams Letters, LOV; Nathaniel Venable Watkins to wife, April 18, 1862, Watkins Papers, CWM.

41. Newton, *Joseph E. Johnston and the Defense of Richmond*, 130–34; William F. Barry to Seth Williams, May 5, 1862, *OR* 11(1):345–46; Symonds, *Joseph E. Johnston*, 152–53.

42. McClellan to Mary Ellen, April 30, May 3, 1862, in Sears, *Civil War Papers of McClellan*, 250, 252.

43. Warner, *Generals in Gray*, 249–50; Ratchford, "More of Gen. Rains and His Torpedoes," 283; Newton, *Joseph E. Johnston and the Defense of Richmond*, 135.

44. "Confederate Use of Subterranean Shells on the Peninsula," 201; William F. Barry to George W. Cullum, August 25, 1863, *OR* 11(1):349; Guiworth, *History of the First Regiment*, 159; *History of the Fifth Massachusetts Battery*, 246–48.

45. Oliver Otis Howard, *Autobiography*, 1:218; Charles E. Halsey to sister, May 4, 1862, Miller Papers, SCL-DU; James McQuade to Fitz John Porter, May 4, 1862, *OR* 11(1):401; William F. Barry to George W. Cullum, August 25, 1863, *OR* 11(1):350; Guiworth, *History of the First Regiment*, 159; McClellan to Edwin Stanton, May 4, 1862, in Sears, *Civil War Papers of McClellan*, 254.

46. *History of the Fifth Massachusetts Battery*, 244, 248; Oliver Otis Howard, *Autobiography*, 1:222; Guiworth, *History of the First Regiment*, 159.

47. Nevins, *Diary of Battle*, 45; Donald, *Gone for a Soldier*, 64; Bryan and Lankford, *Eye of the Storm*, 64; Johnston, "Manassas to Seven Pines," 205; William F. Barry to George W. Cullum, August 25, 1863, *OR* 11(1):350.

48. William F. Barry to George W. Cullum, August 25, 1863, *OR* 11(1):349–50; McClellan to Stanton, May 4, 1862, in Sears, *Civil War Papers of McClellan*, 254; Malles, *Bridge Building in Wartime*, 65.

49. "Confederate Use of Subterranean Shells on the Peninsula," 201.

50. Warner, *Generals in Gray*, 250.

51. William F. Barry to Seth Williams, May 5, 1862, *OR* 11(1):348; John G. Barnard

to Joseph G. Totten, May 6, 1862, *OR* 11(1):320; McClellan to Stanton, May 5, 1862, in *Supplement to the Official Records*, 2:329; Sears, *To the Gates of Richmond*, 66.

52. McClellan to Winfield Scott, May 4, 1862; McClellan to Mary Ellen, May 4, 8, 1862; and McClellan to Ambrose E. Burnside, May 21, 1862, in Sears, *Civil War Papers of McClellan*, 253–54, 255, 260, 269.

53. Sears, *To the Gates of Richmond*, 65–66; Bryan and Lankford, *Eye of the Storm*, 58.

54. H. C. Cabell to John B. Magruder, May 10, 1862, *OR* 11(1):413.

55. John G. Barnard to Joseph G. Totten, May 6, 1862, *OR* 11(1):318; Charles A. Phillips to unknown, May 10, 1862, qtd. in *History of the Fifth Massachusetts Battery*, 249; Henry L. Abbott to Papa, May 8, 1862, in Scott, *Fallen Leaves*, 113–14.

56. John C. Gray to Bessie, June 2, 1863, in Gray and Ropes, *War Letters*, 121–22.

57. Palfrey, "Siege of Yorktown," 141–47. Any effort at a combined operation to reduce either Yorktown or Gloucester Point depended on the navy, and its local commanders were very reluctant to risk their ships. See Reed, *Combined Operations in the Civil War*, 145–47.

58. Robert E. Lee to Benjamin S. Ewell, May 1, 1861, and Lee to John B. Magruder, May 25, 1861, M998, RG109, NARA; Hastings and Hastings, *Pitiless Rain*, 43–45; Benjamin Stoddert Ewell to citizens of James City, York, and Warwick Counties, n.d., and Benjamin Stoddert Ewell, "Reminiscences of Genl. Magruder & of events during Peninsula Campaign," 10–12, Ewell Family Papers, CWM; Lafayette McLaws to children, July 23–25, 1861, and McLaws to wife, July 30, 1861, in Oeffinger, *Soldier's General*, 96–99; Casdorph, *Prince John Magruder*, 119–21.

59. Hastings and Hastings, *Pitiless Rain*, 45–47; Benjamin Stoddert Ewell, "Reminiscences of Genl. Magruder & of events during Peninsula Campaign," 10–12, Ewell Family Papers, CWM; "Map Showing the Position of Williamsburg," RG77, G447, NARA.

60. M. D. McAlester to John G. Barnard, May 6, 1862, in J. G. Barnard, *Report of the Engineer and Artillery Operations*, 204; McClellan to Lorenzo Thomas, August 4, 1863, *OR* 11(1):19; Benton, "From Yorktown to Williamsburg," 216; Nevins, *Diary of Battle*, 59.

61. M. D. McAlester to John G. Barnard, May 6, 1862, in J. G. Barnard, *Report of the Engineer and Artillery Operations*, 205; Donald, *Gone for a Soldier*, 66, 70; McClellan to Lorenzo Thomas, August 4, 1863, *OR* 11(1):19; field visit to Williamsburg, October 17, 1995.

62. Sears, *To the Gates of Richmond*, 70–82.

63. Benjamin Stoddert Ewell to Lizzy, May 4, 1863, Ewell Family Papers, CWM; Richard Stoddert Ewell Letterbook, 1862–1865, 11–12, Ewell Papers, SCL-DU. Many of the works at Williamsburg are in a superb state of preservation. I examined six of

the fourteen works on October 13, 1994, and October 17, 1995. Redoubts No. 1, 2, 3, 11, and 12 are easily accessible, and there may be more that are intact. Fort Magruder is mostly gone. James Tanner, whose 87th New York was positioned in front of the fort during the night following the battle, revisited the area in October 1913. He found that the main road to Richmond had been cut through the work but that most of it was intact. Now there is a small remnant in a city park, which was locked up behind a chain-link fence when I visited the area. See James Tanner to Earle W. Tanner, October 25, 1913, Tanner Papers, CHS. See also a photograph of Fort Magruder in Manning, "Yorktown and Williamsburg Reviewed in 1897," 152. Bryan and Lankford, *Eye of the Storm*, 62–63, 116, has two drawings of Fort Magruder done at the time of the battle and in August 1862, with a map. For descriptions of the fort and Batteries No. 5 and 6 near the end of the war, see J. J. Morrison to Edward O. C. Ord, January 21, 1865, *OR* 46(2):195–96.

Chapter 5

1. Alfred L. Rives to Judah P. Benjamin, March 12, 1862, *OR* 51(2):509–10; Riggs, *Embattled Shrine*, 88, 96.

2. Riggs, *Embattled Shrine*, 2–3, 5, 7.

3. Ibid., 17.

4. Ibid., 20, 25; field visit to Jamestown, October 19, 1995.

5. Riggs, *Embattled Shrine*, 30, 39, 46–47, 142–49.

6. Field visit to Jamestown, October 19, 1995; Robert C. Mabry to friend, June 30, 1861, Mabry Collection, NCDAH.

7. Riggs, *Embattled Shrine*, 46–47. See Bryan, Kelly, and Lankford, *Images from the Storm*, 109, for a drawing of Fort Pocahontas.

8. Robinson, "Drewry's Bluff," 167, 171–74; *Drewry's Bluff*; Thomas H. Wynne to George W. Randolph, April 29, 1862, *OR* 51(2):548–49; Henry Lea Graves to Mrs. Sarah D. Graves, June 13, 1862, in Harwell, *Confederate Marine*, 56; field visit to Drewry's Bluff, August 29, 1995.

9. Alfred L. Rives to Judah P. Benjamin, March 12, 1862, *OR* 51(2):509–10; Rives to Secretary of War, March 12, 1862, M628, RG109, NARA.

10. Jefferson Davis to Confederate House of Representatives, March 20, 1862, *OR* 51(2):507–8; Alfred L. Rives to Henry T. Douglas, March 20, 1862, M628, RG109, NARA.

11. Hunt, "Defending the Citadel of the Confederacy," 306–12; Thomas, *Confederate State of Richmond*, 85; Dickinson, "Union and Confederate Engineering Operations at Chaffin's Bluff," 1–2, RNB. I have not made a thorough attempt to determine if there are any remnants of the Inner Line or the Intermediate Line around Richmond, but I am doubtful if such a search would yield anything significant.

There are several interesting remnants of the Outer Line, but those will be discussed later in this chapter.

12. Brent, *Memoirs of the War between the States*, 128; Gustavus W. Smith, "Two Days of Battle at Seven Pines," 222.

13. Symonds, *Joseph E. Johnston*, 161; Sears, *To the Gates of Richmond*, 124; Newton, *Battle of Seven Pines*, 14.

14. Sears, *To the Gates of Richmond*, 112–13, 277; Miller, "I Only Wait for the River," 48–60.

15. Symonds, *Joseph E. Johnston*, 161, 163, 165; Newton, *Joseph E. Johnston and the Defense of Richmond*, 175–86; Sears, *To the Gates of Richmond*, 118–24.

16. Sears, *To the Gates of Richmond*, 124–45; Newton, *Battle of Seven Pines*, 37, 41, 51–52; John G. Barnard to Randolph B. Marcy, January 26, 1863, *OR* 11(1):113–14; J. G. Barnard, *Report of the Engineer and Artillery Operations*, pl. 15; Gustavus W. Smith, "Two Days of Battle at Seven Pines," 226; Samuel P. Heintzelman to George W. Mindil, June 8, 1874, Mindil Papers, RNB; Miller, "I Only Wait for the River," 52.

17. Hicks and Schultz, *Battlefields of the Civil War*, 63; Gustavus W. Smith, "Two Days of Battle at Seven Pines," 226–27; Johnston, "Manassas to Seven Pines," 215; H. C. Wall, "Thirteenth Regiment of N.C. Infantry," Confederate States of America, Archives, Army Units, SCL-DU. Wall served in the 23rd North Carolina during the Peninsula campaign before his transfer to the 13th North Carolina.

18. Sears, *To the Gates of Richmond*, 124–45; Newton, *Battle of Seven Pines*, 69, 70–81, 88–93, 96; field visit to Seven Pines and Fair Oaks, October 12, 1994. There is nothing left of the Union fortifications here, and virtually nothing is preserved or well marked on the battlefield. A few markers refer to the location of Casey's Redoubt (later renamed Redoubt No. 3), and they locate the second and third Union lines of works. The junction at Seven Pines is now part of the town of Sandston, and a national cemetery is located near the crossroads. The modern town of Fair Oaks has grown over the battlefield, and virtually nothing is marked in this area. One can, however, get a sense of how flat and sandy the terrain is, and there are still several areas on the battlefield that are covered in dense woods.

19. Miller, "I Only Wait for the River," 58; John G. Barnard to Randolph B. Marcy, January 26, 1863, *OR* 11(1):114–16; Barton S. Alexander to John G. Barnard, July 12, 1862, *OR* 11(1):139–40; Sumner, *Diary of Cyrus B. Comstock*, 237; map titled "Line of Entrenchments from Redoubts No. 1 to 6," in J. G. Barnard, *Report of the Engineer and Artillery Operations*, pl. 15; Davis and Wiley, *Photographic History of the Civil War*, 1:585, 588. See also George N. Barnard's photograph of Redoubt No. 3, taken in June 1862, in Sears, *To the Gates of Richmond*, 277, and George N. Barnard, *Photographic Views of Sherman's Campaign*, iv. For a colored drawing of Union works at the Twin Houses at Seven Pines, drawn on June 15, see Bryan and Lankford, *Eye of the Storm*, 66.

20. Thomas, *Robert E. Lee*, 54, 58, 63, 77, 86, 101, 115–42.

21. Brent, *Memoirs of the War between the States*, 153; Lafayette McLaws to Longstreet, April 9, 1879, Longstreet Papers, SCL-DU; Longstreet, *From Manassas to Appomattox*, 113–14.

22. Alfred L. Rives to Walter H. Stevens, June 4, 13, 1862; Rives to Matthew F. Maury, June 10, 1862; Rives to J. F. Whitfield, June 12, 1862; and Rives to Robert E. Lee, June 18, 21, 1862, M628, RG109, NARA; Special Orders No. 23, June 16, 1862, and No. 25, June 23, 1862, in Orders, Rodes's and Battle's Brigades, RG109, NARA.

23. John Wetmore Hinsdale Journal, vol. 2, June 15, 1862, Hinsdale Family Papers, SCL-DU.

24. Longstreet, *From Manassas to Appomattox*, 114; Brent, *Memoirs of the War between the States*, 151; Sears, *To the Gates of Richmond*, 154–55; Thomas, *Robert E. Lee*, 225.

25. June 6, 1862, Haile Diary, MC.

26. Gary W. Gallagher, *Fighting for the Confederacy*, 90–91.

27. Robert E. Lee to Jefferson Davis, June 5, 1862, in Freeman, *Lee's Dispatches*, 6–8.

28. *OR Atlas*, pl. 77, no. 1; Richard M. Lee, *General Lee's City*, 171–72 and map on 88; Grant, "General Grant on the Siege of Petersburg," 574; Jeremy F. Gilmer to W. T. Alexander, March 19, 1863, M628, RG109, NARA. For a 1930s photograph of remnants of the Richmond defenses, probably a segment of the Outer Line, see "Original Breastworks Erected in 1862–63," 1939 World's Fair Photograph Collection, LOV.

29. Dickinson, "Union and Confederate Engineering Operations at Chaffin's Bluff," 1–2, 5, 7, 9, 11–13, 15–17, 22n, 23, 101, RNB.

30. Field visits to Richmond defenses, October 12, 15, 1994, and March 26, 1997. Although small in extent, the remnants of the Outer Line are well preserved and easily accessible. The remnant south of Williamsburg Road (Highway 60) consists of about 300 yards of line on the grounds of the Richmond International Airport, along South Airport Drive. The remnants at Chickahominy Bluffs are preserved as part of the Richmond National Battlefield. See an interesting illustration of them in Hill, "Lee's Attacks North of the Chickahominy," 350. Mechanicsville Pike is now Highway 360. The works at Brook Run are preserved and marked on the grounds of Brook Run Shopping Center. Brook Road is now Highway 1.

31. Imboden, "Stonewall Jackson in the Shenandoah," 285, 285n.

32. Robertson, *Stonewall Jackson*, 45, 54–55, 56–70.

33. Winters, *Battling the Elements*, 118.

34. Imboden, "Stonewall Jackson in the Shenandoah," 283–84.

35. Robert H. Milroy to Mary, April 7, 1862, in Paulus, *Papers of General Robert Huston Milroy*, 1:28.

36. Ibid., April 13, 1862, 29, 31–32; field visit to Shenandoah Mountain, March 22, 29, 1997. Johnson's fortified camp on top of Shenandoah Mountain is within George Washington National Forest and is well preserved, with interpretive markers. It is easily accessible just off Highway 250.

37. Robert H. Milroy to Mary, April 13, 16, May 13, 1862, in Paulus, *Papers of General Robert Huston Milroy*, 1:32, 35–36, 41.

38. Ibid., May 13, 1862, 38, 41; Imboden, "Stonewall Jackson in the Shenandoah," 285–86.

39. Robert H. Milroy to Mary, May 13, 1862, in Paulus, *Papers of General Robert Huston Milroy*, 1:38–40; Imboden, "Stonewall Jackson in the Shenandoah," 285–86; Robertson, *Stonewall Jackson*, 372–77; field visit to McDowell, March 22, 29, 1997.

40. Imboden, "Stonewall Jackson in the Shenandoah," 288. Historians have portrayed Banks as "strongly entrenched" at Strasburg, but the little redoubt there could not have held more than a few hundred troops. See Tanner, *Stonewall in the Valley*, 206. A field visit to Strasburg, June 13, 1994, revealed the redoubt was mostly destroyed by the construction of a water tower, and there are no easily discovered remnants.

41. Imboden, "Stonewall Jackson in the Shenandoah," 290–97.

42. Sears, *George B. McClellan*, 207; Sears, *To the Gates of Richmond*, 195.

43. Brent, *Memoirs of the War between the States*, 158.

44. Porter, "Hanover Court House and Gaines's Mill," 324; Sears, *George B. McClellan*, 201; McClellan telegram to Lincoln, June 20, 1862, and McClellan to Mary Ellen, June 22, 1862, in Sears, *Civil War Papers of McClellan*, 304, 305.

45. McClellan to Randolph B. Marcy, June 25, 1862, in Sears, *Civil War Papers of McClellan*, 311; Edgar M. Newcomb to Charlie, June 25, 1862, in A. B. Weymouth, *Memorial Sketch*, 70; Lyman Blackington to sister, June 24, 1862, Blackington Papers, USAMHI.

46. Porter, "Hanover Court House and Gaines's Mill," 325, 327–28, 353; field visits to Beaver Dam Creek, October 12, 1994, and March 25, 1997; John Wetmore Hinsdale Journal, June 26, 1862, Hinsdale Family Papers, SCL-DU; Johnson and Hartshorn, "Development of Field Fortification in the Civil War," 578; Sears, *To the Gates of Richmond*, 195–209; Burton, *Extraordinary Circumstances*, 66.

47. Sears, *To the Gates of Richmond*, 195–209; Withers, *Autobiography of an Octogenarian*, 184; Strock, "War Sketch," USAMHI.

48. Hill, "Lee's Attacks North of the Chickahominy," 352, 361.

49. Porter, "Hanover Court House and Gaines's Mill," 331.

50. Longstreet, "'Seven Days,'" 398. For a drawing of the battlefield, see Bryan, Kelly, and Lankford, *Images from the Storm*, 80. The battlefield of Mechanicsville is partly preserved. Ellerson's Mill dam and Beaver Dam Creek are much as they were

in 1862, but housing developments have encroached a good deal on the battlefield. A marker, placed in the 1930s, commemorates the battle. Nearly all of Porter's earthworks, except the small remnant described in the text, are gone.

51. Sears, *To the Gates of Richmond*, 213–49; Hicks and Schultz, *Battlefields of the Civil War*, 65; Porter, "Hanover Court House and Gaines's Mill," 331–33; Burton, *Extraordinary Circumstances*, 86–87.

52. Sears, *To the Gates of Richmond*, 213–49; Hill, "Lee's Attacks North of the Chickahominy," 354; Longstreet, *From Manassas to Appomattox*, 126.

53. Porter, "Hanover Court House and Gaines's Mill," 335; Fulton, "Archer's Brigade at Cold Harbor"; Longstreet, *From Manassas to Appomattox*, 126; Hill, "Lee's Attacks North of the Chickahominy," 354; H. S. Campbell to Daniel Butterfield, July 5, 1862, *OR* 11(1):344; Johnson and Hartshorn, "Development of Field Fortification in the Civil War," 578; Hilary A. Herbert, "A Short History of the 8th Alab. Regiment," enclosed in Herbert to McLaws, August 8, 1869, McLaws Papers, SHC-UNC. Herbert claimed that the Federals had dug a ditch six feet wide and four feet deep in front of their first line, but that assertion is not supported by other evidence and is entirely unlikely.

54. William S. Tilton to Fitz John Porter, July 25, 1862, *OR* 11(1):301; Charles W. Roberts to Charles J. Powers, July 5, 1862, *OR* 11(1):296; Turtle, "History of the Engineer Battalion," 6.

55. Sears, *To the Gates of Richmond*, 213–49, 250–51; R. E. L. Krick, "Men Who Carried This Position," 195–99.

56. Warner Reminiscences, RNB.

57. Sears, *To the Gates of Richmond*, 268–74.

58. Edgar M. Newcomb to sister, July 4, 1862, in A. B. Weymouth, *Memorial Sketch*, 72; Mickey Account, 8, SP-MA; Henry K. Burgwyn to mother, July 14, 1862, Burgwyn Family Papers, SHC-UNC; Hess, *Lee's Tar Heels*, 24; Shand Memoir, 29, FB.

59. Sears, *To the Gates of Richmond*, 279–307; Johnson and Hartshorn, "Development of Field Fortification in the Civil War," 579–80; field visits to Glendale and White Oak Swamp, October 12, 15, 1994. Neither battlefield was well marked or preserved when I visited them, but significant preservation efforts were under way at Glendale. Both fields are largely in a natural state, comparable to the landscape and vegetation present in 1862, except for some housing.

60. Hicks and Schultz, *Battlefields of the Civil War*, 66; Sears, *To the Gates of Richmond*, 310–36; field visits to Malvern Hill, October 12, 15, 1994. Malvern Hill is the most rewarding of the Seven Days battlefields for the modern visitor. The core of the field is well preserved and marked as a unit of the Richmond National Battlefield, but encroaching tree lines give the open plateau a narrower appearance than it had in 1862.

61. Sears, *To the Gates of Richmond*, 338–39; field visit to Harrison's Landing,

October 12, 1994. The Harrison family did not own the plantation in 1862, which also was the site of Brig. Gen. Daniel Butterfield's composition of "Taps" that summer. There are no easily accessible remnants of McClellan's earthworks at the landing; but the mansion is in great shape, and a plantation road to the landing, constructed in 1725, is well preserved. See Coski, *Army of the Potomac at Berkeley Plantation*, 1.

62. Sears, *To the Gates of Richmond*, 338–39; Johnson and Hartshorn, "Development of Field Fortification in the Civil War," 580; Coski, *Army of the Potomac at Berkeley Plantation*, 9; John G. Barnard to Randolph B. Marcy, January 26, 1863, *OR* 11(1):1211–22; Barton S. Alexander to John G. Barnard, July 12, 1862, *OR* 11(1):141–42; Donald, *Gone For a Soldier*, 109; R. S. Robertson to father and mother, July 21, 1862, Robertson Letters, FB. There is a superb drawing of the Union works at Harrison's Landing in Averell, "With the Cavalry on the Peninsula," 429. For another good illustration of the line as it bordered Kimage's Creek and a good map of the entire line, see Coski, *Army of the Potomac at Berkeley Plantation*, 8. For superb maps and drawings of the Union defenses at Harrison's Landing, see Bryan, Kelly, and Lankford, *Images from the Storm*, 103, 105, 108–9.

63. Sears, *To the Gates of Richmond*, 341, 343, 355; Coski, *Army of the Potomac at Berkeley Plantation*, 9; Robert E. Lee to Jefferson Davis, July 4, 1862, in Freeman, *Lee's Dispatches*, 26–27.

Chapter 6

1. Hunt, "Defending the Citadel of the Confederacy," 314, 316; R. H. Chilton to W. P. Smith, July 31, 1862, *OR* 11(3):658; Robert E. Lee to Stephen R. Mallory, July 31, 1862, *OR* 11(3):658; Lee to Thomas S. Rhett, July 31, 1862, *OR* 11(3):659.

2. Jeremy Francis Gilmer to Loulie, August 8, 11, 15, 17, 1862, Gilmer Papers, SHC-UNC; Robert E. Lee to Gilmer, August 25, 1862, *OR* 12(3):944–45.

3. Dickinson, "Union and Confederate Engineering Operations at Chaffin's Bluff," 24–28, RNB; William Proctor Smith to Henry A. Wise, July 17, 1862, William Proctor Smith service record, M258, roll 109, RG109, NARA; maps of Chaffin's Bluff defenses, RG77, Z391, NARA.

4. Jefferson Davis to John Letcher, October 10, 1862, *OR* 51(2):633; Jeremy F. Gilmer to George W. Randolph, October 8, 1862, *OR* 51(2):633–34; Gustavus W. Smith to Henry A. Wise, October 11, 1862, *OR* 51(2):634–35; Alfred L. Rives to Lewis E. Harris, July 11, 1862; Rives to Haxall, Crenshaw, and Company, August 7, 1862; Rives to Robert E. Lee, August 7, 1862; Rives to George Randolph, August 11, 1862; Rives to William Proctor Smith, August 14, 1862; Rives to Presiding Justices of Cumberland, Buckingham, Nelson, and Amherst Counties, September 2, 1862; and Jeremy F. Gilmer to William Proctor Smith, December 20, 1862, M628, RG109, NARA.

5. Robert K. Krick, *Stonewall Jackson at Cedar Mountain*, is the best study of the campaign; field visit to Cedar Mountain, March 21, 1996.

6. Hennessy, *Return to Bull Run*, 60–70, 92–95, 96, 100, 122–23, 136, 139, 153–54, 178.

7. Ibid., 200–203; Robertson, *Stonewall Jackson*, 564, 566; field visit to Second Bull Run, March 22, 1996; Hicks and Schultz, *Battlefields of the Civil War*, 75. See *Voices of the Civil War: Second Manassas*, 128, for a photograph of the Deep Cut taken about 1882. Modern, color photographs of the Deep Cut and the ground in front of the railroad grade are in Hennessy, "Second Battle of Manassas," 49–50.

8. Hennessy, *Return to Bull Run*, 200–203.

9. Ibid., 209–14, 245–56.

10. Ibid., 259–67; Jackman, *History of the Sixth New Hampshire*, 78–84.

11. Hennessy, *Return to Bull Run*, 270–86.

12. Ibid., 335–61.

13. Ibid., 362–424; visit to Second Bull Run, March 22, 1996.

14. Johnson and Hartshorn, "Development of Field Fortification in the Civil War," 581.

15. Nichols, *Confederate Engineers*, 86; Alfred L. Rives to Robert E. Lee, September 3, 1863, M628, RG109, NARA.

16. Cooling, *Symbol, Sword, and Shield*, 136, 144–47, 251n; Cooling and Owen, *Mr. Lincoln's Forts*, 11–12; Wilson, "Defenses of Washington," 268–69.

17. Cooling and Owen, *Mr. Lincoln's Forts*, 28–29; Donald, *Gone for a Soldier*, 162.

18. Cooling and Owen, *Mr. Lincoln's Forts*, 11–12; Wilson, "Defenses of Washington," 272; Shiman, "Army Engineers," 49.

19. Cooling, *Symbol, Sword, and Shield*, 151–52, 161, 177, 180. There are many historic photographs of the Washington defenses. See Davis and Wiley, *Photographic History of the Civil War*, 1:1153–58, 1167. See also Donald, *Gone for a Soldier*, 164, for a superb drawing by Alfred Bellard showing the method of constructing a parapet using the wooden frame mentioned in the text and described in the engineer manuals. See also Bryan, Kelly, and Lankford, *Images from the Storm*, 135, for a very detailed, colored map of Fort Lyon. Balicki, "Defending the Capital," 135–47, reports on archaeological digs that reveal garrison life at Fort C. F. Smith.

20. Frye, "Stonewall Attacks!," 10–11, 18; Robertson, *Stonewall Jackson*, 594.

21. *OR Atlas*, pl. 42; Winters, *Battling the Elements*, 119–20, 283n.

22. Winter, "Civil War Fortifications and Campgrounds on Maryland Heights," 104–5, 109; Gilbert, *Walker's Guide to Harpers Ferry*, 86.

23. Frye, "Stonewall Attacks!," 12–13, 16.

24. Ibid., 17.

25. Ibid., 19, 21, 24.

26. Ibid., 25–27; John G. Walker, "Jackson's Capture of Harper's Ferry," 608–9;

William G. Williamson to Jeremy F. Gilmer, October 14, 1862, Williamson Journal, VMI.

27. Frye, "Stonewall Attacks!," 48, 51–52; Robertson, *Stonewall Jackson*, 600–606. There are no historic photographs of the works at Harpers Ferry, but Johnson and Buel, *Battles and Leaders*, 2:608, has a good illustration based on a wartime sketch that shows the cleared area and a log stockade on top of Loudoun Heights. Maryland Heights is well illustrated in the distance, and one can easily see the plateau where the naval battery is located as well as a Union encampment on top of the height.

28. Sears, "Fire on the Mountain," 5, 10–13.

29. Ibid., 13–15, 18, 54; field visit to Fox's Gap, June 28, 1997.

30. Sears, "Fire on the Mountain," 4, 21; field visit to Crampton's Gap, June 28, 1997.

31. Sears, "Fire on the Mountain," 18, 20, 60; field visit to Turner's Gap, June 28, 1997.

32. Hicks and Schultz, *Battlefields of the Civil War*, 86–87; Sears, *Landscape Turned Red*, 175–76; field visit to Antietam, June 28, 1997.

33. Hagerman, "Tactical Thought of R. E. Lee," 32; Hagerman, *American Civil War*, 116–17; Hagerman, "George B. McClellan," 129.

34. Sears, *Landscape Turned Red*, 182, 203, 206; Thomas M. Garrett to J. M. Taylor, October 11, 1862, *OR* 19(1):1043–44.

35. Sears, *Landscape Turned Red*, 236; field visit to Antietam, June 28, 1997.

36. Sears, *Landscape Turned Red*, 236, 244–47, 252. Frassanito, *Antietam*, 204–5, has Alexander Gardner's three photographs of Bloody Lane taken on September 19. They show clearly the lane's profile and how, at least in some sections, it could serve as a trench.

37. Sears, *Landscape Turned Red*, 260–61; field visit to Antietam, June 28, 1997; George B. McClellan to Lorenzo Thomas, October 15, 1862, *OR* 19(1):31; Parker, *History of the 41st Regiment of Pennsylvania*, 226.

38. Sears, *Landscape Turned Red*, 261, 267; field visit to Antietam, June 28, 1997; Frassanito, *Antietam*, 227, 238, 242, has three photographs of Burnside's Bridge, taken by Alexander Gardner on September 21, from different perspectives.

39. C. B. Comstock Field Note Book, 1862–1863, unpaginated, and Comstock to James C. Duane, October 12, 1862, Comstock Papers, LC.

40. C. B. Comstock Field Note Book, 1862–1863, unpaginated, ibid.; Gilbert, *Walker's Guide to Harpers Ferry*, 87, 89–90; Winter, "Civil War Fortifications and Campgrounds on Maryland Heights," 112–15.

41. *OR Atlas*, pl. 42; sketch of the vicinity of Harpers Ferry, October 1862, RG77, F78, NARA; map of works around Harpers Ferry, September 30, 1863, RG77, G135-1, NARA; "Preliminary Sketch of the Defences on Maryland Heights and the Adjacent

Country," August–October 1863, RG77, F106, NARA; Winter, "Civil War Fortifications and Campgrounds on Maryland Heights," 110; Gilbert, *Walker's Guide to Harpers Ferry*, 86, 92, 103. Despite the effort to convert the works into more permanent structures, at least 8,500 sandbags were needed at Harpers Ferry. J. D. Kurtz to J. M. Wilson, March 5, 1863, and Joseph G. Totten to W. F. Reynolds, June 24, 1863, M1113, RG77, NARA.

42. Winter, "Civil War Fortifications and Campgrounds on Maryland Heights," 107; Gilbert, *Walker's Guide to Harpers Ferry*, 96; field visit to Harpers Ferry, June 17, 1994. The remnants of Sheridan's earthworks on Bolivar Heights are very accessible but not extensive. The remnants of the works on Maryland Heights are extensive but very difficult to reach; it is a rough climb up the steep slope to the top.

Chapter 7

1. O'Reilly, *Fredericksburg*, 26–27, 30, 32, 44–48; Sutherland, *Fredericksburg and Chancellorsville*, 12–16, 19.

2. Longstreet, *From Manassas to Appomattox*, 298; Hicks and Schultz, *Battlefields of the Civil War*, 98.

3. William N. Pendleton to Robert E. Lee, March 12, 1863, *OR* 21:563–64.

4. Lee to Samuel Cooper, April 10, 1863, *OR* 21:550–52; Gary W. Gallagher, *Fighting for the Confederacy*, 167–68; Longstreet, *From Manassas to Appomattox*, 299–300.

5. Field visit to Fredericksburg, July 10, 1995.

6. O'Reilly, *Fredericksburg*, 42, 53–54, 59, 61; Sutherland, *Fredericksburg and Chancellorsville*, 29–32; Malles, *Bridge Building in Wartime*, 107–8.

7. Rable, *Fredericksburg!*, 54, 63–65, 74–75, 78–80, 82, 84–85, 87; Sutherland, *Fredericksburg and Chancellorsville*, 34–39; Cyrus B. Comstock to Joseph G. Totten, December 20, 1862, *OR* 21:167–68; Malles, *Bridge Building in Wartime*, 110–14; Daniel P. Woodbury to John G. Parke, December 12, 1862, *OR* 21:171.

8. O'Reilly, *Fredericksburg*, 73; Sutherland, *Fredericksburg and Chancellorsville*, 31; Thienel, *Mr. Lincoln's Bridge Builders*, 79–86; Cyrus B. Comstock to Joseph G. Totten, December 20, 1862, *OR* 21:168; Daniel P. Woodbury to John G. Parke, December 12, 1862, *OR* 21:171. See Johnson and Buel, *Battles and Leaders*, 3:114, for a good illustration by R. F. Zogbaum, made in 1886, of Union infantry crossing the Rappahannock in pontoons to secure the bridgehead.

9. Owen, "Hot Day on Marye's Heights," 97.

10. Daniel P. Woodbury to John G. Parke, December 12, 1862, *OR* 21:171; William L. Davis to S. W. Smyth, December 16, 1862, Davis Collection, MDAH; H. G. O. Weymouth, "Crossing of the Rappahannock," 121; O'Reilly, *Fredericksburg*, 97–98.

11. Cadmus M. Wilcox to Thomas S. Mills, December 24, 1862, *OR* 21:612–13; field visit to Fredericksburg, July 12, 1995.

12. Lafayette McLaws to G. Moxley Sorrel, December 30, 1862, *OR* 21:578, 580; Joseph B. Kershaw to James M. Goggin, December 26, 1862, *OR* 21:588; John K. G. Nance to C. R. Holmes, December 20, 1862, *OR* 21:595; Elbert Bland to C. R. Holmes, December 19, 1862, *OR* 21:597; William L. Davis to S. W. Smyth, December 16, 1862, Davis Collection, MDAH.

13. O'Reilly, *Fredericksburg*, 104–31; Alexander, *Military Memoirs of a Confederate*, 294; Moore, "With Jackson at Hamilton's Crossing," 141; Hagerman, "Tactical Thought of R. E. Lee," 33.

14. Sorrel, *Recollections of a Confederate Staff Officer*, 133.

15. William Farrar Smith, "Franklin's 'Left Grand Division,'" 131–32, 135, 138; O'Reilly, *Fredericksburg*, 129, 152, 167–97, 202–45; George G. Meade to C. Kingsbury Jr., December 20, 1862, *OR* 21:510–13; John F. Goodner to James J. Archer, December 17, 1862, *OR* 21:660; James W. Lockert to Archer, December 19, 1862, *OR* 21:661.

16. Ambrose E. Burnside to Adjutant General, U.S. Army, November 13, 1865, *OR* 21:94; Burnside testimony, in *Report of Joint Committee on the Conduct of the War*, 652–54; Alexander, "Battle of Fredericksburg," 448; Longstreet, *From Manassas to Appomattox*, 316–17.

17. Couch, "Sumner's 'Right Grand Division,'" 111; Rable, *Fredericksburg!*, 219; Winfield S. Hancock to Francis A. Walker, December 25, 1862, *OR* 21:227–29; Alexander, "Battle of Fredericksburg," 447–48; field visit to Fredericksburg, July 13, 1995. Couch, "Sumner's 'Right Grand Division,'" 118, has an illustration based on a good wartime photograph of Marye's Hill taken from the edge of town, with the large brick house evident. The photograph itself, taken seventeen months after the battle, can be seen in Goolrick, *Rebels Resurgent*, 74–75. It shows the ground over which the Federals advanced toward Marye's Hill.

18. Joseph B. Kershaw to James M. Goggin, December 26, 1862, *OR* 21:589; Shand Memoir, 63–64, FB; Longstreet, *From Manassas to Appomattox*, 298; Hagerman, "Tactical Thought of R. E. Lee," 35; O'Reilly, *Fredericksburg*, 106.

19. McLaws, "Battle of Fredericksburg," 77–78; Longstreet, *From Manassas to Appomattox*, 316–17; field visit to Fredericksburg, July 10, 1995. Only 50 yards of the original stone wall exist today, on the left of the 600-yard extent of the wall in 1862. Some 200 yards of the wall farther to the right were reconstructed in the 1930s. See McIntosh, "Ride on Horseback," 10, 14, SHC-UNC, for a description of the battlefield after the turn of the century.

20. O'Reilly, *Fredericksburg*, 254, 275, 305, 322, 329, 351, 366, 387; Rable, *Fredericksburg!*, 229, 232, 239–41; Couch, "Sumner's 'Right Grand Division,'" 111, 113; Gary W. Gallagher, *Fighting for the Confederacy*, 177.

21. O'Reilly, *Fredericksburg*, 296–97, 329; Shand Memoir, 63–64, FB; Joseph B. Kershaw to James M. Goggin, December 26, 1862, *OR* 21:589; Powell Reminiscences, 17, SCL-DU.

22. Couch, "Sumner's 'Right Grand Division,'" 114–15; O'Reilly, *Fredericksburg*, 395, 416; Alexander, "Battle of Fredericksburg," 454–55, 464; McLaws, "Battle of Fredericksburg," 82; Hagerman, "Tactical Thought of R. E. Lee," 35; Sutherland, *Fredericksburg and Chancellorsville*, 52–58.

23. Lee to Samuel Cooper, April 10, 1863, *OR* 21:555–56; Gary W. Gallagher, *Fighting for the Confederacy*, 180; transcript of article by Nathan T. Bartley, in Fredericksburg *Free Lance*, Confederate Veteran Papers, SCL-DU; O'Reilly, *Fredericksburg*, 433; Von Borcke, *Memoirs of the Confederate War*, 2:132.

24. Haskin, *History of the First Regiment of Artillery*, 517; Couch, "Sumner's 'Right Grand Division,'" 117–18; transcript of article by Nathan T. Bartley, in Fredericksburg *Free Lance*, Confederate Veteran Papers, SCL-DU.

25. O'Reilly, *Fredericksburg*, 437, 443; Alexander, "Battle of Fredericksburg," 461–62; Walkup Journal, 28, SCL-DU; James H. Lane to R. C. Morgan, December 23, 1862, *OR* 21:653–56; Oliver E. Mercer to sister, December 19, 1862, in Wyatt, *Reeves, Mercer, New Kirk Families*, 265; Sutherland, *Fredericksburg and Chancellorsville*, 63–68.

26. Alexander, "Battle of Fredericksburg," 451–52; John F. Sale to aunt, January 31, 1863, Sale Papers, LOV; Powell Reminiscences, 17, SCL-DU.

27. Hagerman, "Tactical Thought of R. E. Lee," 34, 36; Hagerman, *American Civil War*, 88–89. In an otherwise sterling book on the battle, Francis Augustin O'Reilly asserts that Longstreet "had erected elaborate defenses and improved them in the weeks leading up to the battle" (*Fredericksburg*, 499).

28. William G. Williamson to Jeremy F. Gilmer, January 7, 1863, Williamson Journal, VMI; Lewis A. Armistead to R. Johnston, February 22, 1863, Letter Book, MC; James Keith Boswell to Rives, January 5, 186[3], Rives Papers, SCL-DU.

29. James Keith Boswell to Rives, January 5, 186[3], Rives Papers, SCL-DU.

30. William G. Williamson to Jeremy F. Gilmer, January 7, 1863, Williamson Journal, VMI.

31. Alexander S. Pendleton letter, April 26, 1863, in Susan P. Lee, *Memoirs of William Nelson Pendleton*, 256n; O'Reilly, *Fredericksburg*, 492.

32. James Longstreet to Thomas J. Jackson, January 18, 1863, *OR* 21:1095–96; Hagerman, "Tactical Thought of R. E. Lee," 36–37.

33. Alexander S. Pendleton letter, April 23, 1863, in Susan P. Lee, *Memoirs of William Nelson Pendleton*, 256n; field visits to Fredericksburg, July 10, 15, 1995; McDonald, *Make Me a Map of the Valley*, 101. Longstreet, "Battle of Fredericksburg," 83, has an illustration based on a wartime photograph of Confederate works on Willis's Hill, now the site of the National Cemetery at Fredericksburg. Another illustration, in McLaws, "Confederate Left at Fredericksburg," 89, also based on a photograph, shows Confederate works at the foot of Willis's Hill. A historic photo-

graph from the foot of Marye's Hill toward Fredericksburg shows a Confederate trench; another taken on top of the hill about May 1864 shows Confederate works. A third photograph, of the stone wall and the sunken portion of Telegraph Road, shows the value of the wall as a defensive position. All are in Davis and Wiley, *Photographic History of the Civil War*, 1:981, 983–84. There are extensive remnants of the Confederate works built after the battle of Fredericksburg, and these are easily accessible today. None of the fortified skirmish line appears to be intact, most of the main line is there, and at least segments of the rear line are visible. Evidence of some of the Confederate regimental camps has also been discovered.

34. Hagerman, "Tactical Thought of R. E. Lee," 37–38; Hagerman, *American Civil War*, 122–25; O'Reilly, *Fredericksburg*, 503.

35. Thompson, *Engineer Battalion*, 30.

36. Jeremy F. Gilmer to John Letcher, March 11, 1863; Gilmer to James A. Seddon, February 9, March 4, 1863; Gilmer to Robert E. Lee, March 9, 1863; and Gilmer to Letcher, March 13, 1863, M628, RG109, NARA.

37. Jeremy F. Gilmer to John McCrady, May 19, 1863; Gilmer to W. M. Brown, March 23, 1863; Gilmer endorsement, March 30, 1862, on recommendation of county delegates to James A. Seddon, ibid.

Chapter 8

1. Sears, *Chancellorsville*, 119–20, 130, 132, 136, 153–59, 179, 181; *Historic Resources along the Rappahannock and Rapidan Rivers*, 93–148, has very good maps of the Confederate works at the Rapidan fords; Hicks and Schultz, *Battlefields of the Civil War*, 122.

2. Hicks and Schultz, *Battlefields of the Civil War*, 123.

3. George S. Greene to Thomas H. Elliott, May 8, 1863, *OR* 25(1):758; Bauer, *Soldiering*, 43–44.

4. Gouverneur K. Warren to Daniel Butterfield, May 12, 1863, *OR* 25(1):199; Bauer, *Soldiering*, 44; Sears, *Chancellorsville*, 197–224.

5. George S. Greene to Thomas H. Elliott, May 8, 1863, *OR* 25(1):758; William Rickards Jr. to Jacob Higgins, May 8, 1863, *OR* 25(1):751; Jacob Higgins to John P. Green, May 10, 1863, *OR* 25(1):756; Simon Litzenberg to John P. Green, May 9, 1863, *OR* 25(1):755; Oliver Ormsby to parents, May 16, 1863, Ormsby Letters and Diary, FB; Sears, *Chancellorsville*, 235–38; field visit to Chancellorsville, July 11, 1995.

6. Field visit to Chancellorsville, July 11, 1995.

7. Hagerman, *American Civil War*, 133; Harry Lewis to Nancy Lewis, May 7, 1863, in Evans, *16th Mississippi*, 155; Sears, *Chancellorsville*, 174–75, 187–88, 198, 239; field visit to Chancellorsville, July 11, 1995. Remnants of Confederate works are in the woods behind Zoan Church.

8. Field visit to Chancellorsville, July 11, 1995.

9. Sears, *Chancellorsville*, 240–43, 246, 257–59.

10. Acken, *Inside the Army of the Potomac*, 239–40.

11. Gouverneur K. Warren to Daniel Butterfield, May 12, 1863, *OR* 25(1):199; Sears, *Chancellorsville*, 260–62, 264–97; Hamlin, *Battle of Chancellorsville*, 75; Adolph von Hartung to Alexander Schimmelfennig, May 4, 1863, *OR* 25(1):665; field visit to Chancellorsville, July 11, 1995.

12. Bauer, *Soldiering*, 52–53; Alpheus Williams to daughter, May 18, 1863, in Quaife, *From the Cannon's Mouth*, 195–202.

13. Field visit to Chancellorsville, July 12, 1995; John F. Reynolds to Seth Williams, May 1863, *OR* 25(1):254–55; Roy Stone to Abner Doubleday, May 9, 1863, *OR* 25(1):296. I am conjecturing a bit in describing the origin of this line of works. The National Park Service identifies it as having been dug by the First Corps; but it appears that this corps was stationed along Hunting Run from its arrival on the battlefield on the night of May 2 until the end of the campaign, and thus it seems unlikely it dug the work. The Fifth Corps was close enough to this area to be concerned about its left and rear, given the success of Jackson's attack that evening. It makes no sense for anyone to have dug this work after the morning of May 3, when Hooker retreated northward to construct his fortified bridgehead to cover the approach to United States Ford; so I conclude the Fifth Corps dug it on the night of May 2. As indicated, the line ends abruptly between the first and second ravines. There is another line that lies farther south of this Fifth Corps work. It runs at right angles to it and faces north. I assume this work was constructed later, on the evening of May 4, by Stuart's men, when they were ordered to dig in and hold the ground they had gained in the tough fighting of May 3. This northward-facing line runs generally west to east but has several shallow angles in it. The angles are not protected by traverses, and there are no artillery emplacements. This is another interesting example of how Union and Confederate fieldworks existed next to each other on this crowded part of the battlefield. The National Park Service has also identified this general area as the ground over which Brig. Gen. Roy Stone conducted a reconnaissance on May 4. Hooker ordered several such probes to the south and west to discover the location of Stuart's left wing, but none of them conclusively gave him that information. I do not believe this area was the location of Stone's probe, for his First Corps brigade headed toward Dowdall's Tavern, a course that should have taken it much farther west than this spot. See Sears, *Chancellorsville*, 315, 322, 405–7, and the reports by Reynolds and Stone already cited in this note.

14. Thomas A. Smyth to William P. Seville, May 7, 1863, and David Barkley McCreary to Nelson A. Miles, December 24, 1863, in *Supplement to the Official Records*, 4:587, 571.

15. Sears, *Chancellorsville*, 316–46; Samuel J. C. Moore to wife, May 4, 1863, Moore Papers, SHC-UNC.

16. Robertson, *Stonewall Brigade*, 186–89.

17. Sears, *Chancellorsville*, 335–36; Weldon Davis to Ma, May 14, 1863, Davis Family Papers, ECU; Bone Reminiscences, 19–20, NCDAH.

18. Silas Colgrove to Thomas H. Ruger, May 10, 1863, *OR* 25(1):711–12; James Johnson Kirkpatrick diary, May 3, 1863, in Evans, *16th Mississippi*, 150.

19. Gary W. Gallagher, *Fighting for the Confederacy*, 204–7; George B. Winslow to Thomas W. Osborn, May 8, 1863, *OR* 25(1):487–88; Osborn to Charles Hamlin, May 8, 1863, *OR* 25(1):483–85; field visit to Chancellorsville, July 11, 1995.

20. Field visit to Chancellorsville, July 11, 1995.

21. Gary W. Gallagher, *Fighting for the Confederacy*, 209; Sears, *Chancellorsville*, 362–63.

22. Sears, *Chancellorsville*, 372.

23. Ibid., 349–57.

24. Henry L. Abbott to Papa, May 5, 1863, in Scott, *Fallen Leaves*, 174–75. We are indebted to Andrew J. Russell for several wonderful photographs documenting the Fredericksburg phase of the Chancellorsville campaign. A captain in the 141st New York on detached duty to photograph the army's railroads, Russell was at Falmouth when the campaign took place. He exposed views before and during the engagement. See Davis and Wiley, *Photographic History of the Civil War*, 1:1210, for a photograph of Union gun emplacements on the Falmouth side of the Rappahannock. They are emplacements for one gun, with no embrasures but with heavy parapets to the front and slight protection on the side. Another Russell photograph, taken in late April, shows Capt. Franklin A. Pratt's Battery M, 1st Connecticut Heavy Artillery, ready to fire from its position on Stafford Heights. The parapet has no revetment, no embrasures, and little flank protection. Obviously the Federal artillery was not much worried about return fire. Another Russell photograph shows New Jersey troops of Brig. Gen. William T. H. Brooks's division of the Sixth Corps and guns of Battery D, 2nd U.S. Artillery, resting in front of occupied Confederate trenches on the flat bottomland south of Fredericksburg just before the battle. The most famous Russell photograph of the campaign, however, was taken on May 3 and shows the sunken segment of Telegraph Road, captured earlier that day. The dead of the 18th Mississippi lay unburied, the debris of battle lies scattered along the road, and the stone wall is clearly visible on the left, its height and profile illustrating its value as a fortification. These last three photographs can be seen in Goolrick, *Rebels Resurgent*, 164–65, 168–70.

25. Sears, *Chancellorsville*, 376–86; unsigned and undated account by a member of Wilcox's brigade, in *Supplement to the Official Records*, 4:677; field visit to Salem Church, July 11, 1995. The original Salem Church is still standing, bullet holes

pockmarking its sides, along with postwar monuments to two different New Jersey regiments. The battlefield around Salem Church is not preserved, and extensive development has marred a great deal of it.

26. Unsigned and undated account by a member of Wilcox's brigade, in *Supplement to the Official Records*, 4:677–78; Sears, *Chancellorsville*, 397–400.

27. Sears, *Chancellorsville*, 411–24; field visit to area of Banks's Ford, July 11, 1995. The ground encompassed by Sedgwick's bridgehead, which is rolling and mostly open now, is not marked or preserved. It is possible to drive to the south side of Banks's Ford, but the earthworks on the north side of the river are gone. These consisted of Confederate works dug prior to April 28, Federal works dug by the Second Corps on the night of April 28, and Federal artillery emplacements dug to protect Sedgwick's retreat. See Luvaas and Nelson, *Guide to the Battles of Chancellorsville and Fredericksburg*, 137–38.

28. Sears, *Chancellorsville*, 372–73, 380.

29. Daniel E. Sickles to Seth Williams, May 20, 1863, *OR* 25(1):393–94; Racine, *"Unspoiled Heart,"* 22.

30. William Rickards Jr. to Jacob Higgins, May 8, 1863, *OR* 25(1):751.

31. Field visit to Chancellorsville, July 11, 1995. These remnants near the apex of Hooker's fortified bridgehead are easily accessible.

32. John Wood quoted in Sears, *Chancellorsville*, 403; Isaac Hardeman to Fletcher T. Snead, May 9, 1863, in *Supplement to the Official Records*, 4:688.

33. Field visit to Chancellorsville, July 11, 1995.

34. Gary W. Gallagher, *Fighting for the Confederacy*, 214, 217; Gouverneur K. Warren to Daniel Butterfield, May 12, 1863, *OR* 25(1):204; Sears, *Chancellorsville*, 426, 428; Fagan, "Battle of Salem Church." The Fagan article is quoted in Fortin, "Colonel Hilary A. Herbert's History of the Eighth Alabama," 108–9. Small remnants of the shorter line laid out by Warren and Comstock inside Hooker's fortified bridgehead are intact.

35. Henry E. Young to Henry, May 16, 1863, Gourdin Papers, EU; William J. Reese to unidentified, May 15, 1863, Walker-Reese Papers, UA; Lancelot M. Blackford to father, August 16, 1863, Blackford Family Papers, UVA; Blackford's letter is reproduced in Michael W. Taylor, "Unmerited Censure of Two Maryland Staff Officers," 81. Journalist John T. Trowbridge toured the battlefield in the summer of 1865 and noted how some soldiers had even used the "old worn planks" of Orange Plank Road in constructing some of the works; see Trowbridge, *Desolate South*, 70.

36. Johnson and Hartshorn, "Development of Field Fortification in the Civil War," 303, and Hagerman, *American Civil War*, 89–92, also emphasize the significance of Chancellorsville in furthering the reliance on hasty entrenchments in the East.

37. Gary W. Gallagher, *Fighting for the Confederacy*, 197.

38. McIntosh, "Ride on Horseback," SHC-UNC.

39. Henry W. Benham to Joseph G. Totten, May 16, 1863, *OR* 25(1):216; James Johnson Kirkpatrick diary, May 3, 1863, in Evans, *16th Mississippi*, 150.

40. Johnson and Hartshorn, "Development of Field Fortification in the Civil War," 584.

41. William D. F. Landon to Greene, May 21, 1864, in Landon, "Fourteenth Indiana Regiment," 92.

Chapter 9

1. Barrett, *Civil War in North Carolina*, 139; John G. Foster to Henry W. Halleck, December 27, 1862, *OR* 18:54; *Kinston, Whitehall and Goldsboro*, 9–10.

2. John G. Foster to Henry W. Halleck, December 27, 1862, *OR* 18:55; Barrett, *Civil War in North Carolina*, 140, 142; *Kinston, Whitehall and Goldsboro*, 11; field visit to Kinston, February 24, 1994. The Confederate works at Southwest Creek are very well preserved.

3. John G. Foster to Henry W. Halleck, December 27, 1862, *OR* 18:55–56.

4. *Kinston, Whitehall and Goldsboro*, 69; Jeremy F. Gilmer to Walter Gwynn, October 22, 25, 30, 1862; Gilmer to Sam A. Melton, October 25, 1862; and Gilmer to J. James Randolph, December 10, 1862, M628, RG109, NARA; field visit to Kinston, February 24, 1994. The river batteries and accompanying infantry works on the north bank of the Neuse River are nicely preserved.

5. John G. Foster to Henry W. Halleck, December 27, 1862, *OR* 18:56–57; Barrett, *Civil War in North Carolina*, 145–46; Hess, *Lee's Tar Heels*, 70–71.

6. John G. Foster to Henry W. Halleck, December 27, 1862, *OR* 18:57–58; Hess, *Lee's Tar Heels*, 72–75; Barrett, *Civil War in North Carolina*, 146–47.

7. Hess, *Lee's Tar Heels*, 80.

8. Samuel G. French to James J. Pettigrew, February 12, 14, 1863, Pettigrew Family Papers, NCDAH; Samuel G. French to James A. Seddon, February 12, 1863, *OR* 18:874–75; Hess, *Lee's Tar Heels*, 82–83.

9. Barrett, *Civil War in North Carolina*, 149–51; Hess, *Lee's Tar Heels*, 86.

10. Barrett, *Civil War in North Carolina*, 151; Hess, *Lee's Tar Heels*, 86–87.

11. Hess, *Lee's Tar Heels*, 86, 89–90; James J. Pettigrew to Daniel H. Hill, March 17, 1863, *OR* 18:193; Barrett, *Civil War in North Carolina*, 154–55.

12. Barrett, *Civil War in North Carolina*, 152, 155; Hess, *Lee's Tar Heels*, 91.

13. Roe, *Twenty-Fourth Regiment Massachusetts*, 132; Chase, *Battery F*, 85.

14. Hess, *Lee's Tar Heels*, 93–94; Barrett, *Civil War in North Carolina*, 157, 159.

15. William G. Lewis to Mitte Parker, April 13, 1863, Lewis Papers, SHC-UNC; Chase, *Battery F*, 85; Hess, *Lee's Tar Heels*, 94–95.

16. John G. Foster to Henry W. Halleck, April 30, 1863, *OR* 18:212–14; Barrett, *Civil War in North Carolina*, 157; Chase, *Battery F*, 85.

17. Hess, *Lee's Tar Heels*, 96–97; Barrett, *Civil War in North Carolina*, 160.

18. Stephen W. Brewer to John J. Paschal, April 11, 1863, Brewer-Paschal Family Papers, SHC-UNC; Hess, *Lee's Tar Heels*, 95, 98.

19. John G. Foster to Henry W. Halleck, April 30, 1863, *OR* 18:215; Barrett, *Civil War in North Carolina*, 161; Hess, *Lee's Tar Heels*, 98. Garnett's artillery emplacements were leveled by the Federals immediately after the siege, and there are no remnants of the Union works at Washington either. The town has long since grown over the defense line, but it was located about where 8th or 9th Street is today. Field visit to Washington, July 29, 1995. There is a historical marker on Highway 33 six miles east of Chocowinity for Fort Hill. Remnants of the fort apparently survive, but they are not easily accessible. Field visit to Washington, October 4, 1995.

20. Hazard Stevens, "Siege of Suffolk," 197–200.

21. Cormier, *Siege of Suffolk*, 22–23, 34–38.

22. Hazard Stevens, "Siege of Suffolk," 200–202; Cormier, *Siege of Suffolk*, 13–15, 47–53, 67, 99–100.

23. Hazard Stevens, "Siege of Suffolk," 204–6, 208–10, 224; Cormier, *Siege of Suffolk*, 99, 101, 119–21; Hazard Stevens to A. D. Bache, April 22, 1863, Stevens Papers, LC.

24. Quoted in Cormier, *Siege of Suffolk*, 79.

25. *OR Atlas*, pl. 26; Weinert, "Suffolk Campaign," 34; Cormier, *Siege of Suffolk*, 99.

26. Lewis A. Armistead to R. Johnston, April 25, 1863, Letter Book, MC; Vaughan, "Diary of Turner Vaughan," 581–82.

27. Cormier, *Siege of Suffolk*, 173–78.

28. Hazard Stevens, "Siege of Suffolk," 201, 211–12; Jordan, "'North Carolinians . . . Must Bear the Blame,'" 313; Vaughan, "Diary of Turner Vaughan," 580.

29. Hazard Stevens, "Siege of Suffolk," 211–16, 218; Cormier, *Siege of Suffolk*, 132–33, 145, 149–50, 153, 156–57; Hazard Stevens to A. D. Bache, April 22, 1863, Stevens Papers, LC.

30. Cormier, *Siege of Suffolk*, 158–61; Jordan, "'North Carolinians . . . Must Bear the Blame,'" 324–25.

31. Hazard Stevens, "Siege of Suffolk," 218–22; Cormier, *Siege of Suffolk*, 272–80.

32. Cormier, *Siege of Suffolk*, 252–53, 281–84, 288; Hazard Stevens, "Siege of Suffolk," 222.

33. Cormier, *Siege of Suffolk*, 181–83, 287; Hazard Stevens, "Siege of Suffolk," 222–24.

34. Hazard Stevens, "Siege of Suffolk," 222, 225; Cormier, *Siege of Suffolk*, 182–83, 288; Hazard Stevens to mother, May 11, 1863, Stevens Papers, LC.

35. Cormier, *Siege of Suffolk*, 294; Hazard Stevens to mother, May 14, September 1, November 22, 1863, Stevens Papers, LC. No remnants of either Union or

Confederate earthworks are accessible at Suffolk, and the Nansemond River today seems more like a narrow creek than a river capable of sustaining gunboat traffic. Field visit to Suffolk, October 16, 1995.

Chapter 10

1. Field visit to Winchester, June 18, 1994.

2. Holsworth, "Quiet Courage," 16, 21–22, 24–25; Maier, *Gateway to Gettysburg*, 10, 12–13.

3. Maier, *Gateway to Gettysburg*, 25; Robert M. Rhodes, "Our Forts"; Grunder and Beck, *Second Battle of Winchester*, 15–16; Maier, *Gateway to Gettysburg*, 197; "Sketch of the Second Battle of Winchester, June 13th, 14th, 15th, 1863," RG77, US253-5, NARA.

4. Grunder and Beck, *Second Battle of Winchester*, 68–72; Maier, *Gateway to Gettysburg*, 115–18, 121–26.

5. Beck and Grunder, *Three Battles of Winchester*, 16–18; Grunder and Beck, *Second Battle of Winchester*, 23, 25, 28–31.

6. Beck and Grunder, *Three Battles of Winchester*, 19–20; Grunder and Beck, *Second Battle of Winchester*, 35–37; Maier, *Gateway to Gettysburg*, 176, 178, 187–88.

7. Grunder and Beck, *Second Battle of Winchester*, 39–40; Maier, *Gateway to Gettysburg*, 192–93.

8. Grunder and Beck, *Second Battle of Winchester*, 36, 38, 41–42; Beck and Grunder, *Three Battles of Winchester*, 2–22; Maier, *Gateway to Gettysburg*, 182, 194–96. See Grunder and Beck, *Second Battle of Winchester*, 59, for a good modern photograph of the undulating ground over which Hays attacked.

9. Grunder and Beck, *Second Battle of Winchester*, 42; Bradwell, "Capture of Winchester," 331; Maier, *Gateway to Gettysburg*, 199, 216.

10. Robert H. Milroy to Mary, June 21, 1863, in Paulus, *Papers of General Robert Huston Milroy*, 1:252; Grunder and Beck, *Second Battle of Winchester*, 45–51; Beck and Grunder, *Three Battles of Winchester*, 22–23; Maier, *Gateway to Gettysburg*, 214, 217, 221, 226, 240, 256.

11. Grunder and Beck, *Second Battle of Winchester*, 63–64; Beck and Grunder, *Three Battles of Winchester*, 23–24; Robert H. Milroy to Mary, June 21, 1863, in Paulus, *Papers of General Robert Huston Milroy*, 1:252, 254. There is a wartime photograph and two postwar photographs that have been identified as probably depicting Fort Milroy. I am not certain I agree, as the topography in the views does not seem to match that around the fort. See Davis and Wiley, *Photographic History of the Civil War*, 2: 747, 770–71. For modern photographs of the remnants of Star Fort and the location of Fort Milroy, see Grunder and Beck, *Second Battle of Winchester*, 58. I have seen the remnants of Star Fort. One corner is well preserved with a gun emplacement, a magazine, and a sally port. There apparently are some

remnants of Fort Milroy, but the remnants of West Fort are inaccessible on private property. The smaller work and infantry parapet connected to West Fort are gone. Field visit to Winchester, June 18, 1994; *Study of Civil War Sites in the Shenandoah Valley*, 73; Grunder and Beck, *Second Battle of Winchester*, 80.

12. McCarthy, "One Month in the Summer of '63," pt. 1, 121–22, 125–26, 128, 130, and pt. 2, 157, 159–69; Cowan, "Fortifying Pittsburg in 1863," 60–61; "Sketch of the Defenses of Pittsburgh," RG77, Dr. 145-9, NARA. Dr. David R. Breed took about thirty photographs of Pittsburgh's defenses in the 1890s. They are among the best such historic documents I have ever seen. See McCarthy, "One Month in the Summer of '63," pt. 2, 156, 158, 161, 162, 165, 166. See also 168 for a photograph of one of the forts by an anonymous photographer taken in 1910.

13. Crist, *Confederate Invasion of the West Shore*, 4–5, 7, 12–14, 16–21, 36; field visit to Harrisburg, March 24, 1990; "Sketch of Defensive Works and Approaches at Harrisburg, Pa," RG77, Dr. 145-10, NARA.

14. Klein, "Meade's Pipe Creek Line," 136–39, 141–43; Koons, "History of Middleburg," GNMP; Klein, "Meade's Pipe Creek Line," 135–36; Church, "Pipe Creek Line," 6, GNMP.

15. Klein, "Meade's Pipe Creek Line," 144–46; Pfanz, *Gettysburg—The First Day*, 336–40; Abner Doubleday Journal, in *Supplement to the Official Records*, 5:88.

16. Pfanz, *Gettysburg—The First Day*, 75, 130; Abner Doubleday to Seth Williams, December 14, 1863, *OR* 27(1):250–51; John C. Robinson to assistant adjutant general, First Corps, July 18, 1863, *OR* 27(1):289; "Report on Field Defenses on the Battlefield of Gettysburg," 4–5, GNMP.

17. Pfanz, *Gettysburg—The First Day*, 76, 85, 87, 104, 106, 109, 114; Vairin Diary, July 1, 1863, MDAH; field visit to Gettysburg, May 31, 1994.

18. Pfanz, *Gettysburg—The First Day*, 122, 158–60, 167, 185; Martin, *Gettysburg*, 214; George Harney to J. William Hofmann, August 16, 1865, in Ladd and Ladd, *Bachelder Papers*, 2:945–46; Ira G. Grover to J. A. Kellogg, July 9, 1863, *OR* 27(1):284.

19. Pfanz, *Gettysburg—The First Day*, 229–68; field visit to Gettysburg, June 14, 1994.

20. Pfanz, *Gettysburg—The First Day*, 295, 298–99, 305–6, 312.

21. Lewis, "Life and Times of Thomas Bailey," 15, 17, GNMP.

22. Pfanz, *Gettysburg—Culp's Hill and Cemetery Hill*, 111–12; field visits to Gettysburg, May 31, June 14, 1994; Frassanito, *Early Photography at Gettysburg*, 195–99, 200 (Dawes quote).

23. Frassanito, *Early Photography at Gettysburg*, 203; Pfanz, *Gettysburg—Culp's Hill and Cemetery Hill*, 112–15; Alpheus S. Williams to daughter, July 6, 1863, in Quaife, *From the Cannon's Mouth*, 226.

24. Frassanito, *Early Photography at Gettysburg*, 140–42, 196. The photograph

of Stewart's artillery emplacements was taken about July 12, 1863, by Frederick Gutekunst. Samuel Fisher Corlies took a photograph of the artillery emplacements on Stevens's Knoll and two photographs of the earthworks constructed by the Iron Brigade about November 1863. All of these views can be seen in ibid. Field visit to Gettysburg, May 31, 1994; R. Bruce Ricketts to Winfield Scott Hancock, December 28, 1885, in Ladd and Ladd, *Bacheler Papers*, 2:1172; "Report on Field Defenses on the Battlefield of Gettysburg," 10–13, GNMP.

25. Reid to Hal, GNMP.

26. Pfanz, *Gettysburg—The Second Day*, 210–11, 229; field visit to Gettysburg, June 16, 1994.

27. Coco, *From Ball's Bluff to Gettysburg*, 198–99; "Report on Field Defenses on the Battlefield of Gettysburg," 16, GNMP.

28. Pfanz, *Gettysburg—Culp's Hill and Cemetery Hill*, 211, 234.

29. "Report on Field Defenses on the Battlefield of Gettysburg," 22–23, GNMP.

30. Ibid., 18A–19, 20–21, GNMP; Frassanito, *Early Photography at Gettysburg*, 164, 255–57, 262–66; field visit to Gettysburg, June 14, 1994. The photographs in Frassanito's book were taken by Alexander Gardner, Peter S. Weaver, Hanson E. Weaver, and Brady and Company about July 7 and 15, 1863, and in 1867. The remnants of the rock breastworks on the Round Tops are very impressive and interesting, but the visitor should be aware that they were rebuilt, probably several times, after the war. Rock breastworks were always hastily thrown together without mortar or the time needed to fit the rocks together in an interlocking way; thus they are subject to rapid deterioration over time. One can assume the modern remnants are still in the same location as the original, but the height, profile, and uniformity of appearance are deceiving.

31. Pfanz, *Gettysburg—Culp's Hill and Cemetery Hill*, 311; Reid to Hal, GNMP; "Report on Field Defenses on the Battlefield of Gettysburg," 16, 18, GNMP; Hess, *Pickett's Charge*, 91–92, 114, 117, 119–20.

32. Hess, *Pickett's Charge*, 393–94; John M. Dunn address, in *Report of Joint Committee to Mark the Positions Occupied*, 16; Henry L. Abbott to Papa, July 6, 1863, in Scott, *Fallen Leaves*, 188.

33. "Report on Field Defenses on the Battlefield of Gettysburg," 5, 11n, GNMP; Frassanito, *Gettysburg*, 70–71; field visit to Gettysburg, June 14, 1994. A stone fence now occupies the site of the breastwork shown in the famous photograph of three Rebel prisoners on Seminary Ridge.

34. George G. Meade to wife, July 5, 1863, in Meade, *Life and Letters*, 2:125; Lewis, "Life and Times of Thomas Bailey," 18, GNMP; Jackson, *First Regiment Engineer Troops*, 8–9; Hess, *Lee's Tar Heels*, 162.

35. Gary W. Gallagher, *Fighting for the Confederacy*, 269–70; field visit to Williamsport, June 20, 1994.

36. Jedediah Hotchkiss Journal, in *Supplement to the Official Records*, 5:383–85.

37. Field visit to Williamsport, June 20, 1994; Waddell Diary, July 11–13, 1863, MC.

38. Gary W. Gallagher, *Fighting for the Confederacy*, 271; *Voices of the Civil War: Gettysburg*, 154; "Map of Hagerstown, Funkstown, & Williamsport," RG77, F97-4, NARA.

39. George G. Meade to wife, July 14, 1863, in Meade, *Life and Letters*, 2:134; Henry L. Abbott to John C. Ropes, August 1, 1863, MOLLUS-Massachusetts Commandery Collection, HU.

40. Entry of July 12, 1863, in Osborne, *Civil War Diaries of Col. Theodore B. Gates*, 95; William Hawley to Jeannie, July 16, 1863, Hawley Collection, SHSI; Francis A. Donaldson to Auntie, July 21, 1863, in Acken, *Inside the Army of the Potomac*, 315.

41. Jedediah Hotchkiss Journal, in *Supplement to the Official Records*, 5:385; Greene, "From Gettysburg to Falling Waters," 189–90; entry of July 14, 1863, in Osborne, *Civil War Diaries of Col. Theodore B. Gates*, 97.

42. Lewis, "Life and Times of Thomas Bailey," 18, GNMP; Young, "Death of Brigadier General J. Johnston Pettigrew," 30–31; Hess, *Lee's Tar Heels*, 162–66.

43. "Report on Field Defenses on the Battlefield of Gettysburg," 27, GNMP.

44. Renfroe to Henderson, GNMP.

45. D. H. Hill to James A. Seddon, July 7, 1863, *OR* 27(3):980; Jeremy F. Gilmer to Walter H. Stevens, July 7, 1863, *OR* 27(3):980–81; Jeremy F. Gilmer to Walter H. Stevens, July 7, 1863, and Jeremy F. Gilmer endorsement on Walter H. Stevens to John Letcher and mayor of Richmond, July 4, 1863, M628, RG109, NARA.

46. Dickinson, "Union and Confederate Engineering Operations at Chaffin's Bluff," 35, 39–40, RNB.

47. Ibid., 41–45, 47, 50–52.

48. Ibid., 41, 43.

49. Ibid., 42, 53–56, 64. Dickinson included superb maps and drawings in his study. See p. 66 for a good map of the alterations to the Chaffin's Bluff works that were done in 1863, p. 49 for a detailed illustration of the stockade at Fort Gilmer, and p. 56 for a detailed map of Fort Harrison as it appeared in November 1863.

50. Jeremy F. Gilmer to Walter H. Stevens, August 5, 6, 1863, and Gilmer endorsement, August 13, 1863, on W. G. Bender to Walter H. Stevens, August 11, 1863, M628, RG109, NARA; Hess, *Lee's Tar Heels*, 109–13.

51. Jeremy F. Gilmer to Walter H. Stevens, August 6, 1863; Alfred L. Rives to Stevens, August 26, 1863; Rives to R. A. Coghill, October 1, 1863; and Rives endorsement, October 2, 1863, on R. A. Coghill letter of September 25, 1863, M628, RG109, NARA; Circular, Engineer Department, Army of Northern Virginia, August 17, 1863, and special requisitions, September 30, 1863, Walter Husted Stevens service record, M331, roll 236, RG109, NARA.

52. Alfred L. Rives to James A. Seddon, January 22, 1864, M628, RG109, NARA.

53. Alfred L. Rives to Jeremy F. Gilmer, February 22, 1864; Rives to John H. Burgess and Company, February 25, 1864; and Rives to John S. Preston, April 22, 1864, M628, RG109, NARA.

Chapter 11

1. Quincy A. Gillmore to Thomas W. Sherman, December 25, 1861, *OR* 6:212–13; Sherman to George B. McClellan, December 26, 1861, *OR* 6:211; Daniel P. Woodbury memo to John G. Barnard, ca. February 1862, *OR* 6:228–35; Barnard to McClellan, February 21, 1862, *OR* 6:227–28.

2. Wise, *Gate of Hell*, 8–10; field visit to Charleston, July 12, 1990. Most of Fort Johnson's Civil War configuration is gone, and the site is currently used for scientific research purposes; but it is worth a visit to this easily accessible and historic spot.

3. Wise, *Gate of Hell*, 12; Ballard, *Pemberton*, 89–90, 93, 98–99; William Porcher Miles to Robert E. Lee, June 11, 1862, *OR* 14:560; John C. Pemberton to Armistead Long, May 21, 1862, *OR* 14:509–10; Brennan, *Secessionville*, 10, 24.

4. Field visit to Charleston, March 21, 1987; *OR Atlas*, pl. 131. Fort Pemberton is well preserved, even though it is in the middle of a large subdivision. In fact, a house now occupies the center of the work.

5. Field visit to Charleston, March 22, 1987; *OR Atlas*, pl. 131; Pierre G. T. Beauregard to William J. Hardee, December 29, 1864, *OR* 53:386. Fort Palmetto is very well preserved, and at least one section of the Mount Pleasant Line remains near Christ Church.

6. November 1863, Manigault Journal, LC; *OR Atlas*, pl. 131; Wilmot G. De Saussure to Beauregard, August 11, 1862, *OR* 14:595–96; States Rights Gist to Roswell S. Ripley, March 3, 1863, *OR* 14:805–7.

7. Brennan, "Battle of Secessionville," 8–11, 16–17, 19; Brennan, *Secessionville*, 68–69, 76–89, 105, 119, 127–36; Hazard Stevens, "Military Operations in South Carolina," 133–34.

8. David Hunter to Henry W. Benham, June 10, 1862, *OR* 14:46; Hunter to Edwin M. Stanton, June 23, 1862, *OR* 14:42–43; Benham to E. W. Smith, June 20, 1862, *OR* 14:45; Isaac I. Stevens to Horatio G. Wright, June 19, 1862, *OR* 14:59; Wilmot G. De Saussure to Beauregard, August 11, 1862, *OR* 14:596; field visit to Secessionville, March 21, 1987; Hazard Stevens, "Military Operations in South Carolina," 138; Brennan, *Secessionville*, 33, 139, 158–59, 161–62.

9. Henry W. Benham to David Hunter, June 16, 1862, *OR* 14:52; Isaac I. Stevens to Hunter, July 8, 1862, *OR* 14:48.

10. Brennan, "Battle of Secessionville," 45–47, 49; Brennan, *Secessionville*, 172–73, 181, 187, 203, 208–9, 217, 220–40, 248, 252–53, 276; Isaac I. Stevens to Hora-

tio G. Wright, June 19, 1862, *OR* 14:59; William M. Fenton to Hazard Stevens, June 17, 1862, *OR* 14:65; David Morrison to Daniel Leasure, June 17, 1862, *OR* 14:75; Joseph R. Hawley to Fenton, June 16, 1862, *OR* 14:67; Leasure to Hazard Stevens, June 17, 1862, *OR* 14:72; Horace Porter to father, June 18, 1862, Porter Papers, LC.

11. T. G. Lamar to John C. Pemberton, n.d., *OR* 14:94–96; Hazard Stevens, "Military Operations in South Carolina," 152; Brennan, "Battle of Secessionville," 53.

12. Hazard Stevens, "Military Operations in South Carolina," 152–53; Brennan, "Battle of Secessionville," 50; Brennan, *Secessionville*, 287–88; David Hunter to Horatio G. Wright, June 27, 1862, *OR* 14:47.

13. Hazard Stevens, "Military Operations in South Carolina," 154–55.

14. Alfred F. Sears to Hazard Stevens, June 17, 1862, *OR* 14:80. Most of Fort Lamar is well preserved and easily accessible.

15. Ballard, *Pemberton*, 105, 107, 110–12; Beauregard, "Defense of Charleston," 1–4; Beauregard memo, September 24, 1862, *OR* 14:610–12; Wilmot G. De Saussure to Beauregard, August 11, 1862, *OR* 14:596; States Rights Gist to Roswell S. Ripley, March 3, 1863, *OR* 14:806; Wise, *Gate of Hell*, 18; General Orders No. 89, Department of South Carolina and Georgia, November 5, 1862, Harris Papers, SCL-DU.

16. Beauregard, "Defense of Charleston," 4–5, 9; Roswell S. Ripley to Thomas Jordan, October 25, 1862, *OR* 14:652; William H. Echols memorandum, November 25, 1862, Harris Papers, SCL-DU; Langdon Cheves to David B. Harris, June 9, 1863, *OR* 14:974; Beauregard to Francis W. Pickens, November 8, 1862, *OR* 14:672.

17. Wise, *Gate of Hell*, 23–27, 30–32.

18. Ibid., 32–34.

19. Gillmore, "Army before Charleston in 1863," 53–56; Wise, *Gate of Hell*, 38, 43–44, 57–58; Reed, *Combined Operations in the Civil War*, 299–301.

20. Charles R. Suter to Quincy A. Gillmore, January 22, 1864, in Gillmore, *Engineer and Artillery Operations*, 294–99; Joseph G. Totten to W. P. Trowbridge, July 8, 1863, M1113, RG77, NARA.

21. Gillmore, "Army before Charleston in 1863," 56–58; Gillmore to George W. Cullum, February 28, 1864, *OR* 28(1):13; Sylvester H. Gray to Joseph Hawley, July 13, 1863, *OR* 28(1):358; casualty return, *OR* 28(1):210; John Johnson, *Defense of Charleston Harbor*, 84.

22. Beauregard, "Defense of Charleston," 13–15; Robert F. Graham to W. F. Nance, July 18, 1863, *OR* 28(1):414; Beauregard to Samuel Cooper, ca. September 18, 1864, *OR* 28(1):71–73; Wise, *Gate of Hell*, 61–76.

23. Wise, *Gate of Hell*, 12–14.

24. John Johnson, *Defense of Charleston Harbor*, 22; Beauregard to Roswell S. Ripley, August 28, 1863, *OR* 28(1):96; William H. Echols to David B. Harris, June 11, 1863, *OR* 14:972; "Charleston Harbor and Its Approaches," RG77, Dr. 64-51, NARA.

25. Gilchrist, *Confederate Defense of Morris Island*, 8; Fuller, "Evacuating Morris Island"; Beauregard, "Defense of Charleston," 22; Wise, *Gate of Hell*, 59–61.

26. Quincy A. Gillmore to George W. Cullum, February 28, 1864, *OR* 28(1):14–15.

27. George C. Strong to Truman Seymour, July 11, 1863, *OR* 28(1):355–56; Sylvester H. Gray to Joseph Hawley, July 13, 1863, *OR* 28(1):360–61; Robert F. Graham to W. F. Nance, July 18, 1863, *OR* 28(1):415; Gilchrist, *Confederate Defense of Morris Island*, 16; Wise, *Gate of Hell*, 76–78.

28. Robert F. Graham to W. F. Nance, July 18, 1863, *OR* 28(1):415; Capers, "Defense of Fort Wagner"; Wise, *Gate of Hell*, 76–78.

29. Wise, *Gate of Hell*, 79; Gillmore to George W. Cullum, February 28, 1864, *OR* 28(1):15; Gillmore, "Army before Charleston in 1863," 58.

30. Beauregard to Samuel Cooper, ca. September 18, 1864, *OR* 28(1):73–75; Thomas Jordan memo, July 12, 1863, *OR* 28(1):62; Beauregard, "Defense of Charleston," 15–16.

31. Beauregard to Samuel Cooper, ca. September 18, 1864, *OR* 28(1):76; William B. Taliaferro to W. F. Nance, July 21, 1863, *OR* 28(1):417; Hector McKethan to W. T. Taliaferro, July 20, 1863, *OR* 28(1):525; Wise, *Gate of Hell*, 92–98.

32. Gillmore, "Army before Charleston in 1863," 59; Gillmore to George W. Cullum, February 28, 1864, *OR* 28(1):15–16; Edward N. Hallowell to Truman Seymour, November 7, 1863, *OR* 28(1):362; Appleton, "That Night at Fort Wagner," 13; Wise, *Gate of Hell*, 102–3.

33. Hector McKethan to W. T. Taliaferro, July 20, 1863, *OR* 28(1):525; Charles W. Knight to Taliaferro, July 20, 1863, *OR* 28(1):524; Beauregard to Samuel Cooper, ca. September 18, 1864, *OR* 28(1):77; Taliaferro to W. F. Nance, July 21, 1863, *OR* 28(1):417–19; Gilchrist, *Confederate Defense of Morris Island*, 20.

34. Sabine Emery to Truman Seymour, November 9, 1863, *OR*, 53:10; Wise, *Gate of Hell*, 105.

35. Josiah I. Plimpton to Seymour, October 20, 1863, *OR* 53:15; Seymour to John W. Turner, November 10, 1863, *OR* 28(1):347–48; Joseph C. Abbott to James A. Gilmore, August 16, 1863, *OR* 28(1):365; Abbott to Seymour, November 6, 1863, *OR* 53:12–13; Lewis Butler to Seymour, February 2, [1864], *OR* 53:6–7; George B. Dandy to assistant adjutant general, Gillmore's headquarters, November 4, 1863, *OR* 53:11; William B. Taliaferro to W. F. Nance, July 21, 1863, *OR* 28(1):419; John Johnson, *Defense of Charleston Harbor*, 105; Wise, *Gate of Hell*, 108.

36. Seymour to John W. Turner, November 10, 1863, *OR* 28(1):348; Josiah I. Plimpton to Seymour, October 20, 1863, *OR* 53:15; Wise, *Gate of Hell*, 108.

37. Gillmore, "Army before Charleston in 1863," 59; Beauregard to Samuel Cooper, ca. September 18, 1864, *OR* 28(1):64, 77; Wilson to folks, FSNM; Wise, *Gate of Hell*, 114.

Chapter 12

1. Gillmore, "Army before Charleston in 1863," 60; Gillmore to George W. Cullum, February 28, 1864, *OR* 28(1):20.

2. Wise, *Gate of Hell*, 139.

3. Ibid., 92, 128; Thomas Jordan to William B. Taliaferro, July 24, 1863, *OR* 28(1):381.

4. Thomas Benton Brooks Journal, *OR* 28(1):271–72; Wise, *Gate of Hell*, 119.

5. Thomas Benton Brooks Journal, *OR* 28(1):274, 279.

6. Gillmore, "Army before Charleston in 1863," 61; Thomas Benton Brooks Journal, *OR* 28(1):275; W. W. H. Davis, "Siege of Morris Island," 102.

7. Thomas Benton Brooks Journal, *OR* 28(1):283–84; W. W. H. Davis, "Siege of Morris Island," 103.

8. Thomas Benton Brooks Journal, *OR* 28(1):281, 292. See *OR* 28(1):334 for an illustration of Union splinterproofs.

9. Gillmore, "Army before Charleston in 1863," 61–62.

10. Thomas Benton Brooks Journal, *OR* 28(1):288–89.

11. Wise, *Gate of Hell*, 173; Thomas Benton Brooks Journal, *OR* 28(1):290–91.

12. Gillmore, "Army before Charleston in 1863," 62; J. T. Champneys to W. H. Echols, September 1, 1863, *OR* 28(1):507; Beauregard to Samuel Cooper, ca. September 18, 1864, *OR* 28(1):85; George P. Harrison to W. F. Nance, August 26, 1863, *OR* 28(1):499–500; Thomas Benton Brooks Journal, *OR* 28(1):295–96; Harrison to Nance, August 27, 1863, *OR* 28(1):501; W. W. H. Davis, "Siege of Morris Island," 103.

13. Thomas Benton Brooks Journal, *OR* 28(1):296.

14. N. 16 to Thomas Benton Brooks Journal, *OR* 28(1):324–25.

15. Thomas Benton Brooks Journal, *OR* 28(1):277–79.

16. N. 1 to Thomas Benton Brooks Journal, *OR* 28(1):303–4. See *OR* 28(1):305 for an illustration of an inclined palisades. See also Davis and Wiley, *Photographic History of the Civil War*, 2:610, for a photograph of a splinterproof that is open on one side and has brush and layers of wood as a roof and walls.

17. Thomas Benton Brooks to Quincy A. Gillmore, August 22, 1863, *OR* 28(1):266; n. 10 to Thomas Benton Brooks Journal, *OR* 28(1):318.

18. Thomas Benton Brooks Journal, *OR* 28(1):277, 284, 293.

19. N. 12 to Thomas Benton Brooks Journal, *OR* 28(1):322–23. See *OR* 28(1):321, for an illustration of the iron embrasure and mantlet.

20. N. 2 to Thomas Benton Brooks Journal, *OR* 28(1):304, 308.

21. Thomas Benton Brooks Journal, *OR* 28(1):285, 327–28.

22. *OR Atlas*, pl. 44; Wise, *Gate of Hell*, 155–61; John W. Turner to Quincy A. Gillmore, November 30, 1863, *OR* 28(1):220, 222; W. W. H. Davis, "Siege of Morris Island," 101.

23. John W. Turner to Quincy A. Gillmore, September 8, November 30, 1863, *OR*

28(1):217, 220–24; Roswell S. Ripley to Thomas Jordan, September 22, 1863, *OR* 28(1):395.

24. Wise, *Gate of Hell*, 148, 170; W. W. H. Davis, "Siege of Morris Island," 100–101. There are two good illustrations of the Marsh Battery in Gillmore, "Army before Charleston in 1863," 66, 71. Robert Knox Sneden also made a watercolor of the battery in Bryan and Lankford, *Eye of the Storm*, 284. See also Davis and Wiley, *Photographic History of the Civil War*, 2:188, for photographs of both the first and second Swamp Angel guns and the emplacement.

25. Davis and Wiley, *Photographic History of the Civil War*, 2:205, 596, 602, 604, 609, 612. See Gillmore, "Army before Charleston in 1863," 52, for an illustration, based on a wartime photograph, of Battery Hays on Morris Island.

26. Wise, *Gate of Hell*, 129; Thomas Benton Brooks Journal, *OR* 28(1):288, 293; George P. Harrison to W. F. Nance, August 15, 1863, *OR* 28(1):497; Edward W. Serrell to Quincy A. Gillmore, September 10, 1863, *OR* 28(1):229.

27. Ripley, *Siege Train*, 19–20, 28–29, 259; Gillmore to Halleck, July 25, 1863, *OR* 28(1):203.

28. Roswell S. Ripley endorsement on Johnson Hagood to Ripley, July 25, 1863, *OR* 28(1):433; Beauregard to Samuel Cooper, ca. September 18, 1864, *OR* 28(1):79; Ripley to Thomas Jordan, August 21, 1863, *OR* 28(1):386; Thomas L. Clingman to Zebulon B. Vance, August 4, 1863, in *Supplement to the Official Records*, 5:496–97; Augustus Hines Iverson to Mary, September 9, 1863, Iverson Papers, FSNM; Wise, *Gate of Hell*, 131.

29. J. T. Champneys to W. H. Echols, September 1, 1863, *OR* 28(1):505–6; Henry Bryan to Alfred Roman, August 9, 24, 1863, *OR* 28(1):410, 412; Thomas Grange Simons to Caroline Bentham, September 9, 1863, Simons Papers, FSNM.

30. Capers, "Defense of Fort Wagner," 195; Wilson to folks, FSNM; Johnson Hagood to W. F. Nance, July 23, 1863, *OR* 28(1):431; Harleston, "Battery Wagner on Morris Island, 1863," 6–7.

31. Harleston, "Battery Wagner on Morris Island, 1863," 3–4.

32. Gilchrist, *Confederate Defense of Morris Island*, 30.

33. Johnson Hagood to W. F. Nance, August 24, 1863, *OR* 28(1):443; Hagood to Nance, August 22, 1863, *OR* 28(1):439; J. T. Champneys to W. H. Echols, September 1, 1863, *OR* 28(1):505, 507; Lawrence M. Keitt to Nance, August 17, 18, 1863, *OR* 28(1):470, 472–73; Kundahl, *Confederate Engineer*, 245; Harleston, "Battery Wagner on Morris Island, 1863," 8.

34. Wise, *Gate of Hell*, 132, 134–35; M. M. Gray to Thomas Jordan, August 12, 1863, *OR* 28(1):523; Roswell S. Ripley to Jordan, September 22, 1863, *OR* 28(1):399.

35. Gillmore, "Army before Charleston in 1863," 62; C. E. Chicester to W. F. Nance, July 31, 1863, *OR* 28(1):512; Lawrence M. Keitt to Nance, September 3, 1863, *OR* 28(1):479; Beauregard to Samuel Cooper, September 30, 1863, *OR* 28(1):92.

36. N. 5, Thomas Benton Brooks Journal, *OR* 28(1):309–11; Palladino, *Diary of a Yankee Engineer*, 34–35. See *OR* 28(1):309 for an illustration of the keg torpedo.

37. Thomas Benton Brooks Journal, *OR* 28(1):296–98; Gillmore to George W. Cullum, February 28, 1864, *OR* 28(1):25–26.

38. N. 13 to Thomas Benton Brooks Journal, *OR* 28(1):323; J. W. Gregorie to P. K. Molony, August 21, 1863, *OR* 28(1):502; Johnson Hagood to W. F. Nance, August 21, 1863, *OR* 28(1):437; Peter S. Michie to Gillmore, February 1, 1863, *OR* 28(1):339. See Davis and Wiley, *Photographic History of the Civil War*, 2:610, for a good photograph demonstrating the sapping process.

39. Gillmore to Cullum, February 28, 1864, *OR* 28(1):25; Thomas Benton Brooks Journal, *OR* 28(1):300; and Peter S. Michie to Gillmore, February 1, 186[4], *OR* 28(1):339–40; Lockwood, "Professor Throws Light"; Joseph G. Totten to W. P. Trowbridge, August 24, 1863, and J. C. Woodruff to Trowbridge, September 5, 1863, M1113, RG77, NARA.

40. Charles Colcock Jones to mother, September 7, 1863, in Bragg, "I Am an Eyewitness," 39.

41. Furness, "Siege of Fort Wagner," 225.

42. Gillmore, "Army before Charleston in 1863," 64.

43. Lawrence M. Keitt to W. F. Nance, September 18, 1863, *OR* 28(1):489; Gilchrist, *Confederate Defense of Morris Island*, 37.

44. T. A. Huguenin Journal, quoted in John Johnson, *Defense of Charleston Harbor*, cxi–cxii; Lawrence M. Keitt to W. F. Nance, September 18, 1863, *OR* 28(1):489; Roswell S. Ripley to Thomas Jordan, September 22, 1863, *OR* 28(1):400–402.

45. T. A. Huguenin Journal, quoted in John Johnson, *Defense of Charleston Harbor*, cxi–cxiii; Lawrence M. Keitt to W. F. Nance, September 18, 1863, *OR* 28(1):489.

46. "Life in Battery Wagner," 352, 354; John Johnson, *Defense of Charleston Harbor*, cxv.

47. "Life in Battery Wagner," 353.

48. Thomas Benton Brooks Journal, *OR* 28(1):300–303; Gillmore, "Army before Charleston in 1863," 64; Wise, *Gate of Hell*, 135.

49. Gillmore, "Army before Charleston in 1863," 64; Gillmore to George W. Cullum, February 28, 1864, *OR* 28(1):27; Wise, *Gate of Hell*, 195–97; W. W. H. Davis, "Siege of Morris Island," 105–6.

50. David B. Harris to Thomas Jordan [September] 6, 1863, *OR* 28(1):103–4; Wise, *Gate of Hell*, 199.

51. Beauregard, "Defense of Charleston," 19–20; Fuller, "Evacuating Morris Island"; Harleston, "Battery Wagner on Morris Island, 1863," 13; Wise, *Gate of Hell*, 199.

52. George Benson Fox to parents, September 9, 1863, Fox Collection, CinnHS;

Gillmore to Cullum, February 28, 1864, *OR* 28(1):27; W. W. H. Davis, "Siege of Morris Island," 105.

53. Gillmore to Cullum, February 28, 1864, *OR* 28(1):137; W. W. H. Davis, "Siege of Morris Island," 106–7.

54. Davis and Wiley, *Photographic History of the Civil War*, 2:183, 185, 205, 602; Wise, *Gate of Hell*, photograph insert. There is very little left of either the Confederate or Federal works on Morris Island. In fact, there is little left of the island itself. The natural rate of sea erosion was great even during the war, but it was accelerated by the construction of jetties to improve the entrance to Charleston harbor after the conflict. The entire sea side of Morris Island was quickly eaten away, and most of the works were destroyed. The only access to what is left of the island is by private boat. Field visit to Charleston, March 22, 1987. See Beauregard, "Defense of Charleston," 8, for an illustration, based on a wartime photograph, of Fort Putnam, the Federal name for Battery Gregg, and of Union Battery Hays on the southern end of Morris Island. Folly Island is intact, but the northern end is inaccessible to the public. Field visit to Folly Island, July 12, 1990.

55. W. W. H. Davis, "Siege of Morris Island," 96, 109–10.

56. Wise, *Gate of Hell*, 206–8; Jeremy Francis Gilmer to Loulie, September 9, 1863, Gilmer Papers, SHC-UNC; Thomas H. Stevens, "Boat Attack on Sumter," 50.

57. John Johnson, "Confederate Defense of Fort Sumter," 26.

58. Gillmore, "Army before Charleston in 1863," 65–67; W. W. H. Davis, "Siege of Morris Island," 107. John Johnson, *Defense of Charleston Harbor*, 116–44, includes clear and detailed sketches and provides the most detailed and fascinating account of how rifled artillery was used to demolish the masonry of Fort Sumter.

59. Gillmore to Halleck, December 15, 1863, *OR* 28(2):129; late November 1863, Manigault Journal, LC. Northern journalist John T. Trowbridge visited Fort Sumter in the fall of 1865. The exterior of the southeast wall "was an irregular, steeply sloping bank of broken bricks, stones and sand—a half-pulverized mountain on which no amount of shelling could have any other effect than to pulverize it still more." Gazing inside the fort from the top of the intact northwest wall, Trowbridge thought it resembled a "huge crater, . . . a sort of irregular amphitheater, with sloping banks of gabions and rubbish on all sides save one" (*Desolate South*, 277–78). Wonderful photographs of the ruined Fort Sumter were taken at the end of the war by George N. Barnard and are reproduced in his *Photographic Views of Sherman's Campaign*, pl. 56 and 57. See also an illustration, based on a wartime photograph, in Beauregard, "Defense of Charleston," 19. There are also a number of photographs of Fort Sumter taken by both northern and southern photographers, many during the last few months of 1863. See Davis and Wiley, *Photographic History of the Civil War*, 2:201–4, 206–7, 212–17, 230. See also illustrations of Fort Sumter,

based on photographs, in *OR Atlas*, pl. 121 and 122; many show the fort in 1861 as well as during the latter part of the war. Fort Sumter is easily accessible by boat, and a visit to the fort pays rich dividends. Only the lower level of the antebellum fortification survives, because the upper two levels were ruined by Union artillery and the rubble fell down to encase the lower level in a protective shield. Much of what remains today still bears numerous signs of the unrelenting fire of Gillmore's guns. Several unexploded projectiles fired from Morris Island are clearly visible and embedded in the interior wall of the face opposite the island. There are numerous holes on this interior wall where other projectiles gouged out chunks of brick. The exterior walls and the inside of the fort show extensive construction, as Sumter's defenses were updated after the war. Field visit to Fort Sumter, March 22, 1987.

60. Gillmore to Halleck, December 5, 1863, *OR* 28(2):129; Gillmore to Cullum, February 28, 1864, *OR* 28(1):38.

61. John Johnson, "Confederate Defense of Fort Sumter," 26; Jeremy Francis Gilmer to Loulie, September 9, 1863, Gilmer Papers, SHC-UNC.

62. Extracts from daily reports of William B. Taliaferro, August 4, 1863, *OR* 28(1):422–24; Beauregard endorsement on Roswell S. Ripley to Thomas Jordan, August 1, 1863, *OR* 28(1):378; Beauregard to Samuel Cooper, ca. September 18, 1864, *OR* 28(1):82; *OR Atlas*, pl. 131.

63. Ripley, *Siege Train*, 236–40; John G. Barnwell to J. R. Waddy, November 4, 1863, *OR* 28(2):485; field visits to Charleston, March 21, 23, 1987. Batteries No. 1 and 2 and the connecting cremailliere line between them are very well preserved and easily accessible.

64. Ripley, *Siege Train*, 227–28; field visit to Charleston, July 12, 1990.

65. "Map of the Defences of Charleston City and Harbor," RG77, I58-1, NARA; Davis and Wiley, *Photographic History of the Civil War*, 2:191–93. We have a rich treasure of at least sixty-six photographs of fortifications around Charleston taken during and after the war. They depict everything from the Union siege works on Morris Island to Fort Sumter, Battery Wagner, Fort Moultrie, Castle Pinckney, Fort Johnson, Fort Marshall on Sullivan's Island, and the artillery emplacements in the city. See also several illustrations of Fort Moultrie and other works on Sullivan's Island, based on photographs, in *OR Atlas*, pl. 121 and 122. Many of the extant photographs are surely the work of S. R. Siebert, a photographer commissioned by the U.S. Engineer Department to record views of various Confederate fortifications at Charleston as soon as the Rebels evacuated the city. Chief Engineer Richard Delafield wanted to study the effects of Union navy and army gunnery on the works, especially on Fort Sumter, but also on the city of Charleston itself. When Delafield learned in June 1865 that William T. Sherman's army had obtained a Confederate journal that recorded the damage done to Sumter, he made efforts to

copy it for department files. See Richard Delafield to S. R. Siebert, February 24, 1865, and Delafield to William T. Sherman, June 2, 1865, M1113, RG77, NARA.

66. Bryan and Lankford, *Eye of the Storm*, 281. The Confederate works that guarded the railroad bridge over the Ashley River, along with Pemberton's old lines on James Island, are long gone.

Chapter 13

1. Henderson, *Road to Bristoe Station*, 15–17, 27–29, 32, 49, 68–69, 70, 72, 84, 104, 140, 167, 169–70, 174–76, 179–80, 182, 194; field visit to Bristoe Station, March 21–22, 1996; Young, "Pettigrew-Kirkland-MacRae Brigade," 562. The Bristoe Station battlefield is partially preserved. There is a heavy growth of small pines covering about half the ground that the Confederates attacked across, and a small town has grown up around the station site; but the rest of the battlefield is much as it was in 1863.

2. Graham and Skoch, *Mine Run*, 4–7, 9–28; Thompson, *Engineer Battalion*, 44–45, 48.

3. Francis Adams Donaldson to brother, November 11, 1863, in Acken, *Inside the Army of the Potomac*, 393; Graham and Skoch, *Mine Run*, 7. See Bryan, Kelly, and Lankford, *Images from the Storm*, 175, 177, for drawings of the Confederate works at Rappahannock Station. The small town of Remington is now at the site of the battle of Rappahannock Station. The railroad bridge still spans the narrow river, with a modern highway bridge next to it. The landscape of the battlefield is still mostly open, but the high ground on which the Confederate earthworks sat is at least partly occupied by houses. There are no easily accessible remnants of fortifications. Field visit to Rappahannock Station, March 21, 1996.

4. Graham and Skoch, *Mine Run*, 31, 38, 44–49, 59, 70–74, 78.

5. Walter H. Taylor to Bettie, December 5, 1863, in Tower, *Lee's Adjutant*, 94–95; Joseph K. Taylor to father, December 6, 1863, in Murphy, *Civil War Letters of Joseph K. Taylor*, 157; James A. Graham to father, December 4, 1863, in Wagstaff, *James A. Graham Papers*, 171.

6. Jones, *Civil War Memoirs of Capt. William J. Seymour*, 97.

7. Early, *War Memoirs*, 323; Samuel D. Buck reminiscences, 87, Buck Papers, SCL-DU.

8. Field visits to Mine Run, March 21, 28, 1996; Luvaas and Nye, "Campaign That History Forgot," 38.

9. John F. L. Hartwell diary, in Britton and Reed, *To My Beloved Wife and Boy at Home*, 166; George Merryweather to parents, December 10, 1863, Merryweather Papers, CHS.

10. Bowen, "Diary of Captain George D. Bowen," 142; Francis A. Walker, *His-*

tory of the Second Army Corps, 383; Simons, One Hundred and Twenty-Fifth New York, 183.

11. Charles A. Upson to grandparents, December 1, 1863, United States Army, Connecticut Volunteers, NYPL.

12. M. R. Johnson, "Those Slips of Paper"; H. S. Stevens, "Those Slips of Paper"; Robert McAllister to Ellen, December 3, 1863, in Robertson, Civil War Letters of General Robert McAllister, 367; Silliker, Rebel Yell and the Yankee Hurrah, 131; Page, History of the Fourteenth Regiment, 202; Livermore, Days and Events, 302; Francis Adams Donaldson to brother, November 25, 1863, in Acken, Inside the Army of the Potomac, 406.

13. Graham and Skoch, Mine Run, 76; Warner, Generals In Blue, 541.

14. Graham and Skoch, Mine Run, 76–83.

15. Benjamin Wesley Justice to wife, December 1, 1863, Justice Papers, EU; James Henry Lane account, in Supplement to the Official Records, 5:597.

16. Graham and Skoch, Mine Run, 76–83; Caldwell, History of a Brigade of South Carolinians, 120. The slight works constructed by Meade's army on the east side of Mine Run on November 30 and December 1 were demolished by Lee's men soon after the campaign.

17. Graham and Skoch, Mine Run, 83.

18. Francis A. Walker, History of the Second Army Corps, 385–86.

19. Walter H. Taylor to Bettie, December 5, 1863, in Tower, Lee's Adjutant, 95.

20. Graham and Skoch, Mine Run, 86–89, 92, 94.

21. Ulysses S. Grant to George G. Meade, April 20, 1864, in Simon, Papers of Ulysses S. Grant, 10:560; Andrew Jackson Crossley to Bradbury, April 30, 1864, Bradbury Papers, SCL-DU; Thompson, Engineer Battalion, 56.

22. Graham and Skoch, Mine Run, 91.

23. Barrett, Civil War in North Carolina, 202–4.

24. John J. Peck to Benjamin F. Butler, April 25, 1864, OR 33:292–93.

25. Seth M. Barton to Charles Pickett, February 21, 1864, OR 33:97–98; Barrett, Civil War in North Carolina, 205–6.

26. Barrett, Civil War in North Carolina, 204–5, 207, 207n–208n; Robert F. Hoke to Maj. Taylor, February 8, 1864, OR 33:96; field visit to New Bern, October 4, 1995. A marker placed where Highway 55 crosses Batchelder's Creek indicates the presence of Union earthwork remnants north of the highway, but they are inaccessible.

27. Barrett, Civil War in North Carolina, 213; Ballard, "Good Time to Pray," 18.

28. Ballard, "Good Time to Pray," 18; "Map of Plymouth and the Defences," RG77, Dr. 143-10, NARA.

29. Ballard, "Good Time to Pray," 20, 22; Barrett, Civil War in North Carolina, 216; Lucien A. Butts to Henry W. Wessells, April 1, 1865, OR 33:301–3.

30. Barrett, *Civil War in North Carolina*, 217–18; Ballard, "Good Time to Pray," 22–23.

31. George S. Hastings account, in J. W. Merrill, *Records of the Twenty-Fourth Independent Battery, New York*, 215–16; William M. Smith, "Siege and Capture of Plymouth," 336.

32. Ballard, "Good Time to Pray," 23–24; E. A. Wright, "Capture of Plymouth."

33. Ballard, "Good Time to Pray," 25; Henry W. Wessells to John J. Peck, August 18, 1864, *OR* 33:299.

34. Ballard, "Good Time to Pray," 25; William M. Smith, "Siege and Capture of Plymouth," 340.

35. Ballard, "Good Time to Pray," 47; Henry W. Wessells to John J. Peck, August 18, 1864, *OR* 33:298–99; Peck to Benjamin F. Butler, April 25, 1864, *OR* 33:293.

36. Ulysses S. Grant to Benjamin F. Butler, April 19, 1864; Grant to Henry W. Halleck, April 22, 1864; and Grant to Butler, April 24, 1864, in Simon, *Papers of Ulysses S. Grant*, 10:328, 337–38, 346; Grant, "Preparing the Campaigns of '64," 108.

37. Barrett, *Civil War in North Carolina*, 220–21, 224; Beauregard, "Defense of Drewry's Bluff," 195–96.

38. J. G. Sills to Pa, May 6 [1864], Howell Collection, NCDAH; Ballard, "Good Time to Pray," 47. There is nothing left of the fortifications at Plymouth, but many historical markers identify the site of key works such as Fort Williams and Fort Wessells. There also are markers identifying the approximate site of the sinking of the *Southfield* and the *Albemarle*. Field visit to Plymouth, October 2, 1995.

Conclusion

1. Nosworthy surveyed the CD-ROM version of the *OR*; while it was not a systematic catalog of all the instances in which fieldworks were used, he did conclude that they appeared more often in the campaigns of 1861–63 than early twentieth-century military writers had assumed. See Nosworthy, *Bloody Crucible of Courage*, 496–518. I used the following to gain insight into the use of fortifications in American warfare before the Civil War: Anderson, *Crucible of War*, 59–60, 118, 120–21, 152, 158, 192, 242–46, 335–37, 348, 364, 394, 499–501; Fischer, *Paul Revere's Ride*, 222–32; Ketchum, *Decisive Day*, 19–24, 78, 111, 117, 120, 127, 142–43, 146, 148–49, 177, 216; Symonds, *Battlefield Atlas*, 16, 21–23, 27, 29, 31–33, 41, 43, 45–47, 49, 51, 53, 55, 57–59, 65, 67–69; John J. Gallagher, *Battle of Brooklyn*, 78–80; Ketchum, *Saratoga*, 117–18, 122–23, 162–80, 188–206, 301, 306–20, 354, 380, 396, 379–80; Lumpkin, *From Savannah to Yorktown*, 12–13, 28–29, 31–32, 34–40, 44–49, 187–205, 236–45; Graves, *Field of Glory*, 95–112; Graves, *Where Right and Glory Lead!*, 83, 91, 134, 151, 177, 211–29; Quimby, *U.S. Army in the War of 1812*, 1:24–28, 30, 32, 37, 40, 43, 45–47, 64, 67–75, 115–18, 132–43, 160–61, 183, 190–95, 204–10, 225–29, 230–35,

238–42, 246–47, 249–51, 274, 277, 280, 285, 327–28, 341–42, 355–60, 385–87, 389, 391–92, 395, 406–10, 2:451–58, 465, 521, 525–27, 538–42, 546–47, 549–55, 560–65, 573, 603, 608, 611, 623, 625, 650, 681, 686, 713–14, 716, 718–22, 770, 779, 809, 817, 821, 831–32, 836, 843–49, 861, 869, 871–72, 874, 881, 891–93, 898, 900–912, 920–22, 940–42; Haecker and Mauck, *On the Prairie of Palo Alto*, 22–23, 27–28, 50–51; Justin H. Smith, *War with Mexico*, 1:158–60, 164–69, 170–78, 230–33, 238–54, 303, 306–13, 382, 385–97, 2:19–36, 42–59, 89–91, 102–3, 110–18, 140, 145, 147–56, 159, 161–63. There are no studies of the use of field fortifications in European history other than some books that deal with trench warfare on the Western Front, but information can be pieced together by looking at a number of campaign and war studies of the various conflicts.

2. Hunt, "Entrenchments and Fortifications," 194, 196; Johnson and Hartshorn, "Development of Field Fortification in the Civil War," 570–71; Wagner, "Hasty Intrenchments in the War of Secession," 149.

3. Hagerman, "From Jomini to Dennis Hart Mahan," 219.

4. For support of this conclusion, see Lowe, "Field Fortifications," 72.

5. Wagner, "Hasty Intrenchments in the War of Secession," 130–31.

6. Hagerman, "Tactical Thought of R. E. Lee," 25–26; Hagerman, "From Jomini to Dennis Hart Mahan," 218; Lowe, "Field Fortifications," 65–66; Griffith, *Battle Tactics of the Civil War*, 73–90, 189; Hess, *Union Soldier in Battle*, 56–57, 65. Nosworthy agrees with Griffith that the rifle musket had far less impact on tactics than has been assumed, but he fails to address how this conclusion relates to the use of field fortifications. Nosworthy makes the unsupportable claim that continuous contact between opposing field armies was the result rather than the cause of the use of field fortifications. See Nosworthy, *Bloody Crucible of Courage*, 542–43, 577, 645–47. Griffith contends that "fashion and book-learning" rather than "improved weaponry" led to the widespread use of field fortifications. This also is unsupportable by the evidence. See Griffith, *Battle Tactics of the Civil War*, 189.

7. David Russell Wright has noted that variations in the design of fieldworks are seen "in the simple breastworks that were 'thrown up' in a quick manner by the soldiers, while the defense of important towns or positions reflect more of the standard system of fortifications" ("Civil War Field Fortifications," 61).

8. Fagan, "Battle of Salem Church"; Pfanz, *Gettysburg—Culp's Hill and Cemetery Hill*, 112–15; James R. Slack to Anne, May 28, 1863, Slack Papers, ID-ISL; Wilder, "Siege of Mumfordville," 298.

9. Johnson and Hartshorn, "Development of Field Fortification in the Civil War," 572, 578; Wagner, "Hasty Intrenchments in the War of Secession," 129–30; Hunt, "Entrenchments and Fortifications," 194.

10. Hagerman, "From Jomini to Dennis Hart Mahan," 213–16.

Appendix 1

1. Barnard, "Journal of the Siege," *OR* 11(1):321; William F. Barry to Seth Williams, May 5, 1862, *OR* 11(1):341–42.

2. James F. Gibson photographs, May 1862, in Davis and Wiley, *Photographic History of the Civil War*, 1:493–95.

3. Malles, *Bridge Building in Wartime*, 60–61; Stephen M. Weld to Hannah, May 1, 1862, in Weld, *War Diary and Letters*, 105; Nevins, *Diary of Battle*, 42; Sears, *To the Gates of Richmond*, 85; James F. Gibson photograph, May 1862, in Davis and Wiley, *Photographic History of the Civil War*, 1:494. See Bryan, Kelly, and Lankford, *Images from the Storm*, 51, for a drawing of Battery No. 4.

4. Field visit to Dam No. 1, October 17–18, 1995; *OR Atlas*, pl. 19, no. 2. The remnants of Union fieldworks opposite Dam No. 1 are around the interpretive center and on the edge of a nearby golf course.

5. William F. Barry to Seth Williams, May 5, 1862, *OR* 11(1):343; John G. Barnard to Joseph G. Totten, May 6, 1862, *OR* 11(1):319.

6. John G. Barnard to Joseph G. Totten, May 6, 1862, *OR* 11(1):319; Barnard, "Journal of the Siege," *OR* 11(1):332–33.

7. John G. Barnard to Joseph G. Totten, May 6, 19862, *OR* 11(1):320.

8. Barnard, "Journal of the Siege," *OR* 11(1):323, 327, 330; John G. Barnard to Randolph B. Marcy, January 26, 1863, *OR* 11(1):127.

9. Henry J. Hunt to William F. Barry, April 27, 1862, *OR* 11(1):351–52; William F. Barry to Seth Williams, May 5, 1862, *OR* 11(1):342.

10. Barnard, "Journal of the Siege," *OR* 11(1):322, 325–27, 329–33, 335–36.

11. William F. Barry to Seth Williams, May 5, 1862, *OR* 11(1):348; Richard Delafield to John G. Barnard, April 22, 1862, in J. G. Barnard, *Report of the Engineer and Artillery Operations*, 224–26. See Delafield, *Report on the Art of War in Europe*, fig. 38, for a superb illustration of the rope mantlets used by the Russians at Sebastopol.

12. Barnard, "Journal of the Siege," *OR* 11(1):333, 335–36; Henry J. Hunt to William F. Barry, May 4, 1862, *OR* 11(1):352; April 21, 1862, White Diary, ALLM; map of Union works at Yorktown, RG77, G106-1, NARA. For a detailed description of the fourteen heavy batteries, see William F. Barry to Seth Williams, May 5, 1862, *OR* 11(1):339–41.

13. William F. Barry to Seth Williams, May 5, 1862, *OR* 11(1):339–41, 343; Alexander Doull to Robert O. Tyler, n.d., *OR* 11(1):356–57.

14. John G. Barnard to Joseph G. Totten, May 6, 1862, *OR* 11(1):317–18; Early, *War Memoirs*, 65–66. I have seen few of the Union remnants at Yorktown, but David W. Lowe has informed me of their existence. Batteries No. 3, 6, 7, 8, 9, and 11 and about half of No. 5 are intact. Battery No. 4 is apparently on the grounds of a coast

guard base and not easily accessible. Redoubts A, B, and D are intact, the latter only half-finished, while Redoubt C is gone except for a section of a covered way leading to the site. Quite a few military roads and infantry parapets are preserved as well. The connecting line that goes westward from Redoubt A toward Batteries 7 and 8 is still there, and the line that goes northeast to Battery 5 is also intact.

15. John G. Barnard to Joseph G. Totten, May 6, 1862, *OR* 11(1):316; *OR Atlas*, pl. 15, no. 1; Palfrey, "Siege of Yorktown," 108–9; Runge, *Four Years in the Confederate Artillery*, 13; Francis Adams Donaldson to Jacob, May 8, 1862, in Acken, *Inside the Army of the Potomac*, 74; George N. Barnard photographs, June 1862, in Davis and Wiley, *Photographic History of the Civil War*, 1:487; "Civil War fortifications that were thrown up during the Siege of 1862 and cover those built by the British in 1781," 1939 World's Fair Photograph Collection, LOV; Bailey, *Forward to Richmond*, 98–99; field visit to Yorktown, October 13, 1994. See Bryan, Kelly, and Lankford, *Images from the Storm*, 52, for a good drawing of the main entrance of the Confederate defenses at Yorktown. The National Park Service at the Yorktown Victory Center understandably preserves and interprets the Revolutionary War history of the site as its primary mission. Yet the extensive Confederate destruction and reworking of the original remnants of Cornwallis's earthworks around Yorktown transformed the place into a Civil War site. One can assume that most of the remnants are of Rebel rather than Royal works and were even reworked by the Civilian Conservation Corps in the 1930s.

16. Palfrey, "Siege of Yorktown," 110; Cyrus B. Comstock to John G. Barnard, May 5, 1862, *OR* 11(1):338; field visit to Gloucester Point, October 16, 1995. The water battery is long gone, but fragments of the huge fort to its rear remain and are easily accessible. Although only a small part of this fort, the remnants are well preserved.

17. John G. Barnard to Joseph G. Totten, May 6, 1862, *OR* 11(1):316–17; *OR Atlas*, pl. 15, no. 3; Palfrey, "Siege of Yorktown," 109–10; Early, *War Memoirs*, 60–61.

18. *OR Atlas*, pl. 19, no. 2; "Map of Yorktown and Vicinity," YB; Bailey, *Forward to Richmond*, 92, has an interesting field sketch by a *Harper's Weekly* artist of a Confederate gun position at Wynn's Mill; field visit to Wynn's Mill, October 17–18, 1995. The remnants here are superb, well protected, and easily accessible.

19. Andrews, *Footprints of a Regiment*, 32; G. H. Houghton photographs, 1862, in Davis and Wiley, *Photographic History of the Civil War*, 2:1016–17; field visit to Dam No. 1, October 17–18, 1995. The works at Dam No. 1 are well preserved and easily accessible. Walk along White Oak Trail to the left, toward Wynn's Mill, to see what remains of the connecting works between those two points, and drive to the campground to the right of Dam No. 1 to see remnants of the connecting works between Garrow's Point and Lee's Mill. The works that traverse the campgrounds are

sadly deteriorated, but those that are hidden in the surrounding brush are well preserved.

20. *OR Atlas*, pl. 19, no. 5; field visit to Lee's Mill and Skiff's Creek Redoubt, October 18, 1995. The works at both places are well preserved. I did not see Fort Crafford on Mulberry Island but was told it is well preserved. Access to the fort is restricted by its location on the compound of Fort Eustis, an active military installation.

21. Cyrus B. Comstock to John G. Barnard, April 12, May 4, 14, 1862, in J. G. Barnard, *Report of the Engineer and Artillery Operations*, 196–97, 201, 203; Henry L. Abbott to mother, April 20, 1862, in Scott, *Fallen Leaves*, 110–11.

22. Alfred L. Rives to Josiah Gorgas, April 14, 1862, M628, RG109, NARA.

Appendix 2

1. Frassanito, *Early Photography at Gettysburg*, 142–46, 200, 255–57; Michael Jacobs quoted in ibid., 203; Trowbridge, *Desolate South*, 7; David Wills quoted in Frassanito, *Early Photography at Gettysburg*, 144; "Report on Field Defenses on the Battlefield of Gettysburg," 24–27, 31–32, GNMP; R. Bruce Ricketts to Winfield S. Hancock, December 28, 1885, in Ladd and Ladd, *Bachelder Papers*, 2:1172.

Glossary

1. There are a number of glossaries in other books about fortifications. I would recommend Cooling and Owen, *Mr. Lincoln's Forts*, 239, and David Russell Wright, "Civil War Field Fortifications," 323–34. Wright also has a very good description of parts of an earthwork on pp. 17–20. One also can find a great deal of information about these matters on the Internet.

2. Stewart, *Camp, March and Battlefield*, 394–95. See also Stephen Minot Weld to Hannah, July 8, 1864, in Weld, *War Diary and Letters*, 335, for a similar comment on the common misuse of the term "rifle pits."

3. David Russell Wright, "Civil War Field Fortifications," 3, uses these terms differently.

4. Anderson, *Crucible of War*, 242. Anderson speculates that the term "abatis" not only derives from the French for "felled trees" but refers to *abattoir*, or slaughterhouse.

5. David Russell Wright, "Civil War Field Fortifications," 327.

6. Mahan, *Treatise on Field Fortification*, 12.

7. Schneck, "Origins of Military Mines," 52.

Bibliography

Archival Sources

Atlanta History Center, Atlanta, Georgia
  L. P. Grant Papers
Burke County Public Library, North Carolina Room, Morganton, North Carolina
  Elam and L. A. Bristol Letters
Chicago Historical Society, Chicago, Illinois
  George Merryweather Papers
  James Tanner Papers
Cincinnati Historical Society, Cincinnati, Ohio
  George Benson Fox Collection
College of William and Mary, Special Collections, Williamsburg, Virginia
  Ewell Family Papers
  Daniel Harvey Hill Papers
  Nathaniel Venable Watkins Papers
Duke University, Special Collections Library, Durham, North Carolina
  Samuel Bradbury Papers
  Samuel D. Buck Papers
  Confederate States of America, Archives, Army Units
  Confederate Veteran Papers
  Benjamin S. and Richard S. Ewell Papers
  David B. Harris Papers
  Hinsdale Family Papers
  Joseph B. Laughton Papers
  James Longstreet Papers
  Bell Halsey Miller Papers
  Stephen Osgood Papers
  Joseph Overcash Papers
  William Nelson Pendleton Papers
  Charles Powell Reminiscences
  William G. Reed Papers
  Alfred Landon Rives Papers
  Thomas D. Snead Papers
  Samuel Hoey Walkup Journal

East Carolina University, East Carolina Manuscript Collection, Greenville,
    North Carolina
    Davis Family Papers
Emory University, Robert W. Woodruff Library, Special Collections,
    Atlanta, Georgia
    Charles M. Duren Papers
    Robert Newman Gourdin Papers
    Benjamin Wesley Justice Papers
Fort Sumter National Monument, Sullivan's Island, South Carolina
    Augustus Hines Iverson Papers
    Thomas Grange Simons Papers
    Wilson to folks, July 23, 1863
Fredericksburg Battlefield, Fredericksburg, Virginia
    Oliver Ormsby Letters and Diary
    R. S. Robertson Letters
    Robert Wallace Shand Memoir
Gettysburg National Military Park, Gettysburg, Pennsylvania
    Ronald A. Church, "The Pipe Creek Line: An Overview," Pipe Creek Line Folder
    James H. Koons, "History of Middleburg," Taneytown, Maryland, *Carroll
        Record*, 1895, Pipe Creek Line Folder
    Mary E. Lewis, "The Life and Times of Thomas Bailey," 47th North Carolina
        Regimental Folder
    Raymond Jenkins Reid to Hal, September 4, 1863, 2nd Florida Regimental
        Folder
    J. J. Renfroe to Brother Henderson, *South Western Baptist*, August 13, 1863,
        10th Alabama Regimental Folder
    "Report on Field Defenses on the Battlefield of Gettysburg," Field Defenses
        Folder
Harvard University, Houghton Library, Cambridge, Massachusetts
    Henry L. Abbott Correspondence, MOLLUS-Massachusetts Commandery
        Collection
Indiana State Library, Indiana Division, Indianapolis
    James R. Slack Papers
Library of Congress, Manuscript Division, Washington, D.C.
    C. B. Comstock Papers
    Louis Manigault Journal
    Horace Porter Papers
    Hazard Stevens Papers

Library of Virginia, Richmond
  1939 World's Fair Photograph Collection
  John F. Sale Papers
  James Peter Williams Letters
Lincoln Memorial University, Abraham Lincoln Library and Museum,
  Harrogate, Tennessee
  Charles Abner White Diary
Mississippi Department of Archives and History, Jackson
  William L. Davis Collection
  A. L. P. Vairin Diary
Moravian Archives, Southern Province, Winston-Salem, North Carolina
  Sam Mickey Account
Museum of the Confederacy, Richmond, Virginia
  "Daily Consolidated Reports of Artillery, Wynn's Mill, Va., April 11–May 2, 1862"
  Robert G. Haile Diary
  Letter Book of Armistead, Barton, and Steuart Brigades, 14 Feb. 1863–19 Nov.
    1864
  Charles E. Waddell Diary
National Archives and Records Administration, Washington, D.C.
  RG77 Records of the Office of the Chief of Engineers
    Map Collection
    M1113 Letters Sent By the Chief of Engineers, 1812–1869
  RG109 War Department Collection of Confederate Records
  Orders, Rodes's and Battle's Brigades, Army of Northern Virginia, 1861–1865,
    chap. 2, vol. 66
  M258 Compiled Service Records of Confederate Soldiers Who Served in
    Organizations Raised Directly By the Confederate Government
  M331 Compiled Service Records of Confederate Generals and Staff Officers and
    Nonregimental Enlisted Men
  M628 Letters and Telegrams Sent By the Engineer Bureau of the Confederate
    War Department, 1861–1864
  M998 Records of the Virginia Forces
New-York Historical Society, New York, New York
  Lawrence O'Bryan Branch Letter
New York Public Library, New York, New York
  United States Army, Connecticut Volunteers
North Carolina Division of Archives and History, Raleigh
  J. W. Bone Reminiscences, Lowry Shuford Collection
  Daniel Harvey Hill Collection

Roy Vernon Howell Collection

Robert C. Mabry Collection

Pettigrew Family Papers

Mary Lee Ticktin Papers

Henry C. Wall Diary

Peabody Essex Museum, Andover, Massachusetts

Herbert E. Valentine Papers

Richmond National Battlefield, Richmond, Virginia

Clifford Dickinson, "Union and Confederate Engineering Operations at
Chaffin's Bluff/Chaffin's Farm, June 1862–April 3, 1865"

George W. Mindil Papers

Adoniram J. Warner Reminiscences

State Historical Society of Iowa, Des Moines

William Hawley Collection

University of Alabama, William Stanley Hoole Special Collections, Tuscaloosa

Walker-Reese Papers

University of North Carolina, Southern Historical Collection, Chapel Hill

Brewer-Paschal Family Papers

Burgwyn Family Papers

Jeremy Francis Gilmer Papers

Eugene Janin Papers

Edmund Walter Jones Papers

Alexander Justice Papers

William Gaston Lewis Papers

Cornelia McGimsey Papers

David Gregg McIntosh, "A Ride on Horseback in the Summer of 1910"

Lafayette McLaws Papers

Samuel J. C. Moore Papers

Christian Thomas Pfohl Papers

Egbert A. Ross Papers

University of Virginia, Special Collections, Charlottesville

Blackford Family Papers

U.S. Army Military History Institute, Carlisle Barracks, Pennsylvania

Lyman and Jacob Blackington Papers

William E. Strock, "War Sketch," Harrisburg Civil War Round Table Collection

Virginia Historical Society, Richmond

Robert Edward Lee Papers

Robert Knox Sneden Collection

Henry M. Talley Papers

Virginia Military Institute, Archives, Lexington
   William G. Williamson Journal
Washington and Lee University, Special Collections, Lexington, Virginia
   William Alexander Gordon Memoirs
   Benjamin Franklin Templeton Papers
Yorktown Battlefield, Colonial National Historical Park, Yorktown, Virginia
   "Map of Yorktown and Vicinity," Coast Artillery School, 1926

Books, Articles, Dissertations, Theses, Archaeological Reports, and Tour Guides

Abbott, Henry L. "The Corps of Engineers." In *The Army of the United States*, edited by Theo. F. Rodenbough and William L. Haskin, 111–25. New York: Argonaut Press, 1966.
Acken, J. Gregory, ed. *Inside the Army of the Potomac: The Civil War Experience of Captain Francis Adams Donaldson*. Mechanicsburg, Pa.: Stackpole Books, 1998.
Alexander, Edward Porter. "The Battle of Fredericksburg." *Southern Historical Society Papers* 10 (1882): 382–92, 445–64.
——. *Military Memoirs of a Confederate*. Bloomington: Indiana University Press, 1962.
Ammen, Daniel. "Du Pont and the Port Royal Expedition." In *Battles and Leaders of the Civil War*, edited by Robert Underwood Johnson and Clarence Clough Buel, 1:671–91. New York: Thomas Yoseloff, 1956.
Anderson, Fred. *Crucible of War: The Seven Years' War and the Fate of Empire in British North America, 1754–1766*. New York: Knopf, 2000.
Andrews, W. H. *Footprints of a Regiment: A Recollection of the 1st Georgia Regulars, 1861–1865*. Atlanta: Longstreet Press, 1992.
Appleton, John W. "That Night at Fort Wagner." *Putnam's Magazine* 4 (1869): 9–16.
Averell, William W. "With the Cavalry on the Peninsula." In *Battles and Leaders of the Civil War*, edited by Robert Underwood Johnson and Clarence Clough Buel, 2:429–33. New York: Thomas Yoseloff, 1956.
Bailey, Ronald H. *Forward to Richmond: McClellan's Peninsular Campaign*. Alexandria, Va.: Time-Life, 1983.
Balicki, Joseph. "Defending the Capital: The Civil War Garrison at Fort C. F. Smith." In *Archaeological Perspectives on the American Civil War*, edited by Clarence R. Geier and Stephen R. Potter, 125–47. Gainesville: University Press of Florida, 2000.

Ballard, Michael B. "A Good Time to Pray: The 1864 Siege of Plymouth." *Civil War Times Illustrated* 25 (1986): 16–25, 47.

——. *Pemberton: A Biography*. Jackson: University Press of Mississippi, 1991.

Balzer, John E., ed. *Buck's Book: A View of the 3rd Vermont Infantry Regiment*. Bolingbroke, Ill.: Balzer and Associates, 1993.

Barnard, George N. *Photographic Views of Sherman's Campaign*. New York: Dover, 1977.

Barnard, J. G. *Report of the Engineer and Artillery Operations of the Army of the Potomac, From Its Organization to the Close of the Peninsula Campaign*. New York: Van Nostrand, 1863.

Barrett, John G. *The Civil War in North Carolina*. Chapel Hill: University of North Carolina Press, 1963.

Bauer, K. Jack, ed. *Soldiering: The Civil War Diary of Rice C. Bull, 123rd New York Volunteer Infantry*. San Rafael, Calif.: Presidio Press, 1977.

Beatty, John. *Memoirs of a Volunteer*. New York: Norton, 1946.

Beauregard, G. T. "The Defense of Charleston." In *Battles and Leaders of the Civil War*, edited by Robert Underwood Johnson and Clarence Clough Buel, 4:1–23. New York: Thomas Yoseloff, 1956.

——. "The Defense of Drewry's Bluff." In *Battles and Leaders of the Civil War*, edited by Robert Underwood Johnson and Clarence Clough Buel, 4:195–205. New York: Thomas Yoseloff, 1956.

Beck, Brandon H., and Charles H. Grunder. *Three Battles of Winchester: A History and Guided Tour*. Berryville, Va.: Country Publishers, 1988.

Beers, Henry Putney. *The Confederacy: A Guide to the Archives of the Government of the Confederate States of America*. Washington, D.C.: National Archives and Records Administration, 1986.

Benton, Reuben C. "From Yorktown to Williamsburg." In *Glimpses of the Nation's Struggle*. 2nd series, *A Series of Papers Read Before the Minnesota Commandery of the Military Order of the Loyal Legion of the United States, 1887–1889*, 204–22. St. Paul: St. Paul Book, 1890.

Billings, John D. *Hardtack and Coffee: The Unwritten Story of Army Life*. Chicago: R. R. Donnelley and Sons, 1960.

Boehm, Robert B. "Battle of Rich Mountain." *Civil War Times Illustrated* 8 (1970): 4–15.

Bowen, George A., ed. "The Diary of Captain George D. Bowen, 12th Regiment New Jersey Volunteers." *Valley Forge Journal* 2 (December 1984): 116–45.

Bradwell, I. G. "Capture of Winchester, VA., and Milroy's Army in June, 1863." *Confederate Veteran* 30 (1922): 330–32.

Bragg, William Harris, ed. "I Am an Eyewitness." *Civil War Times Illustrated* 26 (1988): 38–40.

Branch, Paul. *Fort Macon: A History*. Charleston, S.C.: Nautical and Aviation Publishing, 1999.

Brennan, Patrick. "The Battle of Secessionville: Yankee Debacle at Charleston, South Carolina." *Blue and Gray* 16 (1999): 6–20, 45–53.

———. *Secessionville: Assault on Charleston*. Campbell, Calif.: Savas Publishing, 1996.

Brent, Joseph Lancaster. *Memoirs of the War between the States*. N.p., 1940.

Britton, Ann Hartwell, and Thomas J. Reed, eds. *To My Beloved Wife and Boy at Home: The Letters and Diaries of Orderly Sergeant John F. L. Hartwell*. Madison, N.J.: Fairleigh Dickinson University Press, 1997.

Brown, Daniel A. "Fort Pulaski: April 1862." In *The Civil War Battlefield Guide*, 2nd ed., edited by Frances H. Kennedy, 63–67. Boston: Houghton Mifflin, 1998.

Bryan, Charles F., Jr., and Nelson D. Lankford, eds. *Eye of the Storm: A Civil War Odyssey*. New York: Free Press, 2000.

Bryan, Charles F., Jr., James C. Kelly, and Nelson D. Lankford, eds. *Images from the Storm: Private Robert Knox Sneden*. New York: Free Press, 2001.

Burlingame, John K., comp. *History of the Fifth Regiment Rhode Island Heavy Artillery*. Providence, R.I.: Snow and Farnham, 1892.

Burnside, Ambrose E. "The Burnside Expedition." In *Battles and Leaders of the Civil War*, edited by Robert Underwood Johnson and Clarence Clough Buel, 1:660–69. New York: Thomas Yoseloff, 1956.

Burton, Brian K. *Extraordinary Circumstances: The Seven Days Battles*. Bloomington: Indiana University Press, 2001.

Caldwell, J. F. J. *The History of a Brigade of South Carolinians Known as "Gregg's," and Subsequently as "McGowan's Brigade."* Philadelphia: King and Baird, 1866.

Calver, James L. *Guidebook to the Coastal Plain of Virginia North of the James River*. Charlottesville, Va.: N.p., 1962.

Capers, Henry D. "The Defense of Fort Wagner." *Southern Bivouac*, n.s., 2 (1886): 195–96.

Casdorph, Paul D. *Prince John Magruder: His Life and Campaigns*. New York: John Wiley, 1996.

Chase, Philip Stephen. *Battery F, First Regiment Rhode Island Light Artillery*. Providence, R.I.: Snow and Farnham, 1892.

Coco, Gregory A., ed. *From Ball's Bluff to Gettysburg . . . and Beyond: The Civil War Letters of Private Roland E. Bowen, 15th Massachusetts Infantry, 1861–1864*. Gettysburg, Pa.: Thomas, 1994.

Coffin, Howard. *Full Duty: Vermonters in the Civil War*. Woodstock, Vt.: Countryman Press, 1993.

Cohen, Stan. *The Civil War in West Virginia: A Pictorial History*. Charleston, W.Va.: Pictorial Histories, 1976.

"Confederate Use of Subterranean Shells on the Peninsula." In *Battles and Leaders of the Civil War*, edited by Robert Underwood Johnson and Clarence Clough Buel, 2:201. New York: Thomas Yoseloff, 1956.

Cooling, Benjamin Franklin. *Symbol, Sword, and Shield: Defending Washington during the Civil War*. Hamden, Conn.: Archon, 1975.

Cooling, Benjamin Franklin, and Walton H. Owen. *Mr. Lincoln's Forts: A Guide to the Civil War Defenses of Washington*. Shippensburg, Pa.: White Mane, 1988.

Cormier, Steven A. *The Siege of Suffolk: The Forgotten Campaign, April 11–May 4, 1863*. Lynchburg, Va.: H. E. Howard, 1989.

Coski, John M. *The Army of the Potomac at Berkeley Plantation: The Harrison's Landing Occupation of 1862*. N.p., 1989.

Couch, Darius N. "Sumner's 'Right Grand Division.'" In *Battles and Leaders of the Civil War*, edited by Robert Underwood Johnson and Clarence Clough Buel, 3:105–20. New York: Thomas Yoseloff, 1956.

Cowan, John P. "Fortifying Pittsburg in 1863." *Western Pennsylvania Historical Magazine* 2 (1919): 59–64.

Cox, Jacob D. "McClellan in West Virginia." In *Battles and Leaders of the Civil War*, edited by Robert Underwood Johnson and Clarence Clough Buel, 1:126–48. New York: Thomas Yoseloff, 1956.

———. *Military Reminiscences of the Civil War*. 2 vols. New York: Charles Scribner's Sons, 1900.

Crews, Edward R. "The Battle of Williamsburg." *Colonial Williamsburg* 18 (1996): 14–26.

Crist, Robert Grant. *Confederate Invasion of the West Shore—1863*. Lemoyne, Pa.: Lemoyne Trust Co., 1963.

Crute, Joseph H., Jr. *Units of the Confederate States Army*. Midlothian, Va.: Derwent Books, 1987.

Davis, W. W. H. "The Siege of Morris Island." In *The Annals of the War Written by Leading Participants North and South*, 95–110. Philadelphia: Times Publishing, 1879.

Davis, William C. *Battle at Bull Run*. Baton Rouge: Louisiana State University Press, 1977.

Davis, William C., and Bell I. Wiley, eds. *Photographic History of the Civil War*. 2 vols. New York: Black Dog and Leventhal, 1994.

Delafield, Richard. *Report on the Art of War in Europe in 1854, 1855, and 1856*. Washington, D.C.: George W. Bowman, 1860.

Denson, C. B. "The Corps of Engineers and Engineer Troops." In *Histories of the Several Regiments and Battalions from North Carolina in the Great War, 1861–'65*, edited by Walter Clark, 4:409–32. Goldsboro: Nash Brothers, 1901.

Dix, Mary Seaton, ed. "'And Three Rousing Cheers for the Privates': A Diary of the 1862 Roanoke Island Expedition." *North Carolina Historical Review* 71 (1994): 62–84.

Donald, David Herbert, ed. *Gone for a Soldier: The Civil War Memoirs of Private Alfred Bellard.* Boston: Little, Brown, 1975.

Drewry's Bluff. Richmond National Battlefield Park brochure.

Duane, J. C. *Manual for Engineer Troops.* New York: Van Nostrand, 1862.

Early, Jubal Anderson. *War Memoirs.* Millwood, N.Y.: Kraus, 1981.

Ellis, Robert R. "The Confederate Corps of Engineers." Pt. 1. *Military Engineer* 42 (November–December 1950): 444–47.

——. "The Confederate Corps of Engineers." Pt. 2. *Military Engineer* 43 (January–February 1951): 36–40.

——. "The Confederate Corps of Engineers." Pt. 3. *Military Engineer* 43 (March–April 1951): 120–23.

——. "The Confederate Corps of Engineers." Pt. 4. *Military Engineer* 43 (May–June 1951): 187–91.

Evans, Robert G., ed. *The 16th Mississippi Infantry: Civil War Letters and Reminiscences.* Jackson: University Press of Mississippi, 2002.

Fagan, W. L. "The Battle of Salem Church." *Philadelphia Times,* July 7, 1883.

Farwell, Byron. *Ball's Bluff: A Small Battle and Its Long Shadow.* McLean, Va.: EPM, 1990.

Fischer, David Hackett. *Paul Revere's Ride.* New York: Oxford University Press, 1994.

Fleming, Martin K. "The Northwestern Virginia Campaign of 1861." *Blue & Gray* 10 (1993): 10–17, 48–65.

Fortin, Maurice S., ed. "Colonel Hilary A. Herbert's History of the Eighth Alabama Volunteers Regiment, C.S.A." *Alabama Historical Quarterly* 39 (1977): 5–321.

Frassanito, William A. *Antietam: The Photographic Legacy of America's Bloodiest Day.* New York: Charles Scribner's Sons, 1978.

——. *Early Photography at Gettysburg.* Gettysburg, Pa.: Thomas Publications, 1995.

——. *Gettysburg: A Journey in Time.* New York: Charles Scribner's Sons, 1975.

Freeman, Douglas Southall, ed. *Lee's Dispatches: Unpublished Letters of General Robert E. Lee, C.S.A.* New York: G. P. Putnam's Sons, 1957.

Frye, Dennis E. "Stonewall Attacks!" *Blue & Gray* 5 (1987): 8–63.

Fuller, H. S. "Evacuating Morris Island." *Confederate Veteran* 11 (1903): 519.

Fulton, W. F. "Archer's Brigade at Cold Harbor." *Confederate Veteran* 31 (1923): 300–301.

Furness, William Eliot. "The Siege of Fort Wagner." In *Military Essays and Recollections: Papers Read Before the Commandery of the State of Illinois, Military Order of the Loyal Legion of the United States,* 1:211–29. Chicago: A. C. McClurg, 1891.

Gallagher, Gary W., ed. *Fighting for the Confederacy: The Personal Recollections of General Edward Porter Alexander.* Chapel Hill: University of North Carolina Press, 1989.

Gallagher, John J. *The Battle of Brooklyn, 1776.* New York: Sarpedon, 1995.

Gilbert, Dave. *A Walker's Guide to Harpers Ferry, West Virginia.* Harpers Ferry, W.Va.: Harpers Ferry Historical Association, 1993.

Gilchrist, Robert C. *The Confederate Defense of Morris Island.* Charleston: News and Courier Book Press, 1889.

Gillmore, Quincy A. "The Army before Charleston in 1863." In *Battles and Leaders of the Civil War,* edited by Robert Underwood Johnson and Clarence Clough Buel, 4:52–71. New York: Thomas Yoseloff, 1956.

———. *Engineer and Artillery Operations Against the Defenses of Charleston Harbor in 1863.* New York: Van Nostrand, 1865.

———. "Siege and Capture of Fort Pulaski." In *Battles and Leaders of the Civil War,* edited by Robert Underwood Johnson and Clarence Clough Buel, 2:1–12. New York: Thomas Yoseloff, 1956.

Goolrick, William K. *Rebels Resurgent: Fredericksburg to Chancellorsville.* Alexandria, Va.: Time-Life, 1985.

Grafton, Henry D. *A Treatise on the Camp and March, With Which is Connected the Construction of Field Works and Military Bridges.* New York: Van Nostrand, 1861.

Graham, Martin F., and George F. Skoch. *Mine Run: A Campaign of Lost Opportunities, October 21, 1863–May 1, 1864.* Lynchburg, Va.: H. E. Howard, 1987.

Grant, Ulysses S. "General Grant on the Siege of Petersburg." In *Battles and Leaders of the Civil War,* edited by Robert Underwood Johnson and Clarence Clough Buel, 4:574–79. New York: Thomas Yoseloff, 1956.

———. "Preparing for the Campaigns of '64." In *Battles and Leaders of the Civil War,* edited by Robert Underwood Johnson and Clarence Clough Buel, 4:97–117. New York: Thomas Yoseloff, 1956.

Graves, Donald E. *Field of Glory: The Battle of Crysler's Farm, 1813.* Toronto: Robin Brass Studio, 2000.

———. *Where Right and Glory Lead!: The Battle of Lundy's Lane, 1814.* Toronto: Robin Brass Studio, 1999.

Gray, John Chipman, and John Codman Ropes. *War Letters, 1862–1865.* Boston: Houghton Mifflin, 1927.

Greene, A. Wilson. "From Gettysburg to Falling Waters: Meade's Pursuit of Lee." In *The Third Day at Gettysburg and Beyond,* edited by Gary W. Gallagher, 161–201. Chapel Hill: University of North Carolina Press, 1994.

Griffith, Paddy. *Battle Tactics of the Civil War.* New Haven, Conn.: Yale University Press, 1987.

Grunder, Charles S., and Brandon H. Beck. *The Second Battle of Winchester, June 2–15, 1863.* Lynchburg, Va.: H. E. Howard, 1989.

A Guide to Civil War Maps in the National Archives. Washington, D.C.: National Archives and Records Administration, 1986.

Guiworth, Warren H. *History of the First Regiment (Massachusetts Infantry).* Boston: Walker, Fuller, 1866.

Haecker, Charles M., and Jeffrey G. Mauck. *On the Prairie of Palo Alto: Historical Archaeology of the U.S.-Mexican War Battlefield.* College Station: Texas A&M University Press, 1997.

Hagerman, Edward. *The American Civil War and the Origins of Modern Warfare: Ideas, Organization, and Field Command.* Bloomington: Indiana University Press, 1988.

——. "The Evolution of Trench Warfare in the American Civil War." Ph.D. diss., Duke University, 1965.

——. "From Jomini to Dennis Hart Mahan: The Evolution of Trench Warfare and the American Civil War." *Civil War History* 13 (1967): 197–220.

——. "The Professionalization of George B. McClellan and Early Civil War Field Command." *Civil War History* 22 (1975): 113–35.

——. "The Tactical Thought of R. E. Lee and the Origins of Trench Warfare in the American Civil War, 1861–62." *Historian* 38 (November 1975): 21–38.

Hale, Edward J. "The Bethel Regiment." In *Histories of the Several Regiments and Battalions from North Carolina in the Great War, 1861–'65,* edited by Walter Clark, 1:69–133. Raleigh: E. M. Uzzell, 1901.

Hamlin, Augustus Choate. *The Battle of Chancellorsville.* Bangor, Maine: Author, 1896.

Harleston, John. "Battery Wagner on Morris Island, 1863." *South Carolina Historical Magazine* 57 (1956): 1–13.

Harwell, Richard, ed. *A Confederate Marine: A Sketch of Henry Lea Graves with Excerpts from the Graves Family Correspondence, 1861–1863.* Tuscaloosa: University of Alabama Press, 1963.

Haskin, William L. *The History of the First Regiment of Artillery From Its Organization in 1821, to January 1st, 1876.* Portland, Maine: B. Thurston, 1879.

Hastings, Earl C., Jr., and David S. Hastings. *A Pitiless Rain: The Battle of Williamsburg, 1862.* Shippensburg, Pa.: White Mane, 1997.

Hawkins, Rush C. "Early Coast Operations in North Carolina." In *Battles and Leaders of the Civil War,* edited by Robert Underwood Johnson and Clarence Clough Buel, 1:632–59. New York: Thomas Yoseloff, 1956.

Haynes, Martin A. *History of the Second Regiment New Hampshire Volunteers.* Manchester, N.H.: Charles F. Livingston, 1865.

Henderson, William D. *The Road to Bristoe Station: Campaigning with Lee and Meade, August 1–October 20, 1863*. Lynchburg, Va.: H. E. Howard, 1987.

Hennessy, John. *Return to Bull Run: The Campaign and Battle of Second Manassas*. New York: Simon and Schuster, 1993.

———. "The Second Battle of Manassas." *Blue & Gray* 9 (1992): 11–58.

Hess, Earl J. *Lee's Tar Heels: The Pettigrew-Kirkland-MacRae Brigade*. Chapel Hill: University of North Carolina Press, 2002.

———. *Pickett's Charge—The Last Attack at Gettysburg*. Chapel Hill: University of North Carolina Press, 2001.

———. *The Union Soldier in Battle: Enduring the Ordeal of Combat*. Lawrence: University Press of Kansas, 1997.

Hickenlooper, Andrew. "Our Volunteer Engineers." In *Sketches of War History, 1861–1865: Papers Prepared for the Ohio Commandery of the Military Order of the Loyal Legion of the United States*, 3:301–18. Cincinnati: Robert Clarke, 1890.

Hicks, Roger W., and Frances E. Schultz. *Battlefields of the Civil War*. Topsfield, Mass.: Salem House, 1989.

Hill, Daniel Harvey. *Bethel to Sharpsburg*. Vol. 1. Raleigh: Edwards and Broughton, 1926.

———. "Lee's Attacks North of the Chickahominy." In *Battles and Leaders of the Civil War*, edited by Robert Underwood Johnson and Clarence Clough Buel, 2:347–62. New York: Thomas Yoseloff, 1956.

Historic Resources along the Rappahannock and Rapidan Rivers. Office of Planning and Community Development, City of Fredericksburg, Va.

History of the Fifth Massachusetts Battery. Boston: Luther E. Cowles, 1902.

Hodge, Robert W., ed. *The Civil War Letters of Perry Mayo*. East Lansing: Michigan State University Press, 1967.

Holcombe, William H. "Col. John James Abert." *Professional Memoirs, Corps of Engineers, United States Army and Engineer Department at Large* 7 (1915): 204–5.

Holien, Kim B. "The Battle of Ball's Bluff, October 21, 1861." *Blue & Gray* 7 (1990): 8–18, 46–59.

Holsworth, Jerry W. "Quiet Courage: The Story of Winchester, Va., in the Civil War." *Blue & Gray* 15 (1997): 6–26, 47–54.

Hopkins, George G. "Battle of Newbern as I Saw It." In *Personal Recollections of the War of the Rebellion: Addresses Delivered Before the Commandery of the State of New York, Military Order of the Loyal Legion of the United States*, 138–47. 3rd ser. New York: Knickerbocker Press, 1907.

Howard, Oliver Otis. *Autobiography of Oliver Otis Howard*. 2 vols. New York: Baker and Taylor, 1908.

Howard, William F. *The Battle of Ball's Bluff: "The Leesburg Affair," October 21, 1861.* Lynchburg, Va.: H. E. Howard, 1994.

Hunt, O. E. "Defending the Citadel of the Confederacy." In *The Photographic History of the Civil War*, edited by Francis Trevelyan Miller, 5:304–20. New York: Review of Reviews, 1911.

———. "Entrenchments and Fortifications." In *The Photographic History of the Civil War*, edited by Francis Trevelyan Miller, 5:194–218. New York: Review of Reviews, 1911.

Imboden, John D. "Stonewall Jackson in the Shenandoah." In *Battles and Leaders of the Civil War*, edited by Robert Underwood Johnson and Clarence Clough Buel, 2:282–98. New York: Thomas Yoseloff, 1956.

Jackman, Lyman. *History of the Sixth New Hampshire in the War for the Union.* Concord, N.H.: Republican Press, 1891.

Jackson, Harry L. *First Regiment Engineer Troops, P.A.C.S.: Robert E. Lee's Combat Engineers.* Louisa, Va.: R.A.E. Design and Publishing, 1998.

Johnson, Charles. *The Long Roll.* East Aurora, N.Y.: Roycrofters, 1911.

Johnson, John. "The Confederate Defense of Fort Sumter." In *Battles and Leaders of the Civil War*, edited by Robert Underwood Johnson and Clarence Clough Buel, 4:23–26. New York: Thomas Yoseloff, 1956.

———. *The Defense of Charleston Harbor.* Charleston: Walker, Evans, Cogswell, 1890.

Johnson, M. R. "Those Slips of Paper: Another Graphic Account." *National Tribune,* July 12, 1883.

Johnson, Robert Underwood, and Clarence Clough Buel, eds. *Battles and Leaders of the Civil War.* 4 vols. New York: Thomas Yoseloff, 1956.

Johnson, W. C., and E. S. Hartshorn. "The Development of Field Fortification in the Civil War." *Professional Memoirs of the Corps of Engineers* 7 (1915): 570–602.

Johnston, Joseph E. "Manassas to Seven Pines." In *Battles and Leaders of the Civil War*, edited by Robert Underwood Johnson and Clarence Clough Buel, 2:202–18. New York: Thomas Yoseloff, 1956.

Jones, Terry L., ed. *The Civil War Memoirs of Capt. William J. Seymour: Reminiscences of a Louisiana Tiger.* Baton Rouge: Louisiana State University Press, 1991.

Jordan, Weymouth T., Jr. "'North Carolinians . . . Must Bear the Blame': Calumny, an Affaire d'Honneur, and Expiation for the Fifty-Fifth Regiment North Carolina Troops at the Siege of Suffolk, April–May 1863." *North Carolina Historical Review* 71 (1994): 306–30.

Katcher, Philip, ed. *Building the Victory: The Order Book of the Volunteer Engineer Brigade, Army of the Potomac, October 1863–May 1865.* Shippensburg, Pa.: White Mane, 1998.

Kennedy, Frances H., ed. *The Civil War Battlefield Guide.* 2nd ed. Boston: Houghton Mifflin, 1998.

Ketchum, Richard M. *Decisive Day: The Battle for Bunker Hill.* New York: Henry Holt, 1999.

——. *Saratoga: Turning Point of America's Revolutionary War.* New York: Henry Holt, 1997.

Kimball, William J. "The Little Battle of Big Bethel." *Civil War Times Illustrated* 6 (1967): 28–32.

Kinston, Whitehall and Goldsboro (North Carolina) Expedition, December, 1862. New York: W. W. Howe, 1890.

Klein, Frederic Shriver. "Meade's Pipe Creek Line." *Maryland Historical Magazine* 57 (June 1962): 133–49.

Krick, R. E. L. "The Men Who Carried This Position Were Soldiers Indeed: The Decisive Charge of Whiting's Division at Gaines's Mill." In *The Richmond Campaign of 1862: The Peninsula and the Seven Days*, edited by Gary W. Gallagher, 181–216. Chapel Hill: University of North Carolina Press, 2000.

——. *Staff Officers in Gray: A Biographical Register of the Staff Officers in the Army of Northern Virginia.* Chapel Hill: University of North Carolina Press, 2003.

Krick, Robert K. *Stonewall Jackson at Cedar Mountain.* Chapel Hill: University of North Carolina Press, 1990.

Kundahl, George G. *Confederate Engineer: Training and Campaigning with John Morris Wampler.* Knoxville: University of Tennessee Press, 2000.

Kupperman, Karen Ordahl. *Roanoke: The Abandoned Colony.* Totowa, N.J.: Rowman and Allanheld, 1984.

Ladd, David L., and Audrey J. Ladd, eds. *The Bachelder Papers: Gettysburg in Their Own Words.* 3 vols. Dayton, Ohio: Morningside, 1994–95.

Landon, William D. F. "Fourteenth Indiana Regiment: Letters to the Vincennes Western Sun." *Indiana Magazine of History* 34 (1938): 71–98.

Lee, Richard M. *General Lee's City: An Illustrated Guide to the Historic Sites of Confederate Richmond.* McLean, Va.: EPM Publications, 1987.

Lee, Susan P. *Memoirs of William Nelson Pendleton, D.D.* Philadelphia: J. B. Lippincott, 1893.

Lesser, W. Hunter. "Preliminary Archaeological and Historical Investigations of Cheat Summit Fort." *West Virginia Archaeologist*, no. 31 (1981): 31–37.

Lesser, W. Hunter, Kim A. McBride, and Janet G. Brashler. "Cheat Summit Fort and Camp Allegheny: Early Civil War Encampments in West Virginia." In *Look to the Earth: Historical Archaeology and the American Civil War*, edited by Clarence R. Geier Jr. and Susan E. Winter, 158–70. Knoxville: University of Tennessee Press, 1994.

Lewis, Emanuel Raymond. *Seacoast Fortifications of the United States: An Introductory History*. Missoula, Mont.: Pictorial Histories, 1979.

"Life in Battery Wagner." *Land We Love* 2, no. 5 (March 1867): 351–55.

Little, J. Glenn. "Archaeological Research, Civil War Fort Earthworks: Fort Davis, Fort Mahan, Fort DuPont." Conference on Historic Site Archaeology Papers, 1968.

Livermore, Thomas L. *Days and Events, 1860–1866*. Boston: Houghton Mifflin, 1920.

Lockwood, John. "Professor Throws Light on the Battle Zone." *Washington Times*, March 20, 2004.

Longstreet, James. "The Battle of Fredericksburg." In *Battles and Leaders of the Civil War*, edited by Robert Underwood Johnson and Clarence Clough Buel, 3:70–85. New York: Thomas Yoseloff, 1956.

———. *From Manassas to Appomattox*. Philadelphia: J. B. Lippincott, 1896.

———. " 'The Seven Days,' Including Fayser's Farm." In *Battles and Leaders of the Civil War*, edited by Robert Underwood Johnson and Clarence Clough Buel, 2:396–405. New York: Thomas Yoseloff, 1956.

Lowe, David W. "Field Fortifications in the Civil War." *North and South* 4, no. 6 (August 2001): 58–73.

Lowry, Terry. *September Blood: The Battle of Carnifex Ferry*. Charleston, W.Va.: Pictorial Histories, 1985.

Lumpkin, Henry. *From Savannah to Yorktown: The American Revolution in the South*. New York: Paragon House, 1981.

Luvaas, Jay, and Harold W. Nelson, eds. *Guide to the Battle of Gettysburg*. New York: Harper and Row, 1987.

———. *The U.S. Army War College Guide to the Battle of Antietam: The Maryland Campaign of 1862*. New York: Harper and Row, 1988.

———. *The U.S. Army War College Guide to the Battles of Chancellorsville and Fredericksburg*. New York: Harper and Row, 1988.

Luvaas, Jay, and Wilbur S. Nye. "The Campaign That History Forgot." *Civil War Times Illustrated* 8 (1969): 11–42.

Mahan, D. H. *A Treatise on Field Fortification*. New York: John Wiley, 1863.

Maier, Larry B. *Gateway to Gettysburg: The Second Battle of Winchester*. Shippensburg, Pa.: Burd Street Press, 2002.

Malles, Ed, ed. *Bridge Building in Wartime: Colonel Wesley Brainerd's Memoirs of the 50th New York Volunteer Engineers*. Knoxville: University of Tennessee Press, 1997.

Manning, William C. "Yorktown and Williamsburg Reviewed in 1897." *War Papers Read Before the Commandery of the State of Maine, Military Order of the Loyal Legion of the United States*, 3:139–60. Portland: Lefavor-Tower, 1908.

Martin, David G. *Gettysburg: July 1*. Conshohocken, Pa.: Combined Books, 1995.

Marvin, Edwin E. *The Fifth Regiment Connecticut Volunteers*. Hartford, Conn.: Wiley, Waterman and Eaton, 1889.

McCarthy, Bill. "One Month in the Summer of '63: Pittsburgh Prepares for the Civil War." Pt. 1. *Pittsburgh History* 81 (1998): 118–33.

——. "One Month in the Summer of '63: Pittsburgh Prepares for the Civil War." Pt. 2. *Pittsburgh History* 81 (1998–99): 156–69.

McDonald, Archie P., ed. *Make Me a Map of the Valley: The Civil War Journal of Stonewall Jackson's Topographer*. Dallas: Southern Methodist University Press, 1973.

McKinney, Tim. *Robert E. Lee and the 35th Star*. Charleston W.Va.: Pictorial Histories, 1993.

——. *Robert E. Lee at Sewell Mountain*. Charleston, W.Va.: Pictorial Histories, 1990.

McLaws, Lafayette. "The Battle of Fredericksburg." In *Addresses Delivered Before the Confederate Veterans Association, of Savannah, GA*, 71–93. Savannah: Braid and Hutton, 1893.

——. "The Confederate Left at Fredericksburg." In *Battles and Leaders of the Civil War*, edited by Robert Underwood Johnson and Clarence Clough Buel, 3:86–94. New York: Thomas Yoseloff, 1956.

McWhiney, Grady, and Perry D. Jamieson. *Attack and Die: Civil War Military Tactics and the Southern Heritage*. University: University of Alabama Press, 1982.

Meade, George. *The Life and Letters of George Gordon Meade*. 2 vols. New York: Charles Scribner's Sons, 1913.

Merrill, Catherine. *The Soldier of Indiana in the War for the Union*. Indianapolis: Merrill, 1866.

Merrill, J. W. *Records of the Twenty-Fourth Independent Battery, New York Light Artillery, U.S.V.* Perry, N.Y.: Ladies Cemetery Association, 1870.

Miller, William J. "I Only Wait for the River: McClellan and His Engineers on the Chickahominy." In *The Richmond Campaign of 1862: The Peninsula and the Seven Days*, edited by Gary W. Gallagher, 44–65. Chapel Hill: University of North Carolina Press, 2000.

Moore, J. H. "With Jackson at Hamilton's Crossing." In *Battles and Leaders of the Civil War*, edited by Robert Underwood Johnson and Clarence Clough Buel, 3:139–41. New York: Thomas Yoseloff, 1956.

Morrison, James L., Jr., ed. *The Memoirs of Henry Heth*. Westport, Conn.: Greenwood Press, 1974.

Moten, Matthew. *The Delafield Commission and the American Military Profession*. College Station: Texas A&M University Press, 2000.

Munden, Kenneth W., and Henry Putney Beers. *The Union: A Guide to Federal*

Archives Relating to the Civil War. Washington, D.C.: National Archives and Records Administration, 1986.

Murphy, Kevin C., ed. *The Civil War Letters of Joseph K. Taylor of the Thirty-Seventh Massachusetts Volunteer Infantry*. Lewiston, Maine: Edwin Mellen, 1998.

Nevins, Allan, ed. *A Diary of Battle: The Personal Journals of Colonel Charles S. Wainwright, 1861–1865*. New York: Harcourt, Brace, World, 1962.

Newton, Steven N. *The Battle of Seven Pines, May 31–June 1, 1862*. Lynchburg, Va.: H. E. Howard, 1993.

———. *Joseph E. Johnston and the Defense of Richmond*. Lawrence: University Press of Kansas, 1998.

Nichols, James L. *Confederate Engineers*. Tuscaloosa, Ala.: Confederate Publishing, 1957.

Nosworthy, Brent. *The Bloody Crucible of Courage: Fighting Methods and Combat Experience of the Civil War*. New York: Carroll and Graf, 2003.

Oeffinger, John C., ed. *A Soldier's General: The Civil War Letters of Major General Lafayette McLaws*. Chapel Hill: University of North Carolina Press, 2002.

The Official Military Atlas of the Civil War. New York: Fairfax Press, 1983.

O'Reilly, Francis Augustin. *The Fredericksburg Campaign: Winter War on the Rappahannock*. Baton Rouge: Louisiana State University Press, 2003.

Osborne, Seward R., ed. *The Civil War Diaries of Col. Theodore B. Gates, 20th New York State Militia*. Hightstown, N.J.: Longstreet House, 1991.

Owen, William Miller. "A Hot Day on Marye's Heights." In *Battles and Leaders of the Civil War*, edited by Robert Underwood Johnson and Clarence Clough Buel, 3:97–99. New York: Thomas Yoseloff, 1956.

Page, Charles D. *History of the Fourteenth Regiment, Connecticut Vol. Infantry*. Meriden, Conn.: Horton, 1906.

Palfrey, John C. "The Siege of Yorktown." In *Campaigns in Virginia, 1861–1862: Papers of the Military Historical Society of Massachusetts*, 1:91–152. Boston: Houghton, Mifflin, 1895.

Palladino, Anita, ed. *Diary of a Yankee Engineer: The Civil War Story of John H. Westervelt, Engineer, 1st New York Volunteer Engineer Corps*. New York: Fordham University Press, 1997.

Parker, Thomas H. *History of the 41st Regiment of Pennsylvania Volunteers*. Philadelphia: King and Baird, 1869.

Paulus, Margaret B., comp. *Papers of General Robert Huston Milroy*. 4 vols. N.p., 1965.

Pfanz, Harry W. *Gettysburg—Culp's Hill and Cemetery Hill*. Chapel Hill: University of North Carolina Press, 1993.

———. *Gettysburg—The First Day*. Chapel Hill: University of North Carolina Press, 2001.

———. *Gettysburg—The Second Day.* Chapel Hill: University of North Carolina Press, 1987.

Porter, Fitz John. "Hanover Court House and Gaines's Mill." In *Battles and Leaders of the Civil War,* edited by Robert Underwood Johnson and Clarence Clough Buel, 2:319–43. New York: Thomas Yoseloff, 1956.

Quaife, Milo M., ed. *From the Cannon's Mouth: The Civil War Letters of General Alpheus S. Williams.* Detroit: Wayne State University Press, 1959.

Quimby, Robert S. *The U.S. Army in the War of 1812: An Operational and Command Study.* 2 vols. East Lansing: Michigan State University Press, 1997.

Rable, George C. *Fredericksburg! Fredericksburg!* Chapel Hill: University of North Carolina Press, 2002.

Racine, Philip N., ed. *"Unspoiled Heart": The Journal of Charles Mattocks of the 17th Maine.* Knoxville: University of Tennessee Press, 1994.

Ratchford, J. W. "More of Gen. Rains and His Torpedoes." *Confederate Veteran* 2 (1894): 283.

Reed, Rowena. *Combined Operations in the Civil War.* Annapolis, Md.: Naval Institute Press, 1978.

Report of Joint Committee to Mark the Positions Occupied by the 1st and 2d Delaware Regiments at the Battle of Gettysburg, July 2d and 3d, 1863. Dover: Delawarean Office, 1887.

Report of the Joint Committee on the Conduct of the War. Washington, D.C.: Government Printing Office, 1863.

Report of the Secretary of War Communicating the Report of Captain George B. McClellan, One of the Officers Sent to the Seat of War in Europe in 1855 and 1856. Washington, D.C.: A. O. P. Nicholson, 1857.

Rhodes, Robert M. "Our Forts." In *The Story of Frederick County,* 33. N.p.: Wisecarver's Print Shop, 1989.

Rhodes, Steven B. "Jeremy Gilmer and the Confederate Engineers." M.A. thesis, Virginia Polytechnic Institute and State University, 1983.

Riggs, David F. *Embattled Shrine: Jamestown in the Civil War.* Shippensburg, Pa.: White Mane, 1997.

Ripley, Warren, ed. *Siege Train: The Journal of a Confederate Artilleryman in the Defense of Charleston.* Columbia: University of South Carolina Press, 1986.

Robertson, James I., Jr., ed. *The Civil War Letters of General Robert McAllister.* New Brunswick, N.J.: Rutgers University Press, 1965.

———. *The Stonewall Brigade.* Baton Rouge: Louisiana State University Press, 1963.

———. *Stonewall Jackson: The Man, the Soldier, the Legend.* New York: Macmillan, 1997.

Robinson, William M., Jr. "The Confederate Engineers." *Military Engineer* 22 (July–August 1930): 297–305.

——. "The Confederate Engineers." *Military Engineer* 22 (September–October 1930): 410–19.

——. "The Confederate Engineers." *Military Engineer* 22 (November–December, 1930): 512–17.

——. "Drewry's Bluff: Naval Defense of Richmond, 1862." *Civil War History* 7 (June 1961): 167–75.

Roe, Alfred A. *The Twenty-Fourth Regiment Massachusetts Volunteers, 1861–1866.* Worcester, Mass.: Twenty-Fourth Veteran Association, 1907.

Rowland, Thomas J. *George B. McClellan and Civil War History: In the Shadow of Grant and Sherman.* Kent, Ohio: Kent State University Press, 1998.

Runge, William H., ed. *Four Years in the Confederate Artillery: The Diary of Private Henry Robinson Berkeley.* Richmond: Virginia Historical Society, 1991.

Sauers, Richard A. *"A Succession of Honorable Victories": The Burnside Expedition in North Carolina.* Dayton, Ohio: Morningside, 1996.

Schneck, William C. "The Origins of Military Mines." Pt. 1. *Engineer* 28 (July 1998): 49–55.

Scott, Robert Garth, ed. *Fallen Leaves: The Civil War Letters of Major Henry Livermore Abbott.* Kent, Ohio: Kent State University Press, 1991.

Sears, Stephen W. *Chancellorsville.* Boston: Houghton Mifflin, 1996.

——. "Fire on the Mountain: The Battle of South Mountain, September 14, 1862." *Blue & Gray* 4 (1987): 4–63.

——. *George B. McClellan: The Young Napoleon.* New York: Ticknor and Fields, 1988.

——. *Landscape Turned Red: The Battle of Antietam.* New Haven, Conn.: Ticknor and Fields, 1983.

——. *To the Gates of Richmond: The Peninsula Campaign.* New York: Ticknor and Fields, 1992.

——, ed. *The Civil War Papers of George B. McClellan: Selected Correspondence, 1860–1865.* New York: Ticknor and Fields, 1989.

Shiman, Philip L. "Army Engineers in the War for the Union, 1861–1865." Report to the Office of History, Office of the Chief of Engineers, 1995. Courtesy of the author.

Silliker, Ruth L., ed. *The Rebel Yell and the Yankee Hurrah: The Civil War Journal of a Maine Volunteer.* Camden, Maine: Down East Books, 1985.

Simkins, Francis Butler, Spotswood Hunnicutt, and Sidman P. Poole. *Virginia History, Government, Geography.* New York: Charles Scribner's Sons, 1957.

Simon, John Y., ed. *The Papers of Ulysses S. Grant.* 26 vols. Carbondale: Southern Illinois University Press, 1967–2003.

Simons, Ezra D. *The One Hundred and Twenty-Fifth New York State Volunteers.* New York: Ezra D. Simons, 1888.

Skelton, William B. *An American Profession of Arms: The Army Officer Corps, 1784–1861*. Lawrence: University Press of Kansas, 1992.

Small, Harold Adams, ed. *The Road to Richmond: The Civil War Memoirs of Major Abner R. Small*. New York: Fordham University Press, 2000.

Smith, Gustavus W. "Two Days of Battle at Seven Pines (Fair Oaks)." In *Battles and Leaders of the Civil War*, edited by Robert Underwood Johnson and Clarence Clough Buel, 2:220–63. New York: Thomas Yoseloff, 1956.

Smith, Justin H. *The War with Mexico*. 2 vols. New York: Macmillan, 1919.

Smith, William Farrar. "Franklin's 'Left Grand Division.'" In *Battles and Leaders of the Civil War*, edited by Robert Underwood Johnson and Clarence Clough Buel, 3:128–38. New York: Thomas Yoseloff, 1956.

Smith, William M. "The Siege and Capture of Plymouth." In *Personal Recollections of the War of the Rebellion, New York Commandery of the Loyal Legion of the United States, 1883–1891*, 1:322–43. New York: Commandery, 1891.

Sorrel, G. Moxley. *Recollections of a Confederate Staff Officer*. New York: Smithmark, 1994.

Sprague, A. B. R. "The Burnside Expedition." *Civil War Papers Read Before the Commandery of the State of Massachusetts, Military Order of the Loyal Legion of the United States*, 2:427–44. Boston: F. H. Gilson, 1900.

Stevens, H. S. "Those Slips of Paper: Another Graphic Account." *National Tribune*, July 12, 1883.

Stevens, Hazard. "Military Operations in South Carolina in 1862, Against Charleston, Port Royal Ferry, James Island, Secessionville." In *Operations on the Atlantic Coast, 1861–1865, Virginia, 1862, 1864, Vicksburg: Papers of the Military Historical Society of Massachusetts*, 9:111–58. Boston: Military Historical Society of Massachusetts, 1912.

———. "The Siege of Suffolk, April 11–May 3, 1863." In *Operations on the Atlantic Coast, 1861–1865, Virginia, 1862, 1864, Vicksburg: Papers of the Military Historical Society of Massachusetts*, 9:197–225. Boston: Military Historical Society of Massachusetts, 1912.

Stevens, Thomas H. "The Boat Attack on Sumter." In *Battles and Leaders of the Civil War*, edited by Robert Underwood Johnson and Clarence Clough Buel, 4:47–51. New York: Thomas Yoseloff, 1956.

"Stevens, Walter Husted." In *The National Cyclopaedia of American Biography*, 12:258–59. New York: James T. White, 1904.

Stewart, A. M. *Camp, March and Battlefield; Or, Three Years and a Half with the Army of the Potomac*. Philadelphia: James B. Rodgers, 1865.

Stiles, Robert. *Four Years Under Marse Robert*. New York: Neale, 1904.

Study of Civil War Sites in the Shenandoah Valley of Virginia. Washington, D.C.: National Park Service, U.S. Department of the Interior, 1992.

Sumner, Merlin E., ed. *The Diary of Cyrus B. Comstock*. Dayton, Ohio: Morningside, 1987.

Supplement to the Official Records of the Union and Confederate Armies. 100 vols. Wilmington, N.C.: Broadfoot, 1993–2000.

Sutherland, Daniel E. *Fredericksburg and Chancellorsville: The Dare Mark Campaign*. Lincoln: University of Nebraska Press, 1998.

Symonds, Craig L. *A Battlefield Atlas of the American Revolution*. Baltimore: Nautical and Aviation Publishing, 1991.

———. *Joseph E. Johnston: A Civil War Biography*. New York: Norton, 1992.

"Talcott, Andrew." In *Dictionary of American Biography*, 18:281. New York: Charles Scribner's Sons, 1936.

"Talcott, Andrew." In *The National Cyclopaedia of American Biography*, 13:405. New York: James T. White, 1906.

Talcott, T. M. R. "From Petersburg to Appomattox." *Southern Historical Society Papers* 32 (1904): 67–72.

———. "Reminiscences of the Confederate Engineer Service." In *The Photographic History of the Civil War*, edited by Francis Trevelyan Miller, 5:256–70. New York: Review of Reviews, 1911.

Tanner, Robert G. *Stonewall in the Valley: Thomas J. 'Stonewall' Jackson's Shenandoah Valley Campaign, Spring 1862*. Garden City, N.Y.: Doubleday, 1976.

Taylor, Emerson Gifford. *Gouverneur Kemble Warren: The Life and Letters of an American Soldier, 1830–1882*. Boston: Houghton Mifflin, 1932.

Taylor, Michael W. *To Drive the Enemy from Southern Soil: The Letters of Col. Francis Marion Parker and the History of the 30th Regiment North Carolina Troops*. Dayton, Ohio: Morningside, 1998.

———. "The Unmerited Censure of Two Maryland Staff Officers, Maj. Osmun Latrobe and First Lt. W. Stuart Symington." *Gettysburg Magazine*, no. 13 (1995): 75–88.

Thatcher, Joseph M. "Chevaux-de-Frise: Hardware and Construction." *Military Collector and Historian* 38 (1986): 169–72.

Thienel, Phillip M. "Engineers in the Union Army, 1861–1865." Pt. 1. *Military Engineer* 47 (January–February 1955): 36–41.

———. *Mr. Lincoln's Bridge Builders: The Right Hand of American Genius*. Shippensburg, Pa.: White Mane, 2000.

Thomas, Emory M. *The Confederate State of Richmond*. Austin: University of Texas Press, 1971.

———. *Robert E. Lee*. New York: Norton, 1995.

Thompson, Gilbert. *The Engineer Battalion in the Civil War*. No. 44, Occasional Papers, Engineer School. Washington, D.C.: Press of the Engineer School, 1910.

Tower, R. Lockwood, ed. *Lee's Adjutant: The Wartime Letters of Colonel Walter Herron Taylor, 1862–1865*. Columbia: University of South Carolina Press, 1995.

Trexler, Harrison A. "The Opposition of Planters to the Employment of Slaves as Laborers by the Confederacy." *Mississippi Valley Historical Review* 27 (1940): 211–24.

Trowbridge, John T. *The Desolate South, 1865–1866.* Freeport, N.Y.: Books for Libraries, 1970.

Turtle, Thomas. "History of the Engineer Battalion." *Printed Papers of the Essayons Club of the Corps of Engineers* 1 (1868–72): 1–9.

Vandiver, Frank E. *Ploughshares into Swords: Josiah Gorgas and Confederate Ordnance.* Austin: University of Texas Press, 1952.

Vaughan, Turner. "Diary of Turner Vaughan, Co. 'C,' 4th Alabama Regiment, C.S.A." *Alabama Historical Quarterly* 18 (1956): 573–604.

Viele, Egbert L. *Hand-book for Active Service: Containing Practical Instructions in Campaign Duties, for the Use of Volunteers.* New York: Van Nostrand, 1861.

Voices of the Civil War: Gettysburg. Alexandria, Va.: Time-Life, n.d.

Voices of the Civil War: Second Manassas. Alexandria, Va.: Time-Life, 1995.

Von Borcke, Heros. *Memoirs of the Confederate War for Independence.* 2 vols. New York: Peter Smith, 1938.

Wagner, Arthur L. "Hasty Intrenchments in the War of Secession." In *Civil and Mexican Wars, 1861, 1846: Papers of the Military Historical Society of Massachusetts,* 13:127–53. Boston: Military Historical Society of Massachusetts, 1913.

Wagstaff, H. M., ed. *The James A. Graham Papers, 1861–1864.* Chapel Hill: University of North Carolina Press, 1928.

Walker, Francis A. *History of the Second Army Corps in the Army of the Potomac.* New York: Charles Scribner's Sons, 1887.

Walker, John G. "Jackson's Capture of Harper's Ferry." In *Battles and Leaders of the Civil War,* edited by Robert Underwood Johnson and Clarence Clough Buel, 2:604–11. New York: Thomas Yoseloff, 1956.

Warner, Ezra J. *Generals in Blue: Lives of the Union Commanders.* Baton Rouge: Louisiana State University Press, 1964.

——. *Generals in Gray: Lives of the Confederate Commanders.* Baton Rouge: Louisiana State University Press, 1959.

The War of the Rebellion: A Compilation of the Official Records of the Union and Confederate Armies. 70 vols. in 128. Washington, D.C.: Government Printing Office, 1880–1901.

Weinert, Richard P. "The Suffolk Campaign." *Civil War Times Illustrated* 7 (1969): 31–39.

Welch, William L. *The Burnside Expedition and the Engagement at Roanoke Island.* Providence, R.I.: Published by the Society, 1890.

Weld, Stephen Minot. *War Diary and Letters of Stephen Minot Weld*. 2nd ed. Boston: Massachusetts Historical Society, 1979.

Weymouth, A. B., ed. *A Memorial Sketch of Lieut. Edgar M. Newcomb, of the Nineteenth Mass. Vols.* Malden, Mass.: Alvin G. Brown, 1883.

Weymouth, H. G. O. "The Crossing of the Rappahannock by the 18th Massachusetts." In *Battles and Leaders of the Civil War*, edited by Robert Underwood Johnson and Clarence Clough Buel, 3:121. New York: Thomas Yoseloff, 1956.

Wilder, John T. "The Siege of Mumfordville." In *Sketches of War History, 1861–1865: Papers Prepared for the Commandery of the State of Ohio, Military Order of the Loyal Legion of the United States, 1903–1908*, 6:296–304. Cincinnati: Monfort, 1908.

Wilson, John M. "The Defenses of Washington, 1861–1865." *War Papers: Being Papers Read Before the Commandery of the District of Columbia, Military Order of the Loyal Legion of the United States*, 2:257–80. Wilmington, N.C.: Broadfoot, 1993.

Winter, Susan E. "Civil War Fortifications and Campgrounds on Maryland Heights, the Citadel of Harpers Ferry." In *Look to the Earth: Historical Archaeology and the American Civil War*, edited by Clarence R. Geier Jr. and Susan E. Winter, 101–29. Knoxville: University of Tennessee Press, 1994.

Winters, Harold A. *Battling the Elements: Weather and Terrain in the Conduct of War*. Baltimore: Johns Hopkins University Press, 1998.

Wise, Stephen R. *Gate of Hell: Campaign for Charleston Harbor, 1863*. Columbia: University of South Carolina Press, 1994.

Withers, Robert Enoch. *Autobiography of an Octogenarian*. Roanoke, Va.: Stone, 1907.

Wright, David Russell. "Civil War Field Fortifications: An Analysis of Theory and Practical Application." M.A. thesis, Middle Tennessee State University, 1982.

Wright, E. A. "Capture of Plymouth, N.C." *Confederate Veteran* 24 (1916): 200.

Wyatt, Lillian Reeves. *The Reeves, Mercer, New Kirk Families: A Compilation*. Jacksonville, Fla.: Cooper Press, 1956.

Young, Louis G. "Death of Brigadier General J. Johnston Pettigrew, of North Carolina." *Our Living and Our Dead* 1 (1874): 29–32.

——. "The Pettigrew-Kirkland-MacRae Brigade." In *Histories of the Several Regiments and Battalions from North Carolina in the Great War, 1861–'65*, edited by Walter Clark, 4:555–68. Goldsboro, N.C.: Nash Brothers, 1901.

Zen, E-an, and Alta Walker. *Rocks and War: Geology and the Civil War Campaign of Second Manassas*. Shippensburg, Pa.: White Mane, 2000.

Zinn, Jack. *The Battle of Rich Mountain*. Parsons, W.Va.: McClain, 1971.

Index

Dahlgren, John, 285
Daniel, John M., 111
Daniel, Junius, 131, 203–5
Davis, Jefferson, 19, 21, 24, 68–69, 83,
    100–101, 131, 301
Davis, Joseph R., 223
Davis, Weldon, 182
Davis, William L., 158–59
Davis, William W. H., 281–83
Dawes, Rufus R., 225
Dearing, James, 301–3
Delafield, Richard, 2–4, 319, 384
    (n. 65)
Delafield Commission, 2–5
Delaware units
—infantry
    1st, 232
Demilunes, 296, 335
Denson, Claudius B., 18
De Saussure, Wilmot G., 248
Dismal Swamp Canal, 65
Ditches, 10, 335
Dodge, Richard I., 220
Doles, George, 193
Doubleday, Abner, 222, 233
Drewry's Bluff: fortifications at, 96, 98–
    99
Duane, James C., 11–12, 14, 69, 107
Du Pont, Samuel F., 45, 251
Duren, Charles M., 61

Early, Jubal A., 83, 95, 136, 153, 167, 177,
    185–86, 189, 216–17, 292–93, 320
Echols, William H., 248–50
Ellmaker, Peter C., 292
Embrasures, 2, 330, 336
Engineers: civil, 18–19; Corps of (C.S.),
    17, 20; Corps of (U.S.), 1, 2, 11–14, 17;
    Corps of Topographical (U.S.), 11–
    14, 22; Engineer Bureau (C.S.), 17–
    19, 21, 24, 37, 42, 79, 110, 131; Map
    Bureau (C.S.), 21, 137; staff offficers,
    14, 22, 51; in pre-Civil War America,
    xv; Provisional Corps of (C.S.), 18–
    19; troops (C.S.), 17, 22–23

Evans, Nathan G., 43–44, 200
Ewell, Benjamin Stoddert, 92–93, 95
Ewell, Richard Stoddert, 92, 95, 216,
    218, 292–93

Fagan, W. L., 195
Falling Waters: field fortifications at
    battle of, 236
Fall Line, 25–26
Fardella, Enrico, 305
Farquhar, Francis U., 106, 127
Fascines, 1, 319, 336
Fences as obstructions, 232
Field fortifications: aesthetics of, 86; in
    the Crimean War, 4, 7; dams and,
    80–81, 296; definition of, 9, 336;
    engineers and construction of, 166–
    67; hasty entrenchments, 123, 313;
    living in, 84–86; and manuals, 8–11;
    in Mexican War, 6; and morale, 236–
    37; obstacles in front of, 10; offensive
    vs. defensive role of, 6–7, 308, 314;
    preservtion of, 331–32; reliance on,
    xvii–xviii, 30–31, 308–9, 312; rifle
    musket and, xviii, 3, 7, 311–12, 388
    (n. 6); and tactics, 6–8, 10–11; tools
    used in construction of, 36, 37, 74,
    110, 190, 193, 210–11, 294, 318; use of
    in 1861–63, xvi–xvii; use of slaves
    and free blacks in construction of,
    xii–xiii, xvii, 24, 31, 42, 77, 79–81, 93,
    97, 131, 171, 205, 219, 240, 250; use of
    soldiers in construction of, 175, 192,
    225, 250, 294, 310–11
Firing bays, 176, 191–92
Floyd, John B., 52–54, 57
Ford, Thomas, 142
Fort Anderson, 203–4
Fort Bartow, 59
Fort Blanchard, 59
Fort Boykin, 96
Fort Cerris, 206–7
Fort Crafford, 82, 328
Fort Darling, 98
Fort Defiance, 59–60, 66

White Oak Swamp, battle of, 360
(n. 59)
Whiting, William H. C., 17, 105, 124
Wilcox, Cadmus M., 188–89
Wilder, John T., 312
Williams, Alpheus S., 175, 180, 226
Williams, James Peter, 86
Williamsburg, battle of, 95
Williamsburg Line, 92–95, 355 (n. 63)
Williamson, Thomas H., 32
Williamson, William G., 143, 167
Williamsport: field fortifications at,
233–35
Wills, David, 331
Wilson, John H., 220
Winchester: field fortifications at, 215,
373 (n. 11)
Winter, Susan E., xvi
Wire obstructions, 267
Wisconsin units
—infantry
2nd, 225
5th, 187–88

6th, 223, 225
7th, 225
Wise, Henry A., 49, 51, 53, 59, 113,
130
Wood, John, 193
Wood, John Taylor, 301
Woodbury, Daniel P., 15, 70, 108, 157–
58, 241, 319
Wool, John E., 142
World War I, 310
Wright, Ambrose R., 65
Wright, Horatio, 244, 246
Wynne, Thomas H., 98
Wynn's Mill, 80–81, 83–85, 322–23,
325, 329

Yorktown, battle of, xviii, 19, 28–30, 71,
74–75, 79–81, 86, 89; field fortifications at, 315–30, 389 (nn. 4, 14), 390
(nn. 15, 16, 19), 391 (n. 20)
Young, Henry E., 196
Young's Mill: field fortifications at, 71,
73, 352 (n. 10)